C000052469

DINOSAURS

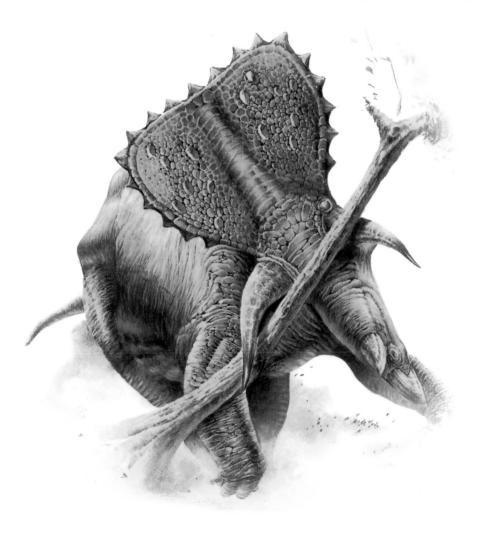

Sandcastle Books

Produced by The Brown Reference Group plc
First Floor
9–17 St. Albans Place
London
N1 0NX
www.brownreference.com

First published © Marshall Cavendish Corporation
1999 as a ten-volume set
Dinosaurs of the World.

ISBN 978-1-906020-16-3

This edition published in 2008 by Sandcastle Books Ltd
The Stables
Sheriffs Lench Court
Sheriffs Lenchs
Worcs WR11 4SN
UK

Printed in Thailand

All rights reserved. No part of this book may be
used or reproduced in any manner whatsoever or
transmitted in any form or by any means,
electronic or mechanical, including photocopying,
recording, or any information storage and
retrieval system, without written permission from
the copyright owner.

Authors

Paul Barrett (University of Cambridge),
Donald Henderson (University of Bristol),
Tom Holtz (University of Maryland), James I.
Kirkland (Dinamation International Society),
Mark Norell (American Museum of Natural
History). With additional material by Liz Cook,
David Gower, Jo Wright (all of the University
of Bristol).

Consultants

Michael Benton is Professor of Vertebrate
Paleontology at the University of Bristol. He
has a Ph.D. from the University of Newcastle
and has had a research career of over 20
years. He works on the origin of the dinosaurs
and other animals of the Triassic period. He
has published 30 books, from popular works
about dinosaurs to textbooks on paleontology.
Tom Holtz is an Assistant Research Scientist
and Lecturer at the University of Maryland,
College Park. He has a Ph.D. from Yale
University and specializes in theropod
evolution. He works on the origin and
behavior of Tyrannosaurus and other
tyrannosaurs. He has published many articles
and technical papers on dinosaurs and has
taken part in dinosaur documentaries in the
U.S. and oversees.

Color illustrations: Arril Johnson, Steve Kirk,
James G. Robins, Steve White (all of The
Dinosaur Society Artists' Guild)
Line art and silhouettes: Guy Smith, Mainline
Design; Denise Blagden and David
Nicholls©Salamander Picture Library

Picture credits
Front Cover: **Shutterstock**: Linda Bucklin

Academy of Natural Science, Philadelphia:
331b; American Museum of Natural History:
Department of Library Services 172, 331t,
Department of Library Services/H.S. Rice 173b,
R.T. Bird 168; **Ardea**: Clem Haagner 165, John
Mason 176; **Corbis**: 287b, 438, Tom Bean 169,
Bettmann 159; Tom Brakefield 248, 424, W.
Perry Conway 332t, FLPA/Terry Whittaker 323,
Michael & Patricia Fogden 344, Robert
Gill/Papilio 315, Clem Haagner 276, Eric &
David Hosking 335, Dave G. Houser 332b,
Layne Kennedy 346, Charles & Josette Lenars
268, Max Gunter 192, Joe McDonald 46, 412,
Mary Ann McDonald 294, Gail Mooney 330,
333, Amos Nachoum 206, David A. Northcott
316, Richard T. Nowitz 286, 289, Laura
Sivell/Papilio 156, UPI/Bettmann 104, Tony
Wharton/FLPA 358; **Dr. W. Desmond
Maxwell**: 428; **FLPA**: Phillip Perry 392; **Mary
Evans Picture Library**: 214b, 287t; Museum
of Natural History: Oxford University 241, 242;
Natural History Museum: Geological Society
178; **Natural History Museum, London**: 210,
214t; NHPA: Anthony Bannister 293, Martin
Harvey 306, David Middleton 227; Prof.
Michael Benton: 288; **Science Photo Library**:
Vaughan Fleming 170, Novosti 173t, Philippe
Plailly 147; **Tony Stone Images**: 130, Chris
Baker 96, Michael Busselle 72, Paul Souders 66.

Contents

articles on ornithischian dinosaurs   articles on saurischian dinosaurs   articles on general topic

How to Use this Book

These two pages explain how to use *Dinosaurs*. The book contains many articles on dinosaurs, groups of dinosaurs, animals that lived alongside the dinosaurs, and other dinosaur-related topics.

Dinosaurs is arranged in alphabetical order. Each entry is two to four pages long and contains a number of different items.

At the start of each entry are the title and a brief description of the dinosaur. Beneath the summary, the main text begins. Prepared by paleontologists, the dinosaur entries explain where and when the dinosaur was found, what type of dinosaur it was, what other dinosaurs it was related to, what it ate, and evidence for how it might have lived.

The central feature of each dinosaur entry is the color illustration, showing the animal as it might have looked when it was alive. Longer entries have extra photographs of recent finds, of paleontologists working in the field, and of modern animals that may have similar habits or features to the dinosaurs.

Extra details about the dinosaurs and their world are provided in fascinating facts boxes. An information panel lists vital statistics such as when and where an animal lived. To find out more, a Check These Out! box guides you to other related topics, many of which can be found within this book.

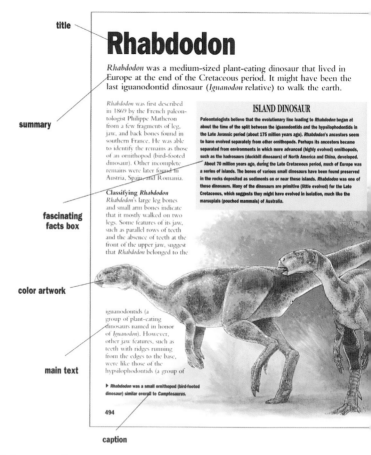

title

Rhabdodon

Rhabdodon was a medium-sized plant-eating dinosaur that lived in Europe at the end of the Cretaceous period. It might have been the last iguanodontid dinosaur (*Iguanodon* relative) to walk the earth.

summary

Rhabdodon was first described in 1869 by the French paleontologist Philippe Matheron from a few fragments of leg, jaw, and back bones found in southern France. He was able to identify the remains as those of an ornithopod (bird-footed dinosaur). Other incomplete remains were later found in Austria, Spain, and Romania.

Classifying *Rhabdodon*
Rhabdodon's large leg bones and small arm bones indicate that it mostly walked on two legs. Some features of its jaw, such as parallel rows of teeth and the absence of teeth at the front of the upper jaw, suggest that *Rhabdodon* belonged to the

ISLAND DINOSAUR

Paleontologists believe that the evolutionary line leading to *Rhabdodon* began at about the time of the split between the iguanodontids and the hypsilophodontids in the Late Jurassic period (about 175 million years ago). *Rhabdodon*'s ancestors seem to have evolved separately from other ornithopods. Perhaps its ancestors became separated from environments in which more advanced (highly evolved) ornithopods, such as the hadrosaurs (duckbill dinosaurs) of North America and China, developed.

About 70 million years ago, during the Late Cretaceous period, much of Europe was a series of islands. The bones of various small dinosaurs have been found preserved in the rocks deposited as sediments on or near these islands. *Rhabdodon* was one of these dinosaurs. Many of the dinosaurs are primitive (little evolved) for the Late Cretaceous, which suggests they might have evolved in isolation, much like the marsupials (pouched mammals) of Australia.

fascinating facts box

color artwork

iguanodontids (a group of plant-eating dinosaurs named in honor of *Iguanodon*). However, other jaw features, such as teeth with ridges running from the edges to the base, were like those of the hypsilophodontids (a group of

main text

▶ *Rhabdodon was a small ornithopod (bird-footed dinosaur) similar overall to Camptosaurus.*

494

caption

Color artwork
The color artwork shows how our team of paleontologists and artists believe the dinosaur might have looked. Dinosaur colors are very controversial. After all, it is impossible to tell that a zebra has stripes just by looking at its skeleton.

photographs

pronunciation

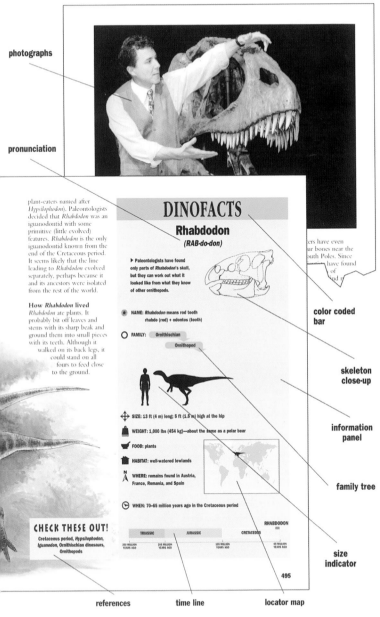

plant-eaters named after *Hypsilophodon*). Paleontologists decided that *Rhabdodon* was an iguanodontid with some primitive (little evolved) features. *Rhabdodon* is the only iguanodontid known from the end of the Cretaceous period. It seems likely that the line leading to *Rhabdodon* evolved separately, perhaps because it and its ancestors were isolated from the rest of the world.

How *Rhabdodon* lived
Rhabdodon ate plants. It probably bit off leaves and stems with its sharp beak and ground them into small pieces with its teeth. Although it walked on its back legs, it could stand on all fours to feed close to the ground.

CHECK THESE OUT!
Cretaceous period, *Hypsilophodon*, *Iguanodon*, Ornithischian dinosaurs, Ornithopods

DINOFACTS

Rhabdodon
(RAB-do-don)

▶ Paleontologists have found only parts of *Rhabdodon*'s skull, but they can work out what it looked like from what they know of other ornithopods.

⬡ **NAME:** *Rhabdodon* means rod tooth
rhabdo (rod) + odontos (tooth)

◯ **FAMILY:** Ornithischian
Ornithopod

✥ **SIZE:** 13 ft (4 m) long; 5 ft (1.5 m) high at the hip

🝳 **WEIGHT:** 1,000 lbs (454 kg)—about the same as a polar bear

🝫 **FOOD:** plants

🏛 **HABITAT:** well-watered lowlands

↑N **WHERE:** remains found in Austria, France, Romania, and Spain

� **WHEN:** 70–65 million years ago in the Cretaceous period

TRIASSIC	JURASSIC	CRETACEOUS	RHABDODON
250 MILLION YEARS AGO	205 MILLION YEARS AGO	135 MILLION YEARS AGO	65 MILLION YEARS AGO

495

...ers have even
...ur bones near the
...outh Poles. Since
...have found
...of
...od

color coded bar

skeleton close-up

information panel

family tree

size indicator

references   **time line**   **locator map**

Photographs
Four-page entries and general entries are illustrated with photographs to show how paleontologists work today.

Information panel
An information panel gives the dinosaur's vital statistics, such as how big it was and what it weighed, what its name means, what it ate, and in what sort of terrain it lived.

Color coded bar
An at-a-glance guide to the subject: blue for saurischian dinosaurs; purple for ornithischians; yellow for other animals and general topics.

Skeleton close-up
These drawings show parts of the dinosaur's skeleton in greater detail.

Family tree
Each dinosaur entry has a small family tree showing the dinosaur's ancestry. Larger trees are found at the front of each volume and in the index volume.

Size indicator
Each entry on an individual dinosaur compares the dinosaur's size to a 6 ft (1.8m) person. Very small animals are shown alongside a house cat.

Locator map
A colorful map shows where the animal's fossil remains were discovered.

Time line
The time line shows when the animal arrived.

Fascinating facts box
Informative boxes provide background about the dinosaur and its world, and compare the dinosaur to modern animals.

References
This box helps you to find out more by listing topics that are related to the entry you have just read.

7

The tree of life

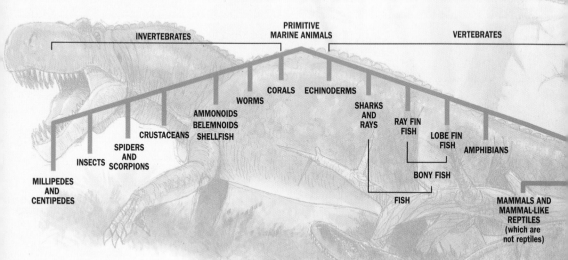

INVERTEBRATES

PRIMITIVE
MARINE ANIMALS

VERTEBRATES

CORALS ECHINODERMS

WORMS

AMMONOIDS
BELEMNOIDS
SHELLFISH

SHARKS
AND
RAYS

RAY FIN
FISH

LOBE FIN
FISH

AMPHIBIANS

CRUSTACEANS

SPIDERS
AND
SCORPIONS

INSECTS

BONY FISH

MILLIPEDES
AND
CENTIPEDES

FISH

MAMMALS AND
MAMMAL-LIKE
REPTILES
(which are
not reptiles)

The history of life looks a bit like an upside-down tree. A common ancestor at the top diverges into different branches, and these branches into even more branches, and so on. The branches represent different groups of life-forms.

Scientists seek to understand just how this tree grew and how life-forms are related to one another. One of their methods is to identify special features. Every living thing has its own unique mix of features, for example, types of bones or numbers of fingers. Some features will be new (they have evolved on their own), and some features will be old (they were inherited from ancestors). By studying these features, or traits, we can climb backward

on the tree of life to find out how different kinds of living things are related.

Let's start with birds. If you examined a bird's skeleton, you would find that it has a flexible neck joint. The first theropod (two-legged meat-eating dinosaur) also had a flexible neck joint. In our tree of life, a group of organisms includes the common ancestor and all of its descendants. For example, the theropod group includes the first theropod and all of its descendants, so scientists identify our bird as a theropod. The bird has a long neck that it inherited from the first saurischian dinosaur, so the bird is also considered a saurischian dinosaur. The bird's hip sockets allow it to walk

with its legs held beneath its body. It inherited these hips from the first dinosaur, so our bird is also considered to be a dinosaur. The holes in its skull in front of its eye sockets came from the first archosaur, so we group it as an archosaur. Our bird has scales around its feet, which it inherited from its reptile ancestors, so it is also part of the reptile branch of the tree of life. Our bird has a backbone inside its body, so, like mammals, amphibians, and fish, it is also a vertebrate.

This diagram shows how groups of animals are linked. By following the tree upward from birds or from any group of animals, you can find out how the different groups of animals are related.

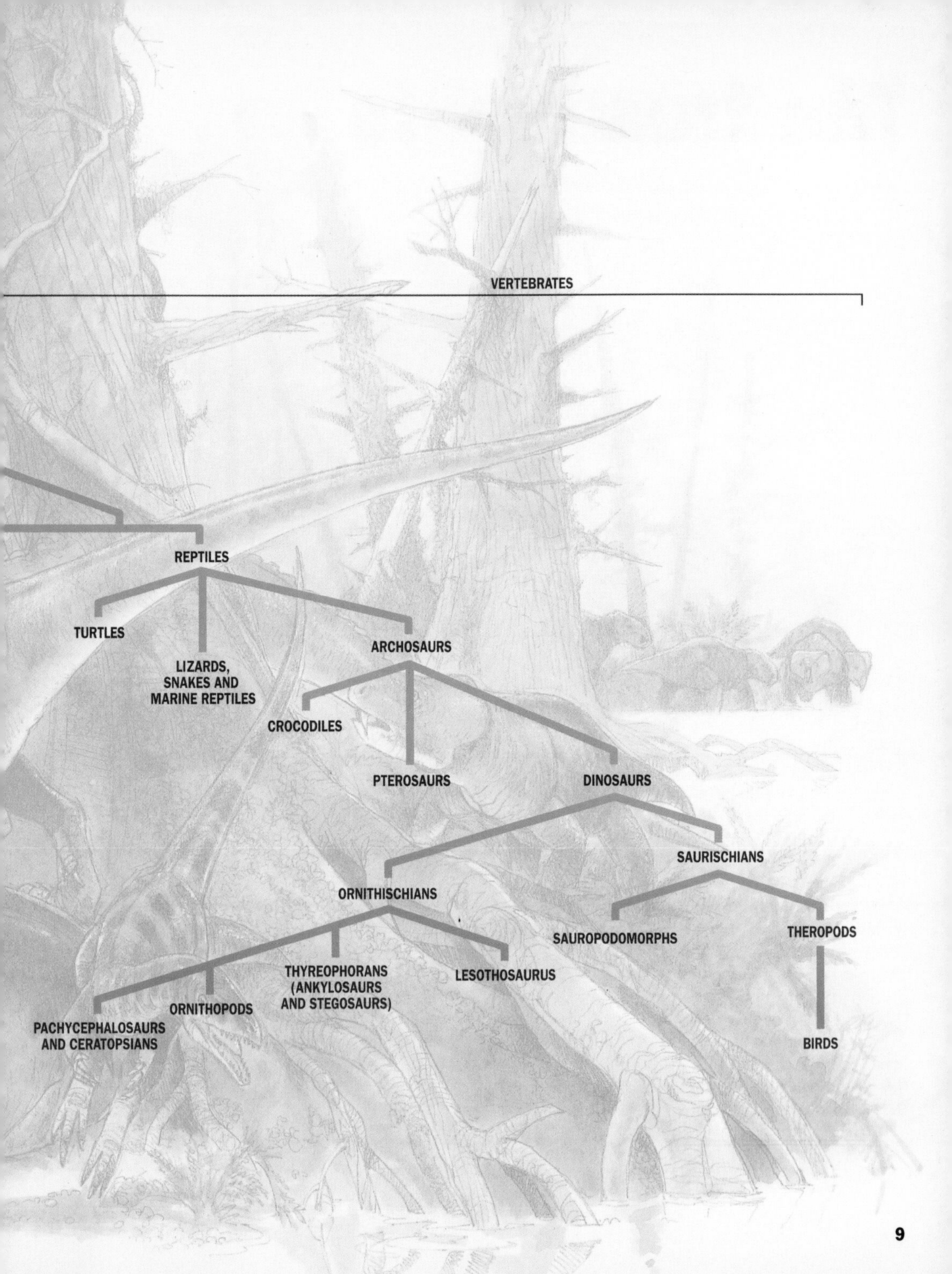

VERTEBRATES

REPTILES

TURTLES

LIZARDS,
SNAKES AND
MARINE REPTILES

ARCHOSAURS

CROCODILES

PTEROSAURS

DINOSAURS

ORNITHISCHIANS

SAURISCHIANS

SAUROPODOMORPHS

THEROPODS

THYREOPHORANS
(ANKYLOSAURS
AND STEGOSAURS)

LESOTHOSAURUS

ORNITHOPODS

PACHYCEPHALOSAURS
AND CERATOPSIANS

BIRDS

9

Abelisaurus

Abelisaurus was a large theropod (two-legged meat-eater) that lived in Argentina. It has given its name to a group of dinosaur predators that ruled the southern hemisphere in the Cretaceous period.

In the 1980s, the skull of a Cretaceous theropod was found in Argentina. The skull was 34 in (86 cm) long with powerful teeth. This was clearly the remains of a very large predator.

OTHER ABELISAURS

Abelisaurus and *Carnotaurus* were the first two abelisaurs recognized by paleontologists, but others are now known. Some, like *Xenotarsosaurus* and *Noasaurus*, also lived in South America. Others such as *Indosaurus* and *Indosuchus* lived in India, while *Majungatholus* (formerly known as *Majungasaurus*) hunted in Madagascar. Recent discoveries of more complete skeletons of *Majungatholus* and *Xenotarsosaurus* will allow scientists to discover what features were shared by all abelisaurs, and which were unique to particular kinds.

Abel's dinosaur

Argentine paleontologists José Bonaparte and Fernando Novas described and named the new dinosaur. In honor of its discoverer, Roberto Abel, they called it *Abelisaurus*.

Abelisaurus's skull had many interesting features. It was very tall and deep, with a ridge of bone over each eye, rather similar to the tyrannosaurs (two-fingered meat-eaters)

▶ *Abelisaurus* probably hunted young sauropods in the forests of Cretaceous South America.

Tyrannosaurus and *Tarbosaurus*. However, *Abelisaurus* was clearly different from the tyrannosaurs in other details of the back and sides of its skull.

The nearest relative that the paleontologists could identify was *Carnotaurus*, which was also from Argentina, but was almost 25 million years older! *Carnotaurus* belonged to the ceratosaurs, a group of four-fingered theropods that also included *Ceratosaurus*, *Coelophysis*, and *Dilophosaurus*.

Because *Abelisaurus* and *Carnotaurus* were more similar to each other than to any other ceratosaur, Bonaparte and Novas placed them in their own group within the ceratosaurs, the abelisaurs. Other abelisaurs were soon discovered in India and in Madagascar, an island off the east coast of Africa.

Top predator
Abelisaurus lived in the last part of the Cretaceous period, at the same time as tyrannosaurs were hunting duckbill and horned dinosaurs in North America and Asia. South of the equator, the abelisaurs hunted sauropods and other plant-eaters, but no one hunted them.

CHECK THESE OUT!

Carnotaurus, Ceratosaurs, Coelophysis, Cretaceous period, Dilophosaurus, Majungatholus, Saurischian dinosaurs, Tyrannosaurs

DINOFACTS

Abelisaurus
(ah-**BELL**-ih-**SORE**-us)

▶ Fossil-hunters have found only *Abelisaurus*'s skull. However, the powerful teeth tell them that this was a meat-eating dinosaur.

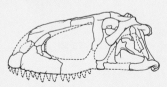

✳ **NAME:** *Abelisaurus* means Abel's lizard
Abel (Roberto Abel, discoverer of the fossil) + sauros (lizard)

○ **FAMILY:**   Saurischian
                    Theropod
                        Ceratosaur

✛ **SIZE:** about 33 ft (10 m) long; about 8 ft (2.4 m) high at the hip

WEIGHT: about 2.5 tons (2.2 tonnes)—about the same as 10 tigers

FOOD: meat

HABITAT: forests

WHERE: remains found in Argentina

🕑 **WHEN:** 71–68 million years ago in the Cretaceous period

			ABELISAURUS
TRIASSIC	JURASSIC	CRETACEOUS	
250 MILLION YEARS AGO	205 MILLION YEARS AGO	135 MILLION YEARS AGO	65 MILLION YEARS AGO

Acrocanthosaurus

Acrocanthosaurus was the biggest predator of the mid–Cretaceous period in North America. It is known from skeletons, teeth, and a set of tracks that may show it hunting sauropods.

In the United States, dinosaurs from both the Late Jurassic period (155–135 million years ago) and from the end of the Late Cretaceous period (80–65 million years ago) have been known for over 100 years. However, very little was known about US dinosaurs between these periods.

The bones of the biggest predator to roam North America between Late Jurassic

ON THE TRACK OF A SAUROPOD

In the early 1940s, American paleontologist Roland T. Bird reported a trackway from the Paluxy River of Texas. These tracks, which were the same age as the rocks in which *Acrocanthosaurus* was found, contained the footprints of a large sauropod (long-necked plant-eater), perhaps a relative of *Brachiosaurus*, and a large theropod. The theropod tracks, which are the right size and shape to have been made by *Acrocanthosaurus*, follow the sauropod tracks.

At one point, the theropod trail shows two right footprints without a left footprint in between. Bird thought that this meant that the theropod (*Acrocanthosaurus*) had grabbed on to the sauropod with its foot in an attack. Because the trackways may not be exact or complete, it is hard to tell precisely what happened 100 million years ago.

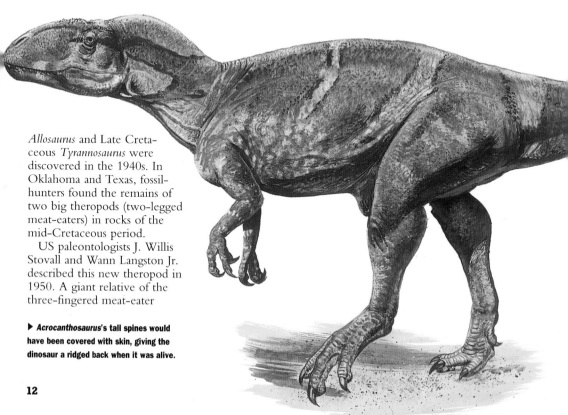

Allosaurus and Late Cretaceous *Tyrannosaurus* were discovered in the 1940s. In Oklahoma and Texas, fossil-hunters found the remains of two big theropods (two-legged meat-eaters) in rocks of the mid-Cretaceous period.

US paleontologists J. Willis Stovall and Wann Langston Jr. described this new theropod in 1950. A giant relative of the three-fingered meat-eater

▶ *Acrocanthosaurus*'s tall spines would have been covered with skin, giving the dinosaur a ridged back when it was alive.

Allosaurus, it mostly resembled that earlier, smaller theropod. However, this new find had tall spines on its neck, back, hip, and tail bones. Because of these spines, Stovall and Langston named it *Acrocanthosaurus*, tall-spined lizard.

For many years, these two skeletons were the only known remains of *Acrocanthosaurus*. Then in Texas and Oklahoma, fossil-hunters found more specimens. In Utah and Maryland, teeth and bones belonging to *Acrocanthosaurus* or to a very similar dinosaur were found. It seems likely that *Acrocanthosaurus* lived across much of North America in the mid-Cretaceous period.

How did it live?
Acrocanthosaurus was a *Tyrannosaurus*-sized hunter. In its shadow lived the dromaeosaur (clawed meat-eater) *Deinonychus*.

While that birdlike dinosaur may have attacked smaller plant-eaters, *Acrocanthosaurus* was four times larger, so it could kill much bigger prey.

CHECK THESE OUT!
Allosaurus, Brachiosaurus, Cretaceous period, Deinonychus, Footprints, Saurischian dinosaurs, Theropods, Tyrannosaurus

DINOFACTS

Acrocanthosaurus
(*AH-crow-CAN-thuh-SORE-us*)

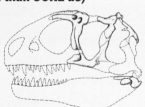

▶ Only fragments of *Acrocanthosaurus*'s skull have been found. Paleontologists think it was fairly like *Allosaurus*'s skull but without the crests in front of the eyes.

☀ **NAME:** *Acrocanthosaurus* means tall-spined lizard
acro (tall) + akantha (spine) + sauros (lizard)

◯ **FAMILY:** Saurischian
→ Theropod
→ Tetanuran

✛ **SIZE:** about 40 ft (12.2 m) long; up to 10 ft (3 m) high at the hip

⚖ **WEIGHT:** up to 4.5 tons (4 tonnes)—about the same as 9–10 polar bears

🥣 **FOOD:** meat

🏠 **HABITAT:** varied, from dry uplands to sea coastlines

N ↑ **WHERE:** remains found in what is now Oklahoma, Texas, Utah, and possibly Maryland

🕐 **WHEN:** 115–105 million years ago in the Cretaceous period

		ACROCANTHOSAURUS
TRIASSIC	JURASSIC	CRETACEOUS
250 MILLION YEARS AGO	205 MILLION YEARS AGO	135 MILLION YEARS AGO

65 MILLION YEARS AGO

Afrovenator

Afrovenator was a general purpose meat-eater that lived in Africa in the Cretaceous period. Even though it had no special features, it is important in understanding the history of African dinosaurs.

In 1990, US paleontologist Paul Sereno joined the British Museum of Natural History on a dinosaur hunt in Africa. While in the desert country of Niger, Sereno spotted a row of bones from a sauropod (long-necked plant-eater) at a location called In Abaka. He could not recover the bones on that expedition, so he made plans to return to Niger.

In 1994, Sereno led an international team of paleontologists and geologists back to In Abaka. There the team found and uncovered the remains of an Early Cretaceous sauropod, which has yet to be officially named or described.

They also found the remains of a new theropod (two-legged meat-eater). Like most meat-eaters, it had bladelike, serrated teeth and large, grasping hands.

SAHARAN DINOSAURS

Besides *Afrovenator*, fossil-hunters have found the remains of other dinosaurs in the Sahara Desert. These include the mid-Cretaceous theropods *Carcharodontosaurus* and *Spinosaurus*, both of them giants. Smaller than these was the sail-backed plant-eater *Ouranosaurus*. A few sauropods (long-necked plant-eaters) have also been discovered in North Africa, but their remains were not very complete. Alongside these dinosaurs lived turtles and huge, 50 ft (15.2 m) crocodiles.

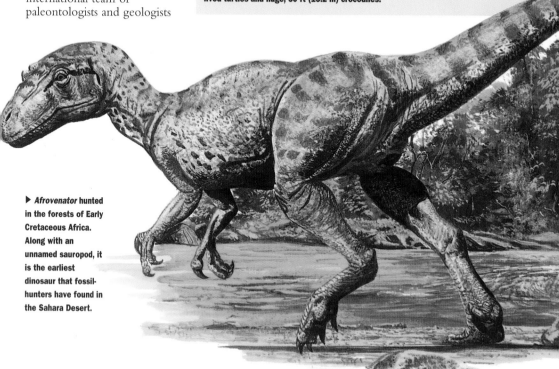

▶ *Afrovenator* hunted in the forests of Early Cretaceous Africa. Along with an unnamed sauropod, it is the earliest dinosaur that fossil-hunters have found in the Sahara Desert.

Because it had three fingers, all of its teeth in front of its eye sockets, and stiffening structures in its tail, Sereno knew that it was a tetanuran (stiff-tailed meat-eater).

African hunter

This was a new theropod, unlike any other known from Africa. The team named it *Afrovenator*, the African hunter. At 27 ft (8.2 m) long, it was not amazingly big. It did not have huge claws or tall spines, and it was not a specialized runner. It was a fairly primitive (little evolved), general purpose tetanuran.

What was important was *Afrovenator*'s age. By comparing the animals and plants found with it to similar fossils from other parts of the world, the scientists figured out that it was from the Early Cretaceous. No dinosaurs had previously been known in all of Africa between the Late Jurassic and the mid-Cretaceous periods, but now two had been found: the sauropod and *Afrovenator*. From these and other remains found in the late 1990s, Sereno and his team are trying to piece together African dinosaur history between the Late Jurassic and the mid-Cretaceous periods.

How did *Afrovenator* live?

Afrovenator was a hunter that roamed what is now one of the largest deserts on earth.

DINOFACTS

Afrovenator

(AF-roh-VEN-ah-tor)

✴ **NAME:** *Afrovenator* means African hunter
Afro (African) + venator (hunter)

○ **FAMILY:** Saurischian
Theropod
Tetanuran

✛ **SIZE:** perhaps about 27 ft (8.2 m) long; perhaps about 5.5 ft (1.7 m) high at the hip

WEIGHT: about 1,760 lbs (800 kg)—about the same as 3–4 tigers

FOOD: meat

HABITAT: forests

WHERE: remains found in Niger, northern Africa

WHEN: 130 million years ago in the Cretaceous period

TRIASSIC	JURASSIC	AFROVENATOR	CRETACEOUS
250 MILLION YEARS AGO	205 MILLION YEARS AGO	135 MILLION YEARS AGO	65 MILLION YEARS AGO

Afrovenator's day the Sahara was covered in forests and rivers. *Afrovenator* probably used its powerful hands to hold onto its victim, while it slashed out lumps of meat with its teeth.

CHECK THESE OUT!

Carcharodontosaurus, Cretaceous period, Ouranosaurus, Spinosaurus, Tetanurans, Theropods

15

Alamosaurus

Alamosaurus was one of the last of the sauropods (long-necked plant-eating dinosaurs). It lived at the very end of the Cretaceous period, and was one of the very last dinosaurs to walk the earth.

Alamosaurus was the last of the titanosaurs (armored sauropods). Titanosaurs were a group of primitive (little evolved) sauropods that survived long after most other sauropods had become extinct. They included *Antarctosaurus,* *Argentinosaurus, Hypselo-saurus,* and *Saltasaurus.*

WHERE THE SAUROPODS ARE

Sauropod footprints and bones are very common in Late Jurassic North American rocks. In the southern hemisphere, many armored sauropod (titanosaur) fossils have been found in later, Cretaceous period rocks. What story do these fossils tell?

Did the sauropods migrate south? Did the sauropods become extinct in Cretaceous North America? Perhaps they died out due to a changing climate, or increased competition for food. Now paleontologists have found *Alamosaurus* in North America at the end of the Cretaceous period. How does this change the story? We would need a lot more evidence to know what happened to the northern sauropods.

▼ **Alamosaurus** steers **clear of** **Quetzalcoatlus,** a huge **pterosaur** (flying reptile) that lived in North **America in** the Late Cretaceous period.

US paleontologist Charles W. Gilmore first discovered *Alamosaurus* in Texas in 1922. Fossil-hunters have since found more remains in Texas, New Mexico, and Utah. They do not have a complete *Alamosaurus* skeleton to study, though: only parts of hips, a tail, a shoulder blade, a front leg and foot, some chest bones, and a few teeth. From these remains, though, they can tell that *Alamosaurus* was pretty big.

Weighty problem

At about 48 ft (14.5 m) long, *Alamosaurus* was large for a titanosaur. Most titanosaurs were about three-quarters its size. Many other kinds of sauropods that grew to great size (for example, *Apatosaurus* and *Diplodocus*) had weight-saving hollows on the sides of each backbone. However, titanosaurs evolved without these hollows. Because most titanosaurs never grew more than about 38 ft (11.6 m) long, body weight was not a serious problem for them.

How *Alamosaurus* lived

No head has yet been found for *Alamosaurus*. Sauropod heads were fairly small and fragile compared to the total size of the dinosaur and were easily crushed and lost after the dinosaur died. However, we can assume that *Alamosaurus* ate plants, as all sauropods did. The size of *Alamosaurus*'s bulky body tells us it held the large guts it needed to break down the food that it swallowed whole.

Like *Titanosaurus*, another titanosaur, *Alamosaurus* probably had small armor plates set in its skin. Fossil-hunters have not yet found any *Alamosaurus* armor, though.

DINOFACTS

Alamosaurus
(AL-*uh*-mow-SORE-*us*)

※ **NAME:** *Alamosaurus* means Alamo lizard
Alamo (place in Texas) + sauros (lizard)

○ **FAMILY:** Saurischian
Sauropodomorph
Sauropod

⊕ **SIZE:** possibly about 48 ft (14.5 m) long; possibly 12 ft (3.6 m) high at the hip

WEIGHT: possibly about 25 tons (22.5 tonnes)—about the same as 5 African elephants

FOOD: plants

HABITAT: broad, low-lying plains with many large rivers

N **WHERE:** remains found in New Mexico, Texas, and Utah

🕐 **WHEN:** 70–65 million years ago in the Cretaceous period

			ALAMOSAURUS
TRIASSIC	JURASSIC	CRETACEOUS	
250 MILLION YEARS AGO	205 MILLION YEARS AGO	135 MILLION YEARS AGO	65 MILLION YEARS AGO

CHECK THESE OUT!

Argentinosaurus, Pterosaurs, Saltasaurus, Sauropods, Titanosaurus

17

Albertosaurus

Albertosaurus was one of North America's most common tyrannosaurs (two-fingered meat-eaters), but was *Albertosaurus* just one kind of tyrannosaur or two kinds? Scientists are not sure.

In the late 1800s, the Geological Survey of Canada brought back many fossils from the badlands of western Canada. Among the fossils they found were two skulls belonging to large theropod (two-legged meat-eating) dinosaurs. US paleontologist E. D. Cope and Canadian paleontologist Lawrence M. Lambe thought they both belonged to the theropod "Laelaps" (now called *Dryptosaurus*) that Cope had discovered.

Meanwhile, Henry Fairfield Osborn of the American Museum of Natural History in New York City was studying a new giant theropod, which he called *Tyrannosaurus rex*. Osborn recognized that the Canadian dinosaurs were not *Dryptosaurus* but relatives of *Tyrannosaurus*. In 1905, Osborn named the Canadian dinosaur *Albertosaurus* in honor of Alberta, where it was found.

Enter *Gorgosaurus*

Then in the summer of 1913, Canadian fossil-hunter Charles H. Sternberg came across an

▲ Like other tyrannosaurs, big-headed *Albertosaurus* probably attacked its prey with its huge jaws and teeth.

ALBERTOSAURUS vs. GORGOSAURUS

Lawrence M. Lambe believed that *Albertosaurus* and *Gorgosaurus* were two different types of tyrannosaurs, and for many years paleontologists agreed with him. Then in 1970, Canadian theropod expert Dale A. Russell suggested that *Albertosaurus* and *Gorgosaurus* were just two different kinds (species) of the same tyrannosaur. He pointed out that they were more similar to each other than to other tyrannosaurs. Most paleontologists accepted this and stopped using the name *Gorgosaurus*.

New evidence in the 1990s, however, showed that *Albertosaurus* and *Gorgosaurus* were as different from each other as from other tyrannosaurs. Some theropod experts said this meant that the two were really completely different tyrannosaurs and the name *Gorgosaurus* should be restored. They say that many museum displays of *Albertosaurus* should really be called *Gorgosaurus*.

almost complete tyrannosaur skeleton near the Red Deer River in Alberta. The rocks in which he found it were a little older than those in which the original *Albertosaurus* skulls were discovered. Lawrence M. Lambe studied it and noticed that the dinosaur's hand had only two fingers. Until then, paleontologists had assumed that tyrannosaurs had three, like *Allosaurus*. After discovering many more fossils, scientists have found that, like *Albertosaurus*, all tyrannosaurs had only two fingers.

Lambe thought this second skeleton was too old to be *Albertosaurus*, so he named it *Gorgosaurus*. Some paleontologists, however, believe that *Gorgosaurus* is just a different kind (species) of *Albertosaurus*.

How *Albertosaurus* lived

Albertosaurus was a smaller version of *Tyrannosaurus*. Its long, slender legs and shock-absorbing feet would have allowed it to outrun its prey: mainly the hadrosaurs (duckbill dinosaurs) and ceratopsians (horned dinosaurs), which were the most common large plant-eaters of its time.

CHECK THESE OUT!

Allosaurus, Cretaceous period, Saurischian dinosaurs, Theropods, Tyrannosaurs, *Tyrannosaurus*

DINOFACT

Albertosaurus
(al-BER-tuh-SORE-us)

▶ ***Albertosaurus*'s** massive skull had openings, or windows, in front of the eye sockets. These openings would have made ***Albertosaurus*'s** head lighter and easier to move without making it any weaker.

☀ **NAME:** *Albertosaurus* means Alberta lizard
  Alberta (province of Canada) + sauros (lizard)

○ **FAMILY:** Saurischian

  Theropod

  Tyrannosaur

✛ **SIZE:** about 28 ft (8.5 m) long; about 9.25 ft (2.8 m) high at the hip

⬛ **WEIGHT:** about 2.75 tons (2.5 tonnes)—about the same as 6 polar bears

🥣 **FOOD:** meat

🏛 **HABITAT:** forests, uplands, riverbanks

N
WHERE: remains found in the western United States and in Canada

🕐 **WHEN:** 80–68 million years ago in the Cretaceous period

			ALBERTOSAURUS
TRIASSIC	JURASSIC	CRETACEOUS	
250 MILLION YEARS AGO	205 MILLION YEARS AGO	135 MILLION YEARS AGO	65 MILLION YEARS AGO

Alectrosaurus

Alectrosaurus is one of the oldest known tyrannosaurs (two-fingered meat-eaters). For many years its bones were mixed up with the bones of another dinosaur, so nobody knew what it was.

Most tyrannosaurs, including *Albertosaurus, Daspletosaurus,* and *Tyrannosaurus* of North America and *Tarbosaurus* of Asia, were very similar. They had powerful skulls, long, slender legs, very short arms, and hands with only two fingers.

All the most famous tyrant dinosaurs lived in the last part of the Late Cretaceous period. In 1923, paleontologists from the American Museum of Natural History discovered the remains of an earlier tyrannosaur in Mongolia.

An odd-looking tyrant
George Olsen and Walter Granger first found some leg, arm, and hip bones. Later, about 100 ft (30 m) away, they found some more arm bones and some tail bones. Granger thought that all the bones belonged to the same dinosaur.

Back in New York, in 1933, paleontologist Charles Gilmore closely examined the bones. He saw that the first bones found were clearly from a tyrannosaur. However, some of the bones found in the second batch of fossils were unusual for a tyrannosaur. The arm bones were larger than those of a typical tyrannosaur, and the finger claws were huge.

▼ *Alectrosaurus* had long, slim legs, so it could probably run fast to catch its prey.

A BEAST WITH SIX HORNS

Another small tyrannosaur found in Mongolia was called *Alioramus*. This was younger than *Alectrosaurus*, and was found in rocks of the same age as those that contained the fossils of *Tarbosaurus*. *Alioramus* is known only from its skull and foot bones. Like *Alectrosaurus*, it had a long, tapered snout. Unlike the older dinosaur, however, *Alioramus* had a row of six bumps or small horns along the top of its snout. Because they would have been too small to be useful weapons, *Alioramus* probably just used its horny bumps for display. *Alloramus* was probably a little longer than *Alectrosaurus*. Its name means other branch because it was thought to represent a separate branch of the tyrannosaur family tree.

Gilmore named this new dinosaur *Alectrosaurus* (the unmarried dinosaur) because it was separate from the rest of the tyrannosaur group.

Mixed–up bones

Many decades later, Mongolian paleontologists discovered new specimens of *Alectrosaurus* that included the dinosaur's skull. Because *Alectrosaurus* was older than most tyrannosaurs, it reveals clues about the tyrannosaurs' ancestors. For example, *Alectrosaurus*'s skull was longer and its snout was more tapered than those of typical tyrannosaurs. American paleontologists then restudied the original *Alectrosaurus* fossils and decided that the arm bones with the huge claws were not from *Alectrosaurus* at all, but from one of the bizarre-looking therizinosaurs like *Segnosaurus* and *Erlikosaurus*.

How did *Alectrosaurus* live?

Like later tyrannosaurs, *Alectrosaurus* ran fast and ate meat. However, like primitive (less evolved) theropods, this early tyrannosaur had a delicate skull and thin teeth. It probably fed by neatly slicing chunks of meat rather than by pulling and tearing as did *Tyrannosaurus* and *Daspletosaurus*.

CHECK THESE OUT!

Cretaceous period,
Daspletosaurus, *Erlikosaurus*,
Segnosaurus, Tyrannosaurs

DINOFACTS

Alectrosaurus
(a-LECK-truh-SORE-us)

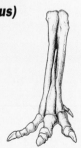

▶ Like other tyrannosaurs, *Alectrosaurus* had a powerful foot with three talons with which it could grab and hold down its prey.

✳ **NAME:** *Alectrosaurus* means unmarried lizard
alectros (unmarried) + sauros (lizard)

○ **FAMILY:** Saurischian
→ Theropod
→ Tyrannosaur

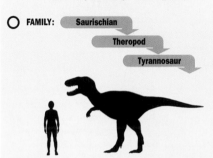

✥ **SIZE:** about 16 ft (5 m) long; about 4 ft (1.2 m) high at the hip

WEIGHT: about 700 lbs (320 kg)—about the size of a large grizzly bear

FOOD: meat

HABITAT: varied, from forests to lake shores to river valleys to dry regions

WHERE: remains found in Mongolia and China

🕐 **WHEN:** 75–73 million years ago in the Cretaceous period

			ALECTROSAURUS
TRIASSIC	JURASSIC	CRETACEOUS	
250 MILLION YEARS AGO	205 MILLION YEARS AGO	135 MILLION YEARS AGO	65 MILLION YEARS AGO

Allosaurus

Allosaurus is the most common and the best known meat-eating dinosaur from the Late Jurassic period. It was a large, fierce predator with eagle-like talons, strong jaws, and fearsome teeth.

The Morrison Formation in the western United States is a series of rock layers stretching from Montana to New Mexico. These rocks are richer in dinosaur skeletons than any other Jurassic rocks.

Morrison dinosaurs

The most common Morrison dinosaurs are the sauropods (long-necked plant-eaters), such as *Apatosaurus, Brachiosaurus,* and *Camarasaurus.* Many ornithischians (bird-hipped plant-eaters) have also been found, such as plate-backed *Stegosaurus* and the ornithopod (bird-footed dinosaur) *Camptosaurus.*

Theropods (two-legged meat-eaters) are rarer. Morrison theropods include horned *Ceratosaurus* and birdlike *Ornitholestes*; however, by far the most common and best known of the Morrison predators is *Allosaurus.*

A petrified horse hoof?

Geologist Ferdinand V. Hayden discovered the first fragment of *Allosaurus* in Colorado in 1869. This was a broken half of a backbone (vertebra), which was jokingly called a petrified horse hoof because of its shape (petrified means turned to stone). This vertebra was described in 1873

by paleontologist Joseph Leidy, who named the fossil *Antrodemus.*

In 1877, paleontologist Othniel C. Marsh's team found a series of theropod bones in the Garden Park quarry of Colorado. They found vertebrae, foot and toe bones, fragments of arm bones, and teeth.

The vertebrae were hourglass shaped rather than spool shaped. Because they were clearly different from any of the other dinosaurs found in the quarry, Marsh named the new creature *Allosaurus*, the strange, or other, lizard.

Complete skeleton

Marsh's team found many more bones of *Allosaurus.* M. P. Felch recovered the best skeleton in Canyon City,

Colorado, in 1883, after a year of digging. His find enabled paleontologists to study almost every part of *Allosaurus*'s skeleton. They discovered that this dinosaur, like most theropods, had bladelike, serrated teeth, powerful three-

▶ **Large numbers of the fierce meat-eater *Allosaurus* roamed the western United States in the Late Jurassic period.**

ALLOSAURUS AROUND THE WORLD?

There have been reports of *Allosaurus* remains discovered outside the Morrison Formation in the US, in places as far away as Africa, Siberia, Japan, and Australia. It is possible that *Allosaurus* did live in some other parts of the world during the Late Jurassic period. Some of the other Morrison dinosaurs, such as *Dryosaurus, Brachiosaurus,* and *Camptosaurus,* have been found in eastern Africa and Europe as well as western North America. Perhaps *Allosaurus* lived in these regions as well.

However, none of the reports of *Allosaurus* remains found outside the United States have been based on fossils that could come only from that dinosaur. Reports based on teeth or a bone or two could refer to many other sorts of tetanurans (stiff-tailed meat-eaters). Although it is possible that someday someone will find true *Allosaurus* remains in another country, for now it is just an American dinosaur.

fingered hands ending in eagle-like talons, strong three-toed feet, and a long tail. *Allosaurus* had a pair of small crests on its snout, and another pair just in front of its eyes.

Cleveland-Lloyd Quarry

After the turn of the century, many other museums began to discover *Allosaurus* specimens in Colorado, Wyoming, Montana, Oklahoma, and elsewhere. These ranged in size from small juveniles to giant adults, some possibly as big as *Tarbosaurus* or *Tyrannosaurus*.

Perhaps the most spectacular discovery was made in Utah, in what is now called the Cleveland-Lloyd Dinosaur Quarry. In 1927, Golden York, an assistant to University of Utah geologist Frederick Pack, found a treasure trove of over 800 dinosaur bones near the town of Cleveland.

Student paleontologist William Lee Stokes of Princeton University reopened the quarry in 1933. Over the next three years more than 1,500 bones were collected. Many years later, after Stokes had become head of the Department of Geology at the University of Utah, he began a new series of digs at the site. By the mid-1970s, thousands more bones had been found. Among these were the remains of at least 44, and possibly more than 50, different individuals of *Allosaurus*!

The typical tetanuran

Unlike most dinosaurs, which are known from incomplete fossils, *Allosaurus* is known from the entire skeleton. By examining its features, we can determine where it fits on the evolutionary tree of life.

Because it has an open hip socket and upright hind limbs that let it stand tall, we can tell that *Allosaurus* was a dinosaur.

In its hand, the second finger is the longest, the thumb claw is larger than the other claws, and the whole thumb sticks out at an angle: these features show that *Allosaurus* was a saurischian (lizard-hipped dinosaur).

As in all true theropods, only the middle three bones of the foot are used to support the creature's weight. The bone in front of the eye rises to the top of the skull (in *Allosaurus*, it supports a crest), and the dinosaur's teeth all lie in front of its eye socket. Its hand has only three fingers, and the tail has stiffening structures toward the back. These features show this dinosaur was a tetanuran (stiff-tailed meat-eater).

Close relations

Among the tetanurans are several other dinosaurs which seem to be closely related to *Allosaurus*. These include the earlier form *Cryolophosaurus*. They also include *Sinraptor*, which lived in China at the same time as *Allosaurus* lived in North America, and the later giants *Carcharodontosaurus*, *Giganotosaurus*, and *Acrocanthosaurus*. All these forms have extra openings in the nose bone and the upper jaw bone. They also have a modified bone at the back of the skull, where the neck joins the head.

All these dinosaurs can be grouped together and called the allosaurs, or three-fingered meat-eaters. Some paleontologists prefer to call these large meat-eaters carnosaurs.

Most paleontologists agree that these dinosaurs are more closely related to each other than to any other group of tetanurans, such as the tyrannosaurs (two-fingered tyrant dinosaurs), the ornithomimosaurs (ostrichlike dinosaurs), or the dromaeosaurs (clawed meat-eaters).

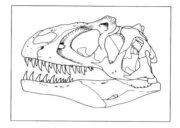

▲ *Allosaurus*'s skull was 3 ft (90 cm) long, and its powerful jaws contained more than 70 serrated teeth, each 3 in (7.6 cm) long.

Finding a wishbone

Scientists thought there was little to be learned from new skeletons of *Allosaurus*. However, even a dinosaur as well studied as *Allosaurus* can sometimes produce surprises. For example, in 1992, allosaur experts Daniel Chure and James Madsen reported that they had discovered a wishbone in *Allosaurus*.

A wishbone (or furcula) is formed when the collarbones of the shoulder join up and

▼ The sharp talons of a bald eagle grasp the top of a tree stump as the bird perches securely. The eagle's talons are remarkably similar to *Allosaurus*'s claws.

fuse together. Some birdlike theropods, such as *Oviraptor*, had wishbones, but this was the first time that an allosaur had been reported with a wishbone.

Why so sure?

Paleontologists could be sure they had discovered a wishbone in *Allosaurus* because they had a skeleton in which very few of the bones had been disturbed after death. Normally after an animal dies but before it gets buried there is some movement of the bones, by wind or water or scavenging animals. In this new specimen of *Allosaurus*, the wishbone was found in place: the shoulder part of the skeleton was still in the original position.

Not belly ribs

Now that they knew what an allosaur wishbone looked like, Chure and Madsen went back to study the *Allosaurus* remains found in the Cleveland-Lloyd Quarry. Among the many thousands of bones discovered in the quarry, they found many wishbones. These had previously been thought to be belly ribs, since paleontologists had not expected to find a wishbone in an allosaur.

The bird connection

Since that time wishbones have been found in many other tetanuran dinosaurs, including tyrannosaurs and dromaeosaurs. The presence of a wishbone in a tetanuran shows that birds are themselves just a specialized branch of the family tree of theropod dinosaurs.

SMITHSONIAN CATCH

One of the best skeletons of *Allosaurus* is on display at the Smithsonian Institution in Washington, DC, even though it was collected by Yale University's Peabody Museum of Natural History. How did this happen?

Yale's paleontologist, Othniel C. Marsh, was working partly for the US government's geological survey. After Marsh died, the government began planning a national museum of natural history. The Peabody Museum agreed to allow many of Marsh's specimens (including the *Allosaurus* skeleton) to be shipped to Washington, where they can still be seen today.

How did *Allosaurus* live?

Allosaurus was without a doubt a meat-eater. It could run very fast on its powerful back legs. It had very large jaws lined with long, bladelike teeth. These would have been useless for grinding plants, but very effective for slicing out chunks of flesh from prey.

Allosaurus's arms were of medium length for a theropod, but very powerfully built, with large areas where arm muscles could attach. The claws are long and curved, and resemble the talons of an eagle. It is likely that these claws were specially adapted for holding squirming prey.

What did it eat?

It is unlikely that even the largest *Allosaurus* could attack an adult sauropod like *Brachiosaurus* or *Apatosaurus*, but it may very well have caught and eaten the young of these dinosaurs. Other, smaller victims may have included *Stegosaurus*, *Camptosaurus*, and the ornithopod *Dryosaurus*. Like most meat-eaters today, *Allosaurus* probably scavenged from any carcass it came across.

DINOFACTS

Allosaurus
(AH-*luh-SORE-us*)

✳ **NAME:** *Allosaurus* means strange lizard
allos (strange, other) + sauros (lizard)

○ **FAMILY:** Saurischian
Theropod
Tetanuran

SIZE: about 28 ft (8.5 m) long; about 7.3 ft (2.2 m) high at the hip

WEIGHT: about 2 tons (1.8 tonnes)—about the same as 8 tigers

FOOD: meat

HABITAT: forests, uplands, lake shores, river valleys

WHERE: remains found in Colorado, Montana, New Mexico, Oklahoma, South Dakota, Utah, and Wyoming

🕑 **WHEN:** 140–135 million years ago in the Jurassic period

ALLOSAURUS

TRIASSIC	JURASSIC	CRETACEOUS
250 MILLION YEARS AGO	205 MILLION YEARS AGO	135 MILLION YEARS AGO / 65 MILLION YEARS AGO

CHECK THESE OUT!

Apatosaurus, Brachiosaurus, Camarasaurus, Camptosaurus, Jurassic period, Oviraptor, Stegosaurus, Theropods

Alxasaurus

Alxasaurus is the oldest of the therizinosaurs, a group of bizarre-looking big-clawed dinosaurs. Its remains showed that therizinosaurs were plant-eating descendants of meat-eating dinosaurs!

In early fall 1988, Chinese and Canadian paleontologists discovered the remains of two individual specimens of a medium-sized dinosaur in Mongolia's Alxa Desert. There were enough bones to make one almost complete skeleton. However, no skull bones were found except a lower jaw.

The new dinosaur was named *Alxasaurus*. It had a long, slender neck, powerful arms with large claws, short, heavy legs, and a short tail.

The Alxa dinosaur
In Beijing, Chinese paleontologist Dong Zhiming and Canadian paleontologist Dale Russell identified *Alxasaurus* as a theropod (two-legged meat-eater). From the shapes of the back, arm, and hip bones, they could tell *Alxasaurus* was one of the odd-looking big-clawed therizinosaurs.

Alxasaurus was also the earliest known therizinosaur. It was found in rocks from the mid-Cretaceous period. Other therizinosaurs had been found only in Late Cretaceous rocks.

The teeth in *Alxasaurus*'s lower jaw were small and had rounded bumps. They were unlike the large, jagged-edged

▶ Like other therizinosaurs, *Alxasaurus* had a stockier body and shorter legs than most theropods. It also had fearsome-looking claws on its hands. However, this scary beast ate only plants.

ALXA'S RELATIVES

Alxasaurus was not the first therizinosaur to be discovered. During the 1970s and early 1980s, the remains of several smaller kinds, such as *Erlikosaurus* and *Segnosaurus*, had been found in Mongolia.

At first, paleontologists were unsure to which dinosaur group these specimens belonged. They were put into their own group, the segnosaurs (named for *Segnosaurus*). However, this did not solve the problem of how they fitted in with dinosaur classification. Because they had long necks and ate plants, some scientists thought that the segnosaurs were related to the prosauropods (early long-necked plant-eaters). The discovery of *Alxasaurus* enabled them to put it, and the segnosaurs, into a new group, the therizinosaurs.

DINOFACTS

Alxasaurus
(ALK-suh-SORE-us)

☀ **NAME:** *Alxasaurus* means Alxa lizard
Alxa (Alxa Desert, where it was found) + sauros (lizard)

○ **FAMILY:**  Saurischian → Theropod → Tetanuran

✛ **SIZE:** about 12.5 ft (3.8 m) long; about 5 ft (1.5 m) high at the hip

⚖ **WEIGHT:** up to 850 lbs (385 kg)—about the same as a zebra

🥣 **FOOD:** plants

🏠 **HABITAT:** forests and lake shores

N ▲ **WHERE:** remains found in Mongolia

🕐 **WHEN:** 112–110 million years ago in the Cretaceous period

		ALXASAURUS ■
TRIASSIC	JURASSIC	CRETACEOUS
250 MILLION YEARS AGO	205 MILLION YEARS AGO	135 MILLION YEARS AGO ... 65 MILLION YEARS AGO

teeth typical of theropods such as the tyrannosaurs. Because of the teeth, scientists decided that even though it belonged to the meat-eating theropods, *Alxasaurus* ate plants.

Study of *Alxasaurus*'s wrist showed that it was related to the maniraptors (long-armed meat-eaters). This meant that *Alxasaurus* was a plant-eater descended from meat-eaters.

How did *Alxasaurus* live?
Digesting plants requires a lot more intestines than digesting meat. Because of this, *Alxa-saurus* had a wider body and shorter legs than most other

theropods. It may have used its strong arms and claws to pull down branches so that it could feed, much as sloths do today. Its claws would also have been useful as defensive weapons.

CHECK THESE OUT!

Cretaceous period, *Erlikosaurus*, Prosauropods, Saurischian dinosaurs, *Segnosaurus*, Theropods, Tyrannosaurs

Amargasaurus

Amargasaurus was a sauropod (long-necked plant-eater) first found in Argentina in the late 20th century. It is remarkable for the long spines along its backbone, which would have looked like a mane.

Fossil-hunters found an almost complete *Amargasaurus* skeleton in La Amarga canyon of Argentina. Like *Dimetrodon* (a mammal-like reptile with a tall back sail), *Amargasaurus* had long spines running along the back of its neck and the top of its back. No one is sure what the spines did.

A colorful flag

Amargasaurus's spines would not have grown from the skin like those of stegosaurs (plate-backed dinosaurs). Instead, *Amargasaurus*'s spines were very long parts of its neck and back bones. All paleontologists agree that these long back spines were not for protection; they were too fragile. Perhaps *Amargasaurus* used the spines for display.

When the dinosaur was alive, the spines would have been covered over by skin. Perhaps the skin was brightly colored as well. Many modern lizards have brightly colored patches and frills under their chins. They nod their heads, or do push-ups with their arms. These signals warn off other lizards or attract mates. Perhaps *Amargasaurus* made signals by showing off its mane.

A SPINY STORY

Amargasaurus was a member of a small group of sauropods called the dicraeosaurids (two-spined lizards). These were related to the diplodocids—dinosaurs like *Diplodocus* and *Apatosaurus*. Both the diplodocids and the dicraeosaurids had very unusual neural spines. The neural spine is the flat bone that sticks up and slightly backward at the very top of every backbone. The diplodocids and dicraeosaurids had a neural spine that split down the middle so that from the front it looked like the letter U. A strong, elastic cable of tissue ran along the base of the U shape and helped to hold up the head and neck. Dicraeosaurids had longer neural spines than those of any diplodocid, and *Amargasaurus*'s neural spines were the longest of all.

How *Amargasaurus* lived

The teeth of *Amargasaurus* tell us that it ate plants. The mane on its neck suggests that *Amargasaurus* lived in groups or small herds. Only animals that live in herds or have territories have evolved such large display structures; think of the horns of deer and antelope, or of the bright colors of many birds.

Like all sauropods, *Amargasaurus* moved on all fours. It probably could not run fast. Small groups of *Amargasaurus* would have moved slowly across open forest areas, feeding on trees and bushes.

▼ *Amargasaurus* may have used its neck ridge to attract a mate or to send signals to other dinosaurs.

CHECK THESE OUT!

Apatosaurus, Cretaceous period, *Diplodocus*, Mammal-like reptiles, Sauropods

DINOFACTS

Amargasaurus
(ah-MAR-gah-SORE-us)

▶ The skeleton of *Amargasaurus* shows the very long spines along the neck, back, and tail.

✳ **NAME:** *Amargasaurus* means Amarga lizard
Amarga (canyon in Argentina) + sauros (lizard)

○ **FAMILY:** Saurischian

Sauropodomorph

Sauropod

✥ **SIZE:** 40–50 ft (12.2–15.2 m) long; 13 ft (4 m) high at the hip

⬛ **WEIGHT:** 10–20 tons (9–18 tonnes)—about the same as 2–4 African elephants

FOOD: plants

HABITAT: broad, forested river valleys

N **WHERE:** remains found in Argentina

🕐 **WHEN:** about 130–120 million years ago in the Cretaceous period

AMARGASAURUS

TRIASSIC	JURASSIC		CRETACEOUS
250 MILLION YEARS AGO	205 MILLION YEARS AGO	135 MILLION YEARS AGO	65 MILLION YEARS AGO

Anatotitan

Anatotitan was a very large hadrosaur (duckbill dinosaur) with an amazingly long skull. It roamed the forests of Montana and South Dakota in the Late Cretaceous period.

The hadrosaurs were a group of ornithischian (bird-hipped) dinosaurs that evolved during the last part of the Cretaceous period. There were many kinds of hadrosaurs. *Anatotitan* was one of several types of very large, but rare, hadrosaurs.

Hadrosaurs are divided into two groups. The lambeosaurines (named for *Lambeosaurus*) had hollow crests; the hadrosaurines (named for *Hadrosaurus*) had small, solid crests or none at all. *Anatotitan* was a hadrosaurine.

Elongated skull

Anatotitan is known from one complete skull and three body skeletons. In 1975, paleontologist Michael Brett-Surman realized that most of the crestless duckbills that had been called *Anatosaurus* were really *Edmontosaurus*. However, one duckbill dinosaur was not like *Edmontosaurus* at all. Its skull was much too long and low. Its limbs were longer than those of

▶ With its wide mouth and strong jaw muscles, *Anatotitan* could munch its way through the toughest plants.

LARGE AND IN CHARGE

Scientists have learned that the amount of food an animal needs does not increase at the same rate as its body size. An elephant that is 1,000 times heavier than a rabbit does not need 1,000 times as much food. As an animal gets larger, the rate at which its body works gets slower. This means that large animals eat relatively less. The body of a tiny shrew works very fast, and this animal will die of starvation in less than a day if it does not eat. An elephant can go for several weeks without feeding.

It is thought that when plant-eating dinosaurs became large their bodies worked at a slower rate. This meant they could survive on much lower-quality plant food like ferns and pine needles. Perhaps being very large helped hadrosaurs like *Anatotitan* and *Edmontosaurus* survive in an increasingly crowded coastal environment.

Edmontosaurus, and it was the only hadrosaur to have teeth in less than half its jaw. In 1990, Brett-Surman named this dinosaur *Anatotitan*.

A wide mouth

All duckbill dinosaurs had a very wide snout that formed a shovel-shaped beak. Because of their wide mouths, the hadrosaurs could scoop up large mouthfuls of plants. Right behind their beaks were fleshy cheeks. *Anatotitan* would have snipped off leaves and stems with its beak, and chewed them up with its flat cheek teeth. Like other ornithopods (bird-footed dinosaurs), *Anatotitan* could swing its upper jaw outward like a hinge to grind its food efficiently.

How *Anatotitan* lived

Most paleontologists think that hadrosaurs lived in herds. Although there is no hard proof, scientists have found trackways that show a number of hadrosaurs moving in the same direction at the same time. Perhaps herds of *Anatotitan* slowly munched their way around the dense forests that covered much of their lowland habitat.

CHECK THESE OUT!

Cretaceous period, *Edmontosaurus*, Hadrosaurs, *Hadrosaurus*, *Lambeosaurus*, Ornithopods

DINOFACTS

Anatotitan

(ah-*NAH*-toe-*TIE*-tan)

▶ *Anatotitan*'s skull was almost 4 ft (1.2 m) long, longer than that of any other hadrosaur. It had no teeth in the front half of its jaws.

✳ NAME: *Anatotitan* means giant duck
anas (duck) + titan (giant)

○ FAMILY:  Ornithischian
Ornithopod
Hadrosaur

✥ SIZE: about 38 ft (11.6 m) long; 14 ft (4.3 m) high at the hip

⚖ WEIGHT: 4–5 tons (3.6–4.5 tonnes)—about the same as 4–5 North American bison

🥣 FOOD: plants

🏠 HABITAT: coasts and forested lowland areas with rivers and lakes

N↑ WHERE: remains found in Montana and South Dakota

🕐 WHEN: 70–65 million years ago in the Cretaceous period

			ANATOTITAN ▪
TRIASSIC	JURASSIC	CRETACEOUS	
250 MILLION YEARS AGO	205 MILLION YEARS AGO	135 MILLION YEARS AGO	65 MILLION YEARS AGO

Anchiceratops

Anchiceratops was a ceratopsian (horned dinosaur) that lived in North America in the Cretaceous period. As well as horns, *Anchiceratops* had a bony frill flaring upward and outward from the back of its head.

In 1912, US fossil–hunter Barnum Brown discovered part of a ceratopsian skull along the Red Deer River in Alberta, Canada. The fossil preserved all of the dinosaur's frill from the back edge to just in front of its eyes. Two years later, in 1914, Brown described the dinosaur. *Anchiceratops*'s frill was decorated with small triangle–shaped horns along the edge, so he named it *Anchiceratops ornatus* (decorated near to horn face).

Its large frill identified *Anchiceratops* as belonging to the chasmosaurine group of ceratopsians. The other main ceratopsian group, the centro-saurines, had smaller frills.

THE SECOND ANCHICERATOPS?

Canadian dinosaur collector Charles M. Sternberg discovered what may have been another kind (species) of *Anchiceratops* in 1929. He named his discovery *Anchiceratops longirostris* (the long-snouted *Anchiceratops*). The new species had smaller horns and a longer snout. As it and *Anchiceratops ornatus* seem to have lived alongside each other, perhaps they were males and females of the same species.

DINOFACTS

Anchiceratops
(ANG-ki-SER-ah-tops)

✳ **NAME:** *Anchiceratops* means near to horn face
anchi (near to) + keratos (horn) + ops (face)

⭕ **FAMILY:** Ornithischian
Ceratopsian

✥ **SIZE:** 15–20 ft (4.6–6 m) long; 6–7.5 ft (1.8–2.25 m) high at the hip

⚖ **WEIGHT:** 2–3 tons (1.8–2.7 tonnes)—about the same as 2–3 North American bison

🥣 **FOOD:** plants

🏠 **HABITAT:** lowland coastal floodplains

🧭 **WHERE:** remains found in Canada

▶ *Anchiceratops's* frill made up half the length of its complete skull.

🕐 **WHEN:** 80–70 million years ago in the Cretaceous period

			ANCHICERATOPS
TRIASSIC	JURASSIC	CRETACEOUS	
250 MILLION YEARS AGO	205 MILLION YEARS AGO	135 MILLION YEARS AGO	65 MILLION YEARS AGO

How did *Anchiceratops* live?
As an ornithischian dinosaur, *Anchiceratops* ate plants. It bit through stems with its beak and chewed them up with its cheek teeth. Like other ceratopsians, it may have lived and traveled in herds. *Anchiceratops* roamed across a wide range of habitats, from wetland cypress swamps to dry evergreen woodlands.

◀ *Anchiceratops* had two long horns above its eyes, a large nose horn, and a tall frill topped with small hornlets.

Anchiceratops would probably have used its frill only for display in mating contests. Its horns may have been used for fighting or defense. Most of the big predators, such as *Albertosaurus*, would usually have left *Anchiceratops* alone. Even the largest predators would have found a healthy *Anchiceratops* a dangerous meal.

CHECK THESE OUT!

Albertosaurus, Centrosaurus, Ceratopsians, Chasmosaurus, Ornithischian dinosaurs

Anchisaurus

Prosauropods (early long-necked plant-eaters) were very common in the Late Triassic period, and some of them managed to live on into the Early Jurassic period. *Anchisaurus* was one of these survivors.

Anchisaurus was a prosauropod from the Jurassic period. It was very like *Thecodontosaurus* from the Late Triassic period, some 20 million years earlier. It is called a primitive prosauropod because it has not evolved much. For *Anchisaurus*, this means that its body, skull, and teeth were more like those we would expect to find in the earliest prosauropods.

Like its ancestors

The ancestors of *Anchisaurus* and other prosauropods lived in the Middle to Late Triassic period and were some of the very first dinosaurs. All dinosaurs evolved from a small, meat-eating animal that walked and ran on its long back legs, and looked a bit like *Eoraptor*.

FOOTPRINTS IN THE MUD

The broad, flat valley floors where *Anchisaurus* lived had many shallow lakes and ponds. The mud and sand around these stretches of water would have become covered in the footprints of dinosaurs and other animals that came to drink. These footprints fossilized because during the Early Jurassic period it seems that Massachusetts and Connecticut had two seasons: dry and wet.

During the dry seasons, the water in the lakes and ponds would dry out, or evaporate. As the lakes got lower and lower, broad stretches of almost dry mud would be exposed to the air. Dinosaurs like *Anchisaurus* would have walked across these mudflats to get water to drink or to move to new feeding grounds. Eventually, the muddy ponds would dry out completely, leaving molded clay footprints. When it rained again, more mud would be washed down to cover and preserve the footprints.

We can see this ancestry clearly in *Anchisaurus* because its back legs are a good bit longer than its front legs. Most likely

▶ At about 8 ft (2.4 m) long, *Anchisaurus* was fairly small for a prosauropod.

DINOFACTS

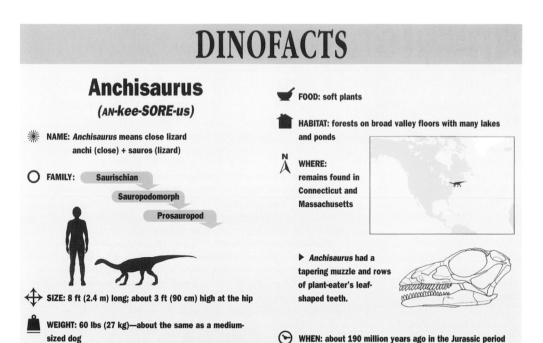

Anchisaurus
(AN-kee-SORE-us)

NAME: *Anchisaurus* means close lizard
anchi (close) + sauros (lizard)

FAMILY: Saurischian
Sauropodomorph
Prosauropod

SIZE: 8 ft (2.4 m) long; about 3 ft (90 cm) high at the hip

WEIGHT: 60 lbs (27 kg)—about the same as a medium-sized dog

FOOD: soft plants

HABITAT: forests on broad valley floors with many lakes and ponds

WHERE: remains found in Connecticut and Massachusetts

▶ *Anchisaurus* had a tapering muzzle and rows of plant-eater's leaf-shaped teeth.

WHEN: about 190 million years ago in the Jurassic period

ANCHISAURUS

TRIASSIC	JURASSIC	CRETACEOUS
250 MILLION YEARS AGO	205 MILLION YEARS AGO	135 MILLION YEARS AGO 65 MILLION YEARS AGO

Anchisaurus was able to run on its hind legs, like *Eoraptor*. It could also have walked on all four legs sometimes.

Because *Anchisaurus* had a very long back and a long neck, it would have been difficult for this dinosaur to keep its balance on just two legs when moving slowly. Think how much easier it is to balance on a bicycle when it is traveling quickly than when it is rolling very slowly. It is probable that the same principle of balance applied to prosauropods like *Anchisaurus*.

How did *Anchisaurus* live?
As a prosauropod, *Anchisaurus* would have eaten plants, but what kind? Scientists can make a few guesses. The fossils of *Anchisaurus* were found in sandstones and mudstones that were deposited in broad, flat valleys. These valleys appear to have had many lakes and ponds. Because of all the water, it seems likely that the plants in these valleys would have had softer, moister leaves than plants found in drier areas. The teeth of *Anchisaurus* do not appear to have been adapted for eating tough leaves and twigs. So it seems likely *Anchisaurus* would have eaten only soft leaves and stems.

CHECK THESE OUT!
Eoraptor, Footprints, Jurassic period,
Prosauropods,
Sauropodomorph dinosaurs,
Triassic period

Ankylosaurs

The ankylosaurs (armored dinosaurs) were plant-eaters of the Jurassic and Cretaceous periods. Although they lived with many meat-eaters, they were protected by their bony armor and massive tail-clubs.

The ankylosaurs (armored dinosaurs) were tanklike plant-eaters that lived in many parts of the world. Paleontologists divide most of them into two groups—the ankylosaurids (named for *Ankylosaurus*), which had bony clubs at the tips of their tails, and the nodosaurids (named for *Nodosaurus*), which had no tail-clubs. All the ankylosaurids lived in the Late Cretaceous, while nodosaurids lived

NO WAY OUT

Fossils of club-tailed ankylosaurs (ankylosaurids) are found only in western North America and in China and Mongolia. Why are ankylosaurid remains never found in eastern North America or in western parts of Asia?

During the Late Cretaceous period, when the ankylosaurids were alive, a large, shallow sea covered the middle of the North American continent. Animals in western North America could not easily cross this sea to go east. Nor could eastern Asian animals move west very easily because of many high mountain ranges.

However, between the North American sea and the Asian mountains, a land bridge linked the North American and Asian continents. Asian animals could move east into North America and North American animals could move west into Asia. Today water covers this ancient land bridge and separates the two continents.

▶ *Euoplocephalus* (an ankylosaurid) and *Edmontonia* (a nodosaurid) visit a waterhole in Late Cretaceous Montana.

Euoplocephalus

Edmontonia

DINOFACTS

Ankylosaurs
(an-KY-lo-SORES)

 NAME: Ankylosaur means fused lizard
ankylo (fused) + sauros (lizard)

 FAMILY: Ornithischian

Thyreophoran

 SIZE: 6.5–33 ft (2–10 m) long; 1–10 ft (30 cm–3 m) high at the hip

WEIGHT: up to 4 tons (3.6 tonnes)—about the same as 4 North American bison

FOOD: plants

HABITAT: forests

WHERE: remains found in North America, Asia, Europe, Australia, and possibly South America and Antarctica

WHEN: from about 185 million years ago in the Jurassic period to 65 million years ago in the Cretaceous period

		ANKYLOSAURS	
TRIASSIC	JURASSIC		CRETACEOUS
250 MILLION YEARS AGO	205 MILLION YEARS AGO	135 MILLION YEARS AGO	65 MILLION YEARS AGO

throughout the Cretaceous, and two kinds lived in the earlier Jurassic period. It is possible that the ankylosaurids evolved from the nodosaurids.

Two kinds of ankylosaurs, however, do not fit in either of these groups. *Minmi*, from Australia, and *Polacanthus*, from England and possibly North America, have features of both ankylosaurids and nodosaurids.

Living tanks

The ankylosaurs' armor was formed of bony plates, or osteoderms, growing in their skins. These large plates covered their heads, backs, parts of their tails, and the ankylosaurids' tail-clubs. The two pairs of osteoderms at the end of the tail grew into egg-shaped lumps fused to each other to form a solid structure.

To swing their clubs, ankylosaurids had very large tail muscles. Ankylosaurids shared their North American and Asian homes with the gigantic tyrannosaurs (two-fingered meat-eaters), so their tail-clubs would have been useful for defense.

How did ankylosaurs live?

As ornithischians (bird-hipped dinosaurs), ankylosaurs ate plants. Their skulls were very wide, and they had a turtle-like beak covering their snouts. Their bulky bodies probably housed large colonies of gut bacteria to help them to digest the large quantities of plants they ate each day.

CHECK THESE OUT!

Ankylosaurus, Cretaceous period, Edmontonia, Euoplocephalus, Hadrosaurs, Minmi, Nodosaurus, Panoplosaurus, Pinacosaurus, Polacanthus, Saichania, Sauropelta, Stegosaurs, Talarurus, Tarchia, Thyreophorans, Tyrannosaurs

37

Ankylosaurus

Ankylosaurus was a large plant-eating dinosaur that must have looked like a walking mountain. It gave its name to the ankylosaur group of dinosaurs, just as the tyrannosaurs are named for *Tyrannosaurus*.

Ankylosaurus was described by American paleontologist Barnum Brown in 1908. *Ankylosaurus* was among the last of the nonflying dinosaurs; it lived during the last two or three million years of the Cretaceous period.

How did *Ankylosaurus* live?
Paleontologists can tell from the shape of *Ankylosaurus*'s bones that it was well adapted

MYSTERIOUS CAVITIES

Like the first archosaurs, the ankylosaurs had many openings in the fronts of their skulls. Most animals have small chambers in their snouts that help them smell. Mammals, however, have greatly enlarged openings. This is because the sense of smell is very important for mammals. They also need to warm the air before they breathe it into their lungs. If a warm-bodied mammal were to breathe cold air deep into its lungs, it would chill its body too much.

Scientists are not sure why ankylosaurs had so many chambers in their snouts. What did they use them for? Was it so that they could smell certain plants and tell if they were edible? Were these dinosaurs warm-blooded, so that they needed to warm up the air before breathing it in? No one knows for sure.

◄ Mighty but slow-moving *Ankylosaurus* had so much armor it had no need to fear attack from hungry predators like the tyrannosaurs.

for a slow pace of life. The patterns of marks where muscles attached to bones show that although *Ankylosaurus*'s muscles were positioned to provide great force, they would have moved its legs and arms very slowly.

With its huge body, *Ankylosaurus* did not have to worry about being attacked. Adult elephants in Africa today are rarely attacked by lions—the largest predators there. In case *Ankylosaurus* ever did feel threatened, it had bony plates covering its neck, back, and the base of its tail.

Ankylosaurus also had a bony club at the end of its tail. *Ankylosaurus*'s strong tail muscles let it swing its clubbed tail quickly like a hammer. This would have been helpful as *Ankylosaurus* lived with the fierce predator *Tyrannosaurus*. *Ankylosaurus* gave its name to two groups of dinosaurs: ankylosaurs (armored dinosaurs) and ankylosaurids, armored dinosaurs that had tail-clubs.

Ankylosaurus had a beak at the front of its mouth to help bite and cut plants. *Ankylosaurus* also had cheeks. So it must have chewed its food a little. However, since its teeth were tiny and found only on the sides of its jaw, it probably ate only soft foods, and did not chew them very much.

CHECK THESE OUT!

Ankylosaurs, Archosaurs, Cretaceous period, Thyreophorans, Tyrannosaurs, *Tyrannosaurus*

DINOFACTS

Ankylosaurus
(an-KY-lo-SORE-us)

▶ *Ankylosaurus*'s tail-club was made of big bony plates fused to the bones at the end of the tail. It was swung from side to side by the strong muscles in the tail and could give a powerful blow.

top view   side view

✷ NAME: *Ankylosaurus* means fused lizard
ankylo (fused) + sauros (lizard)

○ FAMILY: Ornithischian
Thyreophoran
Ankylosaur

✥ SIZE: 33 ft (10 m) long; about 10 ft (3 m) high at the hip

⚖ WEIGHT: 4 tons (3.6 tonnes)—about the same as 4 North American bison

🥣 FOOD: plants

🏠 HABITAT: moist forests

N↑ WHERE: remains found in Montana and Wyoming, and in Alberta, Canada

🕐 WHEN: about 68–65 million years ago in the Cretaceous period

			ANKYLOSAURS ▪
TRIASSIC	JURASSIC	CRETACEOUS	
250 MILLION YEARS AGO	205 MILLION YEARS AGO	135 MILLION YEARS AGO	65 MILLION YEARS AGO

Antarctosaurus

Antarctosaurus was a sauropod (long-necked plant-eater) that lived in South America in the Late Cretaceous period. Paleontologists know it was a big dinosaur, but they do not know just how big.

Of all the Cretaceous sauropods that lived in South America, *Antarctosaurus* seems to have been one of the most widespread. Fossil-hunters have found its remains scattered across four South American countries.

Plant-eating titans

Antarctosaurus belonged to the group of armored sauropods called the titanosaurs. The titanosaurs lived mainly south of the equator in the Cretaceous period, when the northern sauropods, such as *Diplodocus* and its relatives, had died out. Some paleontologists believe that most titanosaurs, like *Saltasaurus*, had armor, although no armor has yet been found for *Antarctosaurus*.

The best specimen of *Antarctosaurus* was an incomplete skeleton found in Argentina. German paleontologist F. von Huene described these remains in 1929. The fossils included parts of the skull that covered the

BITS AND PIECES

When an animal dies in the wild, other animals gather to eat its carcass. These scavengers may pull off pieces and drag them away, spreading bones all over the place. Dinosaurs probably acted the same way, which is why paleontologists often do not recover whole skeletons. Scavengers are not paleontologists' only problem. If a dinosaur's dead body fell into a river, the currents in the river would break it up and scatter it. Also, the flowing water could mix together different bones from several very decayed animals. Sometimes paleontologists cannot tell whether the bones they are studying belong to one, two, or more animals.

Antarctosaurus's bones were just scattered shards. The pieces may belong to more than one type of animal. The ankle bones do not resemble the ankle bones of any other known sauropod. Scientists really need better specimens before they can be sure what *Antarctosaurus* was like.

▶ Like other sauropods, *Antarctosaurus* could have used its long neck to browse on leaves and stems high up in trees.

brain, part of the lower jaw with teeth, a single bit of neck bone, a shoulder blade, some bones from one arm and one leg, and part of the hip.

Antarctosaurus's back and tail bones were not found, so paleontologists do not have a good idea of how long its body would have been. However, scientists found enough arm and leg bones to get a good idea of what its limbs were like. Their size shows that *Antarctosaurus* was a very large animal. Because *Antarctosaurus* also had fairly slim leg and arm bones, this large sauropod was probably not as heavy as others of the same size.

How it lived

Antarctosaurus's teeth show that it ate plants, like all sauropods. *Antarctosaurus* may have lived in small herds as well. Paleontologists think that some kinds of sauropods lived in herds because they have found sauropod trackways that show small groups moving in the same direction. However, scientists have not yet found a group trackway specifically for *Antarctosaurus*.

CHECK THESE OUT!

Cretaceous period, *Diplodocus*, *Saltasaurus*, Saurischian dinosaurs, Sauropods, *Titanosaurus*

DINOFACTS

Antarctosaurus

(ant-ARK-tuh-SORE-us)

▶ Like all sauropods, *Antarctosaurus* had a small skull for its body size. Like *Diplodocus*, it had peglike teeth only at the front of its mouth.

✳ **NAME:** *Antarctosaurus* means Antarctic lizard antarctos (Antarctic) + sauros (lizard)

◯ **FAMILY:** Saurischian

Sauropodomorph

Sauropod

⊕ **SIZE:** perhaps 66–100 ft (20–30 m) long; perhaps 14 ft (4.3 m) high at the hip

⚖ **WEIGHT:** about 20–30 tons (18–27.2 tonnes)—about the same as 4–6 African elephants

⚕ **FOOD:** plants

🏠 **HABITAT:** broad, forested river valleys

N **WHERE:** remains found in Argentina, Brazil, Chile, and Uruguay

🕐 **WHEN:** about 80–65 million years ago in the Cretaceous period

			ANTARCTOSAURUS
TRIASSIC	JURASSIC	CRETACEOUS	
250 MILLION YEARS AGO	205 MILLION YEARS AGO	135 MILLION YEARS AGO	65 MILLION YEARS AGO

41

Apatosaurus

Apatosaurus is one of the most famous dinosaurs in the world, but most people know it by its old name, *Brontosaurus*. This large sauropod (long-necked plant-eater) lived in the Jurassic period.

In 1883, US paleontologist Othniel C. Marsh published the first complete reconstruction of a sauropod. He called it *Brontosaurus*. Unfortunately he used the leg bones and skull of *Camarasaurus*, which gave a false picture of the new dinosaur.

Only later did paleontologists realize that *Brontosaurus* was the same as *Apatosaurus*, a sauropod that Marsh had named in 1877. Because the name *Apatosaurus* had been used first, the name *Brontosaurus* is no longer used.

Diplodocus cousin

Apatosaurus was one of the diplodocid sauropods (closely related to *Diplodocus*). Like other diplodocids it had long, thin, pencil-like teeth crowded

▶ Like other diplodocid sauropods, *Apatosaurus* had a slender-tipped tail that it may have cracked like a whip to scare predators.

together at the front of its mouth, and a long, low head.

Apatosaurus was not as long as *Diplodocus*, but its bones were much thicker and stronger. Shorter, stockier *Apatosaurus* must have weighed more than the taller, leaner *Diplodocus*. Some of *Apatosaurus*'s backbones that

lay between its hipbones were fused. This seems to have strengthened the animal's back.

Some paleontologists have suggested that diplodocids could raise themselves on to their hind legs to feed on taller trees. The strengthening of the backbones at the hips could have helped *Apatosaurus* to support its huge weight on its hind legs.

LIVING TOGETHER

The Late Jurassic rocks of the western United States have produced several different kinds of large sauropods. These different kinds appear to have lived at roughly the same time. There would have been a great struggle for all these large animals to get enough to eat—or would there?

When several kinds of animals share a habitat for a long time, they gradually evolve features that prevent their ways of life from being too similar. If closely related, but slightly different, animals eat different foods, they can all find food to eat in the same habitat. This way many more different types of animals can live together in the same habitat.

It seems that the different types of sauropods found ways to share their Jurassic habitat. Different sized sauropods would have eaten leaves and twigs from different heights. Different types of teeth in different sauropods suggest that each species also ate slightly different types of plants or parts of plants.

How did *Apatosaurus* live?

Fossil trackways show that *Apatosaurus* may have lived in small groups. The trackways show a small number of *Apatosaurus*, not more than about 20 animals, moving together in a single direction.

A group of large plant-eating *Apatosaurus* would soon eat all the plants in a particular area. These dinosaurs must have had to move from place to place to find enough to eat.

Whiplash tails

Apatosaurus's tail had a long, thin tip. In 1997 some scientists suggested that *Apatosaurus* could have cracked its tail like a gigantic whip to scare off attackers, threaten others of its own kind, or attract mates. However, such behavior could have hurt too much to do regularly.

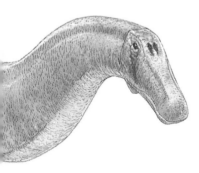

CHECK THESE OUT!

Camarasaurus, Collecting dinosaurs, *Diplodocus*, Footprints, Jurassic period, Sauropods

DINOFACTS

Apatosaurus
(*ah-PAT-oh-SORE-us*)

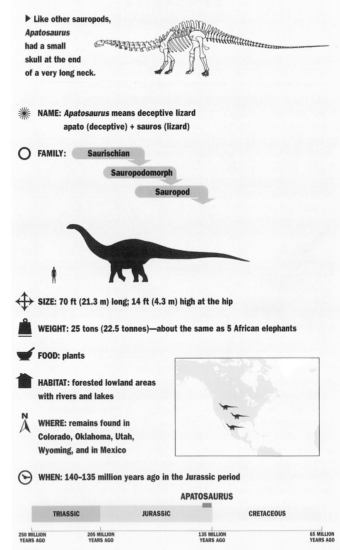

▶ Like other sauropods, **Apatosaurus** had a small skull at the end of a very long neck.

✸ NAME: *Apatosaurus* means deceptive lizard
apato (deceptive) + sauros (lizard)

○ FAMILY: Saurischian

Sauropodomorph

Sauropod

⊕ SIZE: 70 ft (21.3 m) long; 14 ft (4.3 m) high at the hip

⚖ WEIGHT: 25 tons (22.5 tonnes)—about the same as 5 African elephants

FOOD: plants

HABITAT: forested lowland areas with rivers and lakes

N⬆ WHERE: remains found in Colorado, Oklahoma, Utah, Wyoming, and in Mexico

🕐 WHEN: 140–135 million years ago in the Jurassic period

	APATOSAURUS		
TRIASSIC	JURASSIC		CRETACEOUS
250 MILLION YEARS AGO	205 MILLION YEARS AGO	135 MILLION YEARS AGO	65 MILLION YEARS AGO

Archaeopteryx

Archaeopteryx lived in Germany in the Late Jurassic period and was an amazing dinosaur. It was an avialan, a close relative of modern birds. It had feathers and a beak, and it could fly.

The very first *Archaeopteryx* skeleton was found in 1861, just two years after the publication of Charles Darwin's book *On the Origin of Species*, in which Darwin explained his theory of evolution. This theory is now widely accepted, but at that time it was not. The discovery of *Archaeopteryx*, which was halfway between a dinosaur and a modern bird, was important in persuading many people to accept the idea of evolution.

The first hint that anything like *Archaeopteryx* existed was the discovery in 1861 of a single feather in the Solnhofen quarry in Germany. Since then, fossil-hunters have

▶ *Archaeopteryx* takes to the air. It may not have been as good at flying as modern birds, and it may have needed its long tail to help it stay level.

LEARNING TO FLY

Did *Archaeopteryx*'s ancestors first fly by gliding down from trees, or by running really fast on the ground and sticking out their feathery wings? Some paleontologists ask how a two-legged dinosaur could get to the top of a tree in the first place? Also, how could it balance on branches if it did not have the gripping feet of modern birds?

Perhaps, then, *Archaeopteryx*'s ancestors first flew, not from a tree, but from the ground. Perhaps the ancestors of *Archaeopteryx* were fast-running, ground-living animals. The feathers on their wings may have been used to help the animals catch their food, or for display to signal to others of their own kind (species). As these animals ran along the ground, they could have stuck out their feathered arms. The speed of the animal, combined with the air flowing over the wings, may have allowed these running dinosaurs to glide a little bit off the ground. The animals may have eventually discovered that by flapping their arms they could stay in the air, covering greater distances. Over many generations, animals could have evolved with the feathered wings that we see in *Archaeopteryx*.

found seven *Archaeopteryx* skeletons; the last one was found in 1992.

Bird relatives

So what kind of animal was *Archaeopteryx*? *Archaeopteryx* was the earliest known avialan. The avialans are a group of dinosaurs that include birds and their closest relatives.

Avialans belong to a larger groups of dinosaurs called the maniraptors (long-armed dinosaurs). Other maniraptors include the dromaeosaurs

(clawed meat-eaters) such as *Dromaeosaurus* and *Deinonychus*. Dromaeosaurs were close relatives of *Archaeopteryx* and the avialans, and shared several features with them. For example, both dromaeosaurs and avialans had special wrist bones that let them fold their hands away as they ran.

Also, in the hips of most saurischian (lizard-hipped) dinosaurs, the pubis sticks out forward and down from the hip socket. However, in *Dromaeosaurus* and *Deinonychus*, the pubis pointed straight down. In *Archaeopteryx*, it even pointed slightly backward as it does in modern birds.

Turning tail

The tails of *Dromaeosaurus* and *Deinonychus* were different from other dinosaurs' tails, too. They were stiffened with bony rods, and paleontologists think dromaeosaurs used them to turn quickly while running. Modern flying birds use their tails to turn in the air. The only difference is that birds' tails are not bony rods but stiff tail feathers controlled by muscles. *Archaeopteryx*'s long, feathered tail is the perfect halfway point between the short, stiff, feathered tail of modern birds and the long, stiff, unfeathered tail of the dromaeosaurs.

Feathered fossil

The most important feature of *Archaeopteryx* is its feathers. Not only did *Archaeopteryx* have feathers like a bird, but the feathers on its arms were shaped exactly like the feathers of modern flying birds.

All feathers have a central rod (shaft) with soft, flexible bristles (vanes) on either side. In flying birds, the wing feather vanes are wider on one side of the shaft than on the other. *Archaeopteryx*'s wing feathers were shaped the same way. Even under a microscope, *Archaeopteryx*'s feathers look like modern bird feathers.

The feathers of birds and the scales of lizards and snakes are not all that different. Both start out as little bumps in the upper layers of the skin, and both are made from fingernail-like material called keratin. If you look at a bird's foot, you will see that the skin looks like the scales on a lizard's foot.

Why feathers?

Paleontologists wonder why *Archaeopteryx*'s ancestors would have had feathers even though

they did not fly. Some paleontologists think that the feathers trapped in the dinosaurs' body heat and stopped them from getting cold. Others believe that feathers kept sunlight off the dinosaurs' skin and stopped them from overheating.

Whichever explanation is correct, at some time these animals would have discovered that the feathers on their arms allowed them to glide a little through the air. Over millions of years, animals would have evolved with the wings and flight muscles that we see in *Archaeopteryx*.

Although *Archaeopteryx*'s feathers indicate that it could fly, its chest bones were not as strongly built as those of later flying avialans and modern flying birds. These all have a

big, deep, flat breastbone running down the front of their chests to which their powerful flight muscles attach.

▲ A flying squirrel spreads the flaps of skin between its arms and legs and leaps from the treetops. Perhaps *Archaeopteryx* flew something like this.

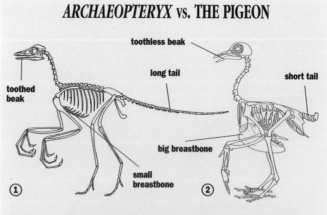

ARCHAEOPTERYX vs. THE PIGEON

toothless beak

long tail

short tail

toothed beak

big breastbone

small breastbone

① ②

The skeletons of *Archaeopteryx* (1) and a pigeon (2) show how birds differ from primitive avialans. *Archaeopteryx* had a toothed beak, a small breastbone, and a long tail. A pigeon has no teeth, a big breastbone for its flight muscles, and a short tail.

46

Birds also have a large wishbone, which helps them to flap their wings. When the flight muscles pull the wings down, the wishbone pushes the wings back up again ready for the next downstroke. *Archaeopteryx* did not have a big breastbone and had only a small wishbone. *Archaeopteryx* could probably flap its wings weakly, but it would not have been a powerful flier.

How *Archaeopteryx* lived
Some paleontologists think that *Archaeopteryx* clambered around in trees, searching for insects to eat. The claws on its fingers would have helped it to climb.

These claws are very similar to the wing claws of young hoatzins. The hoatzin is a tropical South American bird, and its young use their wing claws to help them climb.

Being able to climb trees could also explain how *Archaeopteryx*, or its ancestors, first came to fly. Several kinds (species) of gliding frogs, lizards, and mammals live in trees today. These animals can all form broad, flat surfaces that enable them to jump from the trees and glide through the air.

The gliding frogs have extra-wide hands and feet with webbing between the fingers and toes. The lizards can spread out their ribs to form a flat surface. The mammals, such as flying squirrels, have flaps of skin along their sides that join their arms and legs.

All these gliding animals climb up trees, jump off branches, and glide down to the branches or trunks of other trees. *Archaeopteryx*'s ancestors could have done the same, except that instead of just skin they had feathers to form the surface for gliding. However, there is no way to tell for sure.

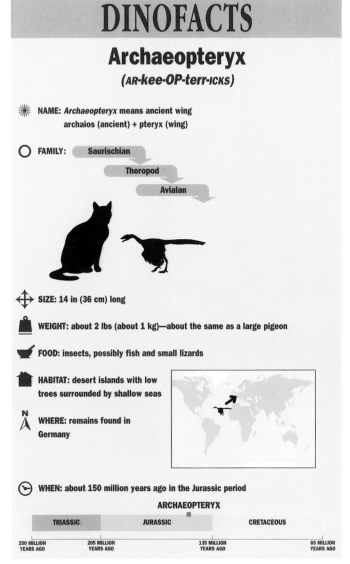

DINOFACTS

Archaeopteryx
(AR-kee-OP-terr-ICKS)

✳ **NAME:** *Archaeopteryx* means ancient wing
archaios (ancient) + pteryx (wing)

○ **FAMILY:** Saurischian
→ Theropod
→ Avialan

✛ **SIZE:** 14 in (36 cm) long

⚖ **WEIGHT:** about 2 lbs (about 1 kg)—about the same as a large pigeon

🥣 **FOOD:** insects, possibly fish and small lizards

🏠 **HABITAT:** desert islands with low trees surrounded by shallow seas

N↑ **WHERE:** remains found in Germany

🕐 **WHEN:** about 150 million years ago in the Jurassic period

ARCHAEOPTERYX

TRIASSIC	JURASSIC	CRETACEOUS
250 MILLION YEARS AGO	205 MILLION YEARS AGO	135 MILLION YEARS AGO · 65 MILLION YEARS AGO

CHECK THESE OUT!
Avialans, Birds, *Deinonychus*, Dromaeosaurs, *Dromaeosaurus*, Jurassic period, Saurischian dinosaurs

Archosaurs

The archosaurs, or ruling lizards, appeared at the boundary between the Permian and Triassic periods, some 250 million years ago. They evolved into the pterosaurs, the crocodiles, and the dinosaurs.

Soon after the largest known extinction, about 250 million years ago, a group of small, meat-eating animals started to evolve into a wide variety of running and flying animals— the archosaurs, the ruling reptiles or lizards. The Mesozoic dinosaurs were the most famous members of this group, but archosaurs are still with us today. We call them crocodiles and birds.

The archosaurs, with the lepidosaurs (scaly reptiles like lizards, snakes, and the tuatara), make up the group of egg-laying animals known as diapsids. Diapsids have two pairs of openings in their skulls behind their eye sockets.

Holes in the head

Archosaurs differ from lepidosaurs in two important ways. The most obvious difference is in their skulls. Besides having openings behind the eye sockets, archosaurs also have a large opening on either side of the skull in front of the eye sockets. Lepidosaurs do not have these extra openings.

Most archosaurs also tend to hold their limbs more upright than lepidosaurs. Their hip and shoulder sockets open more downward instead of sideways as they do in

lizards. When most archosaurs walk, their limbs are held beneath the body. In lepidosaurs, the arms and legs stick out to the sides, and the hands and feet swing out far from the body as the animals move. Having the legs held beneath the body made it easier for the leg muscles of archosaurs to support it. Dinosaurs were archosaurs, and they could never have grown as big as they did if they had not had the archosaur type of legs, hips, and shoulders.

Rulers of the land and air

In the Triassic period, archosaurs evolved many different body forms and lived in many different habitats. Dinosaurs were just one of many

archosaur groups, but they were the most successful. The dinosaurs were the ruling large land animals in the Jurassic and Cretaceous periods.

Archosaurs also evolved flapping flight twice: once as pterosaurs, and again as avialans (birds and their closest relatives). During the Triassic, Jurassic, and Early Cretaceous periods, the pterosaurs were the ruling large flying animals. In the Late Cretaceous period, modern birds took over.

AIR HEADS

The most recognizable feature of archosaurs is the large opening on either side of the skull just in front of the eyes. What did these extra openings do? Perhaps they made the skull lighter without making it any weaker. The snout of the skull was strong enough by itself, and the area around the eyes was also solidly braced.

Perhaps when the archosaurs evolved, most of the world's land was hot and dry. There would not have been a lot of fresh water around for the animals to drink. To get rid of excess salt in their bodies, the archosaurs may have evolved with skull openings to fit special salt-removing glands. Modern seabirds have such glands.

However, many scientists believe the holes held hot air. Many birds and crocodiles also have air vents in their skulls that help them keep a cool head. Scientists think that the extra space near the snout may improve the sense of smell, while space at the back of the skull might improve hearing.

▼ Two *Saurosuchus* spar in Triassic Argentina. *Saurosuchus* was a huge, crocodile-like archosaur and the fiercest land predator of its time.

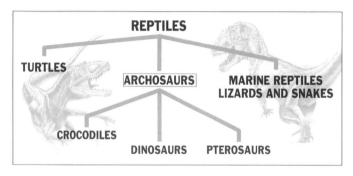

◄ The archosaurs contain the crocodiles, the pterosaurs, and the dinosaurs. Like marine reptiles, lizards, and snakes, archosaurs are diapsid reptiles. Turtles are anapsids, with no hole in the skull behind the eye sockets.

Early archosaurs

The earliest known archosaur was *Archosaurus*, which lived in Russia about 260 million years ago in the Permian period. *Archosaurus* hunted and ate meat or fish, like most of the early archosaurs.

Archosaurus would have lived like modern crocodiles. Its legs would have sprawled out to the sides, and it would have had the same numbers of holes

▼ *Petrolacosaurus* (1) was the earliest known diapsid reptile and the ancestor of the archosaurs. It had openings behind the eye sockets but not in front. It lived in Kansas in the Carboniferous period (360–290 million years ago). *Euparkeria* (2) was a diapsid archosaur that lived in South Africa in the Triassic period. It had openings behind and in front of the eyes.

in its skull as all later diapsid archosaurs. Fossils of close relatives of *Archosaurus* have been discovered in rocks of Early Triassic age in South Africa and China.

South Africa also has very good fossils of an early land-living archosaur called *Euparkeria*. This animal was about 2 ft (60 cm) long and had a large skull with long, sharp teeth. Some paleontologists think that *Euparkeria* could run quickly on its long hind legs, just as the collared lizard of the western United States does today.

Big archosaurs

The first large archosaur fossils also come from Early Triassic rocks of South Africa and

China. These big archosaurs were the erythrosuchians, or crimson crocodiles. Their name comes from the red color of the rocks in which their fossils are found. Despite their name, these were not true crocodiles but only crocodile-like. Their wrists, hips, shoulders, and skulls were slightly different from those of true crocodiles, which first appeared in the Jurassic period.

Erythrosuchians must have been very dangerous hunters. One of them, *Erythrosuchus*, had a skull about 3 ft (90 cm) long! Its total length was almost 16 ft (5 m), and its jaws were lined with long, sharp teeth. *Erythrosuchus* could grow to a large size because its limbs had taken on a more vertical position under its body.

Paleontologists recognize *Erythrosuchus* as the first case of the evolution of large body size in archosaurs. The dinosaurs continued this

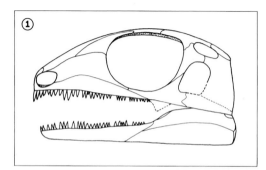

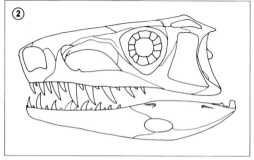

evolution of large bodies tens of millions of years later, eventually giving rise to the giant sauropods (long-necked plant-eaters), such as *Apatosaurus* and *Brachiosaurus*.

Monster archosaurs

During most of the Triassic period, the archosaurs were the ruling meat-eaters. The rauisuchians were a worldwide group of fierce, running, meat-eating archosaurs. They would have looked a bit like long-legged crocodiles, but while most modern crocodile skulls are quite flat, rauisuchian skulls were narrow and deep.

This shape made the skulls of rauisuchians very strong. Because long roots anchored their long, serrated teeth firmly to their jaws, the rauisuchians could rip through the toughest hides. *Saurosuchus* (lizard crocodile) was a 27 ft (8.2 m) rauisuchian from Argentina that would have attacked and eaten just about any land animal it could catch.

In the lakes and rivers of the Triassic period, phytosaurs, or leaf lizards, were the most dangerous predators. They were distant relatives of crocodiles. They looked very similar to the modern gharial, a type of fish-eating crocodile. In crocodiles, the nostrils are at the tip of the snout; in phytosaurs, the nostrils were on a raised bump of bone just in front of the eyes.

Here come the dinosaurs!

While the rauisuchians were prowling the land and the phytosaurs were hunting the

waters, smaller meat-eating archosaurs, such as the ornithosuchids, or bird crocodiles (so named because they walked on two legs and had three-toed feet) also roamed. Ornithosuchid skeletons are very similar to dinosaur skeletons. Some scientists think they might be the ancestors of the dinosaurs. Others think the dinosaurs evolved from the lagosuchids, or lake crocodiles,

a group of small two-legged archosaurs. They lived in Argentina in the Middle Triassic period, just before the first dinosaurs, *Eoraptor* and *Herrerasaurus*, appeared.

CHECK THESE OUT!

Crocodiles, Dinosaurs, *Eoraptor*, *Herrerasaurus*, Pterosaurs, Reptiles, Triassic period

FOSSIL FACTS

Archosaurs
(ARE-keh-SORES)

✴ **NAME:** Archosaur means ruling lizard
archo (ruler) + sauros (lizard)

◯ **FAMILY:** Reptile

✛ **SIZE:** (including birds) huge variation from 2.3 in (5.8 cm) to 120 ft (37 m) or more long

⚖ **WEIGHT:** (including birds) huge variation from 0.06 oz (1.6 g) to 50 tons (45 tonnes) or more—or from a bee hummingbird to 10 African elephants

🥣 **FOOD:** meat, fish, insects, eggs, plants

🏠 **HABITAT:** all habitats, but only birds can live in the polar regions and temperate seas and oceans

🧭 **WHERE:** remains found worldwide

🕐 **WHEN:** from 260 million years ago in the Permian period to today

			ARCHOSAURS →		
DEVONIAN	CARBONIFEROUS	PERMIAN	TRIASSIC	JURASSIC	CRETACEOUS
410 MILLION YEARS AGO	360 MILLION YEARS AGO	290 MILLION YEARS AGO	250 MILLION YEARS AGO / 205 MILLION YEARS AGO	135 MILLION YEARS AGO	65 MILLION YEARS AGO

Argentinosaurus

Argentinosaurus was a huge titanosaur that lived in Argentina in the Cretaceous period. The titanosaurs were armored sauropods (long-necked plant-eaters) that lived mainly south of the equator.

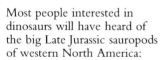

Most people interested in dinosaurs will have heard of the big Late Jurassic sauropods of western North America: animals such as *Brachiosaurus* and *Seismosaurus*. However, these animals were not alone in their great size. The titanosaur *Argentinosaurus* was a giant, but not of the Jurassic period; it lived later, in the Cretaceous period.

Argentine paleontologists José Bonaparte and Rodolfo Coria described *Argentinosaurus* in 1993. Unfortunately, they did not have a complete skeleton, only a few backbones, the tops of the hips, one piece of rib, and one lower leg bone. These pieces do, however, give a good idea of how big *Argentinosaurus* was.

Long bones

The lower leg bone of *Argentinosaurus* was 5 ft (1.5 m) long. Using the leg of another South American sauropod, *Patagosaurus*, as a model, scientists can estimate the total length of *Argentinosaurus*'s legs from the one bone they have found.

Based on *Patagosaurus*, they estimate that the upper leg bone of *Argentinosaurus* was between 7 ft and 8 ft (about 2.4 m) long. Adding on a bit for the length of the ankle and foot bones, scientists have

▶ *Argentinosaurus* was a giant armored sauropod that browsed the forests of Cretaceous South America.

worked out that *Argentinosaurus*'s leg was an astonishing 16 ft (5 m) long, compared with a leg length of about 14 ft (4.3 m) in *Brachiosaurus*. *Seismosaurus*'s leg length has not been estimated because no leg bones have been found.

How it lived

Argentinosaurus was a sauropod, so paleontologists know that it ate plants. However, because no teeth or pieces of jawbone have been found, they cannot tell what sorts of plants it ate. It probably browsed on leaves from the tallest trees, reaching up with its long neck.

LAND OF THE GIANTS

Cretaceous rocks in Patagonia have produced some giant dinosaurs. Besides *Argentinosaurus*, this region has produced the huge meat-eater *Giganotosaurus*, and *Megaraptor*, the largest claw-footed predator ever found. *Megaraptor* may be a dromaeosaur. Scientists are not sure.

The Late Jurassic rocks of western North America are the only other source of giant dinosaur fossils. These rocks are filled with giant sauropods like *Brachiosaurus*, *Supersaurus*, and *Seismosaurus*, and the huge, poorly known predators *Torvosaurus* and *Saurophaganax*. Both places were once dry floodplains with many evergreens. Perhaps this type of setting might have been particularly suitable for large sauropods, which in turn were food for very large predators.

Like *Saltasaurus*, another titanosaur, *Argentinosaurus* probably had small armor plates set in its skin. Fossil-hunters have not yet found any *Argentinosaurus* armor, though.

CHECK THESE OUT!

Brachiosaurus, Cretaceous period, *Patagosaurus*, *Saltasaurus*, Saurischian dinosaurs, *Titanosaurus*

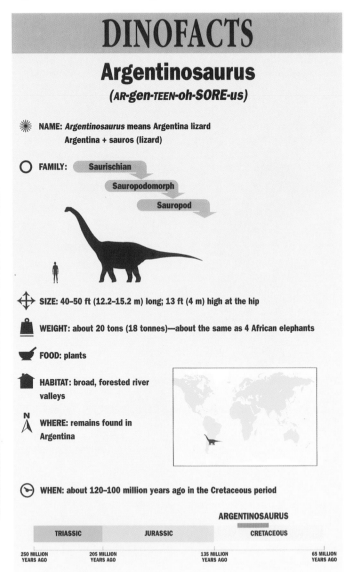

DINOFACTS

Argentinosaurus
(AR-gen-TEEN-oh-SORE-us)

✳ **NAME:** *Argentinosaurus* means Argentina lizard
Argentina + sauros (lizard)

◯ **FAMILY:** Saurischian → Sauropodomorph → Sauropod

⬌ **SIZE:** 40–50 ft (12.2–15.2 m) long; 13 ft (4 m) high at the hip

⚖ **WEIGHT:** about 20 tons (18 tonnes)—about the same as 4 African elephants

🥣 **FOOD:** plants

HABITAT: broad, forested river valleys

Ⓝ **WHERE:** remains found in Argentina

🕑 **WHEN:** about 120–100 million years ago in the Cretaceous period

ARGENTINOSAURUS

TRIASSIC	JURASSIC	CRETACEOUS
250 MILLION YEARS AGO	205 MILLION YEARS AGO	135 MILLION YEARS AGO

65 MILLION YEARS AGO

Avialans

What do you call a dinosaur with wings and feathers? You call it an avialan. Avialans have been around since the Jurassic period. They are still with us today. Modern avialans are called birds.

In 1861, fossil-hunters found the remains of an amazing creature in Germany. It looked a little like a dinosaur. However, the fossil showed the creature had feathers. It also had long arms, which scientists thought may have been wings. They named the creature *Archaeopteryx*. It was the earliest known avialan.

Birds of a feather
Archaeopteryx had feathers and wings, but it wasn't a bird. Although it had some birdlike traits,

Archaeopteryx also had traits that birds do not have. It had teeth and a long tail. Birds do not have teeth, and their tail bones are very short. Birds are just a type of avialan. Although *Archaeopteryx* may not have been the first bird, it was one of the first known avialans.

Avialan moms and dads
Scientists believe avialans evolved from small meat-eating dinosaurs called coelurosaurs. The first avialans had many dinosaur traits, such as teeth, long tails, and solid bones. Later avialans such as

▼ *Iberomesornis* argues with *Concornis*, another avialan. *Iberomesornis* had a fleshy tail. It was shorter than a dinosaur's tail but longer than that of a modern bird.

Concornis

Iberomesornis

Scientists cannot agree on how avialans first flew. Did the first flying dinosaur take off from the ground? Was it perhaps running fast after an insect and then leaped into the air to catch it? Scientists think this explanation is possible.

There is also another explanation. We know *Archaeopteryx* climbed trees. Did the first flyers glide out of the tree tops like modern flying squirrels? Until more fossils are found, scientists cannot tell which explanation is right.

Iberomesornis (shown left) lost these traits. For example, they had a much shorter tail.

During the Cretaceous period, a group of avialans appeared that had short tails and no teeth. Their light, hollow bones made it easier for them to fly. These new kind of avialans were called birds.

How did avialans live?
The first avialans lived much like birds today. *Archaeopteryx* lived in trees beside marshes and fed on insects. Others, such as *Mononykus,* could not fly. It spent most of its time foraging for food on the ground.

Other avialans preferred the sea. *Hesperornis* was like a huge penguin. It also couldn't fly, so it floated on the ocean, diving after fish.

CHECK THESE OUT!

Archaeopteryx, *Avimimus*, Birds, Cretaceous period, *Hesperornis,* Jurassic period, Maniraptors, *Mononykus,* Saurischian dinosaurs, Theropods

DINOFACTS

Avialans
(AY-vee-YAY-lans)

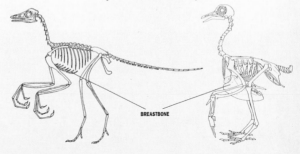

BREASTBONE

▲ The skeleton of *Archaeopteryx.* Look how dinosaurlike it is with its long tail and clawlike fingers.

▲ A pigeon has a huge breastbone to hold its flight muscles. It has no teeth, and its bony tail has almost vanished.

✷ NAME: Avialans means birds
Avis (bird)

○ FAMILY: Saurischian
Theropod
Maniraptor

✥ SIZE: wide variation from 2.5 in (6 cm) to 3.3 ft (1 m) long

FOOD: insects and fish

HABITAT: cliffs, seashores, wetlands

N
↑ WHERE: remains found worldwide

WHEN: 155–65 million years ago in the Jurassic and Cretaceous periods

		AVIALANS	
TRIASSIC	JURASSIC		CRETACEOUS
250 MILLION YEARS AGO	205 MILLION YEARS AGO	135 MILLION YEARS AGO	65 MILLION YEARS AGO

Avimimus

Many dinosaurs looked more like birds than reptiles. *Avimimus*, if it existed, was one of the most birdlike dinosaurs. It would have had a big brain for its size and was probably pretty smart.

In the 1970s, Russian scientist Sergei Kurzanov found some strange fossil bones in Mongolia. He said they belonged to a creature called *Avimimus*. The bones puzzled Kurzanov. They were clearly the bones of a dinosaur.

▶ The picture shows how *Avimimus* may have looked. It had very long legs for a theropod (two-legged walker) and ran very fast.

Yet, this dinosaur had many birdlike traits. Was *Avimimus* a dinosaur or a bird?

Kurzanov studied the bones closely. Many bones were missing, so he had to make guesses.

Wings and feathers

Kurzanov compared the front leg bones of *Avimimus* to the wing bones of a bird. He thought that they were similar. He also found strange scars on the bones that could have held

feathers. Kurzanov wondered: did *Avimimus* have wings and feathers like a modern bird?

This question still puzzles scientists. If *Avimimus* did have wings, they were too small and weak for flying. If *Avimimus* had feathers, they were probably used more for warmth than for flight.

Was *Avimimus* the first bird?

No. *Avimimus* was more a birdlike dinosaur than a bird. Several non-birdlike theropods (two-legged walkers) had

Kurzanov thought that *Avimimus* had feathers. Other scientists disagreed with this idea. Is it bad when scientists disagree? No. Quarrels like this one are usually good for science. Rather than argue, scientists gather evidence to support their idea. Over time, one idea wins the argument; the other idea loses. In the end everyone wins because they learn new knowledge.

feathers, so the presence of feathers in *Avimimus* does not make it a bird.

More importantly, scientists are not sure if *Avimimus* ever lived. They think it may be a hodgepodge of several dinosaurs.

How did *Avimimus* live?

Avimimus, if it ever existed, was a small, saurischian (lizard-hipped) theropod. Theropods were hunters. However, Kurzanov believed *Avimimus* had a beak, so he imagined that the dinosaur ate insects rather than meat.

Avimimus would have been hunted by meat-eating dinosaurs, such as *Troodon* and *Velociraptor*. Amazingly, these predators were also near relatives of *Avimimus*. *Velociraptor* was a fast and successful predator that hunted in packs.

CHECK THESE OUT!

Archaeopteryx, Avialans, Birds, Cretaceous period, Saurischian dinosaurs, Theropods, *Troodon*, *Velociraptor*

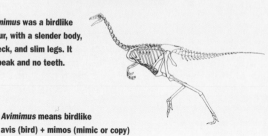

DINOFACTS

Avimimus
(*AAH-vee-MY-mus*)

▶ *Avimimus* was a birdlike dinosaur, with a slender body, long neck, and slim legs. It had a beak and no teeth.

✳ **NAME:** *Avimimus* means birdlike
avis (bird) + mimos (mimic or copy)

◯ **FAMILY:** Saurischian

Theropod

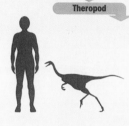

✛ **SIZE:** 5 ft (1.5 m) long; 2 ft (60 cm) high at the hip

WEIGHT: 31 lbs (14 kg)—about the same as a large turkey

FOOD: meat or insects

HABITAT: arid steppe and desert

N ↗ **WHERE:** remains found in Mongolia and China

🕐 **WHEN:** 85–75 million years ago in the Cretaceous period

			AVIMIMUS
TRIASSIC	JURASSIC	CRETACEOUS	
250 MILLION YEARS AGO	205 MILLION YEARS AGO	135 MILLION YEARS AGO	65 MILLION YEARS AGO

Bactrosaurus

When it was discovered, *Bactrosaurus* puzzled scientists. It seemed to be a hadrosaur, or duckbill dinosaur. But something was missing. Where was the crest?

Bactrosaurus was one of the first duckbill dinosaurs. Or was it? Duckbill dinosaurs were a group of plant-eating dinosaurs that lived during the Cretaceous period. Most duckbills had a bump on their head called a crest. Some crests were hollow. Others were solid. *Bactrosaurus* seemed to have no crest. So why was it a duckbill?

To find an answer to this question, scientists looked at other parts of this dinosaur's body. They found that like other hadrosaurs (duckbills), *Bactrosaurus* had no thumbs, no front teeth, it had a duckbill mouth, and it had an *Iguanodon*-shaped body (*Iguanodon* was an earlier plant-eating dinosaur).

Bactrosaurus was an early hadrosaur. It lived at least 10 million years before most other hadrosaurs. *Bactrosaurus* was also smaller and less advanced than some other hadrosaurs.

How did *Bactrosaurus* live?
Bactrosaurus lived in what is now Asia. It was discovered on a trip to the Gobi desert in Mongolia in 1923. *Bactrosaurus* was a browser. It probably ate huge amounts of rough plant material. This may have included twigs and leaves the dinosaur plucked from trees and bushes with its strong beak. The animal would have ground the leaves and twigs with its teeth.

Escaping enemies
Bactrosaurus was not a fighter. Like deer, it had sharp sight, smell, and hearing to look out

HADROSAUR TEETH

All hadrosaurs had many teeth. They were densely arranged on both sides of the upper and lower jaws in rows, each composed of hundreds of teeth. The teeth would have been capable of grinding and breaking even the toughest woody twigs.

▲ The lower jaw had hundreds of teeth; the upper jaw did too.

for predators. When approached by a meat-eating dinosaur, it used its long, powerful legs to run away.

New findings

Recent dinosaur digs have found new head bones for *Bactrosaurus*. These bones show that *Bactrosaurus* may have had a small crest after all.

CHECK THESE OUT!

Cretaceous period, Hadrosaurs, *Iguanodon*, Ornithischian dinosaurs, Ornithopods

◀ *Bactrosaurus* probably spent much of its time on all fours. Scientists also believe it could walk on two legs, too.

DINOFACTS

Bactrosaurus
(BAK-*truh-SORE-us*)

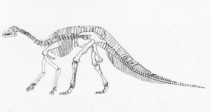

▶ The skeleton of *Bactrosaurus* shows how large the dinosaur's tail was. The tail would have helped it to balance when it moved on two legs.

✳ NAME: *Bactrosaurus* means lizard from Bactria
Bactria (province of Asia) + sauros (lizard)

○ FAMILY: Ornithischian
Ornithopod
Hadrosaur

✛ SIZE: 13–20 ft (4–6 m) long; 5 ft (1.5 m) high at the hip

⚖ WEIGHT: 1–3 tons (0.9–2.7 tonnes)—about the same as 1–3 American bison

🥣 FOOD: plants

HABITAT: dryish upland floodplains

N↑ WHERE: remains found in Mongolia

🕐 WHEN: 95–85 million years ago in the Cretaceous period

BACTROSAURUS

TRIASSIC	JURASSIC	CRETACEOUS
250 MILLION YEARS AGO	205 MILLION YEARS AGO	135 MILLION YEARS AGO 65 MILLION YEARS AGO

Barapasaurus

Barapasaurus was a plant-eating heavyweight that wandered the lowland forests of India in the Early Jurassic period. Fossil-hunters first found remains of this giant in 1959.

Scientists often find it difficult to decide to which group a dinosaur belongs. This happens especially when the dinosaur has traits of more than one group. When scientists first studied *Barapasaurus*, they could not tell if it had been a sauropod or a prosauropod.

Barapasaurus was a lot like the sauropods. Sauropods were huge, long-necked, long-tailed, plant-eating dinosaurs—like *Apatosaurus*, for example.

The fossil was very old, however, so *Barapasaurus* could have been a prosauropod. Prosauropods were the ancestors of the sauropods. They were the first dinosaurs with long enough necks to eat from trees.

NOT THE FIRST SAUROPOD

Although paleontologists believe sauropods evolved in the Late Triassic period, they have not yet found enough fossil remains to prove this theory. *Barapasaurus* is one of the earliest sauropods for which scientists have found fossil remains. It appeared about 40 million years after scientists believe the very first sauropods existed.

Barapasaurus probably looked like most other sauropods, with a long neck and tail, and a bulky body. However its skeleton was different from that of sauropods like *Diplodocus* and *Apatosaurus*, which evolved later. *Barapasaurus* had dents on the outside of its neck and back bones. This adaptation would have made its huge neck bones a little lighter, and easier to lift. Later sauropods like *Diplodocus* and *Apatosaurus* had neck and back bones that had holes in them; these were lighter still.

▶ No one knows exactly what *Barapasaurus* looked like because no complete skulls or feet have been discovered. However, experts can make a good guess from what they know about other similar dinosaurs.

Most were smaller than the sauropods. *Plateosaurus* was a prosauropod.

No head
One way scientists can tell the difference between prosauropods and sauropods is by looking at their heads and feet. Prosauropods had smaller eyes than did sauropods. Their forefeet were like hands; sauropods' forefeet looked like elephant feet.

No one has found a *Barapasaurus* skull, or any of its feet. However, by studying its other bones, scientists found that *Barapasaurus* was not only a sauropod, it was also a close relative of *Cetiosaurus*.

How did *Barapasaurus* live?
Barapasaurus probably spent almost all its time feeding. Lumbering from tree to tree, it picked off pound upon pound of leaves from high branches with its teeth.

Barapasaurus may have lived in herds. In 1961, fossil-hunters found the remains of more than 300 *Barapasaurus* in a small area of southern India. It is unusual to find so many bones in one place. Perhaps a herd of *Barapasaurus* drowned while crossing a river.

DINOFACTS

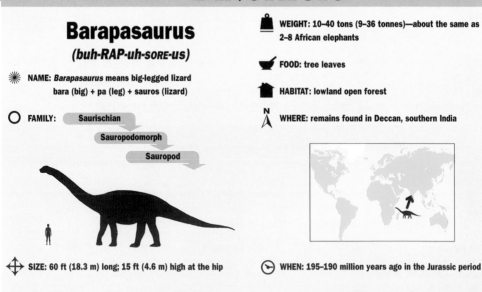

Barapasaurus
(buh-RAP-uh-SORE-us)

✳ **NAME:** *Barapasaurus* means big-legged lizard
bara (big) + pa (leg) + sauros (lizard)

⭕ **FAMILY:** Saurischian
→ Sauropodomorph
→ Sauropod

✥ **SIZE:** 60 ft (18.3 m) long; 15 ft (4.6 m) high at the hip

⚖ **WEIGHT:** 10–40 tons (9–36 tonnes)—about the same as 2–8 African elephants

⚗ **FOOD:** tree leaves

🏠 **HABITAT:** lowland open forest

🧭 **WHERE:** remains found in Deccan, southern India

🕐 **WHEN:** 195–190 million years ago in the Jurassic period

BARAPASAURUS

TRIASSIC	JURASSIC	CRETACEOUS
250 MILLION YEARS AGO	205 MILLION YEARS AGO	135 MILLION YEARS AGO	65 MILLION YEARS AGO

Barosaurus

Barosaurus was a sauropod—a big, long-necked, long-tailed, plant-eating dinosaur. It was named by the American paleontologist Othniel C. Marsh.

American fossil-hunters first found *Barosaurus* in 1890 in South Dakota. They dug up bones that looked a lot like those of another sauropod they already knew, called *Diplodocus*. However, these bones were different. Each neck bone was almost 4 ft (1.2 m) long! This had to be a brand new dinosaur.

Barosaurus had longer neck bones than *Diplodocus*. Not surprisingly, its neck was longer, too—up to 30 ft (9 m) long! That's twice as long as

▼ In 1908, almost 20 years after *Barosaurus* was first discovered in North America, a team found more *Barosaurus* bones in Tanzania in Africa.

most giraffe necks are today. How did such a long neck help *Barosaurus*?

Food! *Barosaurus* lived near many other sauropods. Like a giraffe, because of its longer neck, *Barosaurus* could feed on the leaves that other sauropods could not reach.

Rearing up on hind limbs
Could *Barosaurus* stand on its hind legs? A display in the American Museum of Natural History in New York shows *Barosaurus* doing just that. It is protecting its young from a meat-eating *Allosaurus*. Scientists think *Barosaurus* probably could have reared up. Elephants can stand on their

hind limbs, so why not sauropods? Scientists are not sure *Barosaurus* did rear up, though. They cannot tell from the dinosaur's bones and they have found no *Barosaurus* footprints that prove it.

How did *Barosaurus* live?
Barosaurus wandered through swampy forests. Because of its huge size and small head, it probably spent most of its time feeding so that it could get enough food to stay alive.

CHECK THESE OUT!

Allosaurus, Diplodocus, Jurassic period, Saurischian dinosaurs, Sauropods

ROCKS IN YOUR STOMACH

Scientists discovered 64 polished stones with one *Barosaurus* skeleton from Colorado. What were they doing there? Scientists believe that the dinosaur deliberately swallowed them.

Once inside the animal's stomach, the stones may have helped to grind up the tough plant food that *Barosaurus* ate. *Barosaurus* had teeth, but they were for snipping leaves from trees. The dinosaur swallowed leaves and shoots whole and relied on the stones, or gastroliths, to grind its food up in its stomach.

DINOFACTS

Barosaurus
(BAR-*oh*-*SORE*-us)

▲ *Barosaurus* is very rare. Only five skeletons have been found, and they were all missing pieces. The most complete skeleton was discovered at Dinosaur National Monument in Utah.

❋ **NAME:** *Barosaurus* means heavy lizard
baros (heavy) + sauros (lizard)

◯ **FAMILY:** Saurischian
Sauropodomorph
Sauropod

✚ **SIZE:** 60 ft (18.3 m) long; 15 ft (4.6 m) high at the hip

WEIGHT: 10–40 tons (9–36 tonnes)—about the same as 2–8 African elephants

FOOD: plants

HABITAT: lowland open forest

WHERE: remains found in South Dakota, Wyoming, Colorado in the United States, and Tanzania in East Africa

🕐 **WHEN:** 150–135 million years ago in the Jurassic period

BAROSAURUS

TRIASSIC	JURASSIC	CRETACEOUS
250 MILLION YEARS AGO	205 MILLION YEARS AGO	135 MILLION YEARS AGO / 65 MILLION YEARS AGO

Baryonyx

Scientists first studied *Baryonyx* during the 1980s. Some think it might have been a scavenger. Others believe it hunted fish. Who do you think is right?

When scientists first discovered *Baryonyx*, they soon realized that it looked different from other meat-eating dinosaurs. First, its head was an unusual shape. Meat-eating dinosaurs normally had fairly short snouts. *Baryonyx* had a long snout, though, like a crocodile. The snout turned down slightly at the end, and the animal's nostrils were a long way from the tip of its snout. *Baryonyx* also had many, many small pointed teeth—twice as many teeth as most other meat-eating dinosaurs. Scientists think that *Baryonyx* may have been closely related to *Spinosaurus*, another meat-eating dinosaur that lived in the Cretaceous period, too.

Claws

Besides its snout and teeth, other parts of *Baryonyx* were also unusual for a meat-eater. Hunters such as *Tyrannosaurus* normally had an S-shaped neck. *Baryonyx* had a long neck, which it usually held straight. *Baryonyx* had large, strong arms, too. The most unusual part of *Baryonyx*, though, was the huge claw bone found with the dinosaur's remains. The claw bone was 12 in (30 cm) long. When the dinosaur was alive, the claw bone would have been covered in tough horn, like a huge fingernail. It would have looked twice as long!

The discovery of this bone caused the newspapers to nickname the new dinosaur Claws. The experts were puzzled. Did the claw belong on the animal's hand or on its foot? Also, how many of these claws did

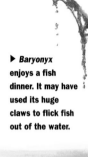

▶ *Baryonyx* enjoys a fish dinner. It may have used its huge claws to flick fish out of the water.

Baryonyx have? *Baryonyx* probably had two claws, one on each hand, but scientists are still not sure.

What *Baryonyx* ate

So why did *Baryonyx* look so unusual? Food! *Baryonyx* could have eaten fish. The long, crocodilelike snout and many pointed teeth would have been ideal for catching slippery fish.

Having nostrils far from the tip of its snout would have made it easier to eat fish, too. *Baryonyx* would have been able to put its head underwater to look for fish and still be able to breathe. It could not have done that if its nostrils had been near the tip of its snout, like those of *Tyrannosaurus*.

The head of *Baryonyx* looked a little like that of a phytosaur, a crocodilelike reptile related to the dinosaurs. Phytosaurs lived in the Triassic period (250–205

MR. WALKER'S *BARYONYX*

Can you imagine having a dinosaur named after you? That is exactly what happened to Mr. William Walker. In January 1983, Mr. Walker made an amazing discovery in southern England. He was a plumber, but he searched for fossils in his spare time. During one of his fossil hunts, he came upon the remains of a huge claw. He guessed the claw must belong to a new kind of dinosaur. He took his find to the Natural History Museum in London.

That spring, the museum sent a team of experts to dig in the area where Mr. Walker had found the claw. The scientists discovered much of the dinosaur's skeleton. They cleaned up the bones and studied what they had. Yes, it was definitely a new dinosaur. The scientists called it *Baryonyx*, and that is what it is usually known as. However, the dinosaur's full name is *Baryonyx walkeri*, in honor of Mr. Walker.

million years ago) and are thought to have eaten fish.

There is more evidence that *Baryonyx* may have eaten fish. Remember the big, strong arms that *Baryonyx* had? Why would a dinosaur need such strong arms when it probably walked on two legs? Or did *Baryonyx* crouch on all fours on river banks as it fished? Some experts think so.

What about the dinosaur's neck? Well, this would probably have helped *Baryonyx* reach down into the water to snap up fish. On top of all this evidence, scientists have even found fish scales in the same rocks as *Baryonyx* remains.

Did it eat fish?

Not necessarily. There are a few things that have not been explained. First, if *Baryonyx* caught fish with its teeth, why did it have claws on its hands? Well, say the scientists who think *Baryonyx* was a fish-eater, they might

have been extra tools for catching fish. *Baryonyx* might have used them to flick fish out of the water. Grizzly bears use their claws in this way to catch salmon today.

That sounds fine, except for one thing. *Baryonyx* could weigh four times as much as the largest grizzly bear ever found. Would it not have been a bit too slow to catch fish? Yes, say a second group of scientists. *Baryonyx* was not a fish-eater, they say. It was a scavenger. In other words, *Baryonyx* fed on the bodies of land animals that were already dead.

A very long nose

What makes these scientists think that *Baryonyx* was a scavenger? Again it has to do with the dinosaur's unusual looks. This second group of scientists explain them differently. They think that *Baryonyx*'s long snout was ideal for poking about inside the bodies of dead dinosaurs. It would have used its small, pointed teeth to grip the slippery guts. It would then have feasted on the soft, gooey bits. The nostrils far back from the tip of its snout would let it breathe while its head was buried deep in the carcass.

What about *Baryonyx*'s strong arms and neck? Those could have been just as useful for scavenging as for catching fish. Standing on all fours meant *Baryonyx* didn't have to bend over to feed on the ground. Its long neck helped it reach its food.

Skin-ripping claws

Why did *Baryonyx* have big claws if it was a scavenger? Simple, reply the second group of scientists. *Baryonyx* probably used its claws to tear open the dead body on which it fed.

The real *Baryonyx*

Did *Baryonyx* hunt for fish, or scavenge for left-overs? Probably both possibilities are right. Scientists are always seeking evidence to support their ideas. Sometimes their ideas are right. Sometimes they discover something new.

▲ Did *Baryonyx* go fishing like modern grizzly bears? Some scientists say yes.

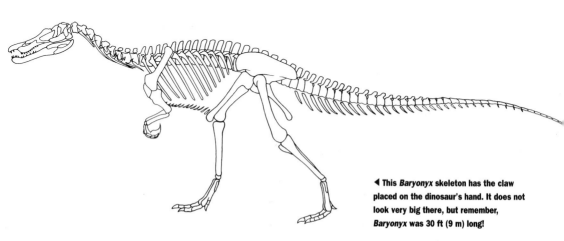

◄ This *Baryonyx* skeleton has the claw placed on the dinosaur's hand. It does not look very big there, but remember, *Baryonyx* was 30 ft (9 m) long!

Baryonyx was too large to live entirely as a scavenger. It certainly could not get by just on soft, gooey guts. However, neither could an animal as big as *Baryonyx* survive on a diet of fish alone.

Baryonyx probably ate a mixture of food. It would have scavenged when it got the chance, as do most meat-eating animals today. *Baryonyx* probably also fed on fish when they were plentiful.

Baryonyx the hunter

Baryonyx could probably have hunted and killed other dinosaurs too. *Baryonyx* lived on river floodplains and in lowlands. It shared its world with dinosaurs such as *Hylaeosaurus*, *Iguanodon*, and *Hypsilophodon*. *Baryonyx* may have fed on these plant-eating animals. Even with its small teeth and weak jaws, *Baryonyx* could probably have killed the youngest, oldest, and weakest of these dinosaurs.

Killer claws

Baryonyx's claws could have been weapons. They were probably big enough to wound or kill a dinosaur. If *Baryonyx* did use its claws as weapons, it means they almost definitely belonged on the dinosaur's hands. *Baryonyx* was too big to jump up and attack with its feet. Raptors such as *Deinonychus* and *Velociraptor* could attack with their feet, but they were smaller and lighter than *Baryonyx*.

CHECK THESE OUT!

Archosaurs, Cretaceous period, Crocodiles, Deinonychus, Hypsilophodon, Iguanodon, Saurischian dinosaurs, Spinosaurus, Theropods, Tetanurans, Velociraptor

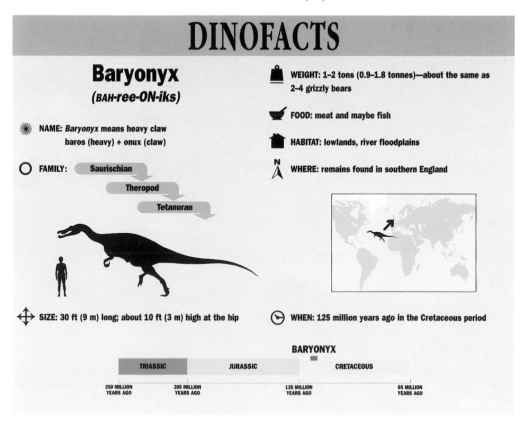

DINOFACTS

Baryonyx
(BAH-ree-ON-iks)

✳ **NAME:** *Baryonyx* means heavy claw
baros (heavy) + onux (claw)

⬤ **FAMILY:** Saurischian
→ Theropod
→ Tetanuran

WEIGHT: 1–2 tons (0.9–1.8 tonnes)—about the same as 2–4 grizzly bears

FOOD: meat and maybe fish

HABITAT: lowlands, river floodplains

WHERE: remains found in southern England

SIZE: 30 ft (9 m) long; about 10 ft (3 m) high at the hip

WHEN: 125 million years ago in the Cretaceous period

BARYONYX

TRIASSIC	JURASSIC	CRETACEOUS
250 MILLION YEARS AGO	205 MILLION YEARS AGO	135 MILLION YEARS AGO · 65 MILLION YEARS AGO

Birds

The dinosaurs died out 65 million years ago—or did they? The last dinosaurs are still with us today in the form of birds. Birds are living, breathing, theropod dinosaurs.

Birds are the only avialans still alive today. They share traits with the extinct avialans, but differ from them in some ways. For example, all living birds have feathers, wings, and beaks. Many avialans, like *Archaeopteryx*, also had feathers, wings, and beaks. However, most early avialans also had teeth; modern birds do not.

Dinosaurs among us
Because birds descended from dinosaurs, we say they are dinosaurs. Just like we say people are primates because, like apes, we descended from primates. From penguins to parakeets, birds are dinosaurs.

Like dinosaur, like bird
Today there are over 10,000 species of birds. This is more than 10 times the number of dinosaur species for which scientists have found remains.

Scientists study birds to discover more about the behavior of these animals' extinct ancestors. Birds build and guard nests because their dinosaur ancestors did. Like today's birds, *Oviraptor* also rearranged and sat on its eggs while they developed.

The first birds
The earliest modern birds we have fossils of lived with *Triceratops*

and *Tyrannosaurus* in the Late Cretaceous period. They were closely related to the grebes and loons of today. Grebes and loons paddle on lakes and dive for fish. Because of their small size and fragile skeletons, fossils of early birds are very rare.

After the Mesozoic Era (the age of dinosaurs), birds became more numerous and widespread. During the Cenozoic Era (the age of mammals, in

▼ *Hesperornis* was a toothy, fish-eating avialan that could not fly. *Presbyornis* was a true bird, it had no teeth. Its closest living relatives are the bird group called screamers.

Presbyornis

Hesperornis

BIRDS AND FEATHERS

Feathers are made from the same material as reptile scales. A typical bird feather has a strong rod in the middle, and thinner, hairy parts called barbs sprouting from it.

Feathers can be found on both birds and more primitive avialans. Although *Archaeopteryx* had feathers, it lived before the first true bird.

which we are living now), some strange birds appeared.

Diatryma was 6.5 ft (2 m) tall. It had a head the size of a horse's, and a toucan-sized, hooklike beak. It could not fly. It lived on the forest floors of North America and Europe 57–45 million years ago. So little is known about *Diatryma* that scientists cannot tell whether it ate meat or plants.

The phoruschracids ate meat. These fierce birds preyed on medium-sized mammals that looked like antelope. Only a few phoruschracids could fly.

Scientists found phoruschracid fossils in South America and Florida in rocks that are between 40 million and 2 million years old. South America was also home to a bird that was as big as a fighter plane. With its 25 ft (7.6 m) wingspan, *Argentavius* was the largest flying bird that ever lived. The heaviest bird of all was the flightless elephant bird, which weighed about 1,200 lbs (545 kg). It lived on the African island of Madagascar until about 10,000 years ago.

CHECK THESE OUT!

Archaeopteryx, Avialans, Eggs and babies, *Hesperornis*, Maniraptors, *Oviraptor*, Saurischian dinosaurs, Theropods

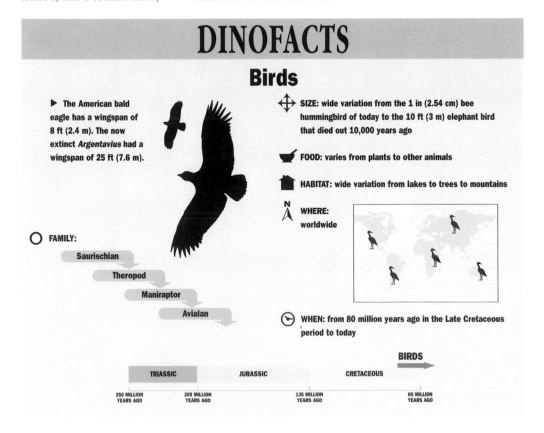

DINOFACTS
Birds

▶ The American bald eagle has a wingspan of 8 ft (2.4 m). The now extinct *Argentavius* had a wingspan of 25 ft (7.6 m).

○ FAMILY:
- Saurischian
- Theropod
- Maniraptor
- Avialan

✛ SIZE: wide variation from the 1 in (2.54 cm) bee hummingbird of today to the 10 ft (3 m) elephant bird that died out 10,000 years ago

FOOD: varies from plants to other animals

HABITAT: wide variation from lakes to trees to mountains

N WHERE: worldwide

WHEN: from 80 million years ago in the Late Cretaceous period to today

BIRDS

TRIASSIC	JURASSIC	CRETACEOUS	
250 MILLION YEARS AGO	205 MILLION YEARS AGO	135 MILLION YEARS AGO	65 MILLION YEARS AGO

Brachiosaurus

Brachiosaurus was a huge, plant-eating sauropod, with a long neck and tail. It lived in the Jurassic period in what is now North America and Africa. Like all real giants, *Brachiosaurus* was rare.

Believe it or not, scientists once thought *Brachiosaurus* lived mostly in water. Why? Because it was so big.

Scientists thought that *Brachiosaurus* was too heavy to move on land. So, they argued, it must have lived in water. The water would have supported the dinosaur's huge weight. *Brachiosaurus* could then have moved around easily.

Prehistoric snorkeling?

Brachiosaurus had a very long neck. It had huge nostrils near the top of its head. Could the dinosaur have breathed through these nostrils while it walked along the beds of lakes and rivers? Could the nostrils have worked like the snorkels people use when they swim underwater?

Until the 1950s, some scientists thought so. They believed *Brachiosaurus* walked underwater holding the top of its head just above the surface. This way, the dinosaur could breathe as it searched for food.

Scientists now know that *Brachiosaurus* could not have snorkeled. If the dinosaur had walked underwater with its neck held straight up, its body would have been in water almost 40 ft (12.2 m) deep.

Brachiosaurus had a big, strong chest. Even so, the crushing pressure of the water would have been too great for the dinosaur. *Brachiosaurus* would not have had the strength to inflate its lungs. It could not have breathed.

How did it move?

Brachiosaurus was a land animal. It was one of the largest land animals that ever lived. How did the dinosaur survive when it was so huge? How could it carry such a lot of weight around?

Brachiosaurus was not as heavy as its size first suggested. Like many other sauropods, its backbones had holes in them. The bones were still strong, but they were also very light.

Even so, *Brachiosaurus* could not run fast. It could not run like a galloping horse—that is with all four feet off the ground at one time. If the dinosaur had tried, the weight of its enormous body would have broken its legs.

However, *Brachiosaurus* may have been able to trot like an elephant. Even that would have made the ground shake!

How did *Brachiosaurus* live?

Brachiosaurus behaved like an

▶ ***Brachiosaurus* got its name, arm lizard, because its forelegs were longer than its hind legs.**

AN ESCALATOR NECK

There is no doubt that the neck of *Brachiosaurus* was designed to be held straight upward. However, animals whose necks are raised high above their hearts like this are faced with a problem. How do they get blood from their heart all the way up their neck to their brain? Sauropods had deep chests. These contained a powerful heart to pump blood around their massive bodies. Their chests also contained large lungs to make sure there was plenty of oxygen in the blood to help their muscles work properly.

However, sauropod hearts probably needed a little extra help to deliver the blood to their faraway brain. Giraffes have specialized muscles and valves that pump their blood all the way up their neck to their brain. Scientists think sauropods like *Brachiosaurus* probably had similar muscle pumps.

enormous giraffe. The dinosaur's extra-long neck was strong and flexible. Like a giraffe, *Brachiosaurus* could also hold its neck up straight.

Like all sauropods, *Brachiosaurus* ate only plants. The dinosaur spent most of its life moving from tree to tree, biting off leaves and shoots. Its long neck allowed it to get at food that other, smaller sauropods could not reach.

Brachiosaurus may even have reared up on its hind legs to reach juicy leaves in the high branches. However, it is not likely that the dinosaur reared up often. It could already reach very high. Despite its light backbones, *Brachiosaurus* was still a pretty heavy dinosaur. Rearing up like an angry stallion would have put an enormous strain on its legs. Of course, just by looking at the bones of elephants, it would be hard to predict all the tricks they can do in the circus. For example, elephants are very heavy animals, yet they can still stand on their hind legs. Actually, it was easier for *Brachiosaurus* to rear up than it is for an elephant. *Brachiosaurus* carried more weight on its hind legs than on its forelegs. When it reared, its back end acted like the heavy end of a seesaw. Elephants are the opposite. They carry more weight on their forelegs. Elephants have to heave all that weight into the air to rear up onto their hind legs.

The Colorado *Brachiosaurus*
The American fossil-hunter Elmer G. Riggs was the first to discover *Brachiosaurus*. He found the remains of the dinosaur near Fruita, Colorado, in rocks called the Morrison Formation. *Brachiosaurus* was an unusual sauropod, Riggs realized. Its forelegs were much longer than its hind legs. Therefore, the dinosaur's back must have sloped from the front down to its rear.

A dinosaur family tree
Scientists like to put dinosaurs into family trees. It helps them

figure out who evolved from whom. Plus, dinosaur cousins probably acted alike.

Brachiosaurus had two cousins, *Diplodocus* and *Camarasaurus*. Who was *Brachiosaurus* more like?

Diplodocus had a long skull like a giraffe. However, unlike a giraffe, *Diplodocus* had long hind legs and short forelegs. Its back sloped down from rear to front. When *Diplodocus* walked, it held its neck down low.

▶ A giraffe wanders among trees in Africa. Giraffes are more lightly built than *Brachiosaurus* was. However, they are very similar in shape.

Camarasaurus was different. Its hind legs and forelegs were about the same length, so its back was almost straight. Also, *Brachiosaurus*'s skull was a lot like *Camarasaurus*'s. So *Brachiosaurus* was more closely related to *Camarasaurus*.

Intercontinental dinosaur?

Brachiosaurus is one of many dinosaurs whose remains have been found in both North America and Africa. Not long after Riggs first found *Brachiosaurus* remains in Colorado, fossil-hunters found *Brachiosaurus* bones in Tanzania, East Africa. How could *Brachiosaurus* have lived in such widely separated places at one time? Did it swim the Atlantic Ocean?

There was no need. Although Africa and North America moved away from one another in the Jurassic period, and the Atlantic Ocean formed between them, sometimes this new sea was dry. At these times, dinosaurs like *Brachiosaurus* could simply walk overland from continent to continent.

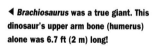

◀ *Brachiosaurus* was a true giant. This dinosaur's upper arm bone (humerus) alone was 6.7 ft (2 m) long!

Different species?

The African *Brachiosaurus* was slightly different from the American *Brachiosaurus*. The African dinosaur was more lightly built. It also had longer forelegs and a shorter body. So how could both these animals be the same kind of dinosaur?

The answer is that they were probably different species of *Brachiosaurus*—like the long-eared African elephant and the short-eared Asian elephant are two different species of elephants. Perhaps even more species of *Brachiosaurus* lived in Jurassic times. We just haven't found them yet.

Ultrasauros

In 1979, the American paleontologist Jim Jensen was digging in Colorado. He found the remains of a huge sauropod. Some scientists thought this dinosaur might have been even bigger than *Brachiosaurus*. Perhaps, they thought, it could have been more than 100 ft (30 m) long and 70 tons (63.5 tonnes) in weight. They called it Ultrasauros.

After more study, though, they discovered that it was really no bigger than the biggest *Brachiosaurus*. They decided that the bones must belong to *Brachiosaurus*. The name Ultrasauros is now as extinct as the sauropods.

CHECK THESE OUT!

Apatosaurus, Bones, Camarasaurus, Continental drift, Diplodocus, Jurassic period, Rocks, Saurischian dinosaurs, Sauropodomorph dinosaurs, Sauropods

DINOFACTS

Brachiosaurus
(BRAAK-ee-o-SORE-us)

☀ **NAME:** *Brachiosaurus* means arm lizard
brachium (arm) + sauros (lizard)

◯ **FAMILY:** Saurischian
Sauropodomorph
Sauropod

⊕ **SIZE:** 75–80 ft (22.9–24.4 m) long; 40–50 ft (12.2–15.2 m) to the top of its head

⚖ **WEIGHT:** 30–35 tons (27.2–31.8 tonnes)—about the same as 6–7 African elephants

🥣 **FOOD:** plants

🏠 **HABITAT:** lowland open forest

N
↑ **WHERE:** remains found in Colorado in the United States and Tanzania in East Africa

🕐 **WHEN:** 150–135 million years ago in the Jurassic period

BRACHIOSAURUS

TRIASSIC	JURASSIC	CRETACEOUS
250 MILLION YEARS AGO	205 MILLION YEARS AGO	135 MILLION YEARS AGO

65 MILLION YEARS AGO

Brachyceratops

Brachyceratops belonged to a group of dinosaurs called the ceratopsians, or horned dinosaurs. It was first discovered by the American paleontologist Charles Whitney Gilmore.

Brachyceratops was a fairly small horned dinosaur. It had short horns over its eyes, and a longer nose horn that gently curved back. *Brachyceratops* looked a little like *Centrosaurus* (which was once thought to be yet another dinosaur—*Monoclonius*). This similarity caused confusion when fossil-hunters discovered the first *Brachyceratops* remains.

Mistaken identity
The first *Brachyceratops* skeletons were found in Montana in 1913. Fossil-hunters discovered five ceratopsian skeletons next to one another. Because the skeletons were small for a ceratopsian, the scientists guessed they were the remains of young dinosaurs. Their horns were in the same place as those of *Centrosaurus*, so the scientists decided the skeletons must have been *Centrosaurus* young.

Right horns, wrong frill
Twenty years later, fossil-hunters dug up a larger ceratopsian skeleton near where the five smaller ones had been. It had similar horns to the smaller skeletons, but the shape of its bony neck frill was different.

Most ceratopsians had these neck frills, and scientists knew they changed shape as a dinosaur got older. However, when the scientists checked this frill against that of *Centrosaurus,* it did not match. That meant the skeletons that had been found in Montana were not *Centrosaurus.* They belonged to a new dinosaur. The scientists named it *Brachyceratops.*

▶ Ceratopsians, or horned dinosaurs, are sometimes grouped by the size of their neck frill. There were long-frilled ceratopsians, and short-frilled ones. *Brachyceratops* is a short-frilled ceratopsian.

AN ANCIENT JIGSAW PUZZLE

The first *Brachyceratops* skull was found shattered in many pieces among the rocks of Montana. These fragmented bits had to be carefully removed from the rocks. Later, scientists pieced them together in a laboratory.

Experts who rebuild new-found dinosaurs use their knowledge of similar dinosaurs to put the pieces together correctly. They need a lot of skill and patience. Much has been learned about the evolution of dinosaurs through the work of these experts.

How did this dinosaur live?

Like all ceratopsians, *Brachyceratops* ate plants. It lived in herds and may have been hunted by a meat-eating dinosaur called *Aublysodon,* a medium-sized relative of the fearsome giant *Tyrannosaurus.*

Dinosaur family

Why would one large skeleton and five small skeletons be in a single place? The answer is a sad one. Scientists think the six dinosaurs may have been a family—perhaps a mother and her young. Somehow, they all died together about 75 million years ago.

CHECK THESE OUT!

Centrosaurus, Ceratopsians, Cretaceous period, Ornithischian dinosaurs, Theropods, Tyrannosaurus

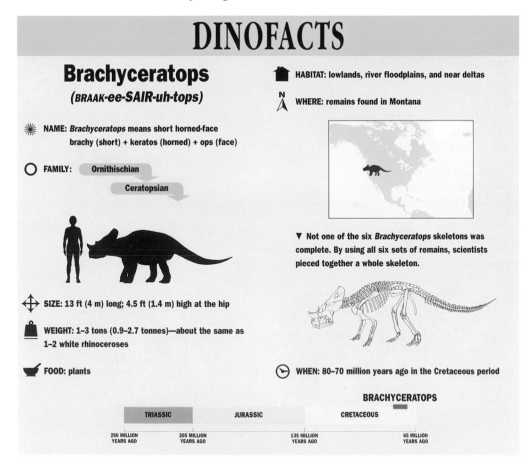

DINOFACTS

Brachyceratops
(BRAAK-ee-SAIR-uh-tops)

※ **NAME:** *Brachyceratops* means short horned-face
brachy (short) + keratos (horned) + ops (face)

○ **FAMILY:** Ornithischian
Ceratopsian

✥ **SIZE:** 13 ft (4 m) long; 4.5 ft (1.4 m) high at the hip

WEIGHT: 1–3 tons (0.9–2.7 tonnes)—about the same as 1–2 white rhinoceroses

FOOD: plants

HABITAT: lowlands, river floodplains, and near deltas

WHERE: remains found in Montana

▼ Not one of the six *Brachyceratops* skeletons was complete. By using all six sets of remains, scientists pieced together a whole skeleton.

WHEN: 80–70 million years ago in the Cretaceous period

BRACHYCERATOPS

TRIASSIC	JURASSIC	CRETACEOUS	
250 MILLION YEARS AGO	205 MILLION YEARS AGO	135 MILLION YEARS AGO	65 MILLION YEARS AGO

Brachylophosaurus

Brachylophosaurus was a hadrosaur, or duckbill dinosaur. Fossil-hunters first found remains of this dinosaur in Alberta, Canada, in 1936. It took until 1953 for scientists to work out exactly what it was.

Brachylophosaurus was a fairly late duckbill dinosaur, but it seems to have looked more like an early one. Many of the later duckbills had amazing crests on their head. *Parasaurolophus* had a huge, curved crest. *Corythosaurus* had an upright, bony disk.

Not *Brachylophosaurus*, though. It did have a crest, but it was just a narrow bar of bone bulging above the nostrils.

▼ *Brachylophosaurus* appeared in the Late Cretaceous period. The closest relative of *Brachylophosaurus* was the duckbill *Maiasaura*.

Hadrosaur relations

Both *Corythosaurus* and *Parasaurolophus* had hollow crests. Hadrosaurs with hollow crests are called lambeosaurines. However, *Brachylophosaurus*'s crest was solid, like that of its close relative *Kritosaurus*. These solid-crested duckbill dinosaurs are called hadrosaurines.

Dinosaur ID?

Why did duckbills have a crest anyway? Well, *Parasaurolophus* had a different shaped crest than *Corythosaurus* or *Brachylophosaurus*. When two duckbills met, they could have

looked at one another's crest to make sure they were both the same duckbill type.

It is even possible that crests were a different shape in male and female duckbills. Some modern animals have clear differences that help males and females tell each other apart. Think of birds. Males of many species have brightly colored feathers. Females are often duller in color. Perhaps male and female *Brachylophosaurus* could tell each other apart by the shape of their crest.

Were duckbill crests only for identification? Scientists think perhaps not. Male *Brachylophosaurus* probably fought one another to find out who was the strongest. During these fights, they butted one another with the flat crests on their heads.

Brachylophosaurus's crest would have been a good weapon. It would also have been a good shield to stop the dinosaurs from getting injured.

How did it live?

Like all duckbill dinosaurs, *Brachylophosaurus* ate plants. Its mouth contained hundreds of teeth to grind up the abundant Cretaceous vegetation.

Brachylophosaurus also had fairly long arms for a hadrosaur. Scientists think it may have spent more time on all fours than other duckbills.

Brachylophosaurus shared its world with tyrannosaurids, including *Albertosaurus* and *Daspletosaurus*. These dinosaurs probably hunted duckbills. *Brachylophosaurus* could not fight them; it ran away.

Duckbills had powerful tails and paddlelike hands. They were probably good swimmers. To escape from a meat-eater, *Brachylopohosaurus* probably rushed into a lake or a nearby swamp.

CHECK THESE OUT!

Albertosaurus, Corythosaurus, Cretaceous period, Daspletosaurus, Hadrosaurs, Kritosaurus, Maiasaura, Ornithischian dinosaurs, Ornithopods, Parasaurolophus, Tyrannosaurus

DINOFACTS

Brachylophosaurus

(BRAAK-*ee-LO-fuh-SORE-us*)

▶ Fossil-hunters found a very good skull of *Brachylophosaurus*. The large hole at the front of the skull is one of the dinosaur's huge nostrils.

✳ **NAME:** *Brachylophosaurus* means short-crested lizard
brachy (short) + lophos (crest) + sauros (lizard)

○ **FAMILY:**   Ornithischian

Ornithopod

Hadrosaur

✛ **SIZE:** 23 ft (7 m) long; 5 ft (1.5 m) high at the hip

WEIGHT: 1–3 tons (0.9–2.7 tonnes)—about the same as 1–3 North American bison

FOOD: plants

HABITAT: lowlands, coastal plains, and near river deltas

WHERE: remains found in Montana in the United States, and Alberta in Canada

◷ **WHEN:** 75 million years ago in the Cretaceous period

BRACHYLOPHOSAURUS

TRIASSIC	JURASSIC		CRETACEOUS	
250 MILLION YEARS AGO	205 MILLION YEARS AGO	135 MILLION YEARS AGO		65 MILLION YEARS AGO

Camarasaurus

Camarasaurus was a sauropod, a large plant-eating dinosaur with a long neck and tail. At the time it was alive, *Camarasaurus* was the most common sauropod in what is now North America.

Because *Camarasaurus* was so common, fossil-hunters have found many of this dinosaur's bones. Many of the skeletons were almost complete. These remains have enabled experts to learn a lot about this dinosaur.

The first bones discovered belonged to young animals. To begin with, scientists did not know that the bones they had found belonged to young dinosaurs. They guessed that *Camarasaurus* was a small sauropod. How did they discover their mistake?

What happened was that fossil-hunters dug up bones that were similar in shape to the early finds—but much larger. The experts realized that these were the bones of a fully grown *Camarasaurus*. It was clear that *Camarasaurus* was not a small sauropod but a very big one. It could be almost as big as *Apatosaurus*.

Even so, *Camarasaurus* looked a little different from *Apatosaurus*. The skull of *Camarasaurus* was blunter and less slender. Where *Apatosaurus* had teeth only at the front of its mouth, *Camarasaurus* had teeth along the sides of its jaws, too. *Camarasaurus* also had a fairly short neck, which made the animal look chunky.

Dinosaur eyes

Scientists studying one *Camarasaurus* skeleton made an amazing discovery. They found small ring bones in the dinosaur's eye sockets. These ring bones helped support the eyes in their sockets. They may also have helped the eyes focus.

Was *Camarasaurus* the only dinosaur to have had these bones? No. Most dinosaurs had them—as did birds.

▶ *Camarasaurus* had a fairly short neck for such a large sauropod. When feeding, it could have reached only the lower branches and leaves of tall trees.

The most complete *Camarasaurus* skeleton found so far was discovered at Dinosaur National Monument, Utah, in 1922. It was the skeleton of a young animal, 17 ft (5.2 m) long. It is now in the Carnegie Museum, Pittsburgh.

When the fossil-hunters found the skeleton, it had a thin covering of carbon. Could this covering be what was left of the dinosaur's skin? Scientists believe so. It is rare to find the remains of dinosaur skin or flesh. The main reason is because soft tissues rot very quickly after death. Another reason is that, soon after an animal died, meat-eating dinosaurs usually ate soft tissues like the skin.

How did *Camarasaurus* live?

Camarasaurus was a plant-eater. It shared its home with other big sauropods, including *Apatosaurus*, *Diplodocus*, and *Barosaurus*. The plate-backed dinosaur *Stegosaurus* also lived alongside *Camarasaurus*.

Despite its huge size, meat-eating dinosaurs like *Allosaurus* may have hunted *Camarasaurus*. No one knows how *Camarasaurus* defended itself. It would have been too big to run away. Its tail would have stopped it from rearing up on its hind legs as other sauropods may have done.

CHECK THESE OUT!

Apatosaurus, Jurassic period, Saurischian dinosaurs, Sauropodomorph dinosaurs, Sauropods, *Stegosaurus*

DINOFACTS

Camarasaurus
(KAM-uh-ruh-SORE-us)

▶ Unlike *Apatosaurus*, *Camarasaurus* had no whiplash tip to its tail. So it probably could not use its tail to defend itself as *Apatosaurus* may have done.

☀ NAME: *Camarasaurus* means chambered lizard
camera (chamber) + sauros (lizard)

○ FAMILY: Saurischian

Sauropodomorph

Sauropod

⊕ SIZE: 60 ft (18.3 m) long; 15 ft (4.6 m) high at the hip

⚖ WEIGHT: 20–25 tons (18–22.5 tonnes)—about the same as 4–5 African elephants

FOOD: plants

HABITAT: lowlands and floodplains

N
A WHERE: remains found in Colorado, Utah, and Wyoming in the United States, and Portugal in Europe

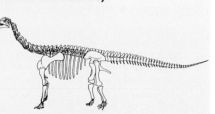

🕐 WHEN: 150–135 million years ago in the Jurassic period

CAMARASAURUS

TRIASSIC		JURASSIC		CRETACEOUS
250 MILLION YEARS AGO	205 MILLION YEARS AGO		135 MILLION YEARS AGO	65 MILLION YEARS AGO

Camptosaurus

Camptosaurus lived in North America and England. No one has ever found a whole *Camptosaurus* skeleton. However, scientists have pieced together enough bits to guess what it was like.

Scientists have found *Camptosaurus* bones in both North America and England. How could one dinosaur live on two continents?

It didn't. In the Jurassic period, North America and Europe were joined as part of one big continent that scientists call Laurasia.

Two legs, or four?

Scientists used to believe that *Camptosaurus* walked on its hind legs like *Tyrannosaurus*. Today they think it walked on all fours. Why did they change their minds? Because of the dinosaur's arms. They were smaller than its hind limbs but still pretty strong.

Why did *Camptosaurus* have such big arms? The scientists had two choices. Either *Camptosaurus* used them for pulling its plant food from the trees, or it walked on them. One look at the dinosaur's hands told the scientists which was the right answer. The hands of *Camptosaurus* were better suited for walking than for grasping. In particular, *Camptosaurus* had small hooves on its fingers, instead of claws. So scientists decided that *Camptosaurus* usually walked on four legs.

How did *Camptosaurus* live?

Like all ornithischian dinosaurs, *Camptosaurus* ate plants. It ate

▶ *Camptosaurus* was a relative of *Iguanodon* and was an ancestor of the hadrosaurs, or duckbill dinosaurs.

FOUR-LEGGED CLUES

Besides its strong arms, there are two other clues that show *Camptosaurus* probably walked on all fours.

The first clue is in the dinosaur's skeleton. On the end of its backbone, near its tail, *Camptosaurus* had tiny extra bones. These bones may have helped the dinosaur hold its tail stiff as it walked. A stiff tail would throw an animal that walked on two legs off balance. So *Camptosaurus* would have had trouble walking on two legs.

The second clue solved the mystery. Scientists found footprints that show *Camptosaurus* walking on four legs.

everything from the ground up to about 6 ft (1.8 m).

Camptosaurus lived alongside the meat-eating dinosaur *Allosaurus*. How did *Camptosaurus* defend itself? Some relatives of *Camptosaurus*, such as *Iguanodon*, had long, sharp, thumb claws to use as weapons. *Camptosaurus*'s thumb claws were short. It could not fight so it probably had to run away.

CHECK THESE OUT!

Allosaurus, Continental drift, Hadrosaurs, *Iguanodon*, Jurassic period, Ornithischian dinosaurs, Ornithopods, *Tenontosaurus*, *Tyrannosaurus*

DINOFACTS

Camptosaurus
(KAMP-*tuh*-SORE-*us*)

▶ *Camptosaurus* usually moved on four legs, but if it needed to run, it switched to two.

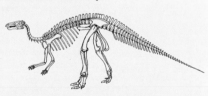

✴ **NAME:** *Camptosaurus* means bent lizard
kamptos (bent) + sauros (lizard)

○ **FAMILY:** Ornithischian

Ornithopod

✛ **SIZE:** 15–20 ft (4.6–6 m) long; 6 ft (1.8 m) high at the hip

WEIGHT: 0.5–1 ton (0.45–0.9 tonnes)—about the same as 1–2 hippopotamuses

FOOD: plants

HABITAT: open plains with plenty of plants

WHERE: remains found in Colorado, South Dakota, Utah, and Wyoming in the United States, and England

WHEN: 150–135 million years ago in the Jurassic period

CAMPTOSAURUS

	TRIASSIC	JURASSIC	CRETACEOUS
250 MILLION YEARS AGO	205 MILLION YEARS AGO	135 MILLION YEARS AGO	65 MILLION YEARS AGO

Carcharodontosaurus

In the Cretaceous period in North Africa, a massive meat-eater was on the loose. Similar in size to *Tyrannosaurus* and *Giganotosaurus*, the shark lizard was one of the most powerful land predators ever.

In 1927, German scientists found the remains of a huge meat-eating dinosaur in Egypt. It was as big as *Tyrannosaurus*. They named the dinosaur *Carcharodontosaurus* and took

its bones to the Munich Museum. During a World War II bombing raid, the museum was hit and the dinosaur's remains were destroyed. It seemed that *Carcharodontosaurus* had disappeared forever.

Then, in 1995, a team from Chicago found the bones of a massive meat-eating dinosaur in

Morocco in North Africa. What could it be? One look at the jaw and they knew. They had stumbled on another *Carcharodontosaurus*.

Land shark

How could the scientists be so sure they had

▶ *Carcharodontosaurus*, the shark lizard, stalks through its Cretaceous home on the lookout for food.

THE CHANGING EARTH

The Chicago fossil-hunting team, led by Paul Sereno, found the remains of *Carcharodontosaurus* in the dry, hot wastes of the Moroccan desert. Believe it or not, when the dinosaur was alive, Morocco could not have looked more different.

Carcharodontosaurus hunted near the delta of a river with treelined banks. Living in the river were crocodiles, turtles, crabs, and shrimps.

found *Carcharodontosaurus*? Because the jaw had teeth like those of a great white shark. Like a shark, *Carcharodontosaurus* had large teeth with jagged edges. The dinosaur got its name because of its teeth. *Troodon* and its relatives also had very jagged teeth.

How did this dinosaur live?

Carcharodontosaurus hunted other dinosaurs. It attacked with its teeth, tearing a huge lump out of its prey. The victim would lose a lot of blood quickly and would collapse.

Scientists have found the remains of a large *Iguanodon*-like animal in the same rocks as *Carcharodontosaurus*. They have also found sauropods—big, long-necked, long-tailed dinosaurs like *Apatosaurus*. *Carcharodontosaurus* probably hunted these plant-eaters.

CHECK THESE OUT!

Apatosaurus, Cretaceous period, *Giganotosaurus*, *Iguanodon*, Saurischian dinosaurs, Sharks, Tetanurans, Theropods, *Troodon*, *Tyrannosaurus*

DINOFACTS

Carcharodontosaurus
(kar-KAR-o-DON-tuh-SORE-us)

▶ *Carcharodontosaurus*'s skull was long and narrow. The dinosaur's lower jaw was never found, but each of the teeth in its upper jaw measured 4 in (10 cm).

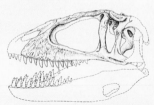

✳ **NAME:** *Carcharodontosaurus* means shark lizard
Carcharodon (great white shark) + sauros (lizard)

○ **FAMILY:** Saurischian
   Theropod
   Tetanuran

✛ **SIZE:** 45 ft (13.7 m) long; 13 ft (4 m) high at the hip

WEIGHT: 15 tons (13.6 tonnes) or more—about the same as 45 tigers

FOOD: meat

HABITAT: swampy lowlands

WHERE: remains found in Algeria, Egypt, and Morocco

🕐 **WHEN:** 115–90 million years ago in the Cretaceous period

		CARCHARODONTOSAURUS	
TRIASSIC	JURASSIC		CRETACEOUS
250 MILLION YEARS AGO	205 MILLION YEARS AGO	135 MILLION YEARS AGO	65 MILLION YEARS AGO

83

Carnotaurus

In 1985, South American paleontologist José Bonaparte discovered the skeleton of a big meat-eating dinosaur in Argentina. It had horns like a bull, but did it charge like a bull?

Carnotaurus was an unusual-looking dinosaur. It was large, it ate meat, and it had two horns on its head, one above each eye. These horns made *Carnotaurus* look a little like a bull, so José Bonaparte named it the meat-eating bull.

Why did it have horns?
Nobody really knows why *Carnotaurus* had horns. Scientists do

not think it used them to attack its prey. *Carnotaurus* probably grabbed its prey with its teeth or kicked at it with its powerful legs. So its horns must have served some other purpose. But what?

Scientists think *Carnotaurus* probably used its horns in head-butting contests with its own kind—perhaps when fighting over food.

▶ *Carnotaurus* was one of the last ceratosaurs. Its closest relative was *Abelisaurus*. Both dinosaurs have been found only in South America.

FOSSIL SKIN

When José Bonaparte found the skeleton of *Carnotaurus*, he also found some interesting marks in the rocks around it. These marks were left by the dinosaur's skin.

Remains of dinosaur skin are rare. Dinosaur skin does not fossilize; it decays. However, sometimes the texture of the skin leaves outlines, or imprints, in the rock. Your footprints leave imprints on a sandy beach. What can skin imprints tell us about a dinosaur's skin?

Well, the *Carnotaurus* skin imprints show that this dinosaur's hide was as rough as a cheese grater and was covered with bony bumps. This would have made the skin very tough.

They may also have helped the dinosaurs recognize each other from far away.

How did *Carnotaurus* live?
Carnotaurus was a ceratosaur. Ceratosaurs were meat-eating dinosaurs that had four fingers on each hand.

Carnotaurus hunted for fresh food. Like most meat-eaters, if it found a dead animal, it would probably have eaten that, too.

Scientists are not sure what animals *Carnotaurus* ate. However, it had small teeth for a meat-eating dinosaur of its size. So perhaps it preferred fairly small prey.

CHECK THESE OUT!

Abelisaurus, Ceratosaurs, Cretaceous period, Fossils, Saurischian dinosaurs, Theropods

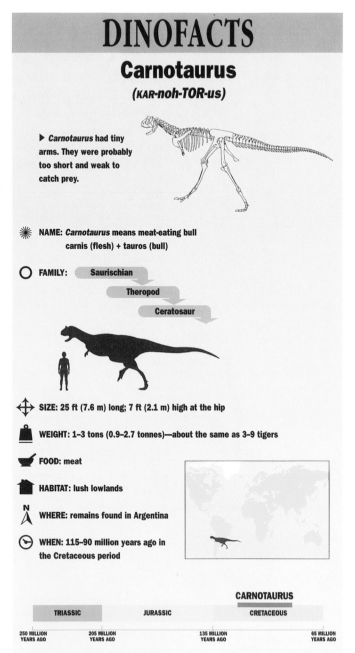

DINOFACTS

Carnotaurus
(KAR-noh-TOR-us)

▶ *Carnotaurus* had tiny arms. They were probably too short and weak to catch prey.

NAME: *Carnotaurus* means meat-eating bull
carnis (flesh) + tauros (bull)

FAMILY: Saurischian
Theropod
Ceratosaur

SIZE: 25 ft (7.6 m) long; 7 ft (2.1 m) high at the hip

WEIGHT: 1–3 tons (0.9–2.7 tonnes)—about the same as 3–9 tigers

FOOD: meat

HABITAT: lush lowlands

WHERE: remains found in Argentina

WHEN: 115–90 million years ago in the Cretaceous period

			CARNOTAURUS	
TRIASSIC		JURASSIC	CRETACEOUS	
250 MILLION YEARS AGO	205 MILLION YEARS AGO	135 MILLION YEARS AGO		65 MILLION YEARS AGO

Centrosaurus

Ceratopsians, or horned dinosaurs, were numerous during the last few million years of the Cretaceous period. Many different kinds evolved in a short time. One very plentiful kind was *Centrosaurus*.

Scientists know *Centrosaurus* was numerous because they sometimes find thousands of its bones at one time. These huge collections of dinosaur fossils are called bone beds. They contain the remains of hundreds of animals. In some places, the rocks contain many bone beds lying one above the other. It seems that large numbers of animals often died at the same time and in the same place.

ALL IN THE FRILL

The large, big-horned ceratopsian dinosaurs belonged to the ceratopsid group. Scientists divide the ceratopsids into two smaller groups—those like *Centrosaurus* (centrosaurines) and those like *Chasmosaurus* (chasmosaurines). The centrosaurines were generally smaller and had shorter neck frills than did the chasmosaurines. *Styracosaurus* was another centrosaurine and a close relative of *Centrosaurus*.

River secrets

Centrosaurus lived in herds, like modern caribou. From time to time, these herds had to cross wide rivers. From watching

herds of modern animals, scientists know that they usually cross rivers at the same spot. *Centrosaurus* herds probably did the same. Sometimes the waters would run high and fast. Crossing a raging river was dangerous and frightening,

even for big dinosaurs. Imagine the scene as the rushing waters swept away some of the terrified herd. Panicking, these animals would have struggled to reach dry land. After a short

▶ Like all centrosaurines, *Centrosaurus* had a long nose horn and little brow horns that were just bumps over each eye.

DINOFACTS

Centrosaurus
(SEN-troh-SORE-us)

 NAME: *Centrosaurus* means well-horned lizard
centro (well-horned) + sauros (lizard)

 FAMILY: Ornithischian
Ceratopsian

SIZE: 20 ft (6 m) long; about 6 ft (1.8 m) high at the hip

WEIGHT: 2–3 tons (1.8–2.7 tonnes)—about the same as 1–2 white rhinoceroses

FOOD: plants

HABITAT: swampy, broad coastal plains

WHERE: remains found in Alberta, Canada

WHEN: 80–70 million years ago in the Cretaceous period

		CENTROSAURUS
TRIASSIC	JURASSIC	CRETACEOUS
250 MILLION YEARS AGO	205 MILLION YEARS AGO	135 MILLION YEARS AGO	65 MILLION YEARS AGO

The bodies would have rotted, and silt and mud would have covered the bones, which eventually turned into fossils. Because the herds always crossed the river at the same place, the dead bodies always washed up at the same place. Pile after pile of bones fossilized one above the other, creating bone beds.

while, they would have tired and drowned. The river would then have washed all the dead bodies downstream and left them in a pile alongside the riverbank.

How did *Centrosaurus* live?
Centrosaurus lived on the coast of a sea that covered the Midwest of North America in the Late Cretaceous period.

Large rivers flowed into this sea, and the land along its edge was covered with forests and swamps. Food was plentiful. Even so, *Centrosaurus* had an enormous appetite, and the herds would have run out of food if they stayed in one place for long. *Centrosaurus* herds were always moving on in search of more plants to eat.

CHECK THESE OUT!
Ceratopsians, *Chasmosaurus*, Cretaceous period, Fossils, Ornithischian dinosaurs, *Styracosaurus*

Ceratopsians

Ceratopsians lived fairly late in the age of the dinosaurs. Some were the last dinosaurs to walk the earth. Ceratopsians came in all shapes and sizes from the tiny *Microceratops* to the mighty *Triceratops*.

Ceratopsians are often called the horned dinosaurs. However, not all ceratopsians had horns. *Psittacosaurus* was a hornless ceratopsian.

So why do scientists call *Psittacosaurus* a ceratopsian if it had no horns? *Psittacosaurus* was an early ceratopsian. The horns appeared only in later animals.

Psittacosaurus lived in the Early Cretaceous period. The big-horned ceratopsians, like *Triceratops*, lived at the end of the Cretaceous period. In between came another group of ceratopsians. These had only small horns and sometimes none at all. *Protoceratops* belonged to the middle group.

How did ceratopsians live?

Ceratopsians were plant-eating dinosaurs. Smaller types, such as *Protoceratops,* would have tried to run away if attacked. However, *Velociraptor* would have caught them.

Scientists believe the large, big-horned ceratopsians used their horns as weapons. A ceratopsian horn could have injured another dinosaur badly.

When threatened, a *Triceratops* may have

▲ *Microceratops* (1) probably walked on four legs and ran on two. *Protoceratops* (2) and large-horned ceratopsians, such as *Styracosaurus* (3) and *Triceratops* (4), moved only on all fours.

CHEEKS AND TEETH

Ceratopsians were unusual dinosaurs because they could chew their food. They could do this because they had cheeks—that is, loose skin around the jaws. Cheeks allow animals to keep food in their mouth while the teeth do their work. Most dinosaurs had no cheeks. Their teeth were at the edge of their mouth. If they had tried to chew, their food would have spilled out. So most dinosaurs had to swallow their food in a single chunk.

dipped its head and charged, like a modern rhinoceros.

Ceratopsians may also have fought one another to show who was strongest. They would lock horns and wrestle, or pretend to charge.

A ceratopsian puzzle
Most horned dinosaurs had bony plates called frills sticking out from their skull. Scientists think that ceratopsians used them as a warning. If another dinosaur got too close, a ceratopsian could wave its huge head and frill to warn, "Stay away. I'm stronger than you."

Frills also had another important job. They held the big jaw muscles ceratopsians needed to chew their food.

CHECK THESE OUT!

Anchiceratops, Arrhinoceratops, Bagaceratops, Brachyceratops, Centrosaurus, Cretaceous period, Einiosaurus, Leptoceratops, Ornithischian dinosaurs, Pachyrhinosaurus, Pentaceratops, Protoceratops, Psittacosaurus, Styracosaurus, Torosaurus, Triceratops, Velociraptor

DINOFACTS

Ceratopsians
(SEH-ruh-TOPE-see-yuns)

▼ Look at the skulls of these ceratopsians below. Can you spot all the differences between them?

1. *Protoceratops* had a horn that was just a little bump on its nose.

2. *Centrosaurus* had a single, large nose horn and bumps over its eyes.

3. *Triceratops* had a small nose horn and a brow horn over each eye.

✴ **NAME:** Ceratopsian means horned-face
keratos (horned) + ops (face)

 FAMILY: Ornithischian

 SIZE: 30 in to 30 ft (76 cm to 9.1 m) long; 1–9 ft (30 cm to 2.7 m) high at the hip

 WEIGHT: huge variation from 9 lb (4 kg) to 10 tons (9 tonnes)

 FOOD: plants

 HABITAT: wide-ranging from semidesert to lush plains

N
↑ **WHERE:** remains found in North America and Asia

🕐 **WHEN:** 130–65 million years ago in the Cretaceous period

		CERATOPSIANS	
TRIASSIC	JURASSIC	CRETACEOUS	
250 MILLION YEARS AGO	205 MILLION YEARS AGO	135 MILLION YEARS AGO	65 MILLION YEARS AGO

Ceratosaurs

Ceratosaurs were theropods—two-legged meat-eating dinosaurs. They were lightly built and had long back legs. The ceratosaurs were very speedy and successful hunters.

The ceratosaur group lived for more than 130 million years. They were the first theropod (two-legged meat-eating) dinosaurs. They survived longer than any other group of theropods.

The ceratosaur group included dinosaurs like *Coelophysis*, *Dilophosaurus*, *Carnotaurus*, and *Ceratosaurus* itself.

Ceratosaurs first appeared in the Late Triassic period more than 220 million years ago. By the Early Jurassic period (about 190 million years ago) the ceratosaurs were the most common theropod dinosaurs around.

Fingers and thumbs
Allosaurus and *Tyrannosaurus* were huge, muscular theropods. Ceratosaurs were smaller and lighter. They also had four fingers on each hand. One of these fingers worked like a human thumb. Scientists think that ceratosaurs, especially small ones, may have used their hands to catch and hold their food.

Ceratosaurs had four fingers because they were primitive theropods. Advanced theropods like *Tyrannosaurus* had only two fingers on each hand and no thumb. They used their huge head and teeth to catch their prey.

Horns and crests
The name *ceratosaur* means "horned lizard." Many ceratosaurs had horns or crests on their head. Mostly, these growths were too weak to use for fighting. So why did ceratosaurs have horns or crests? Scientists think they may have helped one ceratosaur recognize another of its own kind.

How did ceratosaurs live?
Fossil-hunters have found the bones of many ceratosaurs in one clump. They found a clump of

Coelophysis

Dilophosaurus

◄ Ceratosaurs, such as **Dilophosaurus** and **Coelophysis** (one of the earliest dinosaurs), were fast, powerful runners. There were few plant-eaters that were quick enough to outrun them.

Coelophysis in New Mexico, and a clump of *Syntarsus* in southern Africa. Scientists think these discoveries show that ceratosaurs lived in groups.

Why would ceratosaurs have lived in groups? By hunting in packs, they may have been able to kill larger prey than a single ceratosaur could.

CHECK THESE OUT!

Abelisaurus, Allosaurus, Carnotaurus, Ceratosaurus, Coelophysis, Cretaceous period, *Dilophosaurus, Elaphrosaurus,* Jurassic period, *Majungatholus,* Saurischian dinosaurs, Sauropods, *Syntarsus,* Theropods, Triassic period, *Tyrannosaurus*

SHAPE AND SIZE OF CERATOSAURS

Ceratosaurs came in many different sizes. Some, such as *Coelophysis* (top), were no bigger than a large dog. Others, such as *Ceratosaurus* (middle) or *Dilophosaurus* (bottom), were bigger than a grizzly bear.

All ceratosaurs were theropods. While their size varied, their body shapes were similar. The typical ceratosaur had powerful hind legs for running. It had a long tail, a long body, and a long neck. A ceratosaur's long, narrow body would have helped it run fast.

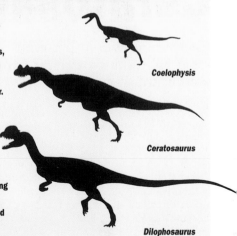

Coelophysis

Ceratosaurus

Dilophosaurus

DINOFACTS

Ceratosaur
(seh-RAT-oh-sore)

☀ **NAME:** Ceratosaur means horned lizard
keratos (horned) + sauros (lizard)

◯ **FAMILY:** Saurischian
Theropod

✛ **SIZE:** 11–20 ft (3.4–6 m) long; 1.5–5 ft (0.5–1.5 m) high at the hip

⚖ **WEIGHT:** large variation from 34 lb (15.4 kg) to 1 ton (0.9 tonnes)—or, from a large dog to 2 grizzly bears

🥄 **FOOD:** meat

🏠 **HABITAT:** fairly arid locations

WHERE: remains found in North America, Europe, southern Africa, and Asia, but ceratosaurs may have lived all over the world

🕐 **WHEN:** 225–70 million years ago in the Late Triassic, the Jurassic, and the Cretaceous periods

CERATOSAURS

	TRIASSIC	JURASSIC	CRETACEOUS
250 MILLION YEARS AGO	205 MILLION YEARS AGO	135 MILLION YEARS AGO	65 MILLION YEARS AGO

Ceratosaurus

Ceratosaurus was a theropod—a two-legged meat-eating dinosaur. Like other large meat-eaters, it had a big head and big teeth. It was the only meat-eater with a horn.

Ceratosaurus belongs to the ceratosaur group of meat-eaters, which also includes *Carnotaurus, Coelophysis,* and *Dilophosaurus.* Fossil-hunters first found the remains of *Ceratosaurus* in Colorado in 1883. Like all meat-eating dinosaurs, it had a big head, big teeth, and

powerful hind legs to chase its prey. It also had a large horn at the end of its snout.

No other meat-eating dinosaur had a nose horn. So why did *Ceratosaurus* have one?

Scientists can only guess. Perhaps the nose horn was used for show. Maybe males used it to attract females during the mating season, as some African antelope do today.

Maybe the nose horn was a kind of dinosaur ID. Perhaps it helped one *Ceratosaurus* recognize another of its own kind. *Ceratosaurus* probably did

◄ A ***Ceratosaurus*** eyes a herd of ***Camarasaurus.*** ***Ceratosaurus*** belongs to the ceratosaur group of meat-eaters, which was named after this dinosaur. The group also includes ***Carnotaurus*** and ***Coelophysis.***

ARMOR PLATING

Besides being the only theropod with a nose horn, *Ceratosaurus* was also the only theropod with armor plates. These small, bony plates were lined along the dinosaur's back.

Why did *Ceratosaurus* have armor plates? Scientists are not sure. The plates were probably too small to give protection. However, the dinosaur may have showed them off like peacock feathers during the mating season.

not use its horn for fighting. The horn was too small for that and not especially strong.

How did *Ceratosaurus* live?
Ceratosaurus was a hunter. It probably wandered in search of animals to eat. It may have hunted in packs, or it may have hunted alone. A pack of *Ceratosaurus* could bring down large sauropods like *Apatosaurus* or *Camarasaurus*. A single *Ceratosaurus* probably could not

have killed an *Apatosaurus*. So if *Ceratosaurus* did work alone, it might have hunted smaller dinosaurs such as *Camptosaurus*, a medium-sized plant-eater.

CHECK THESE OUT!

Apatosaurus, Camarasaurus, Camptosaurus, Carnotaurus, Ceratosaurs, Coelophysis, Dilophosaurus, Jurassic period, Saurischian dinosaurs, Theropods

DINOFACTS

Ceratosaurus
(seh-RAT-oh-SORE-us)

 NAME: *Ceratosaurus* means horned lizard
keratos (horned) + sauros (lizard)

 FAMILY: Saurischian
Theropod
Ceratosaur

 SIZE: 15–20 ft (4.6–6 m) long; 5 ft (1.5 m) high at the hip

 WEIGHT: 0.5–1 ton (0.45–0.9 tonnes)—about the same as 2–4 lions

FOOD: meat

HABITAT: lowland open forest

WHERE: remains found in Colorado in the United States, and East Africa

▼ *Ceratosaurus* had a long, flexible tail. It may have used its tail for swimming.

WHEN: 225–145 million years ago in the Jurassic period

CERATOSAURUS

TRIASSIC	JURASSIC	CRETACEOUS
250 MILLION YEARS AGO	205 MILLION YEARS AGO	135 MILLION YEARS AGO	65 MILLION YEARS AGO

Cetiosaurus

Cetiosaurus was found in the 1830s and was one of the first dinosaurs to be named. Yet for years, scientists did not realize that *Cetiosaurus* was a dinosaur. They believed it was something else entirely.

In 1841, in the early days of paleontology, the British scientist Richard Owen studied the remains of a large plant-eating reptile. (Owen was the man who invented the name *dinosaur,* or "terrible lizard.") When first discovered in the 1830s, the remains had been identified as whale bones. Owen disagreed. He thought the bones belonged to a giant crocodilelike creature. Its back bones were rough, like those of a modern whale, so Owen

called the remains *Cetiosaurus*, or whale lizard.

Thirty years later, fossil-hunters discovered a more complete *Cetiosaurus* skeleton that showed that the animal was neither a whale nor a crocodile. *Cetiosaurus* was a sauropod, a long-necked, long-tailed plant-eating dinosaur with strong, thick legs.

The scientists imagined that *Cetiosaurus* spent most of its time wallowing in water like some prehistoric hippo. How else could it have carried its heavy body around? Scientists now know that *Cetiosaurus* and other sauropods were fully at home on land. *Cetiosaurus* may have wallowed in the water, but it did not have to stay there because of its size.

An average sauropod

Many kinds of sauropods had features that made them stand out from the rest. *Barosaurus* had a very long neck. *Brachiosaurus* had a very long neck and forelegs. *Diplodocus* and its relatives had whiplash tails. *Cetiosaurus* was different. It had a long neck and a short tail. Its forelegs were only slightly longer than its hind legs.

Why did *Cetiosaurus* not have any special traits? Perhaps because it was a primitive sauropod. The sauropods described above did not appear until some time later in the Jurassic period, about 20 million years after the last *Cetiosaurus* had died.

How did *Cetiosaurus* live?

Cetiosaurus was a plant-eating dinosaur. The rocks in

◀ *Cetiosaurus* lived in open Jurassic forests, which would have looked a little like the Florida Everglades today.

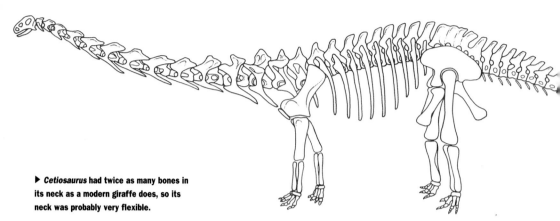

▶ *Cetiosaurus* had twice as many bones in its neck as a modern giraffe does, so its neck was probably very flexible.

which fossil-hunters have found *Cetiosaurus* bones provide many clues about what the dinosaur ate.

Fossil-hunters have discovered the remains of Jurassic plants in these rocks. The plants included horsetails, a type of fern, and conifers. There was also tree pollen.

Cetiosaurus could have eaten all of these foods, or perhaps just some of them.

The dinosaur would have moved slowly from tree to tree, cutting off bunches of rough leaves with its teeth.

A primitive sauropod, *Cetiosaurus* had teeth at the front of its jaws and along the sides as well. Later sauropods had teeth only at the front of their jaws. Sauropods could not chew their food. They swallowed it whole. The loss of teeth may be linked with a

change in feeding habits, although scientists cannot tell if it was the main reason.

Their heads in the clouds?
Scientists disagree over how high *Cetiosaurus* could reach.

Many of them think that *Brachiosaurus* could hold its long neck straight upward. However, unlike *Brachiosaurus*, *Cetiosaurus* might not have had a strong enough heart to pump its blood all the way up its neck to raise its head up high.

Cetiosaurus may have had to carry its neck level with the ground, holding its head down low. A fully grown *Cetiosaurus* might have reached only about 15 ft (4.6 m) up a tree.

Only a sauropod could reach that far while standing on the ground, so *Cetiosaurus* would have had an advantage. Even so, the advantage would have been small.

Too small, according to some paleontologists. They

SAUROPODS' TINY BRAINS

Sauropods seemed to have very small heads. *Cetiosaurus*'s head was the same size as a modern horse's head. It was not really small. It just looked small compared to the rest of the dinosaur.

Sauropods had small brains, though. Their brains were the size of a cat's—a staggering 100,000 times smaller than the dinosaur's body. Sauropods were the least brainy dinosaurs. They did not need to be clever because their size protected them from most meat-eaters.

DINOFACTS

Cetiosaurus
(SEE-tee-oh-SORE-us)

✳ **NAME:** *Cetiosaurus* means whale lizard
ketios (whale) + sauros (lizard)

○ **FAMILY:** Saurischian
→ Sauropodomorph
→ Sauropod

⬌ **SIZE:** 50–60 ft (15.2–18.3 m) long; 15 ft (4.6 m) high at the hip

⚖ **WEIGHT:** 10–40 tons (9–36 tonnes)—about the same as 2–8 African elephants

🥣 **FOOD:** plants

🏠 **HABITAT:** lowland open forest

🧭 **WHERE:** remains found in Morocco, North Africa; and England

🕐 **WHEN:** 180–170 million years ago in the Jurassic period

CETIOSAURUS

TRIASSIC	JURASSIC	CRETACEOUS
250 MILLION YEARS AGO	205 MILLION YEARS AGO	135 MILLION YEARS AGO	65 MILLION YEARS AGO

argue that the only reason plant-eaters have long necks is so they can reach high into trees. A sauropod needed a lot of energy to carry around its long neck. It would have been a waste to have such a long neck just to hold it level with the ground.

That makes sense, too. So who is right? Scientists, like detectives, often make guesses. Then they have to dig for more information to find out what really happened.

The world of *Cetiosaurus*

Who were *Cetiosaurus*'s neighbors? To find the answer, scientists studied a site in England where they had found remains of *Cetiosaurus*. They discovered that the place had been a pond in Jurassic times. It had been full of fish, of course, but turtles and even crocodiles had lived there, too. The scientists also found the bones of lizards, small mam-mals, mammal-like reptiles, and the meat-eating dinosaur *Megalosaurus*, which may have hunted *Cetiosaurus*. Like *Cetiosaurus*, all these animals were probably washed into the pond after they died.

CHECK THESE OUT!

Barosaurus, Brachiosaurus, Crocodiles, Diplodocus, Jurassic period, Lizards and snakes, Mammals, Mammal-like reptiles, Plants, Sauropods, Turtles

97

Chasmosaurus

Remains of *Chasmosaurus* were first discovered in 1901. *Chasmosaurus* was a ceratopsian, or horned dinosaur, and lived in what is now Texas and western Canada near the end of the age of the dinosaurs.

Chasmosaurus, like *Triceratops*, was one of the big-horned ceratopsians that lived at the end of the Cretaceous period. These ceratopsians had bony lumps, or frills, at the back of their head and were divided into short-frilled and long-frilled types.

Chasmosaurus was the earliest long-frilled type, so long-frilled ceratopsians are known as chasmosaurines. *Chasmosaurus*'s body was not very large for a ceratopsian, but its head was 5 ft (1.5 m) long. Its frill was as long as its face.

Different horns
Chasmosaurus usually had a nose horn and two brow horns, one above each eye.

Scientists have studied several *Chasmosaurus* skulls. The brow horns came in different sizes and shapes. Some skulls had small, blunt brow horns. Other skulls had long, pointed brow horns.

Scientists thought that all these different horns meant there were many different species of *Chasmosaurus*.

Girls vs. boys
Just because two skulls

have different horns doesn't always mean they belong to different species. Male and female animals of the same species may also have had different horns. Males and females of modern animals sometimes look different. Think of deer. Males often have huge antlers. Females usually have no antlers at all.

How did *Chasmosaurus* live?
Like all ceratopsians, *Chasmosaurus* was a plant-eater. *Chasmosaurus* probably lived in

▼ A male *Chasmosaurus* (right) shows off his neck frill to a female. Peacocks use their beautiful tail feathers to win mates. Some scientists think that ceratopsians used their frills in the same way.

DINOFACTS

Chasmosaurus
(KAZ-moh-SORE-us)

✳ **NAME:** *Chasmosaurus* means opening lizard
chasma (opening) + sauros (lizard)

○ **FAMILY:** Ornithischian

Ceratopsian

✥ **SIZE:** 17 ft (5.2 m) long; 6 ft (1.8 m) high at the hip

⚖ **WEIGHT:** 2.5 tons (2.3 tonnes)—about the same as a
white rhinoceros

🥣 **FOOD:** plants

🏠 **HABITAT:** lowlands, river floodplains, and near river deltas

↗ **WHERE:** remains found in Alberta, Canada; and Texas

▶ The frill of
Chasmosaurus
had very large
openings in it.
The dinosaur was
named after
these openings.

🕐 **WHEN:** 75–70 million years ago in the Cretaceous period

		CHASMOSAURUS ◾
TRIASSIC	JURASSIC	CRETACEOUS
250 MILLION YEARS AGO	205 MILLION YEARS AGO	135 MILLION YEARS AGO · 65 MILLION YEARS AGO

large herds, as do modern wildebeest or North American bison. When a meat-eating dinosaur appeared, the adult ceratopsians may have formed a defensive circle around their young to keep them safe.

CHECK THESE OUT!

Ceratopsians, Cretaceous period,
Crocodiles, Fossils, Ornithischian
dinosaurs, *Triceratops*

MASS GRAVES

Fossil-hunters often find remains of *Chasmosaurus* in what are called bone beds. Bone beds are like mass graves. They are sections of rock that are full of fossilized bones. Some bone beds have contained the remains of more than 100 dinosaurs of the same *Chasmosaurus* species. How could the skeletons of so many dinosaurs of the same kind come to be in one place?

All the *Chasmosaurus* remains in each bone bed were found close together in rocks of the same age, so scientists decided that all the dinosaurs in each bed died at the same time. Perhaps a herd of *Chasmosaurus* died while crossing a river. Like modern herd animals, *Chasmosaurus* probably moved from place to place searching for food. Today, wildebeest herds suffer many deaths when crossing rivers. Some animals drown. Others are caught by meat-eaters such as crocodiles.

Chirostenotes

The first fossils of *Chirostenotes* were found in 1924. Each hand had three finger bones, but the middle one was much longer than the other two. What did this long finger do?

The first parts of *Chirostenotes* that fossil-hunters found were the dinosaur's hands—and what unusual hands they were! They had three fingers, but the middle finger on each hand was much longer than the others. What sort of creature would have had hands like these?

Fossil-hunters first discovered *Chirostenotes* in the

A DINOSAUR WITH TWO NAMES

Sometimes dinosaurs get named more than once. When fossil-hunters discover a set of bones, scientists may give them a name, not realizing the remains belong to a dinosaur that has already been discovered. This is what happened to *Chirostenotes*. For a while, it had two different names.

Fossil-hunters found the hands of *Chirostenotes* in Canada in the 1920s. Scientists named the dinosaur *Chirostenotes* in 1924. Eight years later, fossil-hunters found a slender foot in the same area of Canada. Scientists did not link this foot with *Chirostenotes* and called the new dinosaur *Macrophalangia* ("big finger"). In 1979, fossil-hunters found another *Macrophalangia* skeleton, but some of its bones were the same as those of *Chirostenotes*. *Macrophalangia* had been the same as *Chirostenotes* all along. All the *Macrophalangia* fossils were renamed *Chirostenotes* since that was the first name to be given.

▼ *Chirostenotes* ate meat. It may have used its long middle finger to pick out creatures from small holes in fallen trees or from the ground.

1920s. Since then teams have dug up more remains. Fossil finds enable scientists to make better guesses at what dinosaurs looked like and how they lived. *Chirostenotes* had long hind legs, which means the dinosaur could probably run fast. All *Chirostenotes* fossils are small, so either they were from a young dinosaur or a small adult. By looking at the bones, scientists could tell it was a small adult.

How did *Chirostenotes* live?

Chirostenotes was a small, long-legged predator. Did it use its unusual hands to help it to catch its prey? Wouldn't a long middle finger get in the way when *Chirostenotes* tried to seize its victim? Not if it hunted tiny prey. Perhaps *Chirostenotes* used its long finger to probe holes in the ground for insects and other small creatures.

One way to guess what an animal ate is to look at its teeth. Unfortunately, fossil-hunters have never found a *Chirostenotes* skull. Scientists believe, though, that *Chirostenotes* probably did not have any teeth at all. From studying the remains they have, paleontologists have decided that *Chirostenotes* was a close relative of the toothless theropod (two-legged walker) *Oviraptor*. *Oviraptor* lived in Mongolia in the Late Cretaceous period, as did *Elmisaurus*, another close relative of *Chirostenotes*.

CHECK THESE OUT!

Cretaceous period, *Elmisaurus*, *Oviraptor*, Saurischian dinosaurs, Tetanurans, Theropods

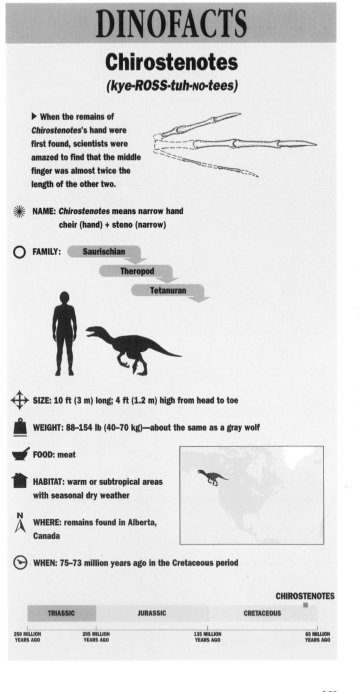

DINOFACTS

Chirostenotes
(kye-ROSS-tuh-no-tees)

▶ When the remains of *Chirostenotes*'s hand were first found, scientists were amazed to find that the middle finger was almost twice the length of the other two.

✳ NAME: *Chirostenotes* means narrow hand cheir (hand) + steno (narrow)

○ FAMILY: Saurischian → Theropod → Tetanuran

✛ SIZE: 10 ft (3 m) long; 4 ft (1.2 m) high from head to toe

⚖ WEIGHT: 88–154 lb (40–70 kg)—about the same as a gray wolf

🥣 FOOD: meat

🏠 HABITAT: warm or subtropical areas with seasonal dry weather

↑N WHERE: remains found in Alberta, Canada

🕐 WHEN: 75–73 million years ago in the Cretaceous period

CHIROSTENOTES

TRIASSIC	JURASSIC	CRETACEOUS
250 MILLION YEARS AGO	205 MILLION YEARS AGO	135 MILLION YEARS AGO	65 MILLION YEARS AGO

Coelophysis

The discovery of several *Coelophysis* skeletons in New Mexico during the 1940s was one of the most exciting dinosaur finds of all time. The first complete Triassic dinosaur had been brought to light.

Coelophysis was one of the first dinosaurs from the Triassic period to be found in North America. Fossil-hunters had discovered the footprints and bones of Triassic dinosaurs in Connecticut early in the 19th century. Then, in 1889, an American collector finally came across the remains of a Triassic dinosaur.

The dinosaur collector David Baldwin found the bones in New Mexico. Baldwin once worked for the paleontologist Othniel C. Marsh, but by 1881 he was collecting for Marsh's great rival, Edward Drinker Cope. Baldwin passed the new

fossils to Cope, who wrote a scientific paper about the new dinosaur in 1889. Cope found that many of the animal's bones were hollow, like those of a modern bird. He named the dinosaur *Coelophysis*, or "hollow form."

What was *Coelophysis*?
The bones that Cope studied were far from being a complete skeleton. However, he had part of the hips, which he recognized as those of a saurischian,

or lizard-hipped, dinosaur. He also had parts of the legs, which were clearly not those of a sauropod (huge, long-necked plant-eater).

He reckoned that if *Coelophysis* was a saurischian dinosaur but not a sauropod it must have been a theropod. If it was a theropod, it must have been a meat-eater, because all theropods were meat-eaters.

▶ *Coelophysis* was a swift hunter. It chased after smaller dinosaurs on its long hind legs and probably caught them in its strong, clawed hands. It may also have fed on flying insects.

THE WORLD OF *COELOPHYSIS*

The world that *Coelophysis* lived in was very different from the one most dinosaurs knew. Most dinosaur skeletons have been found from the Jurassic and Cretaceous periods, when dinosaurs ruled the land. *Coelophysis*, though, was a very early dinosaur. It lived in the Late Triassic period. Since that time, rocks and riverbeds have gone through tremendous changes, and few Triassic fossils have been found.

Giant crocodilelike reptiles roamed Triassic North America at the same time as *Coelophysis*. Some of them may have moved on two legs. *Coelophysis* also shared its world with tritylodonts and haramyids. These were huge mammal-like reptiles. It must have lived in terror of being attacked by these monsters. It had a very different life from its later and bigger relative *Tyrannosaurus*, the fearless king of the Cretaceous.

Later finds of bone, teeth, and claws proved that Cope was right to think *Coelophysis* was a meat-eating dinosaur.

They proved him wrong, though, in one of his beliefs. Cope realized that Baldwin had given him the bones of not one but at least three *Coelophysis*. He worked out that all these dinosaurs had not been the same size. Cope believed he had the remains of three different species, or kinds, of *Coelophysis*. As we shall see later, he did not.

Ghost Ranch

No one found any *Coelophysis* remains for another 60 years. Then, in 1947, a team of fossil-hunters in New Mexico came across some more bits of *Coelophysis* bone. The team was working at Ghost Ranch, near where Baldwin had made his 1881 discovery. Hoping to make a great find, the fossil-hunters kept on digging.

Their hard work paid off. Instead of only bits, the team began to find whole *Coelophysis* bones, even entire skeletons. The remains of hundreds of *Coelophysis* lay together near Ghost Ranch.

Paleontologists have a name for places where they find many dead dinosaurs. They call them dinosaur graveyards. The team at Ghost Ranch was excited by the discovery, because dinosaur graveyards are very rarely found.

Washed away

Why were there so many dinosaurs of the same kind in one place? Paleontologist J. Lynn Gillette has some ideas.

Coelophysis probably lived in herds, like caribou. The bones she studied were caked in hardened red mud. Some of the skeletons were curved, like a carcass that had been baked by the sun. Underneath were some fish bones. Perhaps in a severe drought, the starving *Coelophysis* fed on a few fish before dying.

However, many *Coelophysis* skeletons were tangled together. These bones were in good shape for fossils—they hadn't been baked by the sun or gnawed by scavengers. They might have died quickly, as if in a rush of water and mud. Gillette suggests a flash flood could have buried the rest of the starving pack.

103

THE NAME GAME

When Edward Drinker Cope named *Coelophysis* in 1881, he had very few of the dinosaur's bones to study. After fossil-hunters discovered the Ghost Ranch dinosaurs in 1947, paleontologists had complete *Coelophysis* skeletons to study. At that time, some scientists said they thought Cope had had too few bones to name the dinosaur in 1881. They said the name *Coelophysis* should no longer be used and chose another name for the Ghost Ranch dinosaurs. They called them *Rioarribasaurus*, after Rio Arriba county in which Ghost Ranch lay. Other paleontologists disagree. They say Cope was right, and the name *Coelophysis* should still be used—for the 1881 dinosaur and the 1947 Ghost Ranch fossils. Paleontologists still cannot agree which name should be used.

▲ American paleontologist Edwin H. Colbert and his assistants lift fossils of a *Coelophysis* (or *Rioarribasaurus*) out of the dinosaur graveyard at Ghost Ranch in June 1947.

The amazing finds at Ghost Ranch have helped paleontologists work out exactly what *Coelophysis* looked like. *Coelophysis* was fairly small for a dinosaur, although at 9 ft (2.7 m) long it would seem big enough if you met one. It was a slim, lightly built animal with a long neck and tail and a mouth full of sharp teeth. Like *Ceratosaurus*, *Carnotaurus*, and *Dilophosaurus*, *Coelophysis* was a ceratosaur. The ceratosaurs were meat-eating dinosaurs

▼ The bones of *Coelophysis* were hollow, like the bones of birds. Birds' hollow bones make their skeletons lighter and allow them to fly. Hollow bones would have made *Coelophysis* lighter, too. It would have chased swiftly after its prey.

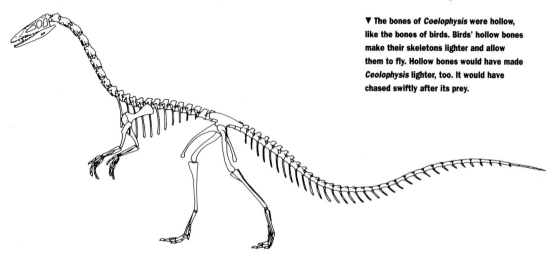

with four-fingered hands. Many ceratosaurs also had horns or crests on their head, although *Coelophysis* did not.

The Ghost Ranch remains included *Coelophysis* of different shapes and sizes. Were there really different species of *Coelophysis*, as Edward Cope had believed?

No. All the Ghost Ranch *Coelophysis* belonged to a single species, as did those that Cope studied in 1881. The small dinosaurs were young *Coelophysis*, and the larger ones were adults. The Ghost Ranch paleontologists had plenty of skeletons to study. Cope had only a few bits of bone to work on, so it is hardly surprising he made a mistake.

How did *Coelophysis* live?
Coelophysis was a fast-running hunter that sped after its prey on its hind legs. It would have fed on small dinosaurs such as *Heterodontosaurus* and *Lesothosaurus* and even smaller animals, including insects.

When *Coelophysis* caught up with a dinosaur, it would probably have grabbed it with its hands. *Coelophysis*'s strong, clawed fingers could have held on to a wriggling creature.

When catching insects, *Coelophysis* could have stretched out its flexible neck and snapped at them with its jaws—a little like a fishing heron does today.

An unusual meal!
Coelophysis may also have been a cannibal and eaten others of its own kind. Some of the Ghost Ranch skeletons had

tiny *Coelophysis* where the dinosaurs' stomachs would have been.

At first, scientists thought these were baby dinosaurs about to be born. However, they were too big. The adult *Coelophysis* must have eaten them, gulping them down in a few large chunks.

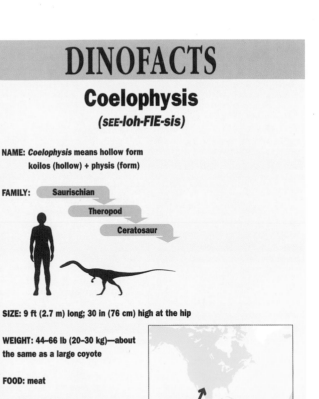

DINOFACTS

Coelophysis
(SEE-loh-FIE-sis)

✳ **NAME:** *Coelophysis* means hollow form
koilos (hollow) + physis (form)

○ **FAMILY:** Saurischian → Theropod → Ceratosaur

✛ **SIZE:** 9 ft (2.7 m) long; 30 in (76 cm) high at the hip

WEIGHT: 44–66 lb (20–30 kg)—about the same as a large coyote

FOOD: meat

HABITAT: dry lowlands

WHERE: remains found in New Mexico, Utah, and Arizona

WHEN: 225–205 million years ago in the Triassic period

COELOPHYSIS		
TRIASSIC	JURASSIC	CRETACEOUS
250 MILLION YEARS AGO 205 MILLION YEARS AGO	135 MILLION YEARS AGO	65 MILLION YEARS AGO

CHECK THESE OUT!
Bony fish, *Carnotaurus*, Ceratosaurs, *Ceratosaurus*, Collecting dinosaurs, Crocodiles, *Dilophosaurus*, Footprints, *Heterodontosaurus*, Insects, *Lesothosaurus*, Mammal-like reptiles, Saurischian dinosaurs, Sauropods, Theropods, Triassic period

Compsognathus

Compsognathus was one of the smallest of all dinosaurs. It was about the size of a pet cat, and like a cat *Compsognathus* was a hunter. It did not attack large animals, though; it was too small for that.

Early fossil-hunters often found only a part of a dinosaur's skeleton; this made it very hard for scientists to figure out what these animals looked like. When they found *Compsognathus*, though, the fossil-hunters hit the jackpot. For the first time, they had come across a dinosaur skeleton that was complete in almost every way. Scientists did not have to guess where the bones went. They were nearly all there, in just the way they would have been when the dinosaur was alive.

How the dinosaur lived

Compsognathus moved on its hind legs; its arms were small and would have been useless as legs. However, the fingers of its hands ended in sharp claws for grabbing prey.

The first *Compsognathus* to be found had small bones in the area where its stomach

A WARM, FEATHERED FRIEND?

Some scientists believe that small theropods such as *Compsognathus* might have been warm-blooded, like cats and dogs. Warm-blooded, or endothermic, means that an animal can control its own body temperature internally. Even when the weather is cold or the sun has gone down, the animal's body remains warm enough for it to move around. Cold-blooded, or ectothermic, animals do not really have cold blood. Ectothermic just means that the animals cannot control their own body temperature internally. They need to move in and out of the sun to warm themselves to just the right temperature. That is why you can often see reptiles, which are ectothermic (cold-blooded), sunning themselves first thing in the morning, trying to warm up.

Most endothermic (warm-blooded) animals have fur, hair, feathers, or blubber (fat) to help keep in their body heat. The scientists who believe *Compsognathus* was endothermic (warm-blooded) think it was also covered in feathers. Fossil-hunters have found the imprints of feathers in the rock around *Archaeopteryx*, a flying dinosaur, or avialan. So the scientists are looking for feather imprints around a *Compsognathus*.

So far they haven't found any. It may not matter. Scientists can also study animals' bones to tell if they were endothermic (warm-blooded) or ectothermic (cold-blooded). They have studied the bones of a Cretaceous bird, and it was probably ectothermic.

Whether or not *Compsognathus* was endothermic or ectothermic, scientists do know that all dinosaurs must have become endothermic at some point. They know because the only living dinosaur relatives are endothermic—birds.

▶ *Compsognathus* speeds after its prey on its long back legs. *Compsognathus* always moved on its hind limbs.

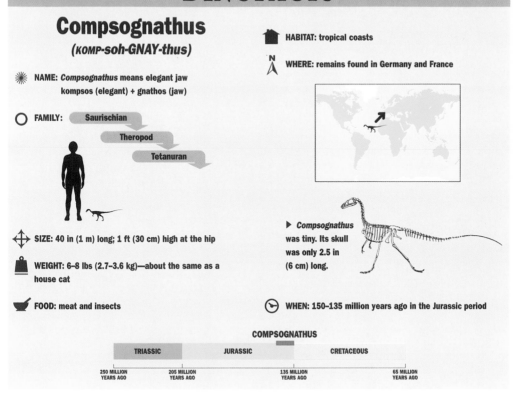

DINOFACTS

Compsognathus
(KOMP-soh-GNAY-thus)

✳ **NAME:** *Compsognathus* means elegant jaw
kompsos (elegant) + gnathos (jaw)

◯ **FAMILY:** Saurischian → Theropod → Tetanuran

⊕ **SIZE:** 40 in (1 m) long; 1 ft (30 cm) high at the hip

⚖ **WEIGHT:** 6–8 lbs (2.7–3.6 kg)—about the same as a house cat

🥣 **FOOD:** meat and insects

🏠 **HABITAT:** tropical coasts

🧭 **WHERE:** remains found in Germany and France

▶ *Compsognathus* was tiny. Its skull was only 2.5 in (6 cm) long.

🕐 **WHEN:** 150–135 million years ago in the Jurassic period

COMPSOGNATHUS

TRIASSIC	JURASSIC		CRETACEOUS
250 MILLION YEARS AGO	205 MILLION YEARS AGO	135 MILLION YEARS AGO	65 MILLION YEARS AGO

would have been. The bones did not belong to the dinosaur, so they must have belonged to something the dinosaur had eaten. They looked like the small bones of a young *Compsognathus*. Was *Compsognathus* a cannibal, an animal that eats others of its own kind? No. These were not dinosaur bones. They were from a small lizard. Lizards were not dinosaurs. This can be confusing, because the word *sauros* in many dinosaur names means lizard. Lizards and dinosaurs are two different types of reptiles.

A relative of *Tyrannosaurus*?
Scientists are not sure where *Compsognathus* fits in the dinosaur family tree. They know it was a theropod (two-legged walker), but most theropods had three fingers on each hand. Ceratosaurs (a kind of theropod) had four. *Compsognathus* had just two.
  The giant tyrannosaurs of the Late Cretaceous were also two-fingered theropods.

Compsognathus lived earlier, in the Jurassic; was it a small, early tyrannosaur? No. It was not enough like *Tyrannosaurus* to be related. However, it was different enough from other Jurassic theropods for scientists to give it its own family.

CHECK THESE OUT!

Archaeopteryx, Avialans, Birds, Ceratosaurs, Jurassic period, Lizards and snakes, Reptiles, Saurischian dinosaurs, Tetanurans, Theropods, Tyrannosaurs, *Tyrannosaurus*

Corythosaurus

Corythosaurus had a huge crest on its head. Because the crest looked like an ancient helmet, scientists called the dinosaur helmet lizard. How *Corythosaurus* used its crest is a mystery.

Corythosaurus was a hadrosaur. Hadrosaurs are also called duckbills because they had a horny beak like a duck's bill.

Scientists divide hadrosaurs into two groups—those with very small crests, and those like *Corythosaurus* with larger, often amazing crests.

▼ *Corythosaurus* **usually moved about slowly on all fours. If chased by a predator, though, it would have taken to its hind legs and run away.**

The American collector Barnum Brown found a *Corythosaurus* skull in Alberta, Canada, in 1914. Scientists do not often find good skulls. Skulls, being hollow, get crushed easily. Luckily, the skull that Brown found was very well preserved.

Corythosaurus had a big crest, like a disk perched on its head. The dinosaur looked as though it were wearing a helmet. (*Corythosaurus* means helmet

lizard.) The crest grew as a dinosaur got older, and males had larger crests than females. *Corythosaurus* might have checked the age and sex of another *Corythosaurus* by looking at its crest.

A sound idea

Corythosaurus's crest may have helped it call loudly. A maze of long breathing tubes filled the disk. These tubes could have worked like a trombone. When *Corythosaurus* hooted, the tubes would have made a loud, deep note.

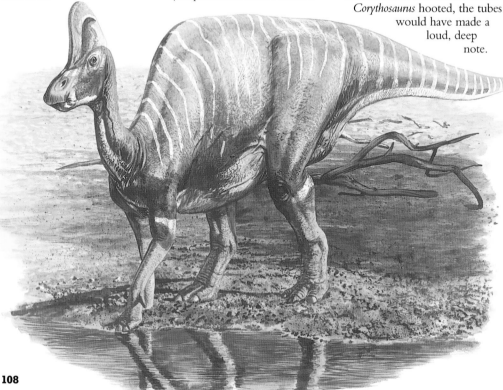

PRICKLY SKIN

It is rare to find evidence of dinosaur skin. This is because the skin usually rots soon after death. Sometimes, however, a skin imprint is left in the rock around the skeleton. Imprints are usually found in old riverbeds. There, when a dinosaur died, its body slipped into the water. Sand quickly covered the skin and preserved an impression.

One *Corythosaurus* skeleton had many small studs in its skin like cut stones. Some studs were rounded, some pyramid-shaped. Scientists think *Corythosaurus* might have had these studs for decoration.

Scientists tested their idea by blowing through a model of a hadrosaur crest; it made sound. Then they studied living animals that are closely related to hadrosaurs. Both crocodiles and birds call to each other. So did *Corythosaurus* make sounds? Scientists cannot tell. They would have to hear a living *Corythosaurus* to know.

How did *Corythosaurus* live?
Like all duckbills, *Corythosaurus* fed on plants. Scientists have found fossilized food in its stomach area. These show that it fed on twigs, seeds, and the needlelike leaves of conifers. Imagine trying to eat Christmas tree needles. *Corythosaurus* could do it easily.

Corythosaurus had about 40 rows of teeth in its upper jaw and about the same in its lower jaw. These rows of teeth were very rough. *Corythosaurus* ground its food between these rows of teeth until it was small enough to swallow.

CHECK THESE OUT!

Cretaceous period, Fossils, Hadrosaurs, Ornithischian dinosaurs, Ornithopods

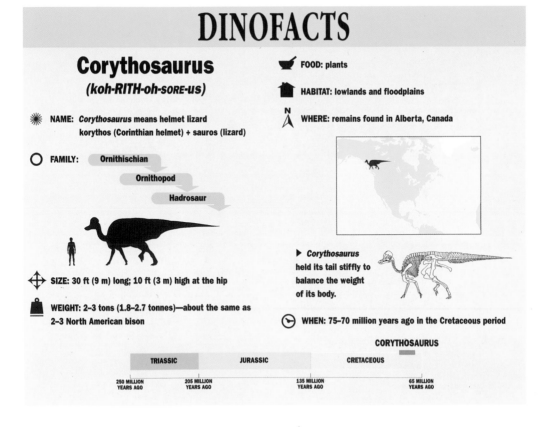

DINOFACTS

Corythosaurus
(koh-RITH-oh-SORE-us)

✳ **NAME:** *Corythosaurus* means helmet lizard
korythos (Corinthian helmet) + sauros (lizard)

○ **FAMILY:** Ornithischian
Ornithopod
Hadrosaur

✛ **SIZE:** 30 ft (9 m) long; 10 ft (3 m) high at the hip

WEIGHT: 2–3 tons (1.8–2.7 tonnes)—about the same as 2–3 North American bison

FOOD: plants

HABITAT: lowlands and floodplains

WHERE: remains found in Alberta, Canada

▶ *Corythosaurus* held its tail stiffly to balance the weight of its body.

◔ **WHEN:** 75–70 million years ago in the Cretaceous period

CORYTHOSAURUS

TRIASSIC	JURASSIC	CRETACEOUS	
250 MILLION YEARS AGO	205 MILLION YEARS AGO	135 MILLION YEARS AGO	65 MILLION YEARS AGO

Cryolophosaurus

Cryolophosaurus is very unusual—it is a dinosaur from the Antarctic. Fossil-hunters found its remains 13,000 ft (4000 m) up Mount Kirkpatrick, only 40 miles (65 km) from the South Pole.

The weather in Antarctica is extremely cold all year long; almost nothing lives there. *Cryolophosaurus* was a fairly large theropod (two-legged walker). How could a meat-eating dinosaur have survived in such conditions?

The answer is that the Antarctic climate was different in the Early Jurassic period when *Cryolophosaurus* was alive. At the time, Antarctica was part of an enormous supercontinent scientists call Gondwanaland. The land was closer to the equator than it is now, so the weather was a little warmer.

▼ Besides dinosaurs, *Cryolophosaurus* may have hunted mammal-like reptiles in Early Jurassic Antarctica.

HOW MANY DINOSAURS?

Just because fossil-hunters find a number of bones close to one another, doesn't mean they all belonged to the same animal. Sometimes they find the bones of several dinosaurs all mixed up in the same place.

For example, when fossil-hunters found *Cryolophosaurus*'s skull in Antarctica, they found some mysterious bones as well. It can take years to sort out which bone goes with which dinosaur. Paleontologists classify dinosaurs into groups based on their similarities—for example, whether they walked on two legs or four. As scientists study all the bones more closely, they will find out whether the remains belonged to one dinosaur, two dinosaurs, or more.

Hat head

Cryolophosaurus's head looked like other theropod heads—it was narrow and deep, and its mouth was full of sharp teeth.

However, it also had a crest, which was unusual for a large theropod. *Cryolophosaurus*'s crest looked silly—it was just a little hook in between its eyes.

No one knows how the crest was used. By watching how modern animals behave, some scientists guess that it was used in display. Male peacocks show off their tails to attract females in the breeding season. Perhaps male *Cryolophosaurus* showed off their crests.

How the dinosaur lived

Cryolophosaurus hunted. It needed a lot of food, so it lived near herds of its prey.

Scientists found the remains of a large prosauropod in Antarctica. Prosauropods were long-necked, long-tailed, plant-eaters like *Plateosaurus*. *Cryolophosaurus* lived at the same time as the prosauropods and would have hunted them.

No one has ever found the arms of *Cryolophosaurus*. However, if it was anything like its meat-eating cousin *Allosaurus*, it would have used its strong forelimbs and jaws to grab a prosauropod, bite its neck, and eat it.

CHECK THESE OUT!

Allosaurus, Continental drift, Jurassic period, Mammal-like reptiles, *Plateosaurus*, Prosauropods, Saurischian dinosaurs, Tetanurans, Theropods

DINOFACTS

Cryolophosaurus
(CRY-oh-LOH-phoh-SORE-us)

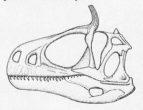

▶ *Cryolophosaurus*'s skull had huge holes, or windows, to make it lighter. In this way it was like the skull of *Allosaurus*, a relative.

✴ **NAME:** *Cryolophosaurus* means cold crested lizard
cry (cold) + loph (crest) + sauros (lizard)

○ **FAMILY:** Saurischian
→ Theropod
→ Tetanuran

✥ **SIZE:** 25 ft (7.6 m) long; 6 ft (1.8 m) high at the hip

WEIGHT: 1,500 lbs (680 kg)—about the same as 3 tigers

FOOD: meat

HABITAT: lowlands where the climate was neither very warm nor very cold

WHERE: remains found in the Transantarctic Mountains in Antarctica

🕑 **WHEN:** 205–178 million years ago in the Jurassic period

CRYOLOPHOSAURUS		
TRIASSIC	JURASSIC	CRETACEOUS
250 MILLION YEARS AGO	205 MILLION YEARS AGO	135 MILLION YEARS AGO	65 MILLION YEARS AGO

111

Dacentrurus

The British paleontologist Richard Owen studied *Dacentrurus* in the 1870s. He was working on a very important fossil. Not only was *Dacentrurus* a new dinosaur, it belonged to a new group of dinosaurs.

Dacentrurus belonged to the stegosaur group of dinosaurs, which had plates and spines on their back and tail. Owen named the dinosaur in 1875 in a scientific paper that described the dinosaur's traits. However, Owen did not name the animal *Dacentrurus*, he called it *Omosaurus*—"upper arm lizard." Why did scientists change its name? Another animal had already been named *Omosaurus*, so in 1902 the American paleontologist Frederick Lucas renamed the new stegosaur *Dacentrurus*, or "pointed tail."

MANY KINDS OF *DACENTRURUS*

Fossil-hunters found the first *Dacentrurus* remains in England in the 1870s. Since then, scientists have discovered further *Dacentrurus* remains in France and Portugal. However, there are slight differences between the various *Dacentrurus* fossils. For example, one has longer, bigger spines than those of the first *Dacentrurus* found.

Do these differences mean that scientists are wrong to believe all the fossils belong to *Dacentrurus*? No. The differences mean that there was more than one species, or kind, of *Dacentrurus*. Today there are many species of cat. There is the lion, the tiger, the leopard, and the jaguar—to name just a few. Each species is different from the rest. In prehistoric times, there were many species of some dinosaurs. Scientists think there may have been four species of *Dacentrurus*, including *Dacentrurus armatus* (armored) and *Dacentrurus hastiger* (spear bearer).

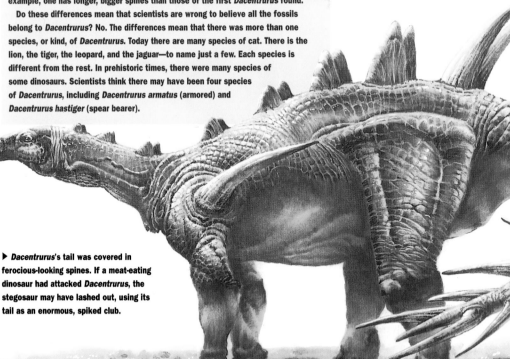

▶ *Dacentrurus*'s tail was covered in ferocious-looking spines. If a meat-eating dinosaur had attacked *Dacentrurus*, the stegosaur may have lashed out, using its tail as an enormous, spiked club.

Not too big, not too small

No one has found a complete *Dacentrurus* skeleton. However, from what they have found, scientists can tell that the dinosaur was a small-to-medium-sized stegosaur.

Dacentrurus was bigger than *Kentrosaurus* but not as large as *Stegosaurus*, the dinosaur after which all stegosaurs are named.

Although fossil-hunters have not found a *Dacentrurus* skull, scientists know the animal had a small head—all stegosaurs did. Inside its small head was a tiny brain, about the size of a walnut. Scientists are still not sure how such a huge animal managed with such a small brain.

Plates and spines

Along its neck, *Dacentrurus* had bony plates. Fossil-hunters have found only one plate. It measured about 6 in (15 cm) along the edge that joined the dinosaur's back.

Scientists guess that *Dacentrurus* had two rows of plates and that the plates stood upright. All plate-backed stegosaurs had double rows of upright plates. At some point on *Dacentrurus*'s back, though, the bony plates turned into long, bony spines. From what they know of other spiny-backed stegosaurs, scientists believe *Dacentrurus* had two rows of spines, too. They reached almost to the tip of its tail.

How *Dacentrurus* lived

Dacentrurus was a four-legged plant-eater, like all stegosaurs. It did not have a long neck, so it would have bitten leaves from low bushes and trees. Meat-eating dinosaurs hunted *Dacentrurus*. However, the stegosaur was not defenseless. Its spine-covered tail was a fearsome weapon.

DINOFACTS

Dacentrurus
(*DAY-sen-TROO-rus*)

NAME: *Dacentrurus* means pointed tail
da (very) + kentron (sharp point) + ourus (tail)

FAMILY: Ornithischian

Thyreophoran

Stegosaur

SIZE: 15 ft (4.6 m) long; 6 ft (1.8 m) high at the hip

WEIGHT: 2 tons (1.8 tonnes)—about the same as 2 North American bison

FOOD: plants

HABITAT: not known

WHERE: remains found in France, Portugal, and southern England

WHEN: 150–135 million years ago in the Jurassic period

DACENTRURUS

TRIASSIC	JURASSIC		CRETACEOUS
250 MILLION YEARS AGO	205 MILLION YEARS AGO	135 MILLION YEARS AGO	65 MILLION YEARS AGO

CHECK THESE OUT!

Collecting dinosaurs, Jurassic period, *Kentrosaurus*, Ornithischian dinosaurs, Stegosaurs, *Stegosaurus*, Thyreophorans

Daspletosaurus

Daspletosaurus was a large, heavy meat-eater. It had a set of huge, jagged teeth to match its size. Like the later *Tyrannosaurus*, it probably chased after the big horned dinosaurs of its day.

Daspletosaurus was closely related to *Tyrannosaurus*, but lived a little earlier. The American paleontologist Charles M. Sternberg named *Daspletosaurus* in the 1920s. He found the skeleton and skull of this large theropod (two-legged walker) in the Red Deer River in Alberta in 1921. These were not the first *Daspletosaurus* remains to be discovered. However, they were in better condition than earlier finds.

Daspletosaurus was a ferocious meat-eating dinosaur. Like all tyrannosaurs, its head was big for its body, and its powerful, flesh-tearing jaws were armed with huge, jagged teeth. Sternberg first thought that he had come across the bones of *Albertosaurus*, another tyrannosaur. However, he soon realized that this dinosaur was too heavy to be *Albertosaurus*.

How *Daspletosaurus* lived

Daspletosaurus had fewer teeth than other tyrannosaurs, but the teeth it had were very big. Scientists have studied other meat-eating dinosaurs that had a few large teeth instead of many smaller ones. These dinosaurs hunted animals much larger than themselves, so *Daspletosaurus* probably did the same. Like *Tyrannosaurus*, *Daspletosaurus* would have attacked head first, biting a lump out of its victim.

Daspletosaurus was not the only tyrannosaur living in Alberta 75-70 million years ago. *Albertosaurus* was there too. The two were able to share the same habitat because they did not compete for food. *Albertosaurus*, a lightly built animal, chased the fast-running

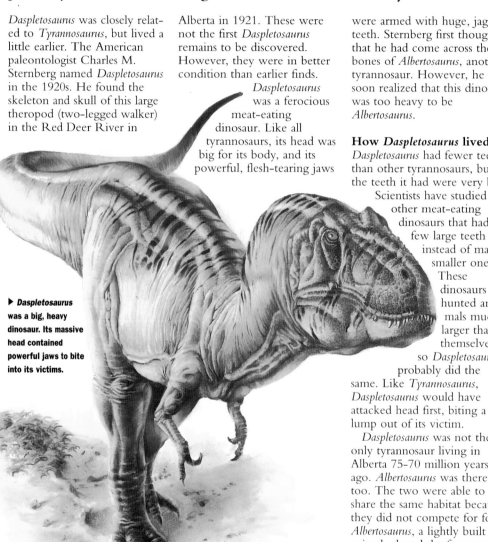

▶ *Daspletosaurus* was a big, heavy dinosaur. Its massive head contained powerful jaws to bite into its victims.

TOO CLOSE FOR COMFORT

How closely related were *Daspletosaurus* and its fellow tyrannosaurs *Tyrannosaurus* and *Tarbosaurus*? Pretty closely, scientists reckon. Some paleontologists think they are such close relatives that their scientific names should be changed.

When scientists name an animal, they give it a name with two parts. The first part indicates the larger group to which the animal belongs—for example, *Canis*. The second part is the animal's name—for example, *lupus*. The two parts together—*Canis lupus*—form the animal's full scientific name. *Canis lupus* is the scientific name for the gray wolf. Other animals in its group (*Canis*) are closely related to it—such as the coyote (*Canis latrans*) and the golden jackal (*Canis aureus*).

Some scientists think *Daspletosaurus*, *Tarbosaurus*, and *Tyrannosaurus* are as similar to each other as wolves, coyotes, and jackals. They think all these dinosaurs should be put into the *Tyrannosaurus* group. Other scientists think each dinosaur is so different from the others that it should keep its own name. It's all right for scientists to disagree. Rather than argue, scientists look for evidence to support their ideas. Eventually they will find enough information to answer their question.

hadrosaurs (duckbills). *Daspletosaurus* hunted giant horned dinosaurs (ceratopsians) such as *Styracosaurus* and *Centrosaurus*. Some scientists think that, like a vulture, *Daspletosaurus* may have also eaten from kills left by other meat-eating dinosaurs.

CHECK THESE OUT!

Albertosaurus, Ceratopsians, Cretaceous period, Hadrosaurs, Saurischian dinosaurs, *Styracosaurus*, *Tarbosaurus*, Tetanurans, Theropods, Tyrannosaurs, *Tyrannosaurus*

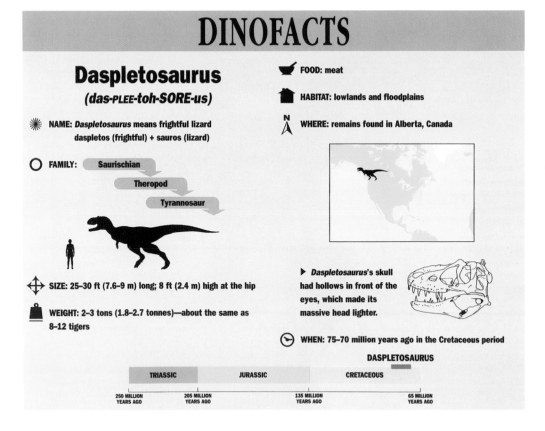

DINOFACTS

Daspletosaurus
(das-PLEE-toh-SORE-us)

☀ **NAME:** *Daspletosaurus* means frightful lizard
daspletos (frightful) + sauros (lizard)

○ **FAMILY:** Saurischian
→ Theropod
→ Tyrannosaur

✛ **SIZE:** 25–30 ft (7.6–9 m) long; 8 ft (2.4 m) high at the hip

⚖ **WEIGHT:** 2–3 tons (1.8–2.7 tonnes)—about the same as 8–12 tigers

🥄 **FOOD:** meat

🏠 **HABITAT:** lowlands and floodplains

WHERE: remains found in Alberta, Canada

▶ *Daspletosaurus*'s skull had hollows in front of the eyes, which made its massive head lighter.

🕐 **WHEN:** 75–70 million years ago in the Cretaceous period

DASPLETOSAURUS

TRIASSIC	JURASSIC	CRETACEOUS
250 MILLION YEARS AGO	205 MILLION YEARS AGO	135 MILLION YEARS AGO / 65 MILLION YEARS AGO

Datousaurus

Datousaurus was an early plant-eating dinosaur. It was enormous, with a very long neck for reaching up to chew leaves from trees. It would have towered over the meat-eating dinosaurs of its day.

Chinese paleontologists first found *Datousaurus* in 1970 in Sichuan Province. They realized they had found a new kind of sauropod, a plant-eating dinosaur with a long neck and tail.

However, the skull was unusual—it was very heavily built. Most sauropod dinosaurs had small, lightly built skulls. These skulls are difficult to find today. Most of them got crushed and lost after the animals died. With its big head, *Datousaurus* must have looked different from other sauropods.

Datousaurus was an early sauropod. It lived at a time when these giant plant-eaters had not yet become widespread or numerous.

Datousaurus tells scientists what early sauropods were like. By comparing it with later sauropods, paleontologists can

▶ *Datousaurus* had to spend a lot of its time feeding because its body was so big. It would have lived in lowland areas with plenty of plants to eat.

VERY DISTANT RELATIVES

Dinosaurs did not have to live in the same part of the world to be closely related. Scientists think that *Datousaurus* may have been related to *Cetiosaurus*, a sauropod that lived in England. How could dinosaurs that lived so far apart be related?

During the millions of years that dinosaurs walked the earth, the shape of the continents changed many times. Lands that are now separated by oceans were once joined. Sometimes, even after continents moved apart, sea levels fell. Strips of land would be exposed, linking one continent with another. Dinosaurs could move easily from one area of the world to another. When sea levels rose again, groups of dinosaurs became stranded. Separated from others of their own kind, they evolved in slightly different ways. New species of dinosaurs appeared.

Perhaps the ancestors of *Datousaurus* and *Cetiosaurus* belonged to groups of the same kind of dinosaur that became separated. Over millions of years, one group eventually gave rise to *Datousaurus*, the other to *Cetiosaurus*.

learn more about how all sauropods evolved.

How did *Datousaurus* live?

Datousaurus was enormous. It needed to eat a huge amount of leaves and shoots, so it spent most of its time feeding.

Datousaurus lived in China at the same time as the sauropod *Shunosaurus* and the stegosaur (plate-backed dinosaur) *Huayangosaurus*. There were also meat-eaters, including *Gasosaurus* and *Xuanhanosaurus*. These theropods (two-legged walkers) would have been too small to kill a fully grown *Datousaurus*, but they would have tried to take young ones. The mother *Datousaurus* would have come to her baby's rescue to fight off the attacker. Unlike *Diplodocus*, *Datousaurus* did not have a whiplash tail to use as a weapon. The mother probably could rear up on her hind legs and strike out with her forelegs. Each of her forefeet probably had a sharp claw that could have badly injured a theropod that got too close.

CHECK THESE OUT!

Cetiosaurus, Continental drift, *Diplodocus*, *Huayangosaurus*, Jurassic period, Rocks, Saurischian dinosaurs, Sauropodomorph dinosaurs, Sauropods, Theropods

DINOFACTS

Datousaurus
(DAH-*toh*-SORE-us)

▶ *Datousaurus* had a massive, heavy skull. Its chunky, spoon-shaped teeth were used for crushing bushels of plants and shoots.

✳ NAME: *Datousaurus* means big-headed lizard
　da (big) + tou (head) + sauros (lizard)

○ FAMILY:　Saurischian

Sauropodomorph

Sauropod

✛ SIZE: 50 ft (15.2 m) long; 8 ft (2.4 m) high at the hip

⚖ WEIGHT: about 22–27.5 tons (20–25 tonnes)— about the same as 4–6 African elephants

FOOD: plants

HABITAT: leafy lowlands

N
↑ WHERE: remains found in China

🕑 WHEN: 170 million years ago in the Jurassic period

DATOUSAURUS		
TRIASSIC	JURASSIC	CRETACEOUS
250 MILLION YEARS AGO	205 MILLION YEARS AGO	135 MILLION YEARS AGO　　65 MILLION YEARS AGO

Deinocheirus

This dinosaur is known only from a few bits and pieces—and a huge pair of arms. Scientists are still not sure whether *Deinocheirus* was a peaceful insect-eater or a terrifying dinosaur-hunter with killer claws.

While digging in Mongolia in 1965, the Polish paleontologist Zofia Kielan-Jaworowska found a pair of huge arms. They were 8 ft (2.4 m) long. Each hand had three clawed fingers. The claws were 1 ft (30 cm) long. The claws would originally have been twice as long, with a casing of horn. Kielan-Jaworowska also found shoulder blades and a few ribs. The ribs showed that the animal must have been about the size of *Tyrannosaurus*. What sort of monster could have owned those huge arms?

A superhunter?
In 1970, two scientists wrote a paper describing the dinosaur as a meat-eater. They named it *Deinocheirus*, or "terrible hand." They believed it was most closely related to the megalosaurids. Megalosaurids were large theropods (two-legged walkers) that clawed other dinosaurs to death.

Like *Deinocheirus*, mega-losaurids had three-fingered hands. However, their arms were small for their body. *Deinocheirus*'s arms were too long for its body. Also, its

▶ Judging by the size of its ribs, scientists think *Deinocheirus* could have been as big as *Tyrannosaurus*.

SLOTHFUL DINOSAURS?

When it was alive, *Deinocheirus* held its arms with its hands turned inward. Today, sloths hold their arms in a similar way. Sloths are fruit-eating mammals from South America that live in trees. Sloths also have curved claws. Could *Deinocheirus* have lived in trees like a sloth?

A young *Deinocheirus* might have. However, an adult could weigh over 7 tons (6.3 tonnes). No tree could have held that weight. So perhaps the adults lived on the ground, pulling down branches with their claws to bring food to their mouth.

claws don't seem sharp enough for killing.

Deinocheirus's fingers were also like those of the ornithomimosaurs, or bird mimics. The ornithomimosaurs were speedy, mainly toothless dinosaurs such as *Ornithomimus* and *Struthiomimus*. They ate insects and other small animals. Like *Deinocheirus*, they had three fingers of equal length on each hand.

However, *Deinocheirus* wasn't exactly like the ornithomimosaurs either. It had stronger claws than the bird mimics; unlike them, however, it could not hold things in its hands. Was *Deinocheirus* a huge bird mimic? Scientists will not know until they find more *Deinocheirus* remains.

CHECK THESE OUT!

Cretaceous period, *Megalosaurus*, *Ornithomimus*, Saurischian dinosaurs, *Struthiomimus*, Theropods, *Tyrannosaurus*

DINOFACTS

Deinocheirus
(DIE-noh-KYE-rus)

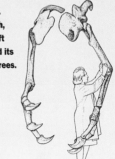

▶ *Deinocheirus* had arms 8 ft (2.4 m) long. Each hand had three fingers of equal length, and each finger had a curved claw up to 2 ft (60 cm) long. The dinosaur might have used its claws to hook down the branches of fruit trees.

✳ NAME: *Deinocheirus* means terrible hand
deinos (terrible) + cheir (hand)

○ FAMILY: Saurischian
Theropod

⊕ SIZE: not known, but probably large

⚖ WEIGHT: perhaps about 7–13 tons (6.3–11.8 tonnes)

⊙ FOOD: not known

🏠 HABITAT: semiarid plains with scattered trees

Ⓝ WHERE: remains found in Mongolia

🕐 WHEN: 75–65 million years ago in the Cretaceous period

DEINOCHEIRUS

TRIASSIC	JURASSIC	CRETACEOUS
250 MILLION YEARS AGO	205 MILLION YEARS AGO	135 MILLION YEARS AGO	65 MILLION YEARS AGO

Deinonychus

Deinonychus was one of the deadliest of all dinosaurs. Small and swift, it was armed with sharp claws to slash its prey. Its discovery led scientists to study the links between dinosaurs and birds.

Deinonychus was first discovered in Montana in the 1930s by the American paleontologist Barnum Brown. Then in 1964 John Ostrom came across more remains in Montana and Wyoming. In 1969 Ostrom became the first scientist to write a scientific paper describing the dinosaur.

Deinonychus was small and fierce with sharp teeth. It also had a large brain. Scientists used to think all dinosaurs were slow and not too bright. The discovery of big-brained *Deinonychus* meant that some dinosaurs had been at least as smart as modern reptiles and birds.

Deinonychus had strong hind legs, which showed it could run fast. When it ran, it used its long, stiff tail to steer. Like a cheetah, swift *Deinonychus* could turn fast.

Killer claws

Besides its speed and brains, the most striking features of *Deinonychus* were the killer claws that gave the dinosaur its name (*Deinonychus* means terrible claw).

▲ Some experts believe that this small but deadly dinosaur was an intelligent killer that hunted in packs.

Like most theropods (two-legged walkers), *Deinonychus* had four toes on each foot. The second toe on each foot was unusually long—up to 5 in (12.7 cm).

These claws were curved and razor-sharp. Their shape showed that they were killing weapons. They would have ripped through dinosaur skin like a knife through butter.

Deinonychus would probably have walked with its second toes bent backward to keep its claws from scraping along the ground and becoming blunt.

How *Deinonychus* lived

Deinonychus killed and ate plant-eating dinosaurs such as ankylosaurs (armored dinosaurs) and young

MY COUSIN THE BIRD

MY COUSIN THE BIRD

The American paleontologist John Ostrom discovered many things from studying *Deinonychus* fossils. For example, when he later studied *Archaeopteryx*, one of the first avialans, Ostrom noticed it was a lot like *Deinonychus*.

Certain parts of *Archaeopteryx*'s skeleton—like the wrist joint, the air spaces in the skull, and the thin, hollow bones—were similar to those of both modern birds and *Deinonychus*. He wondered if birds and dinosaurs were actually related.

Today, most scientists believe birds descended from theropod dinosaurs. *Deinonychus*'s cousin *Velociraptor* was birdlike. So was the theropod *Saurornithoides* ("birdlike lizard"). Scientists think these dinosaurs were closely related to the first birds. Perhaps while they bounded along on two feet, their cousins soared and glided overhead.

DINOFACTS

Deinonychus
(die-NOH-ni-kus)

▶ Swift *Deinonychus* used its long, stiff tail to turn on a dime.

✴ **NAME:** *Deinonychus* means terrible claw
deinos (terrible) + onux (claw)

◯ **FAMILY:** Saurischian
Theropod
Dromaeosaur

✛ **SIZE:** 10 ft (3 m) long; 3.5 ft (1 m) high at the hip

⚖ **WEIGHT:** about 200 lbs (91 kg)—about the same as a large leopard

🥣 **FOOD:** meat

🏔 **HABITAT:** lowlands

⇧ **WHERE:** remains found in Montana and Wyoming

🕐 **WHEN:** 120–90 million years ago in the Cretaceous period

			DEINONYCHUS	
TRIASSIC		JURASSIC		CRETACEOUS
250 MILLION YEARS AGO	205 MILLION YEARS AGO		135 MILLION YEARS AGO	65 MILLION YEARS AGO

sauropods (long-necked, long-tailed plant-eaters). *Deinonychus* was agile enough to catch most plant-eating dinosaurs that tried to run away.

Pack hunter

When Barnum Brown first discovered *Deinonychus* in the 1930s, he made an interesting discovery. He stumbled across several of the dinosaurs lying near a *Tenontosaurus*, a large, plant-eating dinosaur.

How did all these dinosaurs come to die in the same place at the same time? It is possible that *Deinonychus* hunted in packs like modern wolves to bring down large prey. Perhaps the *Tenontosaurus* bones Brown found were the remains of a kill made by a *Deinonychus* pack.

CHECK THESE OUT!

Ankylosaurs, *Archaeopteryx*, Avialans, Birds, Cretaceous period, Dromaeosaurs, Saurischian dinosaurs, Sauropods, *Saurornithoides*, *Tenontosaurus*, Theropods, *Velociraptor*

Dilophosaurus

Dilophosaurus was a large, meat-eating dinosaur that roamed the Early Jurassic landscape. Did it hunt in packs, or did it eat the remains of dead animals? Scientists have yet to decide.

Paleontologists know that *Dilophosaurus* was large and ate meat. However, they disagree on how the dinosaur hunted and what it ate.

Most large theropods (two-legged walkers) hunted large, plant-eating dinosaurs. They charged head first, striking their victims with terrible force. They had very strong skulls.

▼ **Dilophosaurus was a large, crested, meat-eating theropod (two-legged walker). Many scientists believe that Dilophosaurus hunted in packs, attacking large plant-eating dinosaurs.**

Dilophosaurus, though, had a much more delicate skull than larger theropods. Could *Dilophosaurus* have hunted in the same way?

Some scientists say no. If *Dilophosaurus* had crashed head first into a large plant-eating dinosaur, the bones in its skull would have shattered. Perhaps *Dilophosaurus* scavenged on the bodies of big animals it found already dead. It could also have hunted prey smaller than itself, like *Massospondylus*.

To catch small animals *Dilophosaurus* would have had to be fast on its feet. It would not need a strong skull, large teeth, or powerful jaws.

Like some other meat-eaters, *Dilophosaurus* had long arms to help it catch and kill its prey. It belonged to the ceratosaur group of theropods. All ceratosaurs had four sharp-clawed fingers on each hand.

Some scientists, though, believe that the dinosaur's skull was more robust

DOUBLE-CRESTED DINOSAUR

Ceratosaurs, such as *Dilophosaurus*, had horns or crests on their heads. Many plant-eating dinosaurs had horns and crests, as did many theropods, like avialans. *Dilophosaurus* had two huge, fan-shaped crests covering the top of its head from its eyes to the tip of its snout. What were they for?

Paleontologists base their ideas on the fossils they find, and by studying the behavior of living animals.

Perhaps *Dilophosaurus* used its crest like deer use their antlers. Did a male *Dilophosaurus* clash heads with another male to see which was the stronger, like male deer do today? Or were the bony crests so weak that they would have broken with the first headbutt? It's hard to test how strong very old bones could have been.

Perhaps the crest was for show. Maybe males had different-sized crests than females. Or maybe an older dinosaur had a larger crest to let younger dinosaurs know who was in charge.

Making up theories is fun, but good scientists also have to test their ideas thoroughly to find out if they are true. Of course, it's much easier to study how living animals behave today than to work out how extinct dinosaurs may have acted millions of years ago. Perhaps one day a paleontologist will find fossil evidence. Perhaps that paleontologist will be you.

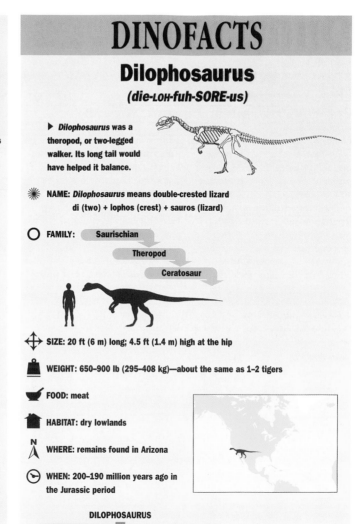

DINOFACTS

Dilophosaurus
(die-LOH-fuh-SORE-us)

▶ *Dilophosaurus* was a theropod, or two-legged walker. Its long tail would have helped it balance.

✳ NAME: *Dilophosaurus* means double-crested lizard
di (two) + lophos (crest) + sauros (lizard)

○ FAMILY: Saurischian
Theropod
Ceratosaur

✥ SIZE: 20 ft (6 m) long; 4.5 ft (1.4 m) high at the hip

⚖ WEIGHT: 650–900 lb (295–408 kg)—about the same as 1–2 tigers

🥣 FOOD: meat

🏠 HABITAT: dry lowlands

N
↑ WHERE: remains found in Arizona

🕐 WHEN: 200–190 million years ago in the Jurassic period

DILOPHOSAURUS

TRIASSIC	JURASSIC	CRETACEOUS
250 MILLION YEARS AGO	205 MILLION YEARS AGO	135 MILLION YEARS AGO / 65 MILLION YEARS AGO

than it looked and its teeth were big enough to kill large dinosaurs. They point to lightly built Komodo dragons (big lizards living in Indonesia) that can take down a water buffalo.

Fossil-hunters also came across the remains of three *Dilophosaurus* in one place. So perhaps *Dilophosaurus* hunted in packs like wild dogs to tackle large prey.

CHECK THESE OUT!

Avialans, Ceratosaurs, Jurassic period, *Massospondylus*, Saurischian dinosaurs, Theropods, Triassic period

Dinosaurs

Dinosaurs were one of the most amazing groups of animals to live on earth. For 165 million years they ruled the land. Some dinosaurs are still alive today. We call them birds!

Dinosaurs are so familiar today that we often forget there was a time when no one knew about them. When people found strange bones and footprints, they thought they had found the remains of dragons, trolls, or elephants.

It was not until the late 1700s that Georges Cuvier, the father of modern paleontology, realized that some fossils came from very different kinds of animals—kinds that were extinct. Some of the first fossils recognized were not dinosaurs, but dinosaur-aged flying and sea-living reptiles. They included flying pterosaurs, and swimming mosasaurs, plesiosaurs, and ichthyosaurs.

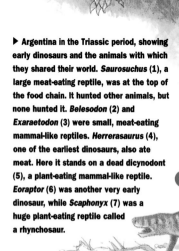

▶ Argentina in the Triassic period, showing early dinosaurs and the animals with which they shared their world. *Saurosuchus* (1), a large meat-eating reptile, was at the top of the food chain. It hunted other animals, but none hunted it. *Belesodon* (2) and *Exaraetodon* (3) were small, meat-eating mammal-like reptiles. *Herrerasaurus* (4), one of the earliest dinosaurs, also ate meat. Here it stands on a dead dicynodont (5), a plant-eating mammal-like reptile. *Eoraptor* (6) was another very early dinosaur, while *Scaphonyx* (7) was a huge plant-eating reptile called a rhynchosaur.

The first dinosaur fossils were found and named in the early 1800s. Among these were land-dwelling *Megalosaurus*, a Jurassic meat-eater, and *Iguanodon* and *Hylaeosaurus*, both Early Cretaceous plant-eaters. Because these first dinosaurs were all land-dwellers, scientists thought that all dinosaurs must live on land.

Dinosaurs get their name

In the 1840s, the British paleontologist Richard Owen described all the fossil reptiles

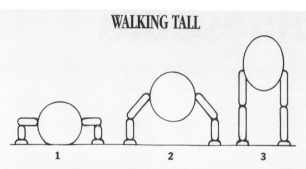

WALKING TALL

1   **2**   **3**

This diagram shows how dinosaurs and other animals stand and walk. Most living reptiles walk with a sprawling gait (1). Some early archosaurs (dinosaur ancestors) walked with their legs half-bent and half-straight (2), as crocodiles do today. Birds and mammals walk with their legs straight (3); so did the dinosaurs.

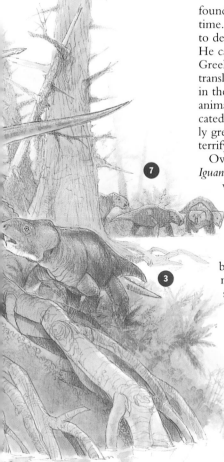

found in England up to that time. Owen invented a name to describe these ancient forms. He called them *dinosaurs*. The Greek word *deinos* is often translated as terrible when used in the names of prehistoric animals. Owen, though, indicated that *deinos* means fearfully great—not simply scary, but terrifyingly big!

Owen saw that *Megalosaurus*, *Iguanodon*, and *Hylaeosaurus* were not like other reptiles. They held their hind limbs beneath their body, as do birds and land mammals. Their hips had extra backbones, like birds and mammals. They even had similar ribs to a bird or mammal. Perhaps they were also warm-blooded, like birds and mammals.

New finds, new kinds

As time went by, new fossils from other parts of the world showed

that dinosaurs were more varied than Owen could have imagined.

For example, Owen thought that all dinosaurs walked on all four legs. Later, paleontologists found the skeleton of a dinosaur that could walk on its two hind legs—*Hadrosaurus*.

Little *Compsognathus*, not much larger than a pet cat, showed that some dinosaurs could be quite small. Until their fossils were found, no one expected that any creature as unusual as three-horned *Triceratops*, or as huge as *Brachiosaurus*, really existed.

Different opinions

By the late 1800s, most paleontologists disagreed with Owen. They thought that the dinosaurs did not make a real group. They thought that these forms were all too different to be closely related.

It didn't matter to them that many dinosaur fossils looked alike. The scientists simply argued that different groups of animals had developed the same features separately. For example, both dolphins and ichthyosaurs clearly had fins. If the two groups developed their fins on their own, then they could not be related.

Owen's dinosaurs

Later discoveries showed that Owen was right after all. Although later dinosaurs appeared different from each other, early dinosaurs were all similar. For example, although *Styracosaurus* and *Amargasaurus* looked very different from each other, their distant ancestors *Lesothosaurus* and *Thecodontosaurus* looked alike.

It's a hip thing

Scientists found how dinosaurs fit into one big group by looking at the dinosaurs' hips. Most modern reptiles walk with their legs sprawled out. Dinosaur hip sockets have a special hole that lets them walk with their legs straight underneath them, just as Owen observed. Also, most reptiles have only two backbones in their hips. Dinosaurs have at least three.

Scientists now agree that the dinosaurs are a proper group. They believe that all dinosaurs are descended from a single ancestor. This is like saying that you and your cousin both belong to one family group because you both have the same grandparents.

Pterosaurs aren't dinosaurs

Using this rule, scientists can decide which kinds of animals are dinosaurs, and which are not. For example, if the pterosaurs (flying reptiles) were to be called dinosaurs, scientists would have to prove that pterosaurs descended from the

▼ The dinosaur family tree. Turtles, archosaurs, and lizards all descended from the first reptile, so they are reptiles too. Dinosaurs are both archosaurs and reptiles. The dinosaur family is divided into two major groups—the ornithischian (bird-hipped) dinosaurs and the saurischian (lizard-hipped) dinosaurs.

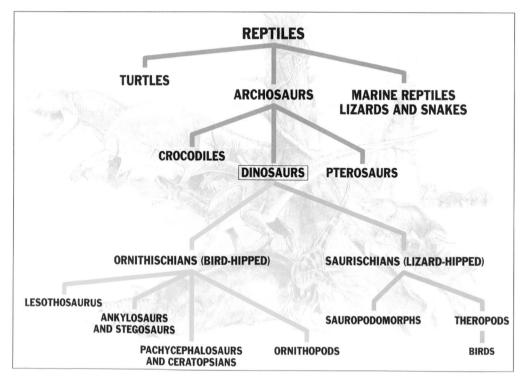

DINOFACTS

Dinosaurs

 NAME: Dinosaur means fearfully great lizard
deinos (fearfully great, terrible) + sauros (lizard)

 SIZE: During the Mesozoic Era, 30 in (76 cm) to 88 ft
(26.8 m) long; 1 ft (30 cm) high at the hip to 50 ft (15.2 m)
high at the top of the head

 WEIGHT: huge variation from 9 lb (4 kg) to 35 tons (31.8
tonnes) or more

FOOD: varies, from plants to insects to meat

HABITAT: varies,
from deserts to
swamps and
floodplains

N **WHERE:** remains
found worldwide

 WHEN: from 230 million years ago in the Triassic period
to today (since birds are dinosaurs)

DINOSAURS

TRIASSIC	JURASSIC	CRETACEOUS
250 MILLION YEARS AGO	205 MILLION YEARS AGO	135 MILLION YEARS AGO / 65 MILLION YEARS AGO

common dinosaur ancestor. Scientists believe that pterosaurs did not descend from this ancestor and so are not dinosaurs. Like dinosaurs, though, and crocodiles, pterosaurs belong to the group of reptiles called archosaurs.

Birds have lizard hips

This new way of grouping dinosaurs has produced an interesting result. Because birds share certain features with theropod dinosaurs, it seems that birds descended from theropods. Therefore, birds descended from the common ancestor of the dinosaurs and are true dinosaurs. Birds fall into the category of lizard-hipped dinosaurs.

Our new understanding of dinosaurs might have surprised Richard Owen. His term

dinosaur once referred to only three British fossil reptiles. We now know that dinosaurs existed in many forms, from the largest meat-eaters and plant-eaters ever to live on land, to today's birds.

Lizard hips and bird hips

Dinosaurs are divided into two major family branches. One branch is the ornithischian, or bird-hipped, dinosaurs.

In most of these animals, the pubis (the front bone of the lower hip) points backward, and the lower jaw includes an extra bone.

Ornithischians were all plant-eaters. They include the armored and plate-backed dinosaurs, or thyreophorans, such as *Ankylosaurus* and *Stegosaurus*. The group also includes the ornithopods, such

as *Iguanodon* and the hadrosaurs, as well as the ceratopsians (horned dinosaurs) and the pachycephalosaurs (thick-headed dinosaurs).

The other major branch is the saurischian, or lizard-hipped, dinosaurs. In most saurischians, the pubis points forward, and their thumb claws are large.

Saurischians include the long-necked, plant-eating sauropodomorphs (pro-sauropods and sauropods) and the theropods (two-legged walkers)—including birds.

CHECK THESE OUT!

Archosaurs, Birds, Collecting dinosaurs, Crocodiles, Evolution, Ornithischian dinosaurs, Reptiles, Saurischian dinosaurs, Triassic period

Diplodocus

Diplodocus was one of the mighty sauropods—giants with a long neck and long tail. That neck, supported inside by a stretchy, ropelike cord, would have been useful for eating leaves from tall trees.

In the early 1900s, the Carnegie Museum in Pittsburgh, Pennsylvania, displayed a huge dinosaur skeleton. Almost 90 ft (27 m) long and more than twice as tall as a person, *Diplodocus* was the new star of the show. It was one of the first large dinosaurs ever displayed.

Scientists had known about *Diplodocus* for many years. Samuel Wendell Williston, an American fossil collector, first found *Diplodocus* remains in 1877 in Colorado. The American paleontologist Othniel C. Marsh wrote a scientific paper on the dinosaur the following year. However, Williston found only a few parts of *Diplodocus*. Not until 1899 did fossil-hunters find a complete skeleton.

That year, O. A. Peterson, also an American, came across two partial skeletons in Wyoming. Put together, these formed the skeleton put on show in Pittsburgh in 1900.

What was *Diplodocus*?
Diplodocus was a very large sauropod. Sauropods were long-necked, long-tailed plant-eating dinosaurs that lived in the Jurassic and Cretaceous periods. At almost

ANDREW CARNEGIE AND *DIPLODOCUS*

Andrew Carnegie, the businessman who founded the Carnegie Museum, was so proud of his museum's *Diplodocus* that he paid an artist to paint pictures of it. The British king, Edward VII, saw one of these paintings. He wanted Britain to have a similar dinosaur skeleton. Carnegie offered to make a model of his *Diplodocus* skeleton for the king. Two years later, the model was finished, and Carnegie sent it to the British Museum of Natural History in London. Carnegie then made more models of *Diplodocus* and sent them to other museums around the world.

However, one part of all the models was wrong. When the artists made the first model, they used the wrong forefeet. Instead of the forefeet of *Diplodocus*, they modeled the hind feet of *Camarasaurus*. It was not their fault. A paleontologist had put the wrong bones on the skeleton. The bones of the two animals look a lot alike. Even today, it is easy to make mistakes when identifying dinosaur bones. For example, the skull of a young *Diplodocus* looks quite like the skull of a fully grown *Barosaurus* (a smaller sauropod).

90 ft (27 m), *Diplodocus* was one of the longest of all the dinosaurs. Its slender neck and tail and the slim build of its body would have made *Diplodocus* look even longer than it really was. The distance between the dinosaur's hips and its shoulders was only 12 ft (4 m). The other 76 ft (23 m) or so were neck and tail. Because its body was so slim, *Diplodocus* was fairly light

◀ *Diplodocus* keeps an eye on a group of *Allosaurus*. These were ferocious meat-eaters with sharp claws and teeth.

for a sauropod.

Diplodocus shared its world with another sauropod called *Apatosaurus*. *Diplodocus* was slightly longer than *Apatosaurus*, but its bones were a little more slender. Taller, skinnier *Diplodocus* was probably lighter than the shorter, chunkier *Apatosaurus*.

Walking tall

How could *Diplodocus* move about when it had such a long neck and tail? In the early 1900s, scientists thought that *Diplodocus* walked with its legs splayed out to the sides, like a crocodile. Moving like this, *Diplodocus* could have dragged most of its long neck and its tail along the ground like a lizard.

However, W. J. Holland, then the director of the Carnegie Museum, showed that this idea was not correct. He explained that *Diplodocus* could not have walked with its legs splayed out. The dinosaur was just too bulky. If *Diplodocus* had tried to walk like a crocodile, its huge, round body would have scraped along the ground!

Besides, the dinosaur's ankles, knees, shoulders, and hips could not have taken the strain of walking like a crocodile. They would have sprung out of place. No. *Diplodocus* walked on straight legs that were tucked beneath its body like those of a rhinoceros or elephant. As it walked, it held its neck and tail high.

Rubber band neck

Diplodocus had an amazingly strong, muscular cord running from the top of its neck all the way along its back to the tip of its tail. The cord was as thick as a rope. Like a huge rubber band, it held the dinosaur's neck and tail up. When the dinosaur put its head down toward the ground, the cord would stretch too—otherwise its tail would snap straight up!

Scientists can test their ideas about how dinosaurs walked. They look at trackways—the fossilized footprints left by dinosaurs. If sauropods like *Diplodocus* and *Apatosaurus* had dragged their tail on the ground, there would be a wavy mark with the footprints. No tail marks have been found in the trackways of sauropods.

How did *Diplodocus* live?

Diplodocus had a huge body but a tiny mouth. It must have spent most of its time feeding to get enough food into its stomach to stay alive.

What did *Diplodocus* eat?
Diplodocus skulls have very loose, pencil-shaped teeth. Scientists once thought that because the teeth were so loose, they must also be weak. Perhaps the dinosaur could only eat soft water plants.

Later, scientists discovered the teeth were loose because

▼ We can get an idea of how *Diplodocus* walked by looking at an elephant. Like the elephant, the dinosaur walked on all fours, supporting its weight on barrel-like legs.

they were being pushed out by new teeth. Anthony Fiorillo of the Dallas Museum of Natural History examined some *Diplodocus* teeth under a strong microscope. The teeth were in perfect condition, except for one thing. They were scraped as if the dinosaur had been flossing! *Diplodocus* must have used its teeth like rakes, or combs. When it fed, it closed its teeth around a leafy branch. Then it pulled back, raking the leaves into its mouth.

Diplodocus had no cheeks and no teeth along the sides of its mouth, so it could not chew. It swallowed its food whole.

Plant food is difficult to digest, especially whole leaves. This is because the cells in leaves are made of a tough material called cellulose.

Even today, leaf-eating mammals have to rely on special ways of digesting cellulose. For example, cows chew their food twice, and have several parts to their stomach to help

digestion. Birds swallow small stones to grind their food in their stomachs. However, no one has found any such stones in the stomach of *Diplodocus*.

Reaching up

Besides *Apatosaurus*, *Diplodocus* lived alongside two other large sauropods, *Brachiosaurus* and *Camarasaurus*. *Camarasaurus* had a short neck for a sauropod, and may have fed on leaves midway up trees. *Brachiosaurus* had a very long neck and could reach high into the trees.

As for *Diplodocus*, scientists think it could stand up on its hind legs. By doing that, *Diplodocus* could have reached farther up into the trees even than *Brachiosaurus*.

However, there is no proof that *Diplodocus* stood on its hind legs. Scientists have found no trackways or footprints that show *Diplodocus* or any sauropod standing on its hind legs alone. Paleontologists cannot tell by looking at a dinosaur's skeleton whether it reared up on its hind legs or not.

All they can say is that there is no reason why *Diplodocus* could not have stood on its hind legs. Look at elephants. They are heavy, four-legged animals that can rear up on their hind legs, and even do handstands on their forelegs.

CHECK THESE OUT!

Allosaurus, Apatosaurus, Barosaurus, Brachiosaurus, Camarasaurus, Footprints, Jurassic period, Saurischian dinosaurs, Sauropodomorph dinosaurs, Sauropods

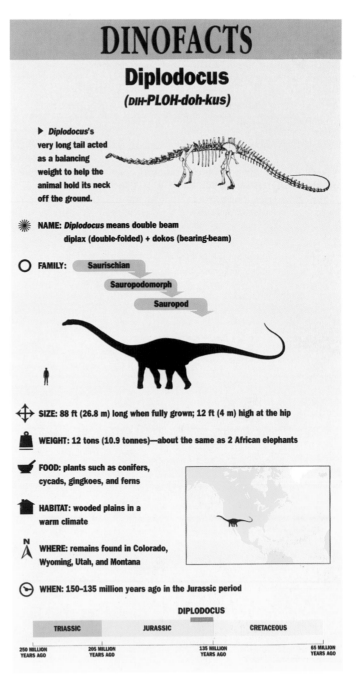

DINOFACTS

Diplodocus
(DIH-PLOH-doh-kus)

▶ *Diplodocus*'s very long tail acted as a balancing weight to help the animal hold its neck off the ground.

NAME: *Diplodocus* means double beam
diplax (double-folded) + dokos (bearing-beam)

FAMILY: Saurischian
Sauropodomorph
Sauropod

SIZE: 88 ft (26.8 m) long when fully grown; 12 ft (4 m) high at the hip

WEIGHT: 12 tons (10.9 tonnes)—about the same as 2 African elephants

FOOD: plants such as conifers, cycads, gingkoes, and ferns

HABITAT: wooded plains in a warm climate

N
WHERE: remains found in Colorado, Wyoming, Utah, and Montana

WHEN: 150–135 million years ago in the Jurassic period

	DIPLODOCUS		
TRIASSIC	JURASSIC		CRETACEOUS
250 MILLION YEARS AGO	205 MILLION YEARS AGO	135 MILLION YEARS AGO	65 MILLION YEARS AGO

Dromaeosaurs

Although not the largest meat-eating dinosaurs, dromaeosaurs were among the fiercest. They may also have been among the most intelligent and most closely related to birds.

All dromaeosaurs ate meat. Some were dog-sized, while others were as large as polar bears. They were all fierce.

The dromaeosaur group got its name in 1969. That year, Edwin H. Colbert of the American Museum of Natural History (AMNH) and Canadian paleontologist

Dale Russell described some new *Dromaeosaurus* specimens. Colbert and Russell decided to place this dinosaur in a new family, which they named the dromaeosaurs. This family also contains *Deinonychus*, *Utahraptor*, and *Velociraptor*.

Slashing claw

All dromaeosaurs have a curved, razor-sharp claw on each foot. Yale University

paleontologist John Ostrom pointed out the traits that helped dromaeosaurs to make the best use of their deadly claws.

Dromaeosaurs had special joints in their feet. As a dromaeosaur walked, its claws stayed off the ground, so they remained nice and sharp. When a dromaeosaur attacked, though, it could flick its claws forward like switchblades.

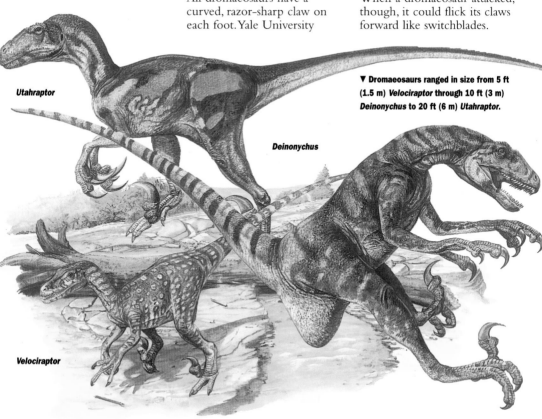

Utahraptor

▼ Dromaeosaurs ranged in size from 5 ft (1.5 m) *Velociraptor* through 10 ft (3 m) *Deinonychus* to 20 ft (6 m) *Utahraptor*.

Deinonychus

Velociraptor

Paleontologists divide dromaeosaurs into two groups: dromaeosaurines and velociraptorines. Dromaeosaurines are more heavily built and have fairly straight, jagged teeth with even-sized jags (serrations) on their back and front edges. Velociraptorines have strongly curved teeth with much larger serrations on their back edges.

Dromaeosaurus belonged to the dromaeosaurine group. *Deinonychus*, *Velociraptor*, and *Utahraptor* were all velociraptorines.

How dromaeosaurs lived

Because dromaeosaurs had jagged teeth, paleontologists know they hunted and ate other dinosaurs.

Compared to most other theropods (two-legged meat-eaters), the dromaeosaurs' bodies made them much more agile. Their large brain suggests that they were intelligent. Their muscular legs helped them chase their prey quickly, while their stiff tails acted like balancing poles to let them turn on a dime.

Once they had caught up with their prey, dromaeosaurs would have grabbed it with their long arms and kicked it to death with the sickle claws on their hind feet. Then they tore off lumps of food with their jagged teeth.

CHECK THESE OUT!

Cretaceous period, *Deinonychus*, *Dromaeosaurus*, Maniraptors, Saurischian dinosaurs, Theropods, *Utahraptor*, *Velociraptor*

DINOFACTS

Dromaeosaurs
(DROE-mee-oh-SORES)

▶ Dromaeosaur claws were lethal weapons. *Utahraptor*'s claw bone was about 8 in (20 cm) long. In life it was covered in tough horn and may have been 10.5 in (26 cm) long.

✳ **NAME:** Dromaeosaur means swift-running lizard
dromaios (swift running) + sauros (lizard)

○ **FAMILY:** Saurischian
→ Theropod
→ Maniraptor

✛ **SIZE:** 5–20 ft (1.5–6 m) long; 2.5–7.5 ft (76 cm–2.3 m) high at the hip

⬛ **WEIGHT:** large variation from 20 lbs (9 kg) to 1,000 lbs (454 kg)—from a small dog to a polar bear

FOOD: meat

HABITAT: wide variation from desert to savanna to coastal forest

N **WHERE:** remains found in North and South America, Asia, Europe, and North Africa

🕐 **WHEN:** 125–65 million years ago in the Cretaceous period

			DROMAEOSAURS
TRIASSIC	JURASSIC		CRETACEOUS
250 MILLION YEARS AGO	205 MILLION YEARS AGO	135 MILLION YEARS AGO	65 MILLION YEARS AGO

Dromaeosaurus

Dromaeosaurus was a small relative of *Deinonychus* and *Utahraptor*. Like them, it was armed with an especially long, sharp, curved claw on each hind foot. It probably used this claw to rip into its prey.

The American fossil collector Barnum Brown first discovered remains of *Dromaeosaurus* in 1914 near the Red Deer River in Canada. Unfortunately, Brown did not find a whole *Dromaeosaurus* skeleton. He found only a fairly complete skull and a few foot bones.

Little or large?

When *Dromaeosaurus* was first described in 1922, it puzzled scientists. Because it had sharp, back-curving teeth in a large skull like the mighty *Tyrannosaurus*, some scientists thought that it was a small

tyrannosaur. Others pointed out its small size. They thought it was related to *Compsognathus*, which was only the size of a house cat and one of the tiniest meat-eating dinosaurs. Who had the right answer? Several

years passed before the mystery was solved.

In the 1960s, American paleontologist John Ostrom discovered lots of dinosaur bones in Wyoming. He found

AN IMPORTANT SKULL

Although few remains of *Dromaeosaurus* have been found, they are very important. When John Ostrom discovered *Deinonychus* in the 1960s, he was better able to describe it because he had studied *Dromaeosaurus*.

Parts of *Deinonychus*'s skull were missing, but *Dromaeosaurus*'s skull was almost complete. Because *Deinonychus* and *Dromaeosaurus* were so similar in other ways, Ostrom believed the two dinosaurs' skulls were also probably similar. So *Dromaeosaurus* gave Ostrom a good idea of what *Deinonychus*'s skull was like.

▼ *Dromaeosaurus* had an extra-long, curved claw on each hind foot. It held these killer claws off the ground when walking, to keep them sharp.

skeletons of *Deinonychus* and noticed that *Deinonychus* looked like *Dromaeosaurus*. Like *Dromaeosaurus*, it had a large skull, so it probably had a big brain. It also had deep jaws full of back-curved teeth, as well as strong arms. Scientists thought *Deinonychus* was a fast-running dinosaur because it had long legs. *Dromaeosaurus* was

likewise probably speedy. Scientists named these small, swift dinosaurs dromaeosaurs in honor of *Dromaeosaurus*, which was the first of the group to be discovered. *Velociraptor* is another dromaeosaur.

How did *Dromaeosaurus* live?
Scientists think *Dromaeosaurus* was a smart and agile hunter. Each of its hind feet was armed with a sharp, curved claw. *Dromaeosaurus* probably leaped on its prey and slashed at it with these vicious talons. *Dromaeosaurus* also had a lightweight skull that may have

allowed it to move its head about rapidly to grab prey.

Dromaeosaurus probably hunted ornithopods, plant-eating dinosaurs such as *Tenontosaurus* or *Camptosaurus*. Its meat-eating neighbors would have included *Deinonychus* and *Troodon*.

CHECK THESE OUT!

Camptosaurus, Cretaceous period, *Deinonychus*, Dromaeosaurs, Ornithopods, Reconstructing dinosaurs, Saurischian dinosaurs, *Tenontosaurus*, Theropods, *Troodon*, *Velociraptor*

DINOFACTS

Dromaeosaurus
(DROE-me-o-SORE-us)

✳ **NAME:** *Dromaeosaurus* means swift-running lizard
dromaios (swift running) + sauros (lizard)

○ **FAMILY:** Saurischian
Theropod
Dromaeosaur

✛ **SIZE:** 6 ft (1.8 m) long; 2.5 ft (76 cm) high at the hip

WEIGHT: 35 lbs (16 kg)—about the same as a coyote

FOOD: meat

🏠 **HABITAT:** dry lowlands

WHERE: remains found in Alberta, Canada

▶ *Dromaeosaurus*'s skull had holes, or windows, in it. The bones formed a framework that was light but still strong.

🕐 **WHEN:** 75–70 million years ago in the Cretaceous period

DROMAEOSAURUS

TRIASSIC	JURASSIC	CRETACEOUS
250 MILLION YEARS AGO	205 MILLION YEARS AGO	135 MILLION YEARS AGO ... 65 MILLION YEARS AGO

Dromiceiomimus

Dromiceiomimus had many of the features of modern flightless birds such as the emu and ostrich. It ran fast on its long hind legs, and also had huge eyes and a large brain.

Dromiceiomimus was an ornithomimid, or "ostrichlike dinosaur," like *Ornithomimus*, *Gallimimus*, and *Struthiomimus*. Ornithomimids were much like modern emus and ostriches. Like ostriches and emus, they probably ran fast on their long,

OSTRICH DINOSAURS

Scientists compare the ornithomimids (ostrichlike dinosaurs) to modern flightless birds—like ostriches. The world's tallest, heaviest, and fastest-running bird, the ostrich can run over 30 mph (50 km/h). The emu is another big flightless bird. It lives in Australia. Although we will never know just how fast ornithomimids ran, we can make a guess and then test it with an experiment. We could measure the track (the space between the footprints) of an ostrich when it runs. By comparing the bird's track to the fossil footprints of an ornithomimid, we would have a rough idea of the dinosaur's speed. Of course, we would also need a very clear set of fossil tracks.

◀ *Dromiceiomimus* probably bounded along like a huge roadrunner. Running fast would have helped it to escape from meat-eaters.

hind legs. *Dromiceiomimus* was especially long-legged for an ornithomimid; it had longer arms than its cousins', too.

Besides having muscular, long legs, ostrichlike dinosaurs also had big eyes and big brains. *Dromiceiomimus* had enormous eyes. Its eye sockets were nearly 3 in (7.6 cm) across! These features suggest that *Dromiceiomimus* may have been able to see in color.

Live young?

Although ornithomimids had narrow bodies, they had wide hips. Some scientists have suggested that *Dromiceiomimus* and its cousins had such wide hips because they gave birth to live young. However, there is no hard evidence that they did this. It is more likely that ornithomimids had wide hips so they could lay very large eggs, as ostriches do today.

What did it eat?

Dromiceiomimus was a theropod (two-legged meat-eater), like all ornithomimids. Most theropods had teeth for eating meat. Ornithomimids, though, had no teeth, only a sharp, bony beak. Could they have eaten meat? Yes, say some scientists, they could have used their beak to eat meat—like birds of prey do today.

Did *Dromiceiomimus* hunt, though? Perhaps not. Its hands were probably not strong enough to grab live prey. The hands could have been used to pick up food from the ground. If *Dromiceiomimus* ate meat, it probably scavenged leftovers from other dinosaurs' kills.

Other scientists are not so sure if *Dromiceiomimus* ate meat after all. They think ornithomimids may have used their beaks for eating plants, like tortoises do today. Yet another group of scientists believe ornithomimids used their beaks to eat a variety of meat and plants.

CHECK THESE OUT!

Cretaceous period, Eggs and babies, *Gallimimus*, *Ornithomimus*, Saurischian dinosaurs, *Struthiomimus*, Tetanurans, Theropods

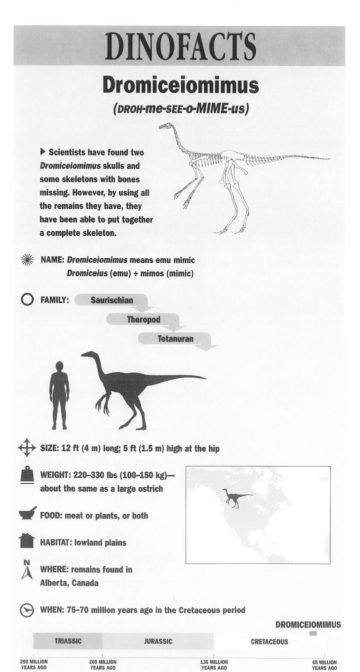

DINOFACTS

Dromiceiomimus
(DROH-me-SEE-o-MIME-us)

▶ Scientists have found two *Dromiceiomimus* skulls and some skeletons with bones missing. However, by using all the remains they have, they have been able to put together a complete skeleton.

✹ **NAME:** *Dromiceiomimus* means emu mimic
Dromiceius (emu) + mimos (mimic)

◯ **FAMILY:** Saurischian
Theropod
Tetanuran

✥ **SIZE:** 12 ft (4 m) long; 5 ft (1.5 m) high at the hip

⚖ **WEIGHT:** 220–330 lbs (100–150 kg)— about the same as a large ostrich

FOOD: meat or plants, or both

⌂ **HABITAT:** lowland plains

↑ **WHERE:** remains found in Alberta, Canada

◔ **WHEN:** 75–70 million years ago in the Cretaceous period

DROMICEIOMIMUS

TRIASSIC	JURASSIC	CRETACEOUS
250 MILLION YEARS AGO	205 MILLION YEARS AGO	135 MILLION YEARS AGO	65 MILLION YEARS AGO

Dryosaurus

Scientists think that speedy *Dryosaurus* might have lived as antelopes or horses do today. As a medium-sized plant-eater, it would have been attacked by meat-eaters—if they ran fast enough!

Fossil-hunters have found an almost complete *Dryosaurus* skeleton in North America, as well as seven partial skeletons. They have also discovered a few pieces of *Dryosaurus* bones at Tendaguru in East Africa.

How could the same dinosaur live on both sides of the Atlantic Ocean? When *Dryosaurus* was alive in the Jurassic period, the Atlantic Ocean had only begun to open. Dinosaurs could cross on dry land from North America to Europe or Africa.

Jurassic speedsters
Dryosaurus was closely related to *Hypsilophodon*, *Valdosaurus*, and *Zephyrosaurus*. All of these dinosaurs ate plants and were fast runners. How do paleontologists know this? By looking at the dinosaurs' hind legs. The three long toe bones on each of *Dryosaurus*'s hind feet were hollow, so they were light and quick.

Like most fast runners, *Dryosaurus*'s upper leg bones were shorter than its lower leg bones. On the upper bones,

▶ ***Dryosaurus* used its beaklike mouth to nibble on low-growing plants. When threatened by meat-eating dinosaurs, it could speed off on its long legs.**

HOME ON THE RANGE

How did *Dryosaurus* live? Well, with its big eyes, it could spot meat-eating dinosaurs from afar. We know it could run fast to escape these killers.

We also know the front of its jaw had no teeth; instead it had a hard beak. *Dryosaurus* was a browser. It used its beak to nip the leaves off trees and bushes, then used its cheek teeth to chew its tough food. Today, sheep and goats eat tough plant food. They do not have beaks, but they crop food by grabbing it between their lower front teeth and the bony pad that they have instead of upper teeth.

big muscles moved the legs back and forth. These muscles made the legs

very powerful. The lower leg bone was not heavily muscled. Instead, strong cords (tendons) pulled it back and forth. Because it had slim tendons instead of big muscles, the lower leg bone was lighter and easier to move. Because it was extra long, the bone also gave *Dryosaurus* a long stride. Look at horses and antelopes. Their lower legs are long and slender. Horses and antelopes can run fast, as could *Dryosaurus*.

CHECK THESE OUT!

Hypsilophodon, Jurassic period, Ornithischian dinosaurs, Ornithopods, *Zephyrosaurus*

DINOFACTS

Dryosaurus
(DRY-oh-SORE-us)

▶ *Dryosaurus* had a slender body. Its hind legs were developed for running fast.

✷ **NAME:** *Dryosaurus* means oak lizard
dryos (oak) + sauros (lizard)

○ **FAMILY:** Ornithischian
Ornithopod

✛ **SIZE:** 10–13 ft (3–4 m) long; 5 ft (1.5 m) high at the hip

WEIGHT: about 175 lbs (80 kg)—about the same as a man

FOOD: leaves from low-growing trees and bushes

HABITAT: wooded plains

WHERE: remains found in Colorado, Wyoming, and Utah in North America, and Tanzania in East Africa.

WHEN: 156–135 million years ago in the Jurassic period

		DRYOSAURUS	
TRIASSIC	JURASSIC		CRETACEOUS
250 MILLION YEARS AGO	205 MILLION YEARS AGO	135 MILLION YEARS AGO	65 MILLION YEARS AGO

Edmontonia

With its armor plating and sharp shoulder spines, the plant-eating *Edmontonia* was superbly protected against its enemies. It would have needed its tough coating to fend off marauding tyrannosaurs.

Canadian paleontologist Charles M. Sternberg described *Edmontonia* in 1928 from remains he found in the Red Deer River area of Alberta, Canada, in 1917. *Edmontonia*, he said, belonged to a group of plant-eaters called ankylosaurs (armored dinosaurs).

There were two groups of ankylosaurs. One group was the ankylosaurids, named in honor of *Ankylosaurus*. Ankylosaurids had a heavy lump of bone, like a club, at the tip of their tail. They may have swung the tail club at attacking meat-eaters, although scientists cannot prove this.

Edmontonia belonged to the other set—the nodosaurids, named in honor of *Nodosaurus*. Like other nodosaurids, *Edmontonia* did not have a tail club. However, it did have something else. Sticking out from its shoulders were long,

CHILLY WINTERS

No ankylosaur lived farther north (or south) than *Edmontonia*. In 1995, Alaskan scientist Roland Gangloff wrote a paper about an *Edmontonia* skull found in Alaska. Although the world was warmer in the Cretaceous than it is today, Alaska was still pretty cool—especially in winter!

With its short legs, *Edmontonia* would have found it difficult to migrate south to warmer areas, so it probably toughed out the winter in Alaska.

▶ *Edmontonia* was as big as a small truck. Its thick, bumpy armor plating would have been a tough mouthful for an attacking tyrannosaur!

DINOFACTS

Edmontonia

(ED-mon-TONE-ee-uh)

☀ NAME: *Edmontonia* means from Edmonton Formation, Alberta, Canada

○ FAMILY: Ornithischian

Thyreophoran

Ankylosaur

🍶 FOOD: low-growing plants

🏠 HABITAT: low-lying floodplains similar to the modern Gulf Coast of the United States

🧭 WHERE: remains found in western North America, from Alaska southward into western Texas.

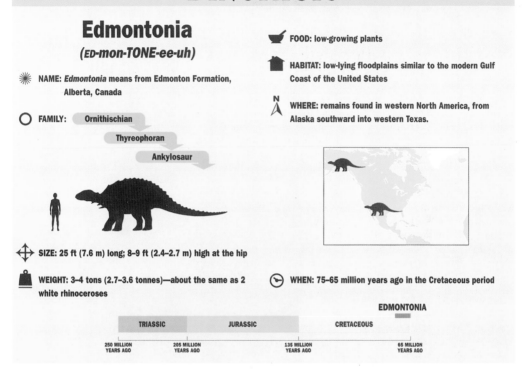

✥ SIZE: 25 ft (7.6 m) long; 8–9 ft (2.4–2.7 m) high at the hip

⚖ WEIGHT: 3–4 tons (2.7–3.6 tonnes)—about the same as 2 white rhinoceroses

🕐 WHEN: 75–65 million years ago in the Cretaceous period

EDMONTONIA

TRIASSIC	JURASSIC	CRETACEOUS	
250 MILLION YEARS AGO	205 MILLION YEARS AGO	135 MILLION YEARS AGO	65 MILLION YEARS AGO

sharp spines. *Edmontonia* was the only nodosaurid to have such forward-pointing spines.

The last nodosaurid?

Most *Edmontonia* remains have been found in rocks 70–75 million years old. In 1988, a scientist found an *Edmontonia* skull in younger rocks in South Dakota. Judging by the age of the rocks, paleontologists think *Edmontonia* was the last known nodosaurid on earth.

How did *Edmontonia* live?

With its small, leaf-shaped teeth, short legs, and low-slung head, *Edmontonia* was clearly a slow-moving plant-eater. It ate fairly soft, low-growing plants.

Many big Cretaceous plant-eaters lived in herds—but not *Edmontonia*. Its heavy armor protected it against enemies, so *Edmontonia* did not need to be in a herd to stay safe.

Edmontonia probably tried to avoid fighting, especially with the bigger meat-eaters. We can imagine it hunkering down among the vegetation and hoping not to be spotted by any nearby tyrannosaurs, such as *Albertosaurus* or even mighty *Tyrannosaurus*.

Did *Edmontonia* use its shoulder spines for fighting off tyrannosaurs? Probably not. Paleontologists imagine instead that two *Edmontonia* might have locked their spines in shoving matches to win the right to territory or mates. However, there is no way to prove this idea.

CHECK THESE OUT!

Albertosaurus, Ankylosaurs, *Ankylosaurus*, Cretaceous period, *Nodosaurus*, Ornithischian dinosaurs, Thyreophorans, *Tyrannosaurus*

141

Edmontosaurus

Edmontosaurus was a hadrosaur, or duckbill, that lived in North America in Late Cretaceous times. Some superb specimens of this dinosaur have been found; it is one of the best-known hadrosaurs.

Canadian scientist Charles H. Sternberg and his sons first found *Edmontosaurus* in Montana in 1908. They also found something very rare—dinosaur skin!

Mummified remains

Although it had lost its tail and hind feet, Sternberg's find was in amazingly good condition. This was because the body had been mummified.

When the dinosaur died, it lay in the open. The sun and wind dried the soft parts (the muscles and organs) before they could rot. The skin became leathery and shrank around the bones. Later, the body was washed into a river, where it was soon buried under layers of silt and sand.

Mummified dinosaurs are very rare. Usually the soft parts rot soon after death, and the bones

crumble away before they can be buried under sand. Because the skin had been preserved for so long, it left an imprint in the rock. *Edmontosaurus*'s skin was thin. It was studded with small, horny bumps (tubercles) on the neck, sides, and back.

Charles Sternberg later found a second *Edmontosaurus* skeleton in Wyoming, although it was in less good condition than the first.

How *Edmontosaurus* lived

Edmontosaurus was a plant-eater, like all the hadrosaurs. We have a good idea what type of plant food it ate, too. Inside the second *Edmontosaurus* found

by Sternberg, scientists found fossilized needles from conifer trees, as well as seeds and fruits. These are probably the remains of its last meal.

Edmontosaurus could have walked on all fours, but might have risen on its hind legs to run. Its tail bones (vertebrae) were linked by bony cords (tendons), which stiffened its spine and tail. When it ran, its stiff tail helped it to balance.

WATER OR LAND?

When they studied Sternberg's *Edmontosaurus*, paleontologists saw that the dinosaur's hands and feet had mittenlike skin coverings.

For years they thought the skin between the fingers and toes was webbed—like ducks' feet. Perhaps *Edmontosaurus* lived in water.

Hadrosaur footprints do not show signs of webbed feet, though. Also, *Edmontosaurus* had thick hind legs with strong ankles and three spreading toes on each foot. These features are good for supporting weight on land, but not so useful in water. The forelegs were small, with short fingers and hooflike claws. These, too, would have been useful on land.

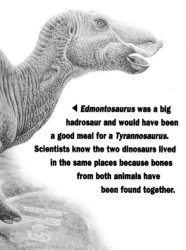

◀ *Edmontosaurus* was a big hadrosaur and would have been a good meal for a *Tyrannosaurus*. Scientists know the two dinosaurs lived in the same places because bones from both animals have been found together.

CHECK THESE OUT!

Cretaceous period, Fossils, Hadrosaurs, Ornithischian dinosaurs, Ornithopods, *Tyrannosaurus*

DINOFACTS

Edmontosaurus
(ed-MON-toh-SORE-us)

▶ Like all duckbill dinosaurs, *Edmontosaurus* had hundreds of teeth. They were arranged in rows and were excellent for crushing and grinding food.

✳ **NAME:** *Edmontosaurus* means Edmonton lizard
Edmonton (rock formation in Alberta, Canada) + sauros (lizard)

○ **FAMILY:** Ornithischian
Ornithopod
Hadrosaur

✛ **SIZE:** 33–40 ft (10–12.2 m) long; 12–14 ft (3.6–4.3 m) high at the hip

WEIGHT: 1–4 tons (0.9–3.6 tonnes)—about the same as 1–4 American bison

FOOD: plants, including evergreen cones, needles, and twigs

HABITAT: forests or plains with patches of woodland

N
↑ **WHERE:** remains found in Colorado, Montana, and South Dakota in the United States, and Alberta and Saskatchewan in Canada

↻ **WHEN:** 73–65 million years ago in the Cretaceous period

EDMONTOSAURUS

TRIASSIC	JURASSIC	CRETACEOUS
250 MILLION YEARS AGO	205 MILLION YEARS AGO	135 MILLION YEARS AGO	65 MILLION YEARS AGO

Eggs and babies

Like modern reptiles and birds, the dinosaurs of the Mesozoic Era also laid eggs. Scientists have found fossil eggs and babies that show that dinosaurs cared for their young.

In the 1850s and 1860s, paleontologists discovered fossilized eggs in France. Some of these were 14 in (36 cm) across—as big as volleyballs. No one knew what sort of creature had laid them.

In 1923, Roy Chapman Andrews of the American Museum of Natural History (AMNH) found a nest of fossil eggs in Mongolia. The ridged shells were 8 in (20 cm) long. He found them among many dinosaur remains, including those of *Protoceratops*, a small horned dinosaur. Andrews thought *Protoceratops* had laid the eggs. Andrews later found dinosaur remains on another nest. He thought the nest belonged to a *Protoceratops*, and that the other dinosaur was stealing *Protoceratops*'s eggs. He called the dinosaur *Oviraptor*— egg thief. It now seemed likely that dinosaurs had laid the strange volleyball-sized eggs.

Dinosaur eggs have since been found in many parts of the world, including France, India, China, Mongolia, Argentina, and the western United States. Most egg sites are found in Late Jurassic and Cretaceous rocks. The oldest dinosaur eggs are from the Late Triassic of Argentina.

Whose eggs are these?
Using microscopes, scientists can see the tiny differences between eggshell structures, so they can now place dinosaur eggs in very general groups. However, scientists can rarely say which dinosaur laid which egg, unless the egg contains an unhatched baby (embryo) that they can identify. Embryo skeletons are very small and fragile. They easily get mixed up with the mud or sand in which they were buried. Also, embryos have not yet grown teeth or armor, which help scientists to identify dinosaurs.

Mistaken identity
In the 1990s, Russian scientist Konstantin Mikhailov studied Andrews's eggs. Mikhailov did not believe *Protoceratops* had laid them because the eggs looked like those of modern birds. Birds are theropod dinosaurs, so Mikhailov suggested these eggs were from a theropod (two-legged meat-eater), too.

SUNNY-SIDE UP

A few reptiles, like garter snakes, give birth to live young; ichthyosaurs and mosasaurs (Mesozoic marine reptiles) did so, too. However, most reptiles and birds lay eggs, as did the Mesozoic Era dinosaurs. Like birds' eggs do now, a dinosaur egg contained a yolk that fed the growing embryo. The shell was thin and easily broken, unlike the leathery cases of modern crocodile eggs. The outside of the shell was covered in bumps, grooves, or ridges, and had lots of tiny holes (pores). Because even the tiniest crack in an eggshell causes the insides to rot, dinosaur embryos are very rare.

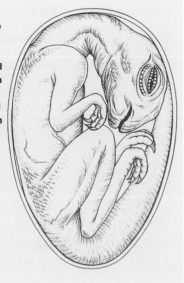

▶ A tiny *Oviraptor*, a Cretaceous theropod dinosaur, ready to hatch.

▶ A mother *Camarasaurus* watches over her newly hatched young in North America during the Jurassic period.

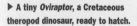

▲ Eggs found in Mongolia in 1925. The dinosaur—possibly *Oviraptor*—arranged its eggs with their narrow ends pointing out from the nest, as some birds do today.

In 1993, Mark Norell of the AMNH found another egg like those found by Andrews. Amazingly, there was still a tiny embryo in the egg. The embryo was not *Protoceratops*, but *Oviraptor*—a theropod. Mikhailov had been right!

The following year, Norell found *Oviraptor* remains on a clutch of its eggs. Birds sit on (brood) their eggs to keep them warm. Did theropods do so, too? It is possible. Fossil-hunters have since found more *Oviraptor* remains on nests. These show at least that *Oviraptor* would get onto its

nest from time to time— perhaps to protect its young from the weather.

Bringing up baby
In 1979, Montana scientists Jack Horner and Robert Makela found several nest sites of *Maiasaura*, a hadrosaur (duckbill dinosaur). Horner named the dinosaur *Maiasaura* (good mother lizard) because he was sure that the dinosaur cared for its babies.

The nests were spaced about 30 ft (9 m) apart, or the length of one mother *Maiasaura*. This showed that the dinosaurs nested in colonies, as sea gulls do today. Similar nests in older rocks in the area proved that *Maiasaura* used the same nesting sites each year.

Horner found *Maiasaura* babies in their nest. They were not in their shells, so Horner thought they had hatched. Because their joints were not fully formed, he believed the babies had to sit in the nest, waiting to be fed by their parents. However, the skeleton of a tiny baby looks a lot like the skeleton of an embryo, so we cannot be sure if the babies had hatched or their eggs had just broken open.

Horner also found eggs on a site in Montana called Egg Mountain. They were smaller and more elongated than the

▶ Most eggs are found in pieces. However, scientists are getting better and better at recognizing fossil eggshell fragments and sticking them back together.

Maiasaura eggs. Then Horner made the same mistake that Andrews made with his eggs. There were many fossils of the ornithopod (bird-footed dinosaur) *Orodromeus* in the area, so Horner thought the eggs must have belonged to *Orodromeus*, too.

In 1997, Horner and David Varricchio decided the eggs belonged instead to the small theropod *Troodon*. Together with the nests of *Oviraptor*, the *Troodon* discovery showed that meat-eating dinosaurs laid their eggs in nests.

Egg thieves

Rats, snakes, crows, and many other animals eat eggs. Did the nonflying dinosaurs die out because mammals ate all their eggs? Probably not. Mesozoic mammals were too small to open most dinosaur eggs. However, crocodiles and monitor lizards may have taken eggs then, as they do now.

The most common thieves of dinosaur eggs were probably dinosaurs themselves. Small theropods could probably use their hands to carry off and open eggs. Norell found bits of a baby *Velociraptor* (a fierce meat-eating dinosaur) in the Mongolian *Oviraptor* nest. Perhaps *Oviraptor* raided the nests of other dinosaurs to feed its own young.

Follow the leader

Joint Chinese-Canadian expeditions in the 1990s found a group of eight young *Pinacosaurus* in Mongolia's Gobi Desert. *Pinacosaurus* was an ankylosaur (armored dinosaur). From the sandstone around them, it looked as if the eight young had been buried alive in a sandstorm.

The young ankylosaurs were all the same size, and were much too big to be hatchlings. Also, they were not found in a nest. It seems likely that young ankylosaurs stayed together for a time after leaving the nest. Perhaps they were following their mother.

CHECK THESE OUT!

Camarasaurus, Collecting dinosaurs, Maiasaura, Orodromeus, Oviraptor, Pinacosaurus, Protoceratops, Troodon

Elaphrosaurus

Some paleontologists think this mysterious theropod (two-legged meat-eater) was like an ostrich. Others think it was more like *Carnotaurus*, the "meat-eating bull." Which idea is nearer the truth?

Elaphrosaurus was one of many dinosaurs found at Tendaguru in Tanzania, East Africa, from 1909 to 1911. The German expeditions at Tendaguru, led by Werner Janensch, were enormous. Collectors dug up hundreds of tons of bones. They found skeletons of *Barosaurus*, *Brachiosaurus*, *Kentrosaurus*, and others.

Elaphrosaurus was the only theropod they found in good condition—even though the skull was missing. Janensch described the dinosaur in 1920. It was a small coelurosaur, or birdlike theropod.

ARMS ACROSS THE OCEAN?

Connecticut paleontologist Peter Galton found a single upper arm bone (humerus) of a small theropod dinosaur in Garden Park, Colorado. It lay in a Late Jurassic rock bed known as the Morrison Formation. He described it as a specimen of *Elaphrosaurus*. Not many paleontologists believed he was right. Other Morrison dinosaurs, however, including *Brachiosaurus*, *Barosaurus*, and *Dryosaurus*, also turned up with *Elaphrosaurus* in East Africa. Could there be a connection between Late Jurassic African and North American dinosaurs? Perhaps someday a more convincing North American specimen of *Elaphrosaurus* will be found to prove Peter Galton was right.

Ostrich or ceratosaur?

Several scientists have studied *Elaphrosaurus*. Baron Franz Nopsca of Romania and Dale Russell of Canada thought *Elaphrosaurus* was in some ways like the fast-running ornithomimids (ostrichlike dinosaurs). Its legs were shorter than those of typical ornithomimids, so Russell reckoned that

▼ No head has been found for this small meat-eating dinosaur. It is assumed it was similar to that of other small meat-eaters.

DINOFACTS

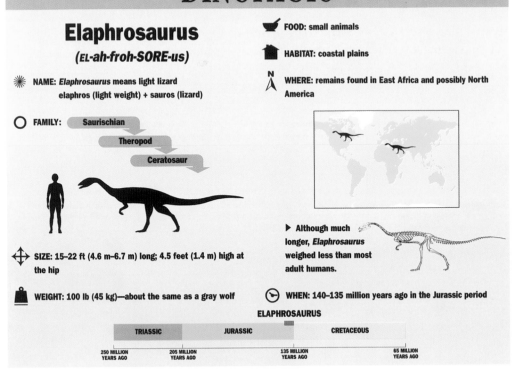

Elaphrosaurus
(EL-ah-froh-SORE-us)

☀ **NAME:** *Elaphrosaurus* means light lizard
elaphros (light weight) + sauros (lizard)

○ **FAMILY:** Saurischian
  Theropod
  Ceratosaur

✛ **SIZE:** 15–22 ft (4.6 m–6.7 m) long; 4.5 feet (1.4 m) high at the hip

⚖ **WEIGHT:** 100 lb (45 kg)—about the same as a gray wolf

🥣 **FOOD:** small animals

🏠 **HABITAT:** coastal plains

🧭 **WHERE:** remains found in East Africa and possibly North America

▶ Although much longer, *Elaphrosaurus* weighed less than most adult humans.

🕐 **WHEN:** 140–135 million years ago in the Jurassic period

ELAPHROSAURUS

TRIASSIC	JURASSIC	CRETACEOUS	
250 MILLION YEARS AGO	205 MILLION YEARS AGO	135 MILLION YEARS AGO	65 MILLION YEARS AGO

Elaphrosaurus would not have been as speedy as they.

Maryland paleontologist Thomas Holtz has studied many theropods. He found that *Elaphrosaurus* had a lot in common with the ceratosaurs, a group of theropods with four-fingered hands that includes *Coelophysis* and *Ceratosaurus*.

In 1994, Holtz suggested *Elaphrosaurus* was related to ceratosaurs like *Carnotaurus*, which lived in the southern hemisphere. He thought *Elaphrosaurus* did not have much in common with the ornithomimids, other than a similar overall body shape.

How did the dinosaur live?
The short answer is that nobody knows. *Elaphrosaurus* is a very mysterious dinosaur. Very little is known about it.

As a theropod, *Elaphrosaurus* would have been able to walk on two legs, and eat meat. It would have used its sharp claws and saw-edged teeth.

Elaphrosaurus has been found with sauropods (long-necked plant-eaters) like *Brachiosaurus*, and the armored dinosaur *Kentrosaurus*. It also lived with some very small animals, such as mammals, lizards, and tiny plant-eating *Dryosaurus*. Did it hunt animals or did it scavenge from other dinosaurs' leftovers? Finding some undigested bones in an *Elaphrosaurus*'s stomach would let us know.

CHECK THESE OUT!

Barosaurus, Brachiosaurus, Carnotaurus, Ceratosaurs, Ceratosaurus, Coelophysis, Dryosaurus, Jurassic period, Kentrosaurus, Ornithomimus, Saurischian dinosaurs, Theropods

Eoraptor

Eoraptor is one of the earliest dinosaurs known. This little hunter probably shows us how the common ancestor of all dinosaurs, from *Tyrannosaurus* to *Triceratops*, looked and acted.

An international team of paleontologists discovered tiny *Eoraptor* in Argentina in 1991. Having found the thigh bone, the team (led by American Paul Sereno) thought they had found a very early crocodile. When they exposed more of the skeleton, they saw it was something much more special.

Primitive dinosaur
When the skull and skeleton were cleaned off, this little creature turned out to be a very, very primitive dinosaur. Scientists had long known that all dinosaurs descended from a common ancestor. They suspected that ancestor was about 3 ft (90 cm) long, had sharp teeth for eating meat, a five-fingered hand, a four-toed foot, a long tail, and walked on its hind legs. Little *Eoraptor* matched the scientists guesses perfectly!

Because there are other dinosaurs known from the same age (*Herrerasaurus* and *Pisanosaurus*), *Eoraptor* lived a little too late in time to be the ancestor of all other dinosaurs. However, the actual common ancestor of all dinosaurs would have been similar to *Eoraptor*. Such an animal would have lived in the middle part of the Triassic period (more than 235 million years ago).

The primitive *Eoraptor* can tell paleontologists a lot about where the dinosaurs came from, how they lived in the early days, and what they were like before they evolved into the fancier forms that lived later in the Mesozoic Era.

We can learn something else from *Eoraptor*. Because we now know what the dinosaur ancestor probably looked like, we can try to imagine why the various groups of dinosaurs—like tetanurans (a group of meat-eating dinosaurs) or sauropods (long-necked plant-eaters)—evolved the way they did.

▶ It is hard to believe that all dinosaurs, from the long-necked, long-tailed sauropods to the plate-backed stegosaurs, evolved from a creature that looked like the tiny *Eoraptor*!

DINOFACTS

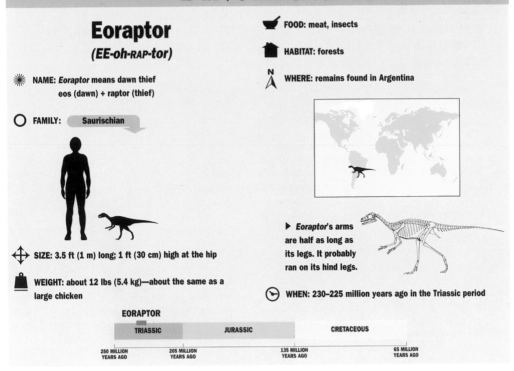

Eoraptor
(EE-oh-RAP-tor)

☀ **NAME:** *Eoraptor* means dawn thief
eos (dawn) + raptor (thief)

○ **FAMILY:** Saurischian

⊕ **SIZE:** 3.5 ft (1 m) long; 1 ft (30 cm) high at the hip

WEIGHT: about 12 lbs (5.4 kg)—about the same as a large chicken

FOOD: meat, insects

HABITAT: forests

WHERE: remains found in Argentina

▶ *Eoraptor*'s arms are half as long as its legs. It probably ran on its hind legs.

WHEN: 230–225 million years ago in the Triassic period

EORAPTOR

TRIASSIC	JURASSIC	CRETACEOUS
250 MILLION YEARS AGO	205 MILLION YEARS AGO ... 135 MILLION YEARS AGO	65 MILLION YEARS AGO

How *Eoraptor* lived

Eoraptor's big eyes, sharp teeth, long legs, and grasping hands show that it was a tiny hunter. Early reptiles, mammals, and amphibians, and large insects, may all have been its main food. Maybe it tried to eat the eggs or babies of the early ornithischian (bird-hipped dinosaur) *Pisanosaurus*. (An adult *Pisanosaurus* was probably too big for *Eoraptor* to eat.)

Eoraptor would have had to look out for the bigger *Herrerasaurus* and the giant meat-eating reptiles that hunted everything else in Triassic period Argentina.

IN A GROUP OF ITS OWN?

Placing *Eoraptor* in a dinosaur group is difficult. Scientists recognize that an animal belongs in a particular group if it shares specialized features with other members of that group. *Eoraptor* shares specialized features of the skull, hands, hips, and legs with other dinosaurs. However, it is so primitive (so similar to the dinosaur ancestor) that it does not have much in common with any particular group of the dinosaurs.

Some paleontologists classify *Eoraptor* with the theropods (two-legged meat-eaters). Others think it is so primitive that they place it in its own group. Further study of this amazing little dinosaur will help us to understand its place in the family tree. Whatever the case turns out to be, *Eoraptor* gives us the best information we have so far about the origins of the dinosaurs.

CHECK THESE OUT!

Dinosaurs, Evolution, *Herrerasaurus*, *Pisanosaurus*, Reptiles, Saurischian dinosaurs, Triassic period

Euhelopus

Euhelopus was one of the first dinosaurs to be discovered in China. It reminded some scientists of the North American dinosaur *Camarasaurus*. Were the two related?

Euhelopus, a medium-sized sauropod (long-necked plant-eating dinosaur), was found in China in 1923 by the Austrian paleontologist Otto Zdansky. Zdansky was a member of a joint European and Chinese fossil-hunting expedition. This expedition was the first to find dinosaur fossils in China. The fossils of *Euhelopus* were found in northern China. This is unusual; most of China's sauropods are from the south.

The remains were first described in 1929 and the dinosaur was given the name *Helopus*. Later, though, it was renamed *Euhelopus* because the name *Helopus* had already been given to another animal.

Similar skulls
Which dinosaurs were the closest relatives of *Euhelopus*? Some scientists say the skull of *Euhelopus* is very similar to that of *Camarasaurus*, a North American sauropod. Both dinosaurs have a short snout and spoon-shaped teeth. They also have nostrils near the top of their head. The scientists say the similarities mean the two dinosaurs must be related.

Other scientists suggest the Chinese sauropods are not so closely related to the North American forms. They think the Chinese dinosaurs belong to a separate sauropod group.

▲ *Euhelopus*'s neck might have been as much as half the total length of its body. Scientists think it may have used its neck as a giraffe does, to reach leaves growing high in the treetops.

152

LONG LEGS

No one has found the tail or forelegs of *Euhelopus*. Fossil-hunters have found dinosaur forelegs near the *Euhelopus* remains, but scientists are not sure they belong to *Euhelopus*.

For one reason, the forelegs seem too long. If the forelegs found near the *Euhelopus* site do belong to this animal, they would have been almost as long as its hind legs. This would mean that *Euhelopus* had longer forelegs in relation to the hind legs than any other sauropod dinosaur except *Brachiosaurus*.

How *Euhelopus* lived

Like all sauropods, *Euhelopus* was a plant-eater. It would have walked from tree to tree, snipping off pound after pound of leaves and stems with its spoon-shaped teeth.

Like all sauropods, *Euhelopus* also swallowed its food whole. Although it had teeth at the front and sides of its jaws, it could not chew. Unlike hadrosaurs (duckbill dinosaurs), for example, sauropods had no cheeks. If they had tried to chew, their food would have spilled out of their mouths.

Euhelopus had a very long neck—perhaps as much as 16 ft (5 m)—with 17 neck bones (vertebrae). This long neck was an adaptation that would have helped the dinosaur pick leaves from the highest branches.

CHECK THESE OUT!

Brachiosaurus, Camarasaurus, Jurassic period, Saurischian dinosaurs, Sauropodomorph dinosaurs, Sauropods

DINOFACTS

Euhelopus
yoo-hel-OH-pus

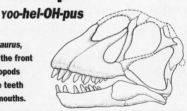

▶ *Euhelopus*, like *Camarasaurus*, had spoon-shaped teeth at the front and sides of its jaws. Sauropods like *Diplodocus* had peglike teeth only at the fronts of their mouths.

✳ **NAME:** *Euhelopus* means good marsh foot
eu (good) + helos (marsh) + pous (foot)

○ **FAMILY:** Saurischian
Sauropodomorph
Sauropod

 SIZE: 34 ft (10 m) long; about 18 ft (5.4 m) high to the top of the head, with the neck raised

 WEIGHT: about 10 tons (9 tonnes)—about the same as 2 African elephants

 FOOD: plants, especially tree leaves

 HABITAT: river floodplains with lots of woodland areas

N **WHERE:** remains found in China

⊙ **WHEN:** 150–135 million years ago in the Jurassic period

	EUHELOPUS	
TRIASSIC	JURASSIC	CRETACEOUS
250 MILLION YEARS AGO	205 MILLION YEARS AGO	135 MILLION YEARS AGO	65 MILLION YEARS AGO

Euoplocephalus

Euoplocephalus was an ankylosaur—an armored dinosaur. Collectors have found several great fossils of this club-tailed, tanklike animal, and they show us clearly how it looked when it was alive.

Canadian scientist Lawrence Lambe first described this dinosaur in 1902. He had studied a partial skull and a few pieces of bony armor found in Alberta in Canada.

Euoplocephalus was an ankylosaur (armored dinosaur). There were two kinds of ankylosaurs—ankylosaurids (such as *Euoplocephalus*) and nodosaurids. Ankylosaurids had a club on the tip of their tail; nodosaurids did not.

One dinosaur, many names
Fossil-hunters have discovered almost 50 *Euoplocephalus* skeletons—more than any other kind of ankylosaur. However, scientists once thought some of these *Euoplocephalus* skeletons belonged to other kinds of ankylosaurs. They mistakenly gave the names *Anodontosaurus*, *Dyoplosaurus*, *Scolosaurus*, and *Stereocephalus* to these skeletons.
    In 1978, New England paleontologist Walter Coombs studied these fossils and

saw that they were all remains of *Euoplocephalus*. The other names are no longer used.

Rebuilding *Euoplocephalus*
With all these skeletons, Denver paleontologist Ken Carpenter was able to rebuild *Euoplocephalus* very accurately in 1982. *Euoplocephalus* had short, powerful legs under a wide

▶ *Euoplocephalus* has been found with its armor intact, so scientists have been able to rebuild this ankylosaur very accurately.

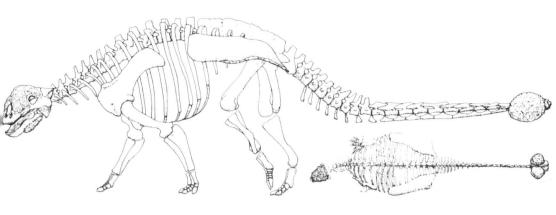

body. Its broad, strong hips supported its heavy armor, and it held its long, clubbed tail off the ground. *Euoplocephalus's* skull was wide and boxy. Horns above and below its eyes made the dinosaur look a little like a horned lizard.

Armor plating

Euoplocephalus's armor was made from a mixture of materials. Bone was set into the skin, and a tough, horny coating covered the bone.

The armor consisted of low, flat plates, high, thin plates and spines, and plates of every shape in between. Mixed armor like this is typical of the advanced (highly evolved) armored dinosaurs of the Late Cretaceous period. *Euoplocephalus* had bands of armor around its neck, across its back, and across much of its tail. Big, stiff armor plates, or scutes, stuck out from *Euoplocephalus's* shoulders and upper back. Smaller scutes studded its front legs. *Euoplocephalus* even had armored eyelids. Scientists know this because some skulls are in such good condition that the eyelids are still attached!

With all this protection, *Euoplocephalus* could fend off most predators. Small meat-eaters such as *Troodon* and

▲ The backbones over *Euoplocephalus's* hips were joined together to support the hip and leg muscles. The lower drawing shows just how broad the tail club was.

Dromaeosaurus may have tried to attack *Euoplocephalus*, but their claws would simply have bounced off its armor.

Large tyrannosaurs, such as *Albertosaurus*, were a deadlier threat. *Euoplocephalus* was too heavy to run away. Perhaps it hunkered down in the brush, hoping not to be seen.

If it had to, though, *Euoplocephalus* could defend itself. Its clublike tail could be used as a fearsome weapon. When a predator appeared, *Euoplocephalus* would have used its forelegs to heave its body around so that its tail was ready for action. Low-slung *Euoplocephalus* would have aimed its club at the feet of a tyrannosaur and swung its tail.

Wrecking ball

A *Euoplocephalus* specimen collected in Alberta, Canada, included the first ankylosaurid tail club ever found. The club is really a pair of huge armor

155

HEADS OR TAILS?

Some scientists have suggested that ankylosaurids might have used their tail club as a decoy. Perhaps there were colored patches on the club that looked like a pair of eyes. When threatened, the ankylosaurid would hunker down in the brush and raise its club. A tyrannosaur would attack the club, believing it to be the head. The ankylosaur would then swing its tail club to crack the tyrannosaur in the head. Although not accepted by most paleontologists, this is certainly an imaginative suggestion. Some creatures today, such as caterpillars and butterflies, have eyelike markings to trick predators into thinking they are another kind of animal.

▲ The peacock pansy butterfly has eyelike spots on its wings to trick predators into thinking they are looking at the head of a much bigger animal.

plates. The plates are fixed to the sides of the tail tip, with a smaller pair behind them.

To give *Euoplocephalus* the strength to swing its tail club, the tail bones (vertebrae) were fused together. Stiff, bony cords, or tendons, wrapped around the bones for extra strength. Thick muscles attached the tendons to the dinosaur's hips. The big club would have dealt a terrible blow when swung by a multi-ton animal. Imagine being struck by a wrecking ball!

Girls vs. boys?
Coombs found that *Euoplocephalus* tail clubs came in lots of different shapes and sizes. He reckoned scientists had found clubs from animals of different ages, sizes, and sexes.

Another explanation is that these different club types belonged to many different kinds of *Euoplocephalus*. If this turns out to be true, then perhaps some of the old names for *Euoplocephalus* may be brought back into use.

Nosey questions
Euoplocephalus's nostrils point forward over its wide mouth. Its nose is very complex, and its skull contains a maze of air passages. Why?

All ankylosaurs had complex noses and airways. Most paleontologists believe the first ankylosaurs came from the center of Asia, where it was very dry. Their noses may have helped to prevent the dinosaurs from drying out. Water vapor in their nostrils could moisten dry air as they breathed it in. Before they breathed out, the long air passages in their skulls could have grabbed the water vapor, keeping it inside their bodies.

However, *Euoplocephalus* lived in a wet place, where it did not need to save moisture. Did its nose give it a better sense of smell? Coombs took a cast, or mold, of the inside of a *Euoplocephalus* skull. He examined the area where the smell-detecting organs had been. They were not especially big, so *Euoplocephalus* probably did not have an extra-sharp sense of smell.

Scientists have suggested the maze of airways helped to strengthen the animal's wide skull. *Euoplocephalus* also had a bony plate across the roof of its mouth. This, too, may have added strength to its skull.

Sunny-side up or overeasy?
Canadian paleontologist Charles M. Sternberg noticed an interesting feature of ankylosaur fossils. They lie in different positions in different

parts of the world. In Asia, ankylosaurs are mostly found upright and in one piece. Perhaps they were crouching down during a sandstorm when they died and were then buried quickly by the sand.

In North America, however, ankylosaur remains turn up either as scattered bones or in an upside-down position. Sternberg suggested that American ankylosaurs had become fossilized close to rivers. When an ankylosaur carcass slid into the water, it would float belly-up. Gases from its rotting guts filled its belly, and its armor weighed down its back. It would float upside-down until it washed ashore or sank and fossilized.

How *Euoplocephalus* lived

Euoplocephalus had a wide beak and short legs, so scientists believe it grazed on low plants. Because its teeth were small, and it had weak jaw muscles for such a large animal, it may have eaten soft plants.

However, *Euoplocephalus* had a huge gut area. This space may have housed a complex stomach and long intestines like those of sheep and cattle. These modern animals can digest really tough plants. Perhaps *Euoplocephalus* could, too, having cropped them with its bony beak instead of its teeth. One day fossil-hunters may find a *Euoplocephalus* skeleton with the remains of its last meal. Then scientists will know better what it ate.

CHECK THESE OUT!

Albertosaurus, Ankylosaurs, *Ankylosaurus*, Cretaceous period, *Dromaeosaurus*, Ornithischian dinosaurs, Thyreophorans, *Troodon*, Tyrannosaurs

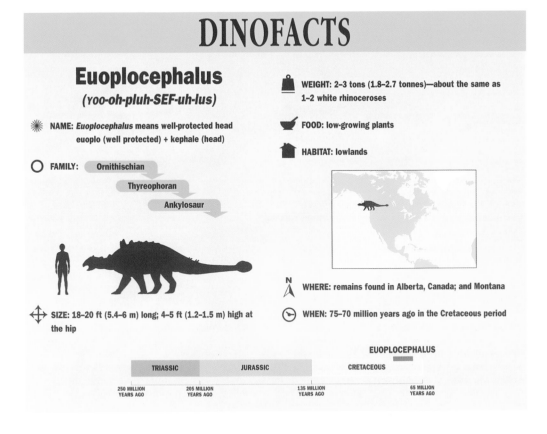

DINOFACTS

Euoplocephalus
(YOO-oh-pluh-SEF-uh-lus)

✳ NAME: *Euoplocephalus* means well-protected head
euoplo (well protected) + kephale (head)

○ FAMILY: Ornithischian
Thyreophoran
Ankylosaur

✛ SIZE: 18–20 ft (5.4–6 m) long; 4–5 ft (1.2–1.5 m) high at the hip

⚖ WEIGHT: 2–3 tons (1.8–2.7 tonnes)—about the same as 1–2 white rhinoceroses

FOOD: low-growing plants

HABITAT: lowlands

N↑ WHERE: remains found in Alberta, Canada; and Montana

◷ WHEN: 75–70 million years ago in the Cretaceous period

EUOPLOCEPHALUS

TRIASSIC	JURASSIC		CRETACEOUS
250 MILLION YEARS AGO	205 MILLION YEARS AGO	135 MILLION YEARS AGO	65 MILLION YEARS AGO

Evolution

Today there are millions of different kinds of animals and plants. From fossils, we know that there were even more kinds in the past. How have so many life-forms come to be? The answer is evolution.

In simple terms, evolution means change through time. To many scientists, it means changes in life-forms through time. It is a way of explaining how animals and plants have developed into the forms that are alive today.

We can see that some kinds of animals look fairly like others: lions look like tigers. Other animals look less similar: cows do not look much like lions or tigers. Scientists started to reason that many similar animals and plants descended from a common ancestor. How and why did these animals and plants change through time and come to be different than their ancestor?

It takes all kinds
Two English biologists came up with an answer. Charles Darwin and Alfred Wallace had both studied plants and animals, and knew about paleontology.

They noticed that animals and plants produce many more offspring than the environment can support. Lack of food or space, as well as predators, disease, and accidents, kill many offspring before they reach adulthood.

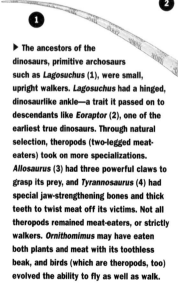

▶ The ancestors of the dinosaurs, primitive archosaurs such as *Lagosuchus* (1), were small, upright walkers. *Lagosuchus* had a hinged, dinosaurlike ankle—a trait it passed on to descendants like *Eoraptor* (2), one of the earliest true dinosaurs. Through natural selection, theropods (two-legged meat-eaters) took on more specializations. *Allosaurus* (3) had three powerful claws to grasp its prey, and *Tyrannosaurus* (4) had special jaw-strengthening bones and thick teeth to twist meat off its victims. Not all theropods remained meat-eaters, or strictly walkers. *Ornithomimus* may have eaten both plants and meat with its toothless beak, and birds (which are theropods, too) evolved the ability to fly as well as walk.

Darwin and Wallace also saw that there are differences (variations) between individuals in any population of animals or plants. Some individuals have useful variations—maybe they are a little taller or stronger, for example, than others of their kind. They will have a slightly better chance of growing up and passing on their useful variations to their offspring.

Natural selection

Over time, the buildup of these slight variations can bring big changes. Take a population of prosauropod dinosaurs (the first long-necked plant-eaters). Some may be a little slower than others, some shorter, some taller. Imagine these prosauropods rearing on their hind legs to reach leaves from trees with their mouths. The taller ones can reach more leaves than the shorter ones, so they have a better chance of living to have offspring of their own. They then pass on their tallness to their offspring.

This process, which Darwin and Wallace called natural selection, is part of evolution. In later generations, there might be more and more tall prosauropods, until eventually the dinosaurs get so big they have to walk on all fours. These new forms would no longer be prosauropods: they would have evolved into sauropods (plant-eaters with long necks and tails).

CHARLES DARWIN

Charles Darwin wrote many books describing how life evolved. As a boy, he enjoyed walking along the shore collecting barnacles and other sea creatures. When he grew up, he sailed around the world to study plants and animals. He visited the Galapagos Islands, off South America, each of which has it own slightly different type of bird. Darwin realized that different environments could cause animals to evolve in different ways. Darwin described his discoveries in his book *On the Origin of Species*.

RELATIVE SIZES

① ② ③ ④

Patterns in evolution

Animals cannot decide to grow larger or faster. This sort of variation happens randomly. Over time, however, we see patterns (trends) in evolution. For example, the earliest ceratopsian (horned) dinosaurs were small, two-legged walkers like *Psittacosaurus*. They did not have frills on their skulls.

Over time, natural selection favored variations of horned dinosaurs which had larger bodies and had developed head frills. Perhaps frills allowed for larger muscles, or showing off in fights, or both. So later ceratopsians, like *Protoceratops*, were bigger and had frills. Frills made their heads heavy, so they walked on all fours.

Later, evolution favored variations with true horns instead of *Protoceratops*'s nose bump, and even larger frills and bodies. These later types— like *Triceratops*—were huge. Therefore, we can talk about an evolutionary trend of increasing body size, frill size, and horn development.

Growing apart

Sometimes, more than one variation is an advantage in a population. One variation may be larger and stronger, another smaller and faster. Both have advantages over all the rest. Over time, the larger ones might get even larger and even stronger, while the smaller variations might get smaller and faster. One common ancestor will have led to two separating (divergent) trends.

The divergences might not alway be great: *Velociraptor* and *Dromaeosaurus* diverged from their own common ancestor but look very like each other.

In time, however, evolution can produce big divergences. All dinosaurs descended from a form similar to *Eoraptor*, a meat-eater the size of a dog. Eventually, dinosaurs grew into forms as varied as ceratopsians, sauropods (long-necked plant-eaters), fierce meat-eating tyrannosaurs, and birds.

Growing together

Sometimes evolution produces similar forms from different ancestors. *Ornithomimus* and its relatives look a bit like today's ostriches. Both groups have toothless beaks and long legs and necks. Are they related?

No. *Ornithomimus* descended from toothed dinosaurs such as *Pelecanimimus*. Ostriches descended from small flying birds. *Pelecanimimus* looks quite unlike a small flying bird. Two different groups evolved to look alike (converged).

The tree of life

The history of life is like a tree. A common ancestor at the root diverges into different branches; these branches grow into more branches, and so on. The branches represent groups of life-forms. Scientists want to know how this tree "grew"— how life-forms grew into one another. One of their methods is to look for features (traits).

Each kind of animal or plant has a unique mix of traits. Some of these traits will pass unchanged to its descendants. All of its descendants inherit these traits. Sometimes natural selection changes a number of other traits. Then the same rule applies: all descendants of the changed forms inherit the changed traits.

Looking at traits helps us to see where dinosaurs fit on the the tree of life. For example, the first dinosaur had an open hole in the hip socket that let it walk upright. Descendants of this first dinosaur all inherited the open hip hole. Through

▼ The first ceratopsian, *Psittacosaurus* (1), walked on two legs and had a small head. Some of its descendants had slightly larger heads and bodies. Because they were more successful, ceratopsians came to be larger, with heavy, frilled skulls—like *Protoceratops* (2). This process of natural selection eventually resulted in huge ceratopsians like *Triceratops* (3).

evolution, they also took on some new traits. For example, the first ornithischians evolved a beak and "bird hips."

Although dinosaurs diverged, they still kept some of these first traits. By studying traits, we can "climb backward" on the tree of life to find out how dinosaur groups are related.

CHECK THESE OUT!

Allosaurus, Ceratopsians, Dinosaurs, *Dromaeosaurus*, *Eoraptor*, Mammal-like reptiles, Ornithischian dinosaurs, *Ornithomimus*, *Pelecanimimus*, Prosauropods, *Protoceratops*, *Psittacosaurus*, Saurischian dinosaurs, Sauropods, Theropods, *Triceratops*, Tyrannosaurus, *Velociraptor*

EVOLUTION FACTS

✳ Every type of animal on this planet evolved from a very simple one-celled creature many millions of years ago. Some paleontologists believe that humans descended from *Lystrosaurus*, a piglike, plant-eating mammal-like reptile from the Permian period (290–250 million years ago).

✳ Many kinds (species) of animals and plants have become extinct during the process of evolution. Scientists estimate between 90 and 99.9 percent of all species that ever lived on earth are now extinct.

✳ Humans are actually driving the evolution of many animals when they create new breeds of animals or plants. This is called domestication, or artificial selection. Because it is a deliberate process, artifical selection happens at a very much faster rate than natural selection. Scientists use artificial selection when, for example, they want to create a sheep with more wool or more meat, or a plant with more fragrant blooms.

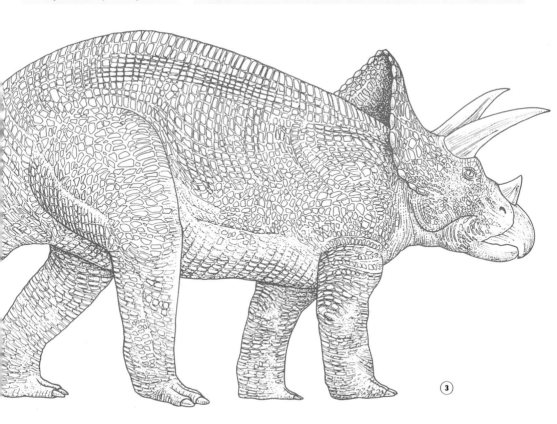

③

Extinction

The dinosaurs were the rulers of the land for 165 million years. Then, together with many kinds of sea-living and flying reptiles, most of the dinosaurs died. What killed all these animals?

The rocks beneath our feet hold fossils of many kinds (species) of animals that are no longer around—woolly mammoths, dinosaur-aged flying and sea-living reptiles, and most kinds of dinosaurs. All these creatures and many others died out without leaving descendants. In other words, they became extinct.

During the millions of years of earth's history, some species of animals have disappeared by themselves. However, there have also been times when many different plant and animal species have become extinct at one time. Scientists can tell this because these species' remains appear together in one layer of rock but are missing from the next layer up. These disappearances of many different plant and animal groups at one time are called mass extinctions.

The Cretaceous extinction

The most famous mass extinction took place at the end of the Mesozoic Era. This event is called the Cretaceous–Tertiary extinction because it marks the end of the Cretaceous and the beginning of the Tertiary period.

Many kinds of sea reptiles died out at the end of the Cretaceous period. Pterosaurs

MASS EXTINCTIONS

The Cretaceous–Tertiary extinction is the most famous mass extinction, but it is not the worst. The most severe extinction was the Permian–Triassic extinction of 250 million years ago. This event marked the end of the Permian period (290-250 million years ago) and the beginning of the Triassic period (250-205 million years ago). It also marked the end of the Paleozoic Era and the beginning of the Mesozoic Era. Scientists estimate that 96 percent of all marine species died out in this extinction—only 60–75 percent are estimated to have died off at the Cretaceous–Tertiary extinction. There were several other mass extinctions during the Paleozoic Era. Some of these were even more severe than the Cretaceous–Tertiary event. There was also a mass extinction at the end of the Triassic period.

(flying reptiles) also became extinct, but the most famous victims of this event were many dinosaurs. Besides the toothless birds, no other dinosaurs survived the end of the Cretaceous. What could have killed all these creatures?

Three guesses

Scientists are trying to figure out what happened. Because so many plants and animals died, on land and in the sea, any guesses must explain what wiped out all of them.

Rocks show three possible causes of extinction. First, scientists have found evidence that an asteroid from outer space struck earth in the Late Cretaceous. Second, there was high volcanic activity at this time. Third, sea levels seem to have fallen at the end of the Cretaceous period.

Visitor from outer space?

It was in 1980 that US scientists Walter and Luis Alvarez discovered evidence of a giant asteroid strike at the end of the Cretaceous period.

They found a thin layer of unusual rock right where the Cretaceous and Tertiary rock layers met. This thin layer contained much of the element iridium. Iridium is very rare on earth, but it is much more common in the chunks of space rock called asteroids.

Walter and Luis Alvarez also came across special kinds of mineral grains around the world where Cretaceous and Tertiary rock layers met. They were grains of shocked quartz, which can be formed only by

▶ The ceratopsians, or horned dinosaurs, were among the last land dinosaurs. Did a huge asteroid end their world?

superhigh temperatures and pressures like those caused by an asteroid impact.

Mexican waves
Scientists also discovered a huge crater in the Yucatan Peninsula in Mexico. Called Chicxulub (CHICH-oh-lob), this crater may be where the asteroid landed.

The Chicxulub crater is no longer visible at the surface, but underground scans show it is probably 110 mi (180 km), and possibly even 175 mi (280 km) across. Such a huge asteroid would have caused severe tidal waves and thrown up a lot of dust!

Scientists worked out that an asteroid only 6 mi (10 km) across would throw up enough dust to block out the sun. Without sunlight, land and sea plants would die. The animals that ate the plants would starve to death, as would the meat-eaters that ate the plant-eaters. Besides, the dust cloud would cool the world by blocking out the sun's warmth before it reached the ground. The cooler temperature would kill even more animals and plants.

Floods of hot rock
However, volcanic activity may have played a part in the extinction at the end of the Cretacous period. In the western part of India lie the Deccan Traps (steps). The Traps are huge staircases of lava, the melted rock that volcanoes spew out when they erupt. Today the lava is solid, but it covers an area bigger than the state of California and is over 8,000 ft (2,450 m) deep. So much lava could not be thrown out in a single eruption. It is the result of many eruptions over 500,000 to 2 million years.

▼ A coin marks the iridium layer sandwiched between Cretaceous and Tertiary rocks. Iridium is very rare on earth but much more common in asteroids.

The eruptions began before the end of the Cretaceous period and continued into the Tertiary period. Scientists know because the iridium layer lies between two layers of lava.

Huge eruptions like this could have produced climate changes around the world. These changes would have led to changes in plant life. Plant-eating animals that could not eat the new plants that grew where they lived would have died off. With no plant-eaters to hunt, the meat-eaters soon would have disappeared, too.

The oceans dry up

The drying up of the seas is the third possible cause of the extinction. For most of the Cretaceous period, shallow seas covered much of the land. For example, western and eastern North America were separated by a shallow sea, and water divided Asia from Europe. These waters were home to many kinds of life. The seas also kept temperatures mild on land. Today coasts have milder climates than do lands in the middle of a continent.

A few million years before the end of the Cretaceous period, these seaways drained away. Scientists do not know why. One cause may have been continental drift, the slow movement of landmasses across the surface of the earth.

The result was that sea creatures that liked warm, shallow water had less of it in which to live. Also, without the shallow waters to keep the weather mild, climates on land changed. The loss of so much

EXTINCTION IS FOREVER

Once an animal becomes extinct, it is gone for good. In science fiction books and movies it might be possible to bring extinct creatures back to life. In real life, though, we do not know how to do that. This is why people are concerned about endangered species, the rare animals and plants that are in serious danger of becoming extinct.

Some animals are in danger because they are overhunted. The white rhinoceros (above) is hunted for its horn, which is used in Chinese medicines. Other animals, such as the lemurs of Madagascar, are endangered because their ancient forest habitats are being destroyed to make way for farms and villages. Sometimes animals and plants are endangered indirectly, because of pollution.

habitat may have helped to kill off some species of sea animals. The effects of the climate changes were probably similar to those caused by the Deccan Traps volcanic activity.

Which of the three?

We have good evidence that all three events occurred. Any of the three may have caused the extinction. A combination of the three is possible, too.

Climate changes caused by draining seaways and the Deccan eruptions would have reduced the areas in which some species of animals and plants could survive. Some places would have been too hot, others too cold or without food. With too few places left to live, many species may have

been already heading for extinction at the end of the Cretaceous period. Perhaps the asteroid then struck and finished them off.

The mystery of the mass extinction at the end of the Cretaceous period is not yet solved. Scientists need more information to figure out exactly what happened. There may be a cause about which we do not yet know.

CHECK THESE OUT!

Birds; Continental drift; Cretaceous period; Dinosaurs; Evolution; Geological time; Ichthyosaurs; Jurassic period; Mosasaurs; Plesiosaurs, pliosaurs, and nothosaurs; Pterosaurs; Rocks; Triassic period

Footprints

Dinosaur footprints have been found on every continent except Antarctica. Some footprints look as fresh today as they first did, millions of years ago, when their makers still walked the earth.

Millions of years ago, dinosaurs left footprints in soft ground. Some of these footprints have survived as fossils. Scientists call footprints trace fossils. They are not true fossils, like bones, but they show a trace of where a dinosaur once was.

Footprints were among the first dinosaur remains ever discovered. A Massachusetts doctor found some prints in the 1830s in the Connecticut River valley. He told US geologist Edward Hitchcock about them. Hitchcock spent the rest of his life studying fossilized footprints.

Giant birds
The Connecticut River footprints were birdlike: each foot had three long, thin toes.

For many years, everyone, including Hitchcock, thought that giant birds had made them. At the time, scientists were convinced that all dinosaurs had been huge, four-legged walkers, like modern rhinoceroses, so they could not have made such birdlike tracks.

Hitchcock died in 1863, still believing his footprints had been made by birds. As we now know, Hitchcock was close to the truth. Theropods

▶ The shadow of a meat-eater falls across the footprints of some far-off sauropods (long-necked plant-eaters). Prints like this make up the dinosaur trackway at the Paluxy River in Texas.

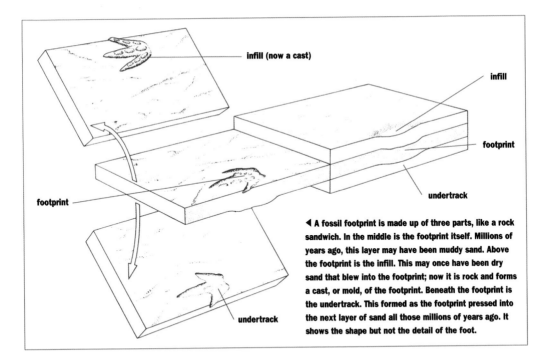

infill (now a cast)

infill

footprint

undertrack

footprint

◀ A fossil footprint is made up of three parts, like a rock sandwich. In the middle is the footprint itself. Millions of years ago, this layer may have been muddy sand. Above the footprint is the infill. This may once have been dry sand that blew into the footprint; now it is rock and forms a cast, or mold, of the footprint. Beneath the footprint is the undertrack. This formed as the footprint pressed into the next layer of sand all those millions of years ago. It shows the shape but not the detail of the foot.

undertrack

(two-legged meat-eaters) left birdlike footprints. We call living theropods birds!

Footprints in the sand
Fossil-hunters find most dinosaur footprints in rocks that were once mud or fine sand. However, for a footprint to become fossilized, the conditions had to be just right.

Imagine a dinosaur walking along a stretch of seashore. As it trod in muddy sand, it would leave its footprints behind. For the footprints to be saved, either the sun had to bake the mud hard, or dry sand needed to blow into the footprints and fill them. More and more sand would have then washed over the footprints and buried them.

Over time, the dinosaur's buried prints would have fossilized (turned to stone).

The best dinosaur footprints clearly show the shape of the animal's foot, including its claws. They also show every detail of the sole of the foot, including wrinkles and the texture of the skin.

Such clear footprints give paleontologists a good chance of telling which kind of dinosaur made them. Most dinosaur footprints, though, are not so clear. Next time you walk along a muddy or sandy track, look back at your footprints. Where you placed your foot firmly, you may see a perfect print of your boots. However, where your foot slipped or twisted, the prints

will probably be blurred. You might find it difficult to recognize your own footprints.

The same is true with dinosaur footprints. If the animal slipped as it ran along muddy ground, it would make a different print than if it had been standing still. The paleontologist has to turn tracker to tell what animal made the print!

Mysteries solved
When paleontologists come across a line of dinosaur footprints, they call it a trackway. Trackways help scientists learn about dinosaur habits. For example, footprints have shown us that hadrosaurs (duckbill dinosaurs) walked on four legs as well as two.

167

For years, scientists thought that *Diplodocus* was so heavy that it must have walked like a crocodile, dragging its neck and tail with its legs splayed out at its sides.

However, *Diplodocus*'s footprints were close together, like those of an elephant, whose legs extend straight under its body. No wavy grooves made by a dragging tail were found. As *Diplodocus* walked, it must have held its neck and tail high.

Trackways also prove that the animal that made them actually traveled over that area in life. The same is not true of dinosaur skeletons. A skeleton may turn up miles from where the animal lived and died.

▲ Some dinosaurs had huge feet! This boy is sitting in the footprint of a sauropod (long-necked, long-tailed plant-eater) on the Paluxy River Trackway site, Texas.

For example, fossil-hunters often find dinosaur skeletons in places that were underwater in dinosaur times. This does not mean that the dinosaur went for a swim! The animal may have died by a river or coast and been washed into the water. The body sank to the bottom and became buried far from where the dinosaur lived.

The best dinosaur trackways are probably in places where animals went only rarely. Scientists have studied modern animals in East Africa. They found that footprints did not last at busy places, like watering holes. Too many animals would trample the mud and blur the prints.

Hand-walking dinosaurs?

Fossilized footprints can wear away over time. American paleontologist R. T. Bird visited the Mayan Ranch Trackway in Texas in the 1930s. This trackway shows

▼ Scott Madsen of the Museum of North Arizona examines dinosaur tracks in Arizona's Painted Desert. The fossils look like the tracks of very large birds.

FOOTPRINT FACTS

✳ Pliny Moody, a Massachusetts farm boy, was the first person ever to find dinosaur footprints. He found them in 1802 while he was plowing a field.

✳ The world's longest single section of dinosaur trackway is in Turkmenistan, Central Asia. It is 1,020 ft (311 m) long. The largest tracksite in the world, by area, is in the Upper Glen Rose Formation of Texas. It covers about 40,000 square mi (100,000 sq km).

✳ The Paluxy River Trackway in Texas shows the tracks of several plant-eating sauropods. On top of them are the prints of three or four meat-eating theropods. Were the meat-eaters hunting the sauropods? It is exciting to imagine so, but we cannot be sure. The theropods might have passed by several days later. Millions of years later, it is impossible to tell.

✳ Some scientists measure the distance between footprints to try to work out how fast a dinosaur was traveling. However, it is almost impossible to find a clear, complete set of tracks that definitely belongs to only one dinosaur.

✳ Some modern animals leave a tail mark on the ground as they walk. The snow leopard, which lives on mountains in Asia, drags its tail in the snow. Very few dinosaur trackways show tail marks. Until recently, scientists believed that long-tailed sauropods like *Diplodocus* dragged their tails along the ground. However, trackways show clearly that dinosaurs held their tails off the ground.

just the forefoot prints of a sauropod, a long-necked plant-eater. Like most paleontologists at the time, Bird believed sauropods lived in water, with just their heads above the surface. Huge sauropods like *Brachiosaurus* would have been too heavy to live on land, they thought. Bird believed that the sauropod had waded along the riverbed on its forefeet, trailing its hind legs behind it.

We now know that the sauropods lived on land. The trackway would once have shown prints of all four feet. The sauropod's forefeet carried more weight than its hind feet, so they left deeper prints than

the hind feet. In time, the trackway wore away, and only the deepest prints remained.

Hard evidence

Footprints give us amazing clues about dinosaur lifestyles. Bones can tell us what shape dinosaurs were, and even whether they could run fast. Footprints, however, show us where they passed and tell us how they may have behaved.

CHECK THESE OUT!

Birds, *Brachiosaurus*, Digging dinosaurs, *Diplodocus*, Hadrosaurs, Rocks, Sauropods, Theropods

Fossils

Almost everything paleontologists know about dinosaurs, they have learned from fossils dug out of the ground. Fossils are the stony remains of ancient animals and plants.

Most fossils of dinosaurs and other prehistoric animals are body bones and skulls. Usually it is only the hard parts, like bones and teeth, that fossilize. It is very rare to find soft parts, like skin or muscle. Also, dead animals usually decay without fossilizing. The dinosaur fossils we see in museums represent just a tiny fraction of all the dinosaurs that lived.

From animal to fossil
Fossils are not made of bone, but of stony minerals. How does an animal turn to stone? Its dead body (carcass) must first survive several stages.

CAUGHT IN THE ACT

Some of the best-preserved fossils are found in hardened tree resin, known as amber. When resin first oozes from a tree, it is sticky, like very thick maple syrup. Insects, plants, and even lizards and frogs get trapped in the sticky liquid. The resin eventually turns to amber, and its captive is stuck fast.

A mosquito trapped in amber for the last 30 million years looks in perfect condition. However, it has actually decayed. It is just a hollow mold with a fine skin of carbon dust. Good sources of amber are the Baltic Sea, Lebanon, the Dominican Republic, and also New Jersey in the United States.

▲ By looking at amber, scientists can study how animals have evolved. These mosquitoes are 30 million years old.

These stages start when the animal dies—from old age, disease, accident, or from the teeth and claws of a hunter. When a predator eats its kill, it may gnaw the bones. We see evidence of this damage today in the form of bite marks on fossilized bones.

Scavengers later pass by to pick the carcass clean. They may damage or destroy the skeleton further, fighting over scraps and scattering the bones.

Other animals passing by might trample the bones, scattering them more widely. Scientists have seen animals do this on the African savanna, which helps explain why so many dinosaurs are known only from partial skeletons.

If bones are left uncovered on the ground, they do not last long. Nighttime cold, the sun's heat, and rainfall cause the outer layers of bones to crack. Eventually the bones break into splinters. Fossil-hunters have found many of these splinters. However, if sand or soil covers a carcass, the skeleton may escape damage.

Washed up and buried
Sometimes, floods or heavy rains wash a carcass into a river. Tumbled in the torrents, the bones become worn as they bump along. Many of the bones shatter.

Some bones, however, are washed up at slow bends on the river. Before long, a new layer of river sediment (silt, sand, or mud) washes over these bones. The sediment buries and protects them. Many of the best bone sites,

▲ Fortunately for fossil-hunters, the body of this dinosaur has been washed into a river. There, the soft body parts soon decay, leaving only the skeleton.

▲ In the gentle water currents on the riverbed, a layer of fine sediment—sand, mud, or silt—drifts over the skeleton. The sediment eventually turns to rock.

▲ The bones decay in one of two ways. Either the soft matter in the bone decays, leaving only the hard matter (left), or the whole skeleton decays to leave a hollow mold (right).

▲ Water filters through the rock. Minerals seep into the gaps left by the decayed soft matter. When they seep into hollow bone molds (right), they completely fill them.

▲ The minerals harden into stone, and the skeleton is now fossilized. Many fossils come to light when volcanic activity pushes fossil-bearing rock layers upward. Wind and water erosion on the earth's surface wear the rock away until the hard fossil is left exposed.

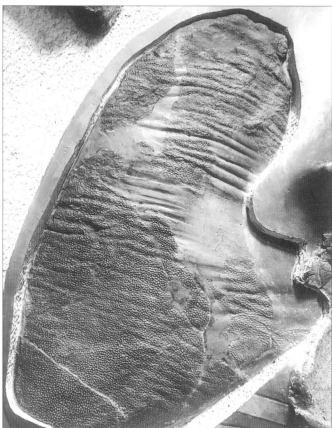

◀ Now we know what dinosaur skin looked like! This is not skin, but a print of skin left in rock by *Corythosaurus*, a Cretaceous hadrosaur (duckbill dinosaur).

into stone. They turn the bone into a stony fossil. In other situations, the whole bone may decay and leave a bone-shaped hollow in the rock. In time, new minerals may trickle in and fill the hollow, making a perfect cast of the bone.

Then the fossil-hunter must find the bone. Fossils may be exposed when rain, seas, rivers, and wind wear away the land. Fossils also turn up when huge pressures fold the land and push fossil-bearing rocks up toward the surface.

Rare finds

The soft tissues (skin and flesh) of an animal usually decay shortly after its death. Very rarely, however, a fossil body shows evidence of soft tissues. These fossils can turn up in amazing places: insects in amber, and woolly mammoths in the frozen soil of Siberia.

Bacteria in the sediment sometimes act on soft tissues. The bacteria preserve the tissues long enough to leave a trace on the rock. Because of bacteria, we can see the webbed feet of the hadrosaur (duckbill) *Edmontosaurus*, or the shape of the wings of a pterosaur (flying reptile). We can even see impressions of a dinosaur's skin.

containing hundreds of bones, lie where rivers ran in the age of the dinosaurs.

Even after the carcass is buried, the sediment itself can still attack it. Acids and tiny organisms, such as bacteria, in the sediment eat away at the bones. If a bone or skeleton survives all of these trials, fossilization can finally happen.

Turning to stone

Over hundreds of thousands of years, the sediment turns to sedimentary rock. Meanwhile,

the buried bone is changing too. Bone contains both organic (carbon-containing) and inorganic (carbon-free) materials. In time, the organic parts decay. The inorganic parts, made of hard mineral crystals, usually remain. They keep a bone in shape.

Water trickling through the sedimentary rock carries minerals with it. The minerals seep into the tiny spaces in the bone where the decayed organic material used to be. There, the minerals harden

Trace fossils

In addition to skeletons, paleontologists also look for less obvious signs of dinosaur

DEEP, DEEP FREEZE

It is so cold in arctic Siberia, northern Asia, that the top layer of the ground is permanently frozen. This layer is called permafrost. It is a bit like a huge freezer. In 1989, Russian scientists found woolly mammoths frozen deep within the permafrost.

Mammoths were mammals related to early forms of elephants. They also looked much like elephants do now, with tusks and a trunk. Mammoths survived until about 10,000 years ago. When the woolly mammoths died in Siberia, the intense cold preserved them; they still had their flesh and fur. The scientists even ate some woolly mammoth steaks!

▲ Scientists dig out a baby woolly mammoth, complete with skin and fur, from the ice.

◀ Fossil-hunters found this *Oviraptor* in Mongolia, Asia. Dinosaur remains are usually scattered, so a nearly complete skeleton is a lucky discovery.

activity—such as footprints, fossilized food remains, nest areas, and fossil dung. These signs are known as trace fossils.

To paleontologists, trace fossils can be just as interesting as bones. From fossilized food and dung, paleontologists can learn what a dinosaur ate. Footprints can show whether a dinosaur lived in a herd and whether it walked on four legs or two. Nests can show if a dinosaur cared for its babies.

CHECK THESE OUT!

Archaeopteryx, Bones, *Corythosaurus*, Digging dinosaurs, *Edmontosaurus*, Eggs and babies, Footprints, Mammals, *Oviraptor*, Pterosaurs, Rocks

Gallimimus

Gallimimus was an ornithomimid—an ostrichlike dinosaur. It looked like an ostrich with a tail, but how did it live?

▶ *Gallimimus* had long legs, and its body was well balanced over its hips. It probably bounded along at speed over the Cretaceous plains of Mongolia.

Gallimimus belonged to the ornithomimids, a group of dinosaurs that resembled modern ostriches. A joint Polish–Mongolian expedition found the first *Gallimimus* remains in 1967 in Mongolia's Gobi Desert.

Since then, fossil-hunters have collected lots of very good skeletons of *Gallimimus*— more than of any other ornithomimid. These skeletons include both adults and the only young ostrichlike dinosaurs yet found.

One small specimen of *Gallimimus* was in very good condition. It was 7 ft (2.1 m) long, 2.5 ft (76 cm) high at the hip, and its skull was 6.5 in (17 cm) in length. Like most young dinosaurs, the juvenile *Gallimimus* had a big head for its body, with large eyes and a short snout. As the dinosaur grew, its snout grew longer and its eyes seemed to get smaller. The eyes actually stayed the same size; it was just its head that got bigger.

Plains runner?

Gallimimus looked much like other ostrichlike dinosaurs, such as *Ornithomimus* and *Struthiomimus*, except that it was bigger. It had a slender, flexible neck and a long tail that stuck out stiffly behind it.

Its powerful hind legs ended in three-toed, birdlike feet. With its long, strong legs, *Gallimimus* was almost certainly a fast runner. With its body thrust forward and its tail held out behind, it could have run quickly. Ostriches today run over 30 mph (50 km/h).

Gallimimus had a long beak with a wide tip, similar to a duck's bill. Like most other ornithomimids, *Gallimimus* had no teeth. Instead, its beak had a horny coating. *Gallimimus*'s beak would have

The Nemegt Basin is a rocky part of the bleak Gobi Desert in Mongolia. Paleontologists love it because it is full of fossils! Polish-Mongolian expeditions visited Nemegt between 1963 and 1971. They found thousands of fossils, including several *Gallimimus* and some new dinosaurs. Many of the skeletons were still in one piece; it is likely that they were discovered in the exact place that they died.

Scientists have collected just a few of the many fossils scattered across this desert. They include many meat-eating dinosaurs, like *Oviraptor*, and Cretaceous mammals.

worn down and grown back throughout the animal's life so that it kept a sharp biting edge.

How did it live?

With its sharp beak, *Gallimimus* could have eaten anything from dead animals and insects to fruits and buds, or even tougher plant parts, such as stems and leaves. Scientists do not know. Only finding a *Gallimimus* with its last meal fossilized inside it would tell paleontologists for sure what the dinosaur ate.

Because of *Gallimimus*'s size, it would have been hunted by larger meat-eaters. *Gallimimus* would have relied on its speed to escape from predators.

CHECK THESE OUT!

Cretaceous period, Mammals, *Ornithomimus*, *Oviraptor*, Saurischian dinosaurs, *Struthiomimus*, Tetanurans, Theropods

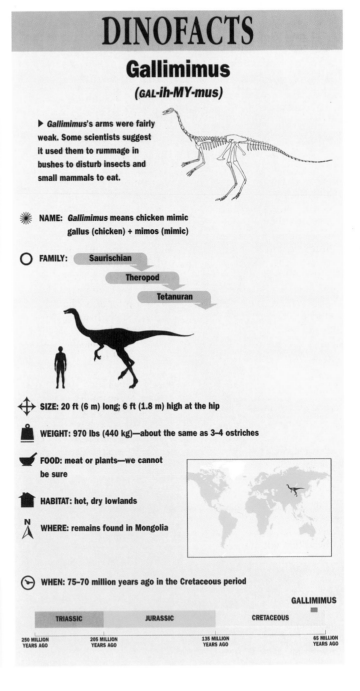

DINOFACTS

Gallimimus
(GAL-*ih-MY-mus*)

▶ *Gallimimus*'s arms were fairly weak. Some scientists suggest it used them to rummage in bushes to disturb insects and small mammals to eat.

✳ **NAME:** *Gallimimus* means chicken mimic gallus (chicken) + mimos (mimic)

○ **FAMILY:** Saurischian
Theropod
Tetanuran

✛ **SIZE:** 20 ft (6 m) long; 6 ft (1.8 m) high at the hip

⚖ **WEIGHT:** 970 lbs (440 kg)—about the same as 3–4 ostriches

FOOD: meat or plants—we cannot be sure

⌂ **HABITAT:** hot, dry lowlands

WHERE: remains found in Mongolia

🕐 **WHEN:** 75–70 million years ago in the Cretaceous period

			GALLIMIMUS
TRIASSIC	JURASSIC	CRETACEOUS	
250 MILLION YEARS AGO	205 MILLION YEARS AGO	135 MILLION YEARS AGO	65 MILLION YEARS AGO

Geological time

Paleontologists use a mixture of modern technology and fossil evidence to work out the huge ages of rocks. They do not describe these ages in years and months; they use a geological timescale.

Planet earth is about 4,600 million years old. We cannot begin to imagine such a huge number of years. So we divide the earth's age into bigger units than years; these bigger units are easier to use. Instead of years, we use a geological timescale. This timescale has a variety of units in different sizes. From the largest to the smallest, these units are called eons, eras, periods, and epochs.

When life began
The most important division in geological time is between the Precambrian Eon and

the Phanerozoic Eon. The Precambrian Eon spans the many millions of years from the planet's birth to the appearance of the first significant life-forms. The Phanerozoic Eon began 550 million years ago; we are still in the Phanerozoic Eon today.

Before the Phanerozoic Eon, only tiny, simple forms of life existed, such as bacteria. At the beginning of the Phanerozoic, animals appeared with hard outer skeletons—like shellfish.

The Phanerozoic Eon is divided into three eras—the Paleozoic, Mesozoic, and

Cenozoic eras. Each era is divided into periods. For example, the Mesozoic Era— the time in which the dinosaurs lived—is made up of the Triassic, Jurassic, and Cretaceous periods. Each period breaks down into several epochs. For instance, the last three epochs of the Cretaceous period are the Santonian, Campanian, and Maastrichtian epochs.

Fossil dating
The long, long history of life on earth is recorded as fossils in the rocks beneath our feet.

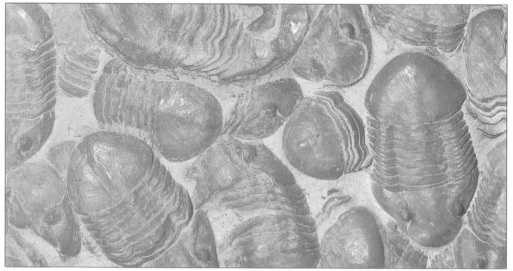

▲ Trilobites appeared more than 500 million years ago in the Cambrian period. They had hard body armor, as did many animals of their day.

THE GEOLOGICAL TIMESCALE

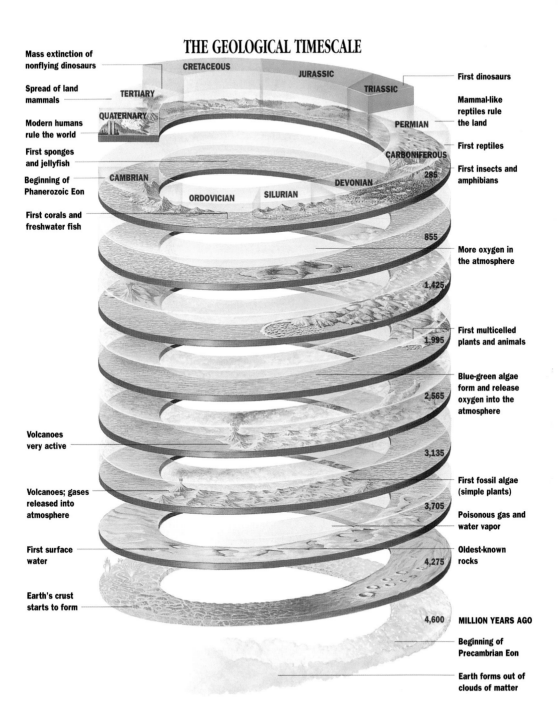

Mass extinction of nonflying dinosaurs

CRETACEOUS

JURASSIC

First dinosaurs

Spread of land mammals

TERTIARY

TRIASSIC

Mammal-like reptiles rule the land

QUATERNARY

PERMIAN

Modern humans rule the world

First reptiles

First sponges and jellyfish

CARBONIFEROUS

CAMBRIAN

First insects and amphibians

285

Beginning of Phanerozoic Eon

DEVONIAN

ORDOVICIAN

SILURIAN

First corals and freshwater fish

855

More oxygen in the atmosphere

1,425

First multicelled plants and animals

1,995

Blue-green algae form and release oxygen into the atmosphere

2,565

Volcanoes very active

3,135

First fossil algae (simple plants)

Volcanoes; gases released into atmosphere

3,705

Poisonous gas and water vapor

First surface water

Oldest-known rocks

4,275

Earth's crust starts to form

4,600   MILLION YEARS AGO

Beginning of Precambrian Eon

Earth forms out of clouds of matter

177

Rock of ages

The first person to show that certain rock types and certain sets of fossils always occurred in a predictable order was William Smith, a British engineer. In 1815, Smith published a map of England and Wales. His map showed that different types and ages of rocks could be recognized by the fossils that could usually be found in them.

Smith's discovery made it possible to compare rocks from different parts of Britain—and later the world—to decide if they belonged to the same part of the geological timescale.

This method of using fossils to measure the relative ages of rocks is called biostratigraphy. Most paleontologists still use biostratigraphy when dating fossils. For example, instead of saying a fossil is 67 million years old, they say it is from the Maastrichtian epoch.

Dating with radioactivity

The reason paleontologists used biostratigraphy is simple. Before the 1920s, it was just not possible to find out the age of rocks in years. All estimates were just guesses, and most guesses were wrong. However, most paleontologists did not worry about the actual age of rocks. As long as they knew the order in which fossils appeared, they could figure out who evolved from whom.

There is only one way to measure the age of rocks in years—by using radiometric dating. Some rock types contain radioactive elements. Certain forms (isotopes) of

Being able to date fossils helps scientists to understand how life developed. It helps them to work out how plants and animals evolved from one form into another. How do scientists know how old rocks are?

Steno's stacks

Most fossils come from rocks made up of hardened sand, silt, and tiny, dead life-forms. These kinds of rocks are called sedimentary rocks. Nicholas Steno, a 17th-century Danish

▲ The engineer William Smith made a map showing the rocks of England and Wales in 1815. He was the first to realize that fossils could show us the different ages of rocks.

naturalist, recognized that all sedimentary rocks were originally laid down in layers, although later events, such as earthquakes, may have moved them around. Steno realized that in a stack of sedimentary rocks, the oldest rocks were at the bottom and the youngest rocks were at the top.

radioactive elements are unstable: they decay (change) into other elements at a steady rate. Different isotopes have different decay rates.

Decay rates are measured in half-lives—the time it takes for half of a certain amount of material to decay. Depending on the isotope, half-lives can be thousands, millions, or even billions of years. Scientists use a wide variety of isotopes to measure the earth's history.

Rock sandwiches

Paleontologists cannot use radiometric dating directly on sedimentary rocks because they do not usually contain radioactive material. Only igneous rocks, such as those thrown out by volcanoes, contain radioactive material.

Sometimes, though, a layer of sedimentary rock may be sandwiched between two layers of igneous rock. By figuring out the ages of the igneous rock layers, scientists can work out the age of the sedimentary rock in between.

However, results from radiometric dating are not completely accurate. That is why paleontologists do not always agree on dates. For example, some say that the Cretaceous period started 135 million years ago; others say 145 million years ago.

CHECK THESE OUT!

Collecting dinosaurs, Cretaceous period, Digging dinosaurs, Evolution, Extinction, Fossils, Jurassic period, Rocks, Triassic period

THE WORLD IN A DAY

Scientists believe that the earth was formed 4.6 billion years ago. Because this is too long a time for us to grasp, we can use simpler ways of looking at geological time. Imagine that all time—from the earth's beginning right up to today—is squeezed into a single day. The earth began in the first split second of the day.

The first life-forms on earth were simple cells, including various kinds of bacteria. They appeared roughly a billion years after the earth began. On our imaginary day, each second lasts more than 50,000 years, and each hour lasts nearly 200 million years. So, life began just before ten to six in the morning.

Around half a billion years ago, creatures with hard shells evolved in the oceans. One hundred million years later, amphibians crawled onto dry land. What about the dinosaurs? They appeared about 230 million years ago. This sounds like a long time ago, but on our clock it is already 10:48 in the evening.

Dinosaurs ruled the earth for about 165 million years. The nonflying dinosaurs died out at the end of the Cretaceous period, 65 million years ago. On our clock, this happens at 11:40 at night. Here the Cenozoic Era starts, the reign of the birds and mammals.

Lots of weird and wonderful mammals have evolved and become extinct during the Cenozoic Era. Humans appeared about two million years ago—just one and a half minutes before midnight on our clock. The wheel was invented, the Egyptians built the pyramids, and people landed on the moon all in the last second of the day.

Giganotosaurus

Giganotosaurus is one of the most famous recent dinosaur discoveries: a meat-eating monster that may have been even bigger than the king of the dinosaurs, the mighty *Tyrannosaurus*!

In 1995, fossil-hunter Ruben Carolini found some huge bones in Neuquén, Argentina. Paleontologists Rodolfo Coria and Leonardo Salgado studied the bones. In many ways, they were like those of *Tyrannosaurus*. Both dinosaurs had relatively short forelimbs, three large claws on each hind foot, and a big, bootshaped tip on the pubic bone.

A new king
However, the longest *Tyrannosaurus* thigh bone ever found was 4.5 ft (1.4 m) long. Because the newfound thigh bone was 4.75 ft (1.45 m) long, Coria and Salgado believed they had discovered

a different dinosaur. They named the new creature *Giganotosaurus*.

There were other differences between *Giganotosaurus* and *Tyrannosaurus*. *Giganotosaurus* had a smaller brain and shorter, stockier hind legs. It was almost certainly not as smart as

▼ *Giganotosaurus* was a huge, fierce predator that stalked the floodplains and forests of South America midway through the Cretaceous period.

WHICH WAS THE BIGGEST MEAT-EATER?

The biggest known meat-eating dinosaurs are *Giganotosaurus*, *Tyrannosaurus*, *Carcharodontosaurus*, and *Spinosaurus*. Of these, *Giganotosaurus* had the biggest head, and *Spinosaurus* the smallest. However, *Tyrannosaurus* and *Spinosaurus* had longer and thicker teeth than *Giganotosaurus* and *Carcharodontosaurus*.

Which had the biggest body? Scientists have not found all the body parts of *Spinosaurus* and *Carcharodontosaurus*, so we cannot tell how big they were. *Giganotosaurus*'s bones were bigger and heavier than those of *Tyrannosaurus*. Does that mean *Giganotosaurus* was the biggest? Not really. We have found so few individuals of each of these dinosaurs. Maybe we have only found the fossils of the smallest individuals. Maybe the largest meat-eaters never became fossils. Maybe there is an even bigger meat-eater still waiting to be discovered.

Tyrannosaurus, and slower on its feet. *Tyrannosaurus* had thick teeth that grew as long as bananas; *Giganotosaurus* had smaller, blade-shaped teeth.

How *Giganotosaurus* lived

Giganotosaurus was one of the last and largest of the allosaurs, a group of mostly big meat-eating dinosaurs. Allosaurs grabbed their prey with their strong claws. They then sliced open their victims with their sharp teeth. *Acrocanthosaurus*, *Carcharodontosaurus*, *Sinraptor*, and *Allosaurus* were allosaurs.

Giganotosaurus hunted the sauropods that lived in Cretaceous Argentina. These included *Titanosaurus* and *Rebbachisaurus*, a huge dinosaur with a high-arched back.

Did *Giganotosaurus* and *Tyrannosaurus* ever meet? No. *Giganotosaurus* died out 25 million years before *Tyranno-saurus*'s giant footsteps first shook the earth.

African cousin

In 1996, paleontologists described a new specimen of *Carcharodontosaurus*, an African dinosaur that lived about the same time as *Giganotosaurus*. Their bones showed that the two dinosaurs were closely related. How could two dinosaurs be so similar, but live so far apart?

In the Jurassic period, South America and Africa were still joined. The ancestors of *Carcharodontosaurus* and *Giganotosaurus* roamed over the whole landmass. In the Cretaceous period, South America and Africa drifted

apart. Only then did the dinosaurs on each landmass begin to develop differently.

Did the two cousins ever meet? Possibly. No one has found *Giganotosaurus* in Africa, or *Carcharodontosaurus* in South America. However, at times, land bridges may still have linked the two continents.

DINOFACTS

Giganotosaurus
(GIH-guh-NO-tuh-SORE-us)

✳ **NAME:** *Giganotosaurus* means giant southern lizard
giga (giant) + notos (southern) + sauros (lizard)

○ **FAMILY:** Saurischian
→ Theropod
→ Tetanuran

⊕ **SIZE:** 46 ft (14 m) long; 11.5 ft (3.5 m) high at the hip

WEIGHT: 8 tons (7.3 tonnes)—about the same as 32 tigers

FOOD: meat

HABITAT: floodplains, forests

WHERE: remains found in Neuquén, Argentina

WHEN: 97–95 million years ago in the Cretaceous period

			GIGANOTOSAURUS
TRIASSIC	JURASSIC		CRETACEOUS
250 MILLION YEARS AGO	205 MILLION YEARS AGO	135 MILLION YEARS AGO	65 MILLION YEARS AGO

CHECK THESE OUT!

Acrocanthosaurus, Allosaurus, Carcharodontosaurus, Continental drift, Cretaceous period, Fossils, Jurassic period, Saltasaurus, Saurischian dinosaurs, Spinosaurus, Tetanurans, Theropods, Titanosaurus, Tyrannosaurus

Gobipteryx

In 1971, a Polish expedition to the Gobi Desert discovered some strange fossil eggshells. The remains inside them were the chicks of an ancestor of modern birds.

Polish paleontologists made many trips to the Gobi Desert in the early 1970s. They were looking for fossils from the Cretaceous period. Among other discoveries, they found seven skeletons of a new avialan. (Avialans are birds and their closest relatives.) They named the avialan *Gobipteryx*—"wing of the Gobi."

Eggs–actly

The paleontologists found *Gobipteryx*'s remains among fragments of fossil eggshell. This led scientists to believe they had found avialan babies almost ready to hatch. The sandstone rock in which the remains were fossilized was also found inside the eggshells. This told the scientists that the eggs had been broken open before they were buried.

The Gobi Desert was the same 80 million years ago as it is today—a hot, dry, windy place with dust storms and sandstorms. A severe sandstorm buried the nest. The eggs' parents were never found. Perhaps they were away from the nest, hunting for food, when the storm broke.

Ancient flier

What was *Gobipteryx*? It was a primitive (little evolved) avialan, an ancestor of modern

▶ *Gobipteryx* scans the desert for signs of prey. This avialan probably snapped up anything that moved, including lizards and insects.

birds. Scientists found birdlike bones in the roof of its mouth. Scientist Andrej Elzanowski described *Gobipteryx* as a close relative of modern large flightless birds, like the ostrich and Australia's cassowary. However, new studies showed that it was an enantiornithine (ih-NAN-tee-OR-nih-theen), or opposite bird, a member of an extinct group from the Cretaceous period.

Born to fly

Gobipteryx must have been able to fly. Fossils show that the arms were very long, a good sign that they were used for flapping and gliding. In one way, though, *Gobipteryx* was unlike most modern flying birds. The wing bones of the unhatched *Gobipteryx* were hard and almost fully grown. This suggests it could fly from its nest soon after hatching. Most newly hatched flying birds rely on their parents for protection and food.

CHECK THESE OUT!

Avialans, Birds, Cretaceous period, Eggs and babies, Lizards and snakes, Mammals, Maniraptors, Rocks, Saurischian dinosaurs, Theropods

THE OPPOSITE BIRDS

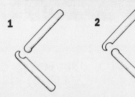

One of the major differences between modern birds and the enantiornithines, or opposite birds, was in their shoulder joints. The diagram shows that modern birds (1) have a hollow in one bone and a knob on the other. The opposite birds (2) had a knob on the first bone and a hollow in the other—the joint was the opposite way around.

After British paleontologist Cyril Walker named the enantiornithines in 1981, fossil-hunters were able to recognize many other opposite birds, like the avialan *Concornis*. So far, scientists have found 15 different kinds of enantiornithines. Some were sparrow-sized; others were huge like *Gobipteryx*.

DINOFACTS

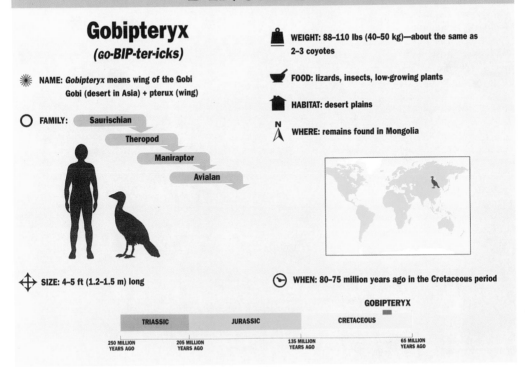

Gobipteryx
(GO-BIP-ter-icks)

☀ **NAME:** *Gobipteryx* means wing of the Gobi
Gobi (desert in Asia) + pterux (wing)

○ **FAMILY:** Saurischian
Theropod
Maniraptor
Avialan

✛ **SIZE:** 4–5 ft (1.2–1.5 m) long

⚖ **WEIGHT:** 88–110 lbs (40–50 kg)—about the same as 2–3 coyotes

🥣 **FOOD:** lizards, insects, low-growing plants

🏠 **HABITAT:** desert plains

🧭 **WHERE:** remains found in Mongolia

🕐 **WHEN:** 80–75 million years ago in the Cretaceous period

GOBIPTERYX

TRIASSIC	JURASSIC	CRETACEOUS
250 MILLION YEARS AGO	205 MILLION YEARS AGO	135 MILLION YEARS AGO · 65 MILLION YEARS AGO

Hadrosaurs

The Late Cretaceous period was filled with many types of hadrosaurs, or duckbill dinosaurs. Some looked like they wore construction hats; others looked like the mythical unicorn.

Hadrosaurs are called duckbills because they had big, toothless beaks. In the Late Cretaceous period, there were more duckbill dinosaurs than any other kind of large land animal. Scientists have found many good specimens of different kinds of hadrosaurs. They have found young and newly hatched babies, as well as eggs, nests, trackways, and even impressions of hadrosaur skin.

THREE-TON DUCKS

For a time, scientists could not tell if hadrosaurs were land animals or water animals. Their feet were webbed like ducks' feet, and they had paddlelike tails. Fossil-hunters found their remains where ancient swamps and rivers used to be. Some even thought lambeosaurines walked underwater, using their hollow crests as breathing tubes.

Paleontologists now know hadrosaurs could not have snorkeled. None of the hadrosaur crests found have holes in them to let in air. Hadrosaurs were land animals. Scientists have found their trackways where land used to be. They have also found fossils with land plants in their stomachs. The animals found on the sites of ancient lakes must have washed into the water after they died. However, scientists believe hadrosaurs liked to wallow in water as modern elephants do. They may also have escaped from predators by running into a nearby lake and swimming away using their webbed feet and paddlelike tails.

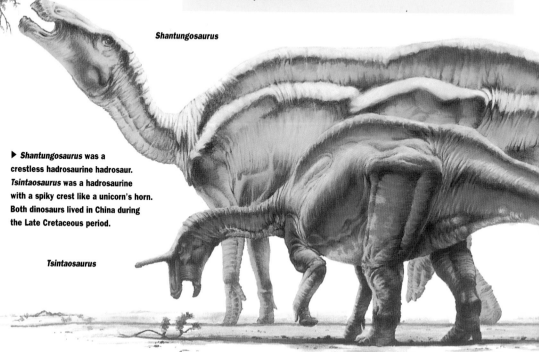

Shantungosaurus

▶ **Shantungosaurus** was a crestless hadrosaurine hadrosaur. **Tsintaosaurus** was a hadrosaurine with a spiky crest like a unicorn's horn. Both dinosaurs lived in China during the Late Cretaceous period.

Tsintaosaurus

184

DINOFACTS

Hadrosaurs
(HAD-ruh-sores)

 SIZE: 21–30 ft (6.4–9 m) long; 7–10 ft (2.1–3 m) high at the hip

 WEIGHT: from 2 to 10 tons (1.8 to 9 tonnes)—or from 2 to 10 North American bison

✳ **NAME:** Hadrosaur means sturdy lizard
hadros (sturdy) + sauros (lizard)

 FOOD: plants

○ **FAMILY:** Ornithischian
Ornithopod

 HABITAT: wide-ranging from low mountains to coastal regions

1   2   3

WHERE: remains found in North and South America, Asia, and Europe

▲ The skulls of *Parasaurolophus* (1), *Lambeosaurus* (2), and *Corythosaurus* (3) show the shapes of some lambeosaurine crests. The crests were hollow, and scientists think these dinosaurs may have blown through them to make sounds.

 WHEN: 100–65 million years ago in the Cretaceous period

		HADROSAURS	
TRIASSIC	JURASSIC	CRETACEOUS	
250 MILLION YEARS AGO	205 MILLION YEARS AGO	135 MILLION YEARS AGO	65 MILLION YEARS AGO

Crests and spikes

Scientists usually divide the hadrosaurs into two groups—the lambeosaurines and the hadrosaurines. Lambeosaurines, like *Corythosaurus*, had hollow crests. Hadrosaurines, such as *Edmontosaurus*, had solid crests or none at all; some, like *Tsintaosaurus*, had a spike.

How they lived

Like all the ornithischian (bird-hipped) dinosaurs, hadrosaurs were plant-eaters. Fossil-hunters found some hadrosaur nests in groups. From this they worked out that hadrosaurs lived in herds. As wildebeest herds in Africa still do today, the hadrosaurs probably moved from place to place during the year searching for food.

CHECK THESE OUT!

Anatosaurus, Bactrosaurus, Brachylophosaurus, Corythosaurus, Cretaceous period, Edmontosaurus, Eggs and babies, Hadrosaurus, Kritosaurus, Lambeosaurus, Maiasaura, Parasaurolophus, Saurolophus, Tsintaosaurus

185

Hadrosaurus

The hadrosaurs, or duckbill dinosaurs, were named in honor of *Hadrosaurus*. It was one of the first dinosaurs to be found in the United States, and scientists learned a great deal from it.

The remains of *Hadrosaurus* were discovered in New Jersey in 1858. Philadelphia zoologist Joseph Leidy studied them. He realized that they belonged to a very large reptile.

Two legs or four?
Because the skeleton was so complete, Leidy was able to reconstruct *Hadrosaurus* accurately. This was a big step forward for paleontology. Until then, scientists had had few bones to work with, and they had made some mistakes in rebuilding dinosaurs.

For example, British scientist and collector Richard Owen figured out that dinosaurs walked with their legs underneath their bodies—not held

out to the sides like those of crocodiles. However, he also believed that all dinosaurs moved on all fours like giant rhinoceroses.

After looking at *Hadrosaurus*, Leidy had other ideas. He saw that this dinosaur looked nothing like a rhinoceros. Its forelegs were too short. He thought it must have stood on its hind legs, like a kangaroo.

Fast and slow
Neither Owen nor Leidy was completely right. Today scientists think that *Hadrosaurus* walked mainly on all fours. Hadrosaurs (duckbill dinosaurs) had strong arms, and their hands had hooflike claws that would have been ideal for

◀ Some hadrosaurs had a hollow crest on their head; others did not. Although no one has found a *Hadrosaurus* skull, the rest of its skeleton looks like that of a hadrosaur with no hollow crest.

STATE FOSSIL

In June 1991, New Jersey declared *Hadrosaurus* its official state fossil. Many other states have also adopted dinosaurs because collectors found them there. For example, South Dakota chose the horned dinosaur *Triceratops*, Utah has the hunter *Allosaurus*, and New Mexico selected *Coelophysis*, a small meat-eater.

walking. However, scientists think hadrosaurs could run on two legs to escape predators.

Although Leidy's ideas were not completely right, they were important. He was one of the first scientists to suggest that some dinosaurs walked on two legs. As we now know, many kinds did—ornithopod (bird-footed) dinosaurs and theropods (two-legged meat-eaters), among others.

How did *Hadrosaurus* live?

Hadrosaurus was a plant-eater. *Corythosaurus*, a cousin of *Hadrosaurus*, ate twigs, seeds, and conifer leaves, so perhaps *Hadrosaurus* ate similar food.

Duckbills had powerful tails and paddlelike hands, so scientists think they may have been strong swimmers. When it was not eating, perhaps *Hadrosaurus* wallowed in water as elephants do today.

CHECK THESE OUT!

Allosaurus, *Coelophysis*, Collecting dinosaurs, *Corythosaurus*, Cretaceous period, Hadrosaurs, Ornithischian dinosaurs, Ornithopods, Theropods, *Triceratops*

DINOFACTS

Hadrosaurus
(*HAD-ruh-SORE-us*)

☀ **NAME:** *Hadrosaurus* means sturdy lizard
hadros (sturdy) + sauros (lizard)

○ **FAMILY:** Ornithischian
Ornithopod
Hadrosaur

✛ **SIZE:** 23 ft (7 m) long; 8 ft (2.4 m) high at the hip

⚖ **WEIGHT:** about 3 tons (2.7 tonnes)—about the same as 3 North American bison

FOOD: plants

HABITAT: subtropical lowlands

WHERE: remains found in New Jersey

🕐 **WHEN:** 76–73 million years ago in the Cretaceous period

			HADROSAURUS
TRIASSIC	JURASSIC	CRETACEOUS	
250 MILLION YEARS AGO	205 MILLION YEARS AGO	135 MILLION YEARS AGO	65 MILLION YEARS AGO

187

Herrerasaurus

Herrerasaurus lived in the Triassic period, not long after the first dinosaurs appeared. It probably looked a lot like the mystery creature from which all the meat-eating dinosaurs descended.

In the late 1950s and early 1960s, several teams of Argentine paleontologists explored the badland rocks called the Ischigualasto Formation. They knew the rocks were from the earliest part of the Late Triassic period, and they hoped to find very early dinosaurs. A local rancher, Don Victorino Herrera, led the scientists to different sites that were rich in fossil bones. They made many new discoveries. In 1963, Argentine paleontologist Osvaldo Reig named one of them *Herrerasaurus* in honor of the rancher.

BEFORE KNIVES AND FORKS

Herrerasaurus's skeleton shows us the basic features, or adaptations, a dinosaur needs to be able to eat meat. *Herrerasaurus*'s teeth are slightly curved and have a row of jagged edges like little knives down their front and back. These teeth are built to slice through meat. The lower jaw of *Herrerasaurus* has a hinge on it to help the dinosaur hold its struggling prey. *Herrerasaurus* could grab its prey with its strong arms, steadying the squirming animal with its long fingers and curved claws to take its first, jagged bite. Later theropods (two-legged meat-eaters) evolved specialized teeth, jaws, claws, and leg muscles.

▼ *Herrerasaurus* hunted, but it also scavenged on dead bodies when it found them.

Jackpot!

Even though *Herrerasaurus* was named in 1963, it was not until the 1980s that scientists realized it was a very special dinosaur. During the 1980s, paleontologists became interested in the origin of the dinosaurs. They looked again at Reig's specimens of *Herrerasaurus*. Scientists recognized that this early meat-eater was one of the most primitive (little evolved) dinosaurs known. It had five fingers on each hand. More advanced (highly evolved) dinosaurs had four, three, or even just two fingers.

Dinosaur dawn

A team of paleontologists visited the Ischigualasto in the late 1980s and early 1990s. The team included Argentine Fernando Novas and American Paul Sereno. Besides finding the meat-eater *Eoraptor*, the team came across more remains of *Herrerasaurus*.

Sereno and Novas began a new study of *Herrerasaurus*. They found it was very close to being the ancestor of all later theropods (two-legged meat-eaters). However, it was more advanced than *Eoraptor*, which lived at the same time. Even *Eoraptor* was not the dinosaur ancestor. Scientists have yet to find that mystery creature's remains.

How did it live?

Herrerasaurus had sharp teeth and strong arms with large, grasping hands. Its powerful legs made it fast. It would have eaten mammals, small reptiles, the plant-eating dinosaur *Pisanosaurus*, and even *Eoraptor*.

Herrerasaurus was itself hunted by other animals. It would have run from the giant *Saurosuchus*, a 27 ft (8.2 m) meat-eating reptile related to the ancestors of the crocodiles.

CHECK THESE OUT!

Crocodiles, Dinosaurs, *Eoraptor*, Mammals, *Pisanosaurus*, Reptiles, Saurischian dinosaurs, Theropods, Triassic period

DINOFACTS

Herrerasaurus
(heh-*RARE*-uh-*SORE*-us)

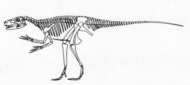

▶ Paleontologists have found only partial skeletons of *Herrerasaurus*, but by taking different bones from each they have built a full skeleton.

❋ **NAME:** *Herrerasaurus* means Herrera's lizard
Herrera (rancher and guide Don Victorino Herrera) + sauros (lizard)

○ **FAMILY:** Saurischian
Theropod

✛ **SIZE:** 8 ft (2.4 m) long; 2.5 ft (76 cm) high at the hip

⚖ **WEIGHT:** about 300 lbs (136 kg)—about the same as 2 large leopards

🥣 **FOOD:** meat

🏠 **HABITAT:** forests

N **WHERE:** remains found in Argentina

🕐 **WHEN:** 230–225 million years ago in the Triassic period

HERRERASAURUS

TRIASSIC	JURASSIC	CRETACEOUS
250 MILLION YEARS AGO	205 MILLION YEARS AGO	135 MILLION YEARS AGO	65 MILLION YEARS AGO

Hesperornis

Hesperornis was a primitive (little evolved) avialan, an ancestor of modern birds. It spent its time fishing in the warm, shallow sea that covered parts of North America in the Late Cretaceous period.

During the Late Cretaceous period, a great inland ocean covered parts of what is now western Canada and the United States. Today, we call this ancient sea the Western Cretaceous Interior Seaway. At one time this waterway stretched from the Arctic Ocean to the Gulf of Mexico. Many interesting animals lived in these warm, very shallow waters.

One of these animals was an avialan called *Hesperornis*. It looked like a modern water bird. It had webbed feet like a duck, a long, slender beak like a heron, and a long, flat body like a penguin. However, *Hesperornis* differed from modern birds. How?

A link in the chain

Hesperornis had teeth! No modern birds have teeth, and toothlessness is one of the features that makes modern birds different from primitive avialans like *Hesperornis*.

Even though *Hesperornis* was not a modern bird, modern birds are descended from creatures like *Hesperornis*. Most paleontologists agree that the ancestor of modern birds was a theropod (two-legged meat-eater)—perhaps a small, fierce hunter like *Velociraptor*.

WATER DINOSAURS, WATER BIRDS

A number of primitive (little evolved) avialans lived near, on, or in water. Ponds, lakes, rivers, seas, and oceans all had kinds of avialans that had features for moving and feeding near or in water. Scientists say they were adapted for this kind of life.

Many modern birds are also adapted for life near, on, or in water. Different groups of water birds share similar traits. Swimming birds usually have webbed feet. Birds such as albatrosses spend days flying over the oceans searching for food. They have long, narrow wings that let them glide for long distances. Gliding is less tiring than flapping. Wading birds that live in lakes and rivers have long legs that let them walk through shallow water. They have long toes to keep them from sinking into the mud.

Different beak shapes tell us what different birds eat. Herons have long, spearing beaks with which to catch fish and frogs. Some ducks find their food by scrabbling about on the bottoms of lakes and rivers. They have shovel-like beaks for digging.

Some water animals like sea snakes can even give birth to live young in the water. They never have to return to land. Birds can never become fully adapted to life in water because they always have to lay their eggs on dry land and keep them warm.

▼ *Hesperornis* strikes. Its teeth were good for holding slippery prey but not for slicing or cutting it. Like modern water birds, *Hesperornis* would have swallowed its fishy meal whole.

It helped that *Hesperornis* still had teeth. *Hesperornis* ate fish, catching them with its beak. Fish are slippery and difficult to hold. Its spiky teeth helped the animal hold a wriggling fish in its beak until it could swallow it.

Some modern fish-eating water birds have little ridges along the edges of their beaks. These birds are called sawbills and are a kind of duck. The little beak ridges are not real teeth like *Hesperornis*'s, but they do a similar job.

Spearfisher

Besides teeth, *Hesperornis* had other features to help it catch its fishy dinner. Its long, slim beak moved easily through water. Its long, flexible neck let it quickly move its head and beak toward a fish. Together, the long, thin beak on the end of a long, flexible neck made *Hesperornis* into something like a person spearfishing. The beak was like the spear, and the neck was like the arm holding the spear.

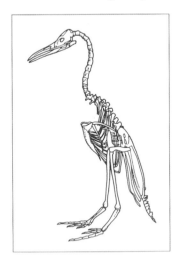

▲ *Hesperornis* had a long neck and a long, pointed bill a little like that of a loon or a heron. Its wing bones were tiny, so it was not able to fly.

Avialans like *Hesperornis* are a link in the chain between theropod dinosaurs and modern birds. Theropods had teeth; *Hesperornis* had teeth. As avialans evolved, however, their teeth vanished and they became modern birds.

Fishy evidence

How do we know *Hesperornis* ate fish and not some other kind of sea creature? We do not. Scientists have, however, found fossilized droppings (coprolites) in the same rocks as *Hesperornis* fossils. The coprolites contain thousands of tiny bones from fish that were eaten and digested by an animal. The coprolites are the right size for an avialan like *Hesperornis* and may belong to it. It is impossible to say for sure, though. Only finding a *Hesperornis* with the remains of its last meal would tell us with certainty what it ate.

What about the wings?

Although *Hesperornis* looks as though it has no wings, it has them. They are tiny, though.

All the bones we normally find in birds' wings were missing from *Hesperornis*, except for one. *Hesperornis*'s only wing bone was the humerus, the upper arm bone. The wings of primitive avialans and modern birds are feathered arms. This bone was just a thin sliver attached to the shoulder joint.

Hesperornis's wings were so weak the animal could not fly. Even so, the wings may have been useful in the water. *Hesperornis* was probably a good swimmer. Like ducks, it had skin stretched between its toes. These webbed feet acted like paddles to drive *Hesperornis* through the water.

While it paddled with its feet, though, *Hesperornis* needed to be able to steer. Perhaps it guided itself with its

▲ The loon is a modern bird that looks like the Cretaceous avialan *Hesperornis*. Loons nest and lay their eggs close to water, so *Hesperornis* probably did the same.

wings. Modern penguins are excellent swimmers; they use their little wings like this.

Ballast bones

Most modern birds have hollow bones. Hollow bones are good for flying animals because they make the animal lighter. *Hesperornis* did not have hollow bones. All its bones were solid and would have made the animal heavier.

It helps if a diving bird is heavier so it can dive more quickly through the water after its prey. *Hesperornis*'s solid bones would have made this avialan only a little heavier, though. It was still able to float on the surface like a duck whenever it wanted to rest.

Island life

Fossil-hunters have found the remains of *Hesperornis* in what were coastal areas in the age of the dinosaurs. *Hesperornis* probably lived along the shores of islands. It probably had a similar lifestyle to the loon, a modern water bird. The two animals may have looked alike, too, although they are not closely related. Like *Hesperornis*, the loon is well suited to catching and eating fish, and is about 3 ft (90 cm) long. Unlike *Hesperornis*, though, the loon can fly.

Like the loon, *Hesperornis* probably nested on islands. Predators would have viewed *Hesperornis* and its young as an easy meal. *Hesperornis*'s paddle feet were great for swimming, but would have been awkward on land. Because it could not fly, *Hesperornis* could escape only by sliding on its belly into the water.

Even in the water, though, *Hesperornis* was not safe. Large ocean-going lizards, the mosasaurs, also lived in the inland waterway. They probably caught and ate *Hesperornis* sometimes. Today, crocodiles and alligators catch and eat water birds.

CHECK THESE OUT!

Avialans, Birds, Bones, Cretaceous period, Maniraptors, Mosasaurs, Saurischian dinosaurs, Theropods, *Velociraptor*

DINOFACTS

Hesperornis
(HESS-per-OR-niss)

✳ **NAME:** *Hesperornis* means western bird
hesper (west) + ornis (bird)

◯ **FAMILY:** Saurischian
Theropod
Maniraptor
Avialan

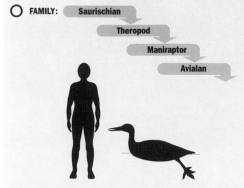

✛ **SIZE:** 3 ft (90 cm) long

WEIGHT: 44 lbs (20 kg)—about the same as a large coyote

FOOD: fish

HABITAT: shallow, near-shore waters of tropical seas

N **WHERE:** remains found in North America, from Alberta to Kansas

🕐 **WHEN:** 88–75 million years ago during the Cretaceous period

			HESPERORNIS
TRIASSIC	JURASSIC	CRETACEOUS	
250 MILLION YEARS AGO	205 MILLION YEARS AGO	135 MILLION YEARS AGO	65 MILLION YEARS AGO

Heterodontosaurus

This small, plant-eating dinosaur's name roughly means "lizard with a mixed bunch of teeth." Its unusual teeth included two pairs of long tusks. How did *Heterodontosaurus* use these tusks?

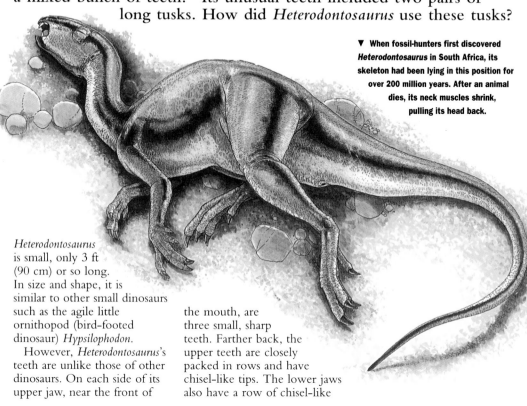

▼ When fossil-hunters first discovered *Heterodontosaurus* in South Africa, its skeleton had been lying in this position for over 200 million years. After an animal dies, its neck muscles shrink, pulling its head back.

Heterodontosaurus is small, only 3 ft (90 cm) or so long. In size and shape, it is similar to other small dinosaurs such as the agile little ornithopod (bird-footed dinosaur) *Hypsilophodon*.

However, *Heterodontosaurus*'s teeth are unlike those of other dinosaurs. On each side of its upper jaw, near the front of the mouth, are three small, sharp teeth. Farther back, the upper teeth are closely packed in rows and have chisel-like tips. The lower jaws also have a row of chisel-like teeth. At the front of the lower and upper jaws are curved tusks, one on each side. No other dinosaur has a mixture of teeth like this.

How did it use the tusks?

There are a number of ways in which the dinosaur could have used its tusks. *Heterodontosaurus* could have defended itself from an attacking predator by biting

RIGHT FOOD, RIGHT TEETH

Biologists studying modern animals have shown that the teeth of an animal determine the kind of food it can eat. For example, cows and horses eat grass and leaves. They have teeth with broad surfaces for grinding down plant food. These teeth are good at grinding plants, but they are not very good at slicing through meat. Meat-eating animals, like lizards and sharks, have teeth with sharp edges. These teeth work like knives. They are great for slicing through flesh but not so good for grinding plants.

Dinosaurs' teeth probably worked in similar ways. Dinosaurs with very sharp teeth, like *Tyrannosaurus*, probably ate meat. Dinosaurs with broad grinding surfaces on their teeth, like *Heterodontosaurus*, probably ate plants.

or slashing with them. Many modern animals, like warthogs or hippopotamuses, use their teeth in defense.

The tusks may have been useful for digging in the soil to find food or water. Warthogs do this, too. Male warthogs also use their tusks to fight for females. *Heterodontosaurus* may have done the same.

A boy and a girl?
Heterodontosaurus belongs to a group of dinosaurs called heterodontosaurs in its honor. Another heterodontosaur, *Abrictosaurus*, was similar to *Heterodontosaurus*, but had no tusks. Female warthogs have much smaller tusks than males. Some scientists think *Abrictosaurus* may have been a female *Heterodontosaurus*.

How *Heterodontosaurus* lived
Heterodontosaurus was an early plant-eating dinosaur. It grabbed branches with its strong arms and long, clawed, flexible fingers. Its horny beak could have nipped leaves and shoots from bushes. The chisel-like cheek teeth of the fossilized *Heterodontosaurus* were worn. The dinosaur would have used these teeth for grinding up plants before it swallowed them.

Heterodontosaurus was lightly built with long hind legs. Antelope have long hind leg bones; they are speedy runners. Perhaps *Heterodontosaurus* was a fast runner, too. Its long tail would have helped it to balance as it walked or ran.

CHECK THESE OUT!

Hypsilophodon, Jurassic period, Ornithischian dinosaurs, Ornithopods, Tyrannosaurus

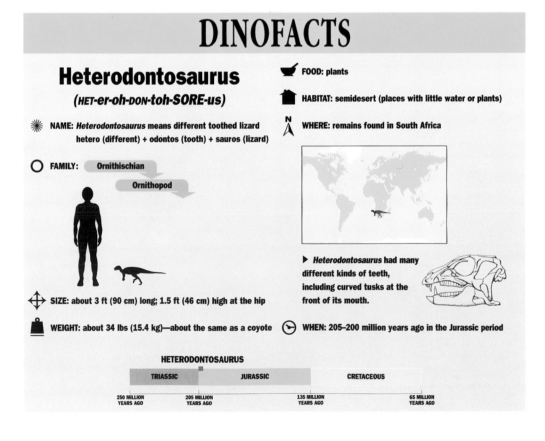

DINOFACTS

Heterodontosaurus
(HET-er-oh-DON-toh-SORE-us)

NAME: *Heterodontosaurus* means different toothed lizard
hetero (different) + odontos (tooth) + sauros (lizard)

FAMILY: Ornithischian
Ornithopod

SIZE: about 3 ft (90 cm) long; 1.5 ft (46 cm) high at the hip

WEIGHT: about 34 lbs (15.4 kg)—about the same as a coyote

FOOD: plants

HABITAT: semidesert (places with little water or plants)

WHERE: remains found in South Africa

▶ *Heterodontosaurus* had many different kinds of teeth, including curved tusks at the front of its mouth.

WHEN: 205–200 million years ago in the Jurassic period

HETERODONTOSAURUS

TRIASSIC	JURASSIC	CRETACEOUS
250 MILLION YEARS AGO	205 MILLION YEARS AGO / 135 MILLION YEARS AGO	65 MILLION YEARS AGO

Huayangosaurus

Huayangosaurus was one of the earliest stegosaurs, or plate-backed dinosaurs. This spiky plant-eater lived in China in the middle of the Jurassic period, about 170 million years ago.

Fossil-hunters first found *Huayangosaurus* in 1980, when they dug up a skull in the mountainous province of Sichuan in central China. Two years later, collectors found more specimens, including some headless skeletons and an almost complete skull.

The first *Huayangosaurus* skull was described by three Chinese scientists in 1982. Ten years later, one of them, Professor Dong Zhiming, worked with

▶ *Huayangosaurus* is the most primitive (little evolved) stegosaur known. It has traits that no other stegosaur has, including wrist bones that are joined together.

BOYS VS. GIRLS

Larger specimens of *Huayangosaurus* have a small horn just above and behind the eye socket. Smaller specimens do not have the horn. Maybe the larger, horned animals were male, and the others were female. Among mammals, scientists usually assume that the male is bigger and has horns, because males often have to fight for females. For example, male deer (stags and bucks) and sheep (rams) have larger horns. The males of some kinds of reptiles are also bigger than the females.

However, in other kinds of reptiles, like some crocodiles, the female is often bigger than the male. This is because the female has to produce lots of eggs, sometimes 20 or more. That takes a lot of energy. Being big helps you lay more eggs—and survive the effort! We cannot say for dinosaurs whether males were always bigger than females. Sometimes the males may have been wimpier!

Chicago paleontologist Paul Sereno, to examine the specimens again.

Plates vs. spikes

Before scientists found *Huayangosaurus*, all the stegosaurs they knew were fairly advanced (highly evolved). Advanced stegosaurs, such as *Stegosaurus*, had a long low head. *Huayangosaurus* had a short, high head. Advanced stegosaurs ripped up plants with their bony beaks. *Huayangosaurus* had no beak, just a few front teeth with which to nibble and pluck.

Advanced stegosaurs had mostly big, flat plates along their backs, and spikes on their tails. Their front legs were much shorter than their back legs. *Huayangosaurus*'s back had some plates but was mostly covered in spikes. Its legs were about the same length.

How *Huayangosaurus* lived

Huayangosaurus fed on leaves and stems growing low to the ground, which it snipped off with its front teeth. It shredded the plants with its cheek teeth before swallowing. Maybe *Huayangosaurus* reared up on its strong hind legs sometimes to snip leaves from higher plants. *Huayangosaurus* was probably not a fast runner, but its spikes and spines would scare off a hungry meat-eater.

CHECK THESE OUT!

Crocodiles, Eggs and babies, Jurassic period, Ornithischian dinosaurs, Reptiles, Stegosaurs, *Stegosaurus*, Thyreophorans, Turtles

DINOFACTS

Huayangosaurus
(hwah-YANG-guh-SORE-us)

▶ *Huayangosaurus* had flattened, bony plates along its neck, but spikes along the rest of its back.

✷ **NAME:** *Huayangosaurus* means lizard from Sichuan
Huayang (old name for Sichuan, province of China) + sauros (lizard)

○ **FAMILY:** Ornithischian
Thyreophoran
Stegosaur

✛ **SIZE:** 13.5 ft (4.1 m) long; 3.5 ft (1 m) high at the hip

WEIGHT: about 2 tons (1.8 tonnes)—about the same as a white rhinoceros

FOOD: plants

HABITAT: subtropical lowlands

N
↑ **WHERE:** remains found in China

WHEN: 170 million years ago in the Jurassic period

	HUAYANGOSAURUS		
TRIASSIC	JURASSIC		CRETACEOUS
250 MILLION YEARS AGO	205 MILLION YEARS AGO	135 MILLION YEARS AGO	65 MILLION YEARS AGO

Hypacrosaurus

A hadrosaur, or duckbill dinosaur, *Hypacrosaurus* roamed Canada in the Cretaceous period. It shared its world with ceratopsians (horned dinosaurs) and pachycephalosaurs (thick-headed dinosaurs).

Collectors have found many *Hypacrosaurus* skeletons. Ten of them are pretty complete; another 10 or 15 are just parts of skeletons. The bones belong to hatchlings, young dinosaurs, and adults, and they show that *Hypacrosaurus* looked much like its close relative *Corythosaurus*. Their heads, including their crests, are almost the same. So why do the two dinosaurs have different names if they looked so similar?

Ridged back
The differences between these two kinds of hadrosaurs are in their backbones (vertebrae). *Hypacrosaurus* had much higher

spines on its backbones than did *Corythosaurus*. That is why *Hypacrosaurus* was named "high-spined lizard."

Hypacrosaurus's high spines ran along its neck, back, and tail. They were surrounded

PLANT-EATERS

Modern plant-eating animals (herbivores) are divided into two groups—grazers and browsers—depending on their way of eating. Grazing animals live on the grasses and soft-leaved herbs that cover the ground. Cattle, sheep, and horses are grazers. They have strong front teeth for nipping up bunches of short grass.

Browsers—such as giraffes, the black rhinoceros, and sloths—eat plant food that grows higher above the ground. They eat leaves, stems, and fruit from bushes and trees. Grazers usually live out on the open grasslands and savannas, while browsers are often smaller and live in woods and forests.

During the Mesozoic Era, all plant-eating animals were browsers. There were no grasslands at all in the Mesozoic Era. Grasses had not evolved yet! They first appeared about 25 million years after the largest dinosaurs had died out. So if you see a painting of a dinosaur eating grass, look out !

◀ *Hypacrosaurus* munches on a twig. Like all hadrosaurs, *Hypacrosaurus* had hundreds of teeth for chewing plant food.

DINOFACTS

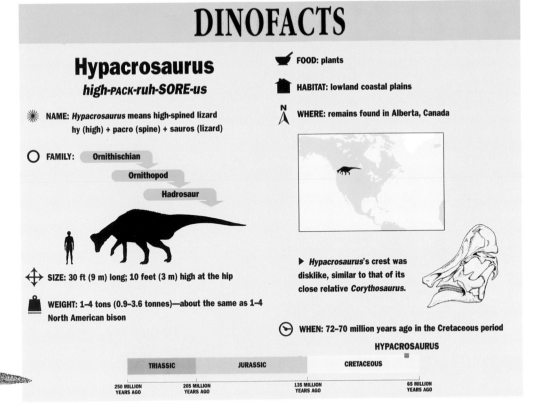

Hypacrosaurus
high-PACK-ruh-SORE-us

※ NAME: *Hypacrosaurus* means high-spined lizard
hy (high) + pacro (spine) + sauros (lizard)

○ FAMILY: Ornithischian

Ornithopod

Hadrosaur

⊕ SIZE: 30 ft (9 m) long; 10 feet (3 m) high at the hip

⚖ WEIGHT: 1–4 tons (0.9–3.6 tonnes)—about the same as 1–4
North American bison

🥣 FOOD: plants

🏠 HABITAT: lowland coastal plains

⇡ WHERE: remains found in Alberta, Canada

▶ *Hypacrosaurus*'s crest was
disklike, similar to that of its
close relative *Corythosaurus*.

🕐 WHEN: 72–70 million years ago in the Cretaceous period

HYPACROSAURUS

TRIASSIC	JURASSIC	CRETACEOUS	
250 MILLION YEARS AGO	205 MILLION YEARS AGO	135 MILLION YEARS AGO	65 MILLION YEARS AGO

by stiff cords, or tendons. The tendons held the spines together, forming a ridge. A layer of skin covered the ridge. Why did *Hypacrosaurus* have a ridge? Scientists are not sure, but one idea is that it was used in display, either to attract a mate or to scare away rivals.

Another idea is that it may have been used in temperature control. The skin over the ridge would have carried many blood vessels. When the animal was too hot, the blood vessels in the ridge gave off heat, and the whole body cooled down. When the

animal was cool, it could take in heat from the sun's rays through its ridge. Elephants use their ears like this today.

Some scientists disagree with this idea. If dinosaurs needed to cool down, then how did those without ridges get by?

How *Hypacrosaurus* lived

Hypacrosaurus was a lambeo-saurine (hollow-crested) hadrosaur. Like all hadrosaurs, it ate plants. It fed on the branches of evergreen trees and bushes. The shape and size of its skeleton suggests that *Hypacrosaurus* ate mostly leaves

and twigs within 3.5–6.5 ft (1–2 m) of the ground, but it could probably reach as high as 13 ft (4 m).

Hypacrosaurus probably moved and stood on all fours when it was feeding. When it needed to move fast, though, it could have taken to its strong hind legs and sped off.

199

Hypsilophodon

Hypsilophodon was a small, two-legged plant-eating dinosaur that lived in England in the Cretaceous period. Scientists used to think it climbed trees, but they now know it lived on the ground.

The first dinosaurs to be named were all found in the southern part of Britain. The scientific study of dinosaurs (paleontology) had just begun when, in 1869, Thomas Henry Huxley, a British geologist, biologist, and a founder of modern paleontology, came across a new dinosaur. He named it *Hypsilophodon*.

Paleontologists have been studying *Hypsilophodon* ever since. Fossil-hunters have discovered about 30 skeletons and numerous separate bones. Paleontologists have had many different ideas about *Hypsilophodon*'s lifestyle. These ideas have changed with the discovery of better material.

Up a tree

Hypsilophodon was a small, agile dinosaur whose only defense against predators was to make a quick getaway. Its long hind legs show that *Hypsilophodon* could run fast. However, some paleontologists suggested *Hypsilophodon* had some even neater tricks to defend itself from meat-eaters.

Because *Hypsilophodon* was so small, they suggested, perhaps it lived by climbing trees and clambering around in the branches. Large meat-eating dinosaurs could not have followed it into the trees. The branches could not have supported their weight. Also, *Hypsilophodon* would have found lots of leaves and stems to eat in the tree tops.

Unfortunately, this lively idea has now been disproved. Early paleontologists believed *Hypsilophodon*'s long-fingered hands and long-toed feet were good for grasping branches and climbing. New studies on *Hypsilophodon*'s finger and toe joints show that they were not very good at grasping. *Hypsilophodon* also had a long, stiff tail, which would have got in the way if it had climbed.

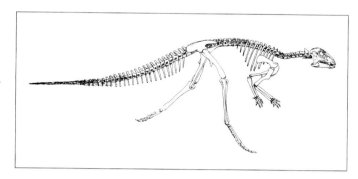

▲ *Hypsilophodon* was a fast runner. Like other speedy dinosaurs, it used its long, stiff tail to balance its body as it ran. Without its tail, *Hypsilophodon* would have fallen flat on its face.

Paleontologists also once guessed that *Hypsilophodon*'s back might have been covered in rows of armor that defended against predators. However, no fossil evidence has been found to back up this idea.

Hypsilophodon definitely had large eyes, though. It probably had sharp eyesight, which it used to spot predators before making a quick dash for safety.

How it lived
Hypsilophodon ate plants. It had many features that helped it to gather and chew food. Its mouth ended in a horny beak with which it could have nipped leaves and stems from low-growing bushes.

Hypsilophodon also had cheeks, like other ornithischian (bird-hipped) dinosaurs such as hadrosaurs (duckbill dinosaurs) and ceratopsians (horned dinosaurs). Cheeks stopped food from falling out of the dinosaur's mouth as it chewed.

Tooth power
Hypsilophodon's teeth had sharp ridges that were great for slicing and grinding plant food. Its jaws worked in an unusual way.

Most reptiles have very simple jaws, which open and close like scissors. Jaws like this can slice flesh and snip leaves from twigs, but they cannot chew from side to side—like the jaws of cattle—to grind up tough plant food.

Hypsilophodon and some closely related dinosaurs had a special type of chewing action. *Hypsilophodon*'s lower jaw still worked like a pair of scissors, but its upper jaw could make small sideways movements. This is unusual because the upper jaws of most animals cannot move at all. The sideways movement of its jaw allowed *Hypsilophodon*'s teeth to rub past each other more efficiently and helped the dinosaur to grind its food more thoroughly before swallowing.

Globe-trotting dinosaur?
Almost all the *Hypsilophodon* remains so far found were discovered in cliffs on the

▲ Because *Hypsilophodon* had a sideways-moving jaw, it was a fairly advanced (highly evolved) ornithischian. It could not have been an ancestor of the ornithischians as some paleontologists once thought.

HYPSILOPHODON AND FAMILY

Hypsilophodon belonged to a group of small, two-legged plant-eating dinosaurs named the hypsilophodontids in its honor. They first appeared in the Middle Jurassic period (about 175 million years ago) and lasted until the end of the Cretaceous (65 million years ago). During this time, they spread far and wide.

The earliest hypsilophodontids were from Europe and China. They included *Yandusaurus* and *Agilisaurus*. The first North American hypsilophodontids—*Othnielia* and *Nanosaurus*—appeared about 140 million years ago. During the Cretaceous, hypsilophodontids spread even farther. *Atlascopcosaurus*, *Leaellynasaura*, and *Fulgurotherium* lived in Australia; *Gasparinisaura* in Argentina. Hypsilophodontids even reached Antarctica. The last hypsilophodontids lived in North America at the very end of the Cretaceous. One of these, *Thescelosaurus*, was large and may not have been a hypsilophodontid at all. No hypsilophodontids have been found in Africa. This is probably because we know very little about the dinosaurs of Africa at the moment. We could expect to find hypsilophodontids there one day.

Hypsilophodontids were widespread and existed for a long time, but only a few remains are known for each type. This may be because they were rare. However, it may be because they rarely fossilized. All hypsilophodontids were small. Small animals are less likely to fossilize than large ones as their skeletons are easily destroyed by scavengers and the weather.

Unfortunately, *Hypsilophodon* remains that have been found outside Britain are usually only isolated bones and teeth. Fossils like these are very difficult to identify. Scientists will have to wait and see if any more complete dinosaur remains are found in these areas before they can be certain that *Hypsilophodon* lived there, too.

Close relatives?
Even though it was small and its remains have been found only in Britain, paleontologists rated *Hypsilophodon* as a very important dinosaur. Scientists thought that by studying *Hypsilophodon*, they could find clues about the evolution of all ornithischian dinosaurs.

Paleontologists once thought that *Hypsilophodon*, or a very similar dinosaur, was the ancestor of almost all of the other ornithischians. New studies, however, have shown that *Hypsilophodon* was actually a fairly advanced dinosaur. It could not have given rise to the other groups of ornithischian dinosaurs.

Bird ancestor?
Paleontologists also once suggested that birds might have descended from dinosaurs like *Hypsilophodon*. As their name suggests, the ornithischian, or bird-hipped, dinosaurs have birdlike hips. Their pubis (the front bone of the lower hip) points backward, as does the pubis of birds.

However, this idea has also been shown to be wrong. Amazingly, birds descended not from the bird-hipped

▲ This early illustration of *Hypsilophodon* shows it perched on the branch of a tree. Paleontologists now know this dinosaur could not have climbed trees.

southern coast of the Isle of Wight in southern England. Some fossil-hunters, however, have claimed they have found remains of *Hypsilophodon* in other parts of the world, including the United States, Spain, and Portugal.

It would not be so surprising to find *Hypsilophodon* in these places. The Cretaceous rocks there contain very similar dinosaurs to English rocks. For example, *Iguanodon*, which lived at the same time as *Hypsilophodon*, is found in Cretaceous rocks in Britain, much of western Europe, and the United States.

ornithischian dinosaurs but from the saurischian, or lizard-hipped, dinosaurs!

Bird-footed cousins

Hypsilophodon is a member of a group of dinosaurs called the hypsilophodontids. They are closely related to *Iguanodon* and the hadrosaurs. All these dinosaurs belong to the larger group called the ornithopods—the bird-footed dinosaurs.

Dinosaur graveyard

The area of the Isle of Wight in which all the *Hypsilophodon* fossils were discovered is called the *Hypsilophodon* bed. Some of the skeletons were so close to one another that they were almost touching. Many of the skeletons were in very good condition, with most of their bones lying just as they had fallen so long ago.

Paleontologists believe the dinosaurs discovered in the *Hypsilophodon* bed were probably buried very quickly after they died. If the bodies had stayed in the open for long, scavengers would have fed on them, and the bones would have been scattered. How were they buried so rapidly? Perhaps a small group of *Hypsilophodon* became trapped in a patch of quicksand. The dinosaurs died together and became buried before scavengers were able to get to the carcasses.

CHECK THESE OUT!

Birds, Ceratopsians, Collecting dinosaurs, Cretaceous period, Fossils, Hadrosaurs, *Iguanodon*, Jurassic period, *Leaellynasaura*, Ornithischian dinosaurs, Ornithopods, Paleontology, Saurischian dinosaurs, *Thescelosaurus*

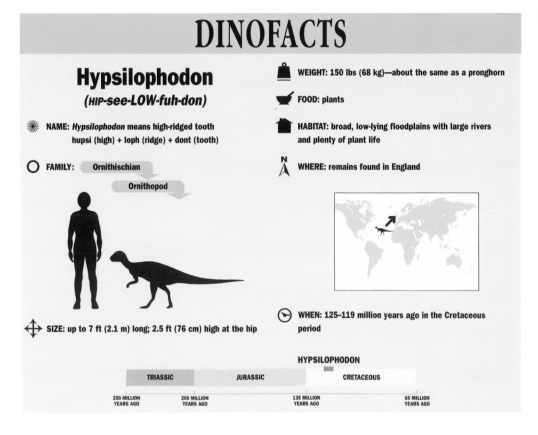

DINOFACTS

Hypsilophodon
(*HIP-see-LOW-fuh-don*)

* **NAME:** *Hypsilophodon* means high-ridged tooth
  hupsi (high) + loph (ridge) + dont (tooth)

○ **FAMILY:** Ornithischian
  Ornithopod

SIZE: up to 7 ft (2.1 m) long; 2.5 ft (76 cm) high at the hip

WEIGHT: 150 lbs (68 kg)—about the same as a pronghorn

FOOD: plants

HABITAT: broad, low-lying floodplains with large rivers and plenty of plant life

WHERE: remains found in England

WHEN: 125–119 million years ago in the Cretaceous period

HYPSILOPHODON

TRIASSIC	JURASSIC	CRETACEOUS
250 MILLION YEARS AGO	205 MILLION YEARS AGO	135 MILLION YEARS AGO · 65 MILLION YEARS AGO

Ichthyornis

Ichthyornis was a primitive (little evolved) avialan, an ancestor of modern birds. Gull-like, it lived by the Niobrara Sea, which covered parts of central North America during the Late Cretaceous period.

Seagulls flapping excitedly over the heads of giant Cretaceous marine lizards and turtles? Not exactly, but some primitive (little evolved) avialans must have looked and sounded just like the seagulls of today.

Ichthyornis was one of these early gull-like creatures. The US paleontologist Othniel C. Marsh discovered its remains in Kansas in 1870. This was about the time that the first good dinosaur skeletons were being discovered in the western United States. Marsh collected as many dinosaur skeletons as he could to beat his rival and one-time friend Edward Drinker Cope.

Muscle power

Ichthyornis was almost certainly a good flier, so its remains tell scientists that flying avialans had evolved by the Cretaceous period. Scientists know that *Ichthyornis* could fly well because of its breastbone.

Modern birds that fly quickly or for long distances have very large wing muscles attached to their chests. These muscles need something rigid to fasten onto. Flying birds have a deep, flat breastbone running down the middle of

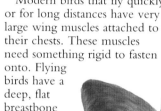
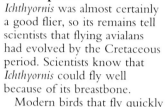

▶ Toothy *Ichthyornis* scavenges on the remains of an ammonoid washed up on the beach of the Niobrara Sea.

their chests on the outside. The breastbone is the rigid structure to which the big flight muscles attach. *Ichthyornis* had a very large breastbone, like most modern birds. This means *Ichthyornis* must have been a good flier.

Archaeopteryx, the earliest known avialan, did not have a large breastbone, so maybe it was not such a good flier.

Wishbone

An important bone in the body of a modern flying bird is the wishbone. Seen from the front, this bone looks like the letter Y. The two upright prongs of this bone each rest against the bird's shoulder joints at the front of its chest.

The wishbone helps to support the chest when the powerful flight muscles pull down on the wings. It also acts like a spring to push the wings back up again ready for the next downstroke.

Marsh found only small parts of *Ichthyornis*'s wishbone, but paleontologists are certain that the bone would have been large. *Ichthyornis* had a big breastbone; it would have needed a strong wishbone, too.

Where's the tail?

Like modern birds, *Ichthyornis* had a very short tail. The early avialan *Archaeopteryx* had a long tail. If it flew, *Archaeopteryx* probably needed a long tail to help it keep in a steady and straight line. Over millions of years, avialans got better at flying, so their tails got shorter. *Ichthyornis*'s very short tail tells us that this avialan was a very

skilled flier. *Ichthyornis* would have been able to make very sharp turns in midair, and take off very quickly.

Bobbing in the waves

How do scientists know that *Ichthyornis* spent time on the sea surface? *Ichthyornis* had long

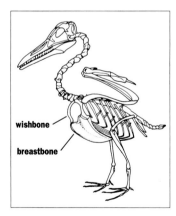

wishbone

breastbone

▲ *Ichthyornis* had a deep, flat breastbone like modern flying birds. It also had a wishbone. Paleontologists therefore think *Ichthyornis* was a strong flier.

toes that spread out widely. Its foot and toe bones are just like those of modern seabirds with webbed feet. These web-footed seabirds often rest on the sea surface. The skin stretched between its toes would have made paddling on the surface of the water very easy for *Ichthyornis*.

Because flying birds are extremely light, *Ichthyornis* could have easily floated on top of the water. It could rest or look in the water for something to eat.

What did *Ichthyornis* eat?

Ichthyornis lived around the Niobrara Sea, part of the shallow inland waterway that divided the western half of North America from the eastern half in the Late Cretaceous period. *Ichthyornis* probably ate fish, and may have eaten squid and squidlike animals, too. Its long, thin beak was shaped like that of a modern seabird, but it was

Most avialans (including modern birds) have very light, delicate skeletons. For this reason, they fossilize very rarely and only under special conditions. They need the very fine sand or mud that collects at the bottom of quiet waters. Only sands and muds are soft enough to preserve the details of the tiny and delicate bones.

Quiet water means that there cannot be any currents or sloshing waves. Moving water breaks up the skeleton of a dead animal, especially the skeleton of an avialan. Avialan skeletons are so fragile because their bones are hollow and very light to allow the animals to fly. Just the slightest motion of water against an avialan skeleton would be enough to scatter the bones. Currents in a river or stream would then tumble and break up any loose bones.

The seven known *Archaeopteryx* skeletons come from fine rocks that formed in very quiet tropical lagoons in Germany. Important avialan fossils also come from Spain and China. In both places, the animals died and fell into deep lakes, with layers of fine, silty mud at the bottom. Some of these muds were so good at preserving the creatures that even some feather patterns can be seen.

▲ A flock of gulls take to the air. Scientists think *Ichthyornis* looked like a gull. It could have had a gull's dark and light coloration.

lined with lots of sharp little teeth. No modern bird has real teeth, although sawbills—a group of ducks—have horny knobs in their beaks. A tooth-filled beak would have been a perfect tool for catching slippery fish and squid.

Stealthy flier

Ichthyornis's skull and skeleton are very similar to the skulls and skeletons of modern seabirds. It also seems that *Ichthyornis* lived in the same sorts of habitats that a lot of modern seabirds live in today. These two major similarities

help scientists reconstruct *Ichthyornis* with more confidence than is possible with most fossil animals.

Many seabirds have strongly contrasting colors—whites and grays—on the body and wings, with dark-colored patches on the head, beak, and legs. Often the belly is white, while the back is gray or brown. These color patterns make it more difficult for other animals to spot seabirds. Most likely *Ichthyornis* would have had color patterns similar to those of modern seagulls.

A fish looking up to the surface of the water would find it hard to see the white belly of a flying *Ichthyornis* against a bright sky. This would have

made it easier for *Ichthyornis* to surprise the fish when it swooped down out of the sky to catch it near the surface.

The darker back and tops of the wings would have made it difficult for flying predators to see *Ichthyornis* against the water or on the ground. *Ichthyornis* shared its habitat with pterosaurs (flying reptiles). Many pterosaurs ate fish, but some kinds may have hunted little *Ichthyornis*.

Hold the salt!

Living near the sea, possibly far from fresh water, means that seabirds have to go without drinking fresh water for long periods. Swallowing salty sea water would make the birds thirsty. Catching sea fish with their mouths makes it hard for seabirds to avoid swallowing some sea water!

Many modern seabirds—such as penguins, albatrosses, and pelicans—have a special gland near their eyes. This gland helps to get rid of the salt in any sea water that they accidentally swallow. *Ichthyornis* has small pits in its skull, near its eyes. These pits probably held the same sorts of special salt-removing glands. This feature suggests that *Ichthyornis* was a true ocean avialan.

Saved by chalk dust

Othniel C. Marsh discovered *Ichthyornis*'s bones in layers of chalk laid down in the Late Cretaceous period.

The chalk is the remains of the shells of billions and billions of tiny sea creatures that floated in the long-gone Niobrara Sea. When these animals died, particles of their tiny shells would sink to the seafloor and form a soft mud. Any larger animal that died and fell into this fine mud would be preserved. Avialans like *Ichthyornis* had extremely delicate bones that would not normally survive to become fossils, but chalk mud was soft enough to save even these.

CHECK THESE OUT!

Ammonoids, *Archaeopteryx*, Avialans, Belemnoids, Birds, Collecting dinosaurs, Continental drift, Cretaceous period, Fish, Fossils, Maniraptors, Pterosaurs, Rocks, Saurischian dinosaurs, Theropods

DINOFACTS

Ichthyornis
(ICK-*thee-OR-niss*)

✳ NAME: *Ichthyornis* means fish bird
ichthy (fish) + ornis (bird)

○ FAMILY: Saurischian
                 Theropod
                    Maniraptor
                       Avialan

✛ SIZE: 8 in (20 cm) high

⚖ WEIGHT: 2 oz (60 g)—about the same as 2–3 sparrows

🥣 FOOD: fish, squid, and squidlike creatures such as belemnoids

🏠 HABITAT: seashores and coastal waters

N⬆ WHERE: remains found in Kansas

🕐 WHEN: 70 million years ago in the Cretaceous period

			ICHTHYORNIS ▪
TRIASSIC	JURASSIC	CRETACEOUS	
250 MILLION YEARS AGO	205 MILLION YEARS AGO	135 MILLION YEARS AGO	65 MILLION YEARS AGO

Ichthyosaurs

Ichthyosaurs appeared in the Triassic period; why did they die out 25 million years before the end of the Cretaceous period?

A time traveler landing in the Early Jurassic period might be surprised to see dolphins swimming in the warm, shallow, tropical seas. If our time traveler stopped to take a closer look at these dolphins, he or she would soon see some important differences.

The most important difference was that the dolphins were not dolphins at all. Dolphins are mammals. The Jurassic creatures were reptiles called ichthyosaurs, or "fish lizards." Ichthyosaurs lived exactly like toothed whales (dolphins, porpoises, and killer whales) do today. They were fast-swimming, intelligent ocean hunters. Ichthyosaurs and toothed whales both descended from animals that lived on land, and both evolved a similar body form for life in water.

Tail swingers

One sign that ichthyosaurs were not mammals was the way their bodies bent when swimming. Dolphins bend their bodies and flat tail fins up and down. Ichthyosaurs swung their bodies and upright tail fins from side to side. Scientists know this from looking at the shapes of the backbones that make up the ichthyosaurs'

▶ Ichthyosaurs came in many shapes and sizes, but most looked and lived more or less like dolphins. These three kinds lived in Europe in the Early Jurassic period. *Stenopterygius* (1) was up to 10 ft (3 m) long, *Eurhinosaurus* (2) was 6.5 ft (2 m) long, and giant *Temnodontosaurus* (3) could reach 30 ft (9 m).

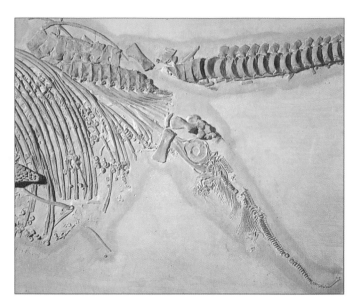

◀ This fossil shows an ichthyosaur being born. Besides being amazing, this fossil is also sad, since the baby and its mother must have died at the moment of the birth.

reptiles need to lay their eggs on land, but some can keep their eggs in their bodies and give birth to live young.

The German fossils show that ichthyosaurs gave birth to live young. One fossil even shows a young ichthyosaur coming out of its mother's body. Like a baby dolphin, the young ichthyosaur is coming out tail first. Ichthyosaurs, like dolphins, breathed air. The baby's head comes out last so it can rush to the surface to take its first breath. If the baby came out head first, it would have to wait until its body popped out before it could swim to the surface. By then, it would have drowned.

▼ The ichthyosaurs were a group of sea-living reptiles. They were not dinosaurs. Dinosaurs pterosaurs (flying reptiles) and crocodiles were all archosaurs. Ichthyosaurs looked like dolphins and lived all over the world.

spinal columns. In the tail area, the backbones are joined in such a way that let the tail move widely from side to side.

Another difference between dolphins and ichthyosaurs is the number and shape of their fins. Both groups of animals have front fins, but only the ichthyosaurs had hind fins. Like dolphins, ichthyosaurs steered with their fins.

Finbacks

Like dolphins and sharks, ichthyosaurs also had a fin on their backs (the dorsal fin). Like other fins, dorsal fins contain bones. However, no ichthyosaur fossils have been found with bones sticking up from their backs. So how do paleontologists know that ichthyosaurs had dorsal fins?

Amazingly, in southern Germany, collectors found the remains of ichthyosaurs with

the outlines of the body preserved as a black, sooty trace. These outlines clearly show a dorsal fin shape in exactly the spot where it would be expected.

Baby ichthyosaurs

Ichthyosaurs could not come ashore to lay eggs, but this did not matter. Most modern

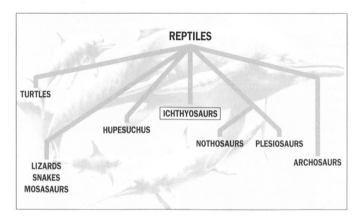

FOSSIL FACTS

Ichthyosaurs
(ICK-thee-o-sores)

▲ Ichthyosaurs' tails turned downward at the tip to support the lower part of their tail fin. When the animal was alive, it had a fleshy upper fin, too, so that it had a tail like a fish.

❋ **NAME:** Ichthyosaur means fish lizard
ichthy (fish) + sauros (lizard)

✛ **SIZE:** wide variation from 3 ft (90 cm) to 45 ft (13.7 m)

🥣 **FOOD:** fish, ammonoids, belemnoids, and shellfish such as clams

🏠 **HABITAT:** warm, shallow, tropical seas, including reefs

N ⇡ **WHERE:** remains found worldwide

🕐 **WHEN:** from 245 million years ago in the Triassic period to 90 million years ago in the Cretaceous period

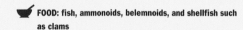

ICHTHYOSAURS		
TRIASSIC	JURASSIC	CRETACEOUS
250 MILLION YEARS AGO	205 MILLION YEARS AGO	135 MILLION YEARS AGO	65 MILLION YEARS AGO

End of the ichthyosaurs

Over the course of 120 million years, ichthyosaurs evolved a wide variety of body forms and sizes. They ranged from little *Mixosaurus*, which was just 3 ft (90 cm) long, to the mighty *Shonisaurus* at 45 ft (13.7 m). Both these animals lived in the Triassic period; the remains of *Mixosaurus* are found all around the world.

Ichthyosaurs were very widespread and numerous. So why did they become extinct in the Cretaceous period, 25 million years before the other marine reptiles and the nonflying dinosaurs?

By the middle of the Cretaceous period, new kinds of sharks evolved. Sharks and ichthyosaurs have similar body shapes and sizes, but their teeth are different. Ichthyosaurs' teeth could only catch and hold food; they could not cut or slice it. Ichthyosaurs swallowed fish, belemnoids, and ammonoids whole. This way of feeding limited the size of prey ichthyosaurs could eat.

Shark warning!

Sharks, though, have many rows of sharp teeth that are great for cutting and slicing prey. Their many sharp teeth allowed the sharks to attack and eat larger animals than the ichthyosaurs could, giving them an advantage.

Other large marine predators evolved by the mid-Cretaceous period, too. These included the mosasaurs. Mosasaurs were huge lizards up to 33 ft (10 m) long, which competed with ichthyosaurs for food.

CHECK THESE OUT!

Ammonoids, Belemnoids, Coral reefs, Cretaceous period, Dinosaurs, Fish, Jurassic period, Mammals, Mosasaurs, Reptiles, Sharks, Triassic period

Iguanodon

Iguanodon was a large plant-eater that lived in the Early Cretaceous period. It walked the earth for 25 million years, making it the longest-surviving dinosaur so far known.

Nineteenth-century British paleontologist Gideon Mantell named *Iguanodon* in 1825. It was only the second dinosaur ever named. The only fossils Mantell had were some teeth. He thought they came from a giant plant-eating lizard.

RUBBER JAW

Iguanodon had a neat trick to grind up the leaves and stems it ate. While one part of its jaw moved up and down, the cheek section moved from side to side. These movements let *Iguanodon*'s teeth rub past each other in a grinding action. We can move our lower jaw from side to side. Now try moving your upper jaw from side to side. You cannot, and neither can any modern mammal. *Iguanodon* could, though, and so could other advanced ornithopod dinosaurs such as the hadrosaurs (duckbills).

▶ *Iguanodon* could stand and move on two legs. However, it could not stand as upright as Belgian scientist Louis Dollo thought.

Others disagreed. French scientist Georges Cuvier, the first paleontologist, thought Mantell's fossils belonged to a later fish or a mammal like a rhinoceros. Mantell insisted they were from the Mesozoic Era. British paleontologist Richard Owen agreed. In 1842, he included *Iguanodon* in his list of dinosaurs. At that time, only two others were on the list!

In 1851, British artist Benjamin Waterhouse Hawkins made a life-sized model *Iguanodon* for an exhibition near London. He followed Mantell's description and created a giant iguanalike animal with upright legs and a horn on the tip of its nose.

The real *Iguanodon*?
Several years later, Belgian paleontologist Louis Dollo wrote a new description of *Iguanodon* that differed from Mantell's. In 1878, near Bernissart in Belgium, coal miners found no fewer than 39 *Iguanodon* skeletons more than 1,000 ft (300 m) underground. Dollo thought the skeletons were like those of kangaroos or flightless birds. He believed *Iguanodon* walked nearly upright on its hind legs, like a kangaroo. As for the nose horn on the model, Dollo found similar horns on the Bernissart dinosaurs.

They were not nose horns at all; they were thumblike spikes on each of *Iguanodon*'s hands.
In the 1970s, paleontologist David Norman from England's Cambridge University, looked

▲ *Iguanodon* had crisscrossed bony struts along its back to help it hold up its tail. Its tail helped to stop *Iguanodon* from toppling forward when it stood on its hind legs.

at the Bernissart *Iguanodon* again. He realized *Iguanodon* could not have stood completely upright on its hind legs. It would have broken its tail! Norman thought *Iguanodon* spent a lot of its time on all fours with its back horizontal. The Bernissart *Iguanodon* had long, sturdy forelimbs suited for walking. Also, *Iguanodon*'s middle three fingers were flattened. They were more like toes for walking on than fingers.

***Iguanodon* herds?**
Were the dinosaurs found at Bernissart a herd of *Iguanodon*? Norman does not believe so. The skeletons lay at slightly different levels. Norman thinks the dinosaurs died and were washed into a swamp over many years.

However, *Iguanodon* was related to the hadrosaurs (duckbill dinosaurs) such as *Corythosaurus*. Trackways show that some hadrosaurs lived in herds. Many *Iguanodon* lived in Europe during the Early

and the United States. An *Iguanodon* from one place is often slightly different from an *Iguanodon* from another.

Scientists give the different kinds, or species, of *Iguanodon* different names. Often they are named for the place where they were found. So, the *Iguanodon* found at Bernissart is called *Iguanodon bernissartensis*, or *Iguanodon* from Bernissart.

How did *Iguanodon* live?
During much of the Early Cretaceous period, *Iguanodon* was the most important large plant-eating dinosaur in the

◀ This is how Louis Dollo thought *Iguanodon* stood. However, its tail is broken where it bends to touch the floor.

▼ Benjamin Waterhouse Hawkins built his life-sized model of *Iguanodon* in 1851. Just before he finished, a group of scientists held a dinner party inside the animal. Today we know that *Iguanodon*'s spike goes not on its nose but on its thumb.

Cretaceous period; perhaps they lived in herds like their relatives. There is no hard evidence that they did, though.

Big-headed dinosaurs
Iguanodon was an ornithopod (bird-footed) dinosaur and belonged to a group of dinosaurs named the iguanodontids in its honor. Other iguanodontids included *Ouranosaurus* and *Camptosaurus*. All these dinosaurs shared similar features, including large skulls for their body size.

Paleontologists have found *Iguanodon* in many parts of Europe, North Africa, Asia,

northern half of the world. Because there were so many *Iguanodon*, and they ate so much, they changed the patterns of plant life in the areas where they lived.

During the Jurassic period, before *Iguanodon*, long-necked sauropods like *Apatosaurus* were the most important plant-eating dinosaurs. They mostly ate the leaves toward the tops of tall trees. *Iguanodon* did not have a long neck. It fed on plants growing closer to the ground. *Iguanodon* ate and killed trees while they were still small. Fewer trees grew up, while the very low-growing plants that *Iguanodon* did not eat flourished.

Chewing machine

Iguanodon had a sharp beak at the front of its mouth for biting off leaves and stems. It also had a groove in the center of its lower beak. This might have let *Iguanodon* stick out its tongue, curl it around a twig, and pull it toward its mouth. Giraffes do this today.

Once the food was in its mouth, *Iguanodon*'s teeth could grind it up thoroughly. Like other ornithopods, such as the hadrosaurs, *Iguanodon* had cheeks. These cheeks stopped its food from falling out of its mouth as it chewed.

CHECK THESE OUT!

Apatosaurus, Camptosaurus, Corythosaurus, Cretaceous period, Hadrosaurs, *Hypsilophodon*, Jurassic period, Ornithischian dinosaurs, Ornithopods, *Ouranosaurus*, Plants, Sauropods

DINOFACTS

Iguanodon
(i-GWAN-uh-don)

 NAME: *Iguanodon* means iguana tooth
iguana (a type of lizard) + odontos (tooth)

 FAMILY: Ornithischian

Ornithopod

 SIZE: 21–33 ft (6.4–10 m) long; up to 9–12 ft (2.7–3.6 m) high at the hip

 WEIGHT: 1–3 tons (0.9–2.7 tonnes)—about the same as 1–3 American bison

 FOOD: plants

 HABITAT: coastal to interior lowlands

 WHERE: remains found in England, Belgium, Germany, Portugal, and Spain in Europe; in Tunisia in North Africa; in Mongolia and China in Asia; and in South Dakota and perhaps Utah in the United States

WHEN: 135–110 million years ago in the Cretaceous period

	IGUANODON		
TRIASSIC	JURASSIC		CRETACEOUS
250 MILLION YEARS AGO	205 MILLION YEARS AGO	135 MILLION YEARS AGO	65 MILLION YEARS AGO

Kentrosaurus

A stegosaur, or plate-backed dinosaur, *Kentrosaurus* roamed East Africa in the Jurassic period. Like many East African dinosaurs, it had close relatives in western North America.

German fossil-hunters found *Kentrosaurus* during their expeditions to East Africa from 1909 to 1912. They discovered its remains in Tendaguru in what is now Tanzania. Believe it or not, similar dinosaurs lived at Tendagaru and in the Morrison Formation of the western United States. Although Africa and North America started moving apart

THE BIGGEST DINOSAUR EXPEDITION

The first *Kentrosaurus* remains were found during one of the biggest ever dinosaur-hunting expeditions. Between 1909 and 1912, a huge expedition was set up by German museums to what was then German East Africa (modern Tanzania). Dozens of paleontologists and hundreds of local workmen worked on the dig. They collected huge bones of sauropods (long-necked plant-eaters) like *Barosaurus* and *Brachiosaurus*, as well as smaller plant-eaters like *Dryosaurus* and *Kentrosaurus*. Most of the material collected by the German dinosaur hunters was taken to the Humboldt Museum in Berlin, Germany. Unfortunately, some of the specimens were destroyed by bombing during World War II. There are still plenty of African remains in Berlin, though, for paleontologists to compare with dinosaurs from elsewhere. Besides sauropods, these remains include skeletons of *Kentrosaurus*.

▼ *Kentrosaurus* had pairs of plates and spikes running along its back and tail. It also had a single spike sticking out from each side of its body.

DINOFACTS

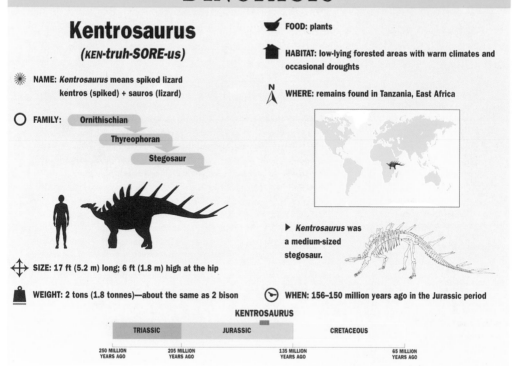

Kentrosaurus
(KEN-truh-SORE-us)

☀ **NAME:** *Kentrosaurus* means spiked lizard
kentros (spiked) + sauros (lizard)

◯ **FAMILY:** Ornithischian
             Thyreophoran
                    Stegosaur

✛ **SIZE:** 17 ft (5.2 m) long; 6 ft (1.8 m) high at the hip

⚖ **WEIGHT:** 2 tons (1.8 tonnes)—about the same as 2 bison

🥣 **FOOD:** plants

🏠 **HABITAT:** low-lying forested areas with warm climates and occasional droughts

🧭 **WHERE:** remains found in Tanzania, East Africa

▶ *Kentrosaurus* was a medium-sized stegosaur.

🕐 **WHEN:** 156–150 million years ago in the Jurassic period

KENTROSAURUS

TRIASSIC	JURASSIC	CRETACEOUS
250 MILLION YEARS AGO	205 MILLION YEARS AGO	135 MILLION YEARS AGO	65 MILLION YEARS AGO

---

in the Jurassic period, the new Atlantic Ocean still barely existed. Dinosaurs could still cross on dry land from North America to Africa. Some dinosaurs, like *Barosaurus*, *Brachiosaurus*, and *Dryosaurus*, were exactly the same in both places. Other African dinosaurs were a bit different from their closest American relatives. *Kentrosaurus*'s closest American relative was *Stegosaurus*.

How did *Kentrosaurus* live?
Kentrosaurus carried its head low to the ground, so it could only have reached the leaves

of ferns and cycads growing 3–6 ft (90 cm–1.8 m) off the ground. Some paleontologists think that *Kentrosaurus* could have reared up on its hind legs to reach to 20 ft (6 m). However, they have not found any trackways that show *Kentrosaurus* stood on its hind legs alone.

Jurassic porcupine?
Predators like *Allosaurus* and *Ceratosaurus* may have hunted *Kentrosaurus*. Its legs were fairly short, so the stegosaur probably could not run very fast. However, it would have been

no easy target. *Kentrosaurus* could have lashed out with its spiky tail. It might even have defended itself like a modern porcupine. A porcupine's quills point backward. When attacked, a porcupine turns its back and pushes its quills into the predator's eyes. Perhaps *Kentrosaurus* could have done the same with its spikes.

CHECK THESE OUT!
Allosaurus, Barosaurus, Brachiosaurus, Ceratosaurus, Continental drift, Dryosaurus, Jurassic period, Stegosaurs, Stegosaurus

Kritosaurus

Kritosaurus was one of the hadrosaurs (duckbill dinosaurs). It lived on lush, leafy plains during the Late Cretaceous period, cropping and crunching plants with its horny beak and tough cheek teeth.

Kritosaurus was one of the biggest and heaviest hadrosaurs. US fossil-hunter Barnum Brown found the first remains of *Kritosaurus* in 1904, while collecting for the American Museum of Natural History.

Kritosaurus had a wide, flat skull. Like other hadrosaurs, it had a broad snout that looked

SKIN AND BONES

Osteoderms are hard, bony plates that are buried in the skin of many reptiles. These plates form a flexible armor that helps protect an animal from attack. Crocodiles are among the best examples of animals living today that have osteoderms. Crocodile osteoderms are shaped like triangles, squares, and diamonds. The underside of an osteoderm is usually smooth. The top is pitted and rough.

Fossilized osteoderms are rarely found in place because they were fixed into the skin layers, not to the main bones of the skeleton. If a dinosaur carcass fell in a river, the skin usually rotted first, scattering the osteoderms all over the place. The paleontologist can only guess where to put the osteoderms. Did the dinosaur have 2 rows of these bony plates or 20? Were the osteoderms along the back, up the neck, along the tail, down the sides? Luckily, when fossil-hunters found *Kritosaurus*, its osteoderms were more or less in place.

◀ *Kritosaurus* belonged to a group of hadrosaurs known as hadrosaurines. Unlike other hadrosaurs, they had no head crests or only small ones. The bump in front of its eyes is sometimes described as a "Roman nose."

like a duck's bill. On its nose was a bump. Females may not have had this bump. If so, males may have used their bumps to show off to females.

A low ridge ran along *Kritosaurus*'s neck, back, and tail. The ridge was made of tall bones that stuck out from its backbones. Stiff cords (tendons) linked the spines, turning them into a smooth ridge. When the animal was alive, the ridge was covered by a layer of skin and small, bony plates called osteoderms. Set into the skin, the osteoderms protected *Kritosaurus* from harm during an attack.

How *Kritosaurus* lived

Kritosaurus lived on plains near the sea where trees and low bushes grew. It had a toothless beak at the front of its mouth, and rows of teeth packed into the sides of its jaws.

Kritosaurus gathered tough leaves and twigs in its beak and chewed them with its cheek teeth. Many dinosaurs could not chew; they had no cheeks so the food would have fallen out of their mouths if they had tried. Ornithopods (bird-footed dinosaurs), such as *Kritosaurus* and *Hadrosaurus*, had cheeks, so they could chew. They could also move their upper jaws from side to side to grind their upper teeth across their lower teeth.

CHECK THESE OUT!

Collecting dinosaurs, Cretaceous period, Hadrosaurs, *Hadrosaurus*, Ornithischian dinosaurs, Ornithopods

DINOFACTS

Kritosaurus
(CRY-*toh*-SORE-us)

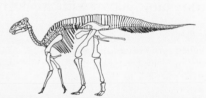

▶ On this skeleton, you can see the ridge of tall bones sticking up from *Kritosaurus*'s backbones.

✳ **NAME:** *Kritosaurus* means noble lizard
kritos (noble) + sauros (lizard)

◯ **FAMILY:** Ornithischian

Ornithopod

Hadrosaur

⊕ **SIZE:** 30 ft (9 m) long; 10 ft (3 m) high at the hip

WEIGHT: about 3 tons (2.7 tonnes)—about the same as 3 North American bison

FOOD: plants

HABITAT: coastal plains with winding rivers and swamps

**N
↑ WHERE:** remains found in New Mexico and Texas, in Argentina, and in Mexico

🕐 **WHEN:** 76–65 million years ago in the Cretaceous period

			KRITOSAURUS
TRIASSIC	JURASSIC	CRETACEOUS	
250 MILLION YEARS AGO	205 MILLION YEARS AGO	135 MILLION YEARS AGO	65 MILLION YEARS AGO

Lambeosaurus

In the Late Cretaceous period, North America was home to many kinds of hadrosaurs, or duckbill dinosaurs. One of the largest of these dinosaurs was *Lambeosaurus* or Lambe's lizard

Lambeosaurus was named in honor of Lawrence Lambe, a Canadian scientist who hunted dinosaurs from 1897 to 1915. Among other dinosaurs, Lambe studied hadrosaurs (duckbills), and that is what *Lambeosaurus* was. Because many good specimens of different sizes, sexes, and ages have been found, *Lambeosaurus* is one of

◀ A *Lambeosaurus* with a disklike crest and another with a double spike. These could be male and female of the same kind (species) of *Lambeosaurus*.

the best-known hadrosaurs. It was also one of the largest. Its strong bones helped this big animal move around.

The head crest
There were two kinds of hadrosaurs—those that had hollow head crests and those that did not. *Lambeosaurus* had a hollow crest, so all hollow-crested duckbills are called lambeosaurines. Duckbills that did not have hollow crests, like *Hadrosaurus*, are called hadrosaurines.

Lambeosaurus had some of the oddest head crests of all. Not all *Lambeosaurus* had similar crests—there were

DINOFACTS

Lambeosaurus
(LAM-bee-oh-SORE-us)

✳ **NAME:** *Lambeosaurus* means Lambe's lizard
Lambe (scientist Lawrence Lambe) + sauros (lizard)

⭕ **FAMILY:** Ornithischian

Ornithopod

Hadrosaur

✥ **SIZE:** 30 ft (9 m) long; 10 ft (3 m) high at the hip

⚖ **WEIGHT:** about 5–10 tons (4.5–9 tonnes)—about the same as 1–2 African elephants

🥣 **FOOD:** plants

🏠 **HABITAT:** dry lowland plains

WHERE: remains found in Montana, in Alberta, Canada, and in Mexico

▶ Many *Lambeosaurus* had large, helmetlike crests. Most of the crest was hollow, but at the back was a backward-pointing spike of solid bone.

🕐 **WHEN:** 76–72 million years ago in the Cretaceous period

LAMBEOSAURUS

TRIASSIC	JURASSIC	CRETACEOUS	
250 MILLION YEARS AGO	205 MILLION YEARS AGO	135 MILLION YEARS AGO	65 MILLION YEARS AGO

TROMBONE NOSE

Much of *Lamboesaurus*'s crest was hollow. Tubes connected it to the dinosaur's nose on the inside. Paleontologists believe that *Lambeosaurus* may have used its crest like a horn. It may have been able to sound off to other *Lambeosaurus* by blowing through it. Because the bony crest could not change shape, it could produce only one type of sound.

Lambeosaurus was probably most closely related to *Corythosaurus* and *Hypacrosaurus*. These two lambeosaurine hadrosaurs also had large, hollow crests.

many different shapes and sizes. Their crests looked like disks, helmets, or double spikes.

Because of the different crests, paleontologists used to think that many kinds of *Lambeosaurus* existed. Later studies, though, suggested that the crests became bigger as *Lambeosaurus* grew older. Adult males' crests may also have been bigger than females' crests. This new information made paleontologists change their ideas. They now think there were perhaps only one or two different kinds of *Lambeosaurus*. The different

crests really belonged to males, females, and young of these same one or two kinds.

How *Lambeosaurus* lived
Like all ornithischians, *Lambeosaurus* ate plants. It lived alongside at least nine other hadrosaurs, including *Corythosaurus*.

CHECK THESE OUT!

Corythosaurus, Cretaceous period, Hadrosaurs, *Hadrosaurus*, *Hypacrosaurus*, Ornithischian dinosaurs, Ornithopods

Leaellynasaura

For a long time, most scientists thought that dinosaurs lived only in warm habitats, but new discoveries prove that dinosaurs lived in cooler places as well. One of these new finds is *Leaellynasaura*.

Fossil-hunters have found many pieces of *Leaellynasaura* remains in quarries in Australia—bits of skulls, tail bones, legs, and toes. From these few scraps, however, scientists can imagine how *Leaellynasaura* looked in life by comparing it to similar, better-known dinosaurs.

How *Leaellynasaura* lived
Leaellynasaura was an ornithischian (bird-hipped) dinosaur. Like all ornithischians

BIG BRAINS, BIG EYES

One special feature of the *Leaellynasaura* fossils is that the skulls contain natural casts, or molds, of the brain formed as the remains fossilized. Scientists can measure the volume of these brain casts, and estimate how intelligent *Leaellynasaura* was. By comparing the brain volume of *Leaellynasaura* with that of lizards, birds, and mammals that are alive today, we see that *Leaellynasaura* was probably smarter than most other dinosaurs, and certainly much smarter than any lizard or crocodile.

Leaellynasaura's brain cast shows us something else, too. The parts of the brain that are important for vision are large. *Leaellynasaura* also seems to have had very large eyes. These two facts suggest that *Leaellynasaura* could see really well. Some scientists think that *Leaellynasaura* may have been able to see well in low light during long, dark winters. If *Leaellynasaura* was adapted for seeing on dull winter days, then perhaps it did not migrate to avoid the winter cold.

▼ *Leaellynasaura* lived in Australia when that country had very cold weather. While some scientists think the dinosaur might have headed for warmer areas during the icy winters, others do not.

it ate plants. Other dinosaurs closely related to *Leaellynasaura*, such as *Hypsilophodon*, had a turtlelike beak, so *Leaellynasaura* probably had a beak, too. A beak can grow faster than teeth can. Because it is also softer than teeth, it can be worn down to just the right shape for nipping leaves off the branches of bushes.

Coping with the cold

This cool-climate dinosaur was found in Australia—a hot, dry country today. During the Cretaceous period, though, the positions of the continents were different than they are now. Australia was much farther south and was joined to Antarctica. It would have had cool, even freezing, winters. How did *Leaellynasaura* deal with the cold weather?

Some scientists think the dinosaur could stand the cold. However, other scientists point out that if it had naked skin, it would have had a hard time keeping warm. Also there would be no food in winter.

These scientists think that *Leaellynasaura* may have migrated every year. It would spend the long summer days feeding on plants close to the South Pole. When the cooler fall and winter weather arrived, *Leaellynasaura* would move closer to the warmer equator.

CHECK THESE OUT!

Continental drift, Cretaceous period, Crocodiles, *Hypsilophodon*, Lizards and snakes, Ornithischian dinosaurs, Ornithopods

DINOFACTS

Leaellynasaura
(LEE-*ah*-LIN-*ah*-SORE-*ah*)

✳ **NAME:** *Leaellynasaura* means Leaellyn's lizard
Leaellyn (the name of a girl who helped dig the fossils) + saura (lizard)

◯ **FAMILY:** Ornithischian
Ornithopod

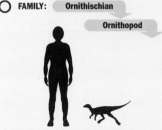

✛ **SIZE:** 3 ft (90 cm) long; perhaps about 1 ft (30 cm) high at the hip

WEIGHT: 10–15 lbs (4.5–7 kg)—about the same as a large chicken or small turkey

FOOD: low-growing plants

HABITAT: well-watered upland valleys

N
WHERE: remains found in Australia

🕑 **WHEN:** about 110 million years ago during the Cretaceous period

LEAELLYNASAURA

TRIASSIC	JURASSIC		CRETACEOUS
250 MILLION YEARS AGO	205 MILLION YEARS AGO	135 MILLION YEARS AGO	65 MILLION YEARS AGO

Leptoceratops

Leptoceratops was a ceratopsian, or horned dinosaur, but it had hardly any of the features that most horned dinosaurs had. Even today, scientists are not sure how to describe it.

US fossil-hunter Barnum Brown first described *Leptoceratops* in 1914 from a partial skeleton and skull found in Alberta, Canada. In the 1940s, Canadian paleontologist Charles M. Sternberg collected some *Leptoceratops* remains that were in better condition.

SWIMMING AGAINST THE TIDE

Scientists see patterns (trends) in the way the horned dinosaurs evolved. Early ceratopsians like *Psittacosaurus* were small, two-legged walkers with simple skulls. Over time, ceratopsians grew horns, neck frills, and much bigger bodies. By the Late Cretaceous period, *Triceratops* had evolved, a horn-faced heavy that could tough it out with big meat-eaters. However, some ceratopsians like *Leptoceratops* and *Microceratops* went against the trend. They stayed simple, small, and fast.

▼ Little *Leptoceratops* had a light body and slender limbs. Scientists are not sure whether it moved only on its hind legs, or only on all fours, or both.

Little ceratopsian

Leptoceratops was a primitive (less evolved) ceratopsian. Most advanced (highly evolved) ceratopsians were large; mighty *Triceratops* was the size of two elephants. More primitive ceratopsians, like *Protoceratops*, *Bagaceratops*, and *Psittacosaurus*, could be smaller than a pig.

DINOFACTS

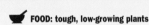

Leptoceratops
(*LEP-toe-SER-ah-tops*)

FOOD: tough, low-growing plants

HABITAT: upland plains

✳ **NAME:** *Leptoceratops* means slender horned face
leptos (slender) + keratos (horned) + ops (face)

WHERE: remains found in Alberta, Canada; and Wyoming

◯ **FAMILY:** Ornithischian

Ceratopsian

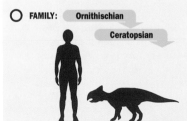

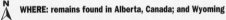

⊕ **SIZE:** 6 ft (1.8 m) long; 2.5 ft (76 cm) high at the hip

WEIGHT: 100–150 lbs (45–68 kg)—about the same as a pronghorn

▶ Like other ceratopsians, *Leptoceratops* had a beak. However, it had only a small neck frill.

🕐 **WHEN:** 70–65 million years ago in the Cretaceous period

			LEPTOCERATOPS
TRIASSIC	JURASSIC	CRETACEOUS	
250 MILLION YEARS AGO	205 MILLION YEARS AGO	135 MILLION YEARS AGO	65 MILLION YEARS AGO

Like these, *Leptoceratops* was small. Advanced ceratopsians had horns on their faces and bony frills on the back of their heads. *Leptoceratops* had no horns, and its head frill was unusually small.

On two legs?

Most Late Cretaceous ceratopsians walked on all fours. Because most of its body weight was in front of its hips, *Leptoceratops* may have walked on all fours, too. However, because its hind legs were longer than its front limbs,

some scientists believe that *Leptoceratops* walked on its hind legs only. Early Cretaceous *Psittacosaurus* also moved around on its hind legs. Because *Leptoceratops* lacked a big frill and might have walked on two legs, some scientists think it might have been as primitive as *Psittacosaurus*.

How *Leptoceratops* lived

All ceratopsians had beak bones at the front of their mouths. In life, horn covered the bone to form the beak. *Leptoceratops* had a beak, and probably had strong jaw

muscles too, which gave it a powerful bite for chopping up tough plant materials.

Leptoceratops would have made a tasty meal for almost any Late Cretaceous meat-eater. It probably ran fast to flee predators or hid in thick bushes to avoid big killers such as *Tyrannosaurus*.

CHECK THESE OUT!

Bagaceratops, Ceratopsians, Cretaceous period, Evolution, Ornithischian dinosaurs, Protoceratops, Psittacosaurus, Triceratops, Tyrannosaurus

Lesothosaurus

When most people hear the word *dinosaur* they think of animals as big as city buses; however, much smaller dinosaurs also existed.

Lesothosaurus was a tiny dinosaur. In life it would not have been more than about 3.3 ft (1 m) long. Even so, *Lesothosaurus* is an important dinosaur because it was one of the earliest members of a group of dinosaurs known as the ornithischian, or bird-hipped, dinosaurs. All the ornithischian dinosaurs were plant-eaters.

The secrets of teeth
Paleontologists know that *Lesothosaurus* ate plants, because of the shape of its teeth. Its teeth were not like the long, serrated blades of the meat-eating dinosaurs, such as *Tyrannosaurus* and *Velociraptor*. *Lesothosaurus*'s front teeth were cone-shaped. The rest of its teeth were like little triangular leaves stuck on top of long, narrow bases, or roots. *Lesothosaurus*'s teeth were about 0.5–0.75 in (1–2 cm) long.

▼ A herd of *Lesothosaurus* on the move. Paleontologists think this dinosaur may have lived in herds, but they have not found any group trackways to prove it.

The longest part of a *Lesothosaurus* tooth was the root. All dinosaurs had teeth with long roots. The roots of the teeth were fixed into deep sockets along the upper and lower edges of the jaws. This made the teeth very strong, and let dinosaurs bite and chew many different foods.

Tearing teeth

The top parts of *Lesothosaurus*'s teeth, the triangular parts, had roughened edges. These rough edges helped *Lesothosaurus* to tear bushes and ferns.

As *Lesothosaurus* closed its jaws, the rough edges of its upper teeth would meet the rough edges of its lower teeth. This chopping and cutting action might have helped to tear its food into pieces small enough to swallow.

Like more advanced (highly evolved) ornithischian dinosaurs, *Lesothosaurus* had cheeks. They were not as muscular as those of advanced ornithischians, but they probably allowed *Lesothosaurus*

▲ Like this tortoise, *Lesothosaurus* had a horny beak. All ornithischian dinosaurs seem to have had beaks for snipping leaves and stems from trees and bushes.

to chew its food a little. Saurischian (lizard-hipped) dinosaurs, such as sauropods (long-necked plant-eaters) and all meat-eaters, had no cheeks. They had to swallow their food whole; it would have spilled out of their mouths if they had tried to chew it.

Beaky dinosaur

Another important feature of ornithischian dinosaurs is that they all had beaks. The beak would have covered the front parts of their upper and lower jaws. It would have been the same as the beaks modern turtles and tortoises have.

Its beak would have helped *Lesothosaurus* to bite off the leaves and soft twigs that it ate. This beak would have been

made of hardened skin, just like our fingernails. Like our fingernails, it would continue to grow throughout the animal's life. The beak would constantly wear down at the edges because of biting. However, because it kept growing, it would stay about the same length.

One further clue tells us *Lesothosaurus* was an ornithischian—it had an extra bone at the front tip of its lower jaw. This bone is seen in all ornithischian dinosaurs. Animals as different as horned *Triceratops*, duckbilled *Edmontosaurus*, and platebacked *Stegosaurus* are all ornithischians, and they all have this extra bone forming part of their chin.

How did it live?

By looking at the differences in length between *Lesothosaurus*'s arms and legs, scientists can see

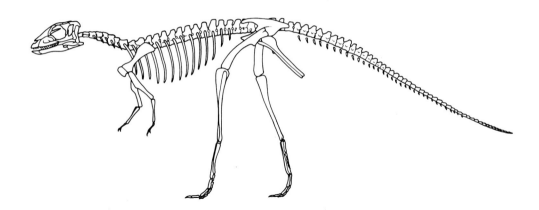

that *Lesothosaurus* was a biped—it would have spent most of its time calmly walking around on its two hind legs like a kangaroo.

Sometimes it would have gotten down on all fours. *Lesothosaurus*'s arms were very short. It would have been difficult to walk quickly on all fours with such short arms. *Lesothosaurus*'s legs were perfect for running, though. Its upper leg bone was shorter than the lower leg bone. Its feet and toes were long and slender. Only animals that need to run fast have this pattern of leg and foot bones. The ostrich, a fast-running bird, has legs and feet

like this; ornithomimosaurs (ostrichlike dinosaurs), such as *Struthiomimus*, did, too.

Fast defense
It is easy to see why little *Lesothosaurus* would have needed to run fast. It did not have sharp teeth or claws. It did not have spikes or any other type of body armor. The only way *Lesothosaurus* could protect itself would be to run away from danger.

If a hungry meat-eating dinosaur chased *Lesothosaurus*, it would have had a very hard time trying to catch it up. In Africa today, lions and cheetahs find it difficult to

▲ *Lesothosaurus* had long legs and slender feet. It was a light dinosaur and almost certainly a fast runner. Its stiff tail would have let it turn sharply at speed.

catch gazelles. Gazelles are very fast runners that are always watching and listening for danger. At the first sign of a big, hungry cat, they run for their lives. Lions and cheetahs only rarely catch a gazelle. Like the gazelles, little *Lesothosaurus* would have been constantly on the lookout for predators and would have run away as soon as one appeared.

Safety in numbers?
Like modern gazelles, *Lesothosaurus* may have lived in herds. A small dinosaur like this may have been safer if it was part of a large group. In a large group there are many more pairs of eyes watching for danger. If one *Lesothosaurus* in a herd saw danger, it could start running first. The other herd members would realize that something was wrong and start running too. This way the whole herd would be safe.

NEW BONES, NEW NAME

Lesothosaurus was originally called *Fabrosaurus* in honor of the French scientist Jean Fabre. The first *Fabrosaurus* fossil was found in 1964, but it was only a part of a jawbone with some teeth—not very useful for identifying a new dinosaur. In 1970, a team of fossil-hunters from London University and the British Museum of Natural History found a new, more complete skeleton of an animal with teeth just like those of *Fabrosaurus*. Paleontologist Tony Thulborn described the new remains, and they were named *Fabrosaurus*, too. Paleontologists then changed their minds. They thought the original 1964 fossil of *Fabrosaurus* was not good enough for identifying future dinosaurs. They renamed the new, more complete skeleton *Lesothosaurus*.

Stubby hands

Only a few *Lesothosaurus* hand and finger bones are known. However, scientists can tell that *Lesothosaurus*'s hands were short, and the fingers were not very flexible. *Lesothosaurus* could not have picked up something off the ground or held its food with its hands. It seems that *Lesothosaurus*'s teeth, jaws, and beak were its main ways of gathering food.

Like its hand, *Lesothosaurus*'s tail is poorly known. Only a few tail bones were found with the skeletons. We do know, though, that *Lesothosaurus*'s tail would have stuck straight out backward. It would never have dragged along the ground.

Rudder tail

Even at high speed, *Lesothosaurus* could have turned on a dime because its stiff tail worked like a rudder. Cheetahs use their tails like this today. *Lesothosaurus*'s tail would have helped it to balance, too. Without the weight of its tail, *Lesothosaurus* would have fallen flat on its face.

Lesothosaurus's backbones tell us it would have held its spine level while it walked. *Lesothosaurus* could have tipped up its body for a look around or to reach up for some leaves to eat, but this would not have been its normal posture.

CHECK THESE OUT!

Edmontosaurus, Hadrosaurs, Jurassic period, Ornithischian dinosaurs, Pisanosaurus, Stegosaurus, Struthiomimus, Triceratops, Tyrannosaurus, Velociraptor

DINOFACTS

Lesothosaurus
(leh-soн-thoh-SORE-us)

✳ **NAME:** *Lesothosaurus* means lizard from Lesotho
Lesotho (country in southern Africa) + sauros (lizard)

○ **FAMILY:** Ornithischian

✛ **SIZE:** 3.3 ft (1 m) long; about 15 in (38 cm) high at the hip

⚖ **WEIGHT:** 10–15 lbs (4.5–7 kg)—about the same as a large chicken or small turkey

🥣 **FOOD:** low-growing plants

🏠 **HABITAT:** semidesert areas

WHERE: remains found in southern Africa

🕐 **WHEN:** 200 million years ago in the Jurassic period

LESOTHOSAURUS

TRIASSIC	JURASSIC	CRETACEOUS
250 MILLION YEARS AGO	205 MILLION YEARS AGO	135 MILLION YEARS AGO	65 MILLION YEARS AGO

Lufengosaurus

Lufengosaurus was a prosauropod, an ancestor of the long-necked, long-tailed plant-eaters called sauropods. This dinosaur's name refers to the fossil-rich place in China where it was discovered.

Chinese paleontologist C. C. Young described *Lufengosaurus* in 1941. The dinosaur was first discovered in some purplish-red mudstones known as the Lufeng Formation, in China.

Paleontologists have found a wealth of fossil remains in Lufeng—amphibians, crocodiles, mammal-like reptiles, and small, primitive (little evolved) mammals.

Other dinosaurs discovered at Lufeng include the stegosaur (plate-backed dinosaur) *Tatisaurus* and the theropod (two-legged meat-eater) *Dilophosaurus.*

Lufengosaurus is one of many prosauropods (ancestors of sauropods) found at Lufeng; others include *Yunnanosaurus* and *Anchisaurus.* Some paleontologists think that most

of the Lufeng prosauropods are just different examples of the same dinosaur. However, there are differences in the age of the fossils and in the size and form of some of their bones. These differences suggest to other scientists that the prosauropods really are different kinds. *Lufengosaurus* could well be closely related to *Plateosaurus* from Germany.

▼ Long-necked and long-tailed, *Lufengosaurus* was an Early Jurassic prosauropod, an ancestor of the mighty sauropods.

DINOFACTS

Lufengosaurus
(loo-FUNG-guh-SORE-us)

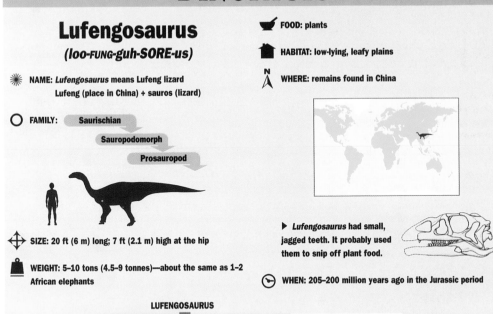

✳ **NAME:** *Lufengosaurus* means Lufeng lizard
Lufeng (place in China) + sauros (lizard)

○ **FAMILY:** Saurischian
Sauropodomorph
Prosauropod

✛ **SIZE:** 20 ft (6 m) long; 7 ft (2.1 m) high at the hip

⚖ **WEIGHT:** 5–10 tons (4.5–9 tonnes)—about the same as 1–2 African elephants

🍶 **FOOD:** plants

🏠 **HABITAT:** low-lying, leafy plains

🧭 **WHERE:** remains found in China

▶ *Lufengosaurus* had small, jagged teeth. It probably used them to snip off plant food.

🕐 **WHEN:** 205–200 million years ago in the Jurassic period

LUFENGOSAURUS

TRIASSIC	JURASSIC	CRETACEOUS
250 MILLION YEARS AGO	205 MILLION YEARS AGO	135 MILLION YEARS AGO / 65 MILLION YEARS AGO

TWO LEGS OR FOUR?

Like all prosauropods, *Lufengosaurus* had much longer back legs than front legs. This suggests that *Lufengosaurus* might sometimes have stood up on its back legs, just as it was first shown in Chinese museums. Standing on its back legs, *Lufengosaurus* could have reached up and eaten foliage from the tops of tall trees. When walking or running, though, *Lufengosaurus* might have used all four of its legs. Its long neck and body would probably have made it difficult for the dinosaur to keep its balance while moving around only on its back legs.

In 1958, *Lufengosaurus* became the first ever Chinese dinosaur to have its complete skeleton displayed in a museum. China celebrated the event by issuing a postage stamp showing the skeleton.

How *Lufengosaurus* lived
Like other prosauropods, *Lufengosaurus* had small, widely spaced teeth with jagged edges. Scientists think it used these teeth to eat plants, but they are not sure. However, they point out that because prosauropods are the most common fossils in Lufeng, they must have been plant-eaters. Plant-eaters are more common than meat-eaters in any food chain; otherwise there would not be enough of them for the meat-eaters to eat! We see this today in Africa, where plant-eating zebra and antelope are more common than lions or hyenas.

CHECK THESE OUT!
Amphibians, *Anchisaurus*, Crocodiles, *Dilophosaurus*, Jurassic period, Mammal-like reptiles, Mammals, *Plateosaurus*, Prosauropods, Rocks, Saurischian dinosaurs, Sauropods, Theropods

Maiasaura

The discovery of *Maiasaura* is one of the most exciting dinosaur finds of all time. It revealed to paleontologists for the first time that dinosaurs may have actively looked after their young.

American paleontologist Jack Horner dug up an adult hadrosaur (duckbill dinosaur) in Montana in 1979. With it were the skeletons of 11 baby hadrosaurs. The babies were near a dishlike dip in the rock. Scientists believe this dip was a dinosaur nest. Nearby were several bits of fossil eggshells, so scientists could tell the babies had already hatched.

Since 1979, paleontologists have found many fossils of *Maiasaura*, as the dinosaur became known. There are lots of complete skeletons of animals of different ages, so that scientists can see how *Maiasaura* grew and developed.

Solid crest

Maiasaura's skull was broad at the front, with a wide, bill-like mouth. It had a crest on its head—not a big, hollow one like many hadrosaurs, but a low, solid ridge. *Maiasaura* had strong back legs and smaller front limbs; this suggested to

GOOD MOTHER

Maiasaura means good mother lizard. Horner gave the dinosaur this name because it seemed that the adult *Maiasaura* cared for its babies. Why do scientists think this? Some of the babies Horner found were newly hatched; others were up to a month old. Because the older babies had stayed in the nest, one or both parents must have brought food to them. Perhaps the parents also protected their nestbound babies from predators.

scientists that the dinosaur sometimes moved on its back legs. *Maiasaura* also had a long tail. Perhaps it used its tail like a rudder when it ran so it could turn quickly.

How *Maiasaura* lived
Some scientists think *Maiasaura* moved from place to place depending on the time of year. For example, zebra and wildebeest migrate today on the African plains.

For part of the year, the dinosaurs lived in leafy areas. Once a year they returned to river floodplains to lay their eggs. Each mother scraped a hollow in the dirt to use as a nest. She laid the oval-shaped eggs in the nest. She may have covered the eggs in rotting leaves to keep them warm.

◀ It seems *Maiasaura* looked after its babies. Scientists do not know when young *Maiasaura* started to look after themselves.

CHECK THESE OUT!
Cretaceous period, Digging dinosaurs, Eggs and babies, Hadrosaurs, Ornithischian dinosaurs

DINOFACTS

Maiasaura
(MY-*uh-SORE-uh*)

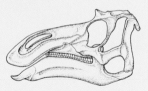

▶ *Maiasaura* was a hadrosaur, but unlike many hadrosaurs it did not have a large crest on the top of its head—just a low ridge.

✳ NAME: *Maiasaura* means good mother lizard
maia (good mother) + saura (lizard)

◯ FAMILY: Ornithischian
Ornithopod
Hadrosaur

✛ SIZE: 37 ft (11.3 m) long; 12 ft (3.6 m) high at the hip

⚖ WEIGHT: 4–7 tons (3.6–6.3 tonnes)—about the same as 4–7 North American bison

🥣 FOOD: plants

🏠 HABITAT: dry lowland plains

N↑ WHERE: remains found in Montana

🕐 WHEN: 77–73 million years ago in the Cretaceous period

			MAIASAURA ▪
TRIASSIC	JURASSIC		CRETACEOUS
250 MILLION YEARS AGO	205 MILLION YEARS AGO	135 MILLION YEARS AGO	65 MILLION YEARS AGO

Mamenchisaurus

Sauropod dinosaurs are famous for their long necks, but one sauropod had a neck that was more than half its total body length! Named *Mamenchisaurus*, it lived in China in the Jurassic period.

Chinese paleontologist C.C. Young named this dinosaur when he described its fossil remains in 1954. Of a total body length of up to 82 ft (25 m), *Mamenchisaurus* could have had a 50 ft (15.2 m) neck. From the Late Triassic period to the end of the Cretaceous, different groups of sauropods evolved very long necks. These adaptations gave them special advantages, such as being able to reach food that other dinosaurs could not.

How did it live?

Mamenchisaurus could have used its super-long neck to eat all the low-growing plants in a large field without moving its feet. With a long neck, the animal did not have to move its huge body much—just its head and neck. It could also have reached up into tall trees.

Sometimes having a long neck can be a hassle. Your heart has to pump really hard to get your blood all the way up to your head. Modern giraffes have necks about 10 ft (3 m) long. They have extra muscles in their necks to help to squeeze the blood up to their heads. They also have a

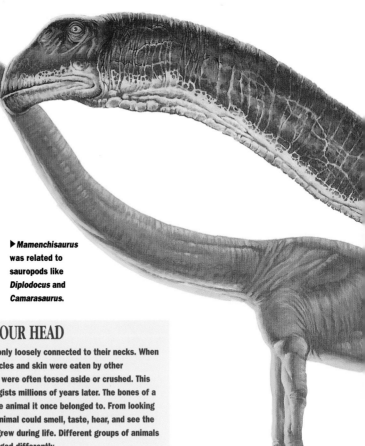

▶ *Mamenchisaurus* was related to sauropods like *Diplodocus* and *Camarasaurus*.

LOSING YOUR HEAD

Sauropods seem to have had their heads only loosely connected to their necks. When they died, their bodies rotted or their muscles and skin were eaten by other dinosaurs. Like animals today, their heads were often tossed aside or crushed. This has caused great problems for paleontologists millions of years later. The bones of a skull contain a lot of information about the animal it once belonged to. From looking at its skull, scientists can learn how the animal could smell, taste, hear, and see the world. The skull can show how an animal grew during life. Different groups of animals have their skull bones and jawbones arranged differently.

heart the size of a basketball. No one knows how *Mamenchisaurus* managed.

Message to brain
Another problem with a really long neck is getting messages between the brain and the rest of the body. Nerves from the brain carry signals to muscles in the arms, legs, and tail. Think how long it would take for nerves in *Mamenchisaurus*'s foot to feel pain, signal the brain, then have the brain send a message to tell the leg muscles to move the foot.

CHECK THESE OUT!

Camarasaurus, Cretaceous period, *Diplodocus*, Jurassic period, Saurischian dinosaurs, Sauropods, Triassic period

DINOFACTS

Mamenchisaurus
(ma-MEN-chee-SORE-us)

▶ *Mamenchisaurus* is the largest dinosaur ever found in Asia and has the longest neck of any dinosaur.

✳ NAME: *Mamenchisaurus* means lizard from Mamen Brook
   Mamen (name of stream) + chi (brook) + sauros (lizard)

○ FAMILY: Saurischian
   Sauropodomorph
   Sauropod

⊕ SIZE: 82 ft (25 m) long; 15–18 ft (4.6–5.4 m) high at the hip

⚖ WEIGHT: 10–40 tons (9–36 tonnes)—about the same as 2–8 African elephants

🥣 FOOD: plants

🏠 HABITAT: lowland open forest

N↑ WHERE: remains found in China

🕐 WHEN: 160 million years ago in the Jurassic period

MAMENCHISAURUS

TRIASSIC	JURASSIC	CRETACEOUS
250 MILLION YEARS AGO	205 MILLION YEARS AGO ... 135 MILLION YEARS AGO	65 MILLION YEARS AGO

Maniraptors

Birds and their closest dinosaur relatives form a group called the maniraptors. Unlike other dinosaurs, they could fold their hands out of the way against their bodies as they ran.

By studying *Dromaeosaurus*, Yale University paleontologist John Ostrom proved that birds descended from small meat-eating dinosaurs called coeluro-saurs. In the 1970s, Ostrom showed that coelurosaurs and birds shared many features that no other creatures had.

In the early 1980s, Yale's Jacques Gauthier listed all the features shared by birds and other dinosaurs. His study showed not only that birds evolved from dinosaurs, but that some coelurosaurs were more closely related to birds than to other coelurosaurs. For example, dromaeosaurs (clawed meat-eaters), like *Velociraptor*, and oviraptorosaurs (egg-thief dinosaurs), such as *Oviraptor*, were more closely related to birds than to ornithomimosaurs (ostrichlike dinosaurs), such as *Struthiomimus*.

Utahraptor

Archaeopteryx

◄ Maniraptors varied from the early avialan (bird relative) *Archaeopteryx* to *Utahraptor*, the largest of the dromaeosaurs (clawed meat-eaters).

DINOFACTS

Maniraptors
(MAN-ee-RAP-tors)

 NAME: Maniraptor means hand snatcher
manus (hand) + raptor (snatcher, thief)

 FAMILY: Saurischian
→ Theropod
→ Tetanuran

SIZE: huge variation from the 2.3 in (5.8 cm) bee hummingbird of today to the 20 ft (6.5 m) *Utahraptor*

WEIGHT: huge variation from about 0.06 oz (1.6 g) to about 1,000 lbs (454 kg)

 FOOD: varies, from plants to insects to meat

HABITAT: wide variation, from deserts to swamps and oceans

N **WHERE:** remains found worldwide

WHEN: from about 165 million years ago in the Jurassic period to today (because birds are maniraptors)

		MANIRAPTORS →	
TRIASSIC	JURASSIC	CRETACEOUS	
250 MILLION YEARS AGO	205 MILLION YEARS AGO	135 MILLION YEARS AGO	65 MILLION YEARS AGO

MANIRAPTOR OR NOT?

The true maniraptors are the dromaeosaurs, oviraptorosaurs, troodontids (big-eyed brainy meat-eaters), avialans, and modern birds. Yet there are other groups of coelurosaurs which may also be maniraptors. The bizarre, big-clawed therizinosaurs, such as *Erlikosaurus*, have similar hands to those of dromaeosaurs and oviraptorosaurs. Ornithomimosaurs and tyrannosaurs lack the special maniraptor wrist, but their ancestors probably had it. Together, true maniraptors, therizinosaurs, ornithomimosaurs, and tyrannosaurs form the group maniraptoriformes.

Hands that fly

Dromaeosaurs, oviraptorosaurs, and modern birds all have similar forelimbs. Their wrist bones and elbow joints allowed dromaeosaurs and oviraptorosaurs to fold their hands out of the way against their bodies as they ran. The same features let them shoot their arms forward to grab prey. These wrists and elbows also enabled birds to fly. They allowed them to beat their wings, driving them through the air.

How did (and do) they live?

Dromaeosaurs and troodontids were smart predators. Oviraptorosaurs were toothless and may have eaten both meat and plants. Birds are the most varied group of all.

Modern birds range from tiny hummingbirds to the fast-running ostrich. In part, birds have survived because they could fly. Their wings would not work as they do today if they had not evolved from a maniraptor wrist.

CHECK THESE OUT!

Archaeopteryx, Avialans, Birds, Dromaeosaurs, *Erlikosaurus*, *Oviraptor*, Oviraptorosaurs, Saurischian dinosaurs, *Struthiomimus*, Theropods, *Troodon*, Tyrannosaurs, *Utahraptor*, *Velociraptor*

Massospondylus

Richard Owen, the British scientist who invented the word *dinosaur*, named *Massospondylus* in 1854. He had only a single tail bone to study. Today paleontologists have many *Massospondylus* skeletons.

Massospondylus belonged to a group of long-necked dinosaurs called the prosauropods. They were ancestors of the sauropods, the big, long-necked, long-tailed plant-eaters like *Apatosaurus*.

Massospondylus was a fairly large prosauropod, although smaller than *Lufengosaurus* and *Plateosaurus*. It was common in southern Africa at the beginning of the Jurassic period.

SEE HOW THEY GROW

Most dinosaurs are known from only a handful of specimens. In these cases, it is often impossible to tell the difference between males and females or to see how the dinosaurs grew. However, collectors have found many specimens of *Massospondylus*, so paleontologists are able to study how it grew. Fossil-hunters have found some very small specimens of *Massospondylus*. These were probably juveniles. Juveniles had big eyes and few teeth. Larger specimens show us that as *Massospondylus* grew, the head caught up with the eyes and more teeth grew in. Some paleontologists think they can tell the difference between male and female *Massospondylus*. They think males had stronger skulls, with thickened bones above their eyes and in their upper jaws.

◀ Besides reaching high into trees, *Massospondylus*'s long neck would have helped the dinosaur to feed over a wide area of ground while standing still.

How did it live?

Like all prosauropods, *Massospondylus* ate plants. However, it lived in fairly dry areas with little vegetation. Some paleontologists believe it may have eaten small animals from time to time when it was short of plant food.

Footprints indicate that most prosauropods usually walked on all fours. *Massospondylus*'s hind legs were bigger than its forelegs, so it probably walked on two legs, too. This ability let *Massospondylus* reach higher into the trees for food.

Like other prosauropods, *Massospondylus* had a large claw on each thumb. It may have used these claws to dig for food and water or to defend against meat-eating dinosaurs.

A transatlantic dinosaur?

Besides southern Africa, *Massospondylus* remains have also been discovered in Arizona. How did it cross the Atlantic Ocean? It did not need to. In the Early Jurassic period, the earth's continents were much closer together than they are today. The Atlantic had only just begun to open, and northwest Africa and eastern North America were still joined. Dinosaurs could cross on dry land between the two continents.

CHECK THESE OUT!

Apatosaurus, Collecting dinosaurs, Continental drift, Jurassic period, *Lufengosaurus*, *Plateosaurus*, Prosauropods, Saurischian dinosaurs, Sauropods

---

DINOFACTS

Massospondylus
(MASS-oh-SPON-die-lus)

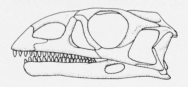

▶ Like other primitive (little evolved) plant-eating dinosaurs, *Massospondylus* had a single row of teeth. More highly evolved plant-eaters had many rows.

✳ NAME: *Massospondylus* means massive vertebra
masso (massive) + spondyl (vertebra)

◯ FAMILY: Saurischian
→ Sauropodomorph
→ Prosauropod

✛ SIZE: up to 12 ft (3.6 m) long; up to about 4 ft (1.2 m) high at the hip

WEIGHT: up to 450 lbs (200 kg)—about the same as a caribou

FOOD: plants and perhaps small animals

HABITAT: semidesert or desert areas with little surface water

N↑ WHERE: remains found in Arizona and southern Africa

🕐 WHEN: 205–190 million years ago in the Jurassic period

MASSOSPONDYLUS			
TRIASSIC	JURASSIC		CRETACEOUS
250 MILLION YEARS AGO	205 MILLION YEARS AGO	135 MILLION YEARS AGO	65 MILLION YEARS AGO

Megalosaurus

Megalosaurus was the first dinosaur ever described. The scientists who first studied it knew almost nothing about dinosaurs, and even today, paleontologists scratch their heads over this puzzling find.

In 1677, Englishman Robert Plot wrote a nature book. In it he described a fossil bone, found in England, which he believed came from an ancient giant human. Scientists are now fairly sure that the fossil that Plot described was the end of a leg bone from the dinosaur *Megalosaurus*.

leg bones. English scientist William Buckland first described *Megalosaurus* from these newly discovered bones in 1824, although it was another English scientist, James Parkinson, who made up the dinosaur's name, *Megalosaurus*, which means "the great lizard," two years before that in 1822.

Mission impossible
Even though *Megalosaurus* was the first dinosaur known to science, it is by no means the best known. Scientists know that it walked on two legs and ate meat, but they are unsure about almost everything else.

Buckland did not have enough good quality bones to

First-known dinosaur
In the early 19th century, *Megalosaurus* became the first dinosaur known to science. In 1818, some more giant bones were discovered in an English quarry. They included a lower jaw with large, jagged-edged teeth, some backbones, the right shoulder, an arm bone, parts of the hips, and several

▲ Scientists know little for certain about *Megalosaurus*, except that it was a large meat-eating dinosaur that moved on its long, strong hind legs.

▶ Because *Megalosaurus* was so poorly known, scientists gave its name to many similar-looking fossils. One such fossil is now called *Eustreptospondylus*.

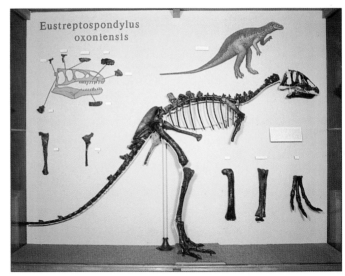

Eustreptospondylus oxoniensis

make an accurate description. Also, the science of identifying and describing animals and plants was then still fairly new.

Today when scientists study a new set of dinosaur bones, they can compare them to bones of already-known dinosaurs. In 1824, though, the *Megalosaurus* bones were all that scientists had to begin describing a totally new group of animals. Buckland and others had a tough time, because they had nothing with which to compare *Megalosaurus*.

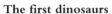

The first dinosaurs

Megalosaurus was an extremely important find. It was soon followed by two other English discoveries, *Iguanodon* and *Hylaeosaurus*. The 19th-century scientists who studied these animals' remains realized their bones were different from any they had seen before. However, they did not call them dinosaurs at first. It was English scientist Richard Owen who first called them dinosaurs. He saw that the bones of these three large animals shared some features. In 1842, he placed them in a new group of animals—the dinosaurs, or terrible lizards.

Megalosaurus, *Iguanodon*, and *Hylaeosaurus* became the first dinosaurs. When Owen called them terrible, he meant dinosaurs were frighteningly big. At that time no one knew how many types of dinosaurs there were.

Strange relations

Since *Megalosaurus* was first described more than 150 years ago, there have been as many as 26 more *Megalosaurus* finds reported. If these fossils are all *Megalosaurus*, then it lived all over the world.

THE LANGUAGE OF SCIENCE

To be recognized scientifically, an animal or plant has to have its description and name published in a scientific journal. Scientists write articles in scientific journals for other scientists. They use complicated scientific language. By using technical words and phrases in journal articles, scientists can communicate quickly with each other. A few big words are equal to many sentences, or even paragraphs, of everyday speech. Scientific language also lets scientists describe their ideas and results as accurately as possible. Different branches of science, like paleontology or astronomy (the study of stars and planets), each have their own sets of words and ideas that every paleontologist or astronomer knows about. Everyone reading complicated technical words in journals also agrees on what those words mean too.

Publishing the name of a newfound animal or plant, and showing drawings or photographs of it (or its remains), lets the whole world learn about a new discovery. When possible, scientists name an animal using the most complete specimen. Sometimes they cannot get a complete animal or plant. For example, dinosaurs are identified from their bones. Even today, some sea animals are known only from parts of their bodies—the largest giant squid is known only from pieces of giant tentacle.

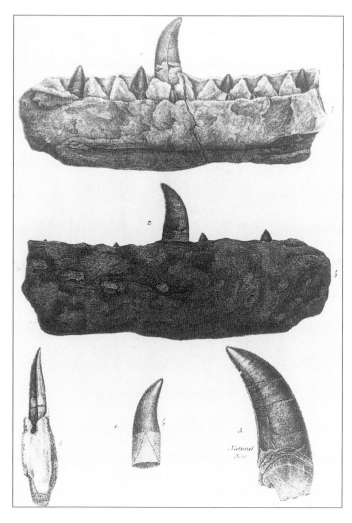

▲ The right lower jaw and teeth of meat-eating *Megalosaurus*. The daggerlike teeth have jagged edges that could have ripped through a victim's skin, muscle, and bone.

dinosaur *Eustreptospondylus*, which means "well-curved backbone."

An American brother?

Mysterious *Megalosaurus* may have lived in North America. Some paleontologists believe *Torvosaurus* may be a kind of *Megalosaurus*. *Torvosaurus* was found in Late Jurassic rocks in Colorado and Wyoming. It is known only from a few bits and pieces of bone and skull.

However, so far all definite *Megalosaurus* remains come from Europe. So does that mean *Torvosaurus* cannot be a kind of *Megalosaurus* because it lived in North America? No. During much of the Mesozoic Era, the earth's continents were in different positions from those of today. During the Jurassic period, the Atlantic Ocean was only just beginning to form. Western Europe and North America were joined together in a single landmass.

A French cousin?

Another dinosaur very similar to *Megalosaurus* lived in Europe during the Jurassic period. Called *Poekilopleuron*, it lived in France and may have been a close relative of *Megalosaurus* and *Torvosaurus*.

Today a seaway called the English Channel separates England and France. However, just as North America and Western Europe were joined in the Jurassic, so were England and France. The English Channel did not exist. Dinosaurs could wander to and fro between England and the rest of Europe.

However, paleontologists are not sure if these fossils are all *Megalosaurus*. They may belong to other meat-eating dinosaurs.

For example, in the 19th century, fossil-hunters found the remains of a large theropod (two-legged meat-eater). Early paleontologists thought it was another *Megalosaurus*. Scientists accepted this description for more than 100 years. In 1964, however, English scientist Alick Walker showed that this dinosaur was different from Buckland's *Megalosaurus*. Walker named the new

Unfortunately, the bones of *Poekilopleuron* were destroyed during World War II. We will have to wait for new finds to see if *Poekilopleuron* really was a close relative of *Megalosaurus*.

How *Megalosaurus* lived
Like most meat-eating dinosaurs, *Megalosaurus* would probably have killed and eaten other large dinosaurs. We would have to find a skeleton that clearly held the remains of its last meal to be sure.

Like the later tyrannosaurs, to which it was not closely related, *Megalosaurus* had short arms. These would have been useless for grabbing prey, although the dinosaur may have been able to pick at remains from other dinosaurs' kills. Like the tyrannosaurs, *Megalosaurus* also had a big head and long teeth. Its head contained large, powerful muscles to work the jaws.

Scientists have worked out how the jaw muscles were arranged in the skull. They can tell that *Megalosaurus* was able to snap its jaws shut very quickly to bite prey. Like a crocodile's, its bite would have been deadly. The jaws of a large modern crocodile can bite an antelope clean in two! *Megalosaurus*'s could have crunched through thick dinosaur bones.

Megalosaurus's teeth had jagged edges (serrations), a bit like the blades of a saw. These serrations would have helped the teeth to slice through a plant-eater's skin and muscles. *Megalosaurus* did not chew its food; it had no cheeks with

which to chew. If *Megalosaurus* had tried to chew, the meat would have spilled out of the sides of its mouth. Instead, the dinosaur sheared off bite-sized chunks from its prey and swallowed them whole.

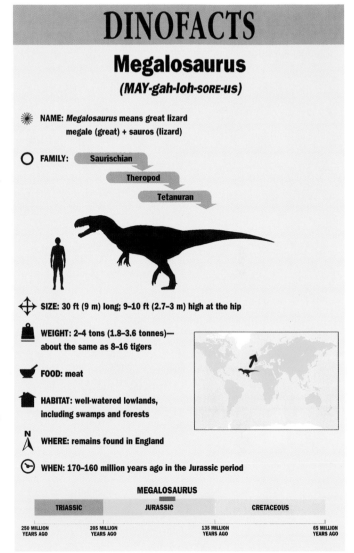

DINOFACTS
Megalosaurus
(MAY-gah-loh-SORE-us)

✳ **NAME:** *Megalosaurus* means great lizard
  megale (great) + sauros (lizard)

○ **FAMILY:** Saurischian
  Theropod
  Tetanuran

✥ **SIZE:** 30 ft (9 m) long; 9–10 ft (2.7–3 m) high at the hip

WEIGHT: 2–4 tons (1.8–3.6 tonnes)— about the same as 8–16 tigers

FOOD: meat

HABITAT: well-watered lowlands, including swamps and forests

WHERE: remains found in England

WHEN: 170–160 million years ago in the Jurassic period

MEGALOSAURUS		
TRIASSIC	JURASSIC	CRETACEOUS
250 MILLION YEARS AGO	205 MILLION YEARS AGO · 135 MILLION YEARS AGO	65 MILLION YEARS AGO

CHECK THESE OUT!
Bones, Collecting dinosaurs, Continental drift, Dinosaurs, *Iguanodon*, Jurassic period, Saurischian dinosaurs, Tetanurans, Theropods, Tyrannosaurs

Minmi

Tanklike *Minmi* was an ankylosaur (armored dinosaur) that lived in Australia during the Early Cretaceous period. It is the most complete dinosaur so far discovered in Australia.

Australian scientist Ralph Molnar named *Minmi* after studying a partial skeleton in 1977. Unlike other dinosaurs, this ankylosaur had extra platelike bones lying along its spine under its skin.

In 1989, rancher Ian Ievers discovered a second *Minmi* specimen. This skeleton was in

SINK OR FLOAT

Both *Minmi* specimens fossilized in silt and mud at the bottom of the ocean. How did they get there? There are two likely explanations, but either way the dinosaurs died on land. First, *Minmi* may have died, dried out, and then been washed into the sea. Eventually it would have filled with water and sunk. Second, *Minmi* washed out to sea just after it died. Gases in its body would have kept it afloat. In the end, though, the carcass would have burst. The gas would have been released and the body would have sunk to the bottom.

▶ *Minmi* was a low-slung, slow-moving plant-eater that lived along rivers near the coast. It was more lightly armored than most of its ankylosaur cousins.

better condition than the first. It was missing only its feet and the last two thirds of its tail. Molnar studied the new specimen. It was about the same size as the first and had the same unusual backbones. Molnar now thinks it may be a new kind of *Minmi*.

Australian tank

Minmi had a broad, low skull with a short, pointed snout. Like all ankylosaurs, *Minmi* had a wide body.

Minmi had 20 rows of small armor plates, or scutes, running from its neck to its hips. Bony triangular plates ran down the sides of its tail. These plates could have hurt an attacking meat-eater if *Minmi* had lashed out with its tail.

Early model

Minmi seems to have been a primitive (little evolved) ankylosaur. *Minmi*'s ancestors may have been stranded in the world's southern landmasses when Pangaea broke up in the Jurassic period. Far from other ankylosaurs, these *Minmi* ancestors would have evolved in different ways.

CHECK THESE OUT!

Ankylosaurs, *Ankylosaurus*, Continental drift, Cretaceous period, Jurassic period, Ornithischian dinosaurs, Thyreophorans

DINOFACTS

Minmi
(MIN-mee)

✳ **NAME:** *Minmi* is named in honor of the Minmi Crossing, Australia, where it was first found

⃝ **FAMILY:** Ornithischian

Thyreophoran

Ankylosaur

✛ **SIZE:** 9–10 ft (2.7–3 m) long; 4 ft (1.2 m) high at the hip

⬛ **WEIGHT:** 400–600 lbs (180–270 kg)—about the same as a brown bear

⬛ **FOOD:** low-growing vegetation

⬛ **HABITAT:** coastal lowland

N **WHERE:** remains found in Australia

🕐 **WHEN:** 115–105 million years ago in the Cretaceous period

			MINMI	
TRIASSIC	JURASSIC			CRETACEOUS
250 MILLION YEARS AGO	205 MILLION YEARS AGO		135 MILLION YEARS AGO	65 MILLION YEARS AGO

Mononykus

This Late Cretaceous dinosaur has got scientists puzzled. It probably ran fast, and may have been an early bird, but how did it use its tiny arms and single-clawed hands?

In 1987, a joint Soviet and Mongolian fossil-hunting expedition found a small skeleton in Mongolia's Gobi Desert. The skeleton lay in Late Cretaceous rocks. The paleontologists found the back of the animal's head, most of its backbone, its forelimbs, its hind legs, its shoulders, and portions of its hips. From its long, strong hind legs, they could see the dinosaur was a two-legged walker.

In 1992, Malcolm McKenna, an expert on mammals at the American Museum of Natural History (AMNH), found part of a smaller dinosaur skeleton in Mongolia. It lay in older rocks but may be the same kind of dinosaur as the larger, 1987 find.

Single claw

Mongolian paleontologist Perle Altangerel, along with Mark Norell, Luis Chiappe, and Jim Clark of the AMNH, described these two skeletons in 1993. These scientists reckoned both belonged to the same kind of dinosaur. They named it *Mononykus* (single claw), because it had only one claw on each hand.

Mononykus had a long neck and tail, long, slender legs, and a small head. Its upper jaw was

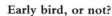

mostly toothless. Although *Mononykus* was birdlike it clearly could not fly. Its thick, stumpy arms were too short to work as wings.

Scientists think *Mononykus* was more closely related to modern birds than was *Archaeopteryx*, the earliest-known of the avialans (the group including birds and their closest relatives). Like modern birds, *Mononykus* had a long, ridged breastbone. The bone supports birds' powerful flight muscles. *Mononykus* had other birdlike features, too. Its lower leg bones narrowed to thin points near its ankles. Part of the upper pelvic bone in its hips was very wide. The way *Mononykus*'s thigh muscles were attached to its leg bones was also birdlike. The scientists who described *Mononykus* decided it was a primitive (little evolved), flightless early bird.

Early bird, or not?

Not all scientists agree that *Mononykus* was an early bird. Yale University's John Ostrom is a pioneer in bird–dinosaur relationships and an expert on *Archaeopteryx* and the dromaeosaur (clawed

▼ *Mononykus* had short, thick arms. Its long legs would have helped it to run at speed. How *Mononykus* used its arms is still a mystery.

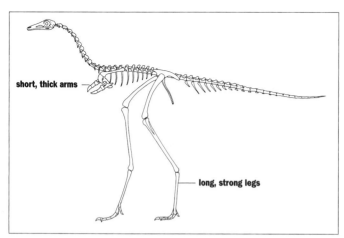

short, thick arms

long, strong legs

hunter) *Deinonychus*. He does not think that *Mononykus* was an early bird. He believes instead that it evolved birdlike features separately from birds.

Ostrom thinks *Mononykus*'s breastbone became enlarged as the animal's arms got thicker and stronger. He believes that the birdlike features in the hips and legs evolved to help

▼ The earliest birds had teeth and long tails. Even if *Mononykus* really could not fly, it probably would have had feathers.

Mononykus to run fast. Some other fossil bird experts agree with Ostrom.

In 1994, fossil-hunters found a *Mononykus* specimen with a complete skull. Although paleontologists have not yet described it, researchers at the AMNH have seen some more birdlike features in this skull.

What was *Mononykus*?
Based on how animals are described and grouped today, all dinosaurs can be traced back to a common ancestor. All dinosaurs, whether saurischian (lizard-hipped) or ornithischian (bird-hipped), descended from this common ancestor. Most scientists now agree that birds descended from theropod (two-legged meat-eating) dinosaurs. This means all birds are theropod dinosaurs, but not all theropods are birds.

Scientists used to place all birds in the group called Aves, with *Archaeopteryx* as the first bird. Today, however, only modern birds are Aves. Modern birds have a short tail and no teeth. The Aves group now includes the common ancestor of all modern bird groups and all its descendants. *Archaeopteryx* and all of its early bird descendants are avialans.

BEATEN BY A BEETLE

Mononykus was first described as *Mononychus*. Later the paleontologists learned that the name *Mononychus* had already been used for a beetle. With animal names, it is first come, first served. Because the beetle was named first, it kept the name *Mononychus*. In a second paper, the paleontologists renamed their dinosaur *Mononykus*. Considering that several million kinds of animals have lived on earth, it is easy to see why naming all those animals gets so complicated.

The avialan group includes both early and modern birds. Therefore all birds are avialans, but not all avialans are modern birds. So what was *Mononykus*? It was a theropod dinosaur. It was probably an avialan, too. However, either way, toothy, long-tailed *Mononykus* was not a modern bird.

Unusual arms
Although many theropods have evolved shorter arms, it is very rare to see theropod arms get shorter *and* thicker. *Mononykus* had short, thick arms. Its arm bones had big fixing points to hold its powerful muscles.

Mononykus's palm bones were joined into one short, solid bone. Its strong, well-developed thumb had a large

claw. *Mononykus* means single claw, but there are places on its hand where there may have been two more tiny fingers.

Burrowing bird?
Almost all paleontologists agree that *Mononykus*'s arms were shaped like the arms of burrowing animals like moles. The large muscle attachments, efficient joints, and thick bones suggest a powerful digging arm. However, scientists cannot imagine a burrowing animal shaped like *Mononykus*. Standing on its long legs, it could not easily have reached the ground with its short arms!

Some scientists think that *Mononykus* may have used its claws to rip open termite mounds, just as giant anteaters do today in South America.

▲ Anteaters use their long, thick, sharp claws to tear open anthills and termite nests in order to eat the insects. Perhaps *Mononykus* did the same.

Termites are small insects that live together in huge colonies. The termite colonies build mounds and towers of dirt. Baked in the sun, the dirt becomes as hard as stone. It is not easy to open a termite mound unless you have very thick, sharp claws.

The first *Mononykus*
Following the 1987 discovery of *Mononykus*, paleontologists realized they had had a *Mononykus* specimen all along! In 1923, a party led by American fossil-hunter Roy Chapman Andrews had collected several bones at the

Flaming Cliffs in Mongolia. Amid their collection of mammals, dinosaur eggs, small theropods, and the small ceratopsian (horned dinosaur) *Protoceratops*, were the pelvis and leg of *Mononykus*. However, no one knew about *Mononykus* in 1923, so Andrews had labeled it simply a birdlike dinosaur.

Mononykus relatives

Argentine paleontologist Fernando Novas found close relatives of *Mononykus* in Cretaceous rocks in Argentina, South America. How did these early birds get from Asia to South America?

In the Mesozoic Era, the earth's landmasses were not in the same positions as they are today. Sea levels changed, and at times, land bridges linked areas that are now separated by ocean. Dinosaurs could move from one continent to another. Scientists believe *Mononykus*-like dinosaurs probably lived in Europe and Africa, as well as in Asia and South America.

How *Mononykus* lived

Mononykus had long, strong legs, so it could have run fast over the desert sand dunes and wooded plains of Mongolia. It probably ate insects and small lizards and mammals.

CHECK THESE OUT!

Archaeopteryx, Avialans, Birds, Continental drift, Cretaceous period, *Deinonychus*, Eggs and babies, Evolution, *Protoceratops*, Saurischian dinosaurs, Theropods

DINOFACTS

Mononykus
(MON-*uh*-NIKE-*us*)

✳ **NAME:** *Mononykus* means single claw
mono (single) + onux (claw)

○ **FAMILY:** Saurischian
→ Theropod
→ Avialan

✥ **SIZE:** 3 ft (90 cm) long; 1.5 ft (50 cm) high at the hip

⚖ **WEIGHT:** 22 lbs (10 kg)—about the same as a turkey

FOOD: probably insects, small mammals, and lizards

🏠 **HABITAT:** dry desert and wooded plains

🧭 **WHERE:** remains found in Mongolia

🕐 **WHEN:** 85–70 million years ago in the Cretaceous period

			MONONYKUS
TRIASSIC	JURASSIC	CRETACEOUS	
250 MILLION YEARS AGO	205 MILLION YEARS AGO	135 MILLION YEARS AGO	65 MILLION YEARS AGO

Mosasaurs

Mosasaurs were not dinosaurs, but they hunted the other animals that shared the coastal waters of the warm Late Cretaceous seas. Some kinds reached 30 ft (9 m), longer than a great white shark!

During most of the Cretaceous period the oceans were much higher than they are today. The sea flooded large areas of what is now dry land. It was in these warm, shallow seas that the mosasaurs swam.

Mosasaurs were reptiles, but not dinosaurs. Their ancestors were probably big land lizards related to modern animals like the 10 ft (3 m) Komodo dragon of Asia. Mosasaurs' cousins were the snakes.

Over millions of years, mosasaurs slowly evolved into better swimmers and hunters.

▼ Mosasaurs in action. A huge, fanged *Tylosaurus* swoops between *Clidastes* (top) and *Platecarpus* (bottom).

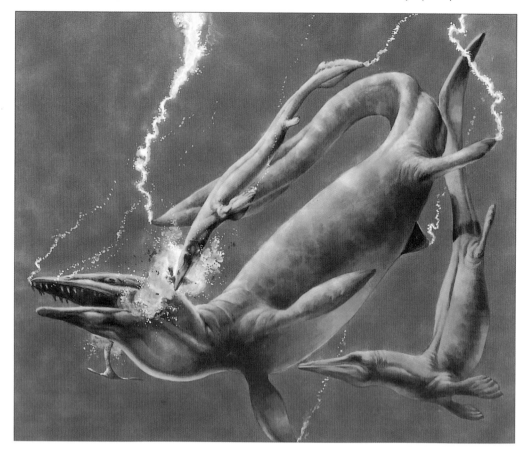

WHY DID THEY DIE?

Like the nonflying dinosaurs, the mosasaurs became extinct at the end of the Cretaceous. Why did they die out when animals like lizards, turtles, birds, and mammals survived?

Mosasaurs lived in coastal waters. When sea levels dropped, these areas became dry land. The mosasaurs had nowhere to live. Differences between winter and summer temperatures also became greater at this time. Perhaps mosasaurs could not survive cooler winter temperatures.

Their bodies became long and eel-like. Like eels, they swam by swinging their bodies from side to side. Their arms and legs evolved into paddles, and their fingers and toes became covered by mittens of muscle.

How did mosasaurs live?

Mosasaurs ate fish and squid-like animals called ammonoids. Collectors have found large ammonoid shells scarred with the V-shaped teeth marks that a mosasaur would make.

Because they were firmly set in deep sockets, like those of the meat-eating dinosaurs, mosasaurs' teeth were much stronger than those of their lizard ancestors. Mosasaurs shared the seas with other fierce hunters, the ichthyosaurs and the plesiosaurs.

CHECK THESE OUT!

Ammonoids; Coral reefs; Cretaceous period; Dinosaurs; Evolution; Extinction; Fish; Ichthyosaurs; Lizards and snakes; Plesiosaurs, pliosaurs, and nothosaurs; Reptiles

FOSSIL FACTS

Mosasaurs
(MOH-zuh-sores)

▲ Collectors have found hundreds of mosasaur skeletons all over the world. *Platecarpus*—14 ft (4.3 m) long—lived in Belgium and the United States.

✳ **NAME:** Mosasaur means lizard from the Meuse
Mosa (form of the name of the Meuse River in Belgium) + sauros (lizard)

◯ **FAMILY:** Reptile

✛ **SIZE:** up to 30 ft (9 m) long

FOOD: fish, small marine reptiles, ammonoids, belemnoids, shellfish

HABITAT: warm, shallow, coastal seas

WHERE: remains found in Belgium, Canada, Netherlands, New Zealand, North Africa, and the United States

⊙ **WHEN:** 75—65 million years ago in the Cretaceous period

			MOSASAURS
TRIASSIC	JURASSIC	CRETACEOUS	
250 MILLION YEARS AGO	205 MILLION YEARS AGO	135 MILLION YEARS AGO	65 MILLION YEARS AGO

Mussaurus

Mussaurus was a fairly early dinosaur. Paleontologists have only found the bones of young *Mussaurus*, but they think it was an ancestor of the sauropods, the big, long-necked plant-eaters.

In the late 1970s, Argentine paleontologists José Bonaparte and Martin Vince found a very small dinosaur skeleton in Late Triassic rocks in Patagonia, southern Argentina. They also discovered enough bones to assemble nine more skeletons.

Because they were so small and found so close together, Bonaparte and Vince thought the fossils belonged to baby dinosaurs that had died close to their nest.

Mouse lizard

The new dinosaur's skeleton fits comfortably in the palm of a man's hand. Bonaparte and Vince named the animal *Mussaurus*, or mouse lizard.

The tiny bones of very young dinosaurs are difficult to find and identify. They blend in with the dirt. Also, they have not yet formed all the special features that help paleontologists to tell to which kind of dinosaur they belong.

CUTE LIZARD

Mussaurus is one of the few dinosaurs for which scientists have a complete juvenile skeleton. Like a human baby, *Mussaurus* had a big head and a short neck. It had a short nose and big, round eyes. Biologists believe babies evolved to look cute so their mothers will always take care of them, however annoying their crying and messes might be. Perhaps baby dinosaurs were cute for the same reason.

▼ A *Mussaurus* stands next to the egg from which it has just hatched. This tiny, wide-eyed creature looks like a dinosaur but was only about the size of a puppy!

Mussaurus's skull had a short snout like that of a sauropod. Sauropods were long-necked, long-tailed, plant-eating dinosaurs like *Apatosaurus*, *Brachiosaurus*, and *Camarasaurus*.

However, the rest of *Mussaurus*'s skeleton from its neck to the tip of its tail was very similar to that of a prosauropod. Prosauropods, such as *Lufengosaurus* and *Massospondylus*, lived from the Late Triassic period to the Early Jurassic period. They were the ancestors of the sauropods (*prosauropod* means "before sauropods").

Like the sauropods, the prosauropods had long necks and tails and ate plants. However, while sauropods walked on all fours, some kinds of prosauropods could walk on just their hind legs.

Is *Mussaurus* a prosauropod?
Paleontologists think so. They have a set of prosauropod skeletons from hatchling to adult which show how prosauropods grew. This set shows that *Mussaurus* could have grown up to be a prosauropod like the sturdy, Late Triassic *Plateosaurus*.

Because no one knows for sure what an adult *Mussaurus* was like, scientists can only guess how this animal lived. If *Mussaurus* was a prosauropod, we can assume it ate plants.

CHECK THESE OUT!

Eggs and babies, *Lufengosaurus*, *Massospondylus*, Plants, *Plateosaurus*, Prosauropods, Saurischian dinosaurs, Sauropods, Triassic period

DINOFACTS

Mussaurus
(muh-SORE-us)

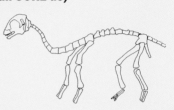

▶ ***Mussaurus*** is known only from its young. If someone finds a fully grown mouse lizard, perhaps its name will need to be changed.

✳ NAME: *Mussaurus* means mouse lizard
mus (mouse) + sauros (lizard)

◯ FAMILY: Saurischian
Sauropodomorph
Prosauropod

✥ SIZE: (as a baby) 16 in (40 cm) long; 2.2 in (5.7 cm) high at the hip

⚖ WEIGHT: 3.5–14 oz (100–400 g)—about the same as 1–2 ground squirrels

🥣 FOOD: plants

🏠 HABITAT: unknown

⬆ WHERE: remains found in Argentina

🕐 WHEN: 215 million years ago in the Triassic period

MUSSAURUS

TRIASSIC	JURASSIC	CRETACEOUS
250 MILLION YEARS AGO	205 MILLION YEARS AGO	135 MILLION YEARS AGO	65 MILLION YEARS AGO

Muttaburrasaurus

In 1981, a new plant-eating dinosaur was named: *Muttaburrasaurus*. This animal is especially interesting because it was discovered in Australia, a continent that has not yet produced many dinosaurs.

That *Muttaburrasaurus* comes from Australia is important for two reasons. The first reason is that dinosaurs are only rarely discovered in Australia. The second reason is that *Muttaburrasaurus* is an iguanodontid, one of the plant-eating dinosaurs with spiky thumbs named after *Iguanodon*. Iguanodontids have been found in Early Cretaceous rocks in Africa, Asia, Europe, and North America. Finding one in Australia shows how widespread this group of dinosaurs became.

Bird-hipped dinosaurs

The iguanodontids belonged to a larger group called ornithischian, or bird-hipped, dinosaurs. Most ornithischians had a pubis (the front bone of the lower hip) that pointed backward. Their lower jaw had an extra bone that is absent from the jaws of saurischian (lizard-hipped) dinosaurs, the other main dinosaur group.

▶ *Muttaburrasaurus* had a hollow bump on its snout. Scientists do not know what this bump was used for. Perhaps the dinosaur could blow through this bump to make sounds. Perhaps the bump just gave the dinosaur a great sense of smell.

EMPTY DESERTS

Australia is a large continent and is mostly desert. Dry, treeless desert areas are usually good places to look for fossils. That way, nothing (not buildings, not trees, not even soil) will hide them. The large areas of desert in Australia have not produced many dinosaur fossils, though. Why is this?

First, northern lands, like Europe and North America, have freezing cold winters. Many years of freezing and thawing cause rocks to splinter and crack, exposing fossils. The climate of Australia, however, does not produce severe winter weather.

Second, it seems that the Australian climate has been dry for many thousands of years. For fossils to be exposed at the earth's surface, the top layer of rocks has to be worn down by wind and rain. Streams and rivers need to flow for many years to cut into cliffs and mountains. Only when the rocky areas are worn down and cleared of sands and gravels can people see parts of skeletons poking out of the ground.

Odd one out

Muttaburrasaurus was an unusual iguanodontid, though. A special feature of the iguanodontids was their jaw. Before the iguanodontids, dinosaur jaws opened and closed like scissors. Most iguanodontids' jaws were different than this. Their lower jaw still moved up and down, but their upper jaw could move from side to side. This movement allowed their teeth to rub past each other to grind food thoroughly.

Muttaburrasaurus's upper jaws could not make sideways movements. Its jaws worked like scissors, as did those of meat-eating dinosaurs and early plant-eaters. However, paleontologists still think it was an iguanodontid. Like others in that group, it had a large skull for its body size and big, bony thumb spikes on its hands.

How did it live?

Like other iguanodontids, *Muttaburrasaurus* ate plants. Like all advanced (highly evolved) ornithischians, it had muscular cheeks, which allowed it to chew leaves and stems. Less evolved plant-eaters had less well developed cheeks and had to swallow their food whole or almost whole.

Besides this, scientists know little of *Muttaburrasaurus*'s lifestyle. They need more of its fossils. However, dinosaur remains are so rare in Australia, that it may be many years before we know more about mysterious *Muttaburrasaurus*.

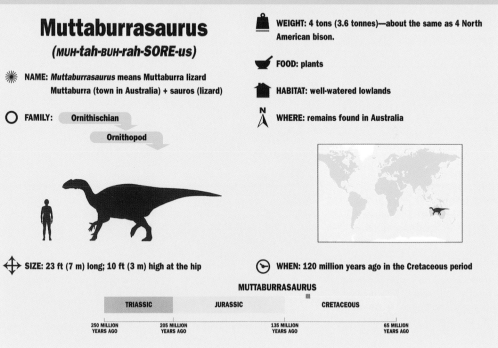

DINOFACTS

Muttaburrasaurus
(MUH-tah-BUH-rah-SORE-us)

✳ NAME: *Muttaburrasaurus* means Muttaburra lizard
Muttaburra (town in Australia) + sauros (lizard)

○ FAMILY: Ornithischian
Ornithopod

SIZE: 23 ft (7 m) long; 10 ft (3 m) high at the hip

WEIGHT: 4 tons (3.6 tonnes)—about the same as 4 North American bison.

FOOD: plants

HABITAT: well-watered lowlands

WHERE: remains found in Australia

WHEN: 120 million years ago in the Cretaceous period

MUTTABURRASAURUS

TRIASSIC	JURASSIC	CRETACEOUS
250 MILLION YEARS AGO	205 MILLION YEARS AGO	135 MILLION YEARS AGO

65 MILLION YEARS AGO

Nanotyrannus

Known only from a fossil skull, *Nanotyrannus* is now thought by many paleontologists to be a juvenile (young) *Tyrannosaurus*. However, it just might be a tiny cousin of the king of predators.

In 1942, a team from the Cleveland Museum of Natural History discovered the skull of a tyrannosaur in Montana. The skull was just 22 in (57 cm)—small for a tyrannosaur.

Smithsonian Institution paleontologist Charles Gilmore thought the skull might have belonged to a young tyrannosaur like *Tyrannosaurus*. In the end, though, Gilmore decided it was an adult of a new kind of *Gorgosaurus*, another tyrannosaur. One of the main reasons he thought it was an adult was that some of the skull bones were fused together, as they were in most adult dinosaurs.

The little tyrant
In the mid-1980s, US paleontologists Robert Bakker, Philip Currie, and Michael Williams reexamined the skull. Because of the fused bones, they agreed that it was an adult tyrannosaur's skull, but not a *Gorgosaurus*'s. The skull is much wider at the back than at the front. The only tyrannosaur with a skull that shape was *Tyrannosaurus*. The skull is too small for an adult

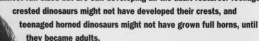

FROM EGG TO ADULT

Like other animals, dinosaurs passed through a number of stages on their way to becoming adults. Most paleontologists recognize four main growth stages—embryo, juvenile, subadult, and adult. Embryos are unhatched babies still in their eggs. Juveniles include all dinosaurs from hatchlings (ones that just broke out of their eggs) to those that are close to being fully grown. Just before adulthood, dinosaurs become subadults. Subadults are the "teenagers" of the dinosaur world. They are almost full sized but are still developing all the adult features. Teenaged crested dinosaurs might not have developed their crests, and teenaged horned dinosaurs might not have grown full horns, until they became adults.

Tyrannosaurus, so it must belong to a new tyrannosaur. The team named the dinosaur *Nanotyrannus*, the dwarf tyrant.

Not all paleontologists agree that *Nanotyrannus* was a small but adult tyrannosaur. Most believe it was a juvenile *Tyrannosaurus*. Paleontologists need to find good remains of an adult and juvenile *Tyrannosaurus* together. They could then compare the young dinosaur's skull with *Nanotyrannus*'s.

However, one day paleontologists may find the remains of a large *Nanotyrannus* and discover that the dinosaur they already have is just a juvenile *Nanotyrannus*.

◀ Was *Nanotyrannus* a young *Tyrannosaurus* or the smallest of the tyrannosaurs? Scientists need more information before they can say for sure.

CHECK THESE OUT!

Cretaceous period, Saurischian dinosaurs, Tetanurans, Theropods, Tyrannosaurs, *Tyrannosaurus*

DINOFACTS

Nanotyrannus
(NAN-oh-ty-RAN-us)

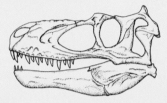

▶ Whether it was a juvenile or an adult, *Nanotyrannus* clearly ate meat. Just look at those daggerlike teeth!

✳ **NAME:** *Nanotyrannus* means dwarf tyrant
nanus (dwarf) + tyrannus (tyrant)

○ **FAMILY:**   Saurischian
            Theropod
               Tyrannosaur

✛ **SIZE:** perhaps 16 ft (5 m) long; perhaps 4 ft (1.2 m) high at the hip

⚖ **WEIGHT:** about 880 lbs (400 kg)—about the same as a polar bear

FOOD: meat

HABITAT: forests

N
A **WHERE:** remains found in Montana

⏱ **WHEN:** 69–65 million years ago in the Cretaceous period

NANOTYRANNUS

TRIASSIC	JURASSIC	CRETACEOUS
250 MILLION YEARS AGO	205 MILLION YEARS AGO	135 MILLION YEARS AGO	65 MILLION YEARS AGO

257

Nodosaurus

Nodosaurus was an armored dinosaur that roamed North America in the Early Cretaceous period. Unlike some armored dinosaurs it had no club on its tail. Its tanklike armor was a good defense, though.

Paleontologist and dinosaur collector Othniel Marsh described *Nodosaurus* in 1889. One of Marsh's collectors found *Nodosaurus* during an expedition to Wyoming. The collector was returning to camp one night when he spotted some dinosaur remains.

The specimen was not complete. It included bits of the forearm, hind legs, the upper part of the hips, part of the tail and back, and some armored bumps. Marsh

recognized that these pieces of bony armor formed rows of small bumps and larger, flat-lying plates across the dinosaur's back. Scientists still

do not know whether *Nodosaurus* had bony spines sticking out of its side, as some other nodosaurids, such as *Edmontonia*, did.

THE FAMILY NAME

Because *Nodosaurus* is known only from a few bits and pieces, there is some debate among scientists whether there is enough material on which to base a dinosaur name. Unfortunately the nodosaurid group (armored dinosaurs with no tail clubs) is based on this one specimen. Since it is missing most of the parts that define the group, someday it might be necessary to base the group on a different dinosaur. That would mean the family name would have to be changed.

▼ Collectors have found only parts of *Nodosaurus*'s body; they have never found its skull. Scientists and artists reconstruct the dinosaur by looking at other nodosaurids, such as *Sauropelta*.

Clubtails and bare tails

Nodosaurus was the first ankylosaur (armored dinosaur) ever discovered. There are two groups of ankylosaurs. Ankylosaurids, named in honor of *Ankylosaurus*, have tails that end in clubs. Nodosaurids, named in honor of *Nodosaurus*, have no tail clubs.

Lumpers and splitters

Scientists disagree about how *Nodosaurus* is related to other nodosaurids. New England paleontologist Walter Coombs has lumped it together with other nodosaurids, including *Sauropelta*. He believes all these nodosaurids are the same dinosaur. Other researchers such as Denver Museum's Ken Carpenter think only Marsh's 1889 specimen is *Nodosaurus*. They believe the others are different kinds of nodosaurids. Scientists need to find good nodosaurid skeletons to help them solve this puzzle.

How did *Nodosaurus* live?

Nodosaurus probably ate low-growing plants. It probably escaped meat-eating dinosaurs by hiding from them. If found, its armor could withstand an attack by small meat-eaters and perhaps even by larger dinosaurs.

CHECK THESE OUT!

Ankylosaurs, *Ankylosaurus*,
Collecting dinosaurs, Cretaceous
period, Ichthyosaurs, *Sauropelta*,
Thyreophorans

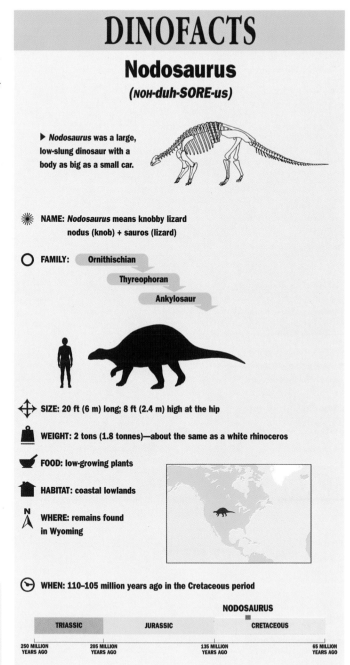

DINOFACTS

Nodosaurus
(*NOH-duh-SORE-us*)

▶ *Nodosaurus* was a large, low-slung dinosaur with a body as big as a small car.

✳ NAME: *Nodosaurus* means knobby lizard
   nodus (knob) + sauros (lizard)

⦿ FAMILY: Ornithischian
   Thyreophoran
   Ankylosaur

✛ SIZE: 20 ft (6 m) long; 8 ft (2.4 m) high at the hip

⚖ WEIGHT: 2 tons (1.8 tonnes)—about the same as a white rhinoceros

FOOD: low-growing plants

HABITAT: coastal lowlands

Ⓝ WHERE: remains found
   in Wyoming

🕐 WHEN: 110–105 million years ago in the Cretaceous period

NODOSAURUS

TRIASSIC	JURASSIC	CRETACEOUS
250 MILLION YEARS AGO	205 MILLION YEARS AGO	135 MILLION YEARS AGO	65 MILLION YEARS AGO

Opisthocoelicaudia

Recent finds show that the sauropods (long-necked plant-eaters) survived to the end of the Cretaceous period. *Opisthocoelicaudia* was an unusual member of one of the last-surviving sauropod groups.

In 1965 a Polish–Mongolian expedition was prospecting for dinosaurs in the Mongolian Gobi Desert. Among the many fossils they discovered were remains of a heavily built sauropod dinosaur.

Although the head and most of the neck were missing, the rest of the skeleton was almost complete. Scientists thought that this animal was related to the Late Jurassic sauropod *Camarasaurus*. When *Camarasaurus* was alive, it was the most common sauropod in North America.

One special feature of *Opisthocoelicaudia* was its very unusual

tail. The tail was so different that the animal was named for its tail. *Opisthocoelicaudia* means "tail bones hollow at the back."

What was it about the tail that so interested paleontologists? Most dinosaur tail

bones are flattened on their ends. In *Opisthocoelicaudia*, the back ends of the tail bones are dish-shaped, while the front ends are domed. The domes and dishes fit together snugly to make *Opisthocoelicaudia*'s tail very flexible and strong.

▲ The golden age of the sauropods was the Jurassic period, but many kinds, including *Opisthocoelicaudia*, lived in the Cretaceous period.

TOUGH TEETH

Sauropod fossils are found around the world. Sauropods were a widespread and numerous group that lived from the Early Jurassic (*Barapasaurus*) to the Late Cretaceous periods (*Titanosaurus* and the camarasaurs).

Opisthocoelicaudia was first thought to be one of the camarasaurs, a very successful group that lived a long time. The camarasaurs were named in honor of *Camarasaurus*. Camarasaurs had much larger teeth than most other sauropods such as the peg-toothed *Diplodocus*. They also had teeth along the sides and front of their jaws. *Diplodocus* and its relatives had teeth only at the front.

New evidence, however, suggests that *Opisthocoelicaudia* belonged to the titanosaurs, a sauropod group named in honor of *Titanosaurus*. The titanosaurs lived mainly in the southern hemisphere, and had very small teeth.

How it lived

Like all sauropods, *Opisthocoelicaudia* ate plants. It could have stood on its hind legs, and used its short, sturdy tail as a prop to help it balance while it reached up into trees. Then it could bite and pull down large leafy branches to eat.

CHECK THESE OUT!

Barapasaurus, Camarasaurus, Cretaceous period, *Diplodocus*, Saurischian dinosaurs, Sauropodomorph dinosaurs, Sauropods, *Titanosaurus*

DINOFACTS

Opisthocoelicaudia
(o-PIS-tho-SEEL-i-CAWD-ee-ah)

▶ When fossil-hunters found *Opisthocoelicaudia*, it was missing its head and neck. The rest of the skeleton was almost complete.

✳ **NAME:** *Opisthocoelicaudia* means tail bones hollow at the back
opistho (the back or behind) + coel (hollow) + caudia (of the tail)

◯ **FAMILY:** Saurischian
Sauropodomorph
Sauropod

✛ **SIZE:** 39 ft (12 m) long; 10–14 ft (3–4.3 m) high at the hip

WEIGHT: 10–40 tons (9–36 tonnes)—about the same as 2–8 African elephants

FOOD: plants

HABITAT: dry woodlands, semidesert areas

WHERE: remains found in Mongolia

🕒 **WHEN:** 70 million years ago in the Cretaceous period

			OPISTHOCOELICAUDIA ▪
TRIASSIC	JURASSIC	CRETACEOUS	
250 MILLION YEARS AGO	205 MILLION YEARS AGO	135 MILLION YEARS AGO	65 MILLION YEARS AGO

Ornithischian dinosaurs

So-called because of the shape of their hips, the ornithischian (bird-hipped) dinosaurs are one of the two main dinosaur groups. The lizard-hipped saurischians make up the other group.

In 1887, soon after scientists studied the first dinosaurs, British geologist Harry Seeley saw that he could divide all the dinosaurs into two main groups. He based the division mainly on the animals' hips.

It's a hip thing

All amphibians, mammals, birds, and reptiles have three bones in each half of the hip: the ilium, the ischium, and the pubis. Seeley saw that in many dinosaurs, the pubis (or at least a part of it) pointed down and

ORNITHISCHIAN FAMILY TREE

The first ornithischian dinosaurs appeared a few million years after the first saurischians did in the Late Triassic period.

DINOSAURS

ORNITHISCHIANS — SAURISCHIANS

ORNITHOPODS — PACHYCEPHALOSAURS AND CERATOPSIANS — THYREOPHORANS (ANKYLOSAURS AND STEGOSAURS) — LESOTHOSAURUS

HETERODONTOSAURUS

IGUANODON — HADROSAURS

▶ All ornithopods, like *Camptosaurus* (1) and *Dryosaurus* (2), were ornithischians. So were the stegosaurs, like plate-backed *Stegosaurus* (3).

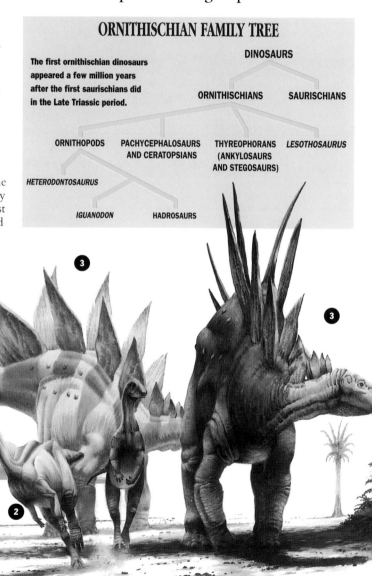

262

backward, as in modern birds. He called these dinosaurs ornithischian, or bird-hipped.

In other dinosaurs, the pubis pointed down and forward. Seeley called them saurischian, or lizard-hipped, because he also saw this hip pattern in lizards, crocodiles, and turtles. Believe it or not, modern birds are saurischians. That means birds descended from lizard-hipped dinosaurs!

Design for plant eating

Ornithischian and saurischian dinosaurs both evolved from a common ancestor which probably looked like the little meat-eater *Eoraptor*. Saurischians developed long necks and better grasping hands. Ornithischians developed a backward pointing pubis and an extra bone at the front of their jaws, with a horny beak.

All ornithischians ate plants, and these two features allowed ornithischians to become even better at eating plants. Their beaks snipped off vegetation, and the angle of their pubis allowed for bigger guts that were needed to digest plants.

Cheeky lizards

Ornithischian dinosaurs also developed cheeks to keep food in their mouths while they chewed. Saurischian dinosaurs lacked cheeks so they had to swallow their food whole. Ornithischians' jaws also had extra fixing points for jaw muscles, so they had very powerful bites.

One group of ornithischians, the ornithopods (bird-footed dinosaurs), developed a sideways-moving upper jaw. The sideways movement allowed them to chew food much more efficiently. One group of ornithopods, the hadrosaurs (duckbill dinosaurs), developed plates of flat teeth to grind tough leaves.

DINOFACTS

Ornithischian dinosaurs
(OR-ni-THISS-KEE-an)

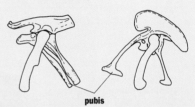

▶ In ornithischians (left), such as *Scelidosaurus*, the pubis points backward. In saurischians (right), such as *Ceratosaurus*, the pubis points forward.

pubis

✳ NAME: Ornithischian means bird-hipped
ornis (bird) + ischian (hipped)

◯ FAMILY: Dinosaur

✛ SIZE: wide variation from 3 ft (90 cm) to about 40 ft (12.2 m) long; from 1 ft (30 cm) to 16 ft (5 m) high at the hip

⬛ WEIGHT: wide variation from 5 lbs (2.3 kg) to 7 tons (6.3 tonnes)

🥣 FOOD: plants

🏠 HABITAT: all types, from woodlands to swamps to deserts

Ⓝ WHERE: remains found worldwide

🕐 WHEN: from 225 million years ago in the Triassic period to 65 million years ago in the Cretaceous period

ORNITHISCHIAN DINOSAURS

TRIASSIC	JURASSIC	CRETACEOUS
250 MILLION YEARS AGO	205 MILLION YEARS AGO	135 MILLION YEARS AGO 65 MILLION YEARS AGO

CHECK THESE OUT!

Ankylosaurs, Ceratopsians, Dinosaurs, Hadrosaurs, *Heterodontosaurus*, Iguanodon, Lesothosaurus, Ornithopods, Pachycephalosaurs, Saurischian dinosaurs, Stegosaurs, Thyreophorans

Ornitholestes

Ornitholestes lived in western North America in the Late Jurassic period. *Ornitholestes* means bird robber. Scientists once believed this dinosaur hunted early birdlike dinosaurs.

Ornitholestes was named in 1903 by US paleontologist Henry Fairfield Osborn. He described it from a nearly complete skull and skeleton collected in 1900 in Wyoming. Fossil-hunters found the remains at the Bone Cabin Quarry, which has produced many famous dinosaur skeletons, such as *Apatosaurus*, *Diplodocus*, and *Camptosaurus*.

Osborn recognized the animal was a small theropod (two-legged meat-eater). Its hands were very long. Its second fingers were its longest ones. Osborn also noted that it had teeth only at the front of its jaws and that they were not jagged. More recent studies,

THE BIRD HUNTER

When Osborn described *Ornitholestes*, he was struck by the lightness of the skeleton, its long tail, its long legs, and its large grasping hands. He suggested that perhaps it had been adapted to hunting early birds, hence its name. Famed dinosaur artist Charles R. Knight painted a picture of *Ornitholestes* leaping into the air after an *Archaeopteryx*, an avialan (bird relative). Although scientists no longer believe this was the way *Ornitholestes* lived, similar reconstructions still appear to this day.

▼ *Ornitholestes* was a small, fast two-legged meat-eating dinosaur.

though, have shown that the teeth are slightly jagged, like those of other theropods.

No other good specimens of *Ornitholestes* have ever been collected—just a few isolated bones from other parts of Wyoming and Colorado.

What was *Ornitholestes*?

Ornitholestes was a primitive (little evolved) coelurosaur, or hollow-tailed dinosaur. It belongs to the large group maniraptoriformes, which includes the tyrannosaurs, the troodontids (big-eyed brainy hunters), the ornithomimosaurs (ostrichlike dinosaurs), the bizarre, big-clawed therizinosaurs, and the maniraptors (long-armed meat-eating dinosaurs).

Ornitholestes was different enough from the other maniraptoriformes to be put in its own group.

How did *Ornitholestes* live?

This swift meat-eating dinosaur might have hunted small prey such as young dinosaurs. With its strong hands *Ornitholestes* could grab its prey before killing it with its bite.

It could also have used its hands to move rocks in its search for prey. If *Ornitholestes* came across a carcass of a large dinosaur, it would certainly have scavenged a meal.

CHECK THESE OUT!

Apatosaurus, *Archaeopteryx*, *Camptosaurus*, *Diplodocus*, Jurassic period, Maniraptors, *Ornithomimus*, Theropods, *Troodon*, *Tyrannosaurus*

DINOFACTS

Ornitholestes
(OR-ni-thuh-LES-teez)

▶ *Ornitholestes* had thick, slightly jagged teeth for biting into its prey after it had caught it with its strong hands.

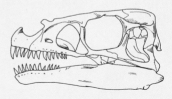

✳ NAME: *Ornitholestes* means bird robber
ornis (bird) + lestes (robber)

○ FAMILY: Saurischian
Theropod
Tetanuran

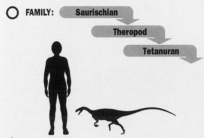

✛ SIZE: 6.5 ft (2 m) long; 3.5 ft (1 m) high at the hip

WEIGHT: 50 lbs (23 kg)—about the same as a large coyote

FOOD: small reptiles or the carcasses of dead animals

HABITAT: lowland areas with rivers and trees

N
↑ WHERE: remains found in Wyoming and perhaps Colorado

🕐 WHEN: 150–145 million years ago in the Jurassic period

ORNITHOLESTES

TRIASSIC	JURASSIC	CRETACEOUS
250 MILLION YEARS AGO	205 MILLION YEARS AGO	135 MILLION YEARS AGO

65 MILLION YEARS AGO

Ornithomimus

Ornithomimus was the first ornithomimosaur, or ostrichlike dinosaur, to be discovered. A long-legged sprinter, it lived in western North America during the Cretaceous period.

In 1889, American dinosaur hunter George Cannon found fossils in Jefferson County, Colorado. He collected the shin bone, foot, and hand of a man-sized dinosaur. Cannon shipped this specimen east, along with the bones of other dinosaurs he had found. He sent all these specimens to Yale University to be studied by Professor Othniel C. Marsh.

Marsh was one of America's leading paleontologists during the late 19th century. When he studied Cannon's new find, Marsh realized he was looking at a very unusual dinosaur.

▶ With its long, slender legs and a compact body, *Ornithomimus* was almost certainly a fast runner. It may have chased small prey across the North American plains.

Pinched toes

One of its oddest features was its hand. All the long bones (metacarpals) of the palm were the same length. They are of different lengths in most other dinosaurs. Also, the middle long bone of the foot, the metatarsal, was pinched between the other two.

Because these structures were different from those of any other dinosaur known at the time, Marsh decided that the fossil needed a new name. The three-toed foot reminded Marsh of a bird's foot, so he called this new dinosaur *Ornithomimus velox*, or swift bird mimic.

What was *Ornithomimus*?

Because of its narrow, three-toed foot, Marsh first thought that *Ornithomimus* might have been an ornithopod (bird-footed plant-eating dinosaur), like *Hypsilophodon* or *Camptosaurus*. (Ornithopods were called bird-footed dinosaurs because, like birds, their feet had three toes.)

As later fragments turned up, though, Marsh realized that *Ornithomimus* was really a theropod (two-legged meat-eating dinosaur).

As it turned out, some of the new specimens that convinced Marsh that *Ornithomimus* was a theropod did not belong to *Ornithomimus* at all, but to tyrannosaurs. Like ornithomimosaurs, tyrannosaurs have pinched middle foot bones.

Today paleontologists know that many smaller theropods have narrow, three-toed feet too. They could have

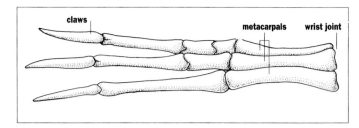

▲ **This is the hand of *Ornithomimus*. You can see the long bones (metacarpals) that surprised Othniel Marsh when he studied the fossil more than a century ago.**

identified *Ornithomimus* a lot more easily than did Marsh. In his day, however, Marsh had much less evidence to study. The best-known theropod feet in the 1880s were those of broad-footed giants like *Ceratosaurus* and *Allosaurus*.

Ostrichlike dinosaurs

Early in the 20th century, soon after Marsh's death, collectors found new fossils of *Ornithomimus* and related forms. American paleontologist Henry Fairfield Osborn described the similar but larger *Struthiomimus*,

found in Canada. When these fossils were taken from the rock, it turned out that Marsh's name—*Ornithomimus,* or bird mimic—was highly suitable. Ostrichlike dinosaurs had a lot in common with their modern bird namesake.

Ornithomimus looked like an ostrich in a number of ways. Unlike other theropods discovered up to that time, *Ornithomimus* did not have any teeth. Instead, it had a beak, just like a bird.

The shape of its head, with its big eyes and large brain, was a lot like that of an ostrich. All the ornithomimosaurs had larger braincases relative to their body sizes than almost any other dinosaur—except for

---

NAMING FRAGMENTS

Ornithomimus velox (swift bird mimic) was named from a very fragmentary fossil. As it turned out, this was a highly suitable name for this very swift, ostrichlike dinosaur. Othniel Marsh and other paleontologists, however, also named several other types (species) of *Ornithomimus* which turned out to be different dinosaurs.

Ornithomimus elegans was named from a foot found in Canada. Later discoveries showed that it was not from an ornithomimosaur (ostrichlike dinosaur), but from the oviraptorosaur (egg-thief dinosaur) *Elmisaurus*. Marsh named *Ornithomimus grandis* from a foot, and later a leg and hip were included in this species. This foot had the same type of pinched middle bone as in true *Ornithomimus*, but ended in sharp claws. Also, the leg was much taller than a man. These specimens turned out to be from a tyrannosaur, possibly *Tyrannosaurus* itself. Marsh also named *Ornithomimus minutus*, from an incomplete foot. Although scientists are not certain at present, this may be from a North American form of the bird relative *Mononykus*.

There were some other important differences between the ancestors of *Ornithomimus* and ostriches. Ostriches descended from birds that were able to fly long ago.

Ornithomimus did not have wings, and its ancestors were never able to fly. Instead, it had arms and three-fingered hands. Also, in all birds and bird relatives more advanced (highly evolved) than *Archaeopteryx*, the bony part of the tail is very short. In *Ornithomimus*, however, the tail is still long.

Convergent evolution

Common ancestry is not the reason for the similarity between *Ornithomimus* and the ostrich. Instead, the similarity is probably the result of convergent evolution. This is a scientific theory that explains how two different, unrelated animals or animal groups may come to look the same because they have similar lifestyles.

The ostrich's small skull and long neck help it pick up bits of food while walking around. Its long legs and trim body enable it to run fast across the African plains. These same features would have been just as useful to a theropod in North America in the Late Cretaceous period. Perhaps *Ornithomimus*, like the ostrich, ran about picking up bits of food. Perhaps that is why it evolved an ostrichlike form.

How *Ornithomimus* lived

With its small, toothless jaws, *Ornithomimus* would have had a hard time killing large prey.

modern birds. Also like an ostrich, *Ornithomimus* had a long, slender neck, its body was short and compact, and its legs were long and slim.

Paleontologists have studied the legs of ostrichlike dinosaurs to see how they might have worked. The results of these studies show that the ornithomimids could have been among the fastest of the Cretaceous dinosaurs, just as ostriches and their relatives are among the fastest modern running birds.

Common ancestors

Although scientists cannot prove *Ornithomimus* ran like an ostrich, it almost certainly looked like an ostrich. How can these two different theropods look so similar?

You might imagine that ostriches and *Ornithomimus* are

▲ *Ornithomimus* probably looked like an ostrich, except it had arms instead of wings and also a very long tail.

closely related. Perhaps they had a common ancestor that looked like both of them.

Paleontologists use the fossil record to test an idea like this. If *Ornithomimus* and ostriches look similar because they are close relatives, then as we trace their roots back, their ancestors should look increasingly alike. Do they? Well, yes, but they do not look much like either *Ornithomimus* or ostriches.

For example, both ostriches and *Ornithomimus* have small, toothless skulls and long, slender necks. However, early avialans (bird relatives), such as *Archaeopteryx*, and early ostrichlike dinosaurs, such as *Harpymimus* and *Pelecanimimus*, had teeth and shorter necks.

However, it could have run after small mammals and lizards, or used its beak to break into eggs.

Some Mesozoic theropods, such as oviraptorosaurs or dromaeosaurs, had grasping hands to grab their prey. The hands of *Ornithomimus* had no grasping thumbs. They were more like the clamping hand of a modern sloth (a tree-dwelling mammal of the Central and South American rainforests). However, *Ornithomimus* could have used its hands to hook branches and pull them down toward its mouth. That way it could feed on fruits or leaves.

Other scientists compare the hands of ostrichlike dinosaurs to those of modern anteaters, that dig into anthills. They have suggested that ostrichlike dinosaurs dug into burrows or insect nests. Today ostriches eat both plants and animals. *Ornithomimus* might have done so, too. Perhaps it also scavenged from kills made by other meat-eating dinosaurs.

Ornithomimus was among the very last of the Cretaceous dinosaurs. It lived alongside *Tyrannosaurus,* and various horned (*Triceratops*), duckbill (*Edmontosaurus*), and armored (*Ankylosaurus*) dinosaurs.

CHECK THESE OUT!

Archaeopteryx, Avialans, Birds, Cretaceous period, Dromaeosaurs, Evolution, *Gallimimus, Harpymimus, Mononykus*, Ornithopods, Oviraptorosaurs, *Pelecanimimus*, Saurischian dinosaurs, *Struthiomimus*, Theropods

DINOFACTS

Ornithomimus

(OR-nith-oh-MY-mus)

☀ **NAME:** *Ornithomimus* means bird mimic
ornis (bird) + mimos (mimic)

○ **FAMILY:**

Saurischian

Theropod

Tetanuran

✥ **SIZE:** 13 ft (4 m) long; up to 5 ft (1.5 m) high at the hip

WEIGHT: 360 lbs (163 kg)—about the same as a very large ostrich

FOOD: possibly meat, eggs, fruit, and leaves

HABITAT: forests and plains

N↑ **WHERE:** remains found in what is now Colorado, Montana, South Dakota, Utah, and Wyoming in the United States, and Alberta, Canada

⊘ **WHEN:** 74–65 million years ago in the Cretaceous period

			ORNITHOMIMUS
TRIASSIC	JURASSIC	CRETACEOUS	
250 MILLION YEARS AGO	205 MILLION YEARS AGO	135 MILLION YEARS AGO	65 MILLION YEARS AGO

Ornithopods

The ornithopods were plant-eating dinosaurs that walked mainly on their hind legs. They appeared in the Early Jurassic period and became very abundant in the Cretaceous period.

In 1881 US paleontologist and fossil collector Othniel Marsh placed all the two-legged plant-eating dinosaurs into one group. He called the group ornithopods, or bird-footed dinosaurs, because like birds these dinosaurs left three-toed tracks. New discoveries have, however, caused scientists to change Marsh's grouping.

Who are the ornithopods?
Today scientists agree that ornithopods are ornithischian (bird-hipped) dinosaurs which have their tooth row above their jaw joint, thicker enamel on one side of their teeth, and a long bump on their thigh bones for the attachment of the leg muscles.

Iguanodon

▶ Ornithopods came in different sizes. Little *Heterodontosaurus* was 3.5 ft (1 m) long; *Hypsilophodon* was up to 7 ft (2.1 m) long; *Iguanodon* was 21–33 ft (6.4–10 m) long; and *Edmontosaurus*, a large hadrosaur, was 33–40 ft (10–12.2 m) long.

Hypsilophodon

Edmontosaurus

Heterodontosaurus

As the ornithopods evolved from the Middle Jurassic period to the end of the Cretaceous period, there was an increase in the number of teeth in their jaws. Their teeth also became more closely packed for better chewing. The grinding surfaces of ornithopod teeth did not work like those of mammal teeth. Instead, hinges developed within the skull so that when the jaws closed the upper jaws rotated outward to grind against the teeth in the lower jaw. In this way, the more advanced iguanodontids and hadrosaurs could grind their way through very tough foods. Having thicker enamel on one side of the teeth meant that the teeth stayed sharp despite constant wear.

DINOFACTS
Ornithopods
(or-NITH-uh-PODS)

▲ Early *Heterodontosaurus* (1) had chisel-like cheek teeth. Later *Edmontosaurus* (2) had many flat teeth that were better for grinding tough plant food.

✳ NAME: Ornithopod means bird foot
   ornis (bird) + pous (foot)

○ FAMILY: Ornithischian

⬥ SIZE: wide variation from about 3 ft (90 cm) to about 40 ft (12.2 m) long; from about 1 ft (30 cm) to 16 ft (5 m) high at the hip

⬛ WEIGHT: huge variation from about 10 lbs (4.5 kg) to 7 tons (6.3 tonnes)

🥣 FOOD: plants

🏠 HABITAT: all types, from woodlands to swamps to deserts

N
↑ WHERE: remains found worldwide

🕐 WHEN: from 205 million years ago in the Jurassic period to 65 million years ago in the Cretaceous period

ORNITHOPODS

TRIASSIC	JURASSIC	CRETACEOUS
250 MILLION YEARS AGO	205 MILLION YEARS AGO	135 MILLION YEARS AGO · 65 MILLION YEARS AGO

There are four major groups of ornithopods: the Jurassic heterodontosaurs (different-toothed dinosaurs), the Middle Jurassic to Late Cretaceous hypsilophodontids (near iguana-tooth dinosaurs), the Late Jurassic to Late Cretaceous iguanodontids (iguana-tooth dinosaurs), and the Late Cretaceous hadrosaurs, or duckbill dinosaurs.

Over time ornithopods become progressively larger and slower. As they got bigger they also began to spend more time on four legs although they retained the ability to walk on only two legs.

How did ornithopods live?

Ornithopods lived in a wide range of habitats and ate a wide variety of plants. Many of the Jurassic kinds, such as *Heterodontosaurus* and *Hypsilophodon*, seem to have lived alone, while many of the Cretaceous types, like hadrosaurs, traveled in herds, with some, like *Maiasaura*, nesting in large colonies.

CHECK THESE OUT!

Edmontosaurus, Hadrosaurs, Heterodontosaurus, Hypsilophodon, Iguanodon, Ornithischian dinosaurs

Ouranosaurus

The iguanodontids (named in honor of *Iguanodon*) were a group of plant-eating dinosaurs that lived in many parts of the world. One of the most unusual iguanodontids was *Ouranosaurus* from Africa.

Ouranosaurus was special because of its backbones (vertebrae). They had tall spines sticking upward to form a sail running from the bottom of the neck to the middle of the tail. What did the sail do?

There are several possible explanations. Perhaps if one *Ouranosaurus* challenged another, the one who had the bigger sail would look larger and stronger. The smaller dinosaur might back off. The sail might have been used to attract a mate as male peacocks' tails are today.

Also, the sail could have acted as a sort of radiator. *Ouranosaurus* could have pumped blood into the arteries and veins under the skin covering the sail. If *Ouranosaurus* was too hot, the warm blood would lose heat through the skin and the animal would cool off quickly. If *Ouranosaurus* was too cool, the blood under the skin of the sail could absorb warmth from the sun. This way *Ouranosaurus* could warm up more quickly.

Many paleontologists, however, do not agree with this idea. They point out that while the idea provides a possible explanation for *Ouranosaurus*'s sail, it does not explain how other dinosaurs

▶ **Ouranosaurus looked similar to *Iguanodon*, but it had a large sail on its back.**

Tall sails along the backbone have evolved several times in dinosaurs and other extinct animals. The earliest backbone sails were seen in mammal-like reptiles like *Dimetrodon*. *Dimetrodon* lived in the heat of Texas about 280 million years ago. Other dinosaurs also evolved large sails. *Spinosaurus*, a theropod (two-legged meat-eater), had a sail almost 6 ft (1.8 m) tall. *Ouranosaurus* and *Spinosaurus* lived in steamy Africa in the Early Cretaceous period, so some scientists think that both animals evolved a sail to cool off.

managed to survive without a sail. If the sail was necessary for *Ouranosaurus*, why was it not necessary for other dinosaurs?

Ouranosaurus's lifestyle

As an ornithopod (bird-footed) dinosaur, *Ouranosaurus* had

muscular cheeks that enabled it to chew tough plant food. Scientists think that some plant–eating dinosaurs may have lived in herds. *Ouranosaurus* might have lived in a herd, but no group trackways have been found to prove this.

CHECK THESE OUT!

Cretaceous period, *Iguanodon*, Mammal-like reptiles, Ornithischian dinosaurs, Ornithopods, *Spinosaurus*

DINOFACTS

Ouranosaurus
(ooh-RAN-oh-SORE-us)

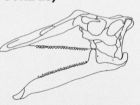

▶ Like all ornithopods, *Ouranosaurus* had a beak to snip leaves and cheek teeth to grind its food.

✳ **NAME:** *Ouranosaurus* means brave lizard
ourano (brave) + sauros (lizard)

⭕ **FAMILY:** Ornithischian

Ornithopod

✛ **SIZE:** 23 ft (7 m) long; 14 ft (4.3 m) high at the hip

⚖ **WEIGHT:** 1–4 tons (0.9–3.6 tonnes)—about the same as 1–4 North American bison

🥣 **FOOD:** plants

🏠 **HABITAT:** dry woodlands, semideserts (dry areas that get more rain than true deserts)

⚐ **WHERE:** remains found in North Africa

🕑 **WHEN:** 110 million years ago in the Cretaceous period

		OURANOSAURUS	
TRIASSIC	JURASSIC	CRETACEOUS	
250 MILLION YEARS AGO	205 MILLION YEARS AGO	135 MILLION YEARS AGO	65 MILLION YEARS AGO

Oviraptor

Oviraptor was one of the more unusual-looking dinosaurs found in Mongolia. Long thought to be an egg stealer, it is now known to have been protecting its own nests.

In July 1923 in the Flaming Cliffs of Mongolia, George Olsen of the American Museum of Natural History (AMNH) discovered the remains of a new kind of dinosaur. He had found the skull and front half of the body of a small theropod (two-legged meat-eater). The skull had an unusual, boxlike shape and no teeth.

Together with two other theropod skeletons also found nearby, it was shipped back to the museum to be examined and described. Henry Osborn studied all three skeletons.

He named the other two dinosaurs, which had long, toothed snouts, *Velociraptor* and *Saurornithoides*. While he was examining the third, toothless, skeleton, Osborn discovered that the sandstone block containing the fossil skull also contained some fossil eggs!

Egg thief?

Osborn thought the fossil eggs belonged to a dinosaur common in the area then, the primitive (little evolved) ceratopsian (horned dinosaur) *Protoceratops*. Because a theropod could not have laid *Protoceratops* eggs, Osborn decided it must have been raiding the nest for food.

A toothless beak would be useful for breaking eggshells, so Osborn named this new theropod *Oviraptor philoceratops*, the egg thief with a fondness for protoceratopsian eggs. *Oviraptor* became famous for

A MATTER OF CRESTS

Sometimes *Oviraptor* is drawn with a tall crest and sometimes it is not. Why the difference? Many different skulls of oviraptorosaurs (egg-thief dinosaurs) have been found in Mongolia. Some have crests and some do not. Some are found attached to skeletons and some are not. Some are very complete, but many more are damaged and eroded. Part of the science of paleontology is trying to put together different bits of evidence, and then testing the ideas against new information. One possibility to explain the presence or absence of crests might be that the different dinosaurs are different sexes (perhaps crested males and crestless females). Another might be that they are different kinds of *Oviraptor* (some with crests, some without). Still another might be that they are different ages (perhaps crestless juveniles and crested adults). Paleontologists in America, Mongolia, and Poland are trying to determine which, if any, of these ideas are true by comparing the form and size of the skulls and skeletons, by noting in what layers and what environments each sort was found, and by comparing *Oviraptor* with modern animals. These studies will provide important information about the lives of these dinosaurs.

◀ *Oviraptor* sits on its nest in Cretaceous Mongolia like a big, ground-nesting bird. It is protecting its eggs from being buried by a sandstorm. This *Oviraptor* had a comblike crest on its snout, so it was probably *Oviraptor philoceratops*.

being found near eggs, but it was soon forgotten as other dinosaurs were discovered.

New ideas

In the 1970s, new *Oviraptor* specimens were discovered by the Polish-Mongolian Paleontological Expedition. The new fossils showed that at least some *Oviraptor* had very tall crests on their snouts. These are sometimes thought to be a separate kind (species), *Oviraptor mongoliensis*. More complete fossils allowed Polish and Mongolian paleontologists to describe much more of these animals' bodies. So much material was found that the expedition's studies are still not finished!

The most famous discoveries of *Oviraptor* in recent years, however, were made by a return trip of the AMNH. A joint Mongolian-American team went back to sites previously studied and also

Oriraptor was lying within a nest that it had made, just as birds do. A later discovery by paleontologist Mark Norell of the AMNH of a very large *Oriraptor* on yet another nest confirmed that these dinosaurs did indeed sit on their nests.

Egg protector

Why did *Oviraptor* sit on its nest? One possibility is to protect its eggs from predators. Today many animals, including modern dinosaurs (birds) and their relatives the crocodiles, will stay near their eggs to chase away mammals, lizards, or other birds that try to eat them. In Cretaceous Mongolia there were many animals which might have tried to eat unprotected *Oviraptor* eggs. The parents might also have been protecting the nests from the effects of sand and sun.

Another possibility is that *Oviraptor* may have been brooding its eggs the way modern birds do: using its body heat to keep the eggs warm. If this were true, then *Oviraptor* might have had a warm covering of some kind. It may also have created its own body heat (that is, it was warm-blooded). Possibly it had

found entirely new localities. One of these sites—Ukhaa Tolgod, or Brown Hills—is one of the best places ever discovered to find fossil mammals, lizards, and small dinosaurs. Among the first discoveries was an egg with the bones of a baby dinosaur. Although it was the same sort

▼ *Oviraptor* skulls varied in shape, perhaps depending on kind (species). Skull (1) has a comblike crest and skull (2) has a bumplike crest on its nose. Paleontologists believe they are both *Oviraptor philoceratops*. Skull (3) has no crest so it may belong to a different species.

▲ Many modern birds make nests that are scraped out of the earth. Scientists believe *Oviraptor* may have done the same.

of egg that Osborn thought had belonged to *Protoceratops*, the skeleton inside was that of a baby *Oviraptor*!

Meanwhile, a joint Chinese-Canadian expedition had found yet another *Oviraptor* in China. This skeleton was also lying on top of eggs. Chinese paleontologist Dong Zhiming and Canadian Philip Currie confirmed that these were definitely *Oviraptor* eggs. They also worked out that the

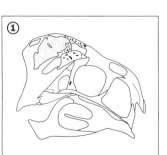

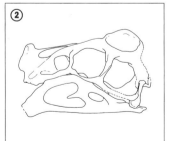

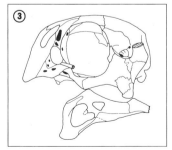

a warm covering and was warm-blooded too.

There are some hints that *Oviraptor* may have provided food for its young. Along with the fossil of the tiny unhatched baby, the first *Oviraptor* nest found at Ukhaa Tolgod also contained the skeletons of two baby dinosaurs.

Mark Norell and his colleagues identified these as dromaeosaurs (clawed meat-eaters), possibly *Velociraptor*. Perhaps they were in the nest because they were *Oviraptor* food. The parent *Oviraptor*, sensing that its eggs were about to hatch, may have brought freshly killed food (the baby dromaeosaurs) to feed its own newly hatched young.

How did *Oviraptor* live?

Figuring out the diet of *Oviraptor* has long been a problem. Some scientists have suggested that *Oviraptor* ate plants, others have suggested it ate shellfish.

The first specimen was found with a small lizard near its stomach. Many birds eat lizards; perhaps *Oviraptor* did too. Even though Osborn was wrong about the identity of the eggs found with the first specimen, the toothless beak of *Oviraptor* might still have been very good at cracking open the eggs of other dinosaurs.

CHECK THESE OUT!

Cretaceous period, Dromaeosaurs, Eggs and babies, Oviraptorosaurs, Protoceratops, Saurischian dinosaurs, Saurornithoides, Theropods, *Velociraptor*

DINOFACTS

Oviraptor
(OH-vee-RAP-tor)

✳ **NAME:** *Oviraptor* means egg thief
ovum (egg) + raptor (thief, snatcher)

○ **FAMILY:** Saurischian
Theropod
Oviraptorosaur

SIZE: up to 15 ft (4.6 m) long; up to 4.6 ft (1.45 m) high at the hip

WEIGHT: up to 400 lbs (180 kg)—about the same as a lioness

FOOD: probably meat, possibly eggs, insects, shellfish, and plants

HABITAT: deserts and edges of deserts

WHERE: remains found in Mongolia and China

WHEN: 80-68 million years ago in the Cretaceous period

OVIRAPTOR

TRIASSIC	JURASSIC	CRETACEOUS	
250 MILLION YEARS AGO	205 MILLION YEARS AGO	135 MILLION YEARS AGO	65 MILLION YEARS AGO

Oviraptorosaurs

Some of the most bizarre-looking dinosaurs were the toothless oviraptorosaurs (egg-thief dinosaurs), which lived across eastern Asia and western North America during the Cretaceous period.

Oviraptorosaurs were theropods (two-legged meat-eaters) that had short toothless beaks, long grasping arms, long legs with long toes, and short tails. For a long time, the only oviraptorosaur that was at all well known was *Oviraptor* itself.

Because it was a toothless theropod, many paleontologists thought *Oviraptor* was a type of ornithomimosaur (ostrichlike dinosaur) such as *Ornithomimus* or *Struthiomimus*.

However, oviraptorosaurs and ornithomimosaurs were distant cousins, and were very different from each other. Ostrichlike dinosaurs had long, pointed snouts, very long necks, and their claws tended to be fairly straight and thick.

Oviraptorosaurs, however, had shorter, blocky skulls with deep snouts. Their necks were shorter, and their claws were more curved and thinner. Mongolian paleontologist Barsbold Rinchen placed

Oviraptor philoceratops

Oviraptor mongoliensis

▶ Oviraptorosaurs were named in honor of *Oviraptor*, the original "egg-thief dinosaur." Paleontologists think there were at least two kinds of *Oviraptor*: *Oviraptor philoceratops* and *Oviraptor mongoliensis*.

TOOTHLESS PROBLEM

When scientists are trying to figure out which dinosaurs lived in a particular place at a particular time, they do not necessarily need complete skeletons. They can tell from just the teeth. The teeth of different dinosaur groups are often very distinctive. All paleontologists need to do is find a tooth or two to determine if a tyrannosaur or ceratopsian (horned dinosaur) was around. However, oviraptorosaurs are much harder to track. Oviraptorosaurs did not have any teeth, so fossil-hunters and paleontologists need to find more complete remains to locate them.

Oviraptor and its relatives in their own group, the oviraptorosaurs, in 1976.

Two families

There are two families of oviraptorosaurs: oviraptorids and caenagnathids. The oviraptorids, like *Oviraptor,* lived only in Asia. The caenagnathids included *Chirostenotes* and *Elmisaurus* and lived in both Asia and North America. No one really knows what the oviraptorosaurs ate, but most scientists agree that they probably ate meat. Only by finding an oviraptorosaur fossil with the remains of its last meal could they be sure.

CHECK THESE OUT!

Ceratopsians, *Chirostenotes,*
Cretaceous period, *Elmisaurus,*
Ingenia, Ornithomimus, Oviraptor,
Saurischian dinosaurs, *Struthiomimus,*
Theropods, Tyrannosaurs

DINOFACTS

Oviraptorosaurs
(OH-vee-rap-TOR-oh-sores)

NAME: Oviraptorosaurs means egg-thief lizards
ovum (egg) + raptor (thief, snatcher) + sauros (lizard)

FAMILY: Saurischian
Theropod
Tetanuran

SIZE: 3–15 ft (90 cm–4.6 m) long;
1–4.6 ft (30 cm–1.45 m) high at the hip

WEIGHT: 7–400 lbs (3–180 kg)—or from a house cat to a lioness

FOOD: probably meat, possibly insects, eggs, and plants

HABITAT: varied, from lake shores to forests to deserts

WHERE: remains found in Mongolia, China, Uzbekistan, the United States, and Canada

WHEN: 115–65 million years ago in the Cretaceous period

			OVIRAPTOROSAURS
TRIASSIC	JURASSIC	CRETACEOUS	
250 MILLION YEARS AGO	205 MILLION YEARS AGO	135 MILLION YEARS AGO	65 MILLION YEARS AGO

Pachycephalosaurs

The name given to this group of dinosaurs means thick-headed lizards; it refers to the incredibly thick caps of bone on the tops of their skulls. Why did these animals need such thick heads?

Remains of pachycephalosaurs, or thick-headed dinosaurs, are usually found in rocks of Late Cretaceous age, although they are quite rare.

It is not hard to guess how these animals got their name—their skulls were covered by an amazingly thick layer of bone. One skull 2 ft (60 cm) long had a layer of bone about 10 in (25 cm) thick! When scientists looked more closely at the skullcap, they saw that it was

MEET THE THICK-HEADED DINOSAURS

Paleontologists have discovered 11 different kinds of pachycephalosaurs in places as far apart as North America, China and Mongolia in Asia, and England in Europe. *Gravitholus, Ornatotholus, Pachycephalosaurus, Stegoceras,* and *Stygimoloch* lived in North America; *Goyocephale, Homalocephale, Prenocephale, Tylocephale,* and—with the longest name of any dinosaur—*Micropachycephalosaurus* lived in Asia; and *Yaverlandia* lived in England.

All pachycephalosaurs had thicker skulls than those of any other dinosaurs, but the thickness varied—from 1.5 in (4 cm) in *Homalocephale* to an incredible 10 in (25 cm) in *Pachycephalosaurus.* The shape of the skull varied, too: domed in some, flat-topped in others. *Goyocephale* and *Stegoceras* also had knobs or bumps on their skulls. Scientists are not sure how these dinosaurs used their bumps.

◀ Spike-headed *Stygimoloch* (1) scuffles with a coup of *Stegoceras* (2) in Late Cretaceous period Montana. Bot these dinosaurs had full, thick domes on their skulls.

made up of an extremely dense growth of bone columns that pointed directly outward from the surface. The bone would have made the skull as tough as a football player's helmet.

How the dinosaurs lived

Some paleontologists think that adult males might have crashed their skulls together when they fought, as sheep and goats do today. In most dinosaurs, the spine connects to the very back of the skull, and the skull projects forward.

In pachycephalosaurs, however, the spine connects directly underneath the skull. Because of this, if two males crashed their heads together, the shock would have traveled down the spine to be soaked up by the whole body.

Unfortunately, because we cannot see how the dinosaurs behaved, we will never know for sure.

Like all ornithischian (bird-hipped) dinosaurs, pachycephalosaurs ate plants. They had cheeks to hold the food in their mouths while they ate, but they did not have the sideways-moving upper jaw of the ornithopods (bird-footed dinosaurs). Pachycephalosaurs could chew to a certain extent, so they did not have to swallow their food whole.

CHECK THESE OUT!

Cretaceous period, *Goyocephale*, *Homalocephale*, Ornithischian dinosaurs, Ornithopods, *Pachycephalosaurus*, *Prenocephale*, *Stegoceras*, *Stygimoloch*

DINOFACTS

Pachycephalosaurs
(PAK-*ee*-SEF-*ah-low*-SORES)

▶ A pachycephalosaur's spine was attached beneath its skull. If these animals fought, they may have lowered their heads and charged. Their spines soaked up the shock.

✳ NAME: Pachycephalosaur means thick-headed lizard
  pachos (thick) + kephale (head) + sauros (lizard)

◯ FAMILY: Ornithischian

✛ SIZE: 3.5–15 ft (1–4.6 m) long;
  1–4 ft (30 cm–1.2 m) high at the hip

WEIGHT: wide variation from 66 lbs (30 kg) to 2 tons (1.8 tonnes)

FOOD: plants

HABITAT: dry forested areas or low-lying, well-watered forests

N
A WHERE: remains found in western North America, Asia, and Europe

🕐 WHEN: 110–65 million years ago in the Cretaceous period

		PACHYCEPHALOSAURS
TRIASSIC	JURASSIC	CRETACEOUS
250 MILLION YEARS AGO	205 MILLION YEARS AGO	135 MILLION YEARS AGO	65 MILLION YEARS AGO

Pachycephalosaurus

This dinosaur gave its name, which means thick-headed lizard, to a whole group of boneheads: the pachycephalosaurs. It was the biggest of them all, and had a thick, tough skull to match.

Pachycephalosaurus is known only from part of its skull and a few other bones, but these remains are enough to tell paleontologists how the dinosaur may have lived.

Biggest of the boneheads

Pachycephalosaurus was the largest known member of the pachycephalosaurs, or thick-headed dinosaurs. These were a group of dinosaurs known for their incredibly thick skulls. *Pachycephalosaurus* had the biggest, boniest head of them all. Its skull was 2 ft (60 cm) long, and had a bony dome more than 10 in (25 cm) thick!

Why did *Pachycephalosaurus* have such a thick skull? To protect its brain from very hard knocks. Paleontologists think male *Pachycephalosaurus* may have fought one another by crashing heads together. Some think that the animals charged head-on at each other. Modern herd-living animals, such as mountain goats, fight like this. They have horns and thick heads to protect their brains. Others think that the animals fought standing still, swinging their heads sideways. Giraffes fight like this today.

▼ KERPOW! Did *Pachycephalosaurus* males settle arguments by crashing heads? We cannot say for sure. This dinosaur may also have headbutted its enemies; here, an adult topples a hungry young tyrannosaur.

TOUGH SURVIVOR

If *Pachycephalosaurus*'s skull were not so big and solid, it might not have survived as a fossil. Then, scientists would know nothing about this animal and its lively lifestyle. Many dinosaurs, like the long-necked plant-eater *Camarasaurus*, had fairly delicate skulls that were easily crushed or lost after the animal died, and their fossil skulls are very rare. Even today, most carcasses get torn apart or crushed when predators scavenge their remains. Only the tiniest fraction of all the animals and plants that have ever lived are preserved as fossils.

However they fought, the extra bone would have helped keep their skulls from caving in. Perhaps the adult males fought for leadership of a herd and for the chance to mate with females.

From strength to strength

Any male *Pachycephalosaurus* whose skull was too thin would soon die in combat. Only the males with the strongest skulls would survive to breed. In this way, males would gradually evolve thicker and thicker skulls over many generations.

How it lived

Like all ornithischian (bird-hipped) dinosaurs, *Pachycephalosaurus* probably ate plants. *Pachycephalosaurus* had fleshy cheeks, so it could chew its food, and it did not have to swallow its food whole. It may have lived in herds in broad river valleys where leafy food was plentiful.

CHECK THESE OUT!

Camarasaurus, Cretaceous period, Fossils, Ornithischian dinosaurs, Pachycephalosaurs

---

DINOFACTS

Pachycephalosaurus
(PACK-ee-SEF-ah-low-SORE-us)

 FOOD: plants

 **HABITAT: forested lowlands near rivers and seas**

✴ **NAME:** *Pachycephalosaurus* means thick-headed lizard
pachos (thick) + kephale (head) + sauros (lizard)

○ **FAMILY:** Ornithischian

Pachycephalosaur

N ↑ **WHERE:** remains found in Alberta, Canada

▶ You can see the huge dome of extra bone on top of *Pachycephalosaurus*'s knobbly skull.

✛ **SIZE: 15 ft (4.6 m) long; 3–4 ft (90 cm–1.2 m) high at the hip**

⚖ **WEIGHT: 1.5–2 tons (1.35–1.8 tonnes)—about the same as 1–2 North American bison**

🕐 **WHEN: 75–70 million years ago in the Cretaceous period**

PACHYCEPHALOSAURUS

TRIASSIC	JURASSIC	CRETACEOUS	
250 MILLION YEARS AGO	205 MILLION YEARS AGO	135 MILLION YEARS AGO	65 MILLION YEARS AGO

Pachyrhinosaurus

Pachyrhinosaurus was a large ceratopsian (horned dinosaur) that lived at the end of the Cretaceous period. Its name means thick-nosed lizard and describes the big, wrinkled lump on its snout.

Canadian paleontologist Charles M. Sternberg described *Pachyrhinosaurus* in 1950 after studying two huge skulls from Alberta, Canada. The skulls had no horns; instead, there was a big lump (boss) of rough bone over the snout area.

The skulls had no neck frills; these had decayed. Because most ceratopsians had neck frills, Sternberg rebuilt them. Boss-nosed *Pachyrhinosaurus* was so unusual that Sternberg put it in its own family.

ARCTIC *PACHYRHINOSAURUS*

In the 1980s, a Berkeley Museum of Paleontology expedition set out to collect remains of the hadrosaur (duckbill dinosaur) *Edmontosaurus* from the Colville River in Alaska. This area lies in the bleak, cold Far North, inside the Arctic Circle. One expedition member, Howard Hutchinson, came across a skull of *Pachyrhinosaurus*—the first ceratopsian (horned dinosaur) ever to have been found in the Arctic. Colville River was even closer to the North Pole during the Cretaceous period. Some paleontologists think *Pachyrhinosaurus* lived in the north in the summer and headed south for the winter to escape the worst of the cold.

◀ *Pachyrhinosaurus* had a bony lump, or boss, on its snout. Charles M. Sternberg thought that when the dinosaur was alive the boss would have been covered in a hornlike material.

The great herds

In 1987, fossil collectors began digging at Pipestone Creek, Alberta. They found hundreds of *Pachyrhinosaurus* skeletons, in ages ranging from youngster to adult. These skeletons enabled scientists to study *Pachyrhinosaurus* in detail.

The skulls from this new site had between one and three small horns pointing forward from the center of their neck frill. Perhaps this is what the frills of Sternberg's dinosaurs would have looked like, or maybe they belonged to a new kind of *Pachyrhinosaurus*. Scientists are not yet sure.

The smallest skulls had hornlets—small, bladelike horns over the nose and eyes. As the animal grew, these hornlets spread to form the big boss. Adult skulls had extra horns along the skull edges.

Why no horns?

The bosses of *Pachyrhinosaurus* came in two forms. The top surface of one was bulging; the other was dished. These might have been separate boss forms for males and females.

Perhaps *Pachyrhinosaurus* males used their bosses in shoving matches to win females or take control of the herd. Perhaps males also had long horns for fighting. Perhaps the boss was only the base for a big horn made of keratin (the material from which fingernails are made). A keratin horn would decay and not fossilize.

How *Pachyrhinosaurus* lived

Pachyrhinosaurus traveled across North America, probably in vast herds, much as caribou do today. These huge animals ate a lot of food. With their strong jaws and shearing teeth, they could chop up tough plants.

CHECK THESE OUT!

Ceratopsians, Cretaceous period, *Edmontosaurus*, Hadrosaurs, Ornithischian dinosaurs

DINOFACTS

Pachyrhinosaurus
(*PACK-ee-RYE-noh-SORE-us*)

▶ Digs during the late 1980s turned up some skulls with their frills intact. Here, you can see the horns fringing the frill, as well as the huge, wrinkled lump on the snout.

✳ NAME: *Pachyrhinosaurus* means thick-nosed lizard
   pachos (thick) + rhinos (nose) + sauros (lizard)

○ FAMILY: Ornithischian
             Ceratopsian

✛ SIZE: 18–21 ft (5.4–6.4 m) long; 6.5 ft (2 m) high at the hip

⬛ WEIGHT: 2–3 tons (1.8–2.7 tonnes)—about the same as 2–3 North American bison

FOOD: tough, low-growing plants

HABITAT: coastal lowlands

N
↑ WHERE: remains found in Alberta, Canada, and in Alaska

⊙ WHEN: 72–68 million years ago in the Cretaceous period

PACHYRHINOSAURUS

TRIASSIC	JURASSIC	CRETACEOUS	
250 MILLION YEARS AGO	205 MILLION YEARS AGO	135 MILLION YEARS AGO	65 MILLION YEARS AGO

Paleontology

Paleontology is the study of ancient life—not only of dinosaurs, but also of all the animals and plants that came before the Mesozoic Era and of many that have lived since.

People have collected fossils since ancient times. Some, such as the philosophers Xenophanes and Pythagoras who lived about 2,500 years ago in Greece, suggested that fossils were the remains of once living creatures. Two hundred years later, Aristotle, another Greek philosopher, suggested that fossils were mistakes of nature. Some people even believed that

fossils were the Devil's work, put in the earth to test people's faith in God.

Origins of paleontology

In 1664, Danish naturalist Nicholas Steno showed that these ideas were not correct. He showed that the so-called Tongue Stones (oddly shaped stones that turned up when farmers were plowing) were really fossil shark teeth. Steno

▲ Two paleontologists carefully measure the length of a fossil before digging it from the ground and taking it back to a laboratory for further study.

proved his theory by comparing the structure of the Tongue Stones with that of modern shark teeth.

At the end of the 18th century, French anatomist Georges Cuvier compared fossil bones found near Paris

▲ Georges Cuvier was one of the founders of modern paleontology. Among other fossils, he studied the bones of woolly mammoths found in France.

with those of modern mammals. He showed that the fossil bones belonged to types of mammals that no longer existed. His studies proved for the first time that animals had once lived that were different from those alive today. These types of animals had since died out—they had become extinct.

Paleontologists date rocks

As scientists learned more about fossils, they discovered that different layers of rock contained different kinds of fossils. They also found that the same fossils were always found in the same rock layer. The study of fossils became widespread after this discovery.

British canal builder William Smith put the discovery to good use during the later part of the 18th century. Smith found that he could predict, by the fossils he found on the surface, which rock layers he would find as he dug. In this way, he could tell where was the best place to dig canals, since some kinds of rock are more difficult to dig through than others. Smith invented biostratigraphy (the use of fossils to tell the age of rocks). Even today, many paleontologists work as biostratigraphers in the worldwide search for oil and minerals.

The history of life

By studying where fossils are found in the earth's rock layers, paleontologists learned that life had begun with simple forms, which changed over time (evolved) into more complex forms.

Biologist Charles Darwin studied both fossils and living animals and plants for his theory of evolution. Darwin believed that animals and plants evolved because of variations.

Animals that had a variation that increased their chances of survival, such as being taller or stronger, were more likely to pass that variation to their offspring. Over time, these variations gradually produced animals that were different enough from their ancestors to be described as a different type (species) of animal.

Fossil record

Scientists can study how living animals are related by comparing their skeletons and body tissue. Scientists can study the history of life, however, only through paleontology.

The fossil record is far from complete, but it provides the only scientific method for deciding how groups of plants and animals developed, and in what order.

▼ Peter Larson, codirector of the Black Hills Institute of Geological Research, carves away the rock from the lower jaw bone of a fossil *Tyrannosaurus* skeleton.

Becoming a paleontologist

To figure out how life evolved on earth, paleontologists need to know about many different areas of science.

Because you cannot study paleontology at college, most paleontologists train as either biologists or geologists. A paleontologist should have a good understanding of biology, geology, chemistry, physics, and math. Paleontologists need to know at least a bit about almost everything.

Paleontologists must be able to write in clear language. They can spend a lot of time writing. This is how they record all the information about a discovery, and put forward their theories.

A paleontologist should also be able to draw fossils. A good drawing can often make a fossil easier to understand. Drawing also helps the paleontologist to remember a fossil and its main features more clearly.

The most important habit a paleontologist can develop is noticing things. In many ways, understanding the present is the key to understanding the past. A paleontologist can never be sure when something he or she has noticed may be useful for studying the past.

Areas of study

Some paleontologists are experts on one section of geological time, such as the Jurassic period; others are experts on one group of fossils, such as dinosaurs.

As well as experts, paleontological museums also have preparators. Preparators assist in digging out fossils. They also work in the laboratory cleaning fossils and preventing them from becoming damaged. Museums have their own scientific illustrators. Besides drawing bones for books, they make reconstructions of ancient animals and their

▲ An illustrator draws a fossil. Whenever a new dinosaur or other ancient animal is discovered, its skeleton must be drawn to show what it looked like.

habitats. Museums also have curators, who organize the fossils so that they can always be found for future study.

Not archaeologists

Many paleontologists like to say "we do not study people." Paleoanthropologists, however, do study the evolution of humans and human ancestors.

Paleontologists study life before the end of the last Ice Age, some 10,000 years ago. This was about the time that ancient peoples first began to build towns with houses made of mud, brick, and stone; some ruins still stand. Archaeologists study human remains that are younger than 10,000 years old. To be more precise in describing their work, paleontologists might instead say "we do not study ruins."

SUBDIVISIONS OF PALEONTOLOGY

Paleontology is a big subject. It is divided into many groups.

Biostratigraphy: using fossils to date rock layers
Ichnology: the study of the traces ancient animals made in sediments, e.g. footprints
Invertebrate paleontology: the study of ancient animals without backbones
Micropaleontology: the study of tiny fossils found by breaking down rock samples
Paleoanthropology: the study of humans before about 8,000 BCE
Paleobiogeography: the study of where ancient animals lived
Paleobiology: the study of the biology of ancient plants and animals
Paleobotany: the study of ancient plants
Paleoclimatology: the study of ancient climates
Paleoecology: the study of how ancient plants and animals fit their environments
Paleopathology: the study of ancient diseases and injuries
Systematics: the study of how different plants and animals are related
Taphonomy: the study of the process of fossilization
Vertebrate paleontology: the study of ancient animals with backbones

PALEONTOLOGY INTO THE 21ST CENTURY

Paleontology is generally a low-tech science. Paleontologists use many of the same methods that were invented more than 100 years ago. However, some new methods have been introduced. The airplane and aerial photography have been used to track down likely areas to search for fossils. Satellite imagery has provided important information on even the most remote areas. Satellite navigation systems have become so small that nearly every paleontologist carries a Global Positioning System (GPS) unit in his or her shirt pocket to record where fossil sites are.

New technologies such as seismic tomography have been used to try and find bones still buried in the ground. With seismic tomography, a small explosion is set off and the echoes through rock are recorded. If the echoes pass through a fossil, they change slightly and the fossil can sometimes be located. These new technologies have not been very successful. Paleontologists still depend on looking for fossils with their eyes. The only dinosaur ever found solely by technology is a new species of ankylosaur (armored dinosaur) discovered by University of Utah radiologist Ramal Jones. He followed the small amounts of radiation the fossil gave off until he found the remains. The dinosaur is being named *Anamantarx ramaljonesi* (Ramal Jones living fortress) in his honor.

Sometimes X-ray photography can tell scientists about a fossil while it is still in the rock. By using CAT scans (computerized axial tomography pictures, which are used in hospitals to safely look inside the human body), paleontologists can create 3-D images of fossil skulls. Paleontologists can get the image on screen and turn it this way and that. Computers have also been used to test how ancient animals moved and how heavy they might have been.

◄ A child helps out at a fossil dig near Egg Mountain in Montana—the place where the eggs and nests of the theropod (two-legged meat-eater) *Troodon* were discovered.

Importance of paleontology

Paleontology is the only way to study the history of life. Paleontologists study and record the different types of plants and animals that have lived on earth. They study the effects of changes to the climate and of the shifting positions of the continents.

Paleontologists study mass extinctions, when many types of plants and animals suddenly die out. We cannot tell what effect people are having on the earth (for example if we are making some animals extinct) without understanding the history of life.

Paleontology has an effect on nearly everyone. Paleontology, especially dinosaur paleontology, is often the first area of science that gets children excited. It lets children see that the world is vastly larger than their own backyard and has a history rich beyond their wildest dreams.

Educators have found that the way paleontologists think is useful in nearly every aspect of modern life. For example, they can use paleontology to teach many different subjects—from geography and geology to computer science and math.

Paleontologists make new discoveries every day. That means if you study real hard, someday you too may make an important discovery in the history of life.

CHECK THESE OUT!

Collecting dinosaurs, Continental drift, Digging dinosaurs, Evolution, Extinction, Fossils, Geological time, Reconstructing dinosaurs, Rocks

Panoplosaurus

Panoplosaurus did not have a lot of the fearsome spikes that adorned most ankylosaurs (armored dinosaurs). This big plant-eater probably hid when faced with large predators.

Canadian paleontologist Charles H. Sternberg found *Panoplosaurus* in 1917 in what is now Dinosaur Provincial Park, Canada. The remains included a well-preserved skull, a partial skeleton, and plenty of armor. Canadian paleontologist Lawrence Lambe described the dinosaur in 1919.

Country cousins

The skull of *Panoplosaurus* looked rather like that of the ankylosaur *Edmontonia*, which had lived in the same region,

but it was shorter and wider.

The whole dinosaur was so similar to *Edmontonia* that New England paleontologist Walter Coombs described both these specimens as *Panoplosaurus*.

However, after Colorado paleontologist Ken Carpenter pointed out several differences in the two sets of remains, Coombs changed his mind. Like Carpenter, he saw they

ARMORED CHEEKS

The ankylosaurs (armored dinosaurs) had bony plates almost all over their bodies—even armored lids over their eyes. In one *Panoplosaurus* fossil, a large, oval armor plate fills the hollow between the upper and lower jaws on each side of the skull. This hollow is found in nearly all ornithischian (bird-hipped) dinosaurs, and for some time scientists have used it as evidence that all bird-hipped dinosaurs had cheeks and even primitive ornithischians could chew their food at least a little. *Panoplosaurus*'s jaw armor is evidence for this; the two jaw plates might have protected the cheeks.

DINOFACTS

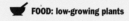

Panoplosaurus
(PAN-o-plo-SORE-us)

☀ **NAME:** *Panoplosaurus* means full-armored lizard
panoplos (full-armored) + sauros (lizard)

○ **FAMILY:** Ornithischian

Thyreophoran

Ankylosaur

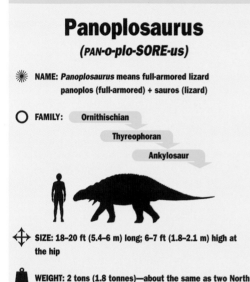

✥ **SIZE:** 18–20 ft (5.4–6 m) long; 6–7 ft (1.8–2.1 m) high at the hip

⚖ **WEIGHT:** 2 tons (1.8 tonnes)—about the same as two North American bison

🥣 **FOOD:** low-growing plants

🏠 **HABITAT:** coastal lowlands, similar to the modern Gulf Coast

WHERE: remains found in Montana and perhaps Texas, and in southern Alberta, Canada

▶ *Panoplosaurus's* skull, seen from below (right) and above (far right), was armor-plated.

🕐 **WHEN:** 75–70 million years ago in the Cretaceous period

			PANOPLOSAURUS
TRIASSIC	JURASSIC	CRETACEOUS	
250 MILLION YEARS AGO	205 MILLION YEARS AGO	135 MILLION YEARS AGO	65 MILLION YEARS AGO

---

were two different dinosaurs.

Spineless nodosaurs?
Paleontologists divide ankylosaurs into two groups. Those with tail-clubs are called ankylosaurids; those without

◀ *Panoplosaurus* was covered in thick armor plating from its snout to the tip of its tail. Small meat-eaters were no match for this tanklike dinosaur.

clubs are called nodosaurids.

Panoplosaurus belonged to the second group. *Panoplosaurus* had armor plates on its back, and like all nodosaurids, it had a cluster of spikes on its shoulders. However, unlike most nodosaurids, *Panoplosaurus* did not have any tall spines on its back. Small nodosaurids found in Texas may also have lacked these spines, but it is hard to tell for sure.

How did *Panoplosaurus* live?
Panoplosaurus was a fairly slow, chunky dinosaur that ate low-growing plants. It is known

only from isolated specimens, so it probably did not live in large herds. *Panoplosaurus's* armor would have protected it from most small meat-eating dinosaurs. Because it had no spines, however, this plump animal would have been easy prey for the large tyrannosaur *Albertosaurus*. Its best defense would have been to hunker down and hide in the bushes.

CHECK THESE OUT!

Albertosaurus, Ankylosaurs, Cretaceous period, *Edmontonia*, Ornithischian dinosaurs, Thyreophorans

Parasaurolophus

Parasaurolophus was a large hadrosaur (duckbilled dinosaur) that lived in North America during the Late Cretaceous period. Paleontologists believe that it used its extraordinary crest to make loud noises.

Did dinosaurs ever honk, tweet, hoot, or screech as modern animals do? New studies inform paleontologists that some dinosaurs almost certainly did make loud sounds. *Parasaurolophus* was probably a very noisy dinosaur. How do we know this?

Supercrest

The first thing you notice about *Parasaurolophus* is the huge, narrow crest sweeping back from its head. This crest was made up of two hollow pipes lying side by side. Most dinosaur crests sat on top of

the head. In *Parasaurolophus*, however, the pipes in the crest ran like a big "U" up from the dinosaur's brow to the tip of its crest and back to its face, ending in the animal's mouth.

The bones of the crest are called the frontals and nasals. In other dinosaurs, these bones lay around the nostrils and the snout. In *Parasaurolophus* and its ancestors, the frontals and nasals had grown bigger than usual to form the two tubes.

When fossil-hunters first discovered *Parasaurolophus* in 1920, the purpose of these U-shaped crest pipes was a

mystery. At the time, scientists were so impressed by the size of dinosaurs that they could not imagine how dinosaurs lived on land. They thought that big dinosaurs must have lived mostly in water.

These ideas not only affected the ways in which scientists reconstructed dinosaur skeletons, they also gave them some peculiar notions about

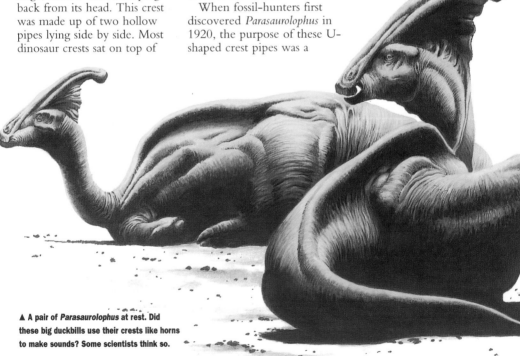

▲ A pair of *Parasaurolophus* at rest. Did these big duckbills use their crests like horns to make sounds? Some scientists think so.

292

dinosaur behavior, too. Some scientists even thought that *Parasaurolophus* fed underwater on soft plants.

Snorkel...

Because *Parasaurolophus*'s crest was connected to its nostrils and mouth, scientists thought it had something to do with breathing. They thought that the crest might have worked like a snorkel, allowing *Parasaurolophus* to breathe as it fed underwater. The problem with this idea is that there is no opening in the tip of the crest to allow air in or out.

...or diving equipment?

Other people thought that the crest held extra air, a bit like a diver's air tank. They thought it let *Parasaurolophus* spend more time underwater, or acted as a float to keep the animal upright in the water.

Unfortunately, the crest would not have held enough air for *Parasaurolophus* to refill its lungs. Nor would there have been enough air to help such a heavy animal float. Still worse, the high pressure underwater would have prevented *Parasaurolophus* from expanding its lungs and filling them with air.

Wrong!

Nobody believes these ideas today. Scientists now realize that the muscles and bones of dinosaurs were very strong. Dinosaurs could have moved easily and quickly on land.

The many hundreds of hard, strong teeth in the mouths of hadrosaurs like *Parasaurolophus*

DINOSAUR SOUNDS

As scientific knowledge grows, scientists' opinions can change. The new idea about *Parasaurolophus*'s musical crest is one example. The use of sound by crocodiles, animals related to dinosaurs, is another.

Zoologists have learned that crocodiles are very good at hearing. Crocodiles also make different types of sound at different stages during their lives. Baby crocodiles just about ready to hatch will start chirping. This tells the mother crocodile to start uncovering the eggs, which are covered by vegetation. Mother crocodiles can alert their swimming babies by making sounds that humans cannot hear. Adult crocodiles also use very low, deep sounds to send signals to one another, such as a warning to one crocodile to keep away from another's territory.

Crocodiles are close living relatives of dinosaurs, and birds are dinosaurs. It is well known that birds use sounds for lots of different purposes. Since both of these groups, birds and crocodiles, make and use sounds, it is quite likely that dinosaurs also used sounds to communicate, but the idea is impossible to test.

▲ Baby crocodiles make sounds to alert their mother that they are about to hatch.

tell paleontologists that these dinosaurs ate tough plants on land, not soft water plants. Now that scientists know this, they have to think again: how did *Parasaurolophus* use its long, hollow crest?

Long and loud

The long, looped tubes of the crest would have worked just like the loops of a horn. The bony crest could not change its shape, so it could have produced only one type of

sound. If *Parasaurolophus* made a sound in its throat, the sound would travel from its mouth into the crest tubes.

The arrangement of the tubes would have made the sound louder, just as the pipes on a church organ make the notes sound louder. The long pipes of *Parasaurolophus*'s crest would have made the note deeper. The crest was about 6 ft (1.8 m) long. A noise in the pipes would have sounded deep, like a ship's horn.

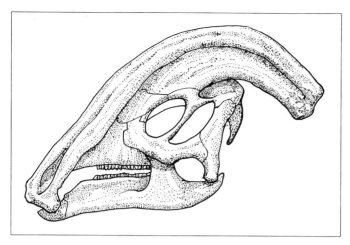

would have used its rasplike teeth to grind up mouthfuls of leaves and soft twigs.

Heard by the herd

The main dinosaur predator in North America during the Late Cretaceous period was the mighty *Tyrannosaurus*. If a member of the herd detected a marauding *Tyrannosaurus*, it could honk or hoot to warn the others. The sounds produced by the long crest tubes would have carried a long way. The lower the note, the less it is weakened when it

▲ *Parasaurolophus*'s skull shows how its nose bones form its crest.

▶ The elephant seal can inflate its nose to trumpet calls that can be heard several miles away.

How *Parasaurolophus* lived

That *Parasaurolophus* might have made sounds suggests that it might have lived in herds. Animals living today in herds or packs or flocks use sounds. Male birds sing to impress other birds and claim nest sites. Monkeys call to alert each other to danger. Male bison bellow threats at each other. Maybe *Parasaurolophus* used its musical crest for similar purposes. Of course, we can never be sure because we were not there to hear it.

Scientists have studied the rocks surrounding the fossils of *Parasaurolophus*. These show that it lived in dense lowland forests. A *Parasaurolophus* herd might have wandered slowly through the forest. Like all hadrosaurs, *Parasaurolophus*

travels over long distances. Modern animals that talk to each other in very low notes include elephants and some types of whales. Some whale songs can travel hundreds of miles through the oceans. The deep rumblings of modern elephants can travel several miles over land.

The low honks of *Parasaurolophus* would have allowed the members of a large, sprawling herd to keep in contact, even if they could not see each other in the thick forest.

Noisy nesting

Scientists believe that another type of hadrosaur, *Maiasaura*, nested in colonies. Its babies might have spent several weeks in the nest before they were able to move and feed on their own. Perhaps *Parasaurolophus* also nested in colonies.

Today many birds, such as gulls and penguins, nest in large colonies. Sound is an important way for birds to communicate. Bird parents talk to their chicks using visual and sound signals.

Parasaurolophus parents might have used their hollow crests to communicate with their offspring. Sounds made by the young dinosaurs would have helped parents find their particular nest among perhaps hundreds of nests that made up the colony.

CHECK THESE OUT!

Cretaceous period, Eggs and babies, Hadrosaurs, *Maiasaura*, Ornithischian dinosaurs, *Tyrannosaurus*

DINOFACTS

Parasaurolophus
(par-ah-SORE-o-LOH-fus)

✳ **NAME:** *Parasaurolophus* means beside *Saurolophus*
    para (beside) + *Saurolophus* (the name of another hadrosaur)

◯ **FAMILY:** Ornithischian

Ornithopod

Hadrosaur

⊕ **SIZE:** 33 ft (10 m) long; 10 ft (3 m) high at the hip

⚖ **WEIGHT:** 2–3 tons (1.8–2.7 tonnes)—about the same as 2–3 North American bison

🥣 **FOOD:** plants

🏠 **HABITAT:** well-watered, lowland forests

⇧N **WHERE:** remains found in Alberta, Canada, and in Alaska

🕐 **WHEN:** 75-70 million years ago in the Cretaceous period

			PARASAUROLOPHUS
TRIASSIC	JURASSIC	CRETACEOUS	
250 MILLION YEARS AGO	205 MILLION YEARS AGO	135 MILLION YEARS AGO	65 MILLION YEARS AGO

Pelecanimimus

Pelecanimimus is the oldest ornithomimosaur (ostrichlike dinosaur) known at present. While most ostrichlike dinosaurs had no teeth, this one had more than any other theropod (two-legged meat-eater)!

In 1993, Spanish fossil-hunter Armando Díaz-Romeral and geologist Santiago Prieto found a small skeleton at Las Hoyas, Spain. The Early Cretaceous rocks at Las Hoyas were once the mud at the bottom of a lake. They have preserved remains of the animals that sank into its depths after they died, including insects, amphibians, fish, lizards, turtles, and early birds.

Pelican mimic

The Spanish scientists found the front half of a small theropod. From its skull, beak, neck bones, and hand (which had palm bones all the same length), they saw it was an ostrichlike dinosaur like *Ornithomimus*.

The fossil had a faint skin print around it, left when the body settled into the mud millions of years ago. From this print, it

▼ *Pelecanimimus* was an early ostrichlike dinosaur. Besides *Harpymimus*, it was the only kind of ornithomimosaur to have teeth.

PLENTY OF BITE

The teeth of *Pelecanimimus* remind scientists of the troodontids *Troodon* and *Sinornithoides*. Troodontids were small theropods (two-legged meat-eaters) with big brains and long legs. They probably ran fast and were clever. They also had lots of teeth: *Troodon* had 122 and *Sinornithoides* had 96. *Pelecanimimus* was one of the few ornithomimosaurs with teeth. Some paleontologists take this as evidence that troodontids and ostrichlike dinosaurs were closely related.

looked as if there was a small pouch beneath the dinosaur's throat, like that of a modern pelican. Because of this pouch, paleontologists called the fossil *Pelecanimimus*, or pelican mimic.

Most of the later ostrichlike dinosaurs had toothless beaks. Old *Harpymimus* still had its teeth, but the only fossil specimen yet discovered was in poor condition so its teeth were hard to study. Now we know *Pelecanimimus* had at least 200 tiny teeth, about twice as many as any other theropod!

How did *Pelecanimimus* live?
Long-legged *Pelecanimimus* might have stalked the shores of the ancient lake at Las Hoyas, snapping up fish and avoiding crocodiles.

CHECK THESE OUT!

Cretaceous period, *Harpymimus*, *Ornithomimus*, Saurischian dinosaurs, *Sinornithoides*, Theropods, *Troodon*

DINOFACTS

Pelecanimimus
(PEL-eh-CAN-ih-MY-mus)

✳ **NAME:** *Pelecanimimus* means pelican mimic
pelecanus (pelican) + mimos (mimic)

○ **FAMILY:** Saurischian
Theropod
Tetanuran

✛ **SIZE:** about 7 ft (2.1 m) long; about 3 ft (90 cm) high at the hip

WEIGHT: about 26 lbs (12 kg)—about the same as a small dog

FOOD: possibly meat, fish, or shellfish

HABITAT: forests and lake shores

WHERE: remains found in Spain

🕐 **WHEN:** 127–121 million years ago in the Cretaceous period

		PELECANIMIMUS	
TRIASSIC	JURASSIC		CRETACEOUS
250 MILLION YEARS AGO	205 MILLION YEARS AGO	135 MILLION YEARS AGO	65 MILLION YEARS AGO

297

Pentaceratops

During the Late Cretaceous period, a handful of mighty ceratopsians (horned dinosaurs) evolved with spectacular horns and frills on their heads. One of the biggest, heaviest, and frilliest was *Pentaceratops*.

Henry Fairfield Osborn of the American Museum of Natural History described *Pentaceratops* in 1923. He had studied a skull and skeleton found in New Mexico in 1922 by Canadian Charles H. Sternberg.

This was no ordinary skull. Fringed by a dozen or more small horns was a shield of a skull 8 ft (2.4 m) long. It was, and still is, one of the biggest skulls of any animal that walked the earth.

Horny head, chunky cheeks

The name *Pentaceratops* means five-horned face, but in truth this dinosaur had only three horns. The other two were its cheek bones. All types of ceratopsians (horned dinosaurs) had big cheek bones, but in *Pentaceratops* they were unusually large.

Another *Pentaceratops*?

In 1930, Swedish scientist Carl Wiman described a second specimen dug up by Sternberg. As did the first find, the second skull had two large windows in the frill that reduced the head weight. Wiman found an extra window; he thought it was one of a pair, and that the skull came from a new kind (species) of *Pentaceratops*.

▼ *Pentaceratops* was elephant-sized. Its skeleton was especially strong around the shoulder area to hold up its heavy head.

It turned out that the window was on one side of the frill only. It was probably a hole made by a horn thrust. There was only one kind of *Pentaceratops* after all.

In the 1970s, scientists in Colorado and New Mexico found some more *Pentaceratops* skulls with well-preserved frills. Each frill had a deep notch in the back edge surrounded by four large, bony spikes.

FIERCE AND FRILLY

Paleontologists divided the advanced (highly evolved) ceratopsians into two groups: short-frilled and long-frilled. You can guess which group included *Pentaceratops*! Other long-frilled types included *Triceratops* and *Torosaurus*. What was the purpose of such a big frill? It provided an anchorage for powerful jaw muscles—but other ceratopsians did just as well with shorter frills. Most scientists think that the frill, with its mighty size and distinctive shape, was used mostly for display. When *Pentaceratops* tilted its head down, the frill would stick up to its full height. Shaking its frill and bellowing, *Pentaceratops* would have been a terrifying sight.

Pentaceratops
(PEN-*tuh-SER-uh-tops*)

▶ *Pentaceratops*'s frill was even longer than the head section of its skull. When the dinosaur was alive, its head may have weighed as much as 1.5 tons (1.35 tonnes).

✳ NAME: *Pentaceratops* means five-horned face
pente (five) + keratos (horned) + ops (face)

○ FAMILY: Ornithischian

Ceratopsian

How did *Pentaceratops* live?

Like other horned dinosaurs, *Pentaceratops* had a toothless but sharp-edged beak at the front of its jaws. Farther back, it had rows of cheek teeth. *Pentaceratops* used its beak to crop mouthfuls of woody, low-growing plants. The upper cheek teeth sheared against the lower cheek teeth, working like scissors to chop the food into smaller portions.

Pentaceratops would have had very few enemies among its Late Cretaceous meat-eating neighbors. Even a big tyrannosaur like *Albertosaurus* would have probably steered clear of *Pentaceratops*.

⊕ SIZE: 25 ft (7.6 m) long; 7 ft (2.1 m) high at the hip

⚖ WEIGHT: 3–4 tons (2.7–3.6 tonnes)—about the same as an Asian elephant

🥣 FOOD: tough, low-growing plants

🏠 HABITAT: coastal floodplains

Ⓝ WHERE: remains found in New Mexico and Colorado

⊘ WHEN: 72–68 million years ago in the Cretaceous period

CHECK THESE OUT!

Albertosaurus, Ceratopsians, Cretaceous period, Ornithischian dinosaurs, *Torosaurus*, *Triceratops*

			PENTACERATOPS
TRIASSIC	JURASSIC	CRETACEOUS	
250 MILLION YEARS AGO	205 MILLION YEARS AGO	135 MILLION YEARS AGO	65 MILLION YEARS AGO

Pinacosaurus

Pinacosaurus was an ankylosaur (armored dinosaur) that lived in Asia in the Cretaceous period. Scientists have found evidence that the young *Pinacosaurus* may have lived together in family groups.

Paleontologist Walter Granger from the American Museum of Natural History found *Pinacosaurus* in southern Mongolia in the 1920s. However, the fossil's skull was badly crushed. In the 1960s Polish expeditions to Mongolia found better material. Paleontologist Teresa Maryanska found that, unlike other ankylosaurs, *Pinacosaurus*

SCUTELINGS!

Baby animals that have just hatched are known as hatchlings. Young birds that have grown their flight feathers are known as fledglings. Researchers at Southern Methodist University recently invented the term scuteling for baby ankylosaurs whose armor plates (scutes) were not fully grown.

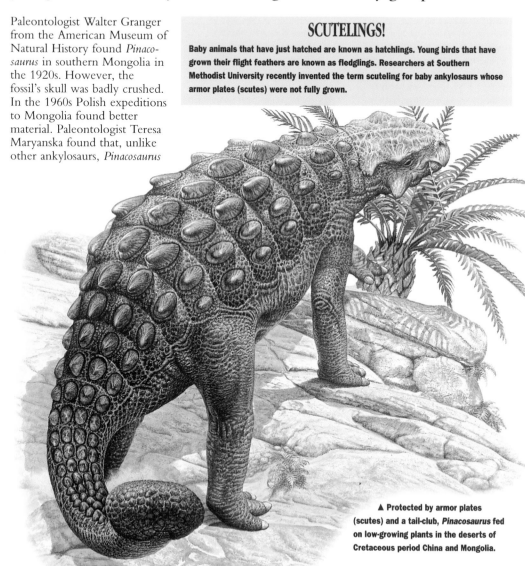

▲ Protected by armor plates (scutes) and a tail-club, *Pinacosaurus* fed on low-growing plants in the deserts of Cretaceous period China and Mongolia.

had slender legs. This suggests that *Pinacosaurus* may have been able to move faster.

The new fossils included the skull of a young *Pinacosaurus*. Since the bones are covered by armor in adult ankylosaurs, this enabled the skull bones of an ankylosaur to be described for the first time.

Family groups?
In recent years, scientists have found the remains of groups of up to 15 young *Pinacosaurus* all of the same age. Based on the size of the young ankylosaurs, this suggests that groups of *Pinacosaurus* hatchlings stayed together for a year or longer.

How did *Pinacosaurus* live?
Pinacosaurus lived along the edges of streams and ponds in desert habitats in Central Asia. It shared its habitat with another ankylosaur, *Saichania*. Like all ornithischians (bird-hipped dinosaurs), low-slung *Pinacosaurus* bit off vegetation with its leaf-shaped teeth.

The armor on an adult *Pinacosaurus* would have protected it from attacks by small theropods (two-legged meat-eaters) such as *Velociraptor*. However, it would have been in danger from large meat-eaters, such as *Tarbosaurus*. If *Pinacosaurus* was attacked, it may have defended itself with its bony tail-club.

CHECK THESE OUT!
Ankylosaurs, Cretaceous period, Ornithischian dinosaurs, *Saichania*, *Tarbosaurus*, *Velociraptor*

DINOFACTS

Pinacosaurus
(PIN-*nack-oh-SORE-us*)

▶ These two views of a young *Pinacosaurus* skull show the individual bones of the skull. In adult ankylosaurs the skull bones were fused together and covered with armor.

✳ NAME: *Pinacosaurus* means broad lizard
pinakos (broad) + sauros (lizard)

◯ FAMILY: Ornithischian
→ Thyreophoran
→ Ankylosaur

✥ SIZE: 15 ft (4.6 m) long; 3–4 ft (90 cm–1.2 m) high at the hip

⚖ WEIGHT: 1–1.5 tons (0.9–1.35 tonnes)—about the same as 1–2 bison

🍽 FOOD: plants

🏠 HABITAT: lowland desert

Ⓝ WHERE: remains found in northern China and southern Mongolia

🕐 WHEN: 80–75 million years ago in the Cretaceous period

			PINACOSAURUS
TRIASSIC	JURASSIC	CRETACEOUS	
250 MILLION YEARS AGO	205 MILLION YEARS AGO	135 MILLION YEARS AGO	65 MILLION YEARS AGO

Pisanosaurus

The Late Triassic rocks of northwestern Argentina have produced many important fossils of dinosaurs and other extinct animals. One of the most important dinosaurs is *Pisanosaurus*.

Pisanosaurus may be the earliest known ornithischian (bird-hipped) dinosaur. It may also be the earliest known ornithopod (bird-footed) dinosaur. Scientists are still unsure because the fossil remains of *Pisanosaurus* are incomplete.

Argentinian paleontologist José Bonaparte studied *Pisanosaurus* in 1976. He had an almost complete right leg, a set of neck bones, the first half of the backbone, part of the pelvis (hipbones), the right side of the lower jaw (with teeth), and a toothed piece of the right upper jaw. From these remains, it was clear that the left side of the skeleton had been worn away by wind and rain long before the paleontologists discovered it.

The hips decide

Scientists divide dinosaurs into one of two groups based on the positions of their hipbones: the saurischians (lizard-hipped dinosaurs) or the ornithischians. Unfortunately, the preserved hipbones

▶ *Pisanosaurus* was an early plant-eating dinosaur, but was it an ornithischian or only an ancestor of the ornithischians?

ORNITHISCHIAN OR NOT?

The broken bits and pieces that make up the remains of *Pisanosaurus* are both good news and bad news for people studying dinosaurs. The good news is that we know that the first plant-eating dinosaurs were alive at the same time as the first meat-eating dinosaurs, *Herrerasaurus* and *Eoraptor*. It is thought that the animals that were the ancestors of dinosaurs were strictly meat-eaters. Finding the jaws and teeth of *Pisanosaurus* tells us that one group of dinosaurs very quickly evolved the teeth and jaws needed to be able to eat plants.

The bad news is that *Pisanosaurus*'s skeleton is not as well preserved as scientists would like. There are doubts about whether it was a true ornithischian. Perhaps *Pisanosaurus* was an ancestor of the true ornithischians. We will have to wait for more complete fossils of *Pisanosaurus* to be discovered to really know.

of *Pisanosaurus* are not really complete enough to say for certain that it really was an ornithischian. However, other features of the skeleton also suggest that *Pisanosaurus* was an ornithischian and maybe even an ornithopod.

Pisanosaurus had typical plant-eater's teeth. *Pisanosaurus*'s lower jaw was shaped a bit like that of another early plant-eating dinosaur, the ornithopod *Hypsilophodon* from England. It is the teeth and jaw that have convinced most, but not all, paleontologists that *Pisanosaurus* was almost certainly an ornithischian dinosaur. However, until an entire fossil pelvis of *Pisanosaurus* is discovered, scientists cannot be sure.

How did it live?

If it was an ornithischian, *Pisanosaurus* probably lived in small herds, quietly feeding on plants. Its teeth show signs of wear that suggest they clamped together as the dinosaur bit off leaves and shoots. By studying the fine-grained rock in which its bones were found, scientists can tell that *Pisanosaurus* probably lived near slow-moving rivers or deltas.

CHECK THESE OUT!

Eoraptor, Herrerasaurus, Hypsilophodon, Ornithischian dinosaurs, Ornithopods, Saurischian dinosaurs, Triassic period

DINOFACTS

Pisanosaurus
(pizz-AH-no-SORE-us)

✳ **NAME:** *Pisanosaurus* means Pisano's lizard
Pisano (person's name) + sauros (lizard)

○ **FAMILY:** Ornithischian

✛ **SIZE:** 3 ft (90 cm) long; 1 ft (30 cm) high at the hip

WEIGHT: 5 lbs (2.3 kg)—about the same as a house cat

FOOD: plants

HABITAT: well-watered lowland areas

N
↑ **WHERE:** remains found in Argentina

🕐 **WHEN:** 230-220 million years ago in the Triassic period

PISANOSAURUS		
TRIASSIC	JURASSIC	CRETACEOUS
250 MILLION YEARS AGO	205 MILLION YEARS AGO	135 MILLION YEARS AGO	65 MILLION YEARS AGO

Plateosaurus

Early in the 20th century, many skeletons of a long-necked, small-headed dinosaur were found in southwestern Germany. These were skeletons of *Plateosaurus*, the earliest of the large dinosaurs.

At the time of the German discoveries, scientists thought that *Plateosaurus* must have lived in hot, dry areas that went for long periods without rain. Fossil-hunters had found many dinosaurs together, so German paleontologist Friedrich Freiherr von Huene thought that a great drought might have caused so many animals to die at the same time. He imagined herds of *Plateosaurus* dying of thirst while searching for water.

A closer look

Did a herd die of thirst 200 million years ago, or is there a different explanation? During the last 20 years of the 20th century scientists carefully studied the rocks in which *Plateosaurus* was buried.

They found that the skeletons had decomposed to different degrees, indicating that the animals had died at different times. Their bodies just happened to collect together after death.

A very early dinosaur

Plateosaurus was one of the earliest dinosaurs to be described by scientists. The first remains of *Plateosaurus* were discovered in 1837.

▼ *Plateosaurus* had a long, flexible neck that enabled it to reach leaves high up in trees. Its long tail would help it to balance when it stood up on its back legs.

The discoveries of many more skeletons of *Plateosaurus* from quarries around southern Germany during the years between 1911 and 1932 gave paleontologists a much better idea of what *Plateosaurus* was like as a living animal.

Plateosaurus was a prosauropod, an ancestor of the giant long-necked, long-tailed sauropods of the Jurassic and Cretaceous periods. *Plateosaurus* was one of the largest prosauropods. It was bigger than China's *Lufengosaurus* and Arizona's *Massospondylus*, but not as big as Argentina's *Riojasaurus*.

Leaf-shaped teeth

Plateosaurus's teeth and jaws tell us that it ate plants. The teeth are leaf shaped with jagged (serrated) edges. These teeth let *Plateosaurus* cut and rip off large mouthfuls of coarse vegetation. However, they would not have been used for chewing food. They were the wrong shape.

Also, to chew its food, an animal needs fleshy cheeks; if an animal had cheeks the skull usually has slight hollows on the outside of the face beside the teeth. Because there is no evidence of these hollows on *Plateosaurus* skulls, paleontologists believe that *Plateosaurus* did not have fleshy cheeks. These two pieces of evidence (roughly serrated teeth and the lack of hollows on the side of the face) tell us that *Plateosaurus* did not chew its food.

Grabbing jaw

If you held the skull and jaw of *Plateosaurus* level with the ground, the jaw joint would lie below the level of the teeth. This is thought to be an

HERDS OF DINOSAURS

When scientists first studied dinosaurs, they realized that they were related to lizards and crocodiles (and later to birds). Lizards and crocodiles were usually thought of as solitary animals, and so were dinosaurs. New studies of dinosaurs, lizards, and crocodiles show that these animals can live in groups, and sometimes even act like mammals that live in herds.

Young crocodiles tend to stay in groups for several days or weeks after hatching. Mother crocodiles keep an eye on their babies to prevent other animals—even other crocodiles—from eating the young ones. Young lizards have also been seen to stay in close groups after hatching. With this new knowledge of how living animals behave, scientists can look at dinosaurs in a new way.

Prosauropods like *Plateosaurus*, hadrosaurs (duckbills) like *Maiasaura*, ceratopsians (horned dinosaurs) like *Centrosaurus*, and some ceratosaurs (four-fingered meat-eaters) are now thought to have spent at least part of their lives living in groups. Plant-eaters, like hadrosaurs, are said to live in herds, while meat-eaters, like the ceratosaurs, are said to live in packs. Herds act as a group to defend themselves against attacks by predators. Packs work as a group to attack larger animals or herds. Of course, many modern dinosaur species (birds) live in groups, or flocks.

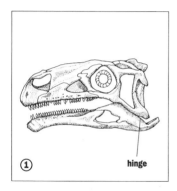

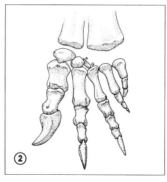

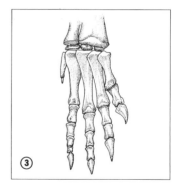

①   **hinge**

②

③

adaptation that let the teeth of the lower jaw move backward as the upper and lower jaws came together. Think about how scissors work. When the scissors are open, the two blades are apart. As soon as the scissor handles are pressed together, the blades begin to meet. As the handles close, the meeting point of the blades moves out toward the tip until the blades are closed.

If the jaws of *Plateosaurus* worked like a pair of scissors, as the animal closed its mouth, and the jaws began to meet, its food would be pushed forward, and out of its mouth. Scientists think the position of the jaw joint evolved so that *Plateosaurus*'s jaw held food firm in its mouth, instead of pushing it out.

A grinding digestion?

If *Plateosaurus*'s mouth and teeth were modified to help it gather food, how did it digest the food? *Plateosaurus* had a

▶ Paleontologists believe that *Plateosaurus* may have lived in herds like zebras and wildebeest do today. Living in a herd protects the animals from predators.

large, barrel-shaped body to house its big stomach and very long intestines. It may also have swallowed stones to help grind its food.

Many living birds swallow sand and gravel to help them grind up seeds and other tough food. Birds have a muscular bag known as the crop (or gizzard) at the front end of their stomachs. Food is swallowed, then ground up small in the crop with gravel.

If *Plateosaurus* did have a crop, paleontologists should someday find small stones in a fossil *Plateosaurus* gizzard.

▲ *Plateosaurus*'s jaws (1) were hinged at a lower level than its teeth to help the animal to eat. *Plateosaurus*'s hand (2) was very flexible—it could be used both for grabbing food and for walking. The foot (3) was very large, making it strong enough for the dinosaur to stand up on its back legs.

Plateosaurus had a specially adapted hand. The thumb bones were large and probably very strong. The thumb claw is especially big. *Plateosaurus* could have used it to pull down vegetation, or as a weapon. As the hand was very flexible, the food-gathering idea seems the most likely.

Plateosaurus also had a long, flexible neck and a small head. With a light head on the end of a slender neck, *Plateosaurus* would have been able to move its head very easily to put food in its mouth. The modified thumb and the mobile neck seem to have evolved together to let *Plateosaurus* feed easily.

Walking on all fours

With a thumb and hand so specialized for feeding, how could *Plateosaurus* have walked on all fours? It has been suggested that *Plateosaurus* could walk only on its back legs. The problem with this idea is that *Plateosaurus*'s body was quite bulky. It seems likely that the animal would always have tipped forward if it had tried to walk on its back legs.

Careful study of the fingers of *Plateosaurus*'s hand showed that they could bend back much further than those of other dinosaurs. This means that *Plateosaurus* could have easily walked on all fours, and its weight would have been carried much more easily by all four limbs.

How did *Plateosaurus* live?

It seems most likely that *Plateosaurus* lived in herds like many other plant-eaters. By itself, *Plateosaurus* did not have any special defenses against attacks by predators. However, in a large herd, life becomes a bit safer.

These herds of *Plateosaurus* would have wandered across the landscape, quietly feeding on any vegetation they could find. The long neck, and the ability to stand up on their back legs, would have enabled *Plateosaurus* to feed both on low-growing plants and on leaves and shoots growing high up in tall trees.

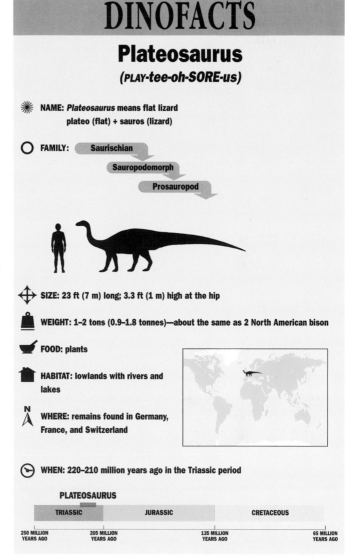

DINOFACTS

Plateosaurus
(PLAY-*tee-oh-SORE-us*)

☀ **NAME:** *Plateosaurus* means flat lizard
plateo (flat) + sauros (lizard)

○ **FAMILY:** Saurischian
Sauropodomorph
Prosauropod

✛ **SIZE:** 23 ft (7 m) long; 3.3 ft (1 m) high at the hip

⚖ **WEIGHT:** 1–2 tons (0.9–1.8 tonnes)—about the same as 2 North American bison

🥣 **FOOD:** plants

🏠 **HABITAT:** lowlands with rivers and lakes

🧭 **WHERE:** remains found in Germany, France, and Switzerland

🕑 **WHEN:** 220–210 million years ago in the Triassic period

PLATEOSAURUS

	TRIASSIC	JURASSIC	CRETACEOUS
	250 MILLION YEARS AGO	205 MILLION YEARS AGO	135 MILLION YEARS AGO	65 MILLION YEARS AGO

CHECK THESE OUT!

Ceratopsians, Ceratosaurs, Hadrosaurs, Prosauropods, Saurischian dinosaurs, Sauropods, Triassic period

Plesiosaurs, pliosaurs, and nothosaurs

Plesiosaurs, pliosaurs, and nothosaurs were not dinosaurs but meat-eating reptiles that lived in the sea at the same time as the dinosaurs lived on land.

The seas of the Mesozoic Era were full of many large, fast, dangerous hunters. Some of these fierce creatures were the large marine reptiles called plesiosaurs, pliosaurs, and nothosaurs. They prowled both the deep oceans and the shallower, coastal waters.

These reptiles were all meat-eaters with large mouths filled with sharp teeth. Along with the ichthyosaurs (fish lizards) and large sharks, the fiercest predators of the seas were the pliosaurs. The largest pliosaurs even hunted other predators like ichthyosaurs and sharks. One pliosaur fossil was found with some remains of a stego-saur (plate-backed dinosaur) inside it! The stegosaur must have died and floated out to sea, where it became food for a hungry pliosaur.

Nothosaurs—first in the sea
The nothosaurs first appeared in the Middle Triassic period, about 240 million years ago. Nothosaurs had bodies like those of large, fat lizards, but with the tail slightly flattened at the sides. The limbs of some nothosaurs had evolved into paddles; others probably had webbed feet. Nothosaurs would have swum by paddling with their front and back legs, and by weaving their bodies from side to side. Their flattened tails would have made swimming easier—the flat sides would have pushed against the water like a paddle blade. Sea snakes today also have flattened tails that help them to swim.

Nothosaurs had longer necks than lizards. This would have helped them catch fish, by letting their heads move about

easily. Nothosaurs would have grabbed fish and squid with their toothy jaws.

Lizard cousins?

The relationship between the nothosaurs and other reptiles is not clear. Most scientists think nothosaurs are related to lepidosaurs, the group that includes the lizards and snakes as well as other marine reptiles such as ichthyosaurs. The nothosaurs were a successful and widespread group, and their remains are found in Europe and Asia. Many different kinds evolved, from 8 in (20 cm) to 13 ft (4 m) in length. Nothosaurs died out in the Late Triassic period.

Most paleontologists think that the nothosaurs were the ancestors of the plesiosaurs and

◀ *Kronosaurus* (1), from Australia, was the largest known pliosaur. Its head was nearly 8 ft (2.4 m) long. The plesiosaur *Cryptocleidus* (2), from England, could be 20 ft (6 m) long.

pliosaurs. However, they are not sure what were the ancestors of the nothosaurs.

Plesiosaurs and pliosaurs

The best fossils of plesiosaurs and pliosaurs come from rocks of the Early Jurassic period (about 200 million years ago) in southern England and western Europe.

Plesiosaurs had long necks and small heads, while pliosaurs had short necks and big heads. These two different body shapes show the very different ways of life of these two groups of animals.

Fish snatchers

The long-necked plesiosaurs probably hunted small fish and squid. They would have quietly paddled along near the surface of the sea, watching for prey to swim within range.

They probably held their long necks in an S-shape while hunting. When some food swam within range, a plesiosaur would have straightened its neck very rapidly, almost throwing its head at its prey like a spear.

The small, light head would have moved as quickly as a rattlesnake striking. Thin, sharp teeth in the plesiosaur's mouth would have made sure that the slipperiest fish or squid had no chance of escape.

▼ The relationship between nothosaurs, plesiosaurs, and pliosaurs and other reptiles is far from clear. Paleontologists know that they were definitely not dinosaurs, which belong to the archosaurs.

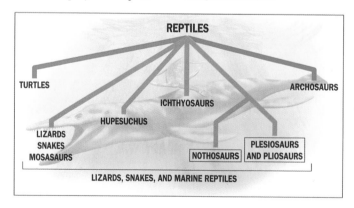

REPTILES

TURTLES

ICHTHYOSAURS

ARCHOSAURS

HUPESUCHUS

LIZARDS
SNAKES
MOSASAURS

NOTHOSAURS

PLESIOSAURS
AND PLIOSAURS

LIZARDS, SNAKES, AND MARINE REPTILES

In Late Cretaceous times, some plesiosaurs had extremely long necks. *Elasmosaurus* had 76 bones in its neck. Humans and all other mammals (even giraffes) have only seven bones in their necks.

Bite and twist

The short-necked pliosaurs fed in a totally different way. Besides their short, strong necks, they had very long, wide, flat skulls. *Liopleurodon,* from the Late Jurassic period, had a skull 9 ft (2.7 m) long on a body 36 ft (11 m) long.

Recent studies by Scottish paleontologist Michael Taylor have shown that the skull and jaws of *Liopleurodon* were specially adapted to resist twisting forces. *Liopleurodon* had teeth only at the front of its mouth. These teeth stuck out pointing forward. The teeth were very strong with deep roots, and the two halves

EGGS AT SEA?

Plesiosaurs, pliosaurs, and nothosaurs had become so adapted to life in the seas that their bodies and skeletons were very different from those of their ancestors. As relatives of lizards, snakes, and turtles, the plesiosaurs, pliosaurs, and nothosaurs are members of the same group of egg-laying animals—the amniotes. If plesiosaurs, pliosaurs, and nothosaurs had become so adapted to an aquatic life, how did they lay their eggs? Or did they lay eggs?

We know from fossils that ichthyosaurs gave birth to live young. The mother held the eggs in her body until they had developed. Modern sea snakes also give birth to live young. What did plesiosaurs, pliosaurs, and nothosaurs do?

The nothosaurs were not as completely adapted for life in water as the later plesiosaurs and pliosaurs. Female nothosaurs probably came ashore, like modern sea turtles, to lay eggs. From looking at their skeletons, we know that the more evolved plesiosaurs and pliosaurs do not appear to have been able to move much on land. Could a long-necked plesiosaur have held its head up when it was out of the water? Could a big, bulky female pliosaur, with a huge, heavy head, have been able to move up a beach to lay eggs above the high tide mark? We will have to wait for more fossil evidence before we can answer these questions.

of the lower jaw were very strongly attached to each other.

Liopleurodon probably fed by grabbing hold of its prey with these front teeth and then rolling its own body sideways. This rolling motion would have twisted large chunks of flesh from its prey. Some modern sharks feed in the same way as *Liopleurodon*, tearing away lumps of flesh.

Underwater swimming

To chase their fast-swimming prey, the plesiosaurs and pliosaurs were also excellent swimmers. Instead of the webbed feet and lightly built paddles of the nothosaurs, the plesiosaurs and pliosaurs had developed strong paddles.

The animals would have moved their paddles up and down like underwater wings. These paddles had the same shape as an airplane wing, which meant that pliosaurs and plesiosaurs would have moved as quickly and easily as if they were flying through the water. The paddles were strengthened by extra bones in the animals' fingers and toes. Some of the plesiosaurs and pliosaurs also evolved extra fingers and toes. These extra bones would have made the paddles very stiff and strong. Plesiosaurs and pliosaurs died out in the Late Cretaceous period, 65 million years ago.

CHECK THESE OUT!
Cretaceous period, Eggs and babies, Fish, Ichthyosaurs, Jurassic period, Lizards and snakes, Reptiles, Sharks, Shellfish, Triassic period, Turtles

FOSSIL FACTS

Plesiosaurs, pliosaurs, and nothosaurs
(PLEE-see-oh-SORES, PLY-oh-SORES, and NO-tho-SORES)

▶ Plesiosaur skulls had a flattened shape and large eye sockets. The jaws contained a single row of sharp, forward-pointing teeth on each side.

✸ NAME: Plesiosaur means near lizard—plesio (near) + sauros (lizard)
Pliosaur means more lizard—plion (more) + sauros (lizard)
Nothosaur means spurious lizard—nothos (spurious) + sauros (lizard)

○ FAMILY: Reptile

✥ SIZE: huge variation from 8 in (20 cm) to 36 ft (11 m) long

🥣 FOOD: plesiosaurs and nothosaurs—fish and squid; pliosaurs—fish, ichthyosaurs and other marine reptiles, dead dinosaurs floating out to sea

🏠 HABITAT: shallow and deep sea water

N↑ WHERE: remains found worldwide

🕐 WHEN: nothosaurs—240–208 million years ago in the Triassic period; plesiosaurs and pliosaurs—200 million years ago in the Jurassic period to 65 million years ago in the Cretaceous period

NOTHOSAURS	PLESIOSAURS AND PLIOSAURS		
TRIASSIC	JURASSIC		CRETACEOUS
250 MILLION YEARS AGO	205 MILLION YEARS AGO	135 MILLION YEARS AGO	65 MILLION YEARS AGO

Polacanthus

Polacanthus was an ankylosaur (armored dinosaur) that lived in England in the Early Cretaceous period. Recent discoveries suggest that another kind of *Polacanthus* lived in North America.

William Fox collected the first fossil of *Polacanthus* in 1865 in southern England. Because of its fused shell, Fox first thought he had discovered a kind of turtle. When British paleontologist James Hulke described the fossil in 1880, he recognized it was an ankylosaur and named it *Polacanthus foxii* in honor of William Fox.

Conflicting features

There are two main groups of ankylosaurs. Ankylosaurids (named for *Ankylosaurus*) had

NODOSAURID OR ANKYLOSAURID?

In the 1990s, Colorado paleontologist James Kirkland and his colleagues uncovered several skeletons of a new type of ankylosaur in the Cedar Mountain Formation in eastern Utah. This ankylosaur is nearly the same age as, and closely related to, *Polacanthus*. It has a shield of armor plates fused together over its hips like *Polacanthus* and the same sort of armor on its shoulders and tail. The dinosaurs differ mainly in the leg and hip bones. The new ankylosaur specimens have not only upright shoulder spines, but also a row of spines sticking out sideways from their shoulders. The triangular plates on the tail also stuck out sideways and not upward. Most importantly, several skulls were preserved showing that the skull of this animal was most like that of an ankylosaurid, while its body was more like that of a nodosaurid.

Scientists classify animals to chart the evolution of life. Both *Polacanthus* and the new ankylosaur fascinate paleontologists because they may redefine what makes a nodosaurid or an ankylosaurid. This is as exciting as relating humans to primates.

▶ *Polacanthus* (many spines) was well named as it was the spiniest of all the armored dinosaurs. Its tail had two rows of sharp triangular armor plates.

no back spines but had bony clubs at the ends of their tails. Nodosaurids (named for *Nodosaurus*) had back spines but no tail-clubs.

Polacanthus puzzles paleontologists because it combines features of both sorts of ankylosaurs. Like most nodosaurids, *Polacanthus* had spines on its back and sides, and the armor plates above its hips were fused together. However, like all ankylosaurids, *Polacanthus* had a bony tail-club. Some paleontologists think *Polacanthus* might represent another, third, group of ankylosaurs.

How did *Polacanthus* live?
Like all ornithischians (bird-hipped dinosaurs), *Polacanthus* ate plants. Its tiny teeth and low-held head suggest that it fed on soft, low-lying plants.

Because *Polacanthus* had short legs, it probably moved fairly slowly. Its long spines would have protected the dinosaur against attack by even the largest predators. Its tail, with armor plates and a club, would have been a dangerous weapon when swung from side to side.

CHECK THESE OUT!

Ankylosaurs, *Ankylosaurus*,
Cretaceous period, *Nodosaurus*,
Ornithischian dinosaurs, Thyreophorans

DINOFACTS

Polacanthus
(*POH-luh-KAN-thus*)

▶ Over its hips, *Polacanthus* had a shield formed of numerous bony armor plates fused together.

shield of fused armor plates

✳ **NAME:** *Polacanthus* means many spines
poly (many) + akantha (spine)

○ **FAMILY:**   Ornithischian

Thyreophoran

Ankylosaur

✛ **SIZE:** 16 ft (5 m) long; 4 ft (1.2 m) high at the hip

⚖ **WEIGHT:** 1.5 tons (1.4 tonnes)—about the same as 1–2 North American bison

🥄 **FOOD:** low-growing plants

🏠 **HABITAT:** lowlands

ᴺ↑ **WHERE:** remains found in southern England and possibly in Utah

🕐 **WHEN:** 125–120 million years ago in the Cretaceous period

POLACANTHUS

TRIASSIC	JURASSIC	CRETACEOUS
250 MILLION YEARS AGO	205 MILLION YEARS AGO	135 MILLION YEARS AGO	65 MILLION YEARS AGO

Prosauropods

Prosauropods were a group of long-necked plant-eating dinosaurs that were probably the ancestors of the gigantic sauropods. Unlike the sauropods, some prosauropods may have walked on two legs.

The prosauropods are a rather neglected group of dinosaurs. They first appeared near the end of the Triassic period, and their remains are extremely common in rocks from the Late Triassic and Early Jurassic periods. During the Triassic period, prosauropods spread all over the world, and their remains have been found on every continent, including Antarctica. Few paleontologists have studied prosauropods in detail, though, so many aspects of this group's biology and evolution are still unknown.

EATEN INTO EXTINCTION?

Although prosauropods were a very widespread group of animals, they all became extinct in the Jurassic period. Paleontologists do not really know why they became extinct, although several ideas have been suggested.

One of these ideas concerns changes in the types of plants that lived alongside the prosauropods. Perhaps the plants which prosauropods could eat became extinct. Other paleontologists think that changes in the weather may have contributed to their decline. Perhaps it became too dry or too warm for them to survive.

Some paleontologists have suggested that prosauropods suffered when the sauropod dinosaurs appeared at the beginning of the Jurassic period. Like prosauropods, sauropods fed mainly on plants. However, the sauropods were much bigger than the prosauropods, so they would have been able to reach higher vegetation. All in all, sauropods seem to have been better at collecting and eating plants than prosauropods. It is difficult to choose between these ideas, and paleontologists need to find more evidence before the reason for prosauropod extinction becomes clear.

Riojasaurus

▲ Prosauropods varied in size. Some like *Riojasaurus* were very large, while others like *Anchisaurus* were fairly small. All were the same basic shape, though.

Anchisaurus

First discovery

The earliest discoveries of prosauropods were made in the 19th century. These finds were often very fragmentary, and it was not clear from which sort of animal the remains came. Some bones found in Connecticut in 1818 were initially thought to be human, although they are now known to belong to the Early Jurassic prosauropod *Anchisaurus*.

The first prosauropod to be named was *Thecodontosaurus*. Henry Riley and Samuel Stutchbury discovered its remains in England in 1836. The specimens included a piece of jaw and other bones from the skeleton, and they could see that *Thecodontosaurus* was a reptile, but it was not clear to which group of reptiles it belonged. It was many years before enough remains of

▲ A gerenuk, a kind of antelope, stands on its hind legs to feed. Could prosauropods do the same? Some scientists think so.

Thecodontosaurus were found to figure out that it was a prosauropod dinosaur.

Better finds were to come: a few years later many complete prosauropod skeletons were found in Europe and North America. Further exploration in the 20th century brought many more skeletons to light in other regions of the world.

Sauropod similarity

There were about 15 different kinds of prosauropods and they all looked rather similar to each other. All prosauropods had very long necks with small heads, large, barrel-like bodies, and extremely long tails.

In terms of shape, prosauropods bear a strong similarity to the sauropod dinosaurs, and it is thought that these two groups may have been closely related. Many paleontologists

have suggested that the prosauropods may have been the ancestors of the sauropods.

Prosauropods ranged in size from fairly small animals, like *Thecodontosaurus,* which was about 8 ft (2.4 m) long, to *Riojasaurus,* which could be as much as 33 ft (10 m) in length. Although 33 ft is not large by dinosaur standards, the prosauropods were the largest land animals until the sauropods appeared at the beginning of the Jurassic period.

How did prosauropods live?

Prosauropod teeth are leaf-shaped, much like the teeth of iguanas. Iguanas eat mostly plants, so it seems likely that the prosauropods may have eaten plants too.

The jaws of prosauropods were rather weak and their teeth did not have the broad grinding surfaces seen on the teeth of animals that spend a long time chewing their food. This, and their lack of fleshy cheeks, suggest that prosauropods could not chew their food particularly well.

Grinding stones

Some prosauropod skeletons have been found with small clumps of pebbles near the animals' stomach. Birds and crocodiles swallow stones to help grind up their food, so paleontologists have suggested that prosauropods also had stomach stones (called gastroliths) to help grind up plant food.

▲ Prosauropod teeth were similar in shape to iguana teeth—spiky with no flat surfaces for grinding up plant food.

Standing tall

The prosauropods' long necks would have let them reach food high in trees that shorter animals could not reach. Some large prosauropods, such as *Plateosaurus,* would have been able to reach branches 10–13 ft (3–4 m) above the ground. Prosauropods could also move their necks from side to side, so they could reach lots of different plants even when standing still.

Some prosauropods may have been able to reach even higher branches by standing on their back legs, using their long tails as a prop.

Walking tall

Paleontologists disagree on how much time prosauropods could have spent walking on their back legs. Some paleontologists think that prosauropods could only rear up on their back legs for very short of periods of time, just long enough to grab a quick mouthful from a tree.

Others think that prosauropods were capable of walking on their back legs all the time, resting on all fours only occasionally. However, you could not guess the range of circus tricks an elephant can do just by studying its skeleton. Thus, until we find prosauropod trackways, it is impossible to be certain.

Handy claw

Prosauropods have very unusual hands. The thumb had a massive claw which could be moved in a number of different ways.

When the hand was on the ground, during walking for example, the thumb could be held clear of the ground so that the claw did not get caught in any plants or in the soft earth.

When a prosauropod reared up on its back legs, the hand would be free for other uses. The large claw may have been used as a weapon to defend against predatory meat-eaters. The claw could also have been used to dig for water or food, much like anteaters do today.

Big thumb

The relative sizes of pro-sauropod fingers are also unusual. In most dinosaurs, the third finger is the longest, while the thumb and the other fingers are much shorter. In prosauropods, the thumb is much larger than the other fingers, a feature not seen in any other dinosaur group.

DINOFACTS

Prosauropods
(PRO-SORE-oh-pods)

✳ **NAME:** Prosauropod means before lizard feet
pro (before) + sauros (lizard) + pous (foot)

○ **FAMILY:** Saurischian
Sauropodomorph

✛ **SIZE:** 8–33 ft (2.4–10 m) long; 3–6 ft (90 cm–1.8 m) high at the hip

WEIGHT: wide variation from 60 lbs (27 kg) to 4 tons (3.6 tonnes)

FOOD: plants

HABITAT: varied, from very dry regions, such as deserts, to well-watered areas near lakes and rivers

WHERE: remains found worldwide

🕑 **WHEN:** from about 230 million years ago in the Triassic period to about 180 million years ago in the Jurassic period

PROSAUROPODS

TRIASSIC	JURASSIC	CRETACEOUS
250 MILLION YEARS AGO	205 MILLION YEARS AGO	135 MILLION YEARS AGO · 65 MILLION YEARS AGO

CHECK THESE OUT!
Anchisaurus, Lufengosaurus, Massospondylus, Mussaurus, Plateosaurus, Riojasaurus, Saurischian dinosaurs, Thecodontosaurus

Protoceratops

Protoceratops was a ceratopsian (horned dinosaur) that lived in Asia in the Cretaceous period. More complete fossils of *Protoceratops*, from hatchlings to adults, have been found than of any other dinosaur.

One of the most famous stories about the American Museum of Natural History's (AMNH) Central Asiatic Expeditions concerns the first discovery of *Protoceratops*.

In 1922, deep in the heart of the Gobi Desert in Mongolia, the expedition stopped along an old caravan route to ask directions. The expedition photographer, J. B. Shackelford, wandered off to inspect some red rocks he had seen to the northwest. He stumbled upon a mass of white fossil bone resting on a tower of red sandstone.

Expedition paleontologist Walter Granger identified it as the skull of a reptile. However, it was not until later in New York that he realized that the skull belonged to a ceratopsian dinosaur. In 1923, the skull was described by Granger and William King Gregory, and named *Protoceratops andrewsi* for the expedition's leader Roy Chapman Andrews.

A fossil bonanza

The beautiful red cliffs of the Djadochta Formation at Bayn Dzak were called the Flaming Cliffs by the expedition, a

PROTOCERATOPS EGGS?

The discovery of dinosaur eggs by Walter Granger at the Flaming Cliffs was the high point of the entire Central Asiatic Expedition. The paleontologists assumed that the eggs belonged to the most common dinosaur in the area, *Protoceratops*. Roy Chapman Andrews and others claimed that bones of an unhatched dinosaur found in the eggs could be identified as belonging to *Protoceratops*. However, the eggs seemed too big to have been laid by a small ornithischian dinosaur like *Protoceratops*, and later studies showed that this identification could not be proved.

In 1991, the Russian paleontologist Konstantin Mikhailov reported that the structure of the eggshells was like that of theropods (two-legged meat-eating dinosaurs), very different from that of ornithischian dinosaurs. Mikhailov identified some smaller eggs as having a structure like that of ornithischian dinosaur eggs. He suggested that these smaller eggs might belong to *Protoceratops*.

Mikhailov's idea gained support in 1993 when the AMNH found an egg of the type found in the 1920s containing an unhatched dinosaur—which turned out to be an *Oviraptor*. So far no eggs have been found that preserve unhatched *Protoceratops*, so it is still impossible to identify *Protoceratops* eggs with any certainty. In 1995, a joint Japanese-Mongolian expedition recovered more than a dozen well-preserved *Protoceratops* hatchlings, but no eggshell fragments were found.

name that would become famous in paleontology. More than 70 skulls and skeletons of *Protoceratops* were found as well as many other fossils including the ankylosaur (armored dinosaur) *Pinacosaurus,* the dromaeosaur (clawed meat-eater) *Velociraptor,* the troodontid (big-eyed brainy hunter) *Saurornithoides,* the egg-thief dinosaur *Oviraptor,* the avialan (bird relative) *Mononykus,* lizards, and the best-preserved Mesozoic mammals ever found.

Stages of growth

Fossil skeletons of *Protoceratops* from hatchlings to adults were found in the Flaming Cliffs. A series of skulls showing how they grew is a highlight of the dinosaur exhibits at the AMNH in New York.

Many specimens of *Protoceratops* have been found perfectly preserved standing with their bodies angled upward so that their beaks point up and their tails point down. These "tail standers" are thought to have been buried alive by collapsing sand dunes and died as they tried to dig their way out.

Protoceratops was a lightly built dinosaur. Its forelegs were much shorter than its hind legs. However, with its large skull making up a quarter of its

▲ *Protoceratops* was a small, primitive (little evolved) ceratopsian. It had a beak and a neck frill, but it had only bumplike horns on its nose and above its eyes.

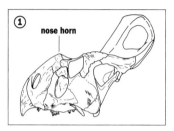

nose horn

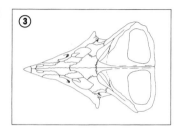

length, it would have walked on all four legs. Its head would have been too heavy for it to walk on two legs.

Its skull was roughly triangular in shape with a beak at the front like all ceratopsians. The skull widened into a broad frill at the back. Its cheeks flared into long points capped with bumplike horns. Some large individuals had a low horn on their snout. *Protoceratops*'s tail made up about half of its total length.

Protoceratops frills
Some paleontologists believe that *Protoceratops*'s frill evolved to protect the animal's neck and shoulders. However, the bone making up the frill was very thin, and the frill had several large openings (windows), so it would not have been very protective.

Some scientists have suggested that powerful jaw muscles attached to the frill through the openings in its base. The muscles then extended across the frill, strengthening it rather like strings strengthen a tennis racket. The jaw muscles are arranged like this in the skulls of the primitive (little evolved) ceratopsians *Psittacosaurus* and *Leptoceratops*.

This arrangement would suggest that *Protoceratops* had a long and powerful set of jaw muscles that gave the animal a very powerful bite.

In 1990, paleontologists Peter Dodson and Phil Currie expressed doubt that long jaw muscles would be stronger than short muscles. They noted that the opening at the base of the frill for the jaw muscles was quite small in most ceratopsians. Also, the frill bones of many ceratopsians were covered with heavy scales. These two things would have limited the area where muscles could attach. Scientists are still not sure how far *Protoceratops*'s jaw muscles ran up its frill.

Male vs. female
Protoceratops may have used its frill to display to others of its kind. In 1977, Australian paleontologist Ralph Molnar suggested that if this were true, then evolution would have led to fancier frills, and also to differences between male and female frills. Scientists believe that they have evidence of differences between male and female *Protoceratops*.

Differences between males and females in size, shape, and coloring are common today

▲ Paleontologists believe they can tell the difference between male and female *Protoceratops* from their skulls. They think skull (1), with its small nose horn and deep face belonged to a male, while the hornless skull (2) belonged to a female. From above (3), you can see the skull's triangular shape and the openings that made it lighter.

among surviving dinosaurs (birds) and other animals. Since the 1920s, scientists have suggested that the same was true for *Protoceratops*. Features such as a wide frill, a deep face, and a nose horn were thought to be male characteristics.

In 1972, Russian paleontologist Sergei Kurzanov showed that there were differences between the heads of male and female *Protoceratops*. A female frill angled up less than 20 degrees from the skull, and flared out to the side less than 30 degrees. In male *Protoceratops*, the frill angled upward more than 40 degrees and flared outward amazingly to more than 70 degrees.

Kurzanov also noted that the faces of male *Protoceratops* widened from the beak much more than female faces, and that only males had a horn on their snout. Though small, this horn would have been better than nothing for fighting.

Checking the evidence

Kurzanov's findings were based on studying *Protoceratops* skulls closely and making some measurements. Peter Dodson decided to make a much more detailed study of the 24 best preserved skulls in the AMNH collection. He made 40 measurements of each skull and then subjected them to a detailed mathematical analysis.

His findings confirmed that Kurzanov had been correct—there were differences between male and female *Protoceratops*. As well as differences in the angle of the frill, and whether there was a nose horn or not, there were differences in the length of the frill, in the size of the openings in the frill, and also in the structure of the eye sockets and nostrils.

Unfortunately there is no way to prove which forms are males and which are females. However, since only one form had nose horns, it seems likely that these were males. Among most modern animals it is the males which often fight with horns to win females as mates.

How it lived

Like all ornithischian (bird-hipped) dinosaurs, *Protoceratops* ate plants. It had strong jaws with teeth arranged so they could cut tough vegetation like a pair of scissors.

Protoceratops lived in a desert habitat, probably feeding on vegetation growing near streams and ponds. The many fossils that have been found show that it was a plentiful animal. It would have been an important food item for meat-eaters. This is shown by the "fighting dinosaurs," a fossil of a *Velociraptor* fighting a *Protoceratops*. The animals were probably preserved when a sand dune collapsed on the struggling pair.

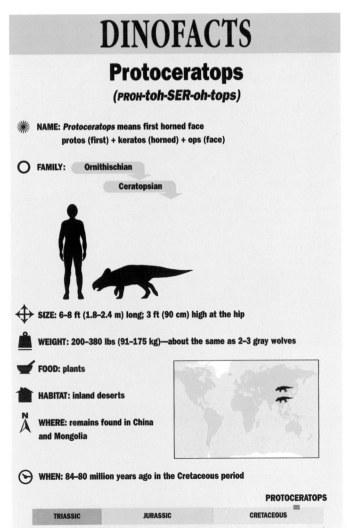

DINOFACTS

Protoceratops
(*PROH-toh-SER-oh-tops*)

✳ **NAME:** *Protoceratops* means first horned face
protos (first) + keratos (horned) + ops (face)

○ **FAMILY:** Ornithischian

Ceratopsian

✛ **SIZE:** 6–8 ft (1.8–2.4 m) long; 3 ft (90 cm) high at the hip

⚖ **WEIGHT:** 200–380 lbs (91–175 kg)—about the same as 2–3 gray wolves

🥣 **FOOD:** plants

🏠 **HABITAT:** inland deserts

WHERE: remains found in China and Mongolia

🕐 **WHEN:** 84–80 million years ago in the Cretaceous period

PROTOCERATOPS

TRIASSIC	JURASSIC	CRETACEOUS
250 MILLION YEARS AGO	205 MILLION YEARS AGO	135 MILLION YEARS AGO ... 65 MILLION YEARS AGO

CHECK THESE OUT!

Ceratopsians, Cretaceous period,
Leptoceratops, Mononykus,
Ornithischian dinosaurs *Oviraptor,
Psittacosaurus, Velociraptor*

Psittacosaurus

Although now one of the best known
dinosaurs, *Psittacosaurus* was for many years
one of the most misunderstood.

In 1922, the Central Asiatic
Expedition of the American
Museum of Natural History
(AMNH) recovered a well-
preserved small dinosaur
skeleton from each of two
Early Cretaceous sites in the
Gobi Desert in Mongolia. The
two sites were about 60 mi
(96 km) apart and were
thought to have rocks of
different ages.

The following year the
AMNH's Henry Fairfield
Osborn described these two
skeletons. He named one
Psittacosaurus mongoliensis for
its narrow parrotlike beak.
He named the other,
which had a less well-
preserved skull,
*Protiguanodon
mongoliensis* as a
possible ancestor of
the iguanodontids
(named in honor
of plant-eating

Iguanodon). Both animals were
about 4 ft (1.2 m) long and 2 ft
(60 cm) high at the hip.
Psittacosaurus seemed to
have thicker bones than
Protiguanodon, and
one of its hip-
bones (the
ilium) was
longer.

▲ A *Psittacosaurus*
and its young search
for food in Asia
during the Early
Cretaceous period.

Osborn recognized that the animals were similar in many ways but placed them in two different new groups: the psittacosaurs (parrot-beaked dinosaurs) and the protiguanodonts (*Iguanodon* ancestors).

Because some fragments of what looked like dinosaur armor had been found, he first thought that *Psittacosaurus* was a primitive ancestor of the ankylosaurs (armored dinosaurs). The following year he changed his mind and placed *Psittacosaurus* with *Protiguanodon* in the ornithopods (bird-footed dinosaurs).

For many years these two skeletons were displayed in New York as different animals. In 1955, the Russian paleontologist A. K. Rozhdestvensky claimed that both *Psittacosaurus* and *Protiguanodon* were really the same kind of dinosaur. The differences in their skeletons were the result of differences in age, or simple variations between individuals.

In 1990, Chicago paleontologist Paul Sereno agreed that both skeletons were of the same kind of dinosaur. He also noted that some of the bones in the *Protiguanodon* skeleton had been distorted during burial, making them appear thicker.

Many species

Perhaps more types (species) of *Psittacosaurus* have been described than of any other dinosaur. At present there are nine described species. This is not completely unexpected because smaller animals usually

STOMACH STONES

Within the rib cage of the "*Protiguanodon*" skeleton at the AMNH, there is a mass of small, smooth stones. Masses of stones have also been found in the rib cages of other species of *Psittacosaurus*. Similar masses of stones found in the rib cages of the sauropod (long-necked plant-eating) saurischian dinosaurs are thought to be stomach stones (or gastroliths). Instead of teeth, modern birds have a muscular crop (or gizzard) in front of their stomachs that holds such stones to grind up food. Because of this, scientists have suggested that a muscular gizzard may have been a feature of all saurischian dinosaurs (not just birds).

However, the presence of stomach stones in *Psittacosaurus* may indicate that a muscular gizzard is a feature shared by all dinosaurs. *Psittacosaurus* is the only ornithischian dinosaur which has been definitely found with stomach stones. Perhaps this feature was independently developed in *Psittacosaurus* to grind tough food. Its deep jaws and enlarged jaw muscles suggest that it fed on very tough plants.

▲ *Psittacosaurus* (parrot lizard) got its name because its beak was like that of the modern parrots.

have more species than larger animals. Among modern animals, for example, there are many species of mice, but only two elephant species. Unlike many other dinosaurs, where new species are often described from a few fragments, most *Psittacosaurus* species are based on complete skeletons.

In 1955, Rozhdestvensky grouped all the *Psittacosaurus*

species named up until then as one species—*Psittacosaurus mongoliensis*. He claimed that the differences between them were the result of differences in age and sex. However, Sereno later pointed out that there really were different species, based on differences in the sizes of the skulls and jaws, and the structure of the teeth. Interestingly, at present, only *Psittacosaurus mongoliensis* has been found in Mongolia.

Primitive ceratopsians

Rozhdestvensky was the first to suggest that *Psittacosaurus* was more closely related to the ceratopsians (horned dinosaurs), such as *Protoceratops*, than to the ornithopods, such as *Iguanodon*. This idea was also supported by a number of other scientists.

However, it was not until 1975 that Polish paleontologists Teresa Maryanska and Halszka Osmólska decided that *Psittacosaurus* should be classified based on the shape of its skull. In their view,

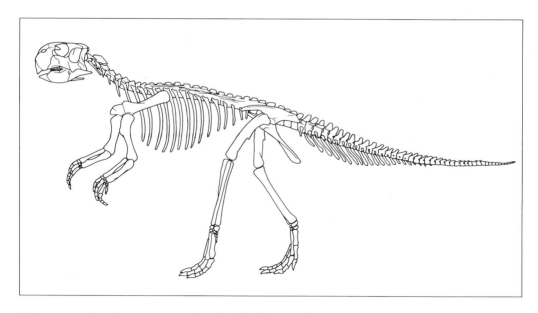

▲ Unlike later ceratopsians, such as *Triceratops*, *Psittacosaurus* probably walked on two legs. Its tail would have helped it to balance and stopped it from falling flat on its face.

Psittacosaurus shared many features of its skull with ceratopsians. It had a narrow snout with a parrotlike beak that widened out, giving the skull a triangular shape seen from the top. Like ceratopsians, *Psittacosaurus* had pointed cheek bones that flared outward.

Maryanska and Osmólska also suggested that Osborn had made a mistake in describing *Psittacosaurus*'s snout. They believed that he had missed the special bone at the front of the upper jaw. This bone supported the upper half of the parrotlike beak. It is also found only in ceratopsian dinosaurs.

The ceratopsian nose bone

The bone that Rozhdestvensky missed is called the rostral bone. The rostral bone is a distinctive bone at the front of the upper jaws of all ceratopsians. Besides forming the upper part of their parrotlike beak, it connects the left and right sides of their upper jaws. Because only ceratopsians have this special, rostral bone, scientists use this bone to define the ceratopsian group and to distinguish it from all other dinosaur groups.

Scientists have suggested that the rostral bone evolved when some tissue holding the beak to the front of the jaws turned into bone. The same process may also have been involved in the evolution of the extra bone (the predentary bone) at the front of the lower beak in all ornithischian dinosaurs.

Baby psittacosaurs

In 1980 and 1982, paleontologist Walter Coombs described a group of tiny dinosaur fossils that had been collected in 1922 by the AMNH's expedition. The fossils were found near to one of the sites that produced the original *Psittacosaurus* specimens. Coombs recognized that these fossils were baby *Psittacosaurus*. He estimated that there were as many as seven individuals in the group and suggested that they were a group of baby dinosaurs that had stayed together after hatching.

The smallest specimen had a skull 1.1 in (2.7 cm) long and measured only 9.8 in (24.8 cm) in length, making this the smallest dinosaur specimen ever found. He noticed that the babies' teeth were worn, indicating they were already eating coarse vegetation. They had features typical of baby dinosaurs, such as large eyes and a short snout. Also, each of the babies' skulls had a rostral bone forming the front part of the upper beak.

The missing finger

Although the psittacosaurs are classified as primitive (little evolved) ceratopsians, it can be shown that the known psittacosaurs could not have been the direct ancestors of the later ceratopsians. This can be demonstrated by the bones of their hands.

The psittacosaurs have completely lost their fifth finger and have a very small fourth finger. The later ceratopsians still have all five fingers on their hands. One of the patterns of evolution is that when a feature, such as a finger, is lost it is rarely regained. Thus, it is best to think of the known psittacosaurs as a sister group of the later ceratopsians, not their direct ancestors.

How *Psittacosaurus* lived

The long legs of *Psittacosaurus* suggest they could run fast, so their best defense against predators would have been to run away. Their sharp beaks, slicing teeth, deep jaws, and powerful jaw muscles indicate they ate tough plants.

CHECK THESE OUT!

Ankylosaurs, Ceratopsians, Cretaceous period, Eggs and Babies, *Iguanodon*, Ornithischian dinosaurs, Ornithopods, *Protoceratops*, Triceratops

DINOFACTS

Psittacosaurus
(SIH-tack-uh-SORE-us)

✳ **NAME:** *Psittacosaurus* means parrot lizard
psittako (parrot) + sauros (lizard)

⭕ **FAMILY:**   Ornithischian
   Ceratopsian

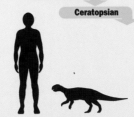

✚ **SIZE:** 3–5 ft (90 cm–1.5 m) long; 1–2 ft (30–60 cm) high at the hip

WEIGHT: 30–80 lbs (13.6–36 kg)—about the same as a medium to large dog

FOOD: plants

HABITAT: dry floodplains often near lakes

WHERE: remains found in China and Mongolia

🕐 **WHEN:** 130–90 million years ago in the Cretaceous period

PSITTACOSAURUS

TRIASSIC	JURASSIC	CRETACEOUS
250 MILLION YEARS AGO	205 MILLION YEARS AGO	135 MILLION YEARS AGO 65 MILLION YEARS AGO

Pterosaurs

The flying pterosaurs were not dinosaurs, but they lived at the same time as the dinosaurs and shared the same ancestors. Fossil pterosaurs are sometimes found alongside fossil dinosaurs.

Three different groups of backboned animals have evolved the ability to fly: birds, bats, and pterosaurs (wing lizards). Birds evolved from small meat-eating dinosaurs, and bats evolved from small insect-eating mammals. Who were the ancestors of the pterosaurs?

Dinosaur cousins

There are two clues that paleontologists have used to solve the mystery of the pterosaurs' ancestors.

The first clue is found in their skulls. There is a big opening on either side of the skull, just in front of the eye sockets and behind the nostrils. The second clue is found in the pterosaurs' ankle bones. Their ankles are simple hinges that let the foot go only backward and forward. The foot could not twist at all.

Dinosaurs have the same openings in their skulls and the same ankles as pterosaurs. This tells paleontologists that pterosaurs are closely related to dinosaurs. However, pterosaurs are not dinosaurs.

Pterosaurs and dinosaurs are both members of a group of animals known as archosaurs that first appeared at the end of the Permian period (290–250 million years ago).

Pterosaurs first appear as fossils in marine rocks of the Late Triassic period, about 220 million years ago. These animals lived on the seacoast. When they died, they fell into the sea and became buried in mud on the seafloor.

One of these early pterosaurs was *Rhamphorhynchus*. This animal was already a specialized flier and fish-eater. It had a long, narrow, pointed head, and a mouth lined with many long, forward-pointing teeth. These teeth were perfect for catching fish.

Rhamphorhynchus would have skimmed over the sea and snatched fish out of the water. Its tail extended far behind its body and had a diamond-shaped flap at its tip. Having the flap on the end of the tail would have helped keep the animal stable while flying. The flap would have been used like the stabilizer fin on an airplane. *Rhamphorhynchus* had long, narrow wings, and it is these wings that make pterosaurs especially interesting.

Long finger

All pterosaurs had four fingers on their hands. The first three fingers were of normal size with strong claws at their tips. However, the fourth finger

---

BEATEN BY BIRDS?

Pterosaurs were most numerous during the Jurassic and Early Cretaceous periods. By the end of the Cretaceous period, however, there were no more pterosaurs. What happened to them?

Avialans (birds and their closest relatives) first appeared in the Late Jurassic period. During the Early Cretaceous period, many types of avialans started to evolve. These avialans, which evolved into modern birds, had very strong flight muscles, strong bones, and feathers forming the wing surface. Feathers were regularly molted and regrown. Like a modern bird, if a Cretaceous avialan lost some feathers, it could regrow them. If a pterosaur tore the thin sheet that formed its wing surface, it would have been unable to fly, unable to find food, and so would have starved to death. Birds and their relatives seem to be better flying animals than pterosaurs—they are faster and stronger, and they can repair their wings by growing new feathers.

▶ *Pteranodon* (1), a pterodactyloid from the Late Cretaceous period, could never have flown in the same skies as *Rhamphorhynchus* (2), which lived 70 million years earlier in the Jurassic period.

was very strange indeed. The bones that made up this finger were easily as long as the bones forming the whole arm.

This huge finger acted like the mast on a ship, with the wings as the sail. A broad sheet of elastic skin stretched from the body out to the very tip of the finger. This sheet of skin formed the wing surface. Bats have a similar sheet forming their wings. In bats, however, all the fingers are equally long and they all help to support the wing surface. In pterosaurs just one "wing finger" supported the whole wing.

Pterosaurs' wings were very delicate, which meant that they were mainly gliders. Strong flapping movements, like those used by modern birds, would have torn the fragile skin of their wings.

Pterosaurs had very light bones and bodies. Most of their bones were as hollow as a pipe. The sides of the bones were usually as thin as a postcard. Thin, crisscrossing rods supported and strengthened the bones where they needed it. Pterosaurs were so light that the slightest breeze would have let them rise into the air when they stretched out their wings. Once aloft they could glide for hours.

327

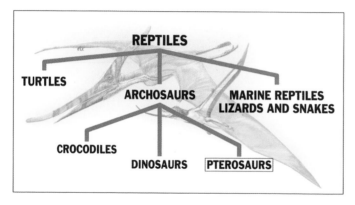

▲ The reptile family tree shows that pterosaurs evolved from the same ancestors as crocodiles and dinosaurs.

Long and short tails

All pterosaurs can be divided into two groups: the long-tailed rhamphorhynchoids (named in honor of *Rhamphorhynchus*) and the short-tailed pterodactyloids (*pterodactyl* means wing finger).

The pterodactyloids evolved from the rhamphorhynchoids sometime in the Middle Jurassic period, about 190–170 million years ago. The short tails meant pterodactyloids were probably more skillful flyers than the rhamphorhynchoids; they did not need a long tail for stability. Some pterodactyloids also became much larger than any of the rhamphorhynchoids.

Texan giant

The largest known flying animal of all time was a pterodactyloid called *Quetzalcoatlus*. Its bones were found in Late Cretaceous period rocks in Texas. The name comes from an ancient Mayan mythical beast that had the body of a snake and the wings of a bird. *Quetzalcoatlus* had a wingspan of 39 ft (12 m), almost the same size as the wings of a small airplane.

How they lived

Most pterosaurs probably ate fish. They had sharp, pointed teeth that would have been ideal for holding slippery fish. Some *Rhamphorhynchus* fossils have been found with fish remains in the stomach.

Pterosaurs may have caught fish by swooping down and snatching them from near the surface of the sea. Many seabirds, such as albatrosses, feed in the same way today.

By the Late Cretaceous period, some pterosaurs had lost their teeth. One of these was *Pteranodon* from the Niobrara Chalks of Kansas, in the western United States. Its name means toothless wing. *Pteranodon* would still have glided out to sea and grabbed fish and squid from the sea surface. Perhaps it had a beaklike covering on its snout with slightly roughened edges. Modern diving birds, such as cormorants and sawbill ducks, that catch fish have rough edges to their bills to help grip their slippery prey.

▼ *Rhamphorhynchus* (1) had a long tail as did all the rhamphorhynchoids. All the pterodactyloids, such as *Pteranodon* (2), were tail-less. Both groups had very long super-fingers supporting their wings.

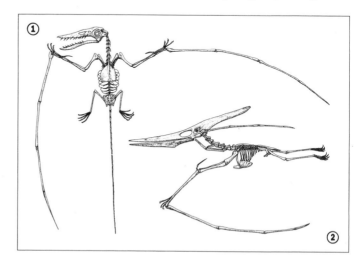

Bristle mouth

The long, narrow snout of *Pterodaustro*, which lived in Brazil in the Early Cretaceous period, had evolved into a sort of comb. *Pterodaustro*'s teeth were long and thin like the bristles of a brush. Many hundreds of bristle-teeth filled its lower jaw.

Scientists think that *Pterodaustro* may have settled beside lakes and ponds that had thousands of tiny shrimps and water fleas living in the shallows. It might have swept its comblike snout through the water to catch food on the bristles. It would have then used its tongue to lick the food off the bristles before swallowing. Modern flamingos feed in a similar way.

Flying food

The small, starling-sized pterosaur *Anurognathus*, from Germany, may have eaten flying food. It had a short, deep face, and a wide mouth with small cone-shaped teeth.

Except for the teeth, these features are very like those of modern birds that specialize in eating flying insects. Its small body would have made *Anurognathus* very agile in the air. Its wide mouth would have let it catch flying insects easily, and its small teeth would have been ideal for holding insects to crunch.

CHECK THESE OUT!

Archosaurs, Avialans, Birds, Cretaceous period, Insects, Jurassic period, Mammals, Triassic period

FOSSIL FACTS

Pterosaurs
(TEH-row-SORES)

▲ The lower jaw of *Pterodaustro* was filled with long bristlelike teeth, which it probably used to comb small shrimps and fleas from the water.

NAME: Pterosaur means wing lizard
ptero (wing) + sauros (lizard)

FAMILY: Reptile
Archosaur

SIZE: huge variation from a 1.7 ft (50 cm) to 39 ft (12 m) wingspan

WEIGHT: huge variation from 3.5 oz (100 g) to 220 lbs (100 kg)—or from a starling to a small adult ostrich

FOOD: fish (mostly), insects, maybe carrion (leftovers of already dead animals)

HABITAT: mostly seacoasts and the shores of large lakes; a few types lived far inland

N **WHERE:** remains found worldwide

WHEN: from 220 million years ago in the Triassic period to 65 million years ago in the Cretaceous period

PTEROSAURS

TRIASSIC	JURASSIC	CRETACEOUS
250 MILLION YEARS AGO	205 MILLION YEARS AGO	135 MILLION YEARS AGO	65 MILLION YEARS AGO

Reconstructing dinosaurs

Reconstructing the appearance of living dinosaurs combines art and science. Putting them in realistic positions and habitats is the final stage in communicating paleontologists' work to the public.

Reconstructing the skeletons of dinosaurs is an important step toward understanding the lives of dinosaurs. Scientists prefer to do their research on complete, perfectly preserved dinosaur skeletons.

For the vast majority of known dinosaurs complete specimens have never been found. However, for every major dinosaur group there are a few exceptionally well-preserved specimens. Examples include *Coelophysis*, *Allosaurus*, *Velociraptor*, *Camarasaurus*, *Heterodontosaurus*, *Iguanodon*, *Corythosaurus*, *Edmontosaurus*, *Stegosaurus*, *Euoplocephalus*, *Protoceratops*, and *Styracosaurus*.

▲ The king of predators *Tyrannosaurus* comes to life—well almost—in the American Museum of Natural History, New York.

For skeletons that are incomplete, paleontologists have to fill in the missing pieces from that dinosaur's better-known relatives. This often works fairly well for animals with only a few missing parts. All too often, a new dinosaur's head is missing or badly damaged. A number of famous mistakes have been made by putting the wrong kind of head on a dinosaur.

When the headless skeleton of *Apatosaurus* was first put on display, it was given a head like that of *Camarasaurus*. Only later did scientists discover that it should have had a head like that of *Diplodocus*.

Posing skeletons

Correctly posing a skeleton can also be difficult even when the skeleton is very well known. For many years *Iguanodon* was posed sitting on its tail like a kangaroo. Careful studies of its hands, tail, and hips by British paleontologist David Norman showed that this idea was incorrect. He showed that *Iguanodon* spent a great deal of its time walking on all fours, and even when walking on its

hind legs, *Iguanodon* walked with its tail up and its back held level.

Working with lightweight casts of the real bones is very useful, as the movements of individual bones can be worked out very accurately. By using casts, scientists can see the surfaces of the bones moving against each other. This lets them work out what movement are possible without dislocating the bones. Some

◄ This 19th-century reconstruction of *Hadrosaurus* used the fossilized bones and a heavy steel frame. The dinosaur was also incorrectly posed in an upright stance.

▲ This superb *Edmontosaurus* specimen, which preserves most of the animal's skin, was dried out (mummified) by natural processes before becoming fossilized.

researchers even create computer models by which they can study a range of possible movements. Of course, paleontologists can only guess how the dinosaurs may have behaved. Think how difficult it would be to imagine all the tricks that a circus elephant can perform just by looking at its skeleton.

Dinosaur trackways have also been very useful in determining how dinosaur

▲ A tiger's stripes make it hard to pick out from the background. Some predatory dinosaurs probably also had some form of camouflage to confuse their prey.

skeletons should be posed. Trackways of nearly every dinosaur group are known. Footprints show that dinosaurs walked with their legs under their bodies, rather than sprawling outward like lizards and crocodiles. Trackways also show that even wide-bodied animals such as ankylosaurs (armored dinosaurs) held their legs underneath their bodies.

For many people, a mounted dinosaur skeleton is the best method of reconstruction. Traditionally, a mounted skeleton consisted of real bones mounted on a steel framework. For a large dinosaur, individual fossil bones can weigh many hundreds of pounds, so life-like mounts are nearly impossible. Also, it is difficult to study a dinosaur once its bones have been mounted because many of the bone

surfaces are hidden from view.

Most modern mounts are of lightweight casts of bones that are mounted with the metal framework inside of them. This allows more lifelike poses, and also saves the original fossils for scientists to study.

Fleshing out a dinosaur

It is fairly straightforward for a good anatomist (a scientist who studies body structure) to

reconstruct the muscles of an animal by studying the skeleton. To develop this skill, paleontologists must study many different types of modern animals to learn the sizes and positions of different muscles in different animals. Since the living birds and crocodiles are closely related to the extinct nonflying dinosaurs, these are the best for understanding dinosaur muscles for reconstruction purposes.

Land animals are remarkably similar in the way that muscles attach to the bones. By examining the position of the points where muscles attach, the exact positions of the muscles can be reconstructed. The size of these attachment points indicate how well developed the muscles were. From this kind of analysis, a paleontologist can, with a high degree of accuracy, reconstruct

▼ A paleontologist reconstructs a stegosaur (plate-backed dinosaur), watched over by the skeleton of a tyrannosaur.

the shape of an extinct animal. It is fortunate that birds and reptiles do not have the heavy layers of fat that obscure the muscles of many mammals.

Dinosaur skin
Pieces of preserved skin have been found for most dinosaur groups. The theropod (two-legged meat-eater) *Carnotaurus* and several kinds of hadrosaurs, most notably *Edmontosaurus*, have been found with most of their skin preserved.

Preserved skin shows paleon-tologists the sizes and patterns of the scales on the surface of the skin. Knowing the pattern of scales on a dinosaur is very important for sculpting lifesized dinosaurs. Most of the scales preserved on dinosaurs are too small to be seen on smaller sculptures or in paintings.

Dinosaur colors
Paleontologists may never know what color dinosaurs really were. However, it is possible for dinosaur artists to make some reasonable guesses.

Artists study modern animals to see under what conditions various color patterns evolved. Some animals have bright colors for display and to attract mates. Equally important are color patterns for camouflage. Both predators and their prey make use of camouflage. There is a great variety of patterns such as stripes, spots, two-tone patterns, and drab greys and browns that blend in with the background.

Different camouflage patterns reflect different behaviors and habitats. For example, some

▲ The sauropod (long-necked plant-eater) *Barosaurus* might have reared up on its hind legs to defend itself or its young.

scientists think that the big dinosaurs looked much like the huge, drab-colored grassland mammals of today, such as brown bison or gray elephants. Others think they may have been more brightly colored. Of course, it would be impossible to tell that zebras had stripes and that horses did not, just by studying their skeletons. Dinosaur skin is extremely rare, but perhaps someday scientists will find enough to solve this mystery.

Is it bad when scientists disagree? Not at all. It just means that they are looking for new and different ways to solve difficult questions.

Reconstructing habitats
Once a dinosaur has been fleshed out it is important that it be placed in its correct habitat. This means including only animals that could have

lived in the same place at the same time. All too many habitat reconstructions include animals from different times and places in the same display.

Getting the plants right
It is also important to include the correct plants that may have lived in that habitat. As with animals, plant species have appeared and become extinct over geological time. Many of the plants that were important in the Triassic or Jurassic periods were gone or rare by the Late Cretaceous period. There are also big differences in the kinds of plants that live in various types of habitats. For example, desert plants are very different from those that grow in swamps.

Sedimentologists, who study sediments such as sand, mud, and silt, can help reconstruct ancient landscapes. Sediments are what bury and preserve fossils. By studying where various types of sediments gather, and examining sediment particles under a microscope, sedimentologists can tell in what sort of habitat the sediment was laid down.

By studying the sediment around a fossil, they can tell whether the landscape was dominated by slow-moving rivers, lakes, swamps, glaciers, a delta, or a desert. The study of fossil soils can also provide evidence about ancient climates.

CHECK THESE OUT!
Bones, Footprints, Fossils, Paleontology, Plants, Rocks

Reptiles

In the classification of animals, dinosaurs belong to the reptile group. However, scientists have recently changed their views about what is and what is not a reptile.

In 1758, the Swedish scientist Carolus Linnaeus published a book, *Systema naturae* (Nature's System), that classified all living things. Linnaeus's system of classification is still used by many scientists, although he was wrong about some things.

Bald eagle

Linnaeus's system was based on grouping animals that share common features. He put all animals in a large group called a kingdom. Within that group he made up smaller groups called phyla (singular: phylum). In one phylum he put all the animals with backbones (the vertebrates). Linnaeus divided this phylum into five parts (classes): mammals, birds, reptiles, amphibians, and fish.

Allosaurus

Pristichampsus

▶ According to modern classification, the bald eagle is as much a reptile as the Carolina box turtle, the Jurassic meat-eating dinosaur *Allosaurus*, and *Pristichampsus*, an extinct crocodile.

In Linnaeus's system, all backboned animals that are cold-blooded and have scales are classified as reptiles. These animals include the turtles, lizards, snakes, crocodiles, and sphenodonts (such as the lizardlike tuatara).

When extinct groups of animals similar to living reptiles were discovered, they too were classified as reptiles. Among these extinct groups were pterosaurs (flying reptiles) and nonflying dinosaurs.

A modern view of reptiles

In 1859, British scientist Charles Darwin published a book, *On the Origin of Species*, that outlined his Theory of Evolution. Darwin showed that all life was interrelated

▲ A tuatara perches on a log. The tuatara, which lives in New Zealand, is the only surviving member of the sphenodonts.

through a long history of development (evolution). His theory is accepted by most scientists today. Darwin's theory pointed toward a new way of classifying animals. Linnaeus's system was based on the similarity between animals, but did not take into account evolutionary relationships between animals.

Carolina box turtle

In 1966 German scientist Willi Hennig proposed a new system of classification in his book *Phylogenetic Systematics*. His system has become accepted by nearly all scientists as the best way to reflect the pattern of evolution in classification.

Hennig's system is based on evolution. It groups animals that share features they have acquired through evolution from a common ancestor.

All reptiles have scales, so in Hennig's system they should be grouped together. However, birds also have

scales. This feature shows that birds and reptiles share a common ancestor.

Birds are reptiles...

By looking at the features that birds and reptiles share, scientists decided that birds descended from the first reptile, so birds are reptiles. Most scientists now accept that birds descended from the first dinosaur. Under Hennig's classification system, this means that birds are dinosaurs. Hennig's evolutionary system, called cladistics, is now widely used.

...mammals are not

Under Hennig's system, a group of animals includes the common ancestor and all of its descendants. For example, all the animals that evolved from the first reptile, from *Tyrannosaurus* to toucans, are reptiles. Similarly, all the animals that evolved from the first vertebrate, from fish to mammals and reptiles, are also considered vertebrates.

Mammals, and their ancestors the mammal-like reptiles, share a common ancestor with reptiles. However, because mammals and mammal-like reptiles branched off before the reptiles' ancestors in the process of evolution, paleontologists do not usually consider them to be reptiles.

Ancient reptiles
The oldest fossil reptiles were found in Scotland in rocks of the Carboniferous period (360–290 million years ago). Very early reptiles had an eardrum supported by a bone near the top of the skull.

Reptiles are usually classified by the number of holes they have in their skulls behind their eye sockets. These ancient reptiles had no holes there so they are called the anapsids (*an* means "no" and *apse* means "arch" or "hole"). They gave rise to the turtles in the Late Triassic period.

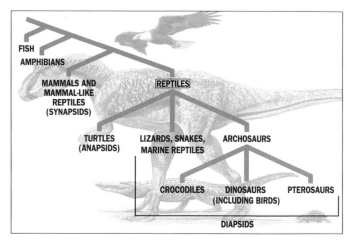

During the Pennsylvanian epoch of the Carboniferous period (322–290 million years ago), a group of reptiles developed two pairs of openings behind their eye sockets to hold their jaw muscles. These reptiles are called the diapsids (*di* means "two"). Many different kinds of reptiles were diapsids, including dinosaurs.

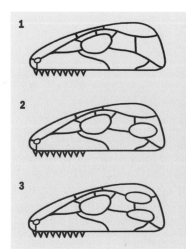

HOLES IN THE HEAD
Reptiles were traditionally classified on the basis of the holes formed at the back of the skull for the better attachment of jaw muscles. The major groups of reptiles were the anapsids (1), such as turtles; synapsids (2), such as mammal-like reptiles; diapsids (3), such as dinosaurs. Each group was given equal rank. However, the new evolutionary system has changed scientists' thinking. According to this system, mammal-like reptiles are not reptiles, but are instead more like mammals. Perhaps they should be renamed reptile-like mammals.

▲ The archosaurs (including dinosaurs), the marine reptiles, lizards, and turtles are all reptiles. The mammals and their ancestors, the mammal-like reptiles, are not reptiles, since they branched off earlier. Close studies of evolution show us that mammal-like reptiles perhaps should be called reptile-like mammals instead.

Lizards and snakes
One group of diapsid reptiles developed a long ear bone and an eardrum supported by a bowed bone at the back of the skull. These reptiles were the neodiapsids. In the Permian period (290–250 million years ago), they split into the lepidosaurs and the archosaurs.

The lepidosaurs had teeth that attached to the inside of the jaws. During the Triassic and Jurassic periods, sphenodonts were the most important lepidosaurs before they nearly became extinct in the mid-Cretaceous. The tuatara is the only sphenodont alive today.

The lizards were also lepidosaurs. They first appeared in the Triassic period but did not become varied and numerous until the sphenodonts had begun to disappear. Snakes evolved from lizards near the beginning of the Cretaceous period, but the snakes became truly numerous only during the Cenozoic Era, the age of the mammals, in which we live today.

The ruling reptiles

The archosaurs, or ruling reptiles, developed an additional skull opening in front of the eyes and in the jaw. They spread amazingly during the Triassic period, when a huge variety of types evolved. Most became extinct at the end of the Triassic period. The groups that survived the Triassic extinction included pterosaurs, crocodiles, ornithischian (bird hipped) dinosaurs, and saurischian (lizard-hipped) dinosaurs. The saurischians gave rise to birds during the Cretaceous period.

The survivors

At the end of the Cretaceous period, many reptile groups became extinct. These included the pterosaurs, the plesiosaurs, the ornithischian dinosaurs, and many groups of saurischian dinosaurs. Of all the many varied reptiles that have arisen on earth in the last 300 million years, only six major groups survive—the turtles, the sphenodonts, the lizards and snakes, the crocodilians, and the birds. However, the birds with their many varied kinds can be considered to be the most successful group of reptiles ever to have lived.

FOSSIL FACTS

Reptiles

 SIZE: huge variation from the 2.3 in (5.8 cm) bee hummingbird to the 120 ft (37 m) or more *Seismosaurus*

 WEIGHT: huge variation from 0.06 oz (1.6 g) to 50 tons (45 tonnes) or more

 FOOD: plants, insects, fish, meat

 HABITAT: all types from the North Pole to oceans to deserts

 WHERE: remains found worldwide

🕐 **WHEN:** from 300 million years ago in the Carboniferous period to today

REPLIES

DEVONIAN	CARBONIFEROUS	PERMIAN	TRIASSIC	JURASSIC	CRETACEOUS
410 MILLION YEARS AGO	360 MILLION YEARS AGO	290 MILLION YEARS AGO	250 MILLION YEARS AGO	205 MILLION YEARS AGO	135 MILLION YEARS AGO	65 MILLION YEARS AGO

How modern reptiles live

Cold-blooded reptiles live from the warm tropics to northern places where the weather does not become too cold. Many smaller reptiles eat insects, while large reptiles eat larger animals like mammals. Some turtles and lizards are largely plant-eaters. While most reptiles live on land in a variety of environments, some like the sea turtles and sea snakes live in the sea.

The modern warm-blooded reptiles are the birds. They live almost everywhere except the South Pole and occupy all kinds of habitats. Using their wings, they can fly to where the food is. Many migrate thousands of miles to better feeding grounds. Like their cold-blooded cousins, they eat a variety of different foods.

CHECK THESE OUT!

Archosaurs, Birds, Crocodiles, Dinosaurs, Evolution, Extinction, Fish, Geological time, Lizards and snakes, Mammal-like reptiles, Mammals, Pterosaurs, Turtles

Rhabdodon

Rhabdodon was a medium-sized plant-eating dinosaur that lived in Europe at the end of the Cretaceous period. It might have been the last iguanodontid dinosaur (*Iguanodon* relative) to walk the earth.

Rhabdodon was first described in 1869 by the French paleontologist Philippe Matheron from a few fragments of leg, jaw, and back bones found in southern France. He was able to identify the remains as those of an ornithopod (bird-footed dinosaur). Other incomplete remains were later found in Austria, Spain, and Romania.

Classifying *Rhabdodon*

Rhabdodon's large leg bones and small arm bones indicate that it mostly walked on two legs. Some features of its jaw, such as parallel rows of teeth and the absence of teeth at the front of the upper jaw, suggest that *Rhabdodon* belonged to the

ISLAND DINOSAUR

Paleontologists believe that the evolutionary line leading to *Rhabdodon* began at about the time of the split between the iguanodontids and the hypsilophodontids in the Late Jurassic period (about 175 million years ago). *Rhabdodon*'s ancestors seem to have evolved separately from other ornithopods. Perhaps its ancestors became separated from environments in which more advanced (highly evolved) ornithopods, such as the hadrosaurs (duckbill dinosaurs) of North America and China, developed.

About 70 million years ago, during the Late Cretaceous period, much of Europe was a series of islands. The bones of various small dinosaurs have been found preserved in the rocks deposited as sediments on or near these islands. *Rhabdodon* was one of these dinosaurs. Many of the dinosaurs are primitive (little evolved) for the Late Cretaceous, which suggests they might have evolved in isolation, much like the marsupials (pouched mammals) of Australia.

iguanodontids (a group of plant-eating dinosaurs named in honor of *Iguanodon*). However, other jaw features, such as teeth with ridges running from the edges to the base, were like those of the hypsilophodontids (a group of

▶ *Rhabdodon* was a small ornithopod (bird-footed dinosaur) similar overall to *Camptosaurus*.

plant-eaters named after *Hypsilophodon*). Paleontologists decided that *Rhabdodon* was an iguanodontid with some primitive (little evolved) features. *Rhabdodon* is the only iguanodontid known from the end of the Cretaceous period. It seems likely that the line leading to *Rhabdodon* evolved separately, perhaps because it and its ancestors were isolated from the rest of the world.

How *Rhabdodon* lived

Rhabdodon ate plants. It probably bit off leaves and stems with its sharp beak and ground them into small pieces with its teeth. Although it walked on its back legs, it could stand on all fours to feed close to the ground.

CHECK THESE OUT!

Cretaceous period, *Hypsilophodon*, *Iguanodon*, Ornithischian dinosaurs, Ornithopods

DINOFACTS

Rhabdodon

(RAB-do-don)

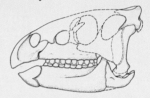

▶ Paleontologists have found only parts of *Rhabdodon*'s skull, but they can work out what it looked like from what they know of other ornithopods.

✳ **NAME:** *Rhabdodon* means rod tooth
rhabdo (rod) + odontos (tooth)

◯ **FAMILY:** Ornithischian

Ornithopod

✥ **SIZE:** 13 ft (4 m) long; 5 ft (1.5 m) high at the hip

⬛ **WEIGHT:** 1,000 lbs (454 kg)—about the same as a polar bear

FOOD: plants

HABITAT: well-watered lowlands

Ⓝ WHERE: remains found in Austria, France, Romania, and Spain

🕐 **WHEN:** 70–65 million years ago in the Cretaceous period

			RHABDODON
TRIASSIC	JURASSIC	CRETACEOUS	
250 MILLION YEARS AGO	205 MILLION YEARS AGO	135 MILLION YEARS AGO	65 MILLION YEARS AGO

Riojasaurus

Riojasaurus was the largest of the prosauropod dinosaurs (early long-necked plant-eaters). *Riojasaurus* lived in Argentina during the Late Triassic period.

▶ *Riojasaurus* probably walked on all fours but may have been able to rear up on its hind legs to feed from tall trees.

The Late Triassic period rocks of Argentina are prized by paleontologists because they contain the remains of the earliest dinosaurs, *Eoraptor* and *Herrerasaurus*. These early dinosaurs are very rare, and are known only from one or two fossil specimens each.

Rocks which were laid down slightly later in the Triassic contain many more dinosaur skeletons. Most of these skeletons belong to prosauropod dinosaurs. The most impressive prosauropod was *Riojasaurus*.

Riojasaurus was the largest of the prosauropod dinosaurs. Adults could reach up to 33 ft (10 m) in length. Although not huge by dinosaur standards, *Riojasaurus* was the largest animal that lived during the Triassic period.

Missing head

Argentinian paleontologist José Bonaparte first discovered remains of *Riojasaurus* in 1962. He later discovered several other skeletons of *Riojasaurus*, some of which were almost complete. Studying these remains enabled paleontologists to learn a great deal about the dinosaur, but one vital piece of the skeletons was missing. Not one of the skeletons had its skull.

The skull of a dinosaur can reveal a lot of information about the animal, including evidence of its diet (which paleontologists can work out from the shape of its teeth and jaws). Paleontologists had to wait until 1986 for fossil-hunters to find a *Riojasaurus* skull, ending a search that had lasted for nearly 25 years.

How did *Riojasaurus* live?

Like all prosauropods, *Riojasaurus* ate plants. It would have used its long neck to reach leaves on high tree branches. Other prosauropods, such as *Mussaurus*, lived alongside *Riojasaurus*. Its large size would have allowed *Riojasaurus* to reach higher than other prosauropods, giving it a wider choice of leaves. Although some prosauropods, such as *Plateosaurus*, were able to walk on their back legs from time to time, *Riojasaurus* probably walked on all fours. It needed to use all its legs to carry its great weight. Even though it was big, *Riojasaurus* still had plenty to fear from nondinosaur hunters such as the crocodile-like *Saurosuchus*, which could grow up to 27 ft (8.2 m) long.

CHECK THESE OUT!

Archosaurs, *Mussaurus*, *Plateosaurus*, Prosauropods, Saurischian dinosaurs, Triassic period

DIFFICULT DIGESTION

Although many different animals live on a diet of plants, plant food is very difficult to digest. This is because plants are made of a very tough material called cellulose. Different animals solve this problem differently. Some animals are able to chew the food into very small pieces. This makes the plants easier to digest, as it helps to break the cellulose apart. This is seen today in animals like cows and horses, and was also the way in which some dinosaurs, such as *Iguanodon*, *Triceratops*, and *Parasaurolophus*, dealt with their food. Paleontologists know this because these dinosaurs had teeth which were heavily worn down, and they all had cheeks, so they could chew food without it falling out of their mouths.

Prosauropod dinosaurs, like *Riojasaurus*, could not chew their food because they had no cheeks. These dinosaurs had large stomachs, which they used to store food for a long time, giving acids and bacteria a chance to break it down. Some sauropod (long-necked plant-eating dinosaur) fossils have been found with what seem to be stomach stones inside them. Like some modern birds, sauropods had a muscular gizzard in front of their stomachs containing stones that were used to grind up food.

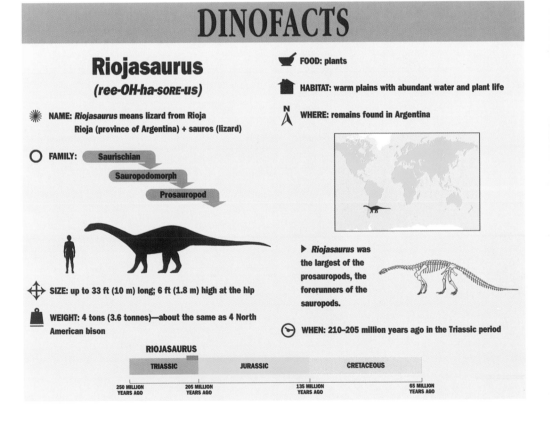

DINOFACTS

Riojasaurus
(ree-OH-ha-SORE-us)

NAME: *Riojasaurus* means lizard from Rioja
Rioja (province of Argentina) + sauros (lizard)

FAMILY: Saurischian → Sauropodomorph → Prosauropod

SIZE: up to 33 ft (10 m) long; 6 ft (1.8 m) high at the hip

WEIGHT: 4 tons (3.6 tonnes)—about the same as 4 North American bison

FOOD: plants

HABITAT: warm plains with abundant water and plant life

WHERE: remains found in Argentina

▶ *Riojasaurus* was the largest of the prosauropods, the forerunners of the sauropods.

WHEN: 210–205 million years ago in the Triassic period

RIOJASAURUS		
TRIASSIC	JURASSIC	CRETACEOUS
250 MILLION YEARS AGO 205 MILLION YEARS AGO	135 MILLION YEARS AGO	65 MILLION YEARS AGO

Saichania

Saichania was a powerful, armor-plated dinosaur. It had triangular, bony horns on its head, and its tail ended in a heavy, bony club, which may have been a good weapon for defense.

In 1971, the Polish–Mongolian Expedition to Mongolia excavated a remarkable skeleton of an ankylosaur (armored dinosaur). The front half of the skeleton was perfectly preserved in the fine red sandstone of the Barun Goyot Formation.

The specimen had a perfect skull followed by two rings of fused armor. Then came rows of low, ridged armor plates extending over the shoulders to the back. Polish paleontologist Teresa Maryanska named *Saichania* in 1977.

GRAZERS AND BROWSERS

Plant-eating animals can be either grazers or browsers. Grazers eat vegetation growing at ground level. Browsers feed on tender shoots, leaves, and twigs they find on shrubs and trees. Among modern plant-eating animals, grazers like wildebeest, zebra, and cattle have broad mouths. Browsers, like deer, antelope, and black rhinoceroses, have narrow mouths. Since ankylosaurids like *Saichania* had broad mouths, paleontologists have concluded they ate low-growing vegetation as do modern cattle. They did not eat grass, though; there was none in the Mesozoic Era.

One tough ankylosaurid

Saichania was an ankylosaurid ankylosaur as it had a bony tail–club. Ankylosaurs without clubs are called nodosaurids. Maryanska found *Saichania* was the strongest of all the ankylosaurids. Unlike other armored dinosaurs, its shoulder blades were fused to its first ribs. Its short legs had places to attach large muscles, indicating

▼ *Saichania* was one of the most heavily armored ankylosaurids. It had tough bony plates covering its legs, sides, back, and even its belly.

DINOFACTS

Saichania
(sye-CHAN-ee-uh)

☀ **NAME:** *Saichania* means from Saichan-tue mountain range in the Gobi Desert, Mongolia

○ **FAMILY:** Ornithischian

Thyreophoran

Ankylosaur

✥ **SIZE:** 20–25 ft (6–7.6 m) long; 6–8 ft (1.8–2.4 m) high at the hip

⚖ **WEIGHT:** 3–4 tons (2.7–3.6 tonnes)—about the same as 3–4 North American bison

🥣 **FOOD:** plants

🏠 **HABITAT:** dry interior lowlands

N ↑ **WHERE:** remains found in Mongolia

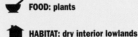

▶ The side view of *Saichania*'s skull shows that it was short, shallow, and had a downturned beak.

🕐 **WHEN:** 80–75 million years ago in the Cretaceous period

SAICHANIA

TRIASSIC	JURASSIC	CRETACEOUS	
250 MILLION YEARS AGO	205 MILLION YEARS AGO	135 MILLION YEARS AGO	65 MILLION YEARS AGO

that its legs were very strong. Recent discoveries have shown that *Saichania*'s front legs may have been covered in armor.

Complicated nose
Desert-dwelling *Saichania* had the most complex nasal passages of any ankylosaurid found in Asia. Perhaps, like camels, they needed to clean and moisten the dusty, dry, desert air they breathed. Perhaps *Saichania* had a very good sense of smell. As its large nostrils point directly forward over its mouth,

Saichania would have been able to smell the ground for food as it walked along.

How did *Saichania* live?
Saichania would have eaten low-growing plants. It may have been able to distinguish between poisonous and nonpoisonous plants by smell.

To defend its territory and win mates, a male *Saichania* may have shaken its head to show off the horns at the back of its skull. This action may have convinced smaller *Saichania* to back off. If the

display failed, the *Saichania* may have engaged in shoving matches with their heads, as modern tortoises often do.

Saichania's armor would have protected it from most predators. If provoked by a tyrannosaur, it may have defended itself by swinging the club at the end of its tail.

CHECK THESE OUT!
Ankylosaurs, *Ankylosaurus*, Cretaceous period, *Nodosaurus*, Ornithischian dinosaurs, Tyrannosaurs

343

Saltasaurus

Saltasaurus was an unusual dinosaur. It was a sauropod, a long-necked plant-eater, but unlike most sauropods it had armor. Why? To protect it from the huge predators that shared its world.

The huge, long-necked, plant-eating sauropods were most numerous and varied during the Late Jurassic period in places like western Europe and North America. However, by the following Cretaceous period, the sauropods had died out in these areas.

Some groups of sauropods, though, like the titanosaurs, did manage to survive right to the end of the Cretaceous in other places in the world. *Saltasaurus* was one of these late titanosaur sauropods.

Armored sauropod

Argentine paleontologists José Bonaparte and Jaime Powell announced *Saltasaurus* to the world in 1980. They had discovered the remains of a small-to-medium sauropod that had a covering of bony armor over its back. This armor was not made up of big plates, though. It was made from scattered lumps of bone called osteoderms (skin bones).

There were two different sizes of osteoderms. The larger ones were about the size of a man's palm. There were only a few tens of these, but they were surrounded by many thousands of pea-sized lumps. All of these osteoderms, large and small, were fixed in the thick skin of the animal's back.

TOUGH GUYS

▲ No predator would want to eat an Australian thorny devil—too prickly!

Many different types of animals have evolved armor to protect themselves. In mammals, armor usually consists of hard, thick patches or broad plates of skin as a defense against predators or protection against rivals of their own kind (species). Think of the thick skin plates of modern rhinoceroses, or the overlapping bands of very tough skin on armadillos. However, it is in the dinosaurs, lizards, and turtles that we see the strangest armor—spikes, plates, and horns. Most people know about spiky dinosaurs like *Styracosaurus* and *Stegosaurus*. What about spiky lizards and turtles?

The Australian thorny devil is a medium-sized lizard about 8 in (20 cm) long that is completely covered by spines. The thorny devil eats ants. It just sits out in the open, lapping them up with its tongue. It does not have to worry about being spotted by a predator like a large goanna lizard or an eagle. No animal would want to try and eat such a spiky mouthful!

Proganochelys is the earliest known turtle. This turtle could not draw its head into its shell as modern turtles can, but it had a line of strong spines all along the back of its neck. *Meiolania*, another turtle, lived in Australia in the Pleistocene epoch (1.8–0.5 million years ago). It had a set of large horns and bumps around the back of its head, and it was covered in spiny armor.

The hadrosaur (duckbill dinosaur) *Corythosaurus* also had osteoderms in its skin, as did the ankylosaurs (armored dinosaurs).

Spiky nails

Saltasaurus's large osteoderms were roundish cones. When the animal was alive, these bony cones would have been covered by an extra layer of horn. This fingernail-like material would have poked out through the skin to form a fairly large, sharp spike.

Modern bison horns grow in a similar way. The bony core of a bison horn is only about one-third to one-half the full length of the horn. Most of the horn is made of the fingernail-like tissue. This softer tissue keeps growing because it is part of the skin. Skin grows more quickly than bone does, so the horn can regrow quickly if it gets damaged.

Late Cretaceous tanks

Paleontologists often find small, isolated osteoderms in Late Cretaceous rocks. They usually have a good idea of which kind of animals these bony lumps came from—ankylosaurs.

Ankylosaurs (armored dinosaurs) were tanklike ornithischians (bird-hipped dinosaurs). Common in the Cretaceous period, they were covered in bony armor that was made up mostly of osteoderms. So when paleontologists find osteoderms in Late Cretaceous rocks, they usually think they belong to ankylosaurs.

Until 1980, scientists thought that the bony lumps they were finding in Argentina were also from ankylosaurs. Bonaparte and Powell, though, were able to show that the Argentine osteoderms came from a

▶ Like other sauropods, armored *Saltasaurus* used its long neck to reach leaves and stems high up in trees. It may have been able to stand on its hind legs, using its tail as a prop, but paleontologists have no proof that it could.

sauropod—*Saltasaurus*. This discovery was a big surprise. Why would sauropods have needed bony armor?

Tough mouthfuls

Animals like turtles, crabs, and some plant-eating dinosaurs (such as ankylosaurs) needed armor as protection from predators. Armor makes it more difficult for a predator to bite and kill an animal. Armor also makes it more difficult for a predator to eat an animal.

If a predator remembered how much trouble it was to kill and eat a well-armored dinosaur, it might not bother to try and kill any more in the future. This would save other armored dinosaurs from attack, because the predator would not want to waste its time on a difficult meal.

Paleontologists suggest that sauropods tended to grow big by natural selection. For example, elephants today are almost never attacked by lions or other predators. They are safe because they are so big; not because they are armored.

A tough little sauropod

So, if sauropods were so big, why did some of them, like *Saltasaurus*, need armor? Part of the reason may be that *Saltasaurus* was less than 40 ft (12.2 m) long. This is small for a sauropod. Of the sauropodomorph dinosaurs, only the prosauropods of the earlier Triassic period were smaller.

The Late Cretaceous period in Argentina was a dangerous place. The land was ruled by a new group of fierce theropods (two-legged meat-eaters) called

▲ Bison horns are made of similar material to *Saltasaurus*'s armor. They have a bony core covered in an outer layer of tough, fingernail-like tissue.

abelisaurs. Abelisaurs were ceratosaurs (four-fingered meat-eaters) and were very large. Like the tyrannosaurs of western North America and eastern Asia, they evolved to catch, kill, and eat large prey.

Maybe *Saltasaurus*'s ancestors were easy animals for these new, large predators to attack. Perhaps some of *Saltasaurus*'s ancestors had some armor. Perhaps this helped them to resist the abelisaurs.

Over time, natural selection would have favored those *Saltasaurus* ancestors with armor. In the end, they would have evolved into armored *Saltasaurus*.

How did *Saltasaurus* live?

Like other sauropods, *Saltasaurus* ate plants. Its long neck would have allowed it to reach leaves and stems high up in trees. It may have been able to rear up on its hind legs, using its tail as a prop. Scientists cannot prove this, though.

Saltasaurus remains seem to be fairly common, and in one case fossil-hunters found the remains of several animals in one place. This discovery may mean that *Saltasaurus* lived in herds. Living in a group would have made life safer. More pairs of eyes could watch out for marauding abelisaurs.

However, finding many skeletons together does not prove that the animals lived in herds. The dinosaurs may have died at different times, slid into a river, and washed up at the same place. Paleontologists need to find trackways of many *Saltasaurus* on the move before they can know for sure that they were herd animals.

Where *Saltasaurus* lived

By studying the sandstones and mudstones in which *Saltasaurus* was found, scientists have worked out that it lived on a broad floodplain close to the sea. There were many lakes and wide, slow rivers. The area was forested, giving *Saltasaurus* plenty of plants to eat.

CHECK THESE OUT!

Abelisaurus, Ankylosaurs, Ceratosaurs, *Corythosaurus*, Cretaceous period, Prosauropods, Saurischian dinosaurs, Sauropods

DINOFACTS

Saltasaurus
(SAL-*ta*-SORE-us)

NAME: *Saltasaurus* means Salta lizard
Salta (province in northwest Argentina) + sauros (lizard)

FAMILY: Saurischian
Sauropodomorph
Sauropod

SIZE: 39 ft (12 m) long; 8 ft (2.4 m) high at the hip

WEIGHT: 10–20 tons (9–18 tonnes)—about the same as 2–4 African elephants

FOOD: plants

HABITAT: low-lying, well-watered floodplains

WHERE: remains found in Argentina and Uruguay in South America

WHEN: about 70–65 million years ago in the Cretaceous period

			SALTASAURUS
TRIASSIC	JURASSIC	CRETACEOUS	
250 MILLION YEARS AGO	205 MILLION YEARS AGO	135 MILLION YEARS AGO	65 MILLION YEARS AGO

Saurischian dinosaurs

The saurischian dinosaurs are divided into two groups: the long-necked, plant-eating sauropodomorphs, and the two-legged, meat-eating theropods, the ancestors of modern birds.

British paleontologist Harry Seeley divided dinosaurs into two groups according to their hip shape: ornithischians (bird-hipped dinosaurs) and saurischians (lizard-hipped dinosaurs). The saurischians had a pubis that pointed downward and to the front, like the pubis of a lizard.

Common ancestor
The saurischians and the ornithischians evolved around the same time from a common

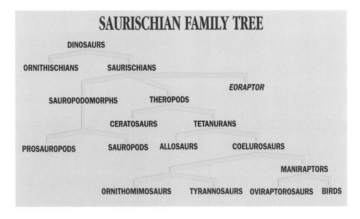

SAURISCHIAN FAMILY TREE

DINOSAURS

ORNITHISCHIANS   SAURISCHIANS

SAUROPODOMORPHS   THEROPODS   EORAPTOR

CERATOSAURS   TETANURANS

PROSAUROPODS   SAUROPODS   ALLOSAURS   COELUROSAURS

MANIRAPTORS

ORNITHOMIMOSAURS   TYRANNOSAURS   OVIRAPTOROSAURS   BIRDS

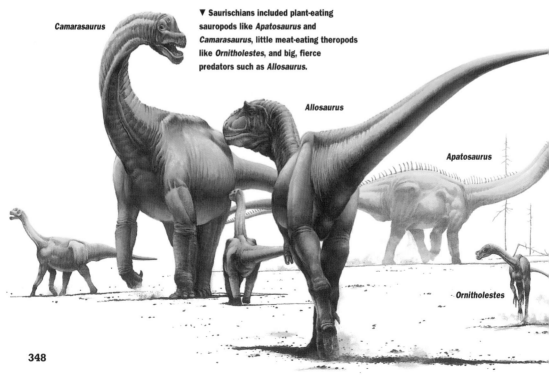

▼ Saurischians included plant-eating sauropods like *Apatosaurus* and *Camarasaurus*, little meat-eating theropods like *Ornitholestes*, and big, fierce predators such as *Allosaurus*.

Camarasaurus

Allosaurus

Apatosaurus

Ornitholestes

ancestor something like the little meat-eater *Eoraptor*. However, the saurischians developed better grasping hands with bigger thumb claws and very long index fingers. They also developed longer, S-shaped necks.

In the Late Triassic, the early saurischians evolved into two major groups: the theropods (two-legged meat-eaters) and the sauropodomorphs (long-necked plant-eaters).

Salads...

The plant-eating sauropod-omorphs were very different from the theropods. Their broad paws helped them to pull down strong branches. Their long necks let them eat the high leaves that the shorter plant-eaters could not reach. They evolved into pro-sauropods (early long-necked plant-eaters) and enormous sauropods (giant long-necked plant-eaters) like *Apatosaurus* and *Brachiosaurus*.

...or steaks

The meat-eating theropods' narrower hands helped them to snatch fleeing prey. Their longer, narrower feet helped them to run fast. The theropods evolved from the tiny ceratosaur (four-fingered meat-eater) *Coelophysis* and primitive tetanurans (stiff-tailed meat-eaters), to the giant three-fingered allosaurs and hollow-tailed coelurosaurs, the mostly toothless ornitho-mimosaurs (ostrichlike dinosaurs) and huge, fierce hunters like *Tyrannosaurus*, and the long-armed maniraptors and oviraptorosaurs (egg-thief dinosaurs). After the largest nonflying dinosaurs died out at the end of the Cretaceous period, the saurischians lived on as birds.

DINOFACTS

Saurischian dinosaurs
(*SORE*-ISK-ee-AN)

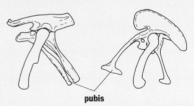

▶ **It's a hip thing—In** ornithischians (left), such as *Scelidosaurus*, the pubis points backward. In saurischians (right), such as *Ceratosaurus*, the pubis points forward.

pubis

 NAME: Saurischian means lizard-hipped sauros (lizard) + ischia (hip)

 FAMILY: Dinosaur

 SIZE: huge variation from 3.3 ft (1 m) to 120 ft (37 m) or more long; from 1 ft (30 cm) to 14 ft (4.3 m) high at the hip

WEIGHT: huge variation from 6 lbs (2.7 kg) to 50 tons (45 tonnes) or more

 FOOD: meat, plants, possibly fish, eggs, insects

HABITAT: all types, from woodlands to plains to swamps to deserts

N
WHERE: remains found worldwide

WHEN: 230 million years ago in the Triassic period to today (since birds are saurischian dinosaurs)

SAURISCHIAN DINOSAURS

TRIASSIC	JURASSIC	CRETACEOUS
250 MILLION YEARS AGO	205 MILLION YEARS AGO	135 MILLION YEARS AGO ··· 65 MILLION YEARS AGO

CHECK THESE OUT!
Dinosaurs, *Eoraptor*, Ornithischian dinosaurs, Sauropodomorph dinosaurs, Theropods

Saurolophus

Saurolophus was the first complete skeleton of a Canadian dinosaur ever found. It was a hadrosaur (duckbill dinosaur) that lived in North America and also Asia during the Late Cretaceous period.

In 1911 Barnum Brown collected the first *Saurolophus* fossil near the Red Deer River in Canada. This skeleton is still the best example of this hadrosaur ever found.

Scientists usually divide the hadrosaurs into two groups: lambeosaurines, which had hollow crests on their heads, and hadrosaurines, with solid or no head crests. *Saurolophus* had a small, solid crest, so it was a hadrosaurine.

Saurolophus in Mongolia
In 1957, Russian paleontologist A. K. Rozhdestvensky described another, larger kind (species) of *Saurolophus* that had been found in Central Asia.

The Central Asian species differed from the North American *Saurolophus* because it had a larger, narrower skull and a longer crest.

HIP PROBLEMS

US fossil-hunter Barnum Brown described the skeleton of *Saurolophus* in 1913. He noted that one of the hipbones, the ischium, was missing from the almost complete Canadian specimen. In its place he described another ischium that had been found at the same site as *Saurolophus*. This substitute bone was very solid and was larger at the bottom than the top.

Brown's use of this other ischium confused scientists when they tried to classify *Saurolophus*. Lambeosaurine hadrosaurs had an ischium that was bigger at the bottom, while the hadrosaurines had an ischium that was bigger at the top. Because of Brown's substitute bone, for many years scientists believed that *Saurolophus* was a lambeosaurine. However, they have now established, on the basis of many other features of the skeleton, that *Saurolophus* was really a hadrosaurine. The ischium that Brown described belonged to a lambeosaurine, such as *Hypacrosaurus*.

▼ Scientists believe hadrosaurs, such as *Saurolophus*, may have spent some time in water. They had paddlelike feet and may have been strong swimmers.

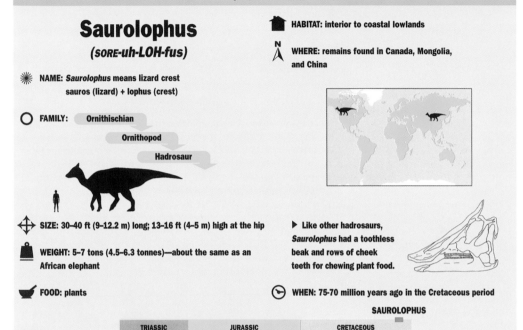

DINOFACTS

Saurolophus
(SORE-uh-LOH-fus)

✳ **NAME:** *Saurolophus* means lizard crest
sauros (lizard) + lophus (crest)

○ **FAMILY:** Ornithischian
→ Ornithopod
→ Hadrosaur

✛ **SIZE:** 30–40 ft (9–12.2 m) long; 13–16 ft (4–5 m) high at the hip

⬛ **WEIGHT:** 5–7 tons (4.5–6.3 tonnes)—about the same as an African elephant

🥣 **FOOD:** plants

🏠 **HABITAT:** interior to coastal lowlands

🧭 **WHERE:** remains found in Canada, Mongolia, and China

▶ Like other hadrosaurs, *Saurolophus* had a toothless beak and rows of cheek teeth for chewing plant food.

🕐 **WHEN:** 75-70 million years ago in the Cretaceous period

SAUROLOPHUS

TRIASSIC	JURASSIC	CRETACEOUS
250 MILLION YEARS AGO	205 MILLION YEARS AGO	135 MILLION YEARS AGO	65 MILLION YEARS AGO

Some specimens of the Asian *Saurolophus* were more than 40 ft (12.2 m) long. This made them as large as the big meat-eaters, such as the tyrannosaur *Tarbosaurus*, that shared the same habitat as *Saurolophus*.

Alaskan land bridge
During the Late Cretaceous, *Saurolophus* and tyrannosaurs lived alongside each other in both Central Asia and North America. This indicates that animals could move between Asia and North America across a land bridge between Alaska and Siberia. This bridge is now covered by the Bering Strait, and animals can cross the frozen sea only in the middle of the coldest winters.

How did *Saurolophus* live?
Central Asia and western Canada were moist lowland habitats in the Late Cretaceous period when *Saurolophus* was alive. Although there is no direct evidence, because many other hadrosaurs traveled in herds, paleontologists think that *Saurolophus* probably did too. Like all ornithischians (bird-hipped dinosaurs), hadrosaurs ate plants. They fed on coarse vegetation, grinding it up with large numbers of small cheek teeth.

The Asian *Saurolophus* was large enough to have pushed down trees to eat, like elephants do today. Both *Saurolophus* species would have been an important source of food for the tyrannosaurs.

CHECK THESE OUT!
Cretaceous period, Hadrosaurs,
Hypacrosaurus, *Lambeosaurus*,
Ornithischian dinosaurs,
Tarbosaurus, Tyrannosaurs

Sauropelta

Tanklike *Sauropelta* was discovered in the 1930s on the Montana-Wyoming border by dinosaur hunter Barnum Brown. It was an armored dinosaur with pairs of massive spines on its neck.

Although *Sauropelta* was first found in the 1930s, scientists did not know what it was at first, except that it was an armored dinosaur. A specimen was even displayed at the American Museum of Natural History as a *Nodosaurus*.

In the 1960s, Yale University's John Ostrom led further expeditions to where the fossils had been found. He found more large armored dinosaur specimens. Ostrom finally described *Sauropelta* in 1970, almost 40 years after its first discovery.

ROUNDED PRINTS

Paleontologist Ken Carpenter recognized that tracks in the Early Cretaceous Bullhead Mountain Formation of British Columbia, Canada, belonged to a large nodosaurid. They had earlier been thought to belong to a ceratopsian (horned dinosaur), but the print was too rounded and the toes were too short. His analysis of these tracks indicated that the feet of *Sauropelta* would fit well within them. The feet appeared to have been covered by heavy skin like those of modern rhinoceroses.

Paleontologists divide most ankylosaurs into two groups: ankylosaurids (with tail-clubs), and nodosaurids (without).

Sauropelta had no tail-club so it was classified as a nodosaurid. It was also a primitive (little evolved) nodosaurid, since it had teeth in its upper beak; more advanced nodosaurids did not. It also did not have a bony layer in the roof of its mouth, as did advanced nodosaurids

Sauropelta
(SORE-uh-PEL-tuh)

❋ **NAME:** *Sauropelta* means small shield lizard
sauros (lizard) + pelta (small shield)

○ **FAMILY:** Ornithischian
> Thyreophoran
>> Ankylosaur

✛ **SIZE:** 30 ft (9 m) long; 8 ft (2.4 m) high at the hip

⚖ **WEIGHT:** 5 tons (4.5 tonnes)—about the same as an African elephant

🥣 **FOOD:** low-growing plants

🏠 **HABITAT:** lowland savannas

WHERE: remains found in Montana, Utah, Wyoming, and perhaps southwestern Arkansas

🕐 **WHEN:** 115–105 million years ago in the Cretaceous period

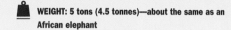

		SAUROPELTA	
TRIASSIC	JURASSIC	CRETACEOUS	
250 MILLION YEARS AGO	205 MILLION YEARS AGO	135 MILLION YEARS AGO	65 MILLION YEARS AGO

◀ ***Sauropelta* was a heavy, armored dinosaur. It had rows of large, ridged armor plates along its back. These were mixed with smaller plates, making its back flexible.**

like *Edmontonia* and *Panoplosaurus* (and mammals). In most ways, however, *Sauropelta* was much like these advanced nodosaurids: it had a long skull, a body covered by ridged armor plates, and back legs longer than its forelegs. *Sauropelta* had three pairs of spines on its neck that got bigger toward the shoulders. On its shoulders it had a pair of huge narrow spines. Along its sides it had spines that got

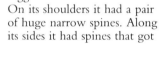

smaller toward the hips. Triangular spines ran down the sides of its tail.

How did *Sauropelta* live?
Sauropelta and its close relatives seem to have been widespread along the edges of the new Western Interior Seaway that covered parts of North America during the Cretaceous period. Their narrow muzzles and small teeth suggest they fed on soft plants. They may have had a complex digestive system, like that of modern plant-eating mammals such as cattle. Their spines, extensive shoulder armor, and long armored tail would have protected them against predators like *Deinonychus*.

CHECK THESE OUT!
Ankylosaurs, Cretaceous period, *Deinonychus, Edmontonia, Nodosaurus, Panoplosaurus*

Sauropodomorph dinosaurs

With their tiny heads, long necks, round bodies, and long tails it is easy to recognize the sauropodomorph dinosaurs. The largest of these plant-eating giants could weigh more than 10 elephants.

The sauropodomorphs were saurischian (lizard-hipped) dinosaurs. They were related to the other main group of saurischians, the theropods (two-legged meat-eaters).

Earliest known dinosaur
The earliest known dinosaur was *Eoraptor*, which lived in Argentina in the Late Triassic period. *Eoraptor* was a small meat-eater similar to a theropod.

The earliest known sauropodomorphs were plant-eaters. No one has found a dinosaur fossil that clearly links

the earliest known plant-eating sauropodomorph to the earliest meat-eating dinosaur.

Although paleontologists are not sure about their exact

A USEFUL CLAW

All sauropodomorphs had a big thumb claw. This was especially big in the prosauropods. What could such a claw have done?

One idea is that it was used to pull down branches of trees. Early sauropodomorphs may have used it this way. However, later sauropodomorphs had very long necks which would have let them poke their heads much higher up into trees than they could reach with the claw.

The claw may have been used as a weapon by males fighting other males or as a defense against predators. The claw may have been a tool to rip off the bark of tree trunks to reach the softer part inside.

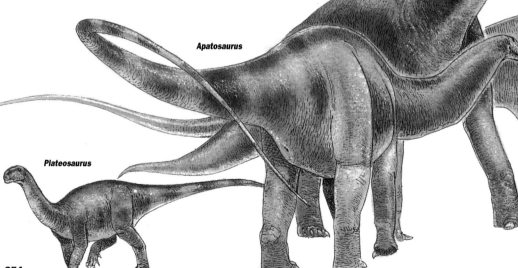

Brachiosaurus

Apatosaurus

Plateosaurus

DINOFACTS

Sauropodomorph dinosaurs

(SORE-uh-POD-uh-MORF)

☀ **NAME:** Sauropodomorph means lizard foot form
sauros (lizard) + pous (foot) + omorph (having the form)

○ **FAMILY:** Saurischian

✛ **SIZE:** huge variation from 8 ft (2.4 m) to 120 ft (37 m) or more long; from 3 ft (90 cm) to 14 ft (4.3 m) high at the hip

⚖ **WEIGHT:** huge variation from about 60 lbs (27 kg) to 50 tons (45 tonnes) or more

🥣 **FOOD:** plants

🏠 **HABITAT:** tropical (dry or wet) and temperate woodlands

WHERE: remains found in Africa, Asia, Europe, India, North America, and South America

🕐 **WHEN:** from 230 million years ago in the Triassic period to 65 million years ago in the Cretaceous period

SAUROPODOMORPHS

TRIASSIC	JURASSIC	CRETACEOUS

| 250 MILLION YEARS AGO | 205 MILLION YEARS AGO | 135 MILLION YEARS AGO | 65 MILLION YEARS AGO |

▼ Sauropods were bigger than prosauropods. One of the largest prosauropods, *Plateosaurus*, was dwarfed by the great sauropod *Seismosaurus*.

Seismosaurus

ancestry, sauropodomorphs share many features with the theropod dinosaurs. The ankles, hips, upper arm bones, and skulls of all sauropodomorphs are very like those of the theropods.

Two groups

Sauropodomorphs are divided into two groups—the medium-sized prosauropods and the gigantic sauropods. The prosauropods were the first to appear in the fossil record and lived during the Late Triassic and Early Jurassic periods. By the Early Jurassic period, the true sauropods appeared. They survived right up to the end of the Cretaceous period.

Although the two groups of dinosaurs were closely related, the prosauropods never got as big as the later sauropods. These giant browsers were the largest land animals ever to have lived on the earth.

CHECK THESE OUT!

Eoraptor, Prosauropods, Saurischian dinosaurs, Sauropods, Theropods

Sauropods

Sauropods (long-necked plant-eaters) were the largest, longest, and heaviest animals ever to walk the earth. Some of these giant dinosaurs weighed as much as an 18-wheeled truck.

A lot of scientific detective work has been carried out to learn about sauropods.

Browsing the treetops
The sauropods got their body plan from their prosauropod (early long-necked plant-eater) relatives. The body plan was specialized for browsing (gathering leaves and twigs with the mouth), swallowing the food quickly because they had no cheeks and could not chew, and then digesting it slowly in a large gut.

The heads of sauropods were basically a large mouth on the end of a long neck. Their long necks

The sauropod dinosaurs were one of the strangest groups of large animals that ever lived on earth. It has taken many years for paleontologists to even begin to fully understand these mysterious animals.

Studying modern birds can give scientists some idea of what the theropod (two-legged meat-eating) dinosaurs might have been like because birds are living theropods.

However, it is a totally different story for the sauropods. They left no living descendants for scientists to compare with the fossil animals.

allowed the animals to reach a wide area of food from one standing position.

Sauropod teeth do not show any features for chewing. However, from looking at the teeth of different kinds of sauropods, scientists can tell that different kinds ate different foods. Diplodocid sauropods, like *Diplodocus* and *Apatosaurus*, from the Late Jurassic period of western North America, had long, pencil-like teeth. These would have been good for raking leaves, pine needles, and shoots from branches. *Camarasaurus*, which lived alongside the

◀ **Brachiosaurus**

Antarctosaurus ▶

diplodocids, had very short, thick, strong teeth. Scientists think that *Camarasaurus*'s teeth were better for biting and pulling much tougher plants.

Long-distance walkers

Sauropods' large bodies were carried by long legs. Large, long-legged animals can walk great distances without getting tired. Modern elephants and giraffes both have long legs, and these animals will walk long distances to find food and water. The sauropods would have needed a lot of food, so they probably would have had to move regularly from place to place to find new feeding grounds. This movement is known as migration.

The sauropods' long limbs would not have bent much at the knee or elbow. It would have been too hard for the animal to support its weight with bent limbs for any length of time. Bones and joints are strongest when the arms and

STAYING IN SHAPE

While the theropods evolved many different body shapes, from tiny *Compsognathus* to giant *Tyrannosaurus*, the sauropods had an almost unchanging body form throughout the 100 million years that they lived on earth. Compare Middle Jurassic *Cetiosaurus* (4) to Late Jurassic *Brachiosaurus* (1) and *Diplodocus* (2) and Cretaceous *Saltasaurus* (3).

◀ The long necks of sauropods may have been used for reaching up into trees for food; or for reaching across for food that was a long way from the dinosaur's feet.

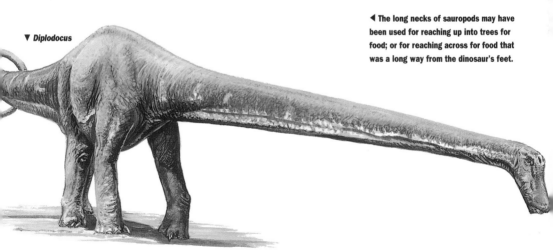

▼ *Diplodocus*

357

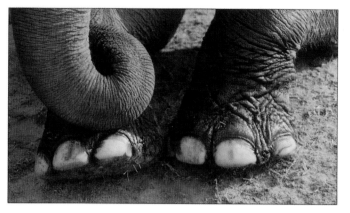

sorts of adaptations that help support their large bodies: legs like pillars, stiff wrists, short toes, and toenails like hooves.

Elephants are a good example of the limitations of supporting a large body weight: they can run for only short periods of time, with a shuffling sort of motion, and they cannot jump. However, they are also a good example of the limitations of studying a skeleton. Who would guess from looking at their bones that elephants could stand on their hands? They can, though.

▲ Elephant feet are similar in many ways to sauropod feet.

legs are close to being straight, and muscles do not have to work too hard. Think how long you can stand with your knees bent. Now imagine that you are 1,000 times heavier! This gives an idea of why it was so important for sauropods to keep their limbs straight.

Also, sauropods would not have swung their limbs back and forth much to take a step. Their legs were long enough that just a small swing would have let the animal walk at a speed of 2-3 mph (3-4 kph).

Not lizard feet

The name *sauropod* means lizard foot, but sauropods' feet were unlike the feet of any lizard. All sauropods had very short fingers and toes (digits). Usually only the first, and sometimes the second, digit had a short claw. The rest of the fingers and toes had a hooflike covering.

Other bones in the hand, such as the bones between the fingers and the wrist, were grouped tightly and looked like little pillars. The wrist

bones were either block shaped or very flat. This meant that the wrists were strong but not very flexible. The ankles were built in the same way. These changes helped to support the huge weight of the sauropod body. Elephants show similar

Weight-saving bones

Although sauropod limbs show adaptations to carrying heavy bodies, some of the more advanced (highly evolved) sauropods had special features that made their bodies lighter. The bones making up the spine between the shoulders

SAUROPODS—A BRIEF HISTORY

The sauropods first appeared in the Early Jurassic period or perhaps even the Late Triassic period. The earliest sauropods that paleontologists know of were *Barapasaurus* from India and *Vulcanodon* from Africa, both of which lived in the Early Jurassic period. Scientists cannot agree whether *Vulcanodon* was a prosauropod (early long-necked plant-eater) or a primitive (little evolved) sauropod.

In the Middle Jurassic period lived the cetiosaurs such as *Cetiosaurus* from England and *Patagosaurus* from Argentina. However, it was in the Late Jurassic period that sauropods were most abundant. During this time, the ridge-backed diplodocids such as *Diplodocus* and *Apatosaurus* roamed North America, as did box-headed *Camarasaurus* and giraffe-necked *Brachiosaurus*. In Asia, tail-clubbed euhelopodid sauropods such as *Euhelopus* and *Mamenchisaurus* were the ruling plant-eaters.

Many kinds of sauropods died out at the end of the Jurassic period, including the diplodocids and the euhelopodids. However, that was not the end of the sauropods. Some unusual forms evolved, such as *Amargasaurus* from Argentina with its strange mane. The most numerous Cretaceous sauropods were the titanosaurs. Most of these, such as *Saltasaurus*, had armor and lived in the southern continents. At the end of the Cretaceous period, there is evidence, such as the remains of *Alamosaurus* found in Texas, that titanosaurs were beginning to move into North America.

and hips of most sauropods were much more lightly built than those of most animals.

The main part of a backbone (vertebra) is called the centrum, and in most animals it is a solid cylinder of bone. Most sauropods, however, had side hollows that made the centrum smaller and lighter. This new form of centrum was almost as strong as a solid one but much lighter. Early sauropods like *Cetiosaurus* from the Middle Jurassic period did not have such improved backbones, but Late Jurassic kinds such as *Apatosaurus* did.

Sauropod decline
The Early Cretaceous period marked major changes in the earth's plant life. Flowering plants appeared, replacing many non–flowering kinds. New plant-eating dinosaurs, the hadrosaurs (duckbill dinosaurs) and ceratopsians (horned dinosaurs), evolved that fed upon the new plants.

In the northern hemisphere, sauropods seem to have declined. Paleontologists have found few sauropod fossils from Cretaceous North America and Europe, although they have recovered several from Asia. It seems that most sauropods either could not digest the new plants, or they could not compete with the smaller ornithischian (bird-hipped) hadrosaurs and ceratopsians. However, in the southern continent sauropods such as the titanosaurs (armored sauropods) thrived and became that region's main plant-eaters.

DINOFACTS

Sauropods
(SORE-uh-PODZ)

☀ **NAME: Sauropod means lizard foot**
sauros (lizard) + pous (foot)

◯ **FAMILY:** Saurischian
Sauropodomorph

✛ **SIZE: 16–120 ft (5–37 m) or more long; 3.5–14 ft (1–4.3 m) high at the hip**

⚖ **WEIGHT: 1–50 tons (0.9–45 tonnes) or more—or from 1 North American bison to 10 African elephants**

🥣 **FOOD: plants**

🏠 **HABITAT: tropical forests and temperate woodlands**

WHERE: remains found in North America, Africa, Asia, Europe, and South America

🕐 **WHEN: from 190 million years ago in the Jurassic period to 65 million years ago in the Cretaceous period**

	SAUROPODS	
TRIASSIC	JURASSIC	CRETACEOUS
250 MILLION YEARS AGO	205 MILLION YEARS AGO	135 MILLION YEARS AGO · 65 MILLION YEARS AGO

CHECK THESE OUT!

Alamosaurus, Amargasaurus, Antarctosaurus, Apatosaurus, Argentinosaurus, Barapasaurus, Barosaurus, Brachiosaurus, Camarasaurus, Cetiosaurus, Datousaurus, Diplodocus, Euhelopus, Hypselosaurus, Mamenchisaurus, Nemegtosaurus, Omeisaurus, Opisthocoelicaudia, Patagosaurus, Saltasaurus, Seismosaurus, Supersaurus, Titanosaurus, Vulcanodon

Saurornithoides

Saurornithoides is one of the best-known troodontids (big-eyed brainy hunters) and roamed Asia in the Cretaceous period. Its saucerlike eyes suggest that it might have been able to see well in poor light.

The skull and partial skeleton of a small theropod (two-legged meat-eating) dinosaur were found in Mongolia in 1923. US paleontologist Henry Fairfield Osborn named them *Saurornithoides*. Two other theropods that he named—*Oviraptor* and *Velociraptor*—became famous, while *Saurornithoides* was forgotten.

In 1969, Canadian paleontologist Dale Russell described the theropod *Troodon,* which shared many features with the forgotten *Saurornithoides.* When more specimens of *Saurornithoides* were discovered in the 1970s, it was seen that *Troodon* and *Saurornithoides* were related and were both troodontids. They

THE FLAMING CLIFFS

Saurornithoides was one of many fossils found at the Flaming Cliffs. This was the name given to badlands in southern Mongolia, because in sunlight the reds and oranges of the sandstone there look like the color of fire. This is one of the richest fossil sites in the world. Among the other dinosaurs first found at the Flaming Cliffs are *Protoceratops, Pinacosaurus, Oviraptor,* and *Velociraptor.*

▼ *Saurornithoides* had good eyesight and long legs, so it was probably good at catching small animals to eat.

were both fairly small theropods with grasping hands and a small claw on the second toe of the foot that could be retracted like a cat's claw.

How *Saurornithoides* lived

From the shape of its skull, we know that *Saurornithoides* had very large eyes. The eyes were directed more forward than to the side, suggesting that *Saurornithoides* had very good forward vision. Also, the spaces where its ears would have been are quite large and specialized, suggesting *Saurornithoides* had very good hearing.

It is likely that *Saurornithoides* hunted small animals. However, the troodontids' teeth were small for the size of their skulls. Their teeth had rough cone-shaped bumps rather than small serrations. These features make them similar to the teeth of other dinosaurs and lizards that ate at least some plants. So *Saurornithoides* may have eaten other things besides meat, possibly insects, eggs, and plants. *Saurornithoides* had very long legs for its size, so it could probably run fast, which is useful for catching small prey.

CHECK THESE OUT!

Cretaceous period, Maniraptors, *Oviraptor, Pinacosaurus, Protoceratops,* Saurischian dinosaurs, Theropods, *Velociraptor*

DINOFACTS

Saurornithoides

(*SORE-or-nee-THOY-deez*)

▶ The skull of *Saurornithoides* had large eye sockets and a long, tapered snout. At first paleontologists thought the dinosaur was an early bird.

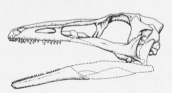

✳ NAME: *Saurornithoides* means lizard bird form
   sauros (lizard) + ornis (bird) + oides (form of)

○ FAMILY:

Saurischian
Theropod
Maniraptor

✛ SIZE: up to 8 ft (2.4 m) long; up to 2.5 ft (76 cm) high at the hip

⚖ WEIGHT: up to 60 lbs (27 kg)—about the same as a large beaver

🥣 FOOD: meat, and possibly insects, eggs, and plants

🏠 HABITAT: deserts and surroundings

⌖N WHERE: remains found in Mongolia and China

🕑 WHEN: 80–68 million years ago in the Cretaceous period

SAURORNITHOIDES

TRIASSIC	JURASSIC	CRETACEOUS
250 MILLION YEARS AGO	205 MILLION YEARS AGO	135 MILLION YEARS AGO	65 MILLION YEARS AGO

361

Scelidosaurus

Scelidosaurus was a heavily built armored dinosaur that plodded along the English seashore in the Early Jurassic period. It was one of the earliest ornithischian (bird-hipped) dinosaurs.

A few scattered *Scelidosaurus* bones were discovered in 1859 in rocks from the Early Jurassic period on the south coast of England. These rocks are famous for preserving the first known ichthyosaur (fish lizard) fossil, which was discovered by fossil-hunter Mary Anning.

British scientist Richard Owen named *Scelidosaurus* in 1861. Two years later, he made a full description based on a nearly complete skeleton that was missing only the front legs and front of the skull.

Owen described *Scelidosaurus* as a four-legged armored dinosaur with a long tail. Its back feet had four toes with fairly sharp claws. Several rows of oval-shape plates

(scutes) of armor ran along the upper part of its body. Just behind the head were a pair of short three-pronged spines. Two rows of low spines ran down the animal's neck and back, with a single row running down its tail. This is very like the arrangement of

▶ **Scelidosaurus lived near the sea. Its skin was covered with small scales and studded with armor plates.**

362

the armor scutes in another Early Jurassic dinosaur: *Scutellosaurus*.

Washed out to sea?

The rocks in which *Scelidosaurus* was found were laid down as sediment at the bottom of a prehistoric sea. This presented Owen with a problem, because he thought *Scelidosaurus* was a land animal. How did it come to be buried at the bottom of the ocean?

Owen believed that *Scelidosaurus* could swim, but he did not think that it had swum out to sea. Instead he proposed that a dead *Scelidosaurus* had floated down a river and into the sea. The carcass could have attracted scavengers, such as sharks, crabs, and

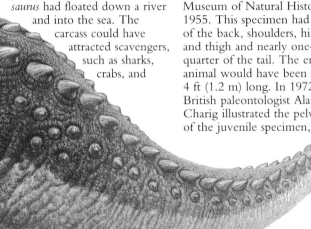

plesiosaurs, which would explain why its legs were missing. After the carcass had been ripped open by the scavengers, it would have sunk and become buried at the bottom of the sea.

AN ACID BATH

Sometimes as bone fossilizes, the surrounding mud can cause hard masses of limestone rock to form around the fossil. Although these stony limestone slabs may preserve the fossils, the slabs can also be very difficult to remove from the fossils. Fossils are usually extracted by carefully chipping the rock away from the bone. When the rock is harder than the bone, this is very difficult to do without damaging the bone. However, limestone and bone react to acetic acid (found in vinegar) differently. If placed in weak acetic acid, limestone can be dissolved away without damaging the bone. The British Museum's juvenile *Scelidosaurus* skeleton was cleaned this way. In 1968, one of the museum's best fossil preparators, A. E. Rixon, published a detailed description of how he had prepared the skeleton. His procedure has become a model for this method of separating fossil bones from limestone.

A young *Scelidosaurus*

A small specimen, identified as a juvenile *Scelidosaurus*, was obtained by the British Museum of Natural History in 1955. This specimen had most of the back, shoulders, hips, and thigh and nearly one-quarter of the tail. The entire animal would have been about 4 ft (1.2 m) long. In 1972, British paleontologist Alan Charig illustrated the pelvis of the juvenile specimen, and his illustration has often been used to show what the pelvis of a primitive (little evolved) ornithischian was like.

Australian paleontologist Tony Thulborn agreed that all primitive ornithischian dinosaurs had a similar pelvis, but disagreed about the identification of the specimen. He pointed out that it was impossible to show that this fossil was *Scelidosaurus*. Thulborn thought that it might have been a primitive ornithopod (bird-footed dinosaur). However, because the specimen had some armor scutes, most paleontologists think it was *Scelidosaurus*.

Classifying *Scelidosaurus*

There has been considerable disagreement over how to classify *Scelidosaurus*. Owen recognized that it was similar to *Hylaeosaurus* in having protective armor. In the 1860s, however, no one knew whether all dinosaurs had armor or not, so it was not clear how important the armor was. After about 1900, most scientists thought that *Scelidosaurus* was a type of stegosaur (plate-backed dinosaur).

In 1968, Harvard paleontologist Alfred Romer decided that it was an ankylosaur (armored dinosaur). Thulborn,

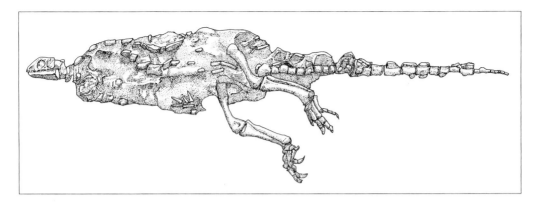

▲ This is how the remains of *Scelidosaurus* looked before being given the acid-bath treatment. Encased in limestone, the bones could not be seen clearly.

however, disagreed with this because at that time there were no known Jurassic ankylosaurs; all were Cretaceous dinosaurs. He classified *Scelidosaurus* as an ornithopod because he believed that some ornithopods had armor. A number of paleontologists disagreed with this idea. In the 1980s, Paul Sereno decided that *Scelidosaurus* was a primitive member of the thyreophoran group (armored and plate-backed dinosaurs), which included both the stegosaurs and the ankylosaurs.

Another new specimen
In 1985, a new specimen of *Scelidosaurus* was discovered near Charmouth in southern England. Although it has not been formally described, British paleontologist David Norman discussed some of the important discoveries learned from this specimen. For the first time the front of the skull

could be studied. This showed that *Scelidosaurus* had a pointed snout with six teeth at the front of its upper jaws.

Parts of the forelimbs and even skin impressions have also been found. The skin impressions show that where the skin was not covered by bony armor, it was covered by small scales. Norman concluded that *Scelidosaurus* was more closely related to the ankylosaurs than to the stegosaurs because it had extensive armor and had armor fused to its skull and jaw bones.

A new relative
In 1990, German paleontologist Hartmut Haubold described a small armored dinosaur. This had been

discovered in rocks about 193 to 187 million years old (from the late Early Jurassic period) in northern Germany— younger rocks than those that contained *Scelidosaurus*. The specimen consisted of a complete skull with parts of the skeleton.

Haubold named this dinosaur *Emausaurus* after his university, Ernst-Moritz-Arndt-Universität (EMAU). *Emausaurus* was similar to *Scelidosaurus* in its overall body form. It was about 6.5 ft (2 m) long. It also had a fairly triangular skull with teeth at

▶ *Scelidosaurus* probably moved on all fours, just as Richard Owen thought. It had longer legs than most thyreophorans and it may have been fairly agile.

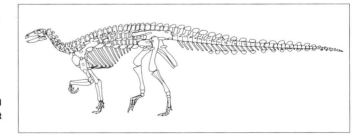

the front of the upper jaws. Its greatest difference from *Scelidosaurus* was that it had no armor fused to its skull. It also had fairly tall armor plates that may have been arranged on its back like those of a stegosaur (plate-backed dinosaur) or along the sides of its body like those of an ankylosaur. Haubold thought that like *Scelidosaurus*, *Emausaurus* was a primitive thyreophoran that could not be placed with either the stegosaurs or the ankylosaurs.

Mysterious armor

In 1989, Berkeley paleontologist Kevin Padian reported that he had found fossil remains of *Scelidosaurus* in the Kayenta Formation of northeastern Arizona. What he had actually found were a few distinctive pieces of armor. This discovery was important because the Kayenta Formation and its dinosaurs (*Scutellosaurus*, *Massospondylus*, *Syntarsus*, and *Dilophosaurus*) had been thought to be Late Triassic in age. Now it seemed they belonged to the Early Jurassic period. However, it is not clear whether the armor belongs to *Scelidosaurus*, *Emausaurus*, or to some other kind of primitive thyreophoran dinosaur that was present in the Early Jurassic period.

How did *Scelidosaurus* live?

Scelidosaurus probably lived on coastal plains. Its narrow mouth would have allowed it to feed selectively on specific plants, which it would have shredded with its leaflike teeth.

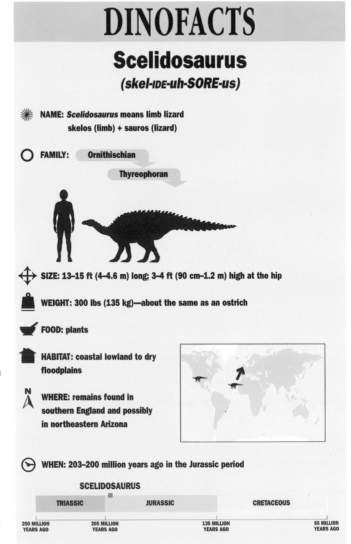

DINOFACTS

Scelidosaurus
(skel-IDE-uh-SORE-us)

NAME: *Scelidosaurus* means limb lizard
skelos (limb) + sauros (lizard)

FAMILY: Ornithischian
Thyreophoran

SIZE: 13–15 ft (4–4.6 m) long; 3–4 ft (90 cm–1.2 m) high at the hip

WEIGHT: 300 lbs (135 kg)—about the same as an ostrich

FOOD: plants

HABITAT: coastal lowland to dry floodplains

WHERE: remains found in southern England and possibly in northeastern Arizona

WHEN: 203–200 million years ago in the Jurassic period

SCELIDOSAURUS

TRIASSIC	JURASSIC	CRETACEOUS
250 MILLION YEARS AGO	205 MILLION YEARS AGO	135 MILLION YEARS AGO ... 65 MILLION YEARS AGO

Although it was an armored dinosaur that walked on four legs, it was lighter and had longer legs than most ankylosaurs and stegosaurs. So it may have been fairly nimble-footed for an armored dinosaur.

CHECK THESE OUT!

Ankylosaurs, *Dilophosaurus*, Jurassic period, Ornithischian dinosaurs, Ornithopods, *Scutellosaurus*, Stegosaurs, Thyreophorans

Seismosaurus

In the 1980s, US paleontologists discovered *Seismosaurus*, a new kind of sauropod (long-necked plant-eating dinosaur). *Seismosaurus* may have been the longest animal that ever lived.

One of the many things that people find amazing about dinosaurs is their great size. *Seismosaurus* was big even by dinosaur standards. Scientists estimate that *Seismosaurus* could have been between 120 and 150 ft (37 and 46 m) long! That is at least 20 ft (6 m)

▶ *Seismosaurus's* tail and neck were both extremely long. Its body was not much larger than the bodies of other big sauropods.

EATEN! DEAD OR ALIVE

The paleontologists digging out *Seismosaurus* found one very interesting clue to how this dinosaur might have died. About 3 ft (90 cm) from one of *Seismosaurus*'s backbones they found a single tooth from a theropod (two-legged meat-eating dinosaur). The original owner of the tooth cannot be identified for certain, but it was probably an *Allosaurus*. There is not enough evidence, however, to tell whether the theropod hunted and killed *Seismosaurus* or just scavenged meat from its dead body.

longer than the longest recorded blue whale, which is the largest animal alive today.

The newly discovered dinosaur was named *Seismosaurus* (shaking lizard) because the ground might have shaken like a small earthquake when this huge animal walked.

Diary of decay
Scientists carefully measured and recorded the position of the dinosaur's bones before digging them from the ground. They also studied the sandstone rock in which the bones had been preserved.

Seismosaurus

(SIZE-mo-SORE-us)

✳ **NAME:** *Seismosaurus* means shaking lizard
seismo (to shake) + sauros (lizard)

○ **FAMILY:** Saurischian

Sauropodomorph

Sauropod

✥ **SIZE:** 120–150 ft (37–46 m) long; 14 ft (4.3 m) high at the hip

⚖ **WEIGHT:** perhaps 50 tons (45 tonnes)—about the same
as 10 African elephants

🥣 **FOOD:** plants

🏠 **HABITAT:** broad, low-lying plains with many large rivers

⇗ **WHERE:** remains found in New Mexico

🕐 **WHEN:** 140 million years ago in the Jurassic period

		SEISMOSAURUS	
TRIASSIC	JURASSIC	▪	CRETACEOUS
250 MILLION YEARS AGO	205 MILLION YEARS AGO	135 MILLION YEARS AGO	65 MILLION YEARS AGO

From their studies, they could tell that the *Seismosaurus* skeleton had lain in a river soon after it died. A meat-eating scavenger may have stripped some of the flesh from the bones. Over several days or weeks, the flow of the river had then broken up the body and carried away the skull, most of the neck bones, the legs, and half of the tail. Fossil-hunters found only some neck, back, and tail bones and the ribs and hips. These bones were enough to tell paleontologists that *Seismosaurus* was a diplodocid sauropod, closely related to *Diplodocus* and *Apatosaurus*.

How did *Seismosaurus* live?
Like other sauropods, *Seismosaurus* probably ate plants. It would have taken a lot of plant material to fill up such a large animal, so it probably spent most of its time feeding.

CHECK THESE OUT!

*Allosaurus, Apatosaurus,
Diplodocus, Jurassic period,
Saurischian dinosaurs,
Sauropodomorph dinosaurs, Sauropods*

367

Shunosaurus

Shunosaurus was a large four-legged dinosaur that browsed in the forests of China in the Middle Jurassic period. It was one of the massive sauropods (long–necked plant–eaters).

Shunosaurus is an important sauropod because it lived in the Middle Jurassic period (178–157 million years ago). Paleontologists know less about this time than any other in the Mesozoic Era, so any new Middle Jurassic fossils give valuable information about this mysterious age.

Finding heads

Sauropod dinosaur skeletons are often found without their heads. Fortunately, there is a dinosaur quarry in Shandong Province of northeast China where many complete sauropod skeletons have been found. *Shunosaurus* is one of these.

About 20 almost complete skeletons of *Shunosaurus* have been discovered, and on five of these the heads were attached. Because the skulls of all animals, whether living or dead, contain a lot of useful information, paleontologists like to find dinosaur heads.

Finding the heads of sauropods is especially important because the body skeletons of different kinds are often quite similar. Finding the head makes identification easier, as the features of the skull help scientists to figure out how *Shunosaurus* was related to other sauropods.

◄ **Unusually for a sauropod dinosaur, *Shunosaurus* had a bony club at the end of its tail, which it could use to swipe an attacker.**

How did *Shunosaurus* live?

Shunosaurus had a fairly short neck for a sauropod. Maybe it did not browse the very tops of trees, as the very long–necked *Brachiosaurus* probably did. Perhaps it ate leaves and twigs that grew partway up the tree trunk. *Shunosaurus* had long jaws that contained many teeth. These teeth were longer and narrower than those of

DINOFACTS

Shunosaurus
(SHOO-no-SORE-us)

✳ **NAME:** *Shunosaurus* means lizard from Sichuan
Shuo (old spelling of Sichuan, province of
China) + sauros (lizard)

FAMILY:

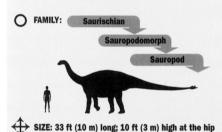

✥ **SIZE:** 33 ft (10 m) long; 10 ft (3 m) high at the hip

⚖ **WEIGHT:** 7–10 tons (6.3–9 tonnes)—about the same as 1–2
African elephants

🥣 **FOOD:** plants

🏠 **HABITAT:** forested lowlands

WHERE:
remains found
in China

🕐 **WHEN:** 175–163 million years ago in the Jurassic period

SHUNOSAURUS

TRIASSIC	JURASSIC	CRETACEOUS
250 MILLION YEARS AGO	205 MILLION YEARS AGO	135 MILLION YEARS AGO · 65 MILLION YEARS AGO

Camarasaurus but shorter than those of *Diplodocus*. Both these sauropods lived in North America during the Late Jurassic period.

Shunosaurus also had more teeth than many other sauropods. Most sauropods had teeth only at the front of their mouth, but in *Shunosaurus* the teeth were arranged at the front and along the sides of the jaws as in *Camarasaurus*. It is easy to imagine *Shunosaurus*

using its long jaws with their many teeth to take in large mouthfuls of vegetation.

One unusual feature of *Shunosaurus* is that it had a bony club on the end of its tail. This appears to have been a weapon. Many ankylosaurs (armored dinosaurs) such as *Saichania* and *Talarurus* had tail-clubs, but *Shunosaurus* is the only known sauropod that definitely had one.

HEADLESS WONDERS

Why should sauropod dinosaurs be found so often without heads? The heads of sauropods were perched on the end of a long neck, and so had to be very small and light. Except for animals like *Shunosaurus* and *Camarasaurus*, the typical sauropod did not have many large teeth in its head. With few teeth, a sauropod head did not weigh very much—it consisted pretty much of a mouth plus eyes and nostrils. The lightly built head did not need many muscles to fasten it to the neck or to work the jaws. When a sauropod died and its body decayed or was pulled apart by scavengers, its lightweight head seems to have been easily crushed.

CHECK THESE OUT!

Ankylosaurs, *Brachiosaurus*,
Camarasaurus, *Diplodocus*, Jurassic
period, *Saichania*, Saurischian
dinosaurs, Sauropods, *Talarurus*

Sinornithoides

Discovered in 1988, *Sinornithoides* is the smallest and most completely preserved troodontid (big-eyed brainy hunter). It probably chased small animal prey in Mongolia during the Cretaceous period.

In 1988, Chinese and Canadian paleontologists discovered the skeleton of a tiny theropod (two-legged meat-eating dinosaur) in the Ordos Basin in northern China. The specimen was found on the surface, and the scientists could see that part of the fossil had been eroded away by the action of frost and sandstorms.

LITTLE BUT QUICK

For its body size, *Sinornithoides* had some of the longest legs in the dinosaur world. Long legs help an animal to cover a lot of distance in a short amount of time; in other words, they help them run faster. However, because *Sinornithoides* was so small, its legs did not cover that much ground in a single stride, so larger long-legged dinosaurs such as *Struthiomimus* could probably cover greater distances faster.

the other troodontids had been discovered. Because of these findings, the paleontologists decided that *Sinornithoides* was a primitive early troodontid.

Primitive troodontid
Paleontologists were able to identify the dinosaur as a small troodontid, a relative of *Saurornithoides* of Asia and *Troodon* of North America. It had the same folding hands, a long snout with small, curved teeth, and long feet with retractable second claws like those of other troodontids.

Paleontologists Dong Zhiming of China and Dale Russell of Canada named the dinosaur *Sinornithoides* (Chinese bird form) in 1993. Dong and Russell thought that *Sinornithoides* was more primitive (less evolved) than other troodontids. Also, the rocks in which it was found were older than those in which

Curled up
One of the most interesting things about the *Sinornithoides* fossil was how complete it was. All of the lower side of the

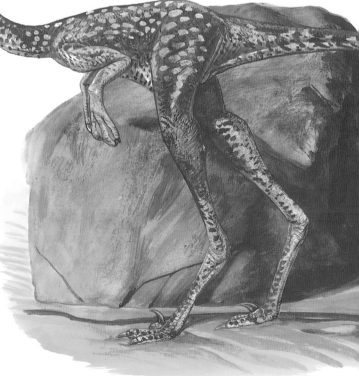

DINOFACTS

Sinornithoides
(SIGH-nor-nih-THOY-deez)

☀ **NAME:** *Sinornithoides* means Chinese bird form
Sino (Chinese) + ornis (bird) + oides (form of)

○ **FAMILY:**

Saurischian
Theropod
Tetanuran

✥ **SIZE:** about 3.5 ft (1 m) long; about 1.5 ft (46 cm) high at the hip

⚖ **WEIGHT:** about 5.5 lbs (2.5 kg)—about the same as a small house cat

🥣 **FOOD:** meat, possibly insects and eggs

🏠 **HABITAT:** forests and lake shores

Ⓝ **WHERE:** remains found in China

▶ *Sinornithoides*'s long tail probably helped the dinosaur to balance when running fast.

🕐 **WHEN:** 112–110 million years ago in the Cretaceous period

		SINORNITHOIDES	
		▪	
TRIASSIC	JURASSIC	CRETACEOUS	
250 MILLION YEARS AGO	205 MILLION YEARS AGO	135 MILLION YEARS AGO	65 MILLION YEARS AGO

body was found. The dinosaur had been curled up, lying on its belly, and all the bones were in the same positions that they were in when it was alive. Its hind legs were folded under its body, the same way that a bird sits today.

Dong and Russell suggested that this little dinosaur had been curled up to protect itself from a sandstorm, but became buried under a blanket of wind-blown sand. Because it was buried so quickly, scavengers were not able to find *Sinornithoides*'s body and tear it apart for food.

◀ *Sinornithoides* was a tiny meat-eating dinosaur that ran fast on its long legs, chasing small prey such as lizards.

How did it live?

Sinornithoides was one of the smallest of all dinosaurs other than birds. It was about 3.5 ft (1 m) long, including its tail, and probably weighed about 5.5 lbs (2.5 kg). Because it was so small, *Sinornithoides* probably hunted small creatures like early mammals and lizards.

CHECK THESE OUT!

Cretaceous period, Saurischian dinosaurs, *Saurornithoides*, *Struthiomimus*, Tetanurans, Theropods, *Troodon*

371

Sinosauropteryx

Little *Sinosauropteryx* was discovered in China in 1996. The fossils are so well preserved that they show *Sinosauropteryx*'s body was covered with hairlike feathers.

Sinosauropteryx was found in Liaoning, China, at a site that had already produced many fossils. The area was once a lake near volcanoes.

The small size of the mud particles in the lake preserved very fine details of the animals that sank to the bottom, including impressions of parts of the body not usually preserved, such as the scales of fish and the feathers of birds.

Chinese paleontologists at first identified *Sinosauropteryx* (Chinese wing lizard) as an early bird because it seemed to

HANDS-ON DETECTIVE WORK

Sinosauropteryx has answered a question about the hand of *Compsognathus*. Since no complete *Compsognathus* hand is known, scientists could not decide whether it had three fingers or only two. The more complete remains of *Sinosauropteryx* (which match what is known of the hands of *Compsognathus*) show that both these dinosaurs probably had three fingers, of which the thumb was the largest.

▼ *Sinosauropteryx* hunted and ate other small animals, such as lizards, mammals, and the early bird *Confuciornis*, which lived in China at the same time.

be covered in feathers. However, these were not true feathers. Instead, its coat was made up of single strands, more like hairs than feathers. Since paleontology has shown that birds are types of theropod (two-legged meat-eating) dinosaurs, these strands might represent a sort of early feather that later evolved into true bird feathers.

Further study of *Sinosauropteryx*'s bones has shown that it was not a bird or even an avialan (bird relative). It was a land-living theropod. It seems to have been closely related to *Compsognathus*, a small theropod that was discovered in Europe. Both animals had very long tails, similar hips and skulls, and fairly short arms.

How it lived

Sinosauropteryx ate meat. One specimen was found with the remains of its last meal in its gut. Like *Compsognathus*, which was also found with its last meal preserved, it had eaten a small lizard. In another fossil *Sinosauropteryx*, paleontologists may have found the bones of an early mammal. So this theropod may also have hunted and eaten mammals.

CHECK THESE OUT!

Avialans, Birds, *Compsognathus*, Cretaceous period, Saurischian dinosaurs, Theropods

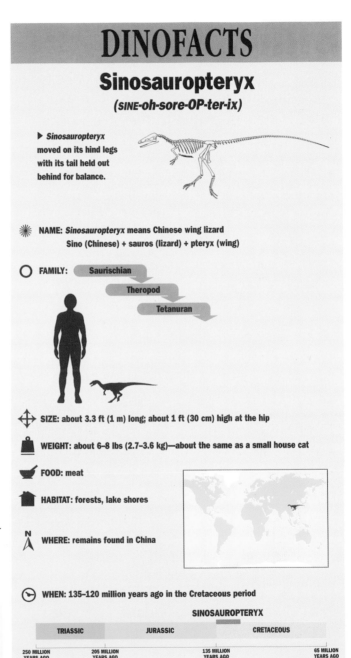

DINOFACTS

Sinosauropteryx
(SINE-oh-sore-OP-ter-ix)

▶ *Sinosauropteryx* moved on its hind legs with its tail held out behind for balance.

✳ NAME: *Sinosauropteryx* means Chinese wing lizard
Sino (Chinese) + sauros (lizard) + pteryx (wing)

○ FAMILY: Saurischian
Theropod
Tetanuran

✥ SIZE: about 3.3 ft (1 m) long; about 1 ft (30 cm) high at the hip

WEIGHT: about 6–8 lbs (2.7–3.6 kg)—about the same as a small house cat

FOOD: meat

HABITAT: forests, lake shores

N WHERE: remains found in China

🕑 WHEN: 135–120 million years ago in the Cretaceous period

		SINOSAUROPTERYX	
TRIASSIC	JURASSIC		CRETACEOUS
250 MILLION YEARS AGO	205 MILLION YEARS AGO	135 MILLION YEARS AGO	65 MILLION YEARS AGO

Sinraptor

During a series of expeditions in the 1980s, Chinese and Canadian paleontologists discovered many new and exciting fossils, including a large meat-eating dinosaur that they named *Sinraptor*.

Sinraptor is an important fossil. It is a theropod (two-legged meat-eating) dinosaur and is related to both the ceratosaurs (four-fingered meat-eaters) and the allosaurs (three-fingered meat-eaters).

The ceratosaurs were the first widespread theropods and include lightly built, small-toothed animals like *Coelophysis* from the Triassic period and the larger *Dilophosaurus* from the Early Jurassic period.

A TEENAGE DINOSAUR

From looking at the shapes of fossil bones and how much they had developed, paleontologists can get a rough idea of how old the animal was when it died. The skull bones of *Sinraptor* were halfway to being fully adult. The lines of contact between the skull bones (the sutures) were very close together but had not started to fuse together as they would in a fully grown adult. Because the sutures were close, this specimen of *Sinraptor* could not have been a very young animal either. Maybe we could think of it as a teenager!

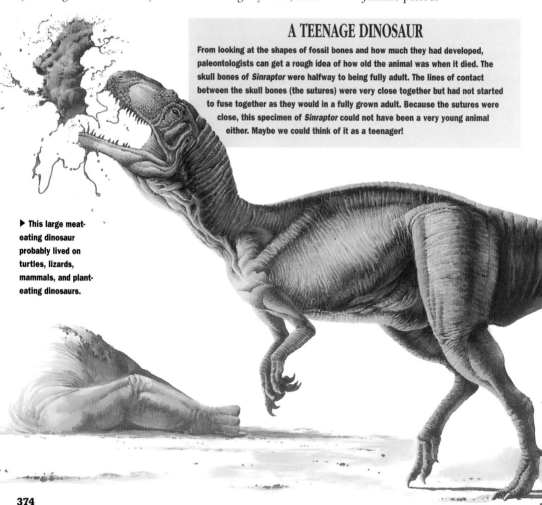

▶ This large meat-eating dinosaur probably lived on turtles, lizards, mammals, and plant-eating dinosaurs.

DINOFACTS

Sinraptor
(SIN-rap-tor)

  NAME: *Sinraptor* means Chinese robber
Sino (Chinese) + raptor (robber)

 FAMILY: Saurischian
→ Theropod
→ Tetanuran

  SIZE: 24 ft (7.3 m) long; about 8 ft (2.4 m) high at the hip

WEIGHT: 1–1.5 tons (0.9–1.35 tonnes)—about the same as 4–6 tigers

FOOD: plant-eating dinosaurs, lizards, mammals

HABITAT: forested lowlands around lakes

 **WHERE:** remains found in China

 ▲ Although the skeleton of *Sinraptor* is incomplete, scientists can guess what it looked like from what they know about other large theropods.

WHEN: 147 million years ago in the Jurassic period

	SINRAPTOR		
TRIASSIC	JURASSIC		CRETACEOUS
250 MILLION YEARS AGO	205 MILLION YEARS AGO	135 MILLION YEARS AGO	65 MILLION YEARS AGO

The allosaurs were the first large, very heavy theropods with big heads and long, slashing teeth. *Allosaurus* of the Late Jurassic period and mid-Cretaceous *Acrocanthosaurus* were both allosaurs. The bones, jaws, and teeth of *Sinraptor* are similar to both those of the ceratosaurs and those of the allosaurs.

Fossil-hunters found only *Sinraptor*'s skull, backbone, pelvic bone, and back legs.

The dinosaur was lying on its right side. Most of the left side of the body had decayed and been washed away before the carcass was buried, and the tail was completely gone. Fortunately the bones that were preserved were of very good quality.

How did *Sinraptor* live?

The fossils were found in an area of rivers leading to a lake. *Sinraptor* probably fed on the other animals found there, like lizards, turtles, and plant-eating dinosaurs such as the *Mamenchisaurus* whose shattered bones were scattered there.

CHECK THESE OUT!

Allosaurus, Ceratosaurs, Coelophysis, Dilophosaurus, Mamenchisaurus, Tetanurans, Theropods

Spinosaurus

Spinosaurus was one of the the largest meat-eaters ever to walk the earth. It was first found in 1915 in Egypt by German paleontologist Ernest Stromer, who named it for the spines along its back.

Spinosaurus was a theropod (two-legged meat-eater) from the middle of the Cretaceous period. It was enormous—over 40 ft (12.2 m) long—and its spines were as long as 5.5 ft (1.7 m) at the center of its back, becoming shorter toward the neck and tail. Its backbones (vertebrae) were 8 in (20 cm)

A GIANT FISH-EATING DINOSAUR

British paleontologists Alan Charig and Angela Milner concluded that both *Spinosaurus* and the theropod *Baryonyx* had jaws very similar to the Indian gharial, the most specialized of all the fish-eating crocodiles. Such thin jaws can snap shut quickly in the water and the long, sharp teeth trap the fish. *Spinosaurus* also had strong front legs like *Baryonyx* that would have permitted it to stand on all fours while it hunted fish with its slender jaws. *Spinosaurus* would have been the largest fish-eating animal ever to live on land.

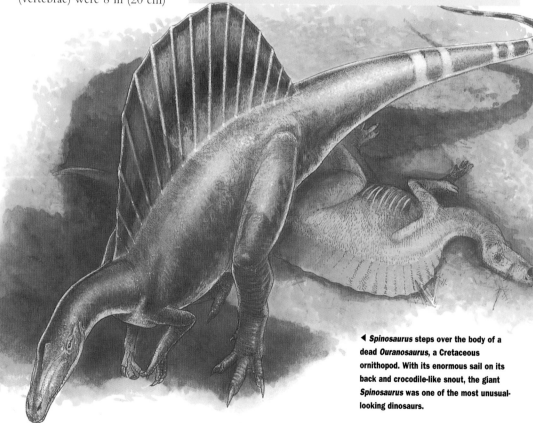

◀ *Spinosaurus* steps over the body of a dead *Ouranosaurus*, a Cretaceous ornithopod. With its enormous sail on its back and crocodile-like snout, the giant *Spinosaurus* was one of the most unusual-looking dinosaurs.

long, 2 in (5 cm) longer than those of the mighty tyrannosaur (two-finger meat-eater) *Tyrannosaurus*, indicating that this was one big dinosaur.

A sail-backed dinosaur.
The spines along the back of *Spinosaurus* were thought to support a tall sail of skin. If richly supplied with blood, this sail could have helped to regulate body temperature. The dinosaur may have been able to warm up by turning sideways to the sun, exposing the full area of its sail. It could have cooled down by turning so only the edge of the sail faced the sun, letting breezes carry heat away from the sail. Similar sails are found in the North African ornithopod (bird-footed) dinosaur *Ouranosaurus*.

Some paleontologists disagree with this idea. If sails were necessary to cope with the heat, they ask, then how did sail-less dinosaurs get by?

Crocodile jaws
Later discoveries of jawbones in rocks of similar age were made by French paleontologists in Morocco. These discoveries eventually led in 1996 to British paleontologist Angela Milner describing the skull of *Spinosaurus*.

Milner decided the skull was long with thin jaws and large, straight teeth, much like the teeth of modern crocodiles. *Spinosaurus* was unusual in having straight teeth without the serrated steak-knife-like edge found in other meat-eating dinosaurs.

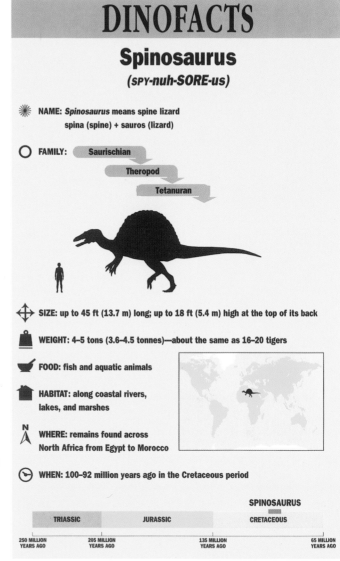

DINOFACTS

Spinosaurus
(SPY-*nuh*-SORE-*us*)

NAME: *Spinosaurus* means spine lizard spina (spine) + sauros (lizard)

FAMILY: Saurischian — Theropod — Tetanuran

SIZE: up to 45 ft (13.7 m) long; up to 18 ft (5.4 m) high at the top of its back

WEIGHT: 4–5 tons (3.6–4.5 tonnes)—about the same as 16–20 tigers

FOOD: fish and aquatic animals

HABITAT: along coastal rivers, lakes, and marshes

WHERE: remains found across North Africa from Egypt to Morocco

WHEN: 100–92 million years ago in the Cretaceous period

		SPINOSAURUS
TRIASSIC	JURASSIC	CRETACEOUS
250 MILLION YEARS AGO	205 MILLION YEARS AGO	135 MILLION YEARS AGO	65 MILLION YEARS AGO

How did *Spinosaurus* live?
Spinosaurus fed on fish along the rivers, lakes, and the coast of North Africa. It could stand on all four legs and grab fish in its long, snoutlike jaws.

CHECK THESE OUT!
Baryonyx, Cretaceous period, *Ouranosaurus,* Saurischian dinosaurs, *Tyrannosaurus*

Stegoceras

Stegoceras was a pachycephalosaur (thick-headed dinosaur) that lived in western North America in the Cretaceous period. No complete skeletons have been found, but scientists can tell a lot from its skull.

Although a complete skeleton of *Stegoceras* has not yet been discovered, paleontologists do have an almost complete skull to study. They also have several other partial skulls and some back and tail bones.

Thick and thin skulls
Like all pachycephalosaurs, *Stegoceras* had very thick bone at the top of its skull. However, some *Stegoceras* skulls are thicker than others.

IN THE TEETH OF THE EVIDENCE

The first *Stegoceras* remains to be discovered were some teeth found in 1902 by the Canadian paleontologist Charles Lambe. He thought that these teeth were similar to some teeth found in 1856 that had been identified as belonging to an extinct monitor lizard that had been named *Troodon*. Lambe also found some thick skull fragments, which he identified as belonging to a new dinosaur that he named *Stegoceras*.

In 1924, US paleontologist Charles Gilmore described a skull and partial skeleton of a dinosaur that had teeth very like those of the lizard identified as *Troodon*. At first these remains were given the name *Troodon* as well. Later, though, it was determined that the teeth and skull belonged to what Lambe had called *Stegoceras*. Additionally, the teeth discovered in 1856 were found to belong not to a lizard but to a small meat-eating dinosaur that is still known as *Troodon*.

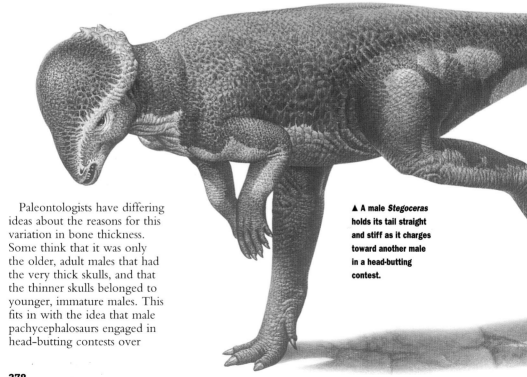

▲ A male *Stegoceras* holds its tail straight and stiff as it charges toward another male in a head-butting contest.

Paleontologists have differing ideas about the reasons for this variation in bone thickness. Some think that it was only the older, adult males that had the very thick skulls, and that the thinner skulls belonged to younger, immature males. This fits in with the idea that male pachycephalosaurs engaged in head-butting contests over mates or territory. Only the fully grown males would have had skulls strong enough to withstand the battering that would be caused by charging each other head-on. Other paleontologists argue that the difference in bone thickness is the difference between male and female *Stegoceras*, with the thinner skulls belonging to females.

Crisscross patterns
Paleontologists also found bones from the rest of *Stegoceras*'s skeleton. Its back and tail bones have bony tendons lying in crisscross patterns along their upper sides. These

tendons would have made its back and the front section of its tail very stiff and strong. The strength of the back and tail may have been related to the head–butting activities of these animals.

How did *Stegoceras* live?
As an ornithischian (bird-hipped) dinosaur, *Stegoceras* ate plants. Like other ornithischians, it had cheeks that could hold food in its mouth while it was chewing. Saurischian (lizard-hipped) dinosaurs had no cheek pouches so they had to swallow their food whole. *Stegoceras*'s snout is quite narrow, and animals with narrow snouts tend to be

browsers. This means that *Stegoceras* may have looked carefully to see which plants were the best to eat rather than just eating everything within reach.

DINOFACTS

Stegoceras
(STEG-uh-SEE-rus)

✳ **NAME:** *Stegoceras* means horny roof
  stegos (roof) + ceras (horny)

◯ **FAMILY:**
  Ornithischian
  Pachycephalosaur

 SIZE: 6 ft (1.8 m) long; 2–3 ft (60–90 cm) high at the hip

WEIGHT: 120 lbs (54 kg)—about the same as a fairly large gray wolf

FOOD: plants

HABITAT: forested lowlands

N **WHERE:** remains found in Montana, and in Alberta, Canada

🕐 **WHEN:** 75–70 million years ago in the Cretaceous period

STEGOCERAS

	TRIASSIC	JURASSIC	CRETACEOUS	
250 MILLION YEARS AGO	205 MILLION YEARS AGO		135 MILLION YEARS AGO	65 MILLION YEARS AGO

CHECK THESE OUT!
Cretaceous period, Ornithischian dinosaurs, Pachycephalosaurs, *Troodon*

Stegosaurs

The stegosaurs were unusual-looking dinosaurs, instantly recognizable by the plates or spines along their backs and the fearsome-looking spikes at the end of their tails.

The stegosaurs (plate-backed dinosaurs) were a fairly numerous and widespread group of dinosaurs. Their remains are found around the world in Jurassic and Cretaceous rocks.

There are only 12 types of stegosaurs known, so they are a clearly defined group of closely related animals. They belong to a larger group called the thyreophorans (armored and plate-backed dinosaurs), which also includes the ankylosaurs (armored dinosaurs). Stegosaurs are different than other thyreophorans because they have spikes over their shoulders and on the ends of their tails, and have upright bony plates running down the middle of their backs.

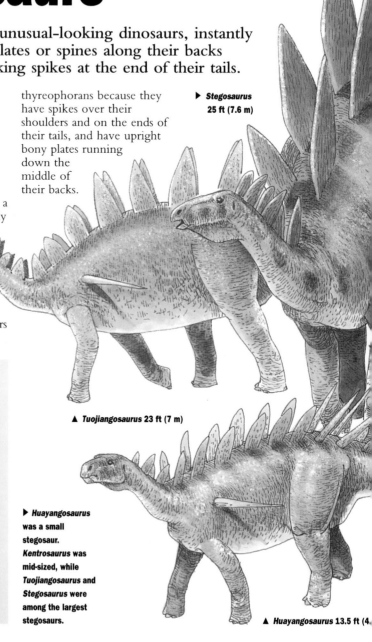

▶ **Stegosaurus 25 ft (7.6 m)**

▲ *Tuojiangosaurus* 23 ft (7 m)

▶ *Huayangosaurus* was a small stegosaur. *Kentrosaurus* was mid-sized, while *Tuojiangosaurus* and *Stegosaurus* were among the largest stegosaurs.

▲ *Huayangosaurus* 13.5 ft (4.

HOT PLATES

Taken all together, the stegosaurs' broad, bony back plates had a large surface area. Some scientists think that the animals could have used this large surface to help them heat up and cool down. The many grooves and channels inside the bony plates may have held blood-pumping veins and arteries. If a stegosaur felt chilly, it could stand sideways to the sun so that it caught the maximum amount of warm sunlight on its plates. Blood circulating just under the surface of the plates would warm up and carry that warmth to other parts of the body. Today, many lizards warm themselves by basking in the sun.

Larger than life

The back plates of stegosaurs are not in the best places to protect against attack, so perhaps stegosaurs used their back plates to communicate with other stegosaurs. The plates would have been covered by a layer of horny, or fingernail-like, material. This outer covering made these back plates seem larger, and it may also have been brightly colored. When seen from the side the plates would have made a stegosaur look much larger than it really was. This illusion could have frightened a rival stegosaur, or it could have helped male stegosaurs to impress females. Different kinds of stegosaurs had different shapes and patterns of plates and spines, much as tigers have stripes and leopards have spots today.

How did stegosaurs live?

As ornithischian (bird-hipped) dinosaurs, stegosaurs ate plants. They had a beaklike covering on their snouts, and most of them had no front teeth. Stegosaurs had cheeks to keep food in their mouths. They had small heads, so they had to feed almost constantly to fill their large bodies.

◀ **Kentrosaurus**
17 ft (5.2 m)

CHECK THESE OUT!

Ankylosaurs, *Chialingosaurus,*
Dacentrurus, Huayangosaurus,
Kentrosaurus, Kritosaurus,
Ornithischian dinosaurs, *Stegosaurus,*
Thyreophorans, *Tuojiangosaurus*

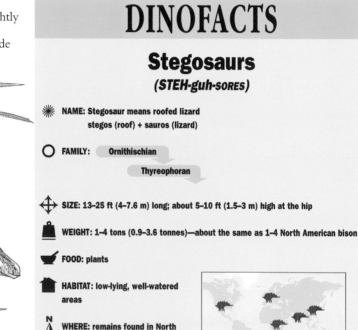

DINOFACTS

Stegosaurs
(STEH-guh-SORES)

✳ NAME: Stegosaur means roofed lizard
stegos (roof) + sauros (lizard)

○ FAMILY: Ornithischian

Thyreophoran

✜ SIZE: 13–25 ft (4–7.6 m) long; about 5–10 ft (1.5–3 m) high at the hip

⚖ WEIGHT: 1–4 tons (0.9–3.6 tonnes)—about the same as 1–4 North American bison

🥣 FOOD: plants

▮ HABITAT: low-lying, well-watered areas

N↑ WHERE: remains found in North America, Africa, China, Europe, India

🕑 WHEN: from 175 million years ago in the Jurassic period to 88 million years ago in the Cretaceous period

	STEGOSAURS		
TRIASSIC	JURASSIC		CRETACEOUS
250 MILLION YEARS AGO	205 MILLION YEARS AGO	135 MILLION YEARS AGO	65 MILLION YEARS AGO

381

Stegosaurus

The best-known of all the stegosaurs (plate-backed dinosaurs), *Stegosaurus* was a large, low-slung plant-eating dinosaur that roamed the plains of North America in the Late Jurassic period.

The first remains of *Stegosaurus* were discovered in the late 1870s in the Rocky Mountain region of Colorado. Pioneering Yale paleontologist Othniel Charles Marsh described the partial skeletons that had been found and named them *Stegosaurus armatus* (armed roof-lizard). He thought the dinosaur was a marine reptile. He decided that the large armor plates found with it were embedded in the skin like the bones in the shell of a sea turtle and that the arms were adapted for swimming.

Many kinds of *Stegosaurus*?
Over the next 50 years, many kinds (species) of *Stegosaurus* were described by Marsh and others. In 1990, Connecticut

paleontologist Peter Galton studied all the different kinds of *Stegosaurus* and decided there were really only four. Unfortunately the original

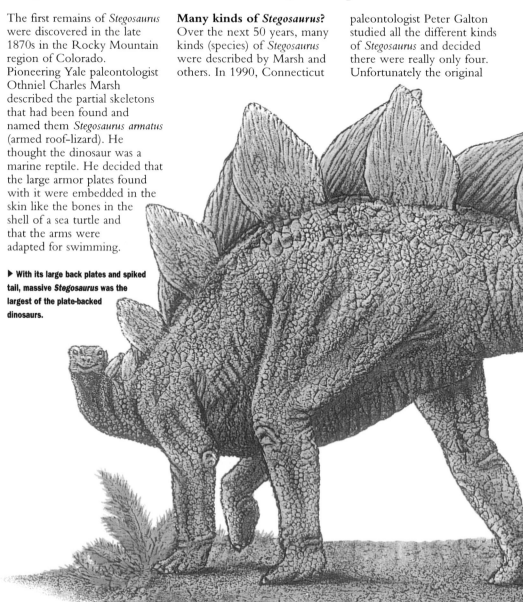

▶ With its large back plates and spiked tail, massive *Stegosaurus* was the largest of the plate-backed dinosaurs.

specimen of *Stegosaurus armatus* was never extracted from the rock, and a detailed description of it has never been published. Scientists really need to be able to compare this first specimen with the other species that have been discovered in order to work out their relationships.

Reconstructing *Stegosaurus*

It was not until 1986 that a nearly complete specimen of *Stegosaurus* was excavated from Felch Quarry, Garden Park, west of Canon City, Colorado. This skeleton became known as the "roadkill" specimen. It

included the first well-preserved skull to be found. The skull was small and slender, with a small, toothless beak and tiny, leaf-shaped teeth along the sides of its mouth. The hind legs of the specimen were much longer than the front legs, and the head was held close to the ground.

Paleontologists learned a lot about *Stegosaurus*'s skeleton from the roadkill specimen. It showed that there

THAGOMIZER

Paleontologists sometimes have fun naming things they discover. In his popular *Far Side* cartoons, Gary Larson once published a cartoon that shows a caveman lecturing about a *Stegosaurus*. Pointing to the tail, the caveman explains that this is called a thagomizer for the late Thag (indicating Thag had been killed by one). As there had never been a specific name proposed for stegosaur tails, it became common for paleontologists to refer to stegosaur tails jokingly as thagomizers. Now the name is official. In 1997, James Farlow and Mike Brett-Surman included the word in the glossary of their massive book on dinosaurs, entitled *The Complete Dinosaur*. Thagomizer is now the correct term for the spikes at the end of a stegosaur's tail.

was a dense chain mail of small bones covering the underside of the neck. It was also evident that *Stegosaurus*'s plates extended upright along the backbone, with the largest plates—as much as 3 ft (90 cm) across—above the hips. These narrow-based plates were smaller along the tail. The long, narrow spikes paleontologists had found clearly belonged near the end of the tail.

Pattern of plates

Scientists have argued for years about how *Stegosaurus*'s back plates were arranged. When Marsh published the first reasonably accurate picture of *Stegosaurus* in 1891, he gave it a single row of 12 plates.

In 1901, Smithsonian paleontologist Frederick Lucas suggested the plates were arranged either in two paired rows or in two alternating rows. Paleontologists still cannot decide if the rows were paired or alternating. Since the plates were not symmetrical, it is agreed that they formed two rows down the back.

In 1987, dinosaur artist Stephen Czerkas studied *Stegosaurus* carefully and decided that the plates formed a single row down the back. The upper parts of the plates overlapped toward the animal's front. More primitive (less evolved) stegosaurs such as *Huayangosaurus*, *Kentrosaurus*, and *Tuojiangosaurus* had armor plates down the right and left sides of the body, and primitive armored archosaurs (dinosaur relatives) commonly had paired armor down their backs. However, Czerkas pointed out that some dinosaurs such as the theropod (two-legged meat-eater) *Ceratosaurus* had only a single row of armor.

Czerkas's view has been followed by many artists and museums. However, in 1992 an even more perfectly preserved specimen of *Stegosaurus* was found in the same age rocks and within a couple of miles of the original roadkill specimen. Denver Museum of Natural History's paleontologists Kenneth Carpenter and Bryan Small reported that this specimen clearly had a total of 17 plates

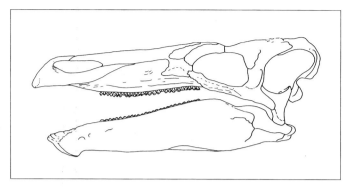

▲ The skull of *Stegosaurus* shows that it had lots of tiny, leaf-shaped teeth with jagged edges, which the dinosaur used to shred its food.

in alternate rows separated by several inches. This pattern is unique among stegosaurs. *Stegosaurus* is also the only stegosaur known to have lost the shoulder spines that more primitive kinds had.

What did the plates do?

No one knows for sure what *Stegosaurus*'s back plates did. In 1976, Indiana paleontologist James Farlow led a team in an experiment. They showed that an alternating arrangement of plates would be the most efficient pattern for getting cool. They recognized that the plates were filled with blood vessels and suggested they were covered in skin so *Stegosaurus* could cool itself. Since it has been shown that the horns of antelope help them to shed heat from their skulls, it seems likely that the plates of *Stegosaurus* could also have been used to get cool.

However, we also know that dinosaur armor was filled with

blood vessels to grow the horn that covered the bone. Additionally the plates of primitive stegosaurs such as *Huayangosaurus*, *Kentrosaurus*, and *Tuojiangosaurus* were very spinelike and were clearly used for defense. The plates of *Stegosaurus* would have been covered in horn for strength and to give them a sharp edge.

Tail spikes

Marsh showed *Stegosaurus* with four pairs of spikes sticking up at the end of its tail. However,

the remains of dinosaurs found with their tails intact have all had only two pairs of spikes. So most drawings of *Stegosaurus* made in the 20th century have shown just two pairs of upright spikes at the end of the tail.

In 1995, Carpenter suggested that *Stegosaurus*'s tail spikes stuck out at the side. He based this idea on the arrangement of spikes found on well-preserved tails. Also, the bases of the spikes were too large to fit side by side on the top of the end of the tail. The spikes needed to be on the sides so they threatened an attacker when *Stegosaurus* swung its tail from side to side. Carpenter also said that *Stegosaurus* had a stiffer tail than had previously been thought.

Two brains?

Stegosaurus had a very small brain, possibly the smallest of any dinosaur, although its senses of sight and smell appear to have been good. Scientists discovered that there was a swelling of the spinal nerve cord in the hips over 20 times larger than the brain itself. This led to the idea that *Stegosaurus*

▶ A well-preserved skeleton of *Stegosaurus* was found lying like this. It seems to show that the back plates were arranged alternately.

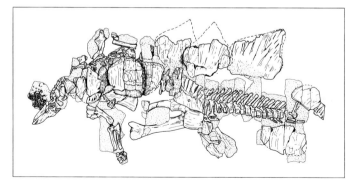

had two brains. One idea was that this swelling controlled the hind legs and tail.

Stegosaurus was not the only animal that had a swelling where the nerves of the legs join the spinal cord. In 1993, Massachusetts scientist Emily Giffin noted that the larger the dinosaur, the larger the swelling in the spinal cord. She suggested that dinosaurs, like birds, had a gland there that contained a substance that made the nerves react more quickly. This would be useful in large animals like stegosaurs.

How did Stegosaurus live?

Stegosaurus was a common dinosaur in the dry grasslands of western North America in the Late Jurassic period. The places where its fossils have been found show that it liked to be near rivers and lakes. Its low-slung head suggests that it probably fed on low-growing plants, which it would snip off with its horny beak and shred with its tiny, leaf-shaped teeth.

Stegosaurus would not have been in much danger from meat-eating dinosaurs. It was too large to be at any risk from small theropods. If it was attacked by large theropods like Allosaurus, it could defend itself by swinging its fearsome spiked tail at them.

CHECK THESE OUT!

Allosaurus, Ceratosaurus, Jurassic period, Huayangosaurus, Kentrosaurus, Ornithischian dinosaurs, Stegosaurs, Thyreophorans, Tuojiangosaurus

DINOFACTS

Stegosaurus
(STEG-uh-SORE-us)

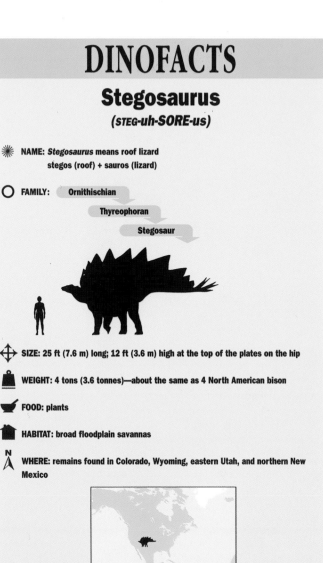

NAME: *Stegosaurus* means roof lizard
stegos (roof) + sauros (lizard)

FAMILY: Ornithischian
Thyreophoran
Stegosaur

SIZE: 25 ft (7.6 m) long; 12 ft (3.6 m) high at the top of the plates on the hip

WEIGHT: 4 tons (3.6 tonnes)—about the same as 4 North American bison

FOOD: plants

HABITAT: broad floodplain savannas

WHERE: remains found in Colorado, Wyoming, eastern Utah, and northern New Mexico

WHEN: 140 million years ago in the Jurassic period

STEGOSAURUS

TRIASSIC	JURASSIC	CRETACEOUS
250 MILLION YEARS AGO	205 MILLION YEARS AGO	135 MILLION YEARS AGO	65 MILLION YEARS AGO

Struthiomimus

Struthiomimus is one of the best known of the ornithomimosaurs (ostrichlike dinosaurs). It scampered over the plains of western Canada in the Late Cretaceous period.

In 1902, a fragmentary skeleton of an ornithomimosaur was found in what is now Dinosaur Provincial Park in Alberta, Canada. Canadian paleontologist Lawrence Lambe described these remains and named them *Ornithomimus altus* (tall bird-mimic).

In 1914, US fossil-hunter Barnum Brown found the most complete ornithomimosaur skeleton discovered up to that point. Paleontologist Henry Fairfield Osborn studied this specimen and decided it belonged to the same species as Lambe's *Ornithomimus altus*.

However, Osborn then found that the fifth foot bone, which was entirely lost in true *Ornithomimus*, was still present as a bony splint in Brown's and Lambe's specimens. So Osborn gave this dinosaur a new name.

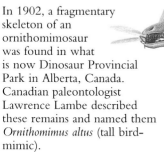

LIFE IN THE FAST LANE

Struthiomimus and other ostrichlike dinosaurs had very specialized feet, as did tyrannosaurs (two-fingered meat-eaters) and troodontids (big-eyed brainy hunters). The middle bone of the foot is wedge shaped at the bottom, instead of being a cylinder shape as in most dinosaurs. The whole foot is very narrow and pinched. This kind of structure would absorb the impact of running better than the more primitive (little evolved) feet of other dinosaurs.

Also, the lower legs of ostrichlike dinosaurs, tyrannosaurs, and troodontids were very long compared to their body sizes. Today animals with long, compressed feet and long lower legs are known to be the fastest runners. So it is likely that these three groups of dinosaurs could run much faster than other dinosaurs of the same size.

▶ *Struthiomimus* munches on a Cretaceous insect. Scientists are not sure what this dinosaur ate, but insects may have been on the menu.

Because it looked so much like an ostrich, he named it *Struthiomimus*—ostrich mimic.

Since then, Brown and other fossil-hunters have found other specimens of *Struthiomimus* in Alberta. A skeleton at least as complete as Brown's famous discovery (still on display at the American Museum of Natural History) was found by a team from Canada's Royal Tyrrell Museum of Palaeontology. This new specimen, still being studied, has the most complete ornithomimosaur skull ever discovered.

How did *Struthiomimus* live?
Struthiomimus was very similar overall to other ostrichlike dinosaurs, such as *Ornithomimus*, *Gallimimus*, and *Dromiceiomimus*. Its small, toothless beak, long, slender neck, and clamplike hands would not have been very good for catching and killing large animals. However, they may have been useful when chasing small prey, digging into nests for eggs, or grabbing onto branches to feed on fruit or leaves. With its very long back legs, *Struthiomimus* could almost certainly run very fast. It was possibly faster than any other dinosaur.

CHECK THESE OUT!

Cretaceous period, *Dromiceiomimus*, *Gallimimus*, *Ornithomimus*, Tetanurans, Theropods, *Troodon*, Tyrannosaurs

DINOFACTS

Struthiomimus
(STROO-thee-oh-MY-mus)

▶ The skeleton of *Struthiomimus* shows its long, slender neck and its very long back legs, which would have enabled it to run very fast.

✷ NAME: *Struthiomimus* means ostrich mimic
struthio (ostrich) + mimos (mimic)

◯ FAMILY: Saurischian
Theropod
Tetanuran

⊕ SIZE: up to 14 ft (4.3 m) long; up to 4.5 ft (1.4 m) high at the hip

⚖ WEIGHT: about 330 lbs (150 kg)—about the same as an ostrich

🥣 FOOD: possibly meat, insects, eggs, fruit, and leaves

🏠 HABITAT: forests and plains

N↑ WHERE: remains found in Alberta, Canada

🕐 WHEN: 80–68 million years ago in the Cretaceous period

STRUTHIOMIMUS

TRIASSIC	JURASSIC	CRETACEOUS
250 MILLION YEARS AGO	205 MILLION YEARS AGO ... 135 MILLION YEARS AGO	65 MILLION YEARS AGO

Stygimoloch

Stygimoloch was a pachycephalosaur (thick-headed dinosaur) that lived in North America in the Cretaceous period. Unlike most other pachycephalosaurs, *Stygimoloch* had horns on the back of its head.

The pachycephalosaurs get their name from their big, thick, strong skulls. Scientists think that males may have used their bony skulls in head-butting contests over mates or territory. Some pachycephalosaurs, however, may have developed a different method of competition. Instead of banging heads, these other pachycephalosaurs may have quietly showed off their elaborate horns and bumps as some lizards do today. *Stygimoloch* was one of these show-off pachycephalosaurs.

Crash or threaten?

Fossil-hunters have found only some fragments of bone from *Stygimoloch*'s skull. Fortunately, these fragments were preserved with enough detail to tell paleontologists that *Stygimoloch* was closely related to the head-crashing pachycephalosaurs but did not live in exactly the same way.

Stygimoloch had several horns 4–5 in (10–12.7 cm) long at the back of its skull and smaller horns and bumps at

▶ Was *Stygimoloch* a show-off? Some scientists think it used its horns to show off to, or even threaten, others of its kind.

MISTAKEN IDENTITY

The isolated pieces of *Stygimoloch*'s skull were first thought to be from a ceratopsian (horned dinosaur) like *Triceratops*. It was US paleontologist O. C. Marsh who made this mistake in 1896. Even experts sometimes have trouble identifying animals from incomplete fossils.

In 1943, some other scientists decided that *Stygimoloch* was an unusual specimen of *Pachycephalosaurus*. It was not until 1983 that paleontologists Peter Galton and Hans-Dieter Sues recognized that the skull fragments of *Stygimoloch* represented a new type of pachycephalosaur that was entitled to its own name.

the base of the bigger horns. These horns would never have survived intact if they had been crashed against the horned head of another *Stygimoloch*. It seems more likely that *Stygimoloch* would have tipped, shaken, or bobbed their heads at one another.

Modern horned lizards from the desert areas of western North America have small horns and crests around their heads very like those of *Stygimoloch*. Horned lizards threaten one another by shaking and bobbing their heads in silent, safe contests. *Stygimoloch* may have behaved in the same way, using their horns to threaten rivals rather than to actually fight with them.

How did *Stygimoloch* live?

As an ornithischian (bird–hipped) dinosaur, *Stygimoloch* ate plants. It would have snipped off leaves with its front teeth and chopped them up with its cheek teeth before swallowing. Like other pachycephalosaurs, it would have walked around on its hind legs, and may have lived in small herds.

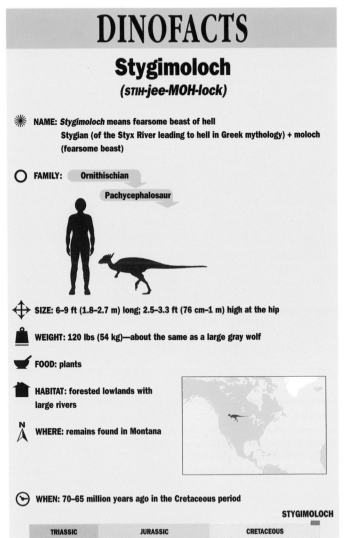

DINOFACTS

Stygimoloch
(STIH-*jee*-MOH-*lock*)

☀ **NAME:** *Stygimoloch* means fearsome beast of hell
Stygian (of the Styx River leading to hell in Greek mythology) + moloch (fearsome beast)

○ **FAMILY:** Ornithischian

Pachycephalosaur

✛ **SIZE:** 6–9 ft (1.8–2.7 m) long; 2.5–3.3 ft (76 cm–1 m) high at the hip

WEIGHT: 120 lbs (54 kg)—about the same as a large gray wolf

FOOD: plants

HABITAT: forested lowlands with large rivers

N
↑ **WHERE:** remains found in Montana

◷ **WHEN:** 70–65 million years ago in the Cretaceous period

STYGIMOLOCH

TRIASSIC	JURASSIC	CRETACEOUS	
250 MILLION YEARS AGO	205 MILLION YEARS AGO	135 MILLION YEARS AGO	65 MILLION YEARS AGO

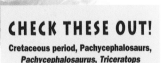

CHECK THESE OUT!

Cretaceous period, Pachycephalosaurs, *Pachycephalosaurus*, *Triceratops*

389

Styracosaurus

Styracosaurus was a ceratopsian (horned dinosaur) that lived in North America in the Cretaceous period. As well as horns on its frill, *Styracosaurus* had a nose horn up to 1.6 ft (50 cm) long.

While prospecting along the Red Deer River in Alberta, Canada, in 1913, fossil-hunter Charles H. Sternberg found a spectacular and almost complete skull of a ceratopsian. The skull was quite different from any of the others he had found. This new fossil was described by paleontologist Lawrence Lambe, who named it *Styracosaurus albertensis* (Alberta's spiked lizard).

Styracosaurus had a huge skull with a deep, toothless beak at the front. Behind the beak, the jaws had the same rows of slicing teeth as those of all large ceratopsians. *Styracosaurus*'s nose had a single straight horn up to 1.6 ft (50 cm) long. There was little evidence of horns above the animal's eyes.

The skull was wider at the back than at the front, giving it a triangular shape. There was also a short frill at the back of the skull with two circular openings. The frill had six long horns along its rear edge, with smaller hornlets running up the sides of the frill. This was one of the most unusual dinosaur skulls ever found.

The centrosaurines

In 1915, Lambe divided the big four-legged ceratopsians into two smaller groups: the

▶ *Styracosaurus* had a dramatic head-on appearance. As well a long nose horn, it had horns and hornlets all around the edges of its bony frill.

centrosaurines (named in honor of *Centrosaurus*), which had short frills and large nose horns, and the chasmosaurines (named in honor of *Chasmosaurus*), which had long frills and large horns above the eyes. *Styracosaurus* was clearly a centrosaurine.

All the centrosaurines that had been discovered by 1915 were from the same period of time (80–75 million years ago) toward the end of the

Cretaceous period. They included *Brachyceratops*, *Centrosaurus*, and *Styracosaurus*. Lambe did not know that some centrosaurines would later be discovered whose nose horns had fallen off, such as *Pachyrhinosaurus*.

A second specimen
Also in 1915, Barnum Brown collected a nearly complete skeleton of *Styracosaurus* from the same part of Canada. This specimen was not described until 1937, when Brown and Erich Schlaikjer

ONE NAME OR TWO?

In the 17th century, Swedish scientist Carolus Linnaeus developed a system of groups to classify all living things. His system is still widely used today. The largest group in Linnaeus's system is the kingdom (such as plant kingdom or animal kingdom), followed by phylum, class, order, family, genus, and species. An animal's scientific name consists of two parts: the genus and the species names. Humans, for example, are classified as *Homo sapiens* (wise people), with *Homo* being the genus name and *sapiens* the species name. Scientific names always use Greek or Latin words (or personal or place names with Greek or Latin endings), and are always written in italics (or underlined) with the genus name having a capital letter.

Most dinosaurs are known from only one species, so it has become very common to refer to most dinosaurs by the genus name alone—*Styracosaurus*, for example. Since most dinosaurs are so little known that it is difficult to identify separate species, and the various species of a genus are usually very similar, using only the genus name for dinosaurs makes a great deal of sense in most cases.

identified it as a new kind (species) of *Styracosaurus*. They named it *Styracosaurus parksi* (Parks's spiked lizard) in honor of paleontologist William Parks.

In 1990, paleontologists Peter Dodson and Phil Currie decided that this second specimen was the same species as *Styracosaurus albertensis*, so the name *Styracosaurus parksi* is no longer used. Brown's specimen is still on display at the American Museum of Natural History in New York. It is one of the few skeletons of a large horned dinosaur that is made up from the bones of a single animal.

Found in Montana
In 1928, Sternberg's son George was collecting fossils along the Milk River in northern Montana. He found a fragmentary *Styracosaurus* specimen. Although it was in poor condition, a large section of the frill was preserved. It showed that the horns on the

frill were arranged differently than on the other known specimens of *Styracosaurus*. This led Charles Gilmore in 1930 to describe this specimen as the new species *Styracosaurus ovatus* (oval spiked lizard).

Einiosaurus from the same region was at first thought to be a new species of *Styracosaurus* with only two long horns at the back of its frill. However, detailed study by paleontologist Scott Sampson in 1995 showed that it was a different kind of ceratopsian.

Styracosaurus bone bed
Few specimens of *Styracosaurus* had been discovered until 1984, when a bone bed was found in Canada with scattered bones from perhaps hundreds of specimens of all ages. Bone beds preserving just one kind of dinosaur may represent part of a dinosaur herd that was caught in a catastrophe that killed many herd members. As well as providing evidence that, like many other

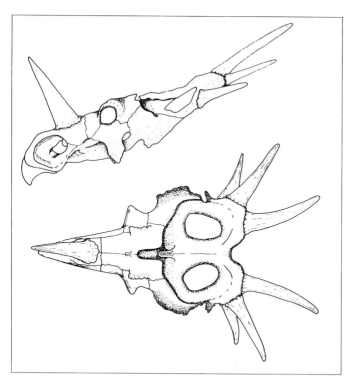

delicately constructed to stand up to much wear and tear. Paleontologists think that the frill served mainly as a means of display. A *Styracosaurus* snorting and shaking its head would certainly have made a dramatic sight. Many modern herding animals, such as deer and antelope, use their antlers and horns in the same way.

Males and females

In 1987, Peter Dodson suggested that *Centrosaurus nasicornis* was really a female *Styracosaurus*. Studies of the Canadian *Styracosaurus* bone bed do not back up this suggestion, because no *Centrosaurus nasicornis* have ever been found there. With so many animals, it is almost certain that at least one adult female would have been preserved there.

Many species

Another function of the spectacular frills among the centrosaurine dinosaurs may have been identification, so

ceratopsians, *Styracosaurus* traveled in herds, this site provides important information on the way *Styracosaurus* grew.

The young animals had no horns, and young *Styracosaurus* looked just like the young of other centrosaurines. The distinctive horns on the frills did not grow until the animal was fully adult.

Frill or spill?

Styracosaurus's long nose horn could undoubtedly have been used for defense. Its frill, however, was much too

▲ *Styracosaurus*'s skull was triangular in shape, with two large openings at the back that reduced the weight of the frill.

▶ Deer, such as this red deer stag, have impressive antlers for attracting mates. Perhaps *Styracosaurus* horns did the same.

that one centrosaurine could recognize another of its own kind. This is important for mating, because animals can breed only with others of their own kind. Modern animals, such as deer and antelope, have physical identification features, antlers and horns. The animals with the best features, the biggest antlers or horns, are the most successful at attracting mates.

Features that attract mates tend to become exaggerated and varied. For example, some individuals may have slightly different-shaped horns. They may pass these different features on to their descendants. Over time, this variation leads to the evolution of a great number of species. This process is responsible for the many kinds of modern deer and antelope with their varied antlers and horns. The same process accounts for the many kinds of ceratopsians, such as *Styracosaurus*, in Late Cretaceous North America.

How *Styracosaurus* lived
Styracosaurus lived on warm, coastal floodplains much like the modern Gulf Coast of North America. Paleontologists can tell this from their studies of the sediments and fossil plants found with its remains. Herds of *Styracosaurus* were less common than herds of *Centrosaurus*, *Chasmosaurus*, and hadrosaurs (duckbill dinosaurs).

As ornithischian dinosaurs, *Styracosaurus* ate plants. They would have fed on tough, low-growing plants that they snipped with their beak and

chopped up with their powerful teeth. Young males might have charged toward each other shaking their heads in play, but few would have dared challenge a big-nosed, frilly-horned adult.

DINOFACTS

Styracosaurus
(STIE-rack-uh-SORE-us)

✳ **NAME:** *Styracosaurus* means spike lizard
styrax (spike) + sauros (lizard)

○ **FAMILY:**   Ornithischian

Ceratopsian

✥ **SIZE:** 18 ft (5.4 m) long; 5.5 ft (1.7 m) high at the hip

⚖ **WEIGHT:** 2 tons (1.8 tonnes)—about the same as 2 North American bison

🍲 **FOOD:** plants

⌂ **HABITAT:** coastal lowlands

WHERE: remains found in Montana and Canada

🕑 **WHEN:** 75–70 million years ago in the Cretaceous period

			STYRACOSAURUS
TRIASSIC	JURASSIC	CRETACEOUS	
250 MILLION YEARS AGO	205 MILLION YEARS AGO	135 MILLION YEARS AGO	65 MILLION YEARS AGO

CHECK THESE OUT!

Brachyceratops, Centrosaurus, Ceratopsians, Chasmosaurus, Cretaceous period, Einiosaurus, Pachyrhinosaurus

Supersaurus

Supersaurus was a giant sauropod (long-necked plant-eater) that lived in western North America during the Jurassic period. It probably used its extremely long neck to reach leaves on the tallest trees.

During the 1970s, US dinosaur hunter James Jensen discovered the incomplete skeletons of several very large sauropods in Colorado. One of these dinosaurs was named *Supersaurus*.

Supersaurus got its name by accident. A journalist writing a story on the fossil discoveries needed a name to use in the story, so he made up the name "Supersaurus." The name was very suitable because the fossil bones of this dinosaur were much larger than those of any other dinosaurs that had then been discovered.

▼ *Supersaurus* browsed. It probably used its teeth to rake leaves from high branches into its mouth.

Supersaurus is not known from a complete skeleton. Paleontologists have 12 of its tail bones, two neck bones, a complete shoulder girdle, and one of its hipbones: the ischium. Luckily, these bones

ONE *SUPERSAURUS* OR TWO?

Paleontologists need to be cautious when they interpret fossil bones. If the bones are arranged roughly the same way that they would have been in life, and the right number of bones are present, they can be reasonably certain that all the bones are from the same animal. However, if the bones are jumbled up it becomes tricky to decide whether they are the remains of one animal or several. Figuring out who's who becomes an even bigger problem if a lot of bones are mixed together and not all the bones needed to make a complete animal are present.

This is the problem with the *Supersaurus* remains, which were found on the bank of an ancient river. The shoulder girdle and the tail bones were not found arranged as they would have been in life. River currents seem to have moved the tail. Do these bones come from the same animal, or were they the bones of two different animals that were swept together after they died?

were enough to let paleontologists decide that *Supersaurus* was a type of diplodocid sauropod; it was a close relative of dinosaurs such as *Apatosaurus* and *Diplodocus*.

The diplodocid sauropods were very long and tall, but they had very lightly built skeletons when compared to other large sauropods like *Camarasaurus* and *Brachiosaurus*.

Paleontologists think that the diplodocids did not have large masses of muscle or fat. They seem to have been very light in weight. This may have allowed them to walk farther or faster in search of food.

How did *Supersaurus* live?
Supersaurus shared its habitat with many other types of sauropods, and like all sauropods it ate plants. How did it survive among all these other plant-eaters?

Supersaurus's large size suggests that it could browse from the highest treetops, which would have been out of the reach of most other sauropods. It would have reached such a large size through natural selection. Perhaps a *Supersaurus* ancestor had a slightly longer neck than the rest. This feature may have given it an advantage in feeding. It may have passed this feature on to its descendants. Over time, a kind of very long-necked sauropod developed—*Supersaurus*. *Supersaurus* may lived in herds, but paleontologists have found no hard evidence that it did.

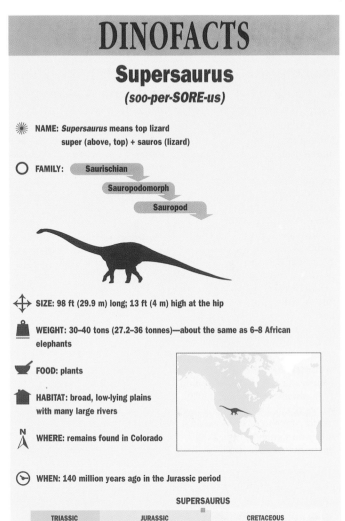

DINOFACTS

Supersaurus
(soo-per-SORE-us)

✳ **NAME:** *Supersaurus* means top lizard
super (above, top) + sauros (lizard)

○ **FAMILY:** Saurischian
Sauropodomorph
Sauropod

✛ **SIZE:** 98 ft (29.9 m) long; 13 ft (4 m) high at the hip

⚖ **WEIGHT:** 30–40 tons (27.2–36 tonnes)—about the same as 6–8 African elephants

🥣 **FOOD:** plants

🏠 **HABITAT:** broad, low-lying plains with many large rivers

N **WHERE:** remains found in Colorado

🕐 **WHEN:** 140 million years ago in the Jurassic period

		SUPERSAURUS	
TRIASSIC	JURASSIC		CRETACEOUS
250 MILLION YEARS AGO	205 MILLION YEARS AGO	135 MILLION YEARS AGO	65 MILLION YEARS AGO

CHECK THESE OUT!

Apatosaurus, Brachiosaurus, Camarasaurus, Diplodocus, Jurassic period, Saurischian dinosaurs, Sauropodomorph dinosaurs, Sauropods

Syntarsus

Little *Syntarsus* was a globe-trotting dinosaur: its remains have been found all over the world. *Syntarsus* was a small theropod (two-legged meat-eater) that lived during the Early Jurassic period.

In 1963, a group of schoolboys from what is now Zimbabwe, in southern Africa, discovered an almost complete dinosaur skeleton. Paleontologist Michael Raath examined the skeleton. From its three-toed feet and pointed snout with sharp teeth, he identified it as a theropod. The skeleton had a long neck and tail and a four-fingered hand, and it looked

JURASSIC GLOBE-TROTTERS

Syntarsus is not the only dinosaur from the early part of the Jurassic period found in many parts of the world. At that time, the continents were joined together into one supercontinent called Pangaea. All sorts of dinosaurs and other animals could travel by land from one region to another. Some of these were the large theropod *Dilophosaurus*, found in Arizona and China; the primitive (little evolved) armored dinosaur *Scelidosaurus*, found in England and Arizona; and the prosauropod *Massospondylus*, found in southern Africa and Arizona.

▼ *Syntarsus* was a small meat-eating dinosaur. It probably chased after fast-moving prey like lizards and early mammals.

very similar to *Coelophysis* from the western United States.

However, some features of its skull, hips, and legs were not like *Coelophysis*, so Raath decided it was a new dinosaur. Because its ankle bones were fused together, he named it *Syntarsus* (fused ankle).

Syntarsus around the world

Fossil-hunters have found additional *Syntarsus* remains in Africa, including a bone bed containing about 30 specimens. This bone bed has allowed

DINOFACTS

Syntarsus
(sin-TAR-sus)

NAME: *Syntarsus* means fused ankle
syn (together) + tarsus (ankle)

FAMILY:
Saurischian
Theropod
Ceratosaur

SIZE: up to 7 ft (2.1 m) long; up to 1.75 ft (53 cm) high at the hip

WEIGHT: up to 30 lbs (13.6 kg)—about the same as a medium-sized raccoon

FOOD: meat

HABITAT: varied from forests to lake shores to deserts

WHERE: remains found in Arizona, England, and southern Africa

▶ Like its relative *Coelophysis*, *Syntarsus* was a small, long, slim meat-eater.

WHEN: 205-192 million years ago in the Jurassic period

	SYNTARSUS		
TRIASSIC	JURASSIC		CRETACEOUS
250 MILLION YEARS AGO	205 MILLION YEARS AGO	135 MILLION YEARS AGO	65 MILLION YEARS AGO

---

paleontologists to study the differences between young and old and between male and female *Syntarsus*.

Syntarsus remains have also been found in other parts of the world. In Arizona, a team of US paleontologists found many specimens of *Syntarsus*. Paleontologist Timothy Rowe recognized differences between the Arizona fossils and those of southern Africa. Those from Arizona each had a pair of crests running down the skull. The African specimens had no crests. More specimens of *Syntarsus* have been found in rocks from England. However, scientists cannot yet be certain if they are the same kind as the US specimens, the same kind as the African specimens, or an entirely new kind of *Syntarsus*.

How did *Syntarsus* live?
Like its relatives *Dilophosaurus* and *Coelophysis*, *Syntarsus* was a meat-eater. Its long neck and long, narrow jaws suggest that it did not try to kill large prey but instead darted after smaller animals. It may have hunted lizards, early mammals, or the young of dinosaurs such as *Lesothosaurus*.

CHECK THESE OUT!

Coelophysis, Continental drift, *Dilophosaurus*, Jurassic period, *Lesothosaurus*

397

Tarbosaurus

Tarbosaurus is the largest known meat-eater from Asia. It was closely related to *Tyrannosaurus*. Some paleontologists think *Tyrannosaurus* and *Tarbosaurus* may even be the same dinosaur.

During the late 1940s, an expedition to Mongolia from the Russian Academy of Sciences discovered rich fossil deposits in the Nemegt Valley. On May 9, 1948, J. Eaglon came across a large skeleton. It turned out to be a tyrannosaur (two-fingered meat-eater), 33 ft (10 m) long. Several more fossils of tyrannosaurs of various sizes were found later that year and in following years.

One or more species?
Some paleontologists thought that these specimens were all a single kind (species), perhaps a new species of *Tyrannosaurus*. Then in 1955, paleontologist E. A. Maleev described the fossils as different kinds of tyrannosaurs.

▼ Two *Tarbosaurus* spar with each other. Like all tyrannosaurs, *Tarbosaurus* had long legs for its body size, and it may have been able to outrun its prey.

The dinosaurs of the Nemegt include the largest found in Mongolia. Unlike those of the Flaming Cliffs (another Mongolian fossil site), many of the dinosaurs were much larger than humans. Why were there so many giants in these rocks?

The reason seems to be the local environment. The fossils of most other sites in Mongolia were formed when those parts of Asia were very dry. The types of rocks of the Nemegt, and the fossils of plants and small animals, show that this region was wetter. More water would allow more plant life, which could support more and larger plant-eaters. In turn, these plant-eaters would allow giant predators such as *Tarbosaurus* to survive.

He thought the biggest bones were a new species of *Tyrannosaurus* (*Tyrannosaurus bataar*), and that the smaller specimens belonged to a new species of *Gorgosaurus*. Maleev believed the medium-sized remains, including Eaglon's skeleton, belonged to an entirely new kind of tyrann-osaur, *Tarbosaurus efremovi*.

How did *Tarbosaurus* live?

Among *Tarbosaurus*'s neighbors were plant-eaters such as hadrosaurs (duckbill dinosaurs), sauropods (long-necked plant-eaters), and ankylosaurs (armored dinosaurs). Small ceratopsians (horned dinosaurs) have also been found in the same region.

Tarbosaurus could have hunted any of these. Baby *Tarbosaurus* would be only a yard or so long and too small to hunt large plant-eating dinosaurs. They probably chased the lizards and mammals of Cretaceous Mongolia, as well as baby dinosaurs, before hunting bigger prey.

DINOFACTS

Tarbosaurus
(TAR-bo-SORE-us)

✳ NAME: *Tarbosaurus* means terrible lizard
tarbos (terrible) + sauros (lizard)

○ FAMILY: Saurischian
→ Theropod
→ Tyrannosaur

✥ SIZE: up to 43 ft (13 m) long; up to 12 ft (3.6 m) high at the hip

⚖ WEIGHT: up to 6 tons (5.4 tonnes)—about the same as 12 polar bears

🍵 FOOD: meat

🏠 HABITAT: warm or subtropical areas with seasonal dry weather

N↑ WHERE: remains found in Mongolia and China

🕐 WHEN: 71–68 million years ago in the Cretaceous period

			TARBOSAURUS ▪
TRIASSIC	JURASSIC		CRETACEOUS
250 MILLION YEARS AGO	205 MILLION YEARS AGO	135 MILLION YEARS AGO	65 MILLION YEARS AGO

CHECK THESE OUT!

Cretaceous period, Saurischian dinosaurs, Sauropods, Tyrannosaurs, *Tyrannosaurus*

Tarchia

Tarchia was a plant-eater that shared its world with *Tarbosaurus*, one of the fiercest predators ever. *Tarchia* had a huge tail-club, which it may have used to defend itself against this massive hunter.

The Polish-Mongolian Expeditions of the late 1960s collected a partial skull of a large ankylosaur (armored dinosaur) from Mongolia's Gobi Desert. It had a higher, squarer skull than *Saichania*, another Mongolian ankylosaur of the same time. In 1977, Polish paleontologist Teresa Maryanska named the new ankylosaur *Tarchia kielanae* for Zofia Kielan-Jaworowska, who

▼ Along with *Ankylosaurus*, which lived in North America with *Tyrannosaurus*, *Tarchia* had the biggest ankylosaur tail-club for its body size.

had led the 1960s expeditions and was the first woman to lead a major dinosaur hunt.

Maryanska then studied the skeletons of another ankylosaur that she thought might be a second kind (species) of *Tarchia*. She proposed naming it *Tarchia gigantea*. In 1990, however, Maryanska and New England paleontologist Walter Coombs decided that *Tarchia kielanae* and *Tarchia gigantea* were the same species.

How did *Tarchia* live?
Tarchia had a square, toothless beak that was well suited to

BIGGEST AND LAST

Tarchia was the largest and the last known of the Asian ankylosaurs. However, it may not have been the last ankylosaur to live in Asia. Scientists studying Cretaceous rocks in Mongolia are convinced that the rocks that were laid down in the last few million years of the Mesozoic Era are missing in central Asia. If so, then there is no way we can know what dinosaurs roamed Asia in the time just before the nonflying dinosaurs became extinct. Perhaps there were even larger Asian ankylosaurs descended from *Tarchia* that we will never find.

cropping off leaves and stems. *Tarchia*'s tiny cheek teeth (molars) only roughly chopped this food, which was broken down in the animal's huge gut.

Short-legged, heavily armored *Tarchia* might have trudged along as slowly as a giant tortoise. *Tarchia*'s armor would have protected it from small meat-eating dinosaurs, but *Tarchia* lived alongside *Tarbosaurus*, a big tyrannosaur (two-fingered meat-eater). How did *Tarchia* defend itself against this huge predator?

Like one group of ankylosaurs, the ankylosaurids, *Tarchia* had a clublike tip to its tail that was formed from big armor plates fused together. Perhaps the ankylosaurs used their tails as weapons. *Tarchia* had strong muscles running down the sides of its tail to pull it from side to side. The last few backbones before the club were locked together and then stiffened by bony rods.

Tarchia's tail would have been like the handle of a club with a knobbly lump at the end. Swung by multiton *Tarchia*, it could have crippled a large tyrannosaur; or it might have broken *Tarchia*'s own tail. We would need clear evidence to prove our theory.

CHECK THESE OUT!

Ankylosaurs, *Ankylosaurus*, Cretaceous period, *Saichania*, *Tarbosaurus*, Tyrannosaurus

DINOFACTS

Tarchia
(TAR-chee-uh)

▶ **Tarchia** had a square skull with bumps and knobs that made it look like a brain.

✳ **NAME:** *Tarchia* comes from the Mongolian word for brain

◯ **FAMILY:** Ornithischian

Thyreophoran

Ankylosaur

✛ **SIZE:** 18–21 ft (5.4–6.4 m) long; 5 ft (1.5 m) high at the hip

⚖ **WEIGHT:** 2.5–3 tons (2.3–2.7 tonnes)—about the same as 2–3 North American bison

🥣 **FOOD:** plants

🏠 **HABITAT:** from arid plains to wetter lowlands

WHERE: remains found in Mongolia

🕐 **WHEN:** 80–70 million years ago in the Cretaceous period

			TARCHIA
TRIASSIC	JURASSIC		CRETACEOUS
250 MILLION YEARS AGO	205 MILLION YEARS AGO	135 MILLION YEARS AGO	65 MILLION YEARS AGO

Tenontosaurus

The large ornithopod (bird-footed dinosaur) *Tenontosaurus* roamed western North America in the Cretaceous period. In many of the sites where it has been found, it is the most abundant dinosaur.

Tenontosaurus was named in 1970 by Yale paleontologist John Ostrom, who was working in the Big Horn Basin on the Montana–Wyoming border. His description was based not only on specimens he had found himself, but also on *Tenontosaurus* specimens collected in the same place in the 1930s by US fossil collector Barnum Brown.

PACK HUNTERS

When Ostrom described the dromaeosaur (clawed meat-eater) *Deinonychus* in 1969, he noted that one fragmentary specimen of *Tenontosaurus* had been found close to fragments of several *Deinonychus*. He wondered whether the meat-eaters were killed when attacking the much larger *Tenontosaurus*. Certainly the discovery of *Deinonychus* teeth with *Tenontosaurus* skeletons suggested that *Deinonychus* ate *Tenontosaurus*, but many paleontologists were still not sure that *Deinonychus* was a pack hunter. In 1995, Ostrom and paleontologist Desmond Maxwell reported on a *Tenontosaurus* skeleton found with 11 *Deinonychus* teeth. Because the *Tenontosaurus* was still in one piece it was unlikely it had been killed by a big predator. Instead, it looked as though several *Deinonychus* had been feeding on a *Tenontosaurus* they had just killed. Even if the large number of teeth found suggests a group of *Deinonychus* fed together, it is hard to prove they hunted in packs.

◀ *Tenontosaurus* was a large ornithopod that probably moved around on all fours as it looked for plants to eat.

Close relatives

Tenontosaurus had a long, stiff tail, so Ostrom identified it as an iguanodontid (a group of large ornithopods named for *Iguanodon*). They had cords, or tendons, crisscrossed over their hips that held their tail stiff.

In some ways, though, *Tenontosaurus* was like the more primitive (less evolved) hypsilophodontids, a group of ornithopods named in honor of *Hypsilophodon*. Like the hypsilophodontids, *Tenonto-saurus* had no thumb spike and had four toes instead of three. However, because it had no front teeth and had a beak instead, most paleontologists still think *Tenontosaurus* was a primitive iguanodontid.

How did *Tenontosaurus* live?

Tenontosaurus could feed on plants growing as high as 10 ft (3 m) above the ground, which it bit off with its toothless beak and chewed up with its cheek teeth. *Tenontosaurus* had no armor. It could only run away from meat-eating dinosaurs such as the dromaeosaur (clawed meat-eater) *Deinonychus*.

CHECK THESE OUT!

Cretaceous period, *Deinonychus*,
Dromaeosaurs, *Hypsilophodon*,
Iguanodon, Ornithischian dinosaurs,
Ornithopods

DINOFACTS

Tenontosaurus
(te-NON-tuh-SORE-us)

▶ Like iguanodontids, *Tenontosaurus* had no teeth at the front of its mouth; hypsilophodontids did.

✳ NAME: *Tenontosaurus* means tendon lizard
tenon (tendon) + sauros (lizard)

◯ FAMILY: Ornithischian

Ornithopod

⬦ SIZE: 18–25 ft (5.4–7.6 m) long; 5–8 ft (1.5–2.4 m) high at the hip

⚖ WEIGHT: 1–2 tons (0.9–1.8 tonnes)—about the same as 1–2 bison

FOOD: plants

🏠 HABITAT: lowlands to coasts

🧭 WHERE: remains found in Idaho, Montana, Oklahoma, Texas, Utah, Wyoming, and perhaps Arizona

🕐 WHEN: 120–100 million years ago in the Cretaceous period

			TENONTOSAURUS
TRIASSIC	JURASSIC		CRETACEOUS
250 MILLION YEARS AGO	205 MILLION YEARS AGO	135 MILLION YEARS AGO	65 MILLION YEARS AGO

Tetanurans

The tetanurans form the large group of theropod (two-legged meat-eating) dinosaurs that includes birds. Some tetanurans, such as hummingbirds, are tiny; others, such as *Giganotosaurus*, were huge.

In the 1970s, Yale University paleontologist John Ostrom showed that only theropod (two-legged meat-eating) dinosaurs had the right combination of features to be the ancestors of modern birds. In the 1980s, paleontologist Jacques Gauthier set out to discover exactly which

TETANURAN FAMILY TREE

The tetanuran group can be divided into two smaller groups: the allosaurs (three-fingered meat-eaters) and the coelurosaurs (hollow-tailed dinosaurs). *Allosaurus* and its relatives make up the allosaurs. The tyrannosaurs (two-fingered meat-eaters), ornithomimosaurs (ostrichlike dinosaurs), troodontids (big-eyed brainy hunters), and maniraptors (long-armed meat-eaters) are all coelurosaurs. *Afrovenator, Baryonyx, Megalosaurus, Piatnitzkysaurus,* and *Spinosaurus* seem to be tetanurans but were more primitive (less evolved) than allosaurs or coelurosaurs.

▶ The tetanuran group contains many different types of theropods, including fish-eating *Baryonyx* (1), allosaurs such as *Giganotosaurus* (2), ostrichlike dinosaurs like *Dromiceiomimus* (3), and avialans (bird relatives) like *Mononykus* (4).

Mesozoic theropods were most closely related to modern birds.

Stiff-tailed dinosaurs
Gauthier examined the features of birds and checked which groups of Mesozoic theropods possessed each of these features. Birds are unusual compared to other dinosaurs in that most of their tail bones are fused together into a stubby, stiffened shaft. Gauthier found that some theropods had stiffened tails. They included dromaeosaurs (clawed meat-eaters), allosaurs (three-fingered meat-eaters), and tyrannosaurs (two-fingered meat-eaters). In forms like *Ceratosaurus*, *Dilophosaurus*, and *Coelophysis*, only the tail tip is a bit stiff. He concluded that the theropods with stiffened tails (including birds) formed one large group; the others formed a second group. He named the bird group the tetanurans, or stiff tails; he named the other group the ceratosaurs for *Ceratosaurus*.

The tetanurans shared other features that the ceratosaurs did not have. For example, they had bigger hands and only two or three working fingers on each; not four as did the ceratosaurs. Tetanurans' teeth were concentrated in the part of the jaws in front of the eyes. Tetanurans also had an extra skull opening in front of the eye but behind the nose. At least some tetanurans, such as allosaurs, tyrannosaurs,

oviraptorosaurs (egg-thief dinosaurs), and birds, had wishbones. They also had special stiffened ankles.

How tetanurans lived
Because the tetanuran group includes many different forms, it is hard to describe a lifestyle for the whole group. Some ate meat, others ate plants, and some ate both. All walked on two legs. The oldest known

tetanuran is *Cryolophosaurus*, which lived in the Early Jurassic period. Birds of course are still alive today.

CHECK THESE OUT!

Afrovenator, Allosaurus, Avialans, Avimimus, Baryonyx, Ceratosaurs, Maniraptors, Megalosaurus, Ornitholestes, Ornithomimus, Piatnitzkysaurus, Spinosaurus, Troodon, Tyrannosaurs

DINOFACTS

Tetanurans
(TET-*uh-NOOR-uns*)

✳ NAME: Tetanuran means stiff-tailed
tetanos (stiff) + ura (tail)

⭕ FAMILY: Saurischian
Theropod

✥ SIZE: up to 46 ft (14 m) long; up to 13 ft (4 m) high at the hip

⬛ WEIGHT: up to 15 tons (13.6 tonnes)—about the same as 3 African elephants

🥣 FOOD: meat, insects, fish, eggs, plants

🏠 HABITAT: all types

⬆ WHERE: remains found worldwide

🕐 WHEN: from 205 million years ago in the Jurassic period to today

	TETANURANS		
TRIASSIC	JURASSIC		CRETACEOUS
250 MILLION YEARS AGO	205 MILLION YEARS AGO	135 MILLION YEARS AGO	65 MILLION YEARS AGO

Thecodontosaurus

Thecodontosaurus was one of the earliest dinosaurs to be discovered and officially named. It is the earliest known prosauropod (early long-necked plant-eater), and lived in Britain in the Triassic period.

Thecodontosaurus was discovered and named in 1836. Over 300 bones of several adults, as well as an almost complete skeleton of a juvenile, were found in southwest England. *Thecodontosaurus* is important because it gives scientists a good idea of what the earliest prosauropods were like. The descendants of the prosauropods

▶ *Thecodontosaurus* probably walked on two legs. Its arms were about half the length of its legs—too short to walk far on all fours.

FILLING IN THE GAPS

The remains of the *Thecodontosaurus* adults were collected from what geologists call fissure fills. During the Triassic period, the climate of southern England was hot and dry. At this time erosion opened up fissures, or deep cracks, in limestones that had formed many millions of years before in the Carbonifereous period (360–290 million years ago). These cracks were filled with the remains of dead animals and sands when flash floods swept across the deserts. The skeletons would have become all jumbled up when the floodwaters carried them in.

were the sauropods (long-necked plant-eaters), such as *Apatosaurus*, which evolved into the largest land animals ever. By looking at *Thecodontosaurus*, paleontologists can see how the body of sauropods had to evolve to be able to grow so large.

DINOFACTS

Thecodontosaurus
(THEE-co-DON-tuh-SORE-us)

 NAME: *Thecodontosaurus* means socket-toothed lizard
theco (socket) + odontos (tooth) + sauros (lizard)

FAMILY:
- Saurischian
- Sauropodomorph
- Prosauropod

SIZE: up to 8 ft (2.4 m) long; about 3 ft (90 cm) high at the hip

WEIGHT: 60 lbs (27 kg)—about the same as a raccoon

 FOOD: plants

HABITAT: semidesert areas

WHERE: remains found in England and Wales

▶ **This juvenile *Thecodontosaurus* was about 3.3 ft (1 m) long.**

WHEN: 210 million years ago in the Triassic period

THECODONTOSAURUS

TRIASSIC	JURASSIC	CRETACEOUS
250 MILLION YEARS AGO	205 MILLION YEARS AGO	135 MILLION YEARS AGO	65 MILLION YEARS AGO

How did it live?

Thecodontosaurus ate plants. Its teeth are very similar to those of living, plant-eating lizards like iguanas. *Thecodontosaurus* gives paleontologists a chance to see how features that became usual in later sauropods got started. Its jaw hinge position was only slightly lower than the tooth rows. In contrast, the later prosauropods (such as *Plateosaurus*) and sauropods had jaw hinges that were well below the level of the tooth rows, so they could use more of a sideways motion to shear their food. *Thecodontosaurus*'s hands had just two fingers and a thumb, which it probably used to gather food. Later prosauropods had larger hands and five fingers as well as longer arms, so they could probably spend more time on all fours than did *Thecodontosaurus*.

CHECK THESE OUT!

Apatosaurus, Plateosaurus, Prosauropods, Sauropodomorph dinosaurs, Sauropods, Triassic period

Therizinosaurus

Therizinosaurus is one of the strangest dinosaurs known. It is the largest of the therizinosaurs, slothlike long-necked plant-eaters with huge curved claws on their hands.

In 1948 a Russian expedition to Mongolia found the huge claws and arms of a fossil reptile in the Nemegt Valley. Later finds showed it was a dinosaur because it clearly held its legs directly beneath its body. Its powerful hind limbs also indicated that it walked on two legs.

With its long, curved claws, *Therizinosaurus* most resembled the "segnosaurs" *Segnosaurus* and *Erlikosaurus*. However, in the 1970s and 1980s, these two dinosaurs were known only from incomplete material, and no one knew where in the dinosaur family tree they fitted.

Then in 1988 fossil-hunters found the "segnosaur" *Alxasaurus*. Its wrist resembled the wrist of a maniraptor (long-armed meat-eater), so paleontologists recognized that it was a theropod (two-legged meat-eater). However, like *Segnosaurus*, *Alxasaurus* had

▶ **Therizinosaurus** was the largest therizinosaur. Its claws were sickle-shaped and its name means reaping lizard.

MONSTER TURTLE

When *Therizinosaurus* was first found, paleontologists did not know what kind of reptile it was. Only the arms, hands, and shoulder bones were found, and they were huge and unlike anything else known at the time.

Russian paleontologist Eugene Maleev thought it might have been a turtle or turtle-like animal because of the broad hand and the shape of the strong arms. Giant sea turtles such as *Archelon* had already been found in Cretaceous rocks in North America. What puzzled Maleev, though, was that Mongolia was far away from the sea in the Cretaceous period, as it is today.

Therizinosaurus

(THER-uh-ZEEN-uh-SORE-us)

 NAME: *Therizinosaurus* means reaping reptile
therizinos (reaping) + sauros (reptile)

○ **FAMILY:**

Saurischian
Theropod
Tetanuran

✛ **SIZE:** about 20 ft (6 m) long; possibly 5 ft (1.5 m) high at the hip

WEIGHT: about 2.5 tons (2.3 tonnes)—about the same as 2–3 North American bison

FOOD: probably plants, possibly insects too

HABITAT: dry uplands

WHERE: remains found in Mongolia

▶ *Therizinosaurus*'s biggest claw was 28 in (70 cm) long; it would have been even longer when the dinosaur was alive. The claw is shown with a child's hand.

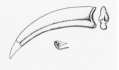

🕐 **WHEN:** 71–68 million years ago in the Cretaceous period

			THERIZINOSAURUS
TRIASSIC	JURASSIC	CRETACEOUS	
250 MILLION YEARS AGO	205 MILLION YEARS AGO	135 MILLION YEARS AGO	65 MILLION YEARS AGO

teeth with rounded bumps instead of bladelike teeth like most meat-eaters. Paleontologists concluded that "segnosaurs" were plant-eating theropods. Since *Therizinosaurus* had been the first of these dinosaurs to be named, paleontologists renamed the "segnosaurs" the therizinosaurs.

How *Therizinosaurus* lived

Like other therizinosaurs, *Therizinosaurus* probably had a toothless beak for snipping off leaves and stems that it chewed with its cheek teeth (molars). It would also have had a fat,

blocky body and short, stumpy legs. It probably moved slowly compared to meat-eating theropods.

Therizinosaurus may have used its huge claws to pull down leafy branches toward its mouth or even as weapons to defend against meat-eaters like the tyrannosaur (two-fingered meat-eater) *Tarbosaurus*.

CHECK THESE OUT!

Alxasaurus, Erlikosaurus, Saurischian dinosaurs, *Segnosaurus, Tarbosaurus,* Theropods, Turtles

Theropods

There are many different kinds of theropods (two-legged meat-eating dinosaurs). They are one of the major groups of dinosaurs and their remains have been found in every continent of the world.

The study of theropods begins with the discovery of their footprints. In the early 19th century, natural historian Edward Hitchcock described many three-toed footprints found in rocks from the Early Jurassic period in New England. Hitchcock thought these were from some sort of giant bird because, like birds, whatever had made the footprint walked on only its three middle toes.

A giant reptile...
About the same time in England, Oxford University geologist William Buckland discovered and described the fossil bones of an enormous reptile. This creature had long, bladelike teeth with serrations down both edges, like those of modern monitor lizards.

Although this fossil was incomplete, it was clearly from an animal much larger than any modern lizard. Furthermore, unlike the other fossil reptiles known at the time, the limb bones showed that this was a land-living creature with strong legs, not a swimmer with flippers. Buckland named this new giant reptile *Megalosaurus*, or great lizard.

In 1842, British paleontologist Richard Owen recognized that *Megalosaurus*

was more similar to other fossil reptiles (particularly the plant-eaters *Iguanodon* and *Hylaeosaurus*) than to any other type of animal. All of these reptiles were large land-living forms with upright, not sprawling, limbs. Owen named this new group of reptiles the dinosaurs, or terrible lizards.

...that walked on two legs
Owen thought that *Megalosaurus* was a giant four-legged creature that looked like a lizard but walked like a bear. Discoveries made in the mid-1800s showed that this idea was wrong. The bones of a related meat-eating dinosaur (*Dryptosaurus*) were found by US paleontologist Edward Drinker Cope in 1866. The

Velociraptor

▶ Most theropods ate meat. Here two *Velociraptor* attack an *Oviraptor* (another kind of theropod) in Cretaceous Mongolia.

A LARGE FAMILY

Besides little *Herrerasaurus*, which is in a group of its own, theropods can be either ceratosaurs (four-fingered meat-eaters) or tetanurans (stiff-tailed meat-eaters). Ceratosaurs include some early long-necked predators like *Coelophysis* and *Dilophosaurus*, and later short-necked carnivores like *Ceratosaurus* and *Carnotaurus*.

Most theropods are tetanurans. Tetanurans include some primitive meat-eaters like *Afrovenator* and *Megalosaurus*, as well as more advanced allosaurs (like *Allosaurus*) and the many sorts of coelurosaurs (hollow-tailed dinosaurs). Some of the coelurosaur groups are the ornithomimosaurs (ostrichlike dinosaurs), the tyrannosaurs (two-fingered meat-eaters), and the maniraptors (long-armed meat-eaters). The maniraptors include such groups as the oviraptorosaurs (egg-thief dinosaurs), the dromaeosaurs (clawed meat-eaters), the big-clawed plant-eating therizinosaurs, and modern birds.

fossil of *Dryptosaurus* included more parts than that of *Megalosaurus*. Because *Dryptosaurus*'s front limb was much shorter than the hind limb, it showed that these dinosaurs must have walked on their back legs only.

Beast foot

Later discoveries of complete meat-eating dinosaur skeletons, such as *Compsognathus* in Germany and *Ceratosaurus* in the United States, confirmed that these creatures walked only on their back legs, and that they grasped with their front limbs. When these new specimens were described, paleontologist Othniel C. Marsh of Yale University coined the term theropod, or beast foot, to describe all these two-legged meat-eaters.

Marsh noted that the theropods all shared various features. In most vertebrates (animals with an internal skeleton), the feet have five toes. In most dinosaurs, the fifth toe (equivalent to our little toe) was lost, but the first toe touched the ground and connected to the ankle.

Curved claws

Marsh's theropods were different from these other dinosaurs. The first toe was reduced, so it did not touch the ground when the dinosaur

Velociraptor

Oviraptor

411

ALL OVER THE WORLD

Theropod fossils are fairly common in almost every sedimentary rock that contains dinosaur bones or footprints. This is because in every environment in which dinosaurs lived, theropods were there, probably eating some of the other dinosaurs. Theropod teeth, bones, and footprints show that of all dinosaur types, their group lasted the longest. Theropods are among the oldest sorts of dinosaurs found and are also found in the very last rocks of the last period of the Mesozoic Era.

Theropods are found in every continent, and in every epoch of the age of dinosaurs. Other sorts of dinosaurs are not as common overall; sauropods, for example, are not found in most of the rocks of the second half of the Cretaceous period in North America. Theropods included small forms (such as *Compsognathus* and *Sinornithoides*), medium-sized animals (*Struthiomimus* and *Deinonychus*), larger creatures (*Afrovenator* and *Allosaurus*), and giants (such as *Carcharodontosaurus* and *Tyrannosaurus*). Most theropods were meat-eaters, but tooth shape (or beak shape, in those without teeth) suggests that some of them may have eaten things other than meat. The toothless theropods included oviraptorosaurs and most ornithomimosaurs, while the bizarre, big-clawed therizinosaurs had plant-eaters' teeth.

walked, and it did not connect to the ankle.

This meant that the dinosaur had only three effective toes, making its foot very similar to that of a bird. Because the theropods also had long, curved claws at the ends of their three main toes, Marsh called them beast-footed.

The jaws that bite
One feature found in all but the most specialized of theropods is a joint in the lower jaw. Between the bones that hold the teeth and the bones that connect the lower and upper jaws is a hinge. Among the dinosaurs, only theropods have this hinge, although similar joints are found in the jaws of certain lizards and snakes.

▶ A snake swallows a mouse almost as big as its own head. Some paleontologists think theropods could swallow big lumps of prey in a similar way. Others are not so sure.

Some paleontologists think that the jaw joint of theropod dinosaurs allowed them to gulp down larger bits of food, in the way that snakes can swallow animals bigger than their heads. However, the bones of theropod jaws do not look as if they were quite that flexible. It is more likely that the jaw joint helped them to feed in a different way. As theropods grabbed their prey, the victims would almost certainly struggle to get away. This struggling would put stresses on the bones of the skull, including the lower jaw. By having a joint in the lower jaw acting as a sort of shock absorber, a theropod could hold onto a struggling animal.

The signs of a theropod
Most theropods have bladelike, serrated teeth, like those of *Megalosaurus*. Other dinosaurs had leaf-shaped teeth with big knobs rather than little serrations. Knobby, leaf-shaped teeth are more useful for chopping up plants than for slicing through meat.

However, bladelike teeth are not special to the theropod group. Many kinds of reptiles have similar teeth. Having bladelike teeth does not make an animal a theropod. The three-toed foot and the special jaw joint, though, do identify an animal as a theropod.

The claws that catch

Besides long, curved claws, theropods tended to have fairly long fingers. Such a hand would be useful for grabbing and holding prey. However, similar claws and fingers are found in some prosauropods (early long-necked plant-eaters) and ornithischian (bird-hipped) dinosaurs, as well as in pterosaurs (Mesozoic flying reptiles). This may indicate that early dinosaurs and their closest relatives all had some sort of grasping ability.

Another feature of theropods is their hollow skeleton. Some other kinds of dinosaurs, such as some sauropods (long-necked plant-eaters), also have hollow spaces in their backbones. However, the theropods, especially the more advanced (highly evolved) ones, have very complex bone hollows. Also, all the long bones of theropods are hollow. This makes them different from big sauropods and ornithischians, and indeed most vertebrates, which have more solidly built bones.

Modern theropods

Marsh and many other paleontologists noticed similarities between modern birds and theropods. Marsh was also one of the first scientists to realize that Hitchcock's tracks were made by theropods.

Both modern birds and theropods have long hind legs with three walking toes and a first toe that does not contact the ankle. Both groups also have hollow bones, and primitive (little evolved) birds have a jaw joint that is like that of a theropod.

Many paleontologists realized that these similarities were not coincidences. Birds had these features because they had inherited them from their theropod ancestors. Birds are the modern representatives of the theropod dinosaurs. This means that theropod dinosaurs are still alive in the modern world and live in habitats stretching from the tropics to the North Pole to the shores of Antarctica.

DINOFACTS

Theropods
(THER-uh-PODS)

☀ **NAME:** Theropod means beast foot
theros (beast) + pous (foot)

○ **FAMILY:** Saurischian

✛ **SIZE:** up to 46 ft (14 m) long; up to 13 ft (4 m) high at the hip

WEIGHT: up to 15 tons (13.6 tonnes)—about the same as 3 African elephants

FOOD: meat, insects, fish, eggs, plants

HABITAT: all types, from deserts to sea shores

N **WHERE:** remains found worldwide

☉ **WHEN:** from 230 million years ago in the Triassic period to today (since birds are theropod dinosaurs)

THEROPODS

TRIASSIC	JURASSIC	CRETACEOUS
250 MILLION YEARS AGO	205 MILLION YEARS AGO	135 MILLION YEARS AGO ... 65 MILLION YEARS AGO

CHECK THESE OUT!

Allosaurus, Birds, Ceratosaurs, Dromaeosaurs, *Herrerasaurus*, *Iguanodon*, Maniraptors, *Megalosaurus*, Saurischian dinosaurs, Tetanurans, Tyrannosaurs

Thescelosaurus

Thescelosaurus lived right at the end of the Mesozoic Era. With its long legs and short arms, it was probably an agile, fast runner that could quickly flee from its predators.

Thescelosaurus neglectus (the neglected marvelous lizard) was described in 1913 by Smithsonian paleontologist Charles Gilmore from specimens collected in 1891 in southeastern Wyoming. It had long legs and short arms, four toes on its hind feet and five on its forefeet. Its long tail was criss-crossed by stiff, bony cords, or tendons. The best specimen had a couple of dark patches that might have been the remains of skin.

Gilmore at first placed *Thescelosaurus* in the same group as *Camptosaurus* (bent lizard), a relative of *Iguanodon* (iguana-toothed dinosaur). In

PARKSOSAURUS

In 1926, Canadian paleontologist William Parks described a new species of *Thescelosaurus* (*Thescelosaurus warreni*) from a skeleton found in Alberta, Canada. In 1937, however, Charles M. Sternberg recognized it was a different kind of dinosaur and named it *Parksosaurus* in Parks's honor.

▶ *Thescelosaurus* was a solitary, fleet-footed ornithopod that used its speed to escape predators.

1915, however, Gilmore changed his mind and placed *Thescelosaurus* in the same group of dinosaurs as *Hypsilophodon*, a small two-legged ornithopod (bird-footed dinosaur). *Hypsilophodon* had sharply ridged cheek teeth and teeth at the front of its mouth that more advanced (highly evolved) ornithopods had lost. In 1995, Connecticut paleon-tologist Peter Galton agreed that *Thescelosaurus* was much more like *Hypsilophodon*, but the roof of its mouth was different.

Another species
In 1940, freelance fossil collector Charles M. Sternberg described a second species, *Thescelosaurus edmontonensis* (marvelous lizard from Edmonton). In 1974, Galton suggested that this specimen was a variant of *Thescelosaurus neglectus*.

How did *Thescelosaurus* live?
Thescelosaurus was a fairly fast dinosaur. It was widespread across the warm lowlands of western North America. Its remains are not very common, so it probably lived alone rather than in herds. Like all ornithischian dinosaurs, *Thescelosaurus* fed on plants, which it chewed up with its leaflike teeth.

Small hunters such as the dromaeosaurs (clawed meat-eaters) may have eaten it, although it was probably too small and agile to be caught by an adult *Tyrannosaurus*.

DINOFACTS

Thescelosaurus
(THES-kel-uh-SORE-us)

✳ **NAME:** *Thescelosaurus* means marvelous lizard
theskelos (marvelous) + sauros (lizard)

◯ **FAMILY:** Ornithischian

Ornithopod

✥ **SIZE:** 12 ft (3.6 m) long; 4 ft (1.2 m) high at the hip

⚖ **WEIGHT:** 500 lbs (227 kg)—about the same as a tiger

⚗ **FOOD:** plants

⌂ **HABITAT:** lowland floodplains

N↑ **WHERE:** remains found in Montana, South Dakota, and Wyoming in the United States, and Alberta and Saskatchewan in Canada

☉ **WHEN:** 75–65 million years ago in the Cretaceous period

			THESCELOSAURUS
TRIASSIC	JURASSIC	CRETACEOUS	
250 MILLION YEARS AGO	205 MILLION YEARS AGO	135 MILLION YEARS AGO	65 MILLION YEARS AGO

CHECK THESE OUT!
Camptosaurus, Cretaceous period, Dromaeosaurs, *Hypsilophodon*, *Iguanodon*, Ornithischian dinosaurs, Ornithopods, *Tyrannosaurus*

415

Thyreophorans

The thyreophorans were the armored and plate-backed dinosaurs. They roamed over most of the world from the Early Jurassic period to the end of the Cretaceous period.

In 1915, Hungarian paleontologist Franz Nopcsa put all the dinosaurs that had armor in a new group, which he called the thyreophorans. In this group, he included the primitive (little evolved) armored dinosaur *Scelidosaurus*, the ankylosaurs (armored dinosaurs), the stegosaurs (plate-backed dinosaurs), and the ceratopsians (horned dinosaurs). At that time, paleontologists believed that ceratopsians had armor. Since then, they have learned that this armor belonged to the ankylosaurs instead.

Paleontologists did not use the name thyreophoran very much until 1986, when Paul Sereno redefined the group. According to Sereno, the thyreophorans included all dinosaurs with the bone below the eye wider than it was tall.

All thyreophorans also had pairs of armor plates running down their backs and rows of armor studs (scutes). Although Sereno decided that the ceratopsians were not thyreophorans, he did include the primitive armored dinosaur *Scutellosaurus* in the group.

Some thyreophorans, such as the stegosaurs, developed with narrow mouths for browsing on trees and bushes, as deer do today. Others, such as some advanced (highly evolved) ankylosaurs, developed with wide mouths for grazing on short vegetation as cows do today.

Both the stegosaurs and the ankylosaurs developed big, barrel-shaped rib cages

Stegosaurus

▲ *Stegosaurus* was a stegosaur. It had two rows of tall plates running down its back, and spikes on its tail. *Mymoorapelta* was an early ankylosaur that had armor plates sticking out from its neck, sides, and tail, and armor studs set in its skin. Scientists do not think it had a tail-club.

SUITS OF ARMOR

Thyreophoran armor evolved throughout the Mesozoic Era. As the stegosaurs evolved, the pairs of armor plates running down their backs gradually got bigger. The size of the ankylosaurs' side armor plates also gradually increased. Among the ankylosaurs, the nodosaurids (named for *Nodosaurus*) developed large shoulder spines; some stegosaurs, such as *Kentrosaurus*, did the same. The males may have poked their spines at each other to decide who was boss or to defend themselves against marauding predators. Most thyreophorans probably defended themselves with their tails as well. Stegosaurs had tail spikes on their tail tips, while the tails of ankylosaurs such as *Sauropelta* and *Polacanthus* had bony blades. The ankylosaurids, a group of armored dinosaurs named for *Ankylosaurus*, had bony tail-clubs.

DINOFACTS

Thyreophorans
(THIH-ree-OH-fuh-rans)

 NAME: Thyreophoran means shield bearer
thyreos (shield) + phoros (bearer)

FAMILY: Ornithischian

SIZE: wide variation from 4 ft (1.2 m) to 33 ft (10 m) long;
from 2 ft (60 cm) to 10 ft (3 m) high at the hip

WEIGHT: huge variation from 30 lbs (13.6 kg) to 4 tons
(3.6 tonnes)

FOOD: plants

HABITAT: valleys and lowland plains

WHERE: remains found worldwide except South America

WHEN: from 200 million years ago in the Jurassic period
to 65 million years ago in the Cretaceous period

THYREOPHORANS

TRIASSIC	JURASSIC	CRETACEOUS
250 MILLION YEARS AGO	205 MILLION YEARS AGO	135 MILLION YEARS AGO ... 65 MILLION YEARS AGO

that probably housed big guts for digesting these plants. They also had spreading toes on their feet to help support their huge bodies as they moved.

Mymoorapelta

How thyreophorans lived
Like other ornithischian (bird-hipped) dinosaurs, thyreophorans ate plants, which they shredded with their simple leaf-shaped teeth. While little *Scutellosaurus* could move on its back legs, the more advanced thyreophorans were so large and heavily armored that they had to walk on all fours. Their front legs were also short, so they could reach only low-growing plants.

CHECK THESE OUT!
Ankylosaurs, Ceratopsians,
Nodosaurus, Polacanthus,
Scelidosaurus, Scutellosaurus,
Stegosaurs, Stegosaurus

417

Titanosaurus

Titanosaurus was a medium-sized sauropod (long-necked plant-eater) first discovered in India. It gave its name to the group of armored sauropods, the titanosaurs.

▼ *Titanosaurus* would have been one of the main plant-eaters in Cretaceous Gondwanaland.

In 1877, at about the time that giant dinosaurs like *Apatosaurus* were being discovered in western North America, English paleontologist Richard Lydekker described a new kind of large dinosaur from India. This new animal was a medium-sized sauropod (long-necked plant-eater) from the Late Cretaceous period. Lydekker named it *Titanosaurus indicus*, which means giant lizard from India.

Fossil-hunters found only tail bones and a thigh bone from the Indian *Titanosaurus*. However, these few remains were enough to tell scientists that the dinosaur belonged to a new group of sauropods, which they called titanosaurs.

Bones that may have belonged to *Titanosaurus* have also been found in Argentina, Madagascar, and France. However, scientists cannot identify them for sure because they have never found a skull bone.

THE GREAT SURVIVORS

During the Cretaceous period, major changes in global climate patterns took place, and new types of plants, the flowering plants, began to take over the landscape. With these new conditions came new plant-eating dinosaurs like the hadrosaurs (duckbill dinosaurs) and ceratopsians (horned dinosaurs). The existing plant-eating dinosaurs, such as the sauropods and the stegosaurs (plate-backed dinosaurs), disappeared from many parts of the world but survived in others.

While the hadrosaurs and ceratopsians became the main plant-eaters in the northern hemisphere, in places like Europe, North America, and Asia, the titanosaurs became the main plant-eaters in the southern hemisphere. South America, India, and Madagascar, the places where most titanosaur remains have been found, were once part of one supercontinent known as Gondwanaland. It seems that the titanosaurs were able to successfully move and live all over Gondwanaland.

Sauropod skulls were fairly small compared to the size of the dinosaurs and often became crushed and scattered before the animals fossilized.

Armored dinosaurs

An important feature of *Titanosaurus* and other titanosaurs was their body armor. Paleontologists suspected that the *Titanosaurus* whose bones were discovered in Madagascar may have had bony plates scattered over its back. However, it was not until the well-preserved fossils of *Saltasaurus* were found in Argentina that paleontologists agreed that *Titanosaurus* and the other titanosaurs had small armor plates, or osteoderms, set into their skin.

How did *Titanosaurus* live?

Because they have found tracks of a number of sauropods moving in the same direction at the same time, paleontologists believe that sauropods may have lived in small herds.

Like all sauropods, *Titanosaurus* would have eaten plants. All sauropods had plant-eaters' barrel-shaped bodies to hold the huge guts needed to digest leaves and stems.

CHECK THESE OUT!

Alamosaurus, Antarctosaurus, Argentinosaurus, Continental drift, Cretaceous period, Hypselosaurus, Opisthocoelicaudia, Saltasaurus, Saurischian dinosaurs, Sauropods

DINOFACTS

Titanosaurus

(TIE-*tah-noh*-SORE-*us*)

▶ By putting together all the *Titanosaurus* bones they have, paleontologists can reconstruct *Titanosaurus's* skeleton fairly accurately.

✳ **NAME:** *Titanosaurus* means titan lizard
titans (giants in Greek mythology) + sauros (lizard)

○ **FAMILY:** Saurischian
  Sauropodomorph
    Sauropod

✥ **SIZE:** 39 ft (12 m) long; 10 ft (3 m) high at the hip

WEIGHT: about 12–14 tons (10.8–12.6 tonnes)—about the same as 2–3 African elephants

FOOD: plants

HABITAT: broad, low-lying plains with many large rivers

N **WHERE:** remains found in Argentina, India, France, and Madagascar

WHEN: 80–65 million years ago in the Cretaceous period

			TITANOSAURUS
TRIASSIC	JURASSIC	CRETACEOUS	
250 MILLION YEARS AGO	205 MILLION YEARS AGO	135 MILLION YEARS AGO	65 MILLION YEARS AGO

Torosaurus

Torosaurus is known only from five incomplete skulls, but from these, paleontologists can work out many details about this huge animal and about the evolution of the horned dinosaurs.

In 1891, John Bell Hatcher, one of US paleontologist O. C. Marsh's field collectors, sent Marsh two almost complete skulls that were discovered in southeastern Wyoming. These skulls were extremely large. One of them was estimated to have been 8 ft (2.4 m) long. This skull was not even from a fully grown animal. By looking at the stage of growth of the bones, paleontologists could see that the animal had not finished growing when it died.

Marsh recognized that these skulls belonged to a new type of ceratopsian, or horned dinosaur. He named the animal *Torosaurus*.

Horns and frills
Torosaurus lived at the same time as *Triceratops*, during the very last stages of the Cretaceous period, but it was never as common as *Triceratops*. *Torosaurus* was one of the chasmosaurine ceratopsians, a group that had an extremely long and wide frill of bone at the back of the skull. The chasmosaurines were named for *Chasmosaurus*, which also had a very long frill; ceratopsians with short frills are called centrosaurines in honor of *Centrosaurus*.

HOLE IN THE HEAD

We do not know why Marsh named *Torosaurus* as he did. However, the Greek word *toro* usually means a perforation, or hole. Perhaps this refers to the weight-saving holes in *Torosaurus*'s frill, which were at first thought to be quite unusual. At the time that *Torosaurus* was described, the only other chasmosaurine known was *Triceratops*, which had a solid frill. The name that Marsh chose therefore probably hints at what he thought was special about the frill of *Torosaurus*.

▶ *Torosaurus* drags itself from a mudbath. Modern rhinoceroses wallow in mud to get rid of parasites. Perhaps ceratopsians did the same.

Torosaurus may have used its frill to signal to other ceratopsians. Unlike the frills of other ceratopsians, *Torosaurus*'s frill did not have little, extra, bony lumps around the edges.

How did *Torosaurus* live?

Like all ceratopsians, *Torosaurus* had a strong beak at the front of its mouth and many rows of grinding and shearing teeth toward the back for eating tough, woody plants.

Torosaurus fossils are so rare that we cannot say if it lived in herds or not. Perhaps it lived like the modern black rhinoceros, an animal that feeds by itself and chases away intruders. Rhinoceroses' nose horns warn other rhinoceroses to keep away. Perhaps the horns and frills of *Torosaurus* sent out similar warnings.

CHECK THESE OUT!

Centrosaurus, Ceratopsians, Chasmosaurus, Cretaceous period, Fossils, Ornithischian dinosaurs, Triceratops

DINOFACTS

Torosaurus
(TOE-roh-SORE-us)

▶ *Torosaurus* had two huge horns above its eyes and a small nose horn. Its frill had large holes in it that made it lighter.

✳ **NAME:** *Torosaurus* means hole lizard
toro (hole, perforation) + sauros (lizard)

○ **FAMILY:** Ornithischian

Ceratopsian

✛ **SIZE:** 24 ft (7.3 m) long; 8 ft (2.4 m) high at the hip

⚖ **WEIGHT:** 3 tons (2.7 tonnes)—about the same as 3 bison

FOOD: plants

HABITAT: broad, low-lying plains with many large rivers

WHERE: remains found in western North America

🕐 **WHEN:** 70–65 million years ago in the Cretaceous period

		TOROSAURUS
TRIASSIC	JURASSIC	CRETACEOUS
250 MILLION YEARS AGO	205 MILLION YEARS AGO	135 MILLION YEARS AGO / 65 MILLION YEARS AGO

Triceratops

With its three horns, *Triceratops* was one of the most distinctive dinosaurs. It was also one of the most common at the end of the Cretaceous period, and perhaps one of the last to survive.

In 1889 Yale paleontologist and fossil collector O. C. Marsh named *Triceratops horridus* from a nearly complete skull found in the Lance Formation, Niobrara County, southeastern Wyoming. It had two massive horns above its eyes, a small nose horn, a large frill of bone sticking out at the back of the skull, and beak-shape jaws.

Triceratops belonged to a group of ceratopsians (horned dinosaurs) called chasmo-saurines in honor of *Chasmosaurus*. Chasmosaurines had large horns over their eyes and a fairly small nose horn. *Triceratops* was a very advanced (highly evolved) ceratopsian. It had very long horns over its eyes. Earlier, less

evolved ceratopsians like *Psittacosaurus* had no horns. *Triceratops* also had a huge bony frill. Primitive (little evolved) ceratopsians like *Bagaceratops* had very tiny frills.

Triceratops was also a very advanced chasmosaurine. *Triceratops*'s frill was solid. Early chasmosaurines, like *Chasmosaurus*, had frills with holes in them under the skin. However, *Triceratops*' frill was shorter than that of most chasmosaurines. Its frill was more like the frills of the centrosaurines, a group of ceratopsians with long nose

▼ The bony cores of *Triceratops*'s horns could be as long as 3 ft (90 cm). When the animal was alive, they were covered in keratin, making them even longer.

horns named in honor of *Centrosaurus*.

No buffalo
Marsh's discovery of *Triceratops* made him rethink earlier finds. Just two years before, he had described a pair of horns collected from the Denver Formation in Colorado. At the time, he thought they belonged to *Bison alticornis*, a kind of bison, but it is more likely they were from *Triceratops* or from *Torosaurus*, another large, horned dinosaur.

How many species?
Triceratops fossils are very common. Between 1902 and 1909 Barnum Brown collected about 500 skulls from Hell Creek in Montana and South Dakota. Over the years, 16 species have been described, based mainly on differences in the horns and frills.

In 1986 and 1990 Yale paleontologist John Ostrom and German paleontologist Peter Wellnhofer proposed there was only one species of *Triceratops*. They pointed out that most individuals of African buffalo vary in the shape of their horns and skull. Certainly if scientists named deer and cows only from the shape of their horns there would be a great many more species.

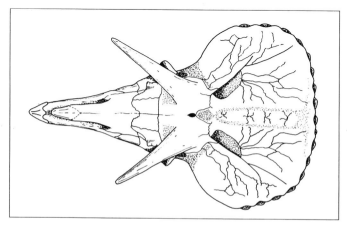

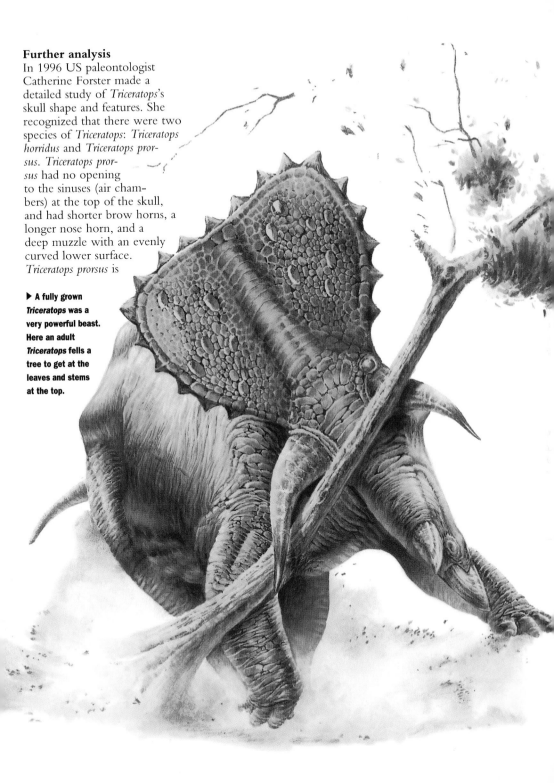

Further analysis

In 1996 US paleontologist
Catherine Forster made a
detailed study of *Triceratops*'s
skull shape and features. She
recognized that there were two
species of *Triceratops*: *Triceratops
horridus* and *Triceratops prorsus*. *Triceratops pror-
sus* had no opening
to the sinuses (air cham-
bers) at the top of the skull,
and had shorter brow horns, a
longer nose horn, and a
deep muzzle with an evenly
curved lower surface.
Triceratops prorsus is

▶ A fully grown
Triceratops was a
very powerful beast.
Here an adult
Triceratops fells a
tree to get at the
leaves and stems
at the top.

much rarer than *Triceratops horridus*, so Forster did not believe that the two could be male and female of the same species. There would have been too many of one sex and not enough of the other.

Catherine Forster also looked again at a skull found in 1905 by Yale paleontologist Richard Swan Lull. It was first described as *Diceratops hatcheri* (Hatcher's two-horned face). Lull had noted that the skull had no nose horn and that the frill had two pairs of openings. In 1933 Lull included the species in *Triceratops*. Ostrom and Wellnhofer later included it in *Triceratops horridus*.

Later, Catherine Forster saw that the nose horn in chasmosaurines like *Triceratops* was a separate bone. Perhaps it had simply fallen off the *Diceratops* specimen. However, she also recognized that *Diceratops*'s frill holes were like a halfway stage between the large openings in the frill of *Torosaurus* and the solid frill of *Triceratops*. *Diceratops* was a separate kind of ceratopsian linking *Torosaurus* and *Triceratops*.

GALLOPING *TRICERATOPS*?

Paleontologists cannot agree on how *Triceratops* held its forelimbs. Traditionally, scientists reconstructed *Triceratops* with its front legs splayed out to the sides. Then in 1987, Wyoming paleontologist Robert Bakker suggested that the robust leg bones and large muscle attachments in *Triceratops* showed that it could gallop like a rhinoceros. This idea was very popular among the public and dinosaur artists, but was questioned by Wisconsin paleontologist Rolf Johnson. He reconstructed the foreleg of *Torosaurus* using ropes to show the positions of the tendons and muscles. His study showed that mechanically these animals had to have sprawling front legs as this was the only way they could be joined to the rest of the skeleton.

However, tracks left by a *Triceratops* near Golden, Colorado, seem to tell a different story. Colorado paleontologist Martin Lockley was able to demonstrate that *Triceratops* left a narrow trackway that would not have been made by an animal with sprawling front legs. Lockley's evidence does not necessarily mean that *Triceratops* could gallop like a rhinoceros, but it certainly suggests that the forelegs of *Triceratops* were more erect than other paleontologists have thought.

▲ A black rhinoceros charges. Paleontologists wonder whether *Triceratops* could too.

Shock absorbers

Paleontologists are not sure whether *Triceratops* used its horns for fighting or just for display. However, scars and broken horns suggest fighting was a major use of the horns.

Another important clue is that ceratopsians developed sinuses, or air chambers, in the skull below the horns and above the brain. The sinuses would have acted like shock absorbers to protect the brain when the horns were being used in battle.

Tyrannosaurus attack

There is no question that *Tyrannosaurus* ate *Triceratops*, as its teeth marks, and in one case a tooth fragment, have been found in *Triceratops* bones. Did *Tyrannosaurus* kill *Triceratops* or did it scavenge the remains?

A *Tyrannosaurus* foolish enough to attack a large, healthy *Triceratops* stood a good chance of being injured or killed. Modern predators such as lions typically attack only young, old, or lame animals in a herd. Not only is this less dangerous for the predator, it also improves the overall health of a herd by weeding out the weak and unhealthy. Perhaps *Tyrannosaurus* preyed on *Triceratops* herds in the same way millions of years ago in North America.

In Late Cretaceous North America, tyrannosaurs were the only meat-eating dinosaurs large enough to kill even a sick ceratopsian. Earlier tyrannosaurs such as *Albertosaurus* were smaller and lived alongside smaller ceratopsians like *Chasmosaurus*, *Styracosaurus*, and *Centrosaurus*. Both *Triceratops* and *Tyrannosaurus* were much larger. This suggests that ceratopsians and tyrannosaurs evolved together, each getting gradually bigger to be able to deal with the other.

How did *Triceratops* live?

Like all horned dinosaurs, *Triceratops* ate plants. It would have snipped off tough leaves and stems with its beak and sliced them up with its sharp cheek teeth.

Triceratops was a very common dinosaur in North America at the end of the Cretaceous period. Although paleontologists have found bone beds for other ceratopsians, including *Centrosaurus*, they have not found any for *Triceratops*. Bone beds are like mass graves where sometimes hundreds of skeletons of the same kind of dinosaur are found at one time. Many paleontologists believe that bone beds show that these animals died together, and if they died together they probably lived together, in herds. One day paleontologists may find hard evidence that *Triceratops* was a herd animal: perhaps a *Triceratops* bone bed, or even better, a trackway showing a herd of *Triceratops* on the move.

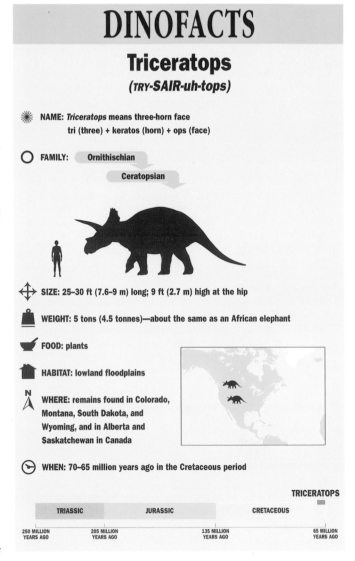

DINOFACTS

Triceratops
(TRY-*SAIR-uh-tops*)

✳ NAME: *Triceratops* means three-horn face
  tri (three) + keratos (horn) + ops (face)

○ FAMILY: Ornithischian
  Ceratopsian

✥ SIZE: 25–30 ft (7.6–9 m) long; 9 ft (2.7 m) high at the hip

⬛ WEIGHT: 5 tons (4.5 tonnes)—about the same as an African elephant

FOOD: plants

HABITAT: lowland floodplains

WHERE: remains found in Colorado, Montana, South Dakota, and Wyoming, and in Alberta and Saskatchewan in Canada

🕐 WHEN: 70–65 million years ago in the Cretaceous period

TRICERATOPS

TRIASSIC	JURASSIC	CRETACEOUS	
250 MILLION YEARS AGO	205 MILLION YEARS AGO	135 MILLION YEARS AGO	65 MILLION YEARS AGO

CHECK THESE OUT!

Centrosaurus, Ceratopsians, Chasmosaurus, Cretaceous period, Ornithischian dinosaurs, Styracosaurus, Tyrannosaurus

Troodon

Troodon was one of the first dinosaurs discovered in North America. It was once thought to be a lizard, then a thick-headed dinosaur, but we now know it was a very birdlike dinosaur.

In 1856, one of the first US paleontologists, Joseph Leidy of Philadelphia, described some specimens of fossil reptile teeth that had been found in what is now the state of Montana. At the time, no dinosaur fossils had been recognized in North America, although their footprints and bones had already been found in New England. Leidy looked at the fossil teeth from Montana and recognized four sorts. Some were fairly small and curved at the tip. There were big serrations down the back edge, but no serrations down the front. Although it was not quite like anything else known at the time, Leidy thought this first group seemed closest to the teeth of modern monitor lizards. Since monitors are mostly meat-eaters, he called these teeth *Troodon*, or wounding tooth.

Not a lizard
For many years *Troodon* was thought to be a lizard. By the beginning of the 20th century, however, paleontologists such

DINOSAUR INTELLIGENCE

Some people claim that *Troodon* was the smartest dinosaur. How can they say that? We will probably never know exactly how smart any particular dinosaur was. Even in the modern world it is very difficult for zoologists to figure out which animals are smarter than which other animals, and by how much.

With fossil species it is even more difficult, because we cannot test the animals by running them through mazes or trying to get them to pick up blocks. The size of the braincase of a fossil, however, can be measured and compared to the size of its body. By comparing the brain-to-body sizes of fossil species and modern animals, we can get a rough idea about how brainy a dinosaur was. *Troodon* had a particularly large brain in relation to the size of its body.

▼ *Troodon* was a very agile and quick theropod, using its long, slender legs to carry it swiftly as it hunted prey or escaped from predators.

as Hungarian Ferenc Nopcsa began to suspect that the teeth came from a small theropod (two-legged meat-eating) dinosaur. Theropods, like monitor lizards, had bladelike, serrated teeth.

Another idea was put forward in 1924 by American paleontologist Charles Whitney Gilmore of the Smithsonian Institution. He noticed that the size of *Troodon* teeth, and the size and shape of the serrations, were similar to those of thick-headed dinosaurs like *Pachycephalosaurus*. He thought that what Leidy had described were neither lizard teeth nor theropod teeth, but the teeth of these plant-eaters.

Thick-headed dinosaurs

Gilmore was at that time describing the first complete thick-headed dinosaur skull ever found. He decided to name this dinosaur *Troodon*. He also decided that the thick-headed dinosaurs should be called the troodontids.

Then in 1945, Canadian paleontologist Charles M. Sternberg examined both Leidy's tooth fossils and the thick-headed dinosaurs. He concluded that the teeth really were not that similar and that it was most likely that *Troodon* was really a theropod dinosaur. Sternberg named the thick-headed dinosaurs "pachycephalosaurs," the name we call them today.

Adding confusion

The story of what *Troodon* really was had one last, confusing twist. In the 1970s, Montana

paleontologist Jack Horner discovered a fossil nest containing the eggs of what he thought was a hypsilophodontid, a dinosaur similar to the small two-legged plant-eater *Hypsilophodon*. However, *Troodon* teeth were found with the nest. Horner suggested that perhaps *Troodon* was a kind of meat-eating hypsilophodontid. He later suggested that perhaps these were the teeth of a nest-raiding *Troodon*.

Troodon's true identity

As it turned out, Horner and his student, David Varricchio, later discovered that the nests were *Troodon* nests and that *Troodon* was neither a hypsilophodontid nor a hypsilophodontid-eater.

Sternberg, who first suggested that *Troodon* was not a thick-headed dinosaur, had found and described bones belonging to *Troodon* in 1932—although he did not know it at the time. Although crushed and incomplete, this skeleton was clearly from a

▲ The fossil nest found by Jack Horner added another confusing piece of evidence to the puzzle about *Troodon*'s true identity.

small theropod dinosaur. An unusual feature of this specimen was the second toe of the foot, which was shorter than the middle and outer toe. Sternberg named the dinosaur *Stenonychosaurus inequalis*, the short-clawed lizard with uneven toes.

More bits and pieces were found over the years. In 1969, Canadian paleontologist Dale Russell described the most complete skeleton of this dinosaur yet found. He recog-

nized that it was a very birdlike form, with grasping hands and long, slim legs. However, he still called it *Stenonychosaurus*.

It was Canadian theropod expert Philip J. Currie who, in 1987, showed that all these teeth and bones belonged to the same kind of dinosaur. Because *Troodon* was the first name given to this dinosaur, that is what we call it today.

Brains not brawn

Most of our modern understanding of *Troodon* comes from the work of Russell, Currie, and Varricchio. *Troodon* seems to be the biggest known of the troodontids, about twice as heavy as *Saurornithoides*, another troodontid. It had a long, tapered snout with many teeth (more than any dinosaur except for the ostrichlike dinosaur *Pelecanimimus*).

The braincase of *Troodon* is very large, and when the size of the brain is compared to the size of the body, *Troodon* is one of the brainiest of all dinosaurs. It is even bigger brained than most of the mammals that lived with it in the Late Cretaceous period. However, it is not especially big brained compared to modern mammals or birds.

TOO MANY NAMES

Troodon is a dinosaur that has had many names over the years. It has also been called *Stenonychosaurus*, *Polydontosaurus*, and *Pectinodon*, and some paleontologists once considered it to be the same as Mongolian *Saurornithoides*.

When a number of names are available, scientists have rules on how to choose among them. Although some of the other names might be more descriptive, only the first valid name can be used. Since these other names were proposed much later than the name *Troodon*, then *Troodon* is the name by which we call this little dinosaur.

Big eyes, long legs

The eyes of *Troodon* were very large, perhaps helping it to see better at night. Like most other maniraptors (the group of theropods to which troodontids belong), *Troodon* had long, grasping hands for grabbing and holding.

Troodon's legs were very long and slender, unlike those of dromaeosaurs, the clawed hunters like *Deinonychus*. Like dromaeosaurs, however, the second toe of the foot had a large claw, although it was not as big or as bladelike as that of *Deinonychus*. Like ornithomimosaurs (ostrichlike dinosaurs) and tyrannosaurs (two-fingered meat-eaters), the middle bone of the foot was pinched, perhaps acting as a shock absorber while running.

How did *Troodon* live?

With its big brain, big eyes, and long, slender legs, *Troodon* was probably very agile and very alert. It would have been an excellent hunter, especially if it was chasing small or fast-moving prey. Its speed and intelligence also helped it to survive in a world of deadlier predators such as dromaeosaurs and tyrannosaurs.

It may be that *Troodon* did not eat only meat. As Gilmore noted, there are some similarities between the teeth of *Troodon* and those of plant-eating dinosaurs and lizards. Perhaps *Troodon* had a varied diet, eating meat, eggs, insects, and even some plants.

Although *Troodon* was one of the first dinosaurs found in the United States, it was one of the last of the dinosaurs of the Mesozoic Era. *Troodon* teeth are found in the very last layers of the Cretaceous period in Wyoming, Montana, and South Dakota.

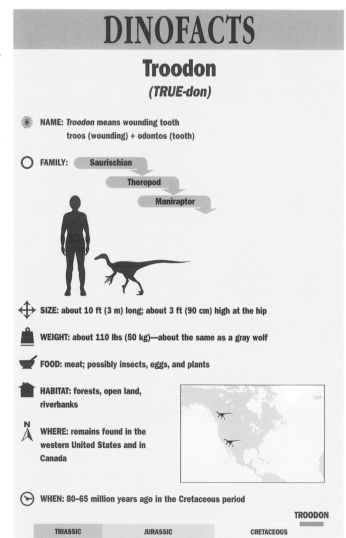

DINOFACTS

Troodon
(TRUE-don)

NAME: *Troodon* means wounding tooth
troos (wounding) + odontos (tooth)

FAMILY: Saurischian → Theropod → Maniraptor

SIZE: about 10 ft (3 m) long; about 3 ft (90 cm) high at the hip

WEIGHT: about 110 lbs (50 kg)—about the same as a gray wolf

FOOD: meat; possibly insects, eggs, and plants

HABITAT: forests, open land, riverbanks

N

WHERE: remains found in the western United States and in Canada

WHEN: 80–65 million years ago in the Cretaceous period

			TROODON
TRIASSIC	JURASSIC	CRETACEOUS	
250 MILLION YEARS AGO	205 MILLION YEARS AGO	135 MILLION YEARS AGO	65 MILLION YEARS AGO

CHECK THESE OUT!

Dromaeosaurs, *Hypsilophodon*,
Pachycephalosaurs, Saurischian
dinosaurs, Theropods, Tyrannosaurs

Tsintaosaurus

Tsintaosaurus, with its long, narrow, solid crest on top of its head, looked much like the legendary unicorn. What could have been the purpose of this strange, single crest?

There are two groups of hadrosaurs (duckbill dinosaurs): the lambeosaurines, such as *Lambeosaurus*, and the hadrosaurines, such as *Hadrosaurus*. The hadrosaurines had a low solid crest on their head or none at all, but the lambeosaurines had very large, hollow crests on their heads, through which they may have hooted. *Tsintaosaurus*'s strange crest seems to have been halfway between a lambeosaurine crest and a hadrosaurine crest.

MYSTERIOUS HADROSAUR

Tsintaosaurus is hard to study for two reasons. First, only a few skulls and body skeletons have been found. Second, some paleontologists think that the skull bones and the body bones may not come from the same animal.

Although scientists know that the bones that have been described as *Tsintaosaurus* are all definitely hadrosaur remains, the strange mix of features shown by the bones of the head make it very difficult to classify *Tsintaosaurus*. Scientists cannot tell if it was related to the hadrosaurs with the tall head crest, the lambeosaurines, or to the saurolophines, a subgroup of the hadrosaurines that had a simple low horn that projected up and backward from the head. Bones from the body skeleton come from at least five different animals that were lambeosaurines, so we might have a reasonable picture of what *Tsintaosaurus* looked like. We will have to wait for more fossils to be found to be certain of what *Tsintaosaurus* was really like.

▶ Was *Tsintaosaurus*'s crest on top of its head or did it stick out the back? Was it solid or hollow? Scientists do not yet have enough evidence to tell.

DINOFACTS

Tsintaosaurus
(CHIN-dow-SORE-us)

☀ **NAME:** *Tsintaosaurus* means Tsintao lizard
Tsintao (Chinese town) + sauros (lizard)

⭕ **FAMILY:** **Ornithischian**
        Ornithopod
           Hadrosaur

✚ **SIZE:** 33 ft (10 m) long; 10 ft (3 m) high at the hip

⚖ **WEIGHT:** 3.7 tons (3.3 tonnes)—about the same as 3–4 North American bison

🥣 **FOOD:** plants

🏠 **HABITAT:** broad, low-lying plains with many large rivers

🧭 **WHERE:** remains found in China

▶ **Did the skeleton of *Tsintaosaurus* look like this, or did some of the bones belong to other dinosaurs?**

🕐 **WHEN:** 75–65 million years ago in the Cretaceous period

			TSINTAOSAURUS
TRIASSIC	**JURASSIC**	**CRETACEOUS**	
250 MILLION YEARS AGO	205 MILLION YEARS AGO	135 MILLION YEARS AGO	65 MILLION YEARS AGO

Tsintaosaurus's fossilized crest was hollow, so some paleontologists think that the crest was hollow when the dinosaur was alive. Others think that the crest was solid when *Tsintaosaurus* was alive and that it is only because the crest was badly preserved as a fossil that it is now hollow.

Whether *Tsintaosaurus*'s crest was solid or hollow, it could have held up a sheet of brightly colored skin in the same way that a ship's mast holds up a sail. *Tsintaosaurus* could have used this sheet of skin to signal to others of its kind. Today, many male lizards have bright patches of skin beneath their chins with which they threaten other males and attract mates. However, because its bones moved out of position before they fossilized, paleontologists are not sure exactly where on its head *Tsintaosaurus* wore its bony crest.

How *Tsintaosaurus* lived
As a hadrosaur, *Tsintaosaurus* ate plants. It would have had hundreds of cheek teeth and a cropping beak. It may have lived in herds that wandered slowly across their Cretaceous home, looking for food.

CHECK THESE OUT!
Cretaceous period, Hadrosaurs, *Hadrosaurus, Lambeosaurus*

431

Tuojiangosaurus

Tuojiangosaurus was a stegosaur (plate-backed dinosaur) from southern China. With its triangular armored plates, it would have been an awesome sight roaming the Late Jurassic Chinese plains.

Fossil-hunters have found only two skeletons of *Tuojiango-saurus*. However, they are both almost complete, so scientists are confident they know what this animal looked like.

Like all other stegosaurs, *Tuojiangosaurus* had bony growths poking out along its back. *Stegosaurus*'s bony growths were large, flat, diamond-shaped plates. The plates on one side of the body

LARGER THAN LIFE

The armored plates sticking up along the back of *Tuojiangosaurus* made it look bigger than it really was. This was probably an advantage for a nonaggressive, plant-eating dinosaur. Many other animals have developed devices to make them look bigger than they really are. For example, many fish will raise their fins so they look larger from the side. This is a great advantage when they want to frighten off a predator or threaten a rival. Some frogs and toads puff up their bodies with air when threatened by a snake. This makes them look like too big a mouthful for the snake to swallow. Some lizards can lower a flap of skin below their jaws to make their heads look bigger. They also raise their bodies up on stretched arms and legs to make themselves look larger and more threatening.

▼ Besides having cone-shaped plates along its back, *Tuojiangosaurus* had spikes on its tail. It may have used its spiked tail as a weapon against attacking meat-eaters.

DINOFACTS

Tuojiangosaurus
(toe-HWANG-oh-SORE-us)

✳ **NAME:** *Tuojiangosaurus* means two river lizard
tuojiang (two rivers) + sauros (lizard)

○ **FAMILY:** Ornithischian

Thyreophoran

Stegosaur

✛ **SIZE:** 23 ft (7 m) long; 7 ft (2.1 m) high at the hip

⚖ **WEIGHT:** 1 ton (0.9 tonnes)—about the same as a North American bison

🥣 **FOOD:** plants

🏠 **HABITAT:** broad, low-lying plains with many large rivers

N ↑ **WHERE:** remains found in China

🕐 **WHEN:** 156 million years ago in the Jurassic period

TUOJIANGOSAURUS

TRIASSIC	JURASSIC	CRETACEOUS
250 MILLION YEARS AGO	205 MILLION YEARS AGO	135 MILLION YEARS AGO

65 MILLION YEARS AGO

did not line up with the plates on the other side. *Tuojiangosaurus*'s bony growths were smaller, triangular, flattened cones. There were 17 pairs of plates, arranged in two rows with each plate of a pair exactly opposite the other.

How *Tuojiangosaurus* lived

Like all stegosaurs, *Tuojiangosaurus* was an ornithischian (bird-hipped) dinosaur that ate plants. It would have spent its time slowly munching its way through low-growing vegetation. Its arms and legs were

quite short for its size, so it probably could not move fast to run away from danger.

Tuojiangosaurus's back plates may have helped scare off predators. The tallest of its plates were just above its hips, the tallest part of its body. This would have made *Tuojiangosaurus* look very large when it was seen from the side.

CHECK THESE OUT!
Jurassic period,
Ornithischian dinosaurs, Stegosaurs,
Stegosaurus, Thyreophorans

Tyrannosaurs

Tyrannosaurs were some of the most spectacular meat-eating dinosaurs of the Cretaceous period. Even the smallest of these tyrant lizards were as large as the largest predators on land today.

The tyrannosaurs, or tyrant lizards, are one of the best-known groups of theropods (two-legged meat-eaters).

They include *Tyranno-saurus* of North America and the very similar *Tarbosaurus* of Asia, as well as slightly smaller forms such as *Daspletosaurus* and *Albertosaurus*.

Piledrivers
Tyrannosaurs all had a very strong skull, although the bones of their braincase were hollow. Scientists believe tyrannosaurs probably ran head-on into their prey and tore off chunks of flesh with their teeth. The shape of the jaws and the back of the skull show that tyrannosaurs had very strong jaw and neck muscles. Their front teeth were shaped like shovels, and were probably used to scrape meat off bones.

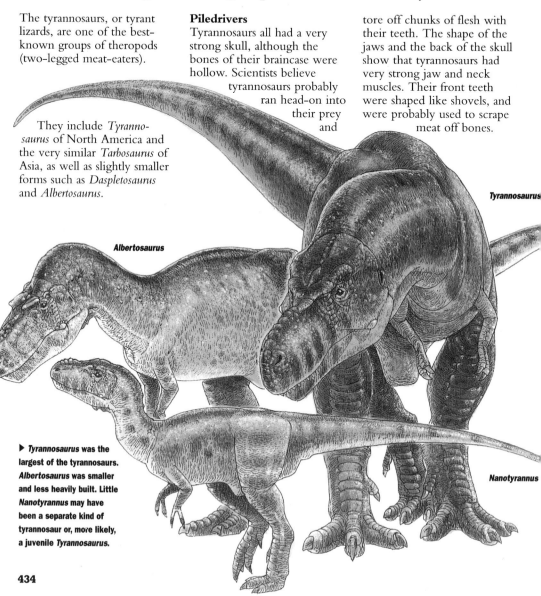

Albertosaurus

Tyrannosaurus

Nanotyrannus

▶ *Tyrannosaurus* was the largest of the tyrannosaurs. *Albertosaurus* was smaller and less heavily built. Little *Nanotyrannus* may have been a separate kind of tyrannosaur or, more likely, a juvenile *Tyrannosaurus*.

TYRANT KINGS

Tyrannosaurs are found only in a few regions of the world: eastern and central Asia and western North America. During the Late Cretaceous period these two regions were joined in a single unit called Asiamerica. Dinosaurs could travel back and forth over what are now Siberia and Alaska.

Tyrannosaurs are the only large predatory dinosaurs known from Late Cretaceous Asiamerica. There were other large theropods in Asia, such as the possible ornithomimosaur (ostrichlike dinosaur) *Deinocheirus* and the bizarre, big-clawed *Therizinosaurus*, but these were probably not hunters. Dromaeosaurs (clawed meat-eaters) and troodontids (big-eyed brainy hunters) also lived in these regions, but these were much smaller than tyrannosaurs. It seems likely that tyrannosaurs were the fiercest predators of their world, since only they seem big enough to have attacked full-grown hadrosaurs (duckbill dinosaurs) or ceratopsians (horned dinosaurs).

Tyrannosaurs
(tie-RAN-oh-sores)

✳ **NAME:** Tyrannosaur means tyrant lizard tyrannos (tyrant) + sauros (lizard)

○ **FAMILY:** Saurischian → Theropod → Tetanuran

✛ **SIZE:** about 16–46 ft (5–14 m) long; about 4–13 ft (1.2–4 m) high at the hip

WEIGHT: wide variation from about 700 lbs to 7.3 tons (320 kg to 6.5 tonnes)— or from a large grizzly bear to about 30 tigers

FOOD: meat

HABITAT: forests, lake shores, river valleys, dry regions

WHERE: remains found in the United States, Canada, China, Japan, Mongolia, and Thailand

🕑 **WHEN:** 127–65 million years ago in the Cretaceous period

TRIASSIC	JURASSIC	CRETACEOUS — TYRANNOSAURS
250 MILLION YEARS AGO	205 MILLION YEARS AGO	135 MILLION YEARS AGO / 65 MILLION YEARS AGO

Two-fingered dinosaurs

The tyrannosaurs have only two fingers on each hand, instead of three or four like most other theropods. Although their arms seem to have been very strong, they were certainly not very long. It is likely that they did not use their arms to grab prey, but to hold their food while their jaws pulled and twisted.

How they lived

One look at the tyrannosaurs' knifelike teeth shows that they were meat-eaters. Some paleontologists think that tyrannosaurs were slow, clumsy animals; others believe they could run faster than their victims. They had a bone in the foot that acted as a shock absorber. This allowed the dinosaur to run fast without hurting its feet.

CHECK THESE OUT!

Albertosaurus, Alectrosaurus, Daspletosaurus, Dromaeosaurs, Nanotyrannus, Saurischian dinosaurs, Siamotyrannus, Tarbosaurus, Tetanurans, Theropods, Tyrannosaurus

Tyrannosaurus

Tyrannosaurus is one of the most famous dinosaurs in the world. The last and largest of the tyrannosaurs (two-fingered meat-eaters), it disappeared in the great extinction around 65 million years ago.

In the 1890s, rival American paleontologists Othniel Charles Marsh and Edward Drinker Cope each tried to name the most new dinosaurs and find the strangest forms. Teams for the two paleontologists shipped fossils back to Marsh's museum at Yale University in New Haven, Connecticut, and to Cope's collections in Phila-delphia. So much material was shipped back that today, over 100 years later, some specimens have yet to be unpacked.

▲ *Tyrannosaurus* crosses a stream. *T. rex* was the largest of the tyrant dinosaurs that prowled North America and Asia in the Cretaceous period.

First specimens

In their haste, Marsh and Cope both managed to let a giant slip by them. In 1890, Marsh described a new dinosaur which he called *Ornithomimus*. This turned out to be a very birdlike theropod (two-legged meat-eater). Some other bones from the same age (the latest part of the Cretaceous period) looked very similar but were much larger. Marsh thought that these were just a new giant species of *Ornithomimus*. He named them *Ornithomimus grandis* and set them aside. He never knew it, but he had just described the first remains found of *Tyrannosaurus*.

Later that year, Cope also described a single backbone, which we now know came from *Tyrannosaurus*. However, he thought it was a new sort of ceratopsian (horned dinosaur), so he set it aside too after mentioning it in a report.

The tyrant recognized

It was Barnum Brown, perhaps the greatest dinosaur hunter of all time, who found the first named specimens of *Tyrannosaurus*. Working in Wyoming in 1900 and in Montana from 1902 to 1905, Brown recovered two skeletons of a gigantic theropod dinosaur. This form was far larger than any previously known meat-eating dinosaur, such as *Allosaurus* or *Ceratosaurus*. The fossils were shipped back to the American Museum of Natural History (AMNH) in New York City.

Giant skeletons

At the American Museum, paleontologist Henry Fairfield Osborn began the task of describing and naming the skeletons. The dinosaurs had been enormous, about 39 ft (12 m) long, holding their head up to 19 ft (5.8 m) off the ground when standing. The teeth were among the largest ever found in a dinosaur, and (unlike those of most meat-eaters) were very thick side to side. The arms, although incomplete, seemed to be fairly small for such large dinosaurs.

Osborn published his first findings in 1905. He thought at first the skeletons were two different forms of dinosaur, one with armor (very unusual for a meat-eater) and one without. The form without armor, the specimen from Montana, he named *Tyrannosaurus rex* (king tyrant lizard). The form he thought had armor, the fossil from Wyoming, he called "*Dynamosaurus imperiosus*" (imperial dynamic lizard).

The next year, Osborn realized he had made a mistake. The armor of "*Dynamosaurus*" was really just the armor of an ankylosaur (armored dinosaur) that had been mixed among the bones of the theropod. Osborn realized that the two skeletons were from the same kind, especially when he compared bones from each as they were uncovered from their stony blocks. Osborn had to choose between the two names for the dinosaur. He decided on *Tyrannosaurus rex*.

Tyrannosaurus in New York

Soon afterward, Brown discovered what for many decades was the most complete and most famous *Tyrannosaurus* fossil of all. This specimen was also shipped back to the AMNH, where it was cleaned up and put on display. The skull was complete and had been only slightly distorted over the 65 million years

PROPER NAMES

Tyrannosaurus rex is one of the very few dinosaurs whose full species name is familiar to just about everybody. However, every species of dinosaur (as well as all other species of animals and plants) has a two-word name. For example, the full names of the two kinds of *Triceratops* are *Triceratops horridus* and *Triceratops prorsus*. The full name of *Velociraptor* is *Velociraptor mongoliensis*.

For some reason, though, it is the name *Tyrannosaurus rex* that is familiar to most people. Perhaps it is because the name is easy to remember. Perhaps it is because most dinosaur books and movies use this name and not the others. Or perhaps it is because Henry Fairfield Osborn gave this "king of the tyrant lizards" a name that seems very appropriate.

during which it was buried. Most of the backbone from the neck through the hips was present, although the tail was known only from fragments. The hands were missing, as were the legs and feet.

Filling the gaps
This specimen, when mounted for display, became one of the most familiar skeletons in the world. Because it was an incomplete fossil, Osborn had to fill in the gaps. This resulted in some errors.

For example, the skeleton was first restored with three fingers (like *Allosaurus*), although later discoveries of more skeletons of *Tyrannosaurus* and other tyrant dinosaurs showed they had only two fingers. The tail was much too long in the display and was shown dragging on the ground; we now know that tyrannosaurs and other dinosaurs held their tails horizontally. Because he did not have any legs from this

Tyrannosaurus to use, Osborn copied those of the original skeleton. Unfortunately that skeleton was from a larger and heavier dinosaur than the new mount, so the legs were too heavy and stocky.

Also, since no complete *Tyrannosaurus* foot was known, Osborn copied an *Allosaurus* foot and made it big enough to fit the tyrant dinosaur. It was later found that *Tyrannosaurus* and all tyrant dinosaurs had a long and slender foot with a

pinched middle bone, different from the short and broad foot of allosaurs.

For all its faults, the display was one of the most famous in the world for many decades, inspiring paleontologists and dinosaur fans for generations. In 1995, the specimen was remounted, and many of the problems were fixed.

Tyrant dinosaurs
In the following years, many new specimens of *Tyrannosaurus* were found all over western North America. Later discoveries of Mongolia's closely related *Tarbosaurus* and North America's *Gorgosaurus*, *Daspletosaurus*, *Albertosaurus*, and *Nanotyrannus* showed that *Tyrannosaurus* was just the last in a long line of tyrant dinosaurs. They all had the same basic body plan: a huge, strong skull, short, two-fingered arms, and long, powerful legs with pinched feet.

TYRANT QUEEN

One very famous specimen of *Tyrannosaurus*, found in 1990, was named Sue after its discoverer, Susan Hendrickson. Paleontologist Peter Larson considered the name very appropriate; based on the shape of the hip and tail bones and on comparison with other theropods, Larson thought that Sue was a female dinosaur.

Sue was also larger than any other *Tyrannosaurus* skeleton yet found. Some people think that this means that female *Tyrannosaurus* were larger than males. While this might be so (it is true for some species of birds, for example), it is impossible to say for certain. Paleontologists still are not sure which specimens of *Tyrannosaurus* were male and which were female. Also, we know of fewer than 30 definite specimens of *Tyrannosaurus*, and only a few of these are nearly complete. More evidence is needed before we can say that the tyrant queens actually grew bigger than the tyrant kings.

Within this family of giants, *Tyrannosaurus* was the most specialized. The back of its skull was very broad, more so than the other forms. This let both eyes face forward, so *Tyrannosaurus* could probably judge distances better than other meat-eating dinosaurs could—useful when hunting and when striking at prey. The broad skull also would give it larger and stronger muscles for twisting and pulling. At up to 6 in (15 cm) long, *Tyrannosaurus*'s teeth were larger than those of other tyrannosaurs.

How did *Tyrannosaurus* live?
Tyrannosaurus ate meat, but some paleontologists question whether it killed its own food. Instead, they think that it was too big and too clumsy to catch its own prey, so it scavenged from carcasses.

Other paleontologists think that *Tyrannosaurus* was a fast-moving (for its size), active hunter, swift enough to capture a ceratopsian or hadrosaur (duckbill dinosaur) and powerful enough to kill it with its massive jaws. However, they agree that, as most predators do today, *Tyrannosaurus* probably scavenged whenever it could. Indeed, by being so huge *Tyrannosaurus* probably could chase any other predator away from its kill!

CHECK THESE OUT!

Albertosaurus, Allosaurus, Ceratosaurus, Daspletosaurus, Nanotyrannus, Ornithomimus, Tarbosaurus, Theropods, Triceratops, Tyrannosaurs, Velociraptor

DINOFACTS

Tyrannosaurus
(tie-*RAN*-oh-*SORE*-us)

✳ **NAME:** *Tyrannosaurus* means tyrant lizard
tyrannos (tyrant) + sauros (lizard)

○ **FAMILY:**

Saurischian

Theropod

Tyrannosaur

✥ **SIZE:** about 46 ft (14 m) long; up to 13 ft (4 m) high at the hip

WEIGHT: up 7.3 tons (6.5 tonnes)—about the same as 30 tigers

FOOD: meat

HABITAT: forests, lake shores, river valleys

N
↑ **WHERE:** remains found in the western United States and in Canada

🕐 **WHEN:** 68–65 million years ago in the Cretaceous period

TYRANNOSAURUS

TRIASSIC	JURASSIC	CRETACEOUS	
250 MILLION YEARS AGO	205 MILLION YEARS AGO	135 MILLION YEARS AGO	65 MILLION YEARS AGO

Utahraptor

About 125 million years ago, a fearsome predator prowled Utah. Armed with sickle-shaped claws and bladelike fingernails, *Utahraptor* was the king of the dromaeosaurs (clawed meat-eaters).

In October 1991, a dinosaur-hunting team led by Dinamation International Society paleontologist James Kirkland and Utah paleontologist Donald Burge was excavating at the Gaston Quarry, Utah. They uncovered parts of a skull and of a large sickle-shaped claw 9 in (23 cm) long. They recognized that these bones belonged to a

SCALING HEIGHTS

Artists often show velociraptorines (smallish dromaeosaurs like *Velociraptor* and *Deinonychus*) as agile hunters that could leap high in the air as they attacked their prey. These animals weighed only 50–200 lbs (23–91 kg) and they quite possibly could attack like that. *Utahraptor* was a very heavy velociraptorine. It weighed about 1,000 lbs (454 kg). Its legs were relatively shorter and thicker than those of *Velociraptor* and *Deinonychus*. This is a matter of scaling. If an animal is twice as long as another animal, it will be about eight times more massive, so it needs thicker legs to carry its weight. *Utahraptor* probably used its foot claws like grappling hooks to climb up the side of its prey, before using its hand claws to slice its victim open.

▲ *Utahraptor*'s large size, massive legs, and bladelike hand claws set it apart from other dromaeosaurs.

dromaeosaur (clawed meat-eater) twice as large as any uncovered before.

The next year, the fossil-hunters uncovered additional parts of the animal's leg and a large, bladelike thumb claw. Kirkland identified still more bones of the same type of dromaeosaur in collections made in the mid-1970s by Brigham Young University's Jim Jensen and Brooks Britt. They had found these bones at a site to the southwest of the Gaston Quarry on the other side of Arches National Park.

Big, bad *Utahraptor*
Kirkland, Burge, and Colorado amateur paleontologist Robert Gaston used all of this material to describe *Utahraptor* in 1993. *Utahraptor* is the oldest known dromaeosaur and the largest. However, features of its skull and claws show that it could not have given rise to any other known dromaeosaur.

The dromaeosaurs are closely related to avialans (birds and their closest relatives). Because *Utahraptor* was not an ancestor of other dromaeosaurs, the dromaeosaurs and the avialans must have descended from an older common ancestor, perhaps in the Jurassic period.

How did *Utahraptor* live?
Utahraptor was the most common large predator in eastern Utah in the Early

DINOFACTS

Utahraptor
(YOO-tah-RAP-tor)

✳ **NAME:** *Utahraptor* means Utah robber
Utah (US state) + raptor (robber)

⭕ **FAMILY:**

Saurischian

Theropod

Dromaeosaur

⬌ **SIZE:** 20 ft (6 m) long; about 8 ft (2.4 m) high at the hip

⚖ **WEIGHT:** 1,000 lbs (454 kg)—about the same as a polar bear

🥄 **FOOD:** meat

HABITAT: lowland floodplains

🧭 **WHERE:** remains found in eastern Utah

🕐 **WHEN:** 125–120 million years ago in the Cretaceous period

UTAHRAPTOR

TRIASSIC	JURASSIC	CRETACEOUS
250 MILLION YEARS AGO	205 MILLION YEARS AGO	135 MILLION YEARS AGO ... 65 MILLION YEARS AGO

Cretaceous period. *Utahraptor* may have hunted in packs. If they did, they could have killed even big sauropods (long-necked plant-eaters) such as *Astrodon*, a Cretaceous relative of *Brachiosaurus*.

CHECK THESE OUT!

Avialans, Birds, *Brachiosaurus*, Cretaceous period, *Deinonychus*, Dromaeosaurs, Saurischian dinosaurs, Theropods, *Velociraptor*

Velociraptor

One of the most remarkable fossil discoveries ever was two dinosaurs caught in what looks like a death struggle. The victim was the horned dinosaur *Protoceratops*; the hunter was *Velociraptor*.

In 1923 the American Museum of Natural History's Central Asiatic Expedition discovered a flattened skull and an isolated finger with a claw in the Gobi Desert of southern Mongolia. Henry Fairfield Osborn named this fossil *Velociraptor mongoliensis* (swift robber from Mongolia) in 1924. He described the dinosaur as a small, fast theropod (two-legged meat-eater). The museum's Edwin H. Colbert and his then student, Canadian paleontol-

ogist Dale Russell, included *Velociraptor* in their new group of theropods, the dromaeosaurs (clawed meat-eaters).

Caught in the act

The most striking features of the dromaeosaurs were the sharp, curved claws on their feet. These were fearsome weapons. In 1971, the Polish-Mongolian Paleontological Expedition uncovered an amazing fossil at Tugrigin Shire, Mongolia. It was a complete skeleton of a

◀ *Velociraptor* was a fast, clever, small predator, with a vicious, curved claw on the second toe of each foot.

Work in the Gobi Desert of Mongolia in the 1990s, led by Michael Novacek and Mark Norell of the American Museum of Natural History (AMNH), has resulted in the discovery of several more *Velociraptor* specimens. One specimen has punctures in the braincase showing that other theropod (meat-eating) dinosaurs fed on *Velociraptor*. In 1997, paleontologists from the AMNH discovered a *Velociraptor* with its wishbone still in place. Many paleontologists have long believed that theropods gave rise to birds and that the dromaeosaurs were the closest relatives of the birds. Finding a wishbone is important evidence that dromaeosaurs are birds' closest relatives.

Velociraptor intertwined with a standing *Protoceratops*, an early ceratopsian (horned dinosaur). It seems they were killed during this life-or-death struggle when a sand dune collapsed on them, burying them alive.

How did *Velociraptor* live?
Velociraptor was a small predator in the Cretaceous deserts of central Asia. It probably fed on a variety of small animals that lived in the region, including the very common *Protoceratops*. Although *Velociraptor* may have hunted in packs, there is no evidence for this behavior.

CHECK THESE OUT!

Ceratopsians, Cretaceous period, Dromaeosaurs, *Protoceratops*, Saurischian dinosaurs, Theropods

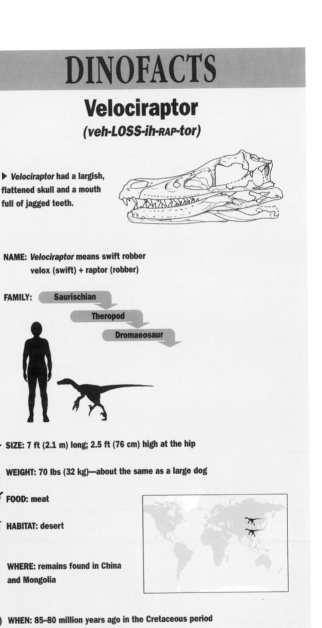

DINOFACTS

Velociraptor
(veh-LOSS-ih-RAP-tor)

▶ *Velociraptor* had a largish, flattened skull and a mouth full of jagged teeth.

✳ NAME: *Velociraptor* means swift robber
velox (swift) + raptor (robber)

○ FAMILY: Saurischian
Theropod
Dromaeosaur

✛ SIZE: 7 ft (2.1 m) long; 2.5 ft (76 cm) high at the hip

⚖ WEIGHT: 70 lbs (32 kg)—about the same as a large dog

FOOD: meat

HABITAT: desert

Ⓝ WHERE: remains found in China and Mongolia

🕐 WHEN: 85–80 million years ago in the Cretaceous period

VELOCIRAPTOR

TRIASSIC	JURASSIC	CRETACEOUS
250 MILLION YEARS AGO	205 MILLION YEARS AGO	135 MILLION YEARS AGO

65 MILLION YEARS AGO

Vulcanodon

Vulcanodon is important for the study of the sauropods (long-necked plant-eating dinosaurs) because it lived at a crucial time in their evolution, just at the beginning of the Jurassic period.

Vulcanodon was discovered in southern Africa and first described in 1972 by South African paleontologist Mike Raath. In 1984, it was redescribed by Mike Cooper when better fossils were found.

Some paleontologists think *Vulcanodon* was a primitive (little evolved) sauropod, a link in the evolutionary chain between the small-to-medium prosauropods (early long-necked plant-eaters) and the later, giant sauropods. Other

MISSING LINK

Fossils of *Vulcanodon* come from rocks that were deposited as sands and muds in Early Jurassic times. *Vulcanodon*'s skeleton was preserved in rocks whose age is just later than the Triassic–Jurassic boundary. The Early Jurassic period is an important time in dinosaur history because all the major groups of dinosaurs began to populate the earth at this time.

Although the long-necked, big-bodied sauropod dinosaurs are easily recognized, it has always been difficult for paleontologists to study the evolutionary history and relationships of sauropods. Their bones are generally so big that it takes years to get them out of the ground, and it is very hard to move them around to study. *Vulcanodon* was living at a time when the first true sauropods were replacing the typical prosauropods that had been common all over the world during the Late Triassic period. Future studies of *Vulcanodon* could give new information about what the earliest true sauropods were like and how they lived.

▼ The few leg bones of *Vulcanodon* that have been found show that its limbs were long and slender, perhaps allowing it to walk long distances to find food and water.

DINOFACTS

Vulcanodon
(vul-KAHN-oh-don)

 FOOD: plants

 **HABITAT:** broad, low-lying plains with many large rivers

✳ **NAME:** *Vulcanodon* means volcano tooth
Vulcan (ancient Roman god associated with volcanoes) + odontos (tooth)

WHERE: remains found in southern Africa

○ **FAMILY:** Saurischian
　　　　　　Sauropodomorph
　　　　　　　Sauropod

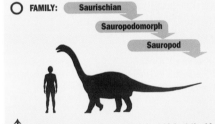

⊕ **SIZE:** 21 ft (6.4 m) long; 7 ft (2.1 m) high at the hip

WEIGHT: 4–5 tons (3.6–4.5 tonnes)—about the same as an African elephant

▶ Finding *Vulcanodon's* skull would help scientists decide to which group of dinosaurs it belonged.

🕐 **WHEN:** 200–195 million years ago in the Jurassic period

VULCANODON		
TRIASSIC	JURASSIC	CRETACEOUS
250 MILLION YEARS AGO	205 MILLION YEARS AGO　135 MILLION YEARS AGO	65 MILLION YEARS AGO

paleontologists think that *Vulcanodon* was simply a very large prosauropod that looked like a sauropod because it was so big.

Unfortunately, the remains of *Vulcanodon* are very far from complete. We only have some broken hipbones, a whole hind leg and foot, bones from the forearm, the front half of the tail, bits and pieces of a shoulder blade and upper arm bone, and a few bones from the hand. Scientists need to find more

Vulcanodon remains before they can say for sure to which group it belonged.

How did *Vulcanodon* live?
Vulcanodon would have eaten leaves, twigs, and the needles of trees similar to modern pine trees. We can say this because all other known sauropods and prosauropods ate plants.

Paleontologists have found examples of footprints made by several sauropods walking in the same direction at the same time. They have also found fossil sites around the world that contain the bones of many

individuals of one kind of sauropod that may have all died together. The trackways and the deaths of many dinosaurs at one time suggest that sauropods may have lived in small groups. Perhaps *Vulcanodon* was a herd animal too. So far, however, paleontologists have found no hard evidence that it was.

CHECK THESE OUT!

Jurassic period, Prosauropods,
Saurischian dinosaurs,
Sauropodomorph dinosaurs,
Sauropods, Triassic period

Zephyrosaurus

Zephyrosaurus was a small North American plant-eater. A primitive (less evolved) ornithopod (bird-footed dinosaur), it could chew like the advanced (highly evolved) ornithopods.

In 1975, Harvard paleontologist Chuck Schaff found part of a skull, some backbones, and some rib fragments in southern Montana. Five years later, paleontologist Hans-Dieter Sues of the Royal Ontario Museum in Toronto, Canada, named the specimen *Zephyrosaurus schaffi* in Schaff's honor.

Sues described *Zephyrosaurus* as a small, lightly built ornithopod with five teeth at the front of its upper jaw and 14–15 cheek teeth (molars). The front cheek teeth were distinctive in lacking sharp cutting edges, and the sides of all the cheek teeth had ridges.

Sues recognized *Zephyrosaurus* was a hypsilophodontid, a kind of primitive (little evolved) ornithopod named

ACROBATIC CHEWING

Can you move your upper jaw sideways without moving your head? *Zephyrosaurus* could. Hans-Dieter Sues noted that there were several flexible points in *Zephyrosaurus*'s skull. The dinosaur's braincase (the covering of the brain) could move relative to its skull roof. Like *Hypsilophodon*, *Zephyrosaurus* also had a hinge across its skull roof. These flexible points allowed the dinosaur to move its muzzle while its braincase remained still. Sues also noted that *Zephyrosaurus*'s upper jaw could move sideways. In the 1980s, paleontologists David Norman and David Weishampel found that this sideways movement let all advanced ornithopods chew very efficiently. While closing their bottom jaws, they could move their top teeth across their bottom teeth to thoroughly grind their food before they swallowed it.

▼ *Zephyrosaurus* is caught in the open by *Deinonychus* in Cretaceous Montana. The ornithopod could only run for its life from these fierce, fast meat-eaters.

Deinonychus

Deinonychus

Zephyrosaurus

for *Hypsilophodon*. Like *Hypsilophodon*, *Zephyrosaurus* had five teeth at the front of its upper jaw. *Zephyrosaurus*'s muzzle was also similar to *Hypsilophodon*'s. However *Zephyrosaurus* had a narrower skull roof.

In 1997, field teams from the Oklahoma Museum of Natural History discovered several more complete *Zephyrosaurus* specimens in Montana. When they have been studied, we shall know more about *Zephyrosaurus*.

How *Zephyrosaurus* lived
Zephyrosaurus was a small two-legged hypsilophodontid that could move swiftly on its long hind legs. It fed on plants, which it bit off with its narrow beak and chewed with its teeth and flexible jaws.

Zephyrosaurus was small enough to hide in the under-growth. If discovered by a predator such as the dromaeosaur (clawed meat-eater) *Deinonychus*, it would have used its speed to escape.

CHECK THESE OUT!

Cretaceous period, *Deinonychus*,
Hypsilophodon, *Iguanodon*,
Ornithischian dinosaurs, Ornithopods

DINOFACTS

Zephyrosaurus
(ZEF-i-ruh-SORE-us)

▶ So far, only a partial skull is known for *Zephyrosaurus*. However, its front teeth were enough for Hans-Dieter Sues to recognize it was a hypsilophodontid.

✳ **NAME:** *Zephyrosaurus* means west wind lizard
zephuros (west wind) + sauros (lizard)

○ **FAMILY:** Ornithischian
Ornithopod

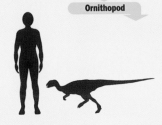

✛ **SIZE:** 6.5 ft (2 m) long; 2.5 ft (76 cm) high at the hip

⚖ **WEIGHT:** 150 lbs (68 kg)—about the same as a pronghorn antelope

FOOD: plants

HABITAT: lowland floodplains

N **WHERE:** remains found in Montana

⊘ **WHEN:** 120–110 million years ago in the Cretaceous period

		ZEPHYROSAURUS
TRIASSIC	JURASSIC	CRETACEOUS
250 MILLION YEARS AGO	205 MILLION YEARS AGO	135 MILLION YEARS AGO	65 MILLION YEARS AGO